A HISTORY OF
JAPAN

THE BLACKWELL HISTORY OF THE WORLD (HOTW)

General Editor: **R. I. Moore**

Published

In Preparation

A HISTORY OF
JAPAN

CONRAD TOTMAN

First published 2000
Reprinted 2000, 2001

Blackwell Publishers Inc.   Blackwell Publishers Ltd
350 Main Street   108 Cowley Road
Malden, Massachusetts 02148   Oxford OX4 1JF
USA   UK

Library of Congress Cataloging-in-Publication Data

Totman, Conrad D.
  A history of Japan / Conrad Totman.
    p.   cm.
  Includes bibliographical references and index.
  ISBN 1–55786–076–9. — ISBN 0–631–21447–X (pbk.)
  1. Japan—History. I. Title.
  DS835. T575 2000
  952—dc21   99–41836
                                                            CIP
British Library Cataloguing in Publication Data
A CIP catalogue record for this book is available from the British Library.

Commissioning Editor: Tessa Harvey
Managing Editor: Louise Spencely
Desk Editor: Anthony Grahame
Production Controller: Brian Johnson

Note on the cover illustration: This woodblock print by Kiyochika, one of the most celebrated artists of the Meiji period, suggests some central themes in the history of Japan. Most immediately the woodblock print, a major art form of the Edo period that still flourishes today, exemplifies the vitality and creative energy of arts and letters. This particular print also illustrates a major thread in modern-day Japanese discourse: the relationship of "East and West", of "past and future". Notice the " traditional" imagery of snow, umbrella, arching bridge, and willow; the "modern", "Western-style" bank building with its roof lines inspired by Japanese temple and castle design; and the "rickshaw", a "modern" Japanese invention of the Meiji period that embodied both "Japanese" and "Western" vehicular elements. More subtly, even the bamboo-ribbed, oil-paper umbrella moves between "old and new" by advertising a drugstore in its surface writing.

Typeset in 10 on 12 pt Plantin by Newgen Imaging Systems (P) Ltd, Chennai, India
Printed in Great Britain by TJ International, Padstow, Cornwall
This book is printed on acid-free paper.

In Memory of

Ikegami Chinpei, village head extraordinaire,
and his son,
Ikegami Taizō, newspaperman, *go* player, and plant lover

CONTENTS

ILLUSTRATIONS

MAPS

FIGURES

TABLES

APPENDIX A: SUPPLEMENTAL TABLES

CONVENTIONS USED

ABBREVIATIONS FOR FREQUENTLY CITED UNIVERSITY PRESSES

CUP   (London; Cambridge): Cambridge University Press
          (New York): Columbia University Press
HUP   Harvard University Press
PUP   Princeton University Press
SUP   Stanford University Press
UCP   (Berkeley): University of California Press
          (Chicago): University of Chicago Press
UHP   University of Hawaii Press
UTP   University of Tokyo Press
YUP   Yale University Press

ABBREVIATIONS FOR JOURNALS MOST COMMONLY CITED IN TEXT

AA   *Acta Asiatica*
HJAS   *Harvard Journal of Asiatic Studies*
JAS   *Journal of Asian Studies*
JJRS   *Japanese Journal of Religious Studies*
JJS   *Journal of Japanese Studies*
MN   *Monumenta Nipponica*
TASJ   *Transactions of the Asiatic Society of Japan*

USAGE FOR JAPANESE NAMES

Japanese names are given in the text in their normal Japanese order, surname first. However, to eliminate inconsistencies, in endnotes and bibliographical citations all authorial names appear in first name–surname sequence.

USAGE FOR BIRTH AND DEATH DATES

Birth and death dates, and alternative readings of names, appear in index entries.

ORTHOGRAPHY

"Long marks," which denote extended-vowel sounds in Japanese, have been omitted from the following commonly-used words: Hokkaidō, Tōkyō, Kyōto, Ōsaka, Kyūshū, Ryūkyū.

SERIES EDITOR'S PREFACE

There is nothing new in the attempt to understand history as a whole. To know how humanity began and how it has come to its present condition is one of the oldest and most universal of human needs, expressed in the religious and philosophical systems of every civilization. But only in the last few decades has it begun to appear both necessary and possible to meet that need by means of a rational and systematic appraisal of current knowledge. History claimed its independence as a field of scholarship with its own subject matter and its own rules and methods, not simply a branch of literature, rhetoric, law, philosophy or religion, in the second half of the nineteenth century. World History has begun to do so only in the second half of the twentieth. Its emergence has been delayed on the one hand by simple ignorance – for the history of enormous stretches of space and time has been known not at all, or so patchily and superficially as not to be worth revisiting – and on the other by the lack of a widely acceptable basis upon which to organize and discuss what is nevertheless the enormous and enormously diverse knowledge that we have.

Both obstacles are now being rapidly overcome. There is almost no part of the world or period of its history that is not the subject of vigorous and sophisticated investigation by archaeologists and historians. It is truer than it has ever been that knowledge is growing and perspectives changing and multiplying more quickly than it is possible to assimilate and record them in synthetic form. Nevertheless the attempt to grasp the human past as a whole can and must be made. Facing a common future of headlong and potentially catastrophic transformation, the world needs its common history. Since we no longer believe that a complete or definitive account is ultimately attainable by the mere accumulation of knowledge we are free to offer the best we can manage at the moment. Since we no longer suppose that it is our business as historians to detect or proclaim "The End of History" in the fruition of any grand design, human or divine, there is no single path to trace, or golden key to turn. There is also a growing wealth of ways in which world history can be written. The oldest and simplest view, that world history is best understood as the history of contacts between peoples previously isolated from one another, from which (some think) all change arises, is now seen to be capable of application since the earliest times. An influential alternative focuses upon the tendency of economic exchanges to create self-sufficient but ever expanding "worlds" which sustain successive systems of power and culture. Others seek to understand the differences between societies and cultures, and therefore the particular character of each, by comparing the ways in which they have developed their values, social relationships and structures of power. The rapidly developing field of ecological history returns to a very ancient tradition of seeing interaction with the physical environment, and with other animals, at the center of the human predicament, while insisting that its understanding demands an approach which is culturally, chronologically and geographically comprehensive.

The Blackwell History of the World does not seek to embody any of these approaches, but to support them all, as it will use them all, by providing a modern, comprehensive and accessible account of the entire human past. Its plan is that of a barrel, in which the indispensable narratives of very long term regional development are bound together by global surveys of the interaction between regions at particular times, and of the great transformations which they have experienced in common, or visited upon one another. Each volume, of course, reflects the idiosyncrasies of its sources and its subjects, as well as the judgment and experience of its author, but in combination they offer a framework in which the history of every part of the world can be viewed, and a basis upon which most aspects of human activity can be compared. A frame imparts perspective. Comparison implies respect for difference. That is the beginning of what the past has to offer the future.

R. I. Moore

SERIES EDITOR'S ACKNOWLEDGMENTS

The Editor is grateful to all of the contributors to the Blackwell History of the World for advice and assistance on the design and contents of the series as a whole as well as on individual volumes. Both Editor and Contributors wish to place on record their immense debt, individually and collectively, to John Davey, formerly of Blackwell Publishers. The series would not have been initiated without his vision and enthusiasm, and could not have been realized without his energy, skill and diplomacy.

PREFACE

The islands of Japan have had, by the usual standards, a fairly long history of human habitation. And this history, like that of any society, community, or individual, has been unique. At the same time, however, it has shared much with human histories elsewhere, most basically a changing relationship to its environmental context, and as a corollary profound changes within society itself. This Preface seeks to situate the Japanese experience in that broader ecological context.

As creatures go, we humans, *Homo sapiens sapiens*, have not been trampling the daisies of this Earth for very long – one or two hundred thousand years perhaps, depending on how one interprets fossil finds. For most of those years our ancestors found niches in the "Old World" biosystem that enabled them to live and reproduce successfully, maintaining the species and slowly, erratically one suspects, extending their presence, generation after generation, millennium after millennium, across Africa, Eurasia, and eventually the Americas and insular South Pacific. Only within the most recent 10,000 years has our species experienced rapid population growth, and only in the last 200–300 years, especially the past fifty, have its numbers exploded exponentially. (See figure 0.2 below.)

Those millennia of a gradually expanding presence reflected the success of humans in fitting their lives to their ecological context. Like all creatures, of course, the humans had an impact on their surroundings. Most notably, our ancestors may have played a decisive role some thirty or forty thousand years ago in the apparent extinction of our cousins, commonly called *Homo neanderthalensis*, and again some twelve thousand years ago in the widespread destruction of large quadruped mammals, such as the giant sloth, woolly mammoth, and great elk. Insofar as humans played a role in those events, moreover, they contributed to wider ranging changes in the ecosystem of the time, because the deaths of great herbivores in turn affected the populations of carnivores, smaller herbivores, plant species, insects, and other biota. Whether these effects served on balance to impoverish or enrich the diversity of the biosystem is probably impossible to say at this remove. Generally, however, the rhythms of hunting and gathering that characterized most of human history produced only local and temporary biotic disruptions, helping to cull the weaker members in other species and essentially leaving the biosystem intact, capable indefinitely of sustaining human life.

Not until ten thousand years ago or less, when humans began to develop what we might call "human-centered biological communities" did they clearly start damaging the global biosystem in substantial and sustained ways, mainly by reducing the diversity of creatures. Through the techniques of agriculture, orchardry, and animal husbandry our ancestors identified sets of plants and animals that would collaborate with them to mutual advantage, widening their communal niche in life by displacing other species from more and more of the Earth's surface. Once devised, the practices of land clearing, pasturage, and "farming" of forest and marine life steadily reduced the areas of land and sea in which other biota could maintain themselves. The commandeered areas were then used to sustain ever larger populations of humans, domesticated plants and animals, and a host of "parasitic" creatures – stigmatized as pests, weeds, vermin, pathogens – that found niches for themselves in the modified terrain. The result of this communal effort by humans and their collaborators was a gradual impoverishment of the biosystem as a handful of preferred species proliferated, squeezing out others, reducing the genetic diversity of the global biome, and in consequence weakening its capacity to cope with chemical, climatic, or other forms of change.

This long-term weakening of the biosystem notwithstanding, for most of the ten thousand years of agriculture, Earth's current production was sufficient to sustain human-centered biological communities on most continents, even though irregularities of climate, vagaries of disease, and local abuses and conflicts led to small-scale collapses and sporadic human hardships. Very recently, however – starting in about the seventeenth or eighteenth century – growth in human numbers in various parts of the world began placing demands of unprecedented severity on available resources, forcing the affected people to intensify old and devise new methods of resource exploitation to sustain themselves.

Several solutions, which varied in their consciousness, effectiveness, and durability, were found to the problem of resource scarcity. The purposeful solutions that we know best are three: (1) the displacement or subordination of weaker human communities by the more powerful, who appropriate for their own use the terrain and resources that previously had sustained the vanquished; (2) the devising of means to exploit more fully the biological productive capacity of areas already being utilized; and (3) the development of techniques for exploiting the biological production – fossil fuels in particular – of past ages. We know these three solutions respectively as conquest or imperialism, agricultural intensification, and industrialization.

A fourth, less coherent solution to the problem of excess demand on the biosystem has been to reduce that demand by reducing the numbers of humans, their collaborating creatures, or both, or by cutting the level of demand per capita. This solution has entailed many planned and unplanned measures, such as replacing draft animals with machines; replacing meat and milch animals with vegetable foodstuffs; reducing parasite populations by trapping, poisoning, etc.; trimming human populations through famine, war, disease, malnutrition, genocide, and purposeful reproductive restraint; and lowering demand per capita by economic contraction, whether selective or universal, or by reductions in technological waste.

Today we find ourselves at a point where the level of human exploitation of the ecosystem appears to be throwing the entire global biome into crisis. The Earth is now home to about six billion people, but in fact this small planet's current biological production is not remotely capable of sustaining those people in the manner to which they are accustomed, much less the manner to which they aspire. This population depends on the production of several Earths: that of the current biosphere; that of past decades and centuries as stored in timber stands, fertile soils, and the existing material property of humankind; and that of past millennia as stored in fossil fuels. The yield of all these Earths is now being consumed at an incalculably rapid rate.

Pell-mell expansion of regions exploited by the human-centered biological community and concurrent injury to other areas of land and sea are undermining the biomass productivity of both terrestrial and oceanic regions and are destroying species and biotic communities at a rate that may have been unparalleled for the past sixty-five, or even two hundred and fifty, million years. Indeed, the processes of physical and chemical manipulation that we associate with industrial society have effects on habitat and reproductive health so threatening to all forms of life that today we can plausibly think of the future not in terms of millennia or even of centuries, but only in decades. This change in our ecological condition and hence in our perspective on life compels us to look anew at the record of our passage. That consideration has prompted me to attempt this book.

ACKNOWLEDGMENTS

From beginning to end this book has been shaped by the writings of scores of scholars, whose hundreds of books and articles provided precious information and insight. Only a small portion of their works are properly acknowledged in endnotes and suggested readings, but many authors will recognize their contributions in the text itself.

I thank the anonymous readers of Blackwell Publishers for helpful corrections and suggestions, though the surviving errors are my own. And I thank the staff and desk editors at Blackwells who were so attentive, helpful, and good humored in seeing this volume through the press. I am grateful to Yale University Library for access to its rich holdings. In particular I thank Hideo Kaneko, Curator of the East Asian Collection, for his generous bibliographical assistance, and Charles Long, Deputy Provost at Yale, for expediting the early retirement that gave me time to complete this volume. And I again thank Michiko for bearing with my mystification and monomania during the years of reading, thinking on, and writing this book.

The author and publishers gratefully acknowledge the following for permission to reproduce copyright material:

Map 4 reproduced by kind permission of The American Geographical Society;

Map 6 from Conrad Totman, *The Green Archipelago: Forestry in Pre-Industrial Japan*. Copyright © 1989 The Regents of the University of California. Used with the permission of the University of California Press;

Figure 0.2 from Colin McEvedy and Richard Jones, *Atlas of World Population History*, Copyright © 1978, Penguin;

Figure 1.1 from Takashi Yoshida, *An Outline of the Geology of Japan, third edition*, copyright © 1976, Kawasaki. Reproduced by kind permission of the Geological Survey of Japan;

Figure 2.1 from D. Denoon, M. Hudson, G. McCormack, and T. Morris-Suzuki (eds.), *Multicultural Japan, Paleolithic to Postmodern*, copyright © 1996, Cambridge University Press;

Figures 2.2, 2.3, 2.4, 2.5, 2.6, and 3.1 from Imamura Keiji, *Prehistoric Japan, New Perspectives on Insular East Asia*, copyright © 1996, UCL Press;

Figure 3.2 from Richard Pearson, *Ancient Japan*, paperback edition, reproduced courtesy of the National Museum of Art, Washington, and Arthur M. Sackler Gallery;

Figure 3.3 from C. Melvin Aikens and Takayasu Higuchi, *Prehistory of Japan*, copyright © 1982, Academic Press Inc. Reproduced by kind permission of C. Melvin Aikens;

Figure 4.2 from Richard Pearson, *Ancient Japan*; art work by Matsumoto Shūji, reproduced courtesy of the Nara Kenritsu Kashihara Kōkogaku Kenkyūjo (Kashihara Archaeological Institute of Nara Prefecture);

Figure 4.3 from Joan R. Piggott, *The Emergence of Japanese Kingship* (1997), Stanford University Press. Originally published in *Nara no Daibutsu* by T. Katori and K. Hozumi (1981), Soshisha Co. Ltd. Reproduced by kind permission of Soshisha Co. Ltd;

Figure 5.1 from "Kyoto as Historical Background" by John W. Hall in *Medieval Japan: Essays in Institutional History*, edited by John W. Hall and Jeffrey P. Mass, reprinted with the permission of the publishers, Stanford University Press (originally published by Yale University Press), copyright © 1974, John W. Hall and Jeffrey P. Mass;

Figure 6.1 from "The Phoenix Hall at Uji and the Symmetries of Replication" by Mimi Hall Yiengpruksawan in *Art Bulletin* 77–4 (Dec. 1995). Reproduced by kind permission of Mimi Hall Yiengspruksawan;

Figure 6.2 from Bradley Smith, *Japan, A History in Art*, copyright © 1964, Doubleday & Co. Inc., from the picture scroll of the Tale of Genji, "Yadorigi II," photo no. 15221.00, courtesy of the Tokugawa Reimeikai Foundation, and Tokugawa Art Museum;

Figures 6.3, 7.1, and 12.1 from Bradley Smith, *Japan, A History in Art*, copyright © 1964, Doubleday & Co. Inc.;

Figure 7.2 from Mary Elizabeth Berry, *The Culture of Civil War in Kyoto*, copyright © 1994, University of California Press. Reproduced by kind permission of University of California Press;

Figure 8.1 from Osamu Mori, *Typical Japanese Gardens*, copyright © 1962, Shibata Publishing Co., Tokyo, p. 19, plate 8. Reproduced by kind permission of Shibata Shoten;

Figure 8.2 from John Hall and Takeshi Toyoda, *Japan in the Muromachi Age*. Copyright © 1977, The Regents of the University of California. Used with the permission of the University of California Press;

Figure 9.1 from Bradley Smith, *Japan, A History in Art*, copyright © 1964, Doubleday & Co. Inc., by kind permission of Kōdaiji;

Figure 10.1 from Morton S. Schmorleitz, *Castles in Japan*, copyright © 1974, Charles E. Tuttle Co. Reproduced by kind permission of Morton S. Schmorleitz;

Figure 11.1 from James W. White *Ikki: Social Conflict and Political Protest in Early Modern Japan*, copyright © 1995. Used by permission of Cornell University Press;

Figure 13.1, 18.1, and 19.2 from *Nihon tōkei nenkan 1950, 1996, 1998 and 1999 (Japan Statistical Yearbook)*, copyright © 1950, 1996, 1998 and 1999, Statistics Bureau, Management and Coordination Agency (annual);

Figure 14.1 from Sharon L. Sievers, *Flowers in Salt, the Beginnings of Feminist Consciousness in Modern Japan*, copyright © 1983, Stanford University Press. Reproduced by kind permission of Mainichi Shinbunsha;

Figure 15.1 from William W. Lockwood, *The Economic Development of Japan*. Copyright © 1954, and renewed 1982, by Princeton University Press. Reprinted by permission of Princeton University Press;

Figure 16.1 reproduced by permission of the publisher from William Johnston, *The Modern Epidemic, A History of Tuberculosis in Japan*. Cambridge, MA: Harvard University Council on East Asian Studies, 1995, p. 39. © The President and Fellows of Harvard College, 1995;

Figure 16.2 from Mariko Inoue, "Kiyokata's *Asasuzu*: The Emergence of the Jogakusei Image," *MN* 51/4 (Winter 1996). Reproduced by kind permission of the Yayoi Art Museum;

Figure 17.1 from William Craig, *The Fall of Japan*, copyright © 1967, The Dial Press;

Figure 18.2 and 18.3 from Andrew Gordon, *Postwar Japan as History*. Copyright © 1993, The Regents of the University of California. Used with the permission of the University of California Press;

Figure 19.1 based on figures from Yano Tsuneta Kinenkai (ed.), *Nippon, A Charted Survey of Japan 1994–95*, copyright © 1994, Kokuseisha;

Figure Epilogue 1 from the Geological Survey of Japan, fact sheet D-3 1998.2. Reproduced by kind permission of the Geological Survey of Japan.

The publishers apologize for any errors or omissions in the above list and would be grateful to be notified of any corrections that should be incorporated in the next edition or reprint of this book.

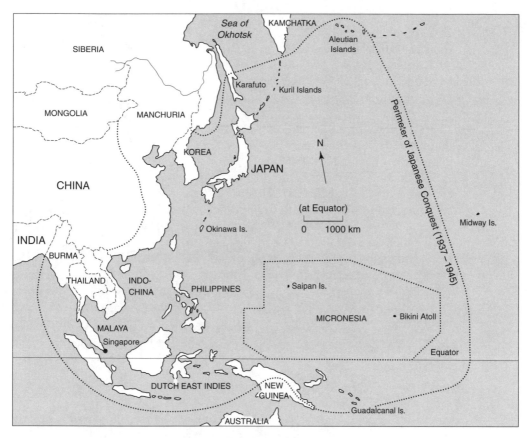

Map 1   East Asia and the Pacific.

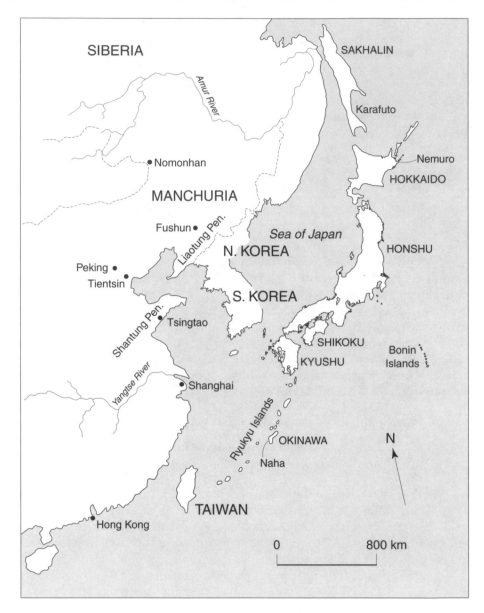

Map 2 Northeast Asia.

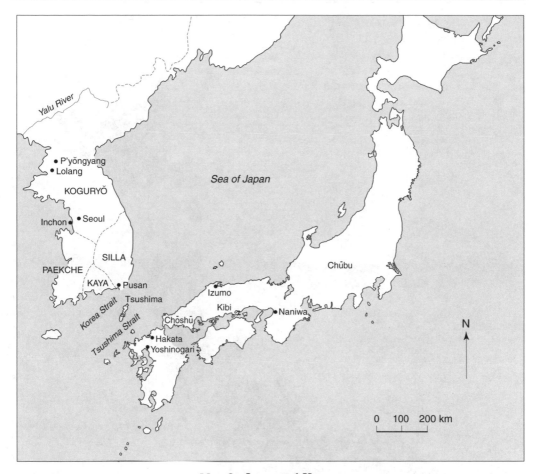

Map 3 Japan and Korea.

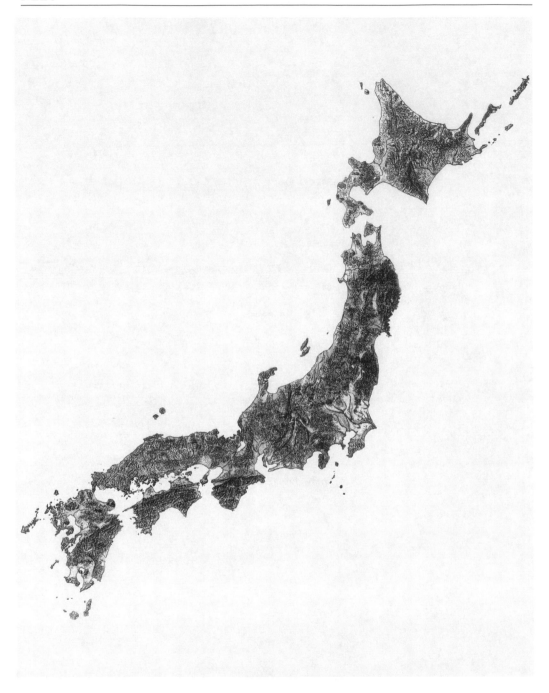

Map 4 Japan: physiographic.

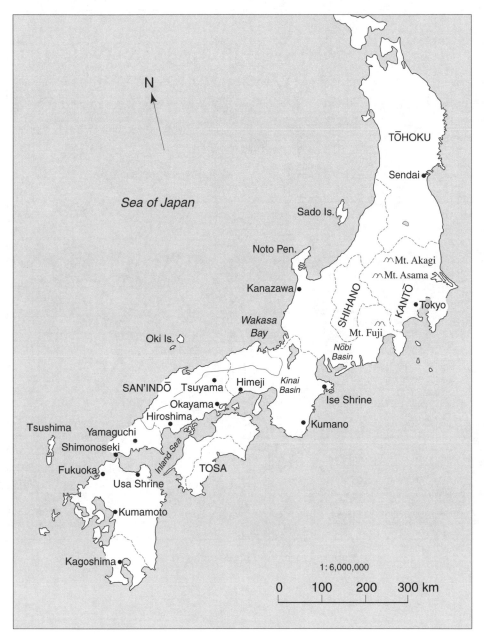

N

Sea of Japan

TŌHOKU

Sendai

Sado Is.

Noto Pen.

Mt. Akagi

Mt. Asama

Kanazawa

SHIHANO

KANTŌ

Tokyo

Wakasa
Bay

Oki Is.

Mt. Fuji

Nōbi
Basin

SAN'INDŌ   Tsuyama   Himeji

Kinai
Basin

Ise Shrine

Okayama

Hiroshima

Kumano

Tsushima

Yamaguchi

Inland Sea

Shimonoseki

TOSA

Fukuoka

Usa Shrine

Kumamoto

Kagoshima

1 : 6,000,000

0   100   200   300 km

Map 5 Japan: general.

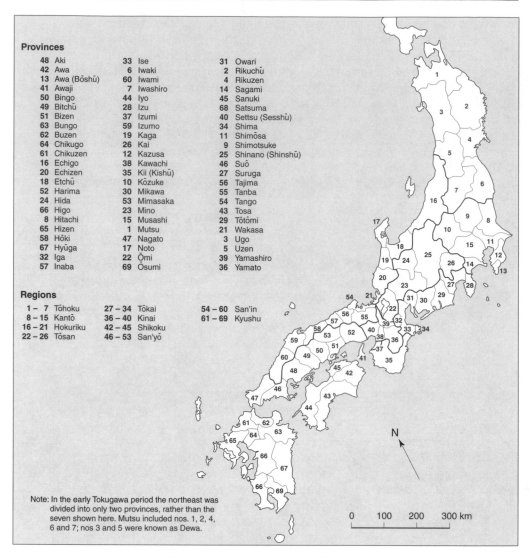

Provinces

48	Aki	33	Ise	31	Owari	
42	Awa	6	Iwaki	2	Rikuchū	
13	Awa (Bōshū)	60	Iwami	4	Rikuzen	
41	Awaji	7	Iwashiro	14	Sagami	
50	Bingo	44	Iyo	45	Sanuki	
49	Bitchū	28	Izu	68	Satsuma	
51	Bizen	37	Izumi	40	Settsu (Sesshū)	
63	Bungo	59	Izumo	34	Shima	
62	Buzen	19	Kaga	11	Shimōsa	
64	Chikugo	26	Kai	9	Shimotsuke	
61	Chikuzen	12	Kazusa	25	Shinano (Shinshū)	
16	Echigo	38	Kawachi	46	Suō	
20	Echizen	35	Kii (Kishū)	27	Suruga	
18	Etchū	10	Kōzuke	56	Tajima	
52	Harima	30	Mikawa	55	Tanba	
24	Hida	53	Mimasaka	54	Tango	
66	Higo	23	Mino	43	Tosa	
8	Hitachi	15	Musashi	29	Tōtōmi	
65	Hizen	1	Mutsu	21	Wakasa	
58	Hōki	47	Nagato	3	Ugo	
67	Hyūga	17	Noto	5	Uzen	
32	Iga	22	Ōmi	39	Yamashiro	
57	Inaba	69	Ōsumi	36	Yamato	

Regions

1 – 7	Tōhoku	27 – 34	Tōkai	54 – 60	San'in
8 – 15	Kantō	36 – 40	Kinai	61 – 69	Kyushu
16 – 21	Hokuriku	42 – 45	Shikoku		
22 – 26	Tōsan	46 – 53	San'yō		

Note: In the early Tokugawa period the northeast was divided into only two provinces, rather than the seven shown here. Mutsu included nos. 1, 2, 4, 6 and 7; nos 3 and 5 were known as Dewa.

N

0   100   200   300 km

Map 6 Provinces of pre-Meiji Japan.

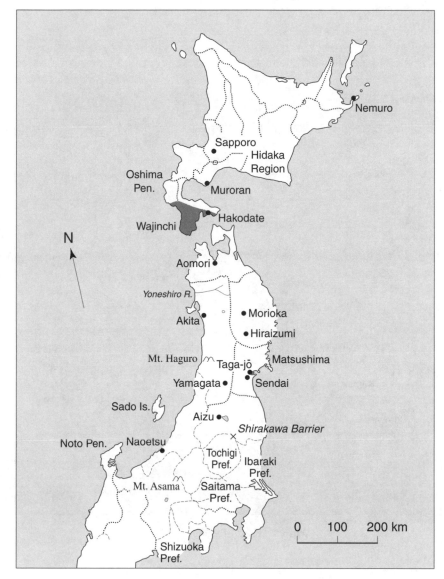

Map 7   Northeast Japan.

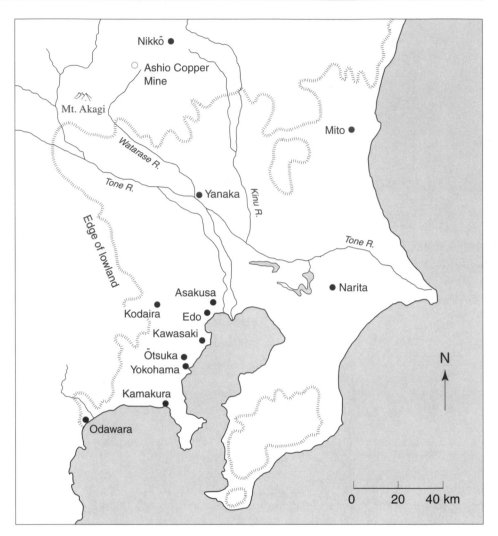

Map 8 Kantō Region.

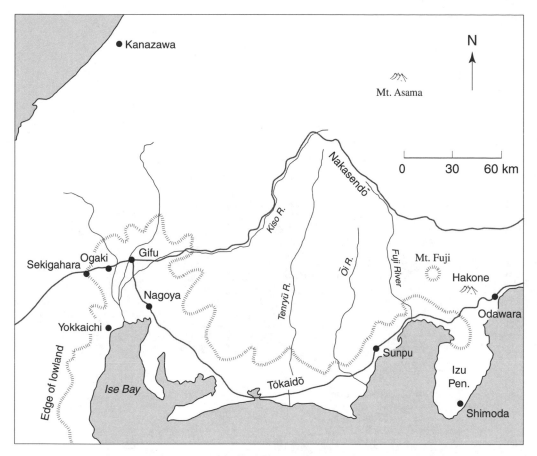

Map 9 Tōkai Region.

Map 10   Kinai Region.

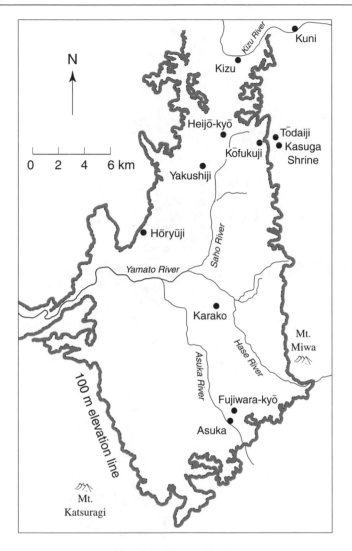

Map 11 Yamato Basin.

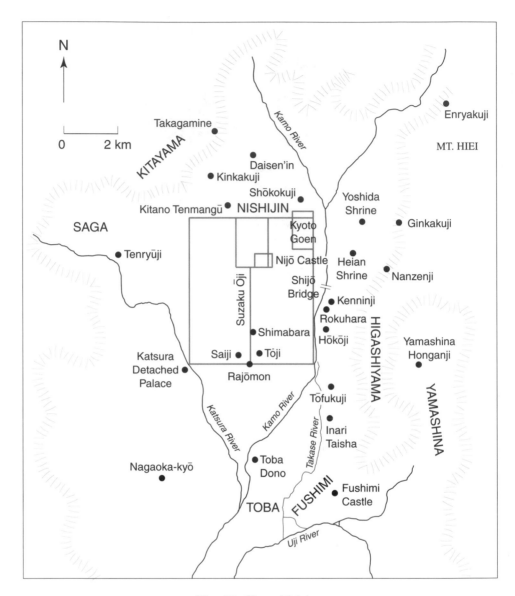

Map 12 Kyoto Vicinity.

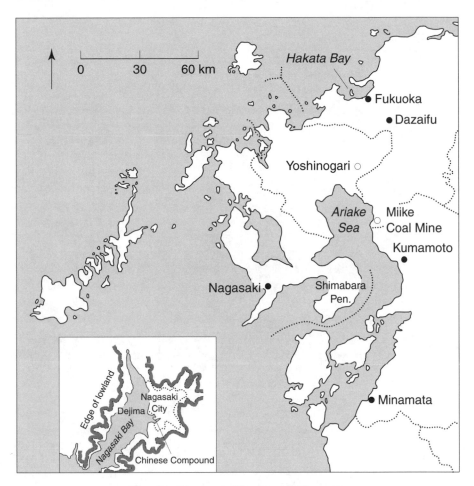

Map 13 Northwest Kyushu and Nagasaki.

INTRODUCTION

From an ecological perspective the history of Japan is particularly interesting. It is unusually accessible thanks to a copious record, and it is manageable because Japan's oceanic boundaries are so clear. In consequence it exemplifies nicely the larger story of humankind's development within a bounded biome from forager (or hunter-gatherer) to agricultural society and thence to the early stage of industrialism that characterizes our own day. In it we can see the durability of forager culture, the formation of a human-centered biotic community, and the usual rhythms of population growth and space utilization. Diverse strategies for coping with the consequences of growth within geographical constraints are visible, as are the fundamental redefinitions of resource base and the corollary changes in techniques of resource usage that are the basic markers of agricultural and industrial society.

Within this broader interpretive context, moreover, the history of Japan exemplifies the panorama of human affairs: the ingenuity of human intellect; the elegance of good taste; the rhetoric of ideological combat; the perversities of politics; and the wonderfully interwoven processes of socioeconomic change. In all these matters, the record is richest and the story most visible and pointed from the mid-sixteenth century onward, but new research is making more and more of the earlier story accessible as well.

It is, however, a story full of ambiguities and one that has not been entirely well served by its tellers – including this one. As with most histories, it has been told mainly as a story of the favored few, their politics, thought, and culture, with the masses consigned to oblivion and the broader ecological context ignored. In part, of course, this situation reflects the striking imbalance of historical documentation. But in part it reflects human hubris, the desire of tale teller and hearer alike to associate with people of weight, the winners in life, as though those who carried the water were of no consequence. And in part it reflects the common wish to give our own lives meaning and worth by finding in the historical record "proof" that the ideas and actions of individuals do indeed have meaning and consequence and that we are not merely creatures of our "context." This text rebalances the few, the masses, and their context only moderately, but it does attempt to keep in mind the limited scope and consequence of elite affairs.

Another characteristic of the historiography that merits particular notice is the problem of "exceptionalism": the tendency of historians to focus on the exceptional qualities of their subject society. At a basic level that tendency may simply reflect human ethnocentrism, the will to distinguish "us" from others, most commonly to limn "our" virtues, if only by highlighting "their" deficiencies. But historians are also driven by a more parochial professional impulse: we commonly focus on a society's particularistic aspects because most of us are trained as specialists in particular societies and we see our task as pointing up those elements that give "our" society its unique, uniquely significant, even attractive character.

In chapter 6 of this text, for example, readers will discover this writer's admiration for the creators and content of classical Japanese higher culture. One could, of course, characterize that aristocratic culture as horrendously parochial, elitist, and decadent; as the creation of a privileged few in a society of appalling economic inequity; or as pathetically superstitious and riddled with belief in such bizarre notions as intrusive deity, salvation, and a hereafter. Then again, on looking about our own societies – or into our own mirrors – we may well find those qualities not so unfamiliar, after all, and perhaps not quite so ridiculous.

Still and all, we historians of Japan seem to have an unusually strong commitment to demonstrating the singularity of its history; hence the focus here on this issue. Three exceptionalist interpretations of history, one of global scope and two that apply specifically to Japan, pose particular problems in this context because they obscure the broader story of Japanese participation in humankind's shared earthly condition.

As we note more fully in Part IV, the global interpretation that for a century now has provided the dominant paradigm for those writing about Japan has perceived as exceptional the historical experience of "the West," "Western man," or "Western civilization." These terms seem to mean somewhat ambiguously the racial/cultural ecumene of Europeans (or at least some Europeans) and those of European extraction, and perhaps any "others" who subscribe to that group's cultural claims. This civilization, we are to understand, is different from all others, deserving but incapable of complete replication, and hence the standard against which all others should be measured. Whether the user of this formulation celebrates the glorious achievements of "Western man" or damns the poor fellow for having singlehandedly made a mess of the world, the paradigm easily leads one to frame analyses in reductionist dyadic terms of the "West" and an alternative, even a rival, ethnocultural ecumene, whether "Japanese," "Oriental," or whatever, and to assume that members of this other ecumene simply react to Westerners, in the process either "succeeding" or "failing" to "Westernize" or to escape Western clutches. It is an approach that can distort priorities, invite oversimplification, and obscure much in the dynamics of the subject society's history.

Of the two exceptionalist interpretations that apply specifically to Japan, one is of domestic origin. Grounded in claims of a unique Japanese legacy, even a link to the gods, this view sets Japan's history apart from all others in terms of origin, character, and significance. For the historian of this persuasion, the task of scholarship is to show the unfolding and implications of this unique legacy. To that end authors usually focus on the central political elite and its cultural accomplishments. Sometimes, however, the project is anthropologized into a discussion of the unique attributes of the Japanese people or Japanese society as a whole or the special virtues of its putatively foundational village communities. And not very long ago it was appropriated by apologists for the industrial elite to explain their allegedly exceptional achievements of the moment.

The other exceptionalist view of Japan is an imported perspective, an adaptation of Western exceptionalism. In this view Japan is held to have experienced a unique set of conditions that led it to industrialize or "modernize" or even "Westernize" in a way that other "non-Western" societies have failed to do. The historian wedded to this perspective, whether in its Marxist or *laissez-faire* "modernizationist" form, seeks to identify and explicate those unique conditions and to show how they have led Japan to its current state, whether that be seen as laudable or lamentable. The indigenous version of Japanese exceptionalism was battered but certainly not broken during the 1940s; the imported version, like its parent, continues to enjoy considerable academic favor.

A problem common to these exceptionalist approaches to history is that the truth they do tell – that Japan, like every society, community, or person, is unique – seems in the larger context of human affairs to be less noteworthy than the other truth, namely, that all societies, like all living creatures, have qualities in common, whether in terms of the contextual conditions of life, the biological equipment with which their members deal with life, the social products (thought and action) of that temporal interplay of context and equipment, or the effects of the ongoing interaction of these three variables. This sense of commonality in the human condition underlies an ecological approach to Japan's history.

Such an approach asks us to look anew at an experience we think we already know. Because we have customarily viewed this history from different perspectives and with different interests in mind, the new look can be disconcerting. Even the basic historical periodization changes. From an ecological perspective – i.e., using the perceived character of the human–environment relationship to determine one's segments – Japan's history can most broadly be divided into the three familiar segments ("periods") of forager, agricultural, and industrial society. The basic distinctions between the three are clearcut, even though on close examination the temporal boundaries become fuzzy and overlapping is evident.

During the forager period humans functioned as autonomous creatures ("top predators") who lived off the naturally recurring yield of the surrounding biosystem. Subsequently, they adopted a survival strategy common to many species, that of the symbiotic relationship. Much as honeybees and flowering plants collaborate to mutual advantage, so humans formed alliances of convenience with collaborating plants and animals, the "human-centered biological communities" mentioned in the Preface, that commandeered terrain and displaced other creatures, thereby advancing their own mutual interests.

In the third period, that of the present day, we humans, functioning as "exploiters of the dead," have reached beyond the living ecosystem to utilize past biotic generations, most crucially in the form of fossil fuels, thereby giving ourselves a gigantic boost in quickly, flexibly usable energy. That boost has enabled us to effect remarkable physical and chemical transformations in our environment. In addition, because those fossil fuels and other resources are distributed unevenly about the globe, the rise of industrialism has shifted humankind from a basic dependence on local resources to a basic dependence on a global resource base. That shift, needless to say, has had unprecedented implications for inter-societal relations and, as a corollary, for the internal organization and ideology of participating societies.

For all its inclusiveness, however, this basic triadic periodization hardly equips us to examine Japanese history because, save for the last few decades, almost the entire knowable record deals with the second, the agricultural period. The basic approach remains useful, however, because one can further divide the history into five phases that permit a more refined examination. These five are early and later forager society, dispersed and intensive agricultural society, and industrial society.

Furthermore, insofar as the record gives us insight, it appears that each of the five phases consisted of two stages, an earlier, longer one of overall social growth and a later, shorter one of stasis or decline. In a manner that resembles, superficially at least, the concept of "punctuated equilibrium" as articulated by Stephen J. Gould and other students of biological history, the stasis in each phase ultimately "ruptured," and basic changes ushered in the subsequent growth stage. For early foragers, the surviving evidence seems too scanty to reveal internal stages, if they occurred. One can only speculate that Pleistocene climatic swings may well have induced parallel fluctuations in population numbers. For later foragers very limited evidence suggests that growth gave way to stasis or even decline around 4,500 years ago. At the other chronological extreme, industrial society, being of such recent provenance, still seems to be in its growth stage; whether it will evolve into a stabilized order remains to be seen. For the dispersed and intensive agricultural orders, however, which together constitute nearly all of Japan's recorded history, the rhythms of growth and stasis are much clearer, with the shift to stasis occurring in the eighth and eighteenth centuries respectively.

Allowing for significant regional variations in timing and detail, these phases and stages encompass the more customary segments of Japanese history as detailed in figure 0.1.

It is probably a truism of history that demographic growth bespeaks, from the viewpoint of the group or species under consideration, relatively benign ecological circumstances while demographic stasis and decline reflect harsher conditions. It may also be a truism that the shift from growth to stasis is inherently a wrenching experience, with a community's preferred day-to-day norms, routines, and expectations being thwarted so persistently that its members adopt new ones of necessity to accommodate the changing circumstances. It does appear, in any case, that in Japan the eighth and eighteenth centuries were periods of severe social stress: not simply political

Top Predator

(1) 130,000 yBP – oldest solid evidence of *early forager society*
    Late Pleistocene; Paleolithic

(2) 13,000 yBP – emergence of *later forager society* (growth: 13,000–4,500; decline: 4,500–3,000)
    Holocene; Mesolithic or Neolithic; Jōmon

Manager of a Human-centered Biological Community

(3) 400 BCE (2,400 yBP) – beginning of *dispersed agricultural society* (growth: 400 BCE–700 CE; stasis: 750–1250)
    400 BCE–250 CE: Yayoi; agricultural
    250–710: Kofun; tomb culture; state building (or Yamato, 300–645)
    710–794: Nara; classical or aristocratic bureaucracy (or *ritsuryō*, 645–900)
    794–1185: Heian; classical or aristocratic bureaucracy (includes Fujiwara, 900–1050; *insei*, 1050–1180; Genpei war, 1180–1185)
    1185–1250: Early Kamakura or Minamoto shogunate; early medieval

(4) 1250 CE – rise of *intensive agricultural society* (growth: 1250–1700; stasis: 1700–1870)
    1250–1333: Later Kamakura
    1333–1600: Muromachi or Ashikaga; late medieval; feudal (includes *nan-bokuchō*, 1336–1392; *sengoku*, 1467–1567; Azuchi-Momoyama, 1568–1600)
    1600–1867: Edo or Tokugawa shogunate; early modern; centralized feudalism
    1868–1890: Early Meiji; start of modern

Exploiter of the Dead

(5) 1890s – start of *industrial society* (growth: 1890–present)
    Imperial Japan (1890–1945) (includes Later Meiji 1890–1912; Taishō, 1925–25; Early Shōwa, 1926–45)
    Entrepreneurial Japan (1945–present) (includes Later Shōwa, 1945–89; Early Heisei, 1989–present)

Figure 0.1 Japanese history: an outline.
Note: For purposes of visual clarity, most dates in this chart are excessively exact: e.g., 250 CE rather than "third century" for the beginning of *kofun*, or 1890s for the start of industrial.

disorder within the elite that generated hardship for lesser folk, as was evident at numerous other times, but a more basic stress that affected the general populace at the elemental level of subsistence. They were times, it appears, that exposed the limits of the ecosystem's "carrying capacity," i.e., its ability to sustain the human-centered biological community as it was then constituted.

It is also arguable, I suppose, that we humans (or is it just we old fogies?) are such creatures of habit that the task of adapting to basic changes in our routines of life is intrinsically traumatic, and hence that the shifts to dispersed and intensive agriculture also were peculiarly disruptive, even though the outcome benefited many people after the fact. At least, one sees ample evidence of social disorder when agricultural practice first spread across Japan and, centuries later, when a more intensive agronomy, which was organized around larger, more complex villages, became established. Nor has industrialism failed to generate its share of discontents among those whose routines of life it has disrupted. In these cases, however, unlike the eighth and eighteenth centuries, one senses that the basic expansion of carrying capacity made possible by technological change created opportunity for "winners" that more than offset the trauma experienced by "losers," thereby enabling the new arrangements to spread and eventually become entrenched.

To make more manageable the many aspects of history that an ecological approach encompasses, it may be useful to think of historical process in terms of three interactive and oftimes synergistic facets. The first is material production, the business of the ecosystem and of humans as participants in that system. Our inquiry seeks to note what is produced, how much, and how that activity relates to the environmental context. The second facet is distribution: the arrangements of society (as expressed in social, economic, and political organization and process) that determine how goods, services, power, and privilege, are allocated. The third facet is representation, the business of higher culture, meaning arts and letters and the ideas that are formulated to represent, explain, justify, and assess reality as it is perceived.

By placing human–environment relations at the center of analysis, this interpretive approach seems to belittle much that we cherish and to dwell at undue length on matters of uncertain import. However, in this book those tendencies are minimized, unfortunately perhaps, by the poverty of the environmental record and the paucity of information on the lowborn. Inevitably, therefore, this volume becomes primarily a study of human affairs. And within that smaller arena, it gives disproportionate attention to the activities of the favored few, who left the fullest records of their passage. Moreover, it concentrates on more recent centuries, for which the record is more intact. In consequence, the story traverses much of the terrain covered by other political, cultural, and economic histories.

This imbalance in favor of the high-born is not entirely inappropriate, however, because the impact that people have on an ecosystem is generally proportional to their wealth and power: the amount of space and biosystem production one consumes, after all, depends primarily on how many goods one can purchase or expropriate. It is true that the lowly do the digging, burning, flooding, planting, nurturing, picking, cutting, capturing, and killing that historically have been humanity's principal ways of dealing with the environment, but how intensively and extensively they do so depends in significant part on the demands of the high-born. Consequently examination of the priorities and policies of the latter sheds appreciable light on the environmental experience of a society.

Nor is imbalance in favor of more recent centuries unreasonable. One can explain it simply enough as a reflection of the ethnocentrism of the "modern": if it's old, it's irrelevant. But there are more defensible reasons for a focus on the recent. If one ascribes equal value to each year of history, of course, then most of it is pre-agricultural. If one's interest lies in the record of elite culture and politics, then one best focus on the favored few of agricultural society. For society as a whole, however, the record, and hence the capacity to speak knowledgeably, is fullest in recent times. Moreover, there is far more to study

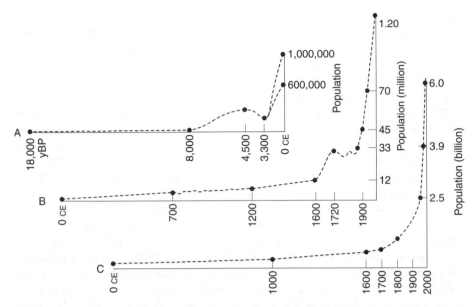

Figure 0.2 Long-term population trends, Japanese and global. The substantial growth and decline in later Jōmon population (Graph A) is concealed by the compressed vertical scale of the graph for more recent millennia (Graph B). The main noteworthy Japanese deviation from the overall global demographic trajectory (Graph C) is the seventeenth-century burst of growth and the subsequent stabilization, which preceded the usual industrial-age population explosion. *Sources*: Global figures: Colin McEvedy and Richard Jones, *Atlas of World Population History* (NY: Penguin, 1978), p. 342. Japanese figures: diverse sources.

because thanks to long-term demographic trends, as the population graphs of figure 0.2 suggest, disproportionately huge numbers of Japanese have lived during the past century or so, whereas comparatively insignificant numbers populated the archipelago during the millennia before written records commenced. Indeed, the numbers remained relatively modest until the seventeenth century: e.g., the population in 1,550 was only about 10 percent of today's. So the story of most Japanese is the story of very recent centuries, and the following pages reflect as much.

One can also argue that for Japan, as for humankind generally, the recent past merits the most attention because that is when the most change has occurred. Readers will have noted that in the periodization used here, each major segment is shorter than the preceding one, with tens of thousands of forager years giving way to thousands of agricultural, and thus far a century or so of industrial. Mindful that both human life spans and the years of childhood and maturation have lengthened substantially as time has passed, especially during recent decades, one might expect inter-generational change to occur more slowly today than ever before. But it actually seems to have speeded up dramatically.

This is so, one suspects, because conjoined trends enable and compel us to do more and adapt more quickly. Thanks to the radically accelerated energy cycling that industrialization has entailed, humans today can "do" more in the course of a day, year, or lifetime – whether as banker, butcher, planter, pundit, bomber pilot, or beanbag producer – than ever before. And because we humans are present in such vastly greater numbers on a planet that is not expanding, we can and do far more quickly "fill up" the niches we occupy, thus presenting ourselves more quickly than ever before with the prospect of implosion. Consequently societies today, Japan included, move far more rapidly than in earlier millennia from the initial development of new socio-technological arrangements through their maturity to exhaustion of their potential, in the process generating pressure to innovate anew. While this process of innovating, utilizing, outgrowing, and being forced to innovate again may characterize all of human history, it is most intensive and most visible in recent times, which prompts this volume to devote its attention accordingly.

Finally, let us mention one aspect of the story that is so transparent we rarely notice it. That is the long-term increase in the portion of earthly surface monopolized by humankind. Population growth itself has contributed mightily to that trend, of course, but there has also occurred a less noticeable but striking increase in space-use per capita. Forager society monopolized almost no space, sharing nearly all areas with other flora and fauna. With the rise of agriculture, substantial areas were shifted to exclusive use of human-centered biological communities, and as agronomic practice intensified, that shift accelerated. Industrialism, however, has produced the most stunning increase in territorial monopolization, as we note in Part IV. From time to time as our story unfolds, we shall observe this general trend as it has played out over the centuries in the context of Japan's geography.

PART I

Beginnings

Introduction to Part I

From the beginnings of Japanese history to the present, the geography of the islands has played a continuous role in shaping their biosystem and the civilization it sustained. Because the influence of geology, climate, and biota has been active and ongoing, it is insufficient to treat these variables as passive context by simply describing them at the outset and disregarding them thereafter. Lest the overall character of the geography be missed, however, it seems helpful to examine it as a whole before plunging into a narrative history that deals predominantly with human affairs. That history begins with foragers, a "pre-history" that can be examined in terms of an earlier, ill-recorded paleolithic culture, a later, much more richly evidenced culture commonly called Jōmon after its pottery, and from about 400 years before the common era (BCE) onward the appearance of an agricultural order that spread eastward across the archipelago from Kyushu.

Chronology of Part I

By 130,000 YBP	Humans present.
32,000 YBP	Evidence of paleolithic culture.
12,700 YBP	Evidence of pottery usage.
4,500 YBP	Jōmon apex.
2,400 YBP (400 BCE)	Rice culture in northwest Kyushu.
400 BCE–250 CE	Agriculture becomes established in Japan.

[1]   GEOLOGY, CLIMATE, AND BIOTA[1]

Knowledge of geography is essential for all historians, and for none more so than students of Japan, because geographical variables have affected all three facets of its history: production, distribution, and representation. In terms of the last, geography is important because place and season are central referents in a wide array of records and creative works. Place names and ecosystem terms are alive with meaning. Words such as *akamatsu* (red pine), *baiu* (rainy season), *yuki* (snow), and *ume* (plum) evoke images of season and condition as well as poem and painting. And place names – Kyoto, Kantō, Nagasaki, Tosa, or Yoshiwara – resonate at many levels, eliciting layer upon layer of significance and sensibility. Not to know those layers denies one access to much of the history's richness and means that one cannot know what that history signifies to those who do.

Much of the charm of geography lies, therefore, in its function in the representation of history. Its more essential quality, however, lies in its key role in shaping patterns of production and distribution. Both general characteristics and specific factors – e.g., Kantō loam, the Kii peninsula's coastline, Mt. Asama's volcanic eruptions, the Inland Sea's location, or Yodo River silting – all in large or small ways have shaped those facets of history.

The basic physical geography of Japan has changed very little during the centuries of its written history, so describing the island chain as it is today pretty much describes it for the past two thousand years. Over the longer duration of its human habitation, however, Japan has experienced major geographic changes, and because those changes not only affected the experience of all creatures living there at the time but also determined the archipelago's present-day character, its geological heritage merits examination. Climate and biota also have played important roles in shaping its history.

JAPAN'S GEOGRAPHY TODAY

Today Japan consists of the four major islands of Hokkaido, Honshu, Kyushu, and Shikoku, a few sizable nearby islands, and innumerable islets, most notably those of the southward-running Ryukyu and Bonin island chains. (See map 2.) The country's gross land area is about 377,000 square kilometers, roughly the size of Germany, Montana, or Zimbabwe. Of that total area, about 56,000 square kilometers are in cultivation while the rest, mostly mountains, are devoted to forest, pasture, or urban uses.

Lying along the eastern edge of Eurasia, Japan extends from about 31° north latitude at the southern tip of Kyushu to 45° near the northern end of Hokkaido. The climate ranges from subtropical to cold temperate, and indigenous forest vegetation ranges similarly from evergreen broadleaf in the south through deciduous broadleaf in much of central Japan to coniferous boreal forest in Hokkaido and at higher elevations in Honshu.

Today, as for the past few thousand years, the bulk of Japan's human population is situated along an east–west axis that runs from northern Kyushu through the Inland Sea to the Kinai basin and the Nobi and Kantō plains, the last of which is the largest area of flat land and the site of megapolitan Tokyo. This elongated strip of central Japan has dominated the country's human history because the Inland Sea provided convenient, reasonably safe transportation and was lined with small but productive and comfortable coastal plains and their richly wooded hinterlands. The Kinai, Nobi, and Kantō plains, all endowed with attractive climates, provided agricultural foundations large and fertile enough to support political organizations that ambitious leaders could employ to conquer outlying populations.

The long-term social domination enjoyed by this Inland–Sea-centered axis has helped sustain ill-defined but enduring regional tensions, most notably that between residents of southwest and northeast Japan. The tension was fostered from early times, it appears, by the entry of diverse continental peoples into Japan via the "land bridges" that periodically linked Kyushu and Sakhalin to the continent, the most recent ones being submerged by rising sea levels about 13,000 years ago. In later millennia the regional distinctions were sustained by differences in the floral composition of Japan's forests. Specifically, the deciduous forests that prevailed from central Japan northeastward enabled that region to sustain a more dense and durable forager culture than could the evergreen stands of the southwest, which proved less supportive and instead encouraged the adoption of rice culture some 2,400 years ago (400 BCE). In subsequent centuries enduring differences in cultural pretensions and economic conditions nurtured regional hostility and outright warfare, most persistently between the "civilized" west and "barbarian" east. Recently the tension was given harsh expression in civil wars of the 1860s, and it has persisted through the twentieth century in the form of political and cultural rivalries and resentments.

THE GEOLOGICAL HERITAGE

From the perspective of the individuals whose passage has produced Japan's human history, the archipelago was and is a large and variegated place in which to live. From a broader global perspective, however, it is a small realm whose character has been determined by the very tectonic processes that shaped the history of the entire planet.

Like earthlings, after all, the Earth does have a history, and Japan's place in it can be outlined briefly. Compared to our universe, with its postulated birthing date of some twelve billion years ago, Earth is a newcomer, taking shape less than half that long ago. By two billion years ago its surface structure of continental and oceanic plates had formed and those plates were embarked on the convoluted journeys that led them eons later, some 250 million years ago, into the great clustered configuration of Pangaea.

The location in Pangaea of that segment of continental plate that we know today as Japan is not certain, but recent soundings indicate that the northerly half was situated on the northwestern margin of the super continent, at the edge of what geologists identify as the North American Plate (see Epilogue 1). As the Earth's internal churnings started disassembling Pangaea some 200 million years ago, that plate was propelled westward, overriding the great Panthallasic Ocean (today's Pacific and Philippine Sea Plates) until its leading edge encountered the northeast section of Pangaea, today's Eurasian Plate. That plate was making a long, pivoting journey southeastward, which drove it roughshod over the Philippine Sea Plate. The area we know as Japan was situated at the intersection of these four colliding continental and oceanic plates. As one can well imagine, the collision generated immense pressures – folding, faulting, and volcanism – and the record of those processes is preserved today in Japan's profoundly complicated geology, most strikingly in the Nagano region where the plates collided with particular directness.

Ever since the post-Pangaea collision started some fifty million or more years ago, Japan has continued to twist and churn, regions irregularly rising and falling as the balance repeatedly shifted between eruptive tectonic pressure and reductive erosion. As figure 1.1 suggests, much of present-day Japan was under water some fifteen million years ago, and not until about five million years ago did the area commence its present orogeny, the rapid mountain building that has formed the archipelago we know today. Compared to the Appalachian and Ural mountains, which are a half-billion or so years old, or the Rockies, Himalayas, and Alps, which date back tens of millions, the mountains of Japan are remarkably young, having gained much of their present height during the past two million years.

About two million years ago (for reasons having to do with atmospheric composition, continental and oceanic configuration, or the tilt of earth's axis and the shape of Earth's solar orbit) the planet entered a period of frequent glaciations that is still in progress. By then, the Pleistocene epoch, Japan consisted of an elongated cluster of intersecting mountain ranges and deposition plains that flanked the continent but was separated from it by a deep depression,

Figure 1.1 The Miocene archipelago (shaded areas). (A reconstruction of terrestrial area, ca. 15 million YBP – Middle Miocene.) Much of present-day Honshu was below sea level fifteen million years ago, and more recent orogenies have completely rearranged topography throughout the archipelago. *Source*: Takashi Yoshida, *An Outline of the Geology of Japan*, 3d edn (Kawasaki: Geological Survey of Japan, 1976), p. 19.

the Sea of Japan. It was bounded by shallow seas to the southwest, deep oceanic trenches to the south and east, and shallow straits in the north. Depending primarily on the ebb and flow of glaciation and the resulting rise and fall of sea level, Japan was isolated periodically as a set of islands or joined to the continent by stretches of coastal lowland – "land bridges" – that extended westward from Kyushu and Sakhalin.

The physical record of early glacial cycles has largely been erased by subsequent fluctuations in sea level, but the rhythm of the most recent cycle is etched clearly all along the archipelago's coastline. As of 75,000 years ago, when a warm interglacial period was ending, Japan was isolated from the continent. Fluctuating but generally colder millennia followed, and by 32,000 years ago land bridges evidently were re-established between Kyushu and Korea and between Hokkaido, Sakhalin, and the Amur region of Siberia. This cold phase, the final stage of the Würm or Wisconsin glaciation, climaxed around 18,000 years ago, with sea level some 130–140 meters below today's. Japan's main islands were united, and southwest Japan was linked to the continent via a coastal plain covered with temperate deciduous forest growth and bisected, one suspects, only by a broad river that drained a body of water twice the size of the Black Sea. (See figure 2.1, p. 21.)

During the millennia when sea level was dropping, the existing coastal plains gradually eroded, leaving residual "terrace deposits" of regolith along the flanks of newly formed river valleys. Later, as global warming occurred, especially between 13,000 and 12,000 years ago, those valleys filled with sea-water and sediment. The ocean's transgression over glacial-age coastal low-lands and valleys once again restored Japan's island character, with the rise in sea level peaking about 6,000 years ago when global temperatures were appreciably higher than at present. By then silting had filled in the former river valleys, and when a new but modest phase of global cooling lowered sea level several meters during the next 2,000–3,000 years, substantial areas of coastal plain re-emerged all along Japan's shoreline. These constituted much of the flat land that is now occupied by cities, towns, and paddy fields.

This geological legacy is evident today. The ceaseless squeezing between continental and oceanic plates has produced an extraordinarily complex series of mountain ranges that extend northward to form Sakhalin and the Kuril Islands and southward to form the Bonin and Ryukyu island arcs. In Japan proper the process has created a mosaic of central ridgelines with branching spurs that constitutes the archipelago's backbone (see map 4). In Honshu, at a key interface of the Eurasian and North American plates, a central cordillera of closely dissected ranges makes Nagano and adjoining prefectures a labyrinth of narrow valleys whose rushing rivers twist and turn between ranges with peaks that rise well beyond the tree line, several exceeding 3,000 meters above sea level.

Because the orogenic activity that created Japan's mountains is so recent, they thrust skyward with exceeding abruptness, culminating in sharp peaks and ridges that are subject to uncommonly rapid erosion. During downpour and snowmelt debris-laden waters thunder down rock-strewn streams and rivers that descend precipitously to the lowlands, where the detritus settles out to form stony alluvial fans and sedimentary flood plains.

The tectonic stresses that fueled Japan's rapid mountain building during the most recent five million years also produced the volcanism that dotted the realm with its large number of volcanoes, lava and ash surfaces, and areas of continuing geothermal activity. Indeed, Japan's 60-odd active volcanoes constitute about 10 percent of those known to be currently active around the globe.[2] Over the millennia the ash that spewed from them washed into lakes and shallow coastal waters, helping form sedimentary plains and maturing into loams supportive of a rich lowland vegetation. The most well known of these ash deposits is a series of deep layers produced during spurts of eruption over the past 350,000 years by the Asama and Akagi volcanoes northwest of Tokyo and by a cluster of other vents in the Hakone region, of which Mt. Fuji is by far the grandest and newest. Ash from these peaks has blown and washed eastward, settling out to produce the rich layers of loam that form the modern Kantō plain.

The mountains produced by tectonic activity constitute about 80 percent of Japan's modern land surface. The other 20 percent is sedimentary terrain of two types. Scattered widely about Japan are residual areas of Pleistocene sedimentation known as diluvium, the eroded remnants of plains formed mainly during inter-glacial periods of high sea level 50,000 or more years ago. Subsequently elevated by crustal movement and volcanic fallout and eroded by renewed stream action, these remnants survive today as terrace deposits – mostly hillocks and low-lying ridges of unconsolidated material that rise anywhere from 10 to 300 meters above adjacent alluvial plains. These latter plains, the bulk of present-day flatland, were formed, as noted above, following the last major glacial period. Most emerged from the sea during the cooling that commenced some five to six thousand years ago.

Two characteristics of this geological legacy merit particular emphasis. First, unlike most large areas of dense human population, Japan lacks tectonic flatlands: i.e., horizontal bedrock of either pre-Cambrian or later origins. Instead, its flatlands are small, sedimentary basins most of which are bounded by steep mountain slopes. This means that beyond the flatland there are almost no gradually rising plains or hill country that can, with somewhat more labor, be turned to human use. Nor are the alluvial fans and diluvial terraces that do exist especially beneficial. Because the mountains rise so sharply and streamflow carries so much debris, fans at the upper ends of valleys phase quickly through loam to sand, gravel, and finally rock-infested soil of little agricultural value. And the terrace deposits frequently are of limited utility because many consist of coarse, leached soils of low fertility, and their slopes are so acute that they erode easily when disturbed, damaging the good land below. Consequently, once a human community has developed the productive potential of its flatlands, it has very little marginal area into which it can expand; the transition from ampleness of resources to ecological overload is an unusually abrupt one.

Second, although late Pleistocene glacial epochs were decisive in shaping Japan's lowlands, the region was not itself covered with ice. Except for a few small mountain glaciers, Japan was not subjected, in the manner of northerly North America and Europe, to the grinding activity of ice that scoured and lowered mountain ridges, leaving bare rock faces and depositing the regolith in irregular patches of glacial till that could disrupt surface and subsurface waterflow. In consequence Japan's mountains have retained their height and sharpness and the shallow, stony soil that supports a fairly even forest cover. For lowlands, the absence of extensive glacial residues means that natural drainage systems have remained more regular in configuration and hydrologic behavior than in areas where glacial activity has occurred. This more orderly lowland topography has fostered uniformity and regularity in land use patterns – notably irrigated rice culture – and in the social arrangements that accompany them.

THE INFLUENCE OF CLIMATE AND OCEAN CURRENTS

At the most general level, two major climatic forces determine Japan's weather. Prevailing westerly winds move across Eurasia, sweep over the archipelago, and continue eastward across the Pacific Ocean. And great cyclonic air flows that arise over the western equatorial Pacific wheel northeastward across Japan and nearby regions. During winter months heavy masses of cold air from Siberia dominate the weather around Japan. Persistent cold winds skim across the Sea of Japan from the northwest, picking up moisture that they deposit as several feet of snow on the western side of Honshu's mountain ranges. As the cold air drops its burden of moisture, it flows over high ridges and down eastern slopes to bring cold, relatively dry weather to intermontane valleys and coastal plains and cities.

In spring the Siberian air mass warms and loses density, enabling atmospheric currents over the Pacific to steer warmer air from south of the Himalayas into northeast Asia. This warm, moisture-laden air blankets Kyushu and overspreads Shikoku and Honshu during June and July. The resulting late spring rains, or *baiu*, then give way to a drier summer that is sufficiently hot and muggy, despite the island chain's northerly latitude, to allow widespread rice cultivation.

Summer heat is followed by the highly unpredictable autumn rains, *shūu*, which accompany typhoons. These cyclonic storms originate over the western Pacific and travel in great clockwise arcs, initially heading west toward the Philippines and southern China, curving northward later in the season, and finally tracking eastward. The first typhoons to reach Japan generally hit the Ryukyus and southern Kyushu, later ones working their way eastward across Shikoku and Honshu as autumn advances, until by November they usually wheel harmlessly across the sea southeast of the archipelago. This eastward shift of cyclonic storm paths is caused by the return of cold weather, which revitalizes the Siberian air mass, enabling it to push out oceanic air, re-establish its dominant winter position over Japan, and usher in a new annual weather cycle.

This yearly cycle has played a key role in shaping Japanese civilization. It has assured the islands ample precipitation, ranging irregularly from more than 200 centimeters annually in parts of the southwest to about 100 in the northeast and averaging 180 for the country as a whole. The moisture enables the islands to support uncommonly lush forest cover, but the combination of precipitous slopes and heavy rainfall also gives the archipelago one of the world's highest rates of natural erosion. That rate, moreover, has been intensified by both human activity and the natural shocks of earthquake and volcanism. These factors have given Japan its wealth of sedimentary basins, but they have also made mountainsides extremely susceptible to erosion and landslides and hence generally unsuitable for agricultural manipulation, even as pasturage. For the country as a whole, climate has thus heightened the abruptness of the transition from potentially arable to non-arable terrain.

The island chain's mountainous backbone and great length from north to south produce climatic diversity that has contributed to the regional differences mentioned earlier. Generally sunny winters along the Pacific seaboard have made habitation there relatively pleasant, especially from the Kantō southwestward. Along the Sea of Japan, on the other hand, and especially from the Noto Peninsula northward, cold, snowy winters have discouraged settlement. Furthermore, although annual precipitation is high in that region, much of it comes as snow and rushes to the sea as spring runoff, providing relatively little moisture for cropping.

Summer weather patterns in northern Honshu, and especially along the Sea of Japan, have also discouraged agriculture. The area is subject to the *yamase* effect, in which cool air from the Sea of Okhotsk sometimes prevails throughout the summer, sharply lowering temperatures and damaging farm production. The impact of the *yamase* effect has been especially great on rice culture because, if it is to grow well, the rice most widely grown in Japan (*Oryza sativa japonica*) requires a mean summer temperature of 20° centigrade or higher.[3] A drop of 2–3° can lead to a 30–50 percent drop in rice yield, and the *yamase* influence is capable of exceeding that level.

This *yamase* effect does not, however, extend very far down the Pacific coast of Tōhoku. There, as further southward, most precipitation comes in the form of rain and the bulk of it in spring, summer, and fall, when most useful for cultivation. Even the autumn typhoons, which deposit most of their moisture along the southern seaboard, are beneficial because they help start the winter crops that have for centuries been grown in southerly Japan.

For the past two millennia, in short, the climate in general and patterns of precipitation in particular have encouraged the Japanese to cluster their settlements along the southern littoral, most densely along the sheltered Inland Sea, moving reluctantly and more recently into the northeast. There the limits that topography imposed on production have been tightened by climate, with the result that agricultural output has been more modest and less reliable, making the risk of crop failure and hardship commensurately greater.

Annual rhythms of climate have thus shaped Japan's agricultural capacity and sharpened regional differences. In the longer run, as well, fluctuations in temperature have affected the archipelago's biota and hence the human culture they could sustain. Longer-term swings played a major role in shaping stone-age culture and may have spurred the rise of organized polities around 200–300 CE. Shorter-term swings had idiosyncratic effects on more recent history, most notably influencing political events of the 1180s and contributing to periodic crop failure and famine (*kikin*) in later centuries. The two most famous of these famines, those of the 1780s and 1830s, were so traumatic that even today the terms "Tenmei *kikin*" and "Tenpō *kikin*" evoke images of social catastrophe and cannibalism.

The general climatological discrimination in favor of the south has been reinforced by the effects of offshore ocean currents. The southern coast is warmed by the *kuroshio* or Japan Current, which carries equatorial water from east of the Philippines northward through the Ryukyus, eastward along Japan's south coast past the Kantō plain, and on into the Pacific. To the north, by way of contrast, the *oyashio* or Chishima Current brings arctic water down along the Kurils, past Hokkaido, to the east coast of northern Honshu, depressing temperature and shortening the growing season. Although both currents have helped sustain marine life all along the coast, giving the archipelago rich and varied sources of fish, shellfish, seaweed, and other marine products, they have also exacerbated the northeast–southwest distinction.

A branch of the warm *kuroshio* passes through Tsushima Strait into the Sea of Japan, but its power to warm that coastline is vitiated by intermixing with cold water that circulates southward from the Sea of Okhotsk. The principal contributions of that current have been to sustain a vital marine life and to promote, with the support of waves generated by westerly winds, patterns of coastal sand movement that regularly clog river mouths and gradually build coastal lowlands. Over the millennia a rhythmic *pas de deux* of river and sea has formed the alternating braids of dune and swamp that line much of the coast north of the Noto Peninsula.

THE BIOTIC INHERITANCE

The geological and climatic patterns of the archipelago, which have done so much to shape its character as habitat for humans, have also determined the region's flora and fauna. Because Japan has been closely linked to the Asian continent for so many millennia, actually being attached to it by dryland corridors and broad coastal plains during cold phases of the Pleistocene epoch, it has acquired the biological repertoire of the adjoining mainland. Before the widespread mammal extinctions of about 12,000 years ago, the East Asian complement of great beasts – including mammoth, elephants, moose, and giant deer, as well as lesser deer, wild cattle, bison, asses, horses, bear, wolves, and tigers – roamed Japan's forests.[4] Later, after a combination of climatic change and human predation destroyed the greatest creatures, diverse smaller fauna, including monkeys, deer, bear, boar, innumerable other land animals, and a grand collection of water and land birds, still filled the island chain.

More impressive than the fauna, perhaps, or at least more central to human life during recent millennia, has been the archipelago's floral repertoire. Again, proximity to the Asian mainland proved a blessing. Before the Pleistocene, Japan appears to have enjoyed long periods of temperate climate intermixed with phases of subtropical warmth that supported a rich biota based on that of the adjacent continent. Later, when the radical swings of ice-age weather endangered woodland communities, plants were able to retreat southward far enough to survive. They could do so for two reasons. First, the main mountain lines trend north-to-south, so inter-generational migration along coastal strips and valley corridors was comparatively easy, enabling species to retreat in the face of intensifying cold and then advance again during periods of inter-glacial warming. Second, as the expansion of polar ice caps lowered sea level, shallow seas evolved into marsh and later into dryland corridor and plain, enabling threatened species to retreat southward along the Ryukyus and even further down the China coast, later to move northward again as global weather warmed. For species that may have been stranded in the south by rising seas, the *kuroshio* could transport seeds or other viable parts on an island-hopping advance that eventually would return them to the archipelago.

The upshot of this floral experience is that Japan has continued to share in East Asia's extraordinary vegetational wealth. Whereas Western Europe hosts about 80 species of commercially useful, indigenous trees, for example, and North America about 250, East Asia, including Japan, numbers some 500.[5] This richness of biological diversity has been important to Japan's civilization because it has given the archipelago an extremely adaptable biosystem, one that offered humans a great variety of resources and one that could make many responses to human encroachment. Unquestionably that biological diversity has been critical to the archipelago's capacity to support a remarkably dense population for centuries on end.

[2] FROM ORIGINS TO AGRICULTURE

CHAPTER SYNOPSIS

EARLY FORAGERS

LATER FORAGERS

THE EMERGENCE OF
AGRICULTURE

In temporal terms most of Japan's human history, like that of all humankind, occurred during the Pleistocene epoch, with its recurrent glaciations and meltoffs. Recent finds suggest that early humans may have been in Japan half a million years ago, and they clearly were there 130,000 years ago. However, extensive evidence of a paleolithic culture dates back only about 32,000 years. Some 13,000 years ago, as Pleistocene gave way to Holocene (the current inter-glacial period), a larger, technologically more elaborate, non-agricultural society became established. Sometimes labeled mesolithic or neolithic, it is most commonly known as Jōmon in recognition of the *jōmon* or "cord-markings" that decorated its pottery.

This Jōmon culture waxed and waned over the course of ten thousand years until some 2,500–2,000 years ago. Around then it was transformed into an agricultural society equipped with iron and bronze tools, becoming a culture known as Yayoi from the name of its original archaeological site in Tokyo. As centuries passed, this agricultural society grew in size and complexity, and by about 250–300 CE it was supporting local polities of sufficient scale that their rulers were being interred in giant burial mounds, *kofun*. That development is used to mark the end of Yayoi and to denote the succeeding Kofun era of political consolidation.

EARLY FORAGERS

Early forager society in Japan is largely unknown. It existed during the Late Pleistocene glacial epoch, ca. 130,000–13,000 years ago. During those millennia, as figure 2.1 suggests, Japan's islands were intermittently joined and the whole connected to mainland Asia by way of northern Sakhalin and western Kyushu, making the area a long terrestrial "arcland" that looped northeastward around a major inland sea, today's Sea of Japan.

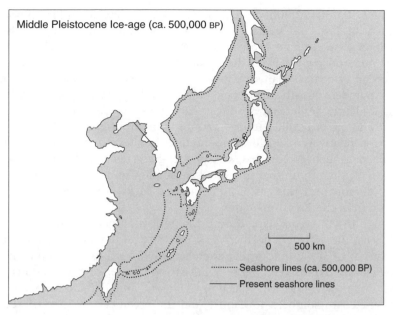

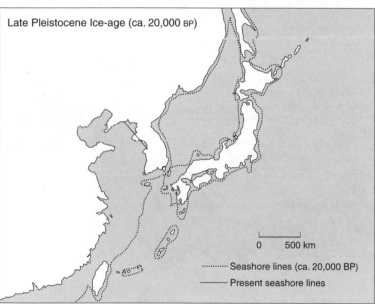

Figure 2.1 The Pleistocene shoreline. (Reconstructions of the arcland, ca. 500,000 and 20,000 YBP.) Ice-age fluctuations in sea level periodically linked Japan and the continent, facilitating faunal and floral migrations, contributing to the region's biodiversity, and probably easing early human ingress. *Source*: Donald Denoon et al., eds., *Multicultural Japan, Paleolithic to Postmodern* (Cambridge: CUP, 1996), p. 20.

Around 30,000–22,000 years ago, during a somewhat milder phase that preceded the last cold surge of the Würm glaciation, the arcland's human population seems to have grown, but it later declined, and possibly as few as several hundred people lived there during the glacial maximum.[1] The later submersion of coastal plains may, however, conceal the evidence of a much greater number. Mostly these paleolithic people lived in rock shelters and caves, evidently preferring southeast-facing slopes and streamsides, from whence clusters of families moved about in pursuit of game and other goods, perhaps in relatively fixed foraging circuits. For food they relied heavily on large animals such as Nauman's elephant, giant deer, and (in Hokkaido at least) woolly mammoth that inhabited coastal lowlands. They appear to have cooked the meat on clusters of hot, fist-sized rocks, a technique that spread eastward from the Kyushu vicinity.

Around 18,000 years ago, during the Würm's final maximum in Latest Pleistocene, the arcland's northern half consisted of boreal forest interspersed with patches of arctic tundra that stretched southward to the mountains west of present-day Tokyo (see figure 2.2). Mixed conifer and deciduous forest of the sort now found in Hokkaido, Tōhoku, and highlands to the south was restricted to southern lowlands. And the broadleaf evergreen forest that

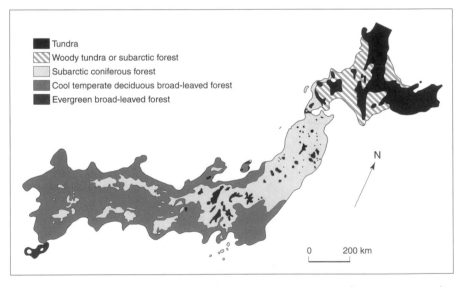

Figure 2.2 Latest Pleistocene vegetation. (A reconstruction of arcland vegetation, ca. 20,000 YBP.) Around 20,000 years ago, during the last cold phase before the present-day (Holocene) interglacial, and when the human population of the arcland probably was miniscule, much of Japan was wreathed in coastal lowlands. Vegetation was roughly divided between tundra and subarctic conifers in the northeast and temperate deciduous forests in the southwest. In central Honshu highlands were coniferous and lowlands deciduous. Evergreen broadleafs, which cover much of southern Japan today, were limited to the Ryukyu vicinity. *Source*: Imamura Keiji, *Prehistoric Japan, New Perspectives on Insular East Asia* (Honolulu: UHP, 1996), p. 30.

prevails today at lower elevations from the Kantō westward retained only a toehold on the coastal plain south of today's Kyushu.

During the several millennia of glacial warming and melt-off that started about then, floral species slowly migrated northward, coastal lowlands shrank, and the population of great mammals declined. Concurrently the human population of northeast Asia was growing, and natural increase in Japan together with in-migration from the west led to population growth in the arcland. Faced by a growing scarcity of big game, this swelling population hunted more intensively, its effort aided by the rising seas that slowly restricted large mammals to valleys where hunters could corner them more readily. In addition foragers improved their success in hunting small game and catching fish by refining their blades, using smaller points, and fitting some to hafts, evidently as arrows or spears. These trends appear to have intensified sharply in response to an abrupt acceleration in global warming around 13,000 years ago.

By then more and more families were living in simple handmade shelters, with some becoming more sedentary and relying more fully for sustenance on nuts and acorns, which they preserved in nearby storage pits. Excavation work has revealed human burial arrangements that suggest a sense of caring for the deceased, or perhaps a religious desire to mollify troubled spirits. And a few objects, notably a doll-like stone figure, betray an interest in art, whether decorative or amuletic in function.

Signs of trade were also appearing, with settled specialists in stone-tool manufacture turning out blades and points in quantity, their products being utilized by others in the surrounding region. These goods and the raw material used in their production not only circulated overland but also overseas, with some items reaching islands in waters to the south of Japan. This ocean-going capacity, based on dugout canoes or rafts, not only facilitated trade and travel within the archipelago itself but also helped sustain occasional contact with the continent despite the post-glacial rise in sea level.

As the final Pleistocene meltoff advanced, the rapid warming and intensified hunting so devastated Japan's great mammals that they, like their fellow creatures elsewhere in the northern hemisphere, were thinned to a level below reproductive effectiveness and thence to extinction by about 12,000 years ago. The thinning and disappearance of great herbivores forced hunters to continue improvising and emulating, which they evidently did successfully, though not, one suspects, without considerable hardship and perhaps inter-group violence. Despite the loss of big game, Japan's human population continued to multiply, in the process giving rise to the later forager or Jōmon society that is sometimes called neolithic despite its essential lack of agriculture.

LATER FORAGERS

Post-Pleistocene warming re-established the predominance of deciduous forest with its generous harvest of beechnuts, acorns, and other edibles and the richer fauna that lived off this bounty. Particularly in the Jōmon heyday, roughly 7,000 to 4,000 years ago, the warmer, well-watered realm supported

biotic communities so rich and diverse that in much of the archipelago people were able to sustain sedentary lives by exploiting regular annual cycles of
natural yield whose particulars varied with the locality.

Perhaps the most noteworthy element in this population's adaptation to a
changing food supply was the use of pottery, which scholars currently date
from about 12,700 years ago. Jōmon pottery is noteworthy not only for its
early appearance, being one of the oldest yet recovered by archaeologists, but
also for the extraordinary diversity and ornamentation that it acquired as
millennia passed (figure 2.3). Utilitarian pieces of many sizes and shapes proliferated, and these were supplemented by others that seem to have served
religious and decorative functions. The pots enabled people to boil diverse
seafoods and land plants, making edible otherwise indigestible varieties of
greens, seeds, and roots. With that adaptation the populace shifted from a
meat-centered to a more vegetable-oriented diet, while also opening marine
resources to fuller exploitation.

Moreover, the pots enabled coastal people to evaporate seawater and
obtain salt, which they traded to groups living inland, thus enabling the latter
to offset any loss of dietary salt that accompanied their heavier reliance on
vegetable foods. This salt was only one of the items whose exchange enhanced
Jōmon well-being. As millennia passed, regional trade continued expanding in
both distance and volume, with people exchanging sea catch, other foodstuffs,
pottery, pigments, and diverse handicraft products that required some special
skill or raw material.

The custom of meat-eating persisted, however. As great mammals grew
scarce, hunters modified their tools to pursue the smaller, fleeter species,
notably bear, boar, and Japanese deer, which flourished in the archipelago's
mountainous terrain. They used hunting dogs, adopted bows and arrows for
the hunt, especially in northern Japan, and raised the pit-trapping of boar to
a fine art. They installed fish weirs in streams and employed harpoons as well
as nets and diverse hooks to catch fish, both inshore and off. Fishing was
made easier by the rise in sea level, which lined the islands with innumerable shallow, silt-bottomed, nutrient-rich inlets, as in the reconstruction
(figure 2.4) of the Kantō coastline, ca. 6,000 years ago.

Under these more favorable circumstances, the human population grew,
especially in central and northeastern Japan. Evidence reveals a striking
increase in the number and size of human settlements, with individual hamlets coming to number a half dozen households or considerably more.
Although there is no reliable way to determine total numbers because the
archaeological evidence is so limited, by one highly tentative estimate,
Japan's population rose to some 22,000 people as of 8,000 years ago and
260,000 by 4,500 years ago.

Some, at least, of these larger settlements had houses laid out in a circular
pattern around a central space that was devoted to shared needs, such as
burial sites for family members or pits for food storage. Besides dwellings,
these hamlets came to include raised storage buildings and, in a few instances,
large structures that may have accommodated some sort of community ceremonial function or signified the presence of a dominating figure.

Figure 2.3 Middle Jōmon pottery. Jōmon pottery styles changed as the centuries passed, and style also varied by region. But Jōmon ware of all times and places showed a delight in lush design, pieces being richly decorated with clay appliqué. *Source*: Imamura Keiji, *Prehistoric Japan, New Perspectives on Insular East Asia* (Honolulu: UHP, 1996), p. 99.

Population growth also led to expansion in the quality and quantity of handmade housing. Caves and rock shelters were relegated to secondary functions, and the rude surface huts of late paleolithic culture gave way to much larger and more substantial pit dwellings whose thatched roofs were

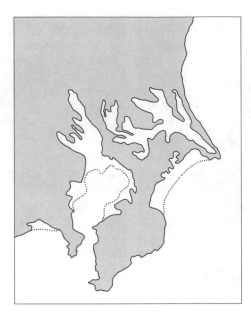

Figure 2.4 Kantō shoreline, ca. 6,000 YBP. On the basis of shell midden sites, archaeologists envisage the Kantō shoreline, during the postglacial sea-level maximum, as intruding well into the Kantō plain, nearly severing the Bōsō Peninsula from Honshu proper. *Source*: Imamura Keiji, *Prehistoric Japan, New Perspectives on Insular East Asia* (Honolulu: UHP, 1996), p. 69.

supported by sturdy posts set well into the ground. Floors commonly rested about a half-meter below ground level, giving occupants more shelter from wind and cold. And the size of houses, commonly three meters or more in diameter, permitted indoor cooking and storage. Recent excavation work along the Sea of Japan littoral has revealed the presence some 4,000 years ago of buildings with raised floors and more rugged framing, which may betray the presence of immigrant groups.[2]

These improvements in housing were accompanied by a proliferation of possessions: besides diverse pots and stone tools, there were wooden bowls, lacquered containers, combs, needles, earrings and other body ornaments, and clothing made of textiles (hemp and ramie) as well as animal skin. Ceremonial practices also seem to have grown more elaborate. Many clay figurines and stone implements betray an interest in sexuality and reproduction and probably in magical protection against the risks of childbirth, illness, and death (figure 2.5).

In all these matters there was regional variation, with artifacts differing by region and trends being more pronounced in some areas than others. These regional variations were grounded most basically in climatic differences between northeast and southwest, but also, it appears, in ethnic diversity that reflected ingress of different groups at different times from the Sakhalin and Kyushu land bridges. They were given added complexity by the emergence of trade arrangements, such as those that linked occupants of the Chūbu highlands to people on the Kantō lowlands.

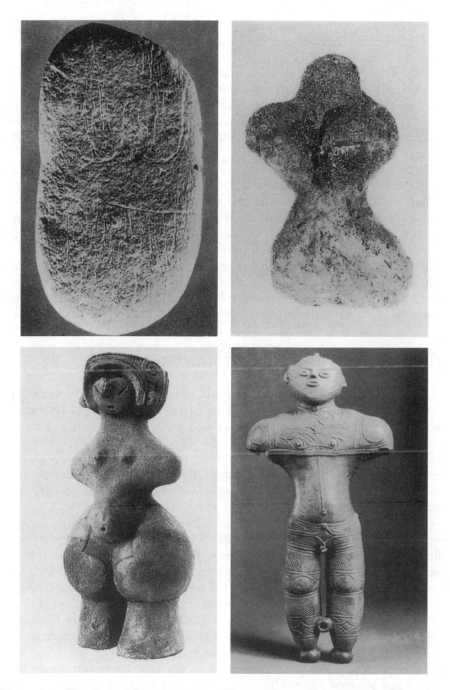

Figure 2.5 Figurines, early-to-late Jōmon. These representations of female figures suggest that Jōmon people practiced rituals to facilitate reproduction and childbirth. Starting with simple outlines scratched on small stones (upper left), they developed into eleborate clay figurines by late Jōmon (lower right). *Source*: Imamura Keiji, *Prehistoric Japan, New Perspectives on Insular East Asia* (Honolulu: UHP, 1996), p. 100.

Such variations notwithstanding, this later forager culture had its limits. Skeletal remains indicate that even during the Jōmon heyday people faced periodic famine, and they commonly died in their thirties. By 4,500 years ago a renewed decline in global temperature was worsening the situation by producing a slow southward and shoreward migration of vulnerable plant and animal species. In intermontane areas of central Japan, where the earlier population growth had been particularly pronounced, conifers displaced nut-producing trees and other broadleaf growth, reducing both the edible vegetable supply and the mammal population it sustained.

As deer and bear became scarce, hunters took more and more small game and immature specimens, but the deepening adversity still forced survivors to abandon interior settlements and relocate to the coast, where maritime food was available. That movement, which may well have generated considerable conflict among communities, led to more intensive exploitation of both marine and coastal life, including fishing on the open sea and the harvest of wild grains and other edible pioneer species that spread over lowlands newly exposed by receding seas. Under these deteriorating conditions the demographic trend seems to have reversed, in central Japan at least, and the population declined, by one estimate, to some 160,000 as of 3,300 years ago.

THE EMERGENCE OF AGRICULTURE

About 3,000–2,500 years ago insular and continental lines of development converged in Japan to start propelling the islanders into an era of agriculture-based civilization. The consumption of wild grain was not new, and the use of fire to modify natural vegetation also appears to trace back to earlier millennia. However, beyond this incipient form of slash-and-burn culture, agriculture in the full sense of purposefully breaking soil, scattering seed, and nurturing the sprouts to grow crops of choice appears to date from about these centuries.

The hardship induced by late Jōmon climatic cooling evidently prompted more and more people to practice simple nurturing of wild grains or other plants that yielded desired fruit, seeds, leaves, roots, or stems: one list includes gourds, beans, *shiso*, *egoma*, hemp, mulberry, colza, burdock, and peach.[3] Doing so entailed bothersome chores, but as people became familiar with the techniques, they evidently concluded that, given the choices facing them, the advantages of cropping outweighed the bother. And in Kyushu, it appears, people began clearing land to grow grain, namely buckwheat and barley, which probably was of continental origin.

Subsequently, in the face of a new warming trend that began re-submerging coastal lowland some 2,500 years ago (500 BCE), the islanders opened more and more inland patches to tillage. In the process they began expanding the portion of the archipelago subject to exploitation by their emergent human-centered biological community, inadvertently putting pressure on other species, thereby starting a trend that has continued down to the present.

At about the same time people in northwest Kyushu began learning about wet-rice cultivation through the introduction of hardy varieties of short-grain rice (*Oryza sativa japonica*), which almost certainly were brought by migrants from peninsular Korea. The character and scale of this in-migration is unclear, but it had profound social and political ramifications, as we note in the next chapter. Suffice here to observe that rice culture, which was present in today's Fukuoka region by about 400 BCE, spread eastward thereafter. It became established at coastal sites all along the Sea of Japan coast, spread through the Inland Sea and beyond as far as the Nōbi Plain, and moved somewhat more slowly from there into central Japan's deciduous woodlands.

The irrigation technique of this Yayoi rice culture varied according to site, with cultivators of swampy areas simply employing drainage ditches to remove excess water whereas those working more elevated fields used both intake canals and outlet drains, as detailed in figure 2.6. As long as appropriate land was ample, comparatively simple methods of paddy tillage, along with other forms of intermittent dry-field cultivation, appear to have prevailed. Villagers also started keeping domesticated pigs, thereby giving themselves another relatively dependable source of food. The labor requirements of this agricultural work were sufficiently modest so that the elderly, women, and children could handle much of the work, perhaps allowing able-bodied

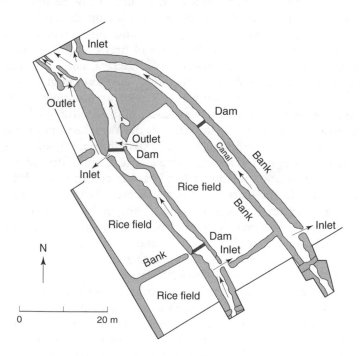

Figure 2.6 Early Yayoi rice fields. At this low-lying, early-Yayoi site in northwest Kyushu a comparatively complex system of canals, dams, paddy-field walls, and water intakes and outlets was employed to achieve optimum levels of paddy flooding. *Source*: Imamura Keiji, *Prehistoric Japan, New Perspectives on Insular East Asia* (Honolulu: UHP, 1996), p. 136.

adult males to pursue hunting or other traditional "manly" activities. And foraging activity continued to provide significant amounts of food, with products of the hunt richly supplemented by acorns, other nuts, tubers, and various other wild plant foods.

The yield from this mixed system of provisioning enabled the archipelago's human population to grow again, rising from the postulated 160,000 in ca. 1,300 BCE, or perhaps even fewer a few centuries later, to an estimated 600,000 to 1,000,000 by 0 CE.[4] As population grew, however, accessible wild food supplies became ever less adequate and reliance on cultigens proportionally greater. When easily irrigable fields or land naturally wet enough for rice production became difficult to locate, tillers used more and more dikes, ditches, and dams to bring water to more elevated fields. Also, by the third century CE, if not earlier, tillers were starting to improve their yield by transplanting rice seedlings from seedbed into paddy field in more orderly and weedable rows. In this more labor-intensive form, which increased both output per hectare and reliability of harvest, rice cropping seems to have demanded the attention of nearly all able-bodied community members, at least seasonally. As a corollary, it reduced the importance of forager activity, giving the Japanese countryside the basic agricultural character it would retain for a millennium.

The productivity of this agricultural regimen was enhanced by the iron tools that came with it. Iron blades and points made cutting tasks much easier; iron tips made wooden hoes and spades much more durable and efficient. Iron axes, chisels, drills, planes, and other woodworking tools greatly facilitated land clearance, lumber and firewood production, and the creation of wooden paddy-field walls, tools, buckets, and other implements. These iron tools came from the continent in finished form or else they were cast from imported pig iron. The quantities in service were severely limited due to scarcity and consequent high cost, but because of their indisputable advantages, their use gradually spread across the realm as the Yayoi centuries advanced.

By late Yayoi a mixed agriculture that consisted primarily of paddy culture but included unirrigated rice-field tillage, intermittent dry-field cropping, and slash-and-burn was spread widely across the country from Kyushu eastward to Tōhoku. In broadest terms lower, wetter, flatter areas were planted to rice while drier areas, such as alluvial fans and terrace deposits, grew buckwheat and other crops. More mountainous areas were used for slash-and-burn, fuel wood, building material, and diverse wild food supplies. In the far northeast, however, reliance on foraging and simpler forms of cultivation continued to prevail until 1,000 CE or later.

This southwestern system of mixed agriculture supported a growing population of cultivators who were dispersed about the countryside in small communities and scattered households as topography dictated. Because so much upland area was too steep for cultivation, the bulk of the populace settled on and around the alluvial plains, giving Japan the overall pattern of human occupancy that has persisted down to the present.

Yayoi hamlets generally contained only a few more houses than did Jōmon, but settlements proliferated, with new ones arising as more areas were opened to cultivation. As time passed, their occupants relied less on storage pits and more on elevated storehouses for preserving the harvest, while simple shaft wells gave them more reliable supplies of water for drinking and household use. Their dwellings retained the basic character of Jōmon antecedents, but they were larger, generally five to seven meters across, and more comfortable. Local notables had significantly more elegant dwellings, with raised wooden floors and with posts and planking more carefully fitted by carpenters.

Other items of daily life also changed. Iron needles facilitated the sewing of clothes, with the better social classes enjoying woven garments of silk and hemp while most people continued to clothe themselves in ramie. The ornately decorated pottery of high Jōmon gave way to a simpler style of earthenware whose thinner, smoother walls were decorated with incised lines rather than cord markings and clay appliqué. By late Yayoi this pottery was increasingly the product of professional potters.

Regarding spiritual life, it seems likely that hamlet practice retained much of its Jōmon character, although immigrants surely added new elements. It is difficult to say, however, because, as we note in the next chapter, Yayoi society became increasingly stratified, and more and more of the archaeological record reflected elite practice rather than that of ordinary villagers. How similar the two were is unclear.

By 250 CE the centuries of low-intensity tillage were transforming the archipelago's landscape by opening many scattered areas of lowland to sunlight. Cultivation was creating new or bigger niches for some species of plants and animals, but it was driving others out of preferred habitats, doubtless causing some unrecorded extinctions and reducing other populations by forcing creatures to survive in less favorable circumstances.

Far more visible were the changes affecting human society, which was experiencing substantial and continuing growth. As the next chapter notes, regional and overseas trade and travel were expanding dramatically. And social stratification was becoming much more pronounced in conjunction with the rise of a privileged political elite and, in the outcome, the formation of a centrally controlled polity, the *ritsuryō* order, with its associated aristocratic culture.

Part II

The Age of Dispersed Agriculturalists
(400 BCE–1250 CE)

Introduction to Part II

The agricultural regimen that became established in Japan during the centuries after about 400 BCE can be characterized as non-intensive, to distinguish it from the much more intensive regimen that took shape from the thirteenth century onward. Or it can be called an era of dispersed agriculturalists, on the basis of its relatively scattered, low density settlement patterns, as distinct from the larger, more densely settled villages that accompanied the rise of intensive agriculture.

This era of dispersed agriculturalists, the third of the five historical "phases" mentioned in the Introduction, consisted in turn of two stages, growth and stasis. During the first, which lasted for a millennium or more until about 700 CE, immigrants kept arriving from the continent, and the archipelago's population, cultivated acreage, commerce, and scale of social organization and activity all grew substantially, with the growth in agricultural output proving sufficient to support a swelling number of local rulers and attendant personnel.

These local rulers were present in northern Kyushu by the third century BCE or earlier and in the Kinai region a couple of centuries later. As their numbers grew, they struggled with one another for control of the producer population, and the more successful among them gradually extended their sway over nearby localities. In the process they became more sharply stratified and were drawn into regional confederations and contests and even overseas entanglements. By the early 700s the victors in this process had established a stabilized, statute-based aristocratic political order headquartered in the Kinai Basin (see map 10),[1] an order known by historians as the *ritsuryō seido* or "system of penal and civil codes." Through it they regularly funneled tribute to their Kinai headquarters from all across the region between Kyushu and the Kantō, but mainly from producers in central Honshu.

The era of stasis that emerged with this political consolidation was thus characterized by centralized rule. However, *ritsuryō* rulers made very few changes in the systems of agriculture and village life that they had inherited, in essence settling for institutional modifications that enhanced tribute extraction. They relied primarily on the Kinai Basin for the timber and other materials that formed and sustained their cities, palaces, and mansions, as well as their Buddhist temples and Shintō shrines (or fanes, to employ a term for religious institutions that, although archaic, is blessedly concise and wonderfully apt). And they drew most of the food for their urban populace from nearby regions. On this material basis a very small, very privileged elite elaborated an elegant higher culture of arts and letters whose accomplishments command respect among the cognoscenti even today.

By the eleventh century human exploitation had stripped the Basin of its old-growth forests and damaged enough soil in the metropolitan region so that the ruling elite, given the limits of its political and material technology, was unable to maintain the level of resource extraction essential to its urban civilization. Heian, the capital city, decayed; the tone of elite cultural production became more somber and conflictive, and as competition for scarce resources grew more intense, disputes became more acrimonious, and political order weakened. For several generations aristocratic leaders staved off the worst by making strategic adaptations that accommodated shifts in power, but during the later thirteenth century Japan's ruling classes entered a season of violence and warfare that ended the age of non-intensive agriculture and the *ritsuryō* order it had sustained.

Before turning our attention to the human history of dispersed agriculture, let us adumbrate the changing character of the human–environment relationship.

The early centuries of land clearance and low-intensity tillage altered the archipelago's biotic composition and, by opening many scattered areas of lowland to sunlight, transformed the landscape's appearance. More worrisome ecological consequences appeared with the introduction of the *ritsuryō* system during the seventh and eighth centuries, as chapter 4 notes more fully. In essence the adoption of Chinese architectural practices and the creation of a succession of densely populated capital cities in the Kinai Basin led to deforestation of the basin, frequent eruption of wildfires that swept through areas of recently created scrub growth, and erosion, gradual degrading of soils, and downstream flooding. Urban construction tapered off sharply after the early 800s, however, and during the next two centuries decay of the imperial regime and decline in the size and opulence of Heian eased human pressure on the Kinai ecosystem.

Cumulatively, as pollen counts reveal, these centuries of logging, land clearance, and spreading agriculture altered in basic ways the archipelago's mix of floral species. Tillers replaced large areas of biologically diverse, old-growth forest with monoculture fields, which soon became exhausted and reverted to brush growth while the depleted soil revived. These changes did not necessarily constitute general ecological deterioration, however; historical records show that enough game animals survived, mostly in less developed regions, so that diverse hides, horn, and other usable animal parts showed up in the marketplaces of Heian.

Given the size of Japan's population and the extent of habitat change, some local biotic communities surely were lost, and some unrecorded extinctions may have occurred. The decline in marketing of animal pelts late in the Heian period may well reflect their growing scarcity. Nevertheless, the principal game animals – deer, boar, and bear – survived into the twentieth century. That outcome can perhaps be attributed in some degree to Buddhist injunctions against killing animals, but the effectiveness of such injunctions among the rural populace as a whole, especially in times of famine, is highly problematic.

Even in the absence of such a doctrinal factor, the conversion of old-growth conifer areas to intermittent arable may on balance have increased species diversity and biomass production by increasing the acreage in fast-growing brush and other deciduous pioneer growth that could feed and shelter both game animals and smaller creatures. In addition, given the tortuous configuration of lowland in the islands, land clearance created miles and miles of forest edge, which provided an environment favorable to faunal diversity. And finally, because so much of Japan is precipitous mountains, most of the realm remained forested in any case, and hence much of the ecosystem remained intact, even though lumbering, hunting, and wildfire did make inroads on it.

If, indeed, these *ritsuryō* centuries of non-intensive agriculture were environmentally benign – beyond the Kinai Basin at least – one reason surely is that overall human demand on the ecosystem expanded relatively little. Living conditions of the general public, and hence the level of material consumption, remained essentially unchanged, and the demands of the ruling elite grew only modestly following the initial surge that accompanied formation of the *ritsuryō* system. In addition the near-stability in demand per capita was matched after 700 CE by near-stability in the numbers being sustained.

There was some regional variation in demographics: the Kantō grew appreciably more populous, but northeast Japan remained sparsely settled, perhaps because the known varieties of rice did poorly there, which helped sustain the appeal of older semi-agricultural arrangements. Nor was population growth out of control in the western and central regions where agriculture was well established. The development of large cities, an extensive tribute and transportation system, and sustained contact with the continent enabled disease organisms, notably the smallpox virus, to appear frequently in these regions. The existing pattern of dispersed rural residence seems, however, to have prevented people from routinely transmitting such pathogens to one another, so general immunities did not develop. Instead, when travelers from the continent brought disease to the islands, epidemics erupted along travel routes and took many lives, serving as a cruel but effectual brake on population growth. In consequence the slow and irregular rise in human population that non-intensive agriculture made possible could be accommodated by an expansion of cultivated territory that occurred gradually enough to give many threatened species time to migrate or adjust their niches, leaving most of Japan's indigenous biosystem intact outside the Kinai Basin.

Chronology of Part II

ca. 400 BCE ff	Rice culture in northwest Kyushu.
ca. 100 BCE–250 CE	Yoshinogari flourishes.
ca. 200–400 CE	Rise of local polities.
238	Himiko despatches mission to headquarters of Wei Dynasty.
ca. 390–410	Wa forces in Korea; repulsed by Koguryŏ.
421	"Ts'an of Wa" recognized by Liu Sung emperor.

ca. 400–500	Heyday of gigantic keyhole tomb construction.
ca. 510–571	Keitai and Kinmei head Yamato regime; Soga gain power.
592–628	Suiko heads Yamato regime.
ca. 600–700	Century of reform eventuates in *ritsuryō* system.
645	Taika coup.
660s	Japanese armada routed by Silla-T'ang forces; Silla unifies Korea.
672	Jinshin Disturbance; Tenmu triumphs.
710s	Genmei *tennō* builds Nara.
720	*Nihon shoki* compiled.
730s	Great smallpox epidemic.
740s	Shōmu *tennō* commences Tōdaiji construction.
759	*Man'yōshū* published.
794	Kanmu *tennō* designates Heian as imperial capital.
ca. 810–830	Saichō and Kūkai introduce Tendai and Shingon teachings.
ca. 890–1050	Heyday of Northern Fujiwara regents.
905	*Kokinshū* published.
ca. 990–1020	Murasaki Shikibu flourishes.
1053	Fujiwara no Yorimichi erects Phoenix Hall of Byōdōin.
1086–1129	Shirakawa dominant as retired emperor.
ca. 1150s ff	Scroll paintings proliferate.
1180s	Genpei wars and Minamoto no Yoritomo founds Kamakura *bakufu*.
ca. 1200ff	Hōjō regents become dominant.
ca. 1200–1250	Shinran and others promote Amidist Buddhism.

[3] *Political Consolidation to 671 CE*

CHAPTER SYNOPSIS

CONTINENTAL INFLUENCES

MATERIAL FOUNDATIONS

THE STRUGGLE FOR HEGEMONY
THE RISE OF A CENTRAL POLITY
STABILIZING CENTRAL CONTROL

From the outset Japan's agricultural order was strongly shaped by continental influences. The immigrants who introduced rice culture also brought iron and bronze tools and other paraphernalia, as well as levels of community organization, social hierarchy, military know-how, and political conflict that greatly exceeded those of Jōmon society. As generations passed, the complicated interaction of immigrants, their progeny, and the descendants of longer-established indigenous households eventuated in the rise of a consolidated polity centered in the Kinai but dominant from Kyushu to the Kantō. That polity, which was sustained by the agricultural production of its subject people, was continually engaged in complex dealings with peripheral peoples and continental regimes. And its rise was marked by even more continual struggle among domestic rivals for power and prestige.

CONTINENTAL INFLUENCES

By seven or eight thousand years ago rice culture was being practiced in central China and dry-field tillage farther north. As millennia passed, the practices became widespread, local political entities arose, and by about 3,000 years ago (1,000 BCE) political leaders were able to impose a weakly unified regime, the Chou dynasty, on much of the realm. By then agricultural practice was also established on the Korean Peninsula, and a low level of trade and contact existed between people on both sides of the Korea Strait.

Maritime contact between Kyushu and the mainland intensified in following centuries as China's warfare engulfed Korea. Conflicts that accompanied political change – Chou decay and collapse, the creation of the Han dynasty

in 206 BCE, its subsequent vicissitudes, and the related disorder that con-
vulsed the Korea–Manchuria region off and on into the fourth century CE –
all produced surges of disorder and migration that repeatedly spilled into
Japan. Most of the movement was directed toward Kyushu, but whether by
choice or because of wind and water currents that sweep northeastward along
the Sea of Japan coast, migrants settled all along Honshu's western coastline,
mostly on the San'in littoral but some even north of Noto Peninsula.

Archaeological finds indicate that by 200 BCE Kyushu contained settlements that were sustained by wet-rice production, protected from hostile
outsiders by moats and embankments, and controlled by local leaders who
enjoyed superior housing and burial treatment. As centuries passed, communities of this sort became established all across Japan at least as far as the
Kantō: *vide* the hilltop settlement of Ōtsuka, near present-day Yokohama
(figure 3.1).

The distinctive characteristics of these fortified sites gradually became
more pronounced. They became larger; their moats multiplied, becoming
wider and deeper; wooden palisades and watch towers were added; and the
homes and burial sites of local magnates became more elegant. Moreover,
evidence from excavations betrays the proliferation of warfare. Growing
numbers of weapons appear – swords, arrowheads, and halberds – together
with skeletons displaying wounds and dismemberment. And metal weapons
increasingly displaced those made of stone. It is also noteworthy that the
moat-making activity appears to have occurred in surges, the timing in
Kyushu and Kinai differing until late Yayoi. This pattern suggests that the
fortification work occurred during periods of political turmoil and that until
late Yayoi such turmoil was largely local or at most regional in extent.

The character of the immigrant–indigene relationship is difficult to ascertain because of the limited evidence. The issue has been further complicated
by its deep entanglement in twentieth-century ethnic politics. From the
limited evidence available, however, it seems best to envisage a variety of
relationships, with immigrants in some situations dominating nearby local
folk, in others being dominated by them, at some sites inhabiting quite clearly
segregated communities, at others developing reasonably amicable working
and exchange relationships. Furthermore, several considerations – the centuries of time the process involved, the continental disorder that marked
those centuries, the tendency of immigrants to scatter rather than settle
"among their own," and the limited evidence of an overwhelming impact on
the indigenes – make it seem likely that the immigrants, though predominantly
Korean, were of diverse origins and ethnic and political affiliations.

In any case, as generations passed, the differences became blurred, and
links to "the old country" or old culture grew weak, were forgotten, or
became romanticized. Pottery types, burial practices, economic arrangements, and patterns of community organization lost their distinctiveness and
a common language prevailed. Fossil DNA evidence suggests the gradual
integration of indigenous and immigrant populations.[1] As one would expect,
given the proximity of Kyushu to Korea, genetic material and its phenotypic
expression in skeletal dimensions reveal much more Korean influence

Figure 3.1 Hilltop settlement site: Ōtsuka. At this defensible site near present-day Yokohama a substantial community of posthole-and-thatch-roof pit-dwellings clustered within the confines of a protective moat. Some house sites overlap others because new houses were built where earlier ones had once stood. *Source*: Imamura Keiji, *Prehistoric Japan, New Perspectives on Insular East Asia* (Honolulu: UHP, 1996), p. 181.

in Kyushu than farther east, where immigrants constituted a much smaller portion of the total population.

The spread of agriculture into Japan fostered continental exchange as well as migration. Most essentially, metal, whether in the form of weapons, tools, and ceremonial items, or in the form of ingots for use by insular metal casters, came from Korea. In addition, diverse other finished goods, including cloth, body ornaments, coins, and most famously Chinese bronze mirrors, were imported. In its entirety the regional exchange extended southward along the Ryukyu Islands, north across Japan to Hokkaido, and westward into China and northeast Asia.

The continental connections also acquired a political dimension. Evidence from burial artifacts as well as from the *Hou Hanshū*, a first-century Chinese source, suggest that a few local magnates in Kyushu (who may well have been recent immigrants or their descendants) were sending diplomatic delegations, "tribute missions" in terminology of the day, to the Han dynasty's outpost of Lolang in northern Korea. Two centuries later, unambiguous records report similar missions in the years just before 250 CE. Later generations of political figures maintained relations with one or another continental regime, using the connections for trade and legitimation. Thus the *Sungshū*, a later dynastic history, records that during the 470s the ruler "Bu" (the Kinai magnate Yūryaku of Japanese accounts) presented himself as a mighty but distant chieftain who sought the Liu Sung emperor's support for his schemes of conquest, specifically requesting the emperor to appoint him

> supreme commander of the campaign, with the status of minister, and to grant to others [among my followers] rank and titles, so that loyalty may be encouraged.[2]

The emperor, having other diplomatic obligations, only awarded Bu part of what he sought, but that part placed him on a par with Korean rulers of the day. In return the emperor presumably acquired a supportive politico-military subordinate.

During the next two centuries continental influence continued pouring into Japan. Immigrants provided expertise on matters political, military, and technological. They brought ideas about political authority and organization along with religious creeds and practices, most notably Buddhism, which was introduced during the sixth century and became well entrenched during the seventh. Finally, and perhaps most importantly, they introduced literacy, and during the seventh and eighth centuries writing in the Chinese manner with its associated arts and letters became normative among males in the ruling elite of the emergent *ritsuryō* regime.

MATERIAL FOUNDATIONS

This emerging political elite was sustained by the general populace, and it could expand only because of growth in society as a whole. The estimated population of a million or fewer in 0 CE rose to some 5,000,000 by 700 CE. A portion were immigrants, but most were the result of domestic fecundity, the offspring of Jōmon descendants and more recent immigrants, social categories that lost their distinctiveness as time passed.

This population was spread across the realm in hamlets that commonly numbered about five to ten houses and 50–75 residents. The settlements that developed into fortified bastions would, of course, grow much larger, numbering hundreds or perhaps one to two thousand people by the end of Yayoi. Supported in part by their role as trade entrepôts, such bastions also derived tribute from nearby hamlets, many of which were branch settlements that they had established by despatching people to cultivate newly opened land.

The most celebrated example of development from hamlet to bastion is Yoshinogari, situated a few kilometers inland from the Ariake Sea in Kyushu. Its growth from a small cluster of settlements to a powerful regional headquarters has been skillfully reconstructed by archaeologists (see figure 3.2). As of 200 BCE inhabitants of the Yoshinogari locality were sustained by a mixed economy of foraging and agriculture, but they gradually gave up hunting and in later generations concentrated on cultivation. Skeletal remains suggest that during this period an immigrant group established itself locally at a defensible site and, as decades passed, extended its control over surrounding hamlets, in part at least through conquest and escalating warfare with rival magnates in the vicinity. As this process unfolded, stone weapons and tools gave way to iron, and moats, walls, watch towers, weapons, and evidence of violent death proliferated. Concurrently members of Yoshinogari's elite enjoyed more and more comforts and luxuries, many of which came to them via trade with the Ryukyus and the continent. By the final century BCE the bastion's magnates were being interred in a large burial mound (*funkyūbō*), a technique that subsequently appeared elsewhere in Japan, and the local pre-eminence of Yoshinogari's rulers persisted at least into the second century CE.

Figure 3.2 A partial reconstruction of Yoshinogari. As envisioned by archaeologists, the long-lived settlement at Yoshinogari eventually acquired moats, raised storage buildings, a substantial settlement, extensive burial areas, and a walled central citadel with watch towers from which any approaching enemy could be observed and countered. *Source*: Richard J. Pearson, *Ancient Japan* (NY: George Braziller, 1992), p. 157.

Not only at large sites such as Yoshinogari, but more generally too, hamlet life changed as the centuries of political consolidation advanced. Ordinary dwellings reflected growing economic disparities. Among dry fields, which were less productive than paddy land, houses continued to be built in the pit-dwelling style and tended to be smaller; those near rice paddies were larger. And the grandest houses, those of the local elite, were equipped with raised, wooden floors and gradually came to include more nearby storage sheds and other outbuildings as well as gates and fences that delineated boundaries of the household plot.

Many aspects of this stratifying society are revealed by the "Commentary on the People of Wa," or *Wajinden* in Japanese pronunciation, a Chinese account of ca. 280–297 CE that appears to describe conditions a few decades earlier.[3] *Wajinden*'s compiler lacked the political and geographical knowledge necessary to record clearly the location of Wa, but the identifiable referents suggest that his information was based primarily on observations of life in the Hakata Bay vicinity of northwest Kyushu. And that area may in fact have been the heartland of the shadowy realm of Wa that seems to have flourished during the two or three centuries prior to 350 CE or so. Archaeological evidence suggests, however, that most *Wajinden* observations probably would have applied elsewhere as well, at least from the Kantō westward.

Wajinden does not always make clear which of its comments apply to common folk and which to their leaders. Insofar as social inequalities did exist, however, one suspects that continental observers would mostly have associated with the more favored classes and based the more intimate parts of their reports on observations of them. In any case, we are told that

> The land of Wa is warm and mild. In winter as in summer the people live on vegetables and go about barefooted. Their houses have rooms; father and mother, elder and younger, sleep separately. They smear their bodies with pink and scarlet, just as the Chinese use powder. They serve meat on bamboo and wooden trays, helping themselves with their fingers.
>
> The men wear a band of cloth around their heads, exposing the top. Their clothing is fastened around the body with little sewing. The women wear their hair in loops. Their clothing is like an unlined coverlet and is worn by slipping the head through an opening in the center.

They appear to have been a productive people. They are, "fond of diving into the water to get fish and shells." Moreover, they

> cultivate grains, rice, hemp, and mulberry trees for sericulture. They spin and weave and produce fine linen and silk fabrics. There are no oxen, horses, [or] sheep…Taxes are collected. There are granaries as well as markets in each province, where necessaries are exchanged under the supervision of the Wa officials.

They also engaged in warfare. "Their weapons are spears, shields, and wooden bows made with short lower part and long upper part; and their bamboo arrows are sometimes tipped with iron or bone."

Successful warfare, it appears, led to conquest. In localities ("provinces") subject to a ruler from elsewhere, "there is a high official stationed especially to exercise surveillance over those provinces, so that they are kept in a state of awe and fear."

Chinese concepts of intra-family status distinctions were not observed, but people were scarcely treated as equals.

> In their meetings and in their deportment, there is no distinction between father and son or between men and women... Ordinarily, men of importance have four or five wives; the lesser ones, two or three... There are class distinctions among the people, and some men are vassals of others... When the lowly meet men of importance on the road, they stop and withdraw to the roadside. In conveying messages to them or addressing them, they either squat or kneel, with both hands on the ground. This is the way they show respect. When responding, they say "ah," which corresponds to the affirmative "yes."

Law and order were maintained.

> Women are not loose in morals or jealous. There is no theft, and litigation is infrequent. In case of violation of law, the light offender loses his wife and children by confiscation; as for the grave offender, the members of his household and also his kinsmen are exterminated.

The leaders of Wa sent embassies to China, we are told, and they did their best to assure success in such dangerous endeavours.

> Whenever they undertake an enterprise and discussion arises, they bake bones and divine in order to tell whether fortune will be good or bad. First they announce the object of divination, using the same manner of speech as in tortoise shell divination; then they examine the cracks made by the fire and tell what is to come to pass.

Besides utilizing such Chinese-like tactics for controlling the fates, they employed shamanistic devices to channel misfortune in tolerable directions.

> When they go on voyages across the sea to visit China, they always select a man who does not arrange his hair, does not rid himself of fleas, lets his clothing get as dirty as it will, does not eat meat, and does not approach women. This man behaves like a mourner and is known as the fortune keeper. When the voyage turns out propitious, they all lavish on him slaves and other valuables. In case there is disease or mishap, they kill him, saying that he was not scrupulous in his duties.

For the most powerful, as noted a bit earlier, there were wives. For the lowliest, slavery. As the passage above indicates, slaves were given domestically as payment for services rendered. They also were sent to China as a form of tribute.

The religious sensibility indicated above was evident elsewhere as well. "In their worship, men of importance simply clap their hands instead of kneeling or bowing." And for coping with death:

> When a person dies, they prepare a single coffin, without an outer one. They cover the graves with sand to make a mound. When death occurs, mourning is observed for more than ten days, during which period they do not eat meat. The head mourners wail and lament, while friends sing, dance, and drink liquor. When the funeral is over, all members of the whole family go into the water to cleanse themselves in a bath of purification.

All in all, our observer found much to admire in the land of Wa.

Items discovered in archaeological sites add to our understanding of the era. Pottery sherds reflect the economic disparities noted in *Wajinden* and also suggest the growing importance of trade. As noted in chapter 2, by late Yayoi pottery production was becoming a specialist's craft, and in following centuries most households came to use a standardized, reddish earthenware known as *hajiki* (Haji ware), which remained the daily-use ware of most people into the twelfth century. In addition, during the fifth century immigrants introduced a new type of pottery, *sueki* (Sue ware), a more highly fired, wheel-thrown stoneware. Produced by professionals using more elaborate equipment and more costly procedures, Sue ware was expensive and became the preferred ware of the ruling classes. So prized was it as a mark of status that despite the cost of replacement, pieces commonly accompanied the deceased in elite burials.

Perhaps the most striking technical change in domestic life was adoption of the *kamado* (figure 3.3), a small cooking stove of continental derivation whose use in Japan dates from about the fifth century. Whereas householders had previously cooked in an adjoining shed or on a hearth near the center of the house, venting smoke through openings in the peak of the roof, the user of a *kamado* placed it against the wall so its flue would vent smoke through a hole to the outdoors. He or she fed fuel into it through the arched opening in front and placed the food to be cooked in a container that nestled in the circular opening at its top. The *kamado* thus enhanced the quality of indoor air while making it easier to control cooking heat. It also improved fuel efficiency, which may have become increasingly important as headquarters settlements grew larger and land clearance eliminated nearby woodland.

It may be tempting to assume that women did the cooking, but in fact evidence regarding gender roles and relationships among the general public is extremely hard to come by. The *Wajinden*, as noted above, indicates that "men of importance have four or five wives; the lesser ones, two or three."[4] Other accounts from later centuries suggest that marriage was rather informal and non-binding in character.[5] Perhaps for that reason a bride commonly remained at her natal home, at least until her offspring were well into childhood and hence of enough value to their father so that he would welcome their presence. That practice may have been intended to protect children from neglect, but one consequence of it was that households tended to

Figure 3.3 A *kamado* (hearth and steamer) of Haji ware. The *kamado* provided an efficient, relatively unsmoky, cooking stove for the preparation of diverse foods and for heating water. Fuel wood was fed into the arched opening in front, heat rose beneath the pot inserted in the top hole, and smoke was vented out the house wall through a rear aperture (not shown). *Source*: C. Melvin Aikens and Takayasu Higuchi, *Prehistory of Japan* (San Diego: Academic Press, Inc., 1982) p. 302.

include more adult siblings. And inter-household relations were more fluid, which facilitated adaptation to fluctuations in household fortune.

Such adaptability was important because the shift to an agricultural base of existence had not come without cost, quite apart from intensified social inequality and political exploitation. Whereas the Jōmon forager system of sustenance had presented the risk of famine in a highly irregular way – depending on whether the acorn crop was good, boar fell to a viral epidemic, schools of fish migrated elsewhere for a time, or some other biotic disruption occurred – agriculture regularized the sequence of plenitude and dearth. It made late winter to early summer the normal period of hardship, with the intensity and duration of this "spring hunger" depending essentially on the prior year's harvest.

Yayoi villagers tried to minimize the risk of spring hunger by growing diverse crops and continuing to hunt and gather. As population grew, however, arable land expanded at the expense of woodland, and more complex systems of irrigation had to be developed and maintained. In consequence the availability of wild foods declined and there was less free time to gather them. Moreover, as ruling elites waxed powerful, they were able to commandeer tribute more effectively, and insofar as they engaged in competitive displays of power and prestige, they were encouraged to maximize their level of expropriation.

In consequence of these trends, as the centuries of political consolidation advanced, spring hunger became a customary condition. The elite rarely faced it directly, but it threatened them indirectly because it could kill and incapacitate the producers who supported them and because famished villagers had compelling reason to eat any rice or other food at hand, which meant consuming seed needed to start the new year's crop. To assure themselves the tribute income that a rice crop would provide, local and regional magnates developed, perhaps in late Yayoi and probably from continental precedents, the practice of loaning seed rice (*suiko*), as well as emergency foodstuffs and tools, to poorer villagers. Doing so assured themselves a modest interest income as well as tribute from the new crop. By the eighth century *suiko* had developed into a regular policy of *ritsuryō* leaders, a policy that combined usury with the appearance of benevolent rule in a way that helped sustain the agricultural production necessary to elite privilege.

THE STRUGGLE FOR HEGEMONY

The process of creating a centralized polity in Japan consumed centuries of time. In broad outline, the years to 500 CE or so passed before a clearly preeminent regime was established, and the generations from then until 671 were consumed by the task of stabilizing the exercise of power within that regime.

THE RISE OF A CENTRAL POLITY

The politics of Wa. By late Yayoi local regimes, such as that of the Yoshinogari magnates, were scattered all across Japan. Their rules of authority and instruments of control are not clear today, but *Wajinden* speaks of decades of warfare in Wa that continued until

> the people agreed upon a woman for their ruler. Her name was Pimiko. She occupied herself with magic and sorcery, bewitching the people. Though mature in age, she remained unmarried. She had a younger brother who assisted her in ruling the country. After she became the ruler, there were few who saw her. She had one thousand women as attendants, but only one man.

> He served her food and drink and acted as a medium of communication. She
> resided in a palace surrounded by towers and stockades, with armed guards in a
> state of constant vigilance.[6]

Wajinden thus suggests, disapprovingly perhaps, both the importance of religious sanction in the exercise of power and the legitimacy of female leadership, at least in some communities. Whether the woman functioned mainly as a shaman or as a figure who fully combined sacred and secular power in her person is unclear, but she was protected by armed force.

As elsewhere in *Wajinden*, the veracity of specifics is problematic, but in the year 238, after Himiko (to use a more common reading of her name) acceded to office, her government did despatch an embassy via Korea to the headquarters of the Wei emperor, where her authority received proper Confucian sanction:

> Herein we address Pimiko, Queen of Wa, whom we now officially call a friend
> of Wei ... [Your ambassadors] have arrived here with your tribute, consisting of
> four male slaves and six female slaves, together with two pieces of cloth with
> designs, each twenty feet in length. You live very far away across the sea; yet
> you have sent an embassy with tribute. Your loyalty and filial piety we appreci-
> ate exceedingly. We confer upon you, therefore, the title "Queen of Wa
> Friendly to Wei," ... We expect you, O Queen, to rule your people in peace and
> to endeavor to be devoted and obedient.

Himiko is thus recorded as receiving the type of tributary status *vis-à-vis* Wei that was customary in Chinese diplomatic practice.

Doubtless Himiko and her lieutenants saw the relationship differently; at least they invoked it on their own behalf when dealing with other magnates. Specifically, by the year 247, Himiko's government was at odds with the "king" of the "country of Kunu," which reportedly lay to the south of Wa, and Himiko solicited imperial support for her cause. The outcome of her effort is unclear, but after she died, probably in the following year,

> a king was placed on the throne, but the people would not obey him.
> Assassination and murder followed; more than one thousand were thus slain.

With Wei approval a thirteen-year-old female relative of Himiko was then named queen and "order was restored."

For reasons having less to do with the ambiguities of *Wajinden* geography than with enduring issues of imperial legitimacy, local pride, and modern-day ethnic sensibility, the location of Himiko's headquarters, usually called Yamatai, has long been a topic of intense debate. In a larger sense, however, it matters little because by 250 CE magnates such as she and the "king" of Kunu were found in much of Japan. The late Yayoi warfare that spurred creation of fortified bastions and local polities occurred all across the country, and some archaeological evidence suggests that it was fostered or intensified by renewed climatic warming, which raised sea level enough to flood coastal paddy fields and settlements.[7] That trend, it is argued, forced cultivators to open more upland, and it pitted magnates against one another as they struggled to seize territories for development or to control new areas of production.

Whether driven by these or other considerations, magnates of the day created their bastions: places such as Yoshinogari and Ōtsuka on their defensible hillocks, the major moated fortress at Yao on the middle reaches of the Yamato River southeast of present-day Osaka, and the powerfully defended Karako to its east in the Yamato Basin. In due course some of these power holders extended their sway sufficiently to create regional hegemonies, most notably in Kyushu, Izumo, Kibi (the Okayama area), and the Kinai region. Himiko's regime, whether headquartered in northern Kyushu, the Kinai, or elsewhere, constituted one such regional hegemony.

As the scale of conflict grew, these local, militarized elites of the third-to-fourth centuries depended for continued success on their control of agricultural production, labor resources, sacral authority, and the equipment of war. Kinai leaders, particularly those in the Yamato Basin, had a key advantage because theirs was the richest agricultural area outside the Kantō, which was still largely forested. That superior resource base made it easier for them to extract more tribute and field larger armies. Concurrently, however, combatants developed greater dependence on iron tools and weapons and hence a greater need for reliable access to the main source of supply, which was in Korea.

That need for Korean iron spurred magnates in the Kinai region to use their greater power to expand westward along the Inland Sea and northern Kyushu, setting in motion a long process of inter-regional conflict and consolidation. It also meant that political developments in the Kinai region and Korean peninsula became entangled as never before, and evidence of that entanglement appears in both places, especially from about 400 CE onward.

During the preceding two centuries northern China had been politically fragmented while the Korean Peninsula was divided among three major regional regimes (Koguryŏ, Paekche, and Silla) and the smaller Kaya. Kaya was a cluster of semi-unified communities that maintained ties to leaders of Wa, ties that may well have involved kinship as well as trade and diplomacy. That political fragmentation fostered conflicts, and by the 350s, both the peninsula and archipelago were racked by political turmoil. During the next few decades that disorder produced recurrent conflict and diplomatic jockeying that spanned the Korea Strait.

By the 390s, it appears from Korean reports, forces of Wa, Kaya, and Paekche were collaborating against the sometimes-allied armies of Silla and Koguryŏ, but in a series of battles between 400 and 407, armies of the Koguryŏ king, Kwanggaet'ŏ routed their opponents, momentarily ending the contest for primacy in Korea. That Koguryŏ triumph evidently was a victory of mounted troops over foot soldiers, and it foreshadowed a major change in warfare and politics in the islands.

Whether the forces of Wa that were involved in this fighting actually came from the islands, or if they did, from where and under whose command, is unclear. The most plausible explanation may be that the leaders of a north Kyushu-centered regime were seeking to preserve useful ancestral connections, perhaps as a way to counter threats from Kinai power holders bent on gaining control over the route to Korea. With defeat in its Korean venture, however, the regime was more vulnerable than ever to conquest from the east. Alternatively, of course, a Kinai chieftain may already have established some sort of position in northern Kyushu and been the one to suffer at the hands of Koguryŏ.[8]

The Kinai's rise to pre-eminence. Surviving evidence does not solve this minor puzzle, but it does suggest that at about this time the political situation in Japan was beginning to change quite dramatically. An impressive body of data – burial mounds and their contents most notably, but also material from other sites and sources – illuminates the process of political consolidation during late Yayoi and following decades. Gaps and inconsistencies persist, but a story one can extract from this material suggests that by about 250–300 CE a Kinai power holder had established some sort of ceremonial suzerainty, probably an alliance system, with select magnates as far west as Kyushu. These arrangements may have proven transient, but later in the century magnates in the Yamato Basin waxed powerful, as evidenced by the ever more gigantic burial mounds (*kofun*) that mark their passage. They gained some level of continental connections, acquired metal, metal smiths, and other artisans, and exchanged goods with local chieftains across the realm from Kantō to Kyushu. They also began pursuing more aggressive policies of consolidation, seeking, it appears, not transient alliances but permanent hegemony.

Written versions of this Yamato story appear in the *Kojiki* and *Nihon shoki*, the two oldest extant Japanese political narratives, which were compiled around 700 CE for reasons discussed in the next chapter. Suffice here to note that what they treat as a chronology of the "imperial lineage" appears to have encompassed at one point an exceedingly shadowy local polity in the southwestern corner of the Yamato Basin near Mt. Katsuragi (Kazuraki) and much more certainly a later regime centered northeast of there at the foot of Mt. Miwa. Scholars adjust the *Nihon shoki*'s implausible chronology to date the former, the "Katsuragi court," to later Yayoi and the latter, the "Miwa court," to the century or more prior to about 350 CE.

From about that date, it appears, some Kinai figures, perhaps the Miwa chieftains, began projecting their power beyond the Yamato Basin. Employing an array of carrots and sticks – gifts, titles, assurances of privilege, religious honors, threats of punishment, and military assault as needed – they extended their control down the Yamato River and by late in the century across Kawachi to Naniwa and the shore of the Inland Sea. From there they deployed forces westward along the Sea, coopting and subduing rivals and eventually securing surer access to the continental sources of iron that equipped armies with up-to-date armor and swords and provided tools for opening and working more farm land.

This outward extension of Kinai influence is evident in the archaeological record. Most visibly, whereas the large tumuli of previous centuries had varied regionally in size, shape, and contents, as the fourth century advanced, a "keyhole-shaped" tumulus style that was first used in the Yamato Basin began to be employed by local magnates elsewhere, even as far away as Echizen and Izumo, and during the fifth century in the Kantō. As the use of keyhole tumuli spread, other elite burial styles disappeared and the contents of chiefly tombs acquired more commonality, coming to include "bronze mirrors, swords, and halberds; stone bracelets; beads; flint; and iron tools."[9]

Religion and diplomacy played key roles in the extension of this regime's influence. As generations passed, the god of Sumiyoshi, who was enshrined at the water's edge at Naniwa to protect seafarers en route to and from the west, acquired more and more new homes at additional shrines scattered along the sea route to Kyushu and Korea. Excavations show that this proliferation of Sumiyoshi shrines paralleled the spread of ceremonial gifts (select types of mirrors, jewels, and swords being the most widely known) that presumably signified the Yamato River regime's political linkage to local magnates along this crucial trade corridor.

Military and economic aspects of the story are also illuminated by archaeological evidence. It reveals that in the southern Yamato Basin immigrant craftsmen of the fifth century operated an iron-smelting, arms-producing industry to manufacture Korean-style swords. And it shows that such craftsmen produced Sue ware and other goods near the headquarters of these rulers, and that trade goods were stored in large warehouses there.

The dominant role of Yamato River hegemons in this socio-political integration is suggested most forcefully by the immense size of their greatest tombs, most famously those officially ascribed to the "emperors" Ōjin and Nintoku. It appears that the moated, 415-meter-long Kondayama tomb (Ōjinryō) was created, probably sometime after 400 CE, not by the older, relatively simple method of reshaping a hillock of diluvium and digging a shaft into it to place the burial materials, but by the vastly more laborious process of excavating an encircling moat, piling up hundreds of tons of soil in the moated area, and mounding it to the desired shape and height around the stone crypt and access tunnel. Not long afterward, or possibly somewhat before, the even more monumental, triple-moated, 486-meter-long Daisen (Nintokuryō) was erected in the same way on the coastal lowland south of Naniwa.

Giant tumuli of this sort, which were carefully shaped and then encircled with parallel lines of ceramic figurines (haniwa) and cylinders – some 20,000 of them at Daisen – appear to have served as sites for grand memorial services. They thus constituted permanent, awe-inspiring testaments to the glory of their occupants. Insofar as official tomb identifications are correct, the Yamato River chieftains who followed Nintoku also received grandiose interment, though less monumental in scale, presumably in keeping with their less monumental accomplishments.

Chinese records also illuminate these fifth-century developments. At the time of Kwanggaet'ŏ's victories in 400–407, the pre-eminent figure in the Kinai region appears to have been the chieftain we know as Nintoku. In 421, when Nintoku still seems to have been in power, the Sungshū reports that a certain "Ts'an of Wa" (Nintoku, one suspects) received diplomatic recognition from the newly established Liu Sung dynasty. He was the first of "five kings of Wa" so recognized. The last of the five was Bu (Yūryaku), whose formal reign dates are credibly given by *Nihon shoki* as 456–479 and who, as earlier noted, secured Wei's recognition as the status equal of Koguryŏ and Paekche leaders.

If, as seems plausible, Kwanggaet'ŏ's triumph badly weakened a Wa hegemon in northern Kyushu, thereby enabling Nintoku to extend Kinai control all the way to the Hakata region, that demise of the hoary Wa regime has been concealed by the continental practice of using the term Wa to identify Japan indiscriminately, which practice continued until late in the seventh century. The persistence of that usage may reveal that Kinai leaders simply were unable to change continental historiographical custom to reflect a new reality. Or they may have found it useful to retain the established diplomatic persona of "Wa." Indeed, they eventually appropriated an elevated form of that name to celebrate their grandeur, employing Chinese characters (*kanji*) that can be read *daiwa* or Great Wa to signify Yamato, their home territory. Whatever the reason, the persistent continental usage of the term Wa concealed changing insular political alignments, and it continues even today to bedevil scholarly attempts to sort them out.

The military lessons of Kwanggaet'ŏ's triumph gradually became visible in Japan as horses, horse gear, and associated armament were imported, reproduced, put to use, and prized as political gifts. By the 450s, it appears, Kinai magnates were engaging in mounted warfare, which permitted longer-distance campaigning and magnified the attacking force's capacity to terrorize those being overrun. Other magnates also adopted the technology when they could, and archaeological sites throughout the archipelago reveal the escalating arms race. The essential effect of mounted warfare was to expand signficantly the range and ferocity of warfare, in effect transforming Japan from a realm in which regional polities could coexist in mutual isolation into a single field of political action that had space only for winners and losers.

Emboldened, perhaps, by the offensive power that horse warfare gave him, around 450 one of the "kings of Wa" (Sai; presumably Ingyō) entered the military fray in Korea to uncertain effect. A few years later, according to *Sungshū*, Bu (Yūryaku) assumed the rulership, and under his energetic direction troops from Wa collaborated with Kaya, Paekche, and others in a decade or more of sporadic warfare, mostly against Koguryŏ. In 475, however, Koguryŏ armies again triumphed. They overran the Paekche capital, throwing the Wa troops into retreat and setting off a massive flow of refugees southward across the strait, and on to the Kinai vicinity. That rout ended another period of Japanese participation in Korea's civil wars, but it also brought rich new talent to the Kinai region.

In the outcome Yūryaku's court turned this newest Korean débâcle to advantage, its success reflected perhaps in his later reputation as a brutal tyrant. He put refugee groups to work opening land and constructing irrigation ponds and canals in Kawachi, Yamashiro, and Ōmi. Artisans produced their specialties, and officials from Paekche and other peninsular regimes provided valuable knowledge about government organization and operation, particularly in regard to land control and tribute collection. The court also continued to utilize those locally influential lineages that accepted its leadership, but it clarified and regularized their roles and relationships by requiring magnates to provide specified services in return for the right to administer and tax designated territories. These favored lineages became known as *uji*, their chiefs as *uji no kami*, and their household deities as *ujigami*.

Some of these *uji* stemmed from immigrants; others were of local ancestry. Unlike earlier magnates, however, they accepted more-or-less permanent roles as subordinates of the Yamato River regime. And their status and function were signified by Korean-type hereditary titles, *kabane* or "bone ranks." As decades passed and Yamato's control extended farther across the realm, its most trusted *uji* chiefs acquired more lands and villages to administer. To counter-balance those chiefs, Yūryaku and his successors also designated more and more clusters of agricultural hamlets as *miyake* or "crown lands." These were administered by appointees of the court who functioned essentially as petty bureaucratic tribute collectors. As the court expanded its realm, these policies enabled its leaders to utilize more and more local figures as well as immigrants and still keep them checkmated by the commensurately growing power of the center.

By 500 CE the Yamato River regime had established an unprecedented level of central control over local magnates from Kyushu to the Kantō. Its core Kinai region bustled with productive activities of diverse sorts, and it was accepted by continental rulers as a regime on a par with those in Korea and the only bona fide government of Japan. Southern Kyushu and Tōhoku lay beyond its reach, and it had not yet fully subdued rulers in the Izumo region, where a tradition of local autonomy traced back centuries. Growing pressure from the Kinai notwithstanding, Izumo magnates maintained their trade links to Kibi and Kyushu, and they continued to practice their own sacral traditions. Within a few years, however, they too were destined to be overwhelmed.

STABILIZING CENTRAL CONTROL

By 500 CE rulers in the Kinai region thus controlled much of Japan through an array of widely scattered allies and subordinates whose cooperation was based on a combination of mutual advantage, fear, and ideological engagement. Following the débâcle of 475, Yamato River rulers had abandoned efforts to project their control onto the continent, if such had been their intent. Foreign relations remained a recurrent concern, however, as did occasional acts of defiance by local magnates in Kyushu and elsewhere.

Still, the major political issue, the primary source of political disorder, lay at the center, where the ruling lineage's closest associates waxed powerful, quarreling, competing for advantage, and scheming to seize the throne. As generations passed, the circle of claimants to royal authority shrank – from allies to in-laws and finally to paternal relatives of the ruler, who was for most of this period headquartered in the Asuka vicinity of Yamato or at Naniwa by the sea. The intensity of elite power struggles remained high, however, culminating in 672 in a succession conflict of unprecedented scale, the Jinshin Disturbance (Jinshin *no ran*) as it is called.

The process of political consolidation had long been smoothed by the use of sacred symbols and ceremonies, which rulers reinforced with secular rituals of respect and reward. During the sixth century new forms of sacred power were introduced, Buddhism in particular, but for several decades they complicated affairs by adding a layer of ideological, or at least rhetorical, conflict to power struggles within the central elite. Eventually, however, doctrinal and organizational means were found to meld the old and new sacred orders in ways supportive of the emerging imperial regime.

A political narrative. A narrative overview of the period will help identify key actors and developments before we focus on a few particularly noteworthy issues of governance: aspects of foreign affairs, challenges by magnates, and religious politics.

Following Yūryaku's death in 479 or thereabouts, the Yamato River regime was increasingly troubled by internal quarrels, and in or around the year 506 dissatisfied chieftains rebelled. They installed as new ruler a regional magnate of their own choosing known to us as Keitai. From then until 571 political life appears to have been dominated, save for an interregnum during the 530s, by Keitai and the later Kinmei, men who mostly governed from headquarters in the Asuka vicinity. Although repeatedly drawn into Korean politics, they managed on most occasions to minimize military participation, devoting their energies instead to domestic affairs. In particular they continued to improve tribute-collection and other income-producing arrangements, thereby helping to sustain their regime's power *vis-à-vis* their allies and followers.

This very process of administrative consolidation, however, served to strengthen successive chiefs of the Soga family, most notably Iname and his son Umako, who acquired pre-eminent roles as masters of Kinmei's fisc. They built themselves a solid landed base in the Asuka vicinity and added to their power by acting as intermediaries to continental figures of consequence and as patrons of immigrant artisans. Most crucially, perhaps, the two acquired a key role as principal in-laws of Kinmei and his progeny. Unsurprisingly this great rise in Soga fortunes generated resentment among other major families, leading to plots and violent confrontations whose intensity was only heightened by Soga espousal of Buddhism, which challenged the courtly religious roles of key rivals.

During the 580s these rivals challenged the Soga militarily but were defeated. Umako consolidated his power and in 592 had his niece Suiko, a daughter of Kinmei, designated head of the ruling house. In addition, the young Prince Shōtoku (Shōtoku *taishi*), a grand-nephew of Umako and grandson of Kinmei, was elevated to an ill-defined role as implicit successor-in-waiting. Shōtoku may, however, simply have furnished male cover for the awkwardness of a female occupant in a customarily male position, making the arrangement conform, superficially at least, to the continental practice of empress dowager and child ruler. In any case, as it worked out, Suiko held her monarchical position until 628, making her reign longer than that of any successor for the next twelve centuries. During that reign and after, Umako, his son Emishi, and grandson Iruka dominated affairs of state, until rivals destroyed them in a violent coup d'état in 645.

The several decades of Soga pre-eminence witnessed notable developments. Like Keitai and Kinmei, Soga leaders managed to limit their involvement in Korean affairs, even though new Chinese dynastic struggles brought more turmoil to the peninsula, causing more refugees and continental cultural influences to flow into Japan. This influx fostered a rapid growth in Buddhist institutions and liturgical activity, leading by the 640s to Buddhism's acceptance as an integral part of elite life. The Soga years also witnessed economic growth, the first despatch of study missions to China, the beginnings of indigenous elite literacy in the Chinese language, the recording of poetry, and the use of more expansive architectural styles. Also the promotion of Confucian principles of governance – as evidenced in new styles of court garb and official rank, the tightening of fiscal and administrative procedures, compilation of law codes, and creation of official court chronicles.

Soga ambitions matched Soga accomplishments, however, which fueled resentments and prompted highly placed rivals to oust them in the brutal palace coup of 645. Among the plotters of that coup, as recorded in *Nihon shoki*, were two of the most notable figures in Japanese history, men known for both their own roles and those of their descendants. One was the young prince Naka no Ōe, who subsequently became the ruler Tenji and begat the later female rulers Jitō and Genmei. The other was Nakatomi no Kamatari, who received on his deathbed the honorific name Fujiwara, which he passed on to his son Fuhito. Fuhito's descendants proliferated, becoming the most sprawling patrilineage in Japan and the dominant source of imperial consorts for centuries thereafter.

All the fury of their assault on Soga chiefs notwithstanding, the coup leaders of 645 kept most of the Soga-era changes intact. Their acceptance of the new was reflected in continued promotion of continental learning, active support of Buddhism, and adoption of the Chinese year-period (*nengō*) type of calender with the claim that their coup initiated the Taika or "Great Change" year period. In that spirit they pursued a number of vigorous policies to consolidate power and strengthen central control of land and magnates.

The new ruling group was riven, however, by harsh personal feuds from which Tenji emerged the bloody winner a few years later. Worse yet, he and his advisors failed to avoid major entanglement in continental politics, which had become exceedingly unstable and threatening. In 663 forces of T'ang and Silla wrecked a major military expedition that they had sent to aid Paekche, giving Kinai leaders their worst military débâcle in Korea in nearly two centuries. For several years after that disaster, Tenji concentrated on preparing defenses against a joint T'ang–Silla invasion, but in the end diplomacy prevailed and war was avoided. That outcome freed him at last to pursue domestic reform and government strengthening, but death cut short his effort in 671.

Tenji's passing precipitated a savage succession dispute between his son and his younger brother Tenmu. The great scale of that dispute reflected both the long-term expansion in war-making capacity of preceding centuries and the high level of armaments and readiness associated with recent continental affairs. Tenmu's victory in this Jinshin Disturbance set the stage for a period of major political consolidation and reform out of which came the *ritsuryō* system of imperial government. That system, an aristocratic bureaucratic arrangement, was foreshadowed by the prior centuries of organizational development. And like them it reflected a continual interplay of insular precedents and conditions and continental influences. To an unprecedented degree, however, it constituted an attempt to adapt a continental political model to the existing society of Japan. The result was imperfect, but – for better or worse – much of it lasted, in modified form, for half a millennium. The creations of few political architects have fared as well.

Issues of governance. Such, in brief, is the central political history of the years 500–671. Turning to foreign relations, they played an important role in Japan's political life throughout the centuries of political consolidation, spurring a wide array of changes and altering particular balances of power among contenders for leadership. The record of those relations is much richer for the period after 500 than for earlier centuries, and only two of the most salient aspects can be noted here. First, the hoary links between Wa and the Kaya vicinity were finally severed. Compromised initially by the Kinai conquest of Kyushu, the links weakened further when the discovery of iron sands in Honshu reduced Japanese need for Korean iron. The ties were finally ruptured during the sixth century when Kaya's neighboring regimes, primarily Silla, seized the area despite noisy protestations and periodic military posturing by Kinai leaders.

Second, whereas regimes and resources in Korea had long been the focus of Japanese continental interest, emergence of the Sui and T'ang dynasties, in 581 and 618 respectively, shifted Kinai attention farther westward by presenting leaders throughout northeast Asia with a unified China for the first time since Himiko was a young woman. That resurgence of Chinese power (especially the T'ang–Silla alliance and Paekche's resulting pleas for assistance) drew Kinai leaders more deeply into continental affairs than they had been at any time since Yūryaku's day. And this time a Chinese, rather than a Korean, regime was perceived as the fundamental threat.

As the scale of T'ang power became evident, nearly all Kinai leaders sought to learn about it, largely in hopes of strengthening their own regime by mastering T'ang's secrets. As continental refugees and Japanese study missions brought more and more knowledge to Naniwa and Asuka, however, the cultural attainments of T'ang also elicited interest in their own right. During the seventh century growing numbers of the Kinai elite studied Chinese language, prose writing, poetry, visual arts, religion, and political thought. In the process they laid a foundation for establishing the *ritsuryō* order.

Domestically, meanwhile, the task of controlling magnates in the hinterland prompted diverse measures. It spurred administrative tightening, the granting of secular rewards such as higher *kabane* rank or more land, the use of religious devices to elicit cooperation, and occasional resort to force. Perhaps the most striking use of sacred devices, as evidenced in *Kojiki*, was the symbolic manipulation that presumably helped Kinai chiefs overcome Izumo's stubborn resistance to their advances. As bartering and battling proceeded, they treated the deities (*kami*) of Izumo magnates with dignity, imbricating them at suitable levels in the hierarchy of their own gods. Most famously, they declared Susano-ō, the ancestral god of the greatest Izumo chiefly lineage, to be the disruptive younger brother of the sun goddess Amaterasu, reputed ancestress of their own lineage. That maneuver placed Izumo chieftains near the very pinnacle of families in terms of godly status and legitimized a number of valued ritual and material perquisites.

In terms of sticks, rather than carrots, the most noteworthy instance of armed suppression occurred in Kyushu. The rebellious magnate there was Tsukushi no Iwai, a man who dominated central Kyushu early in the sixth century and who may well have aspired to restore an independent Wa. During the 520s or thereabouts, when Keitai deployed an army westward, allegedly to aid Kaya and Paekche against Silla, Iwai evidently allied himself with Silla and blocked Keitai's advance, derailing his Korean plans and forcing his generals to turn their attack on their defiant lieutenant. In the end they crushed him. But while that outcome may have prevented a revival of Wa, Iwai's effort helped preserve the memory of Kyushu autonomy and revealed anew a secession potential that periodically troubled Kinai rulers for centuries thereafter.

Turning to political ideology, the century or more to 671 witnessed striking developments, most visibly the use of Buddhism for political legitimation. The essence of the story is suggested by *Nihon shoki*'s apocryphal narrative of Buddhism's introduction to Japan. The king of Paekche sought aid against Silla, we are told, and Kinmei's reluctance to respond prompted the king to despatch a second delegation. That mission presented the Asuka chief with "an image of Shaka Butsu in gold and copper, several flags and umbrellas, and a number of volumes of 'Sutras.'" An accompanying message said,

> This doctrine is amongst all doctrines the most excellent. But it is hard to explain, and hard to comprehend. Even the Duke of Chow and Confucius had not attained to a knowledge of it. This doctrine can create religious merit and retribution without measure and without bounds, and so lead on to a full appreciation of the highest wisdom. Imagine a man in possession of treasures to his heart's content, so that he might satisfy all his wishes in proportion as he used them. Thus it is with the treasure of this wonderful doctrine. Every prayer is fulfilled and naught is wanting. Moreover, from distant India it has extended hither to the three Han, where there are none who do not receive it with reverence as it is preached to them.[10]

Wealth and wisdom, all one's wishes, available to those who believe.

Insofar as records illuminate the matter, Buddhism was thus from its introduction to the Kinai region a creed brought to the elite by emissaries and emigrants from Korea. And it was from the beginning valued by rulers as a political tool and by individuals as a weapon against illness or other misfortune. It served Soga factional interests at first, as noted above, and during the 590s Umako deepened his family's link to Buddhism by building a grand temple, the Hōkōji (Asukadera) on his home territory, just a short walk from where Suiko's handsome new Oharida Palace would be built a few years later. The foundation of Hōkōji's pagoda contained "jewels, horse trappings, and gold and silver baubles similar to goods previously buried in mounded tombs."[11] That use of the pagoda suggests how the ritual functions of key-hole tumuli were being taken over by the new Buddhist ceremonial centers.

In that spirit, during the Soga heyday tomb construction rapidly declined as magnates scrambled to align themselves with their leaders. We are told that they, "vied each with one another in erecting Buddhist shrines for the benefit of their Lords and parents."[12] As the religion prospered, Suiko's administration moved to assure its doctrinal consistency and political reliability by establishing offices to oversee the religious community and staffing them with trusted appointees, commonly immigrant priests. One result of her effort was a religious census in the year 623, which reported the existence of 46 temples, 816 priests, and 569 nuns. One of those temples was Ikarugaji, which later was renamed Hōryūji and stands today as one of Japan's most ancient and cherished historial monuments.

By the 640s Buddhism had gained wide enough acceptance among the elite to transcend factional boundaries, and the architects of the anti-Soga coup in 645 further strengthened the religion's legitimacy. *Nihon shoki* records the newly appointed monarch, Kōtoku, decreeing, shortly after the coup, that priests must be properly instructed in Buddhist doctrine and assistance given where needed to maintain all temples erected by members of the titled elite. He continued:

> We shall also cause Temple Commissioners and Chief Priests to be appointed, who shall make a circuit to all the temples, and having ascertained the actual facts respecting the priests and nuns, their male and female slaves, and the acreage of their cultivated lands, report all the particulars clearly to us.[13]

Since many of these temples had been established by leaders of powerful *uji*, the control of temples became a way to control *uji* chiefs. Kōtoku's interest in doctrinal propriety and institutional health thus merged seamlessly with the new regime's interest in control.

In following decades Buddhism continued to enjoy official favor, acquiring new, grander, and more richly endowed temples, ever more priests, nuns, and adherents, and the introduction from abroad of more and more Buddhist texts (sutras), images, and religious paraphernalia. The prestige of Buddhism and its importance as an element of elite legitimization is evident in both *Nihon shoki* and surviving regulations of the decades around 700 CE, as we note in chapter 4.

By 672, then, the centuries of political consolidation had created a Kinai-centered regime that was pre-eminent in the realm. It had established diplomatic relations with several continental governments, but how stably it could maintain them remained to be seen. Domestically, and especially in the Kinai vicinity, it had become reasonably secure in its control of regional magnates and uppity lieutenants. But whether it could regularize relations among the members of its ruling household was still uncertain. Finally, it was busily developing an elaborate elite culture heavily based on Chinese precedents, but only the future would reveal how solidly it could establish the fiscal foundation such an elite culture required.

[4] *ESTABLISHING THE RITSURYŌ ORDER (672–750)*

CHAPTER SYNOPSIS

A POLITICAL NARRATIVE

THE SOURCES

ESTABLISHING A CAPITAL CITY

FORMING A STATE CHURCH

THE RITSURYŌ STATE AT 750
THE HIERARCHY OF STATE
STAFFING AND FINANCING THE
GOVERNMENT

THE BROADER CONTEXT
THE HUMAN CONDITION
TRENDS IN THE ECOSYSTEM

When viewed from the far future, the Jinshin Disturbance of summer 672 stands out as a major event in Japanese political history, the moment when generations of foreshadowing gave way to decades of fulfillment. In significant part the moment looks that way because our primary source of information, *Nihon shoki*, wishes it to do so. But even when we discount that source's grand hyperbole, shrewd selectivity, and handsome inventiveness, the summer of seventy-two still displays a watershed quality comparable to that of such years as 1185, 1600, 1868, or 1945.

In essence the process of political consolidation that had been slowly proceeding for centuries was pressed to a major form of completion after 672, with establishment of the *ritsuryō seido* or "system of penal and civil codes." This elaborately structured, hereditary aristocratic regime was headquartered in a great palace within a grand capital city and linked to the hinterland producer populace by a bureaucracy of officials stationed at the capital and posted to provincial headquarters to collect tribute and keep the peace.

Several aspects of this political settlement command attention. The major literary sources themselves require note because their very compilation was an act of political legitimization that shaped their contents. The formation of a capital city and the establishment of an elegant state religion merit attention. An overview of the state structure that took shape by 750 will indicate the aristocratic, bureaucratic character of the regime. And a look at the evidence of social and environmental stress will suggest the ecological ramifications of the process of political change. But first, a brief narrative history of the decades will identify key figures and events.

A POLITICAL NARRATIVE

In warfare that swirled across the Kinai region the armies of Tenmu routed those of his 22-year-old nephew in a month of hard summer fighting. During the subsequent fourteen years of his reign Tenmu governed with uncommon success. He pursued policies designed to avoid conflict with newly triumphant Silla and managed to maintain peaceful relations with all the continental Powers. At home he consolidated his control of land and magnates and strengthened his command of armed forces throughout the realm. He tightened his grip on officialdom and ordered the drafting of a legal code to clarify and standardize administrative procedure. He initiated the compiling of historical records to establish his right to rule – a particularly pressing task given the messiness of his ascent to power – and he affirmed his regime's sacral claims by supporting both Buddhist and Shintō institutions and practices. Finally, he addressed, with partial success, a central problem that his seizure of the crown had brutally highlighted: the need for a peaceful means of succession to rulership.

By the time of his illness and death in 686, Tenmu had greatly strengthened his regime. The magnitude of that achievement has been obscured, however, by its lack of physical expression in a great capital city of the sort favored by continental rulers of the day. He had made gestures toward the creation of one, but at his death the Yamato River regime still governed from a simple headquarters. The palace compound included warehouses and other buildings as well as the palace proper, but relatives and officials occupied their own mansion compounds, most of which were situated in the immediate Asuka vicinity but not associated with the palace as elements of an organized, urban setting.

Tenmu was succeeded by his widow, Jitō, a daughter of Tenji, and during her fifteen years of rule she labored to overcome the lack of a suitable capital. Utilizing Chinese precedents and modifying them as seemed helpful, her government constructed the sprawling headquarters compound of a new capital city, Fujiwara-*kyō*, a setting fit for a truly "imperial" government. By 694 she was able to occupy her splendid new palace. It was situated at the north end of an immense rectilinear ground that included not only the palace compound with its great gates and encircling walls but also geometrically arrayed government office buildings, warehouses, ceremonial centers, and official residence compounds, the whole laid out on a scale of unprecedented grandeur.

Jitō's other great achievement was to modulate the cycles of violence within the imperial family enough to maintain reasonable stability at the center. As figure 4.1 indicates, she and Tenmu had produced an heir, Kusakabe, whom they wedded to Jitō's much younger sister Genmei. The young couple soon begat a daughter Genshō and a son Monmu. However, perhaps to avoid the fate of Tenji's son, Kusakabe did not succeed to the throne on

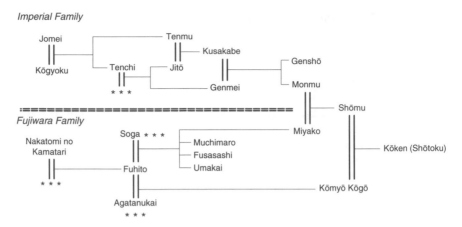

Imperial Family

Fujiwara Family

Figure 4.1 Early *ritsuryō* leaders. The imperial–Fujiwara duopoly entailed a sustained marital association that dated from the age of Fujiwara Fuhito's daughters Miyako and Kōmyō Kōgō. *Note*: *** = spousal family.

Tenmu's death in 686, and he died three years later, still unappointed. Lest his death precipitate a succession struggle, Jitō assumed the throne, being known by the unusual title *tennō*, "Heavenly Sovereign." And a few years later (697), after young Monmu's main potential rival had died, she abdicated in her grandson's favor, guarding him until her own death in 702.

Meanwhile, officials (including the ambitious Fujiwara no Fuhito, who had thrown in his lot with Jitō) pressed ahead with the drafting of law codes, compilation of an official history, and the myriad tasks of routine governance and ceremonial. Indeed, the record of Jitō's rule is striking for its tone of routine and ritual, as though governance had become, thanks to Tenmu's accomplishments, nothing more than systems maintenance. The most celebrated result of her officials' labors was the Taihō Code (Taihō *ryō*) of New Year's 702, a sprawling set of government statutes modeled on Chinese precedents and intended as basic regulations for the *ritsuryō* system.

In her later years Jitō was firmly supported by Fuhito, whose daughter Miyako became Monmu's wife and, in 701, mother to his son, the later Shōmu. Upon Jitō's death the following year, the mature Genmei became Monmu's guardian, and when the young monarch died suddenly in 707, she assumed the title *tennō* for herself, proving to be an even more energetic ruler than Jitō. Like her older sister, Genmei is most well known for the capital she built – Heijō-*kyō*, in present-day Nara. But in conjunction with that project she also undertook Japan's first attempt to monetize the fisc, and she initiated a survey of the realm, which project yielded gazetteers (*fudoki*) that identified localities and their deities, described local customs, and recorded the resources and special products of the provinces.

Genmei kept order within the imperial family in much the manner of Jitō. In 715, allegedly due to illness, she abdicated in favor of her mature daughter Genshō, rather than her grandson Shōmu. Genshō *tennō*, however, seems to have been a less forceful woman, relying mainly on her mother until

Genmei's death in 721 and on Shōmu's maternal relatives, Fujiwara no Fuhito and his sons, as long as they lived.

After the Taihō Code's issuance in 702, numerous changes were made in legal particulars, and in 718 Fuhito headed a commission that updated the entire code, producing a new 20-volume version that is known by its date of compilation as the Yōrō Code (Yōrō *ritsuryō*). As that project made headway, Fuhito also spurred compilers to complete *Nihon shoki*, which was done by 720, eight years after others had finished *Kojiki*.

From 719 onward Genshō involved Shōmu in affairs, and in 724, after weathering another plot among senior imperial family members, she abdicated in his favor. By then Fuhito was dead, but another daughter of his, the later Kōmyō Kōgō, had become Shōmu's primary consort in 716, and in following years Fuhito's sons – half brothers to Kōmyō – rose to powerful office. They allied themselves with Shōmu in opposition to rival claimants to the throne. Together they dominated affairs for a decade, holding rivals at bay and confronting issues of the day.

Shōmu *tennō* himself was one of the most interesting rulers in Japanese history. Learned, devoutly Buddhist, and intensely filial, he subscribed to the notion that peace, prosperity, and an orderly natural order were the result of, and hence signs of, imperial virtue and good governance while social disorder and natural disaster indicated imperial misrule. Unfortunately his reign witnessed some of the most horrific natural disasters in Japanese history, and his conviction that the suffering was a measure of his own failure led him to adopt extreme and erratic policies that only added to the difficulty.

The most prominent quality of Shōmu's rule was its promotion of and reliance on Buddhism as a force for social good. Ironically, however, considering his dedication to compassionate rule, his most successful policy involved the military conquest of central Tōhoku and ouster of the Emishi, as the area's residents were known, from ancestral lands and livelihoods. For generations a growing population of agriculturalists had been moving northward to reclaim more and more land. Many may have done so in hopes of escaping the tribute collector's grasp, but imperial authority followed (and sometimes led) them, extending the collector's reach. Especially during the rule of Genmei and Genshō the court promoted development of Tōhoku, and predictably the settlers collided with Emishi residents, whose lives still retained much Jōmon forager practice.

Doubtless the Emishi reacted to this escalating encroachment in diverse ways, but one response was to arm themselves and resist. In reply the court despatched military expeditions, and by 725 these had "pacified" the eastern coastal region north to the vicinity of present-day Sendai, where commanders erected Taga-jō and other frontier fortresses. As in North America a millennium later, however, the agricultural frontier kept advancing, eliciting yet more Emishi resistance. In 737 Shōmu deployed another major military expedition, which overran more Emishi hamlets and projected imperial influence into the interior valleys north of modern Yamagata. In following years agricultural settlements appeared all across the region between today's Akita and Morioka.

This governmental success in penetrating Emishi ancestral lands was not matched, however, by commensurate success in the Kinai itself. During the 730s the country was racked by epidemic disease on an unprecedented scale, a calamity that slashed the producer populace, especially in western and central Japan. It also decimated the aristocracy, sparing the *tennō* but not his key princely and Fujiwara supporters. In response to the disaster Shōmu reduced tribute and military service obligations and announced a grand array of religious initiatives, mostly Buddhist and Shintō.

He also juggled advisors. In the process, however, he managed to antagonize a grandson of Fuhito, the ambitious Fujiwara survivor, Hirotsugu, whom he exiled to Dazaifu, the court's fortified outpost and regional headquarters in Kyushu. In an action reminiscent of Tsukushi no Iwai some two centuries earlier, the resentful Hirotsugu denounced Shōmu and mobilized the armed forces of Kyushu, reviving yet again the specter of a secessionist Wa supported by a truculent Silla. Shōmu took steps to forestall continental involvement in the quarrel and in 740 despatched an army of suppression, which, after some confusion and considerable dismay, crushed Hirotsugu and resecured the region.

Even as that problem was nearing resolution, Shōmu initiated one of his most cherished schemes, a plan to build a new capital northeast of Nara. That task shortly ran afoul of official resistance and natural disaster, but Shōmu stubbornly pressed ahead. Only after five chaotic years of lurching about the Kinai did he abandon his dream in the face of earthquake and conflagration and return to Nara, a severely weakened ruler who thereafter allowed officialdom to handle most affairs of state. Even then, however, Shōmu pressed on with his most beloved surviving project, the creation of a Buddhist church that would be centered in the capital but embrace the entire realm. And that project, as we note more fully below, came to fruition, in effect completing the association of government and Buddhism that the Soga had begun promoting some two hundred years earlier.

When Shōmu died in 756, the *ritsuryō seido* was at its pinnacle of development. And fittingly, it was headed by another strong-willed woman, Kōken *tennō*, the daughter of Kōmyō Kōgō and Shōmu, and thus a woman who embodied the lineages of Tenji, Tenmu, and Nakatomi no Kamatari, founding fathers of the *ritsuryō* order.

THE SOURCES

As known today, Japan's history down to about 500 CE is essentially a story based on archaeological evidence, with embellishments from literary sources, mainly continental. From about that year onward, however, the balance shifts and literary works become the basic source.[1] A number of works contain useful information, but two Japanese compilations, *Nihon shoki* (Chronicle of Japan, 720) and *Shoku Nihongi* (Chronicle of Japan, Continued, 797) provide the bulk of information for the years to 791. The latter work, as its name indicates, is a continuation of the former, picking up the story in 697 with Monmu's accession. Its format and content reflect that character, but unlike the former it records recent, well documented events and is credible in most detail, whereas *Nihon shoki* is credible only for the last few reigns it treats, notably those of Tenji, Tenmu, and Jitō.

Nihon shoki and the earlier *Kojiki* (Record of Ancient Matters, 712) are the two formative works of Japanese historical scholarship. Together they established an official version of the origins, early development, and character of the imperial institution and the realm it governed. Both works were commenced at Tenmu's behest, presumably to create a record of the past that would rectify any "misunderstanding" and thereby legitimize his regime. The two advanced only slowly, however, not being completed until decades after his death, during Genmei's heyday.

The compilers of *Kojiki* seem to have had two main objectives. One was to elevate the ruling lineage's status by establishing and highlighting its unique linkage to the founding gods of the cosmos. The other was to strengthen its ties to other major families by imbricating their household gods and myths in its own pantheon at levels that would be gratifyingly high to members of those families yet proportional to their power and safely below that of the monarch. Hence *Kojiki* is predominantly a narrative of godly affairs, extraordinarily lush in imagery and rich in complexity, and it focuses on the distant past, when those relationships developed. Its treatment of more recent, this-worldly imperial generations is perfunctory by comparison, and it ends with the death of Suiko in 628.

Nihon shoki was designed much more as a work in the Chinese historiographical tradition, intended to record, and thus establish the legitimacy of, successive rulers down to the present. It recorded the merits of virtuous monarchs, the flaws of the unvirtuous, the effects thereof, and hence the importance of good governance. Its compilers seem to have utilized the roster of sovereigns developed for *Kojiki*, along with the godly stories assembled therein, but they were content to adumbrate the myths while concentrating on more recent centuries, for which they had information in Chinese, Korean, and Japanese sources, many of them no longer extant. Their Chinese model required that they devise a chronology for their history and birth–reign–death dates for their successive rulers. Sources at hand gave them plausible dates back two centuries or so, but beyond that they had to invent. So they did. They employed an overarching scheme of symbolic eras to establish a founding date for the dynasty and then assigned individual reign dates to bring their story down to the point where dating could be derived from other sources. That point appears to have been around the time of the "five kings of Wa."

The immediate task of these creators of history was to legitimize the rule of Tenmu and hence of his descendants. Several strategies helped them attain that objective. Most obviously, they presented Tenmu's triumph in the Jinshin Disturbance as an unparalleled victory of virtue over knavishness. They described it in incomparably loving detail, recounting its one month of warfare day by day. The incident fills nearly twenty pages of text (in English translation), making it by far the longest war story in the *Chronicle*. They also tried to conceal the nature of Tenmu's coup by presenting him as Tenji's immediate successor, completely omitting the brief reign of Tenji's son. That omission was not "rectified" until around 1900, when the hapless young man was designated emperor number 39, Kōbun *tennō*.

From Tenmu via Tenji on back through time the compilers sought to establish a genealogical line leading straight to Jinmu, earthly founder of their "imperial" lineage, and thence to the age of *kami* on the Plain of High Heaven. That task was made necessary – and difficult – by the fact that for centuries succession had been essentially an outcome of ruthless maneuver among powerful households that often were linked only tenuously by mutual interest and the fluid marital arrangements of the day. Not every rupture was successfully concealed, but considering the rough terrain they were dealing with, the compilers did an estimable job of crafting a coherent lineage for their ruling house.

The compilers helped legitimize Tenmu's vigorous measures of political consolidation by treating them as the implementation of policies enunciated after the Taika coup of 645, the so-called Taika Reform. They presented the Reform as a bold, four-point plan, which they clothed richly in Confucian rhetoric and expressions of religious devotion. They added further depth to the policy of consolidation by elevating Prince Shōtoku, nephew and advisor of Suiko, to the level of great cultural progenitor, whom they credited with first promulgating the guiding principles for proper *ritsuryō* governance. *Nihon shoki* presents Shōtoku as precocious, multi-talented, admirably foresighted, and wise beyond human ken. His celebration had the important corollary effect of lowering the visibility of Soga accomplishments, thus elevating the royal family *vis-à-vis* its supporters.

Nihon shoki compilers also took care to demonstrate the regime's role as key player in the East Asian diplomatic field. Rather in the manner of Chinese dynasts, successive *tennō* (as the rulers were retroactively styled) benevolently hosted "barbarian" visitors from afar. For the seventh century, in particular, compilers recorded the details of diplomacy and the many visitors to Asuka and Naniwa. The guest list included Emishi and Sushen from northern Japan, Hayato from southern Kyushu, Yaku, Tane, Amami, and Toka from the Ryukyus, and delegates from Kaya, Paekche, Silla, Koguryŏ, Sui, and T'ang.

Insofar as the compilers were trying to create a continental-style history, they faced one unusual problem: they needed to justify the presence of female rulers. Chinese dynastic histories had not recognized women as appropriate rulers, and when a remarkably gifted imperial concubine was elevated to the title of emperor of T'ang in 690, she – the celebrated Empress Wu – changed the dynastic name, alienated great magnates, ran afoul of various other groups, and after fifteen years of energetic rule was ousted in a coup d'état, evidently unprotected by her devout support of Buddhism. Perhaps reports of those troubling developments, which were unfolding even as *Nihon shoki* compilers were at work, spurred them to reinforce the propriety of female rulers. After all, they were working for Genmei.

One device that served this purpose was the irregular title *tennō*, which had no ascribed gender connotation, having been recently used in China for Empress Wu as well as her male predecessor. In Japan the term appears to have been employed during Tenmu's day, but it showed up most regularly in references to Jitō. Subsequently *Nihon shōki* compilers applied it retrospectively to their roster of "emperors" from Jinmu on, thus asserting that their ruling family's distinctive, ungendered title of authority traced back to the age of the gods.

They found in Suiko's long reign an excellent precedent for a female monarch. And they further enhanced the stature of female rulers by inserting in their genealogy at a point shortly before the "five kings of Wa" a female *tennō*, Jingū, perhaps to accommodate the information on Himiko in *Wajinden*. Characterizing her as intelligent, shrewd, and a beauty to behold, they endowed Jingū with miraculous powers and despatched her to invade and subdue the kingdoms of Korea, which she did with splendid éclat. Beyond Jingū they traced the *tennō* lineage back to the godly time of creation, in which female *kami* had possessed at least as much generative power as males, and in which the female god Amaterasu Ōmikami was grandparent to Jinmu and great foundress of the lineage.

By the time these compilers completed their work, probably in 719 or so, they had constructed a narrative that anchored the current ruling house in a glorious mytho-history. In Prince Shōtoku they had provided a great cultural progenitor for their regime. In the term *tennō* they had found a genderless monarchical title that met their needs while nicely distinguishing their ruling house from those of the continent. And in the tales of godly and human alliance and association they had given their allies and subordinates appropriate positions as honored, hereditary henchmen, whose connections traced back through battles, bargains, and benevolences to the divine beginnings of time.

ESTABLISHING A CAPITAL CITY

The construction of a capital city – indeed, two of them in quick succession – was another major aspect of the *ritsuryō* system's establishment. Several factors contributed to their creation. In essence, changes then occurring in Japanese political life were rendering past headquarters arrangements obsolete, and continental models offered an escape from that obsolescence. That escape, however, ultimately imposed new difficulties of its own.

To elaborate, elite marital practice of preceding centuries, which was an important instrument of political alliance-making, had encouraged rulers to maintain multiple palaces: that of their own family and those of their spouses, who commonly remained at or near their natal family headquarters, at least for some years after marriage. These arrangements had the corollary effect of encouraging frequent changes in royal residence as children matured and marriage alliances changed. The customs of multiple palaces and a moveable court were feasible as long as a ruling group was modest in size and its architectural practices relatively simple.

Moreover, because the pillars and lashing used in customary thatch-roof-and-posthole construction rotted away in a score of years or so, periodic replacement of palaces, shrines, warehouses, gate towers, and fortress walls was essential. The custom of residential mobility was thus not especially wasteful of labor and material resources: when the time came, one simply erected a new building at a new site, reusing valuable timbers as appropriate, and torched the rest. The practical necessity of periodic replacement was given religious sanction via notions of pollution, which eventually decreed regular replacement of shrines and palaces as acts of spiritual cleansing, thereby transmogrifying essential routine into sacred ritual.

As Yamato River rulers of the sixth and seventh centuries expanded their realm, however, they acquired more and more underlings, administrative paraphernalia, weaponry, and tribute goods, and they needed more and more buildings to house them. As the scale of government grew, moreover, it became more important to have these people and resources close at hand where they could be more easily controlled and utilized. Under these circumstances, frequent moves by the court or replacement of buildings became more costly, eventually even prohibitive.

A solution to the problem was at hand, however, and it was advocated by immigrant experts and their domestic supporters. This was the use of continental principles of urban design and techniques of construction. These produced geometrically laid out capital cities whose major gates and buildings employed stone foundations, mortise-and-tenon framing, and tile roofs that largely eliminated the problem of rot and the consequent need for replacement.

On the other hand, to construct cities and buildings of that sort required so much labor and material that their use effectively precluded periodic replacement or the transfer of a royal headquarters from site to site. Nevertheless, the notion of grand buildings and capital cities became immensely attractive to Kinai rulers during the seventh and eighth centuries. Continental regimes, the glorious new Chinese dynasties most notably, had them: they constituted an expression of political triumph, a legitimizing symbol of the first order. Moreover, the architecture was an integral part of Buddhism, and acceptance of the creed willy nilly fostered adoption of its building style.

These several conflicting factors – the need to modify palace and capital arrangements but the difficulty of doing so; the wish to enjoy grandeur but the reluctance to settle for a single, immobile court – all became evident by the mid-seventh century. Change did come, but slowly, and in the end a compromise system was devised. Shintō shrines and many residential buildings continued to be built in the rottable, replaceable posthole style that accommodated religious concerns and taboos, while city gates, major government buildings, and Buddhist temples were built in the continental fashion that met the need for permanence and grandeur. Moreover, the wish of rulers to maintain multiple palaces was abetted by the custom of certain continental regimes that maintained "summer" palaces or other regional capitals to which rulers could periodically sojourn. Those precedents helped justify the maintenance and use of two or more palaces. In toto these compromise arrangements were workable, but they also were costly, and during the eighth century they became a major source of social hardship and political trouble.

During the Soga heyday, as noted earlier, temple construction proceeded apace, and after the Taika coup of 645 it continued. The new rulers also engaged in greatly expanded palace construction, pursuing major projects at both Naniwa and Asuka. As they became entangled in continental politics, moreover, they engaged in frenetic defense work, with Tenji building major fortresses at key points all the way from Kyushu to the Kinai. The corvée labor demands of these several projects generated hardship among the general public and discontent among the ruling elite.

Following the destructive Jinshin Disturbance, Tenmu pursued recon-struction, erecting a handsome palace complex, the Kiyomihara Palace, com-plete with satellite temples, at Asuka. And during the 670s he resolved to build more elaborate headquarters both there and at Naniwa. Even though these efforts were making only modest progress, in 683 he launched plans for a third center, an Eastern Capital, to be built in the mountainous Shinano region. Death cut short his plans, but Jitō revived the main scheme for a grand new headquarters at Asuka. How much of that capital, Fujiwara-*kyō*, was completed during its brief lifetime is still unknown, but excavations sug-gest that its builders produced a central government compound roughly on the scale later realized at Heijō-*kyō* and Heian-*kyō* (see figure 4.2), a layout covering fifty times the area of Tenmu's Kiyomihara Palace complex.

Jitō's builders hauled timber by river and ox cart from Ōmi Province well to the north, which suggests that more accessible forests around the Yamato

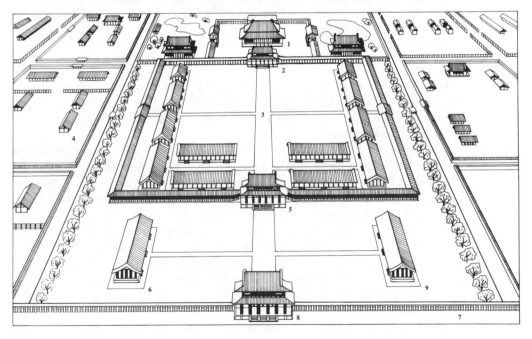

Figure 4.2   A reconstruction of Fujiwara-*kyō*. On the basis of excavation work, archaeologists envision Fujiwara-*kyō* as a rectilinear capital centered on a great boulevard that led due northward via three 2-story gates, past government office buildings, to the imperial palace proper. The residence and out-buildings of officialdom and others flanked the palace's walled enclosures. *Source*: Richard J. Pearson, *Ancient Japan* (NY: George Braziller, 1992), p. 267.
Key: 1. Imperial council hall; 2. official gate; 3. administrative palace; 4. government offices; 5. middle gate; 6. west assembly hall; 7. palace enclosure; 8. main (south) gate; 9. east assembly hall.

Basin no longer had timber of the desired size and quality. Nevertheless the work progressed, and it yielded a geometrically arranged government headquarters complete with great gates and a grand audience hall built in the continental manner, a handsome imperial residence done in the Japanese posthole-and-thatch style, other office buildings, and encircling walls and moats. Beyond the moats builders laid out the avenues and cross streets of the surrounding city, with its aristocratic compounds, temples, market places, and residential areas for a growing commoner population of servants, provisioners, craftsmen, and laborers.

In Fujiwara-*kyō* Jitō had given Japan a great capital city, but the ideals of periodic renewal, multiple palaces, and a mobile court persisted. In 708, after Monmu's death and Genmei's succession, the new *tennō* issued an edict expressing regret that she had "not yet had time to consider a change of Capital."[2] Her relatives and officials, she said, had urged her to proceed in the approved manner, following the dictates of divination, astrology, and geomancy, "thereby making the foundations for establishing the seat of government lasting and strong." She continued:

> Since their feelings are so sincere, it is difficult to oppose their counsel. Moreover, the Capital being the residence of the officials, the place where people from everywhere come together, this is a matter for rejoicing, not for Us alone, and since it is profitable, how could We be opposed to it? In antiquity, the Yin-kings changed their capital five times, and received the name of prosperity-bringer; the king of Chou did it three times, and acquired the name of Great Peace; by means of peaceful changes, a tranquil house was built which lasted a long time.

The construction of a new capital would thus assure the realm peace and prosperity, and Genmei informed her subjects that the proposed site at Nara, some twenty-one kilometers to the north, satisfied the requirements of divination and geomancy.

Her upbeat rhetoric notwithstanding, Genmei was well aware that such a project would be hugely burdensome on aristocrats and commoners alike. She pressed ahead, however, despite the protests that soon arose. To secure the necessary flat-land site, the government ousted villagers from their fields and houses, and laborers cleared the area for use. Workers were conscripted, with some crews felling and hauling timber from the interiors of Ōmi and Iga provinces while others brought diverse materials from elsewhere. Yet others produced roof tile, quarried and shaped foundation stones, sawed, hewed, and chiseled wood to shape, and erected the new buildings. Their combined efforts enabled Genmei to move into her new palace at Heijō-*kyō* during the spring of 710.

Over the next several years policies and problems associated with the construction of Heijō-*kyō* grew increasingly severe, dominating political life. Laborers were continually conscripted, overworked, and underfed, with consequent suffering, sabotage, and flight, which elicited government attempts to manage travel arrangements and land and labor use so as to ameliorate the problems and expedite the project. Aristocrats, unable to prevent the enterprise, mobilized their own work crews to build mansions, household temples, and shrines at the new site, sometimes by diverting labor recruited for government use. And because of the poor accessibility and resultant high cost of satisfactory new timber, they disassembled buildings at Fujiwara-*kyō* and hauled the material northward for reuse.

Genmei, meanwhile, intensified tribute collection to help pay for the work. She also began minting coins and by a variety of ingenious stratagems forced workers and aristocrats alike to accept them as payment for goods and services. She ordered the preparation of provincial gazetteers to identify sources of valuable materials, such as mica, mercury, sulphur, alum, loadstone, and quartz. And gradually, despite the discontent and resistance, the new capital took shape and the city rose around it. By 715 most of the government construction was complete, although aristocrats and commoners continued building for another decade or more. That autumn Genmei abdicated; construction slowed and the attempts to establish a coinage petered out.

Even then the old ideals of multiple capitals and a mobile court were not really abandoned. Actual practice, however, had changed substantially. Whereas earlier rulers had made seemingly permanent moves from one palace or place to another, most commonly at Asuka or Naniwa, Jitō, Genmei, and their eighth-century successors made frequent, short visits to other palaces, whether for vacation, religious retreat, or to "show the flag," while the administrators remained at their offices in Fujiwara-*kyō* and, later, Heijō-*kyō*.

Like Tenmu, however, young Shōmu *tennō* wanted a more elaborate, multiple-capital arrangement. Sometime around 730 he rebuilt Naniwa, which had burned a few decades earlier, and also Heijō, where he erected a new palace on the site of his grandmother's original. Then, during the 740s, as adumbrated above, he moved frenetically about the Kinai, initiating capital projects at Kuni and Shigaraki to the north, at one point settling in Naniwa, and in the end returning to Heijō in humiliation and despair. His successors also moved about, although less frenetically, launching palace construction projects at Hora near Lake Biwa, at Yuge southeast of Naniwa, at Nagaoka, and finally at Heian.

Of these several undertakings, only the last one, Heian-*kyō*, was carried to fruition, and its construction so drained the realm that it was never completed and emperors did not again make such a move. By default rather than design Japan had acquired a permanent capital. In following generations emperors became habituated to residing in a single city even though the vicissitudes of fire and faction kept them moving from palace to palace within it. The ecological imperatives of the new political order and its architecture had finally ended the hoary tradition of multiple capitals and a freely moveable court.

FORMING A STATE CHURCH

As *Kojiki* reveals in its gorgeous Shintō mythology, the Yamato elite's legacy of *kami* stories and practices had proven a usable skeleton around which to construct an elaborate pantheon of deities that helped link the households of local magnates to its political order. And *Nihon shoki* carried that story forward, revealing how Tenmu and other rulers nurtured shrines and their *kami* from the Kantō to Kyushu.

Meanwhile the introduction of continental thought had brought rich new conceptual systems that needed somehow to be integrated into the ideology of rule, and *Nihon shoki* shows that process unfolding. Most famously it presents the cultural progenitor Prince Shōtoku as a master of all learning. But successive monarchs, as well, appear in it as dedicated advocates of elevated thought. Thus Kōtoku, after being installed by leaders of the Taika coup, is shown in this august declaration explaining the Soga comeuppance and warning others to heed the lesson:

> Heaven covers us: Earth upbears us: the Imperial way is but one. But in this last degenerate age, the order of Lord and Vassal was destroyed, until Supreme Heaven by Our hands put to death the traitors. [Henceforth lord and vassal shall be in concord, or else] Heaven will send a curse and earth a plague, demons will slay them, and men will smite them. This is as manifest as the sun and moon.[3]

Ideas and practices of Confucianism, Taoism, and other continental provenance were utilized by these rulers, but Buddhist thought became the predominant element in the *ritsuryō* state church.

Soga leaders promoted Buddhism as conducive to personal health and government security, and by the mid-seventh century Kinai rulers were actively and persistently fostering both Buddhist and Shintō practice without regard to factional changes. Tenmu gave particularly energetic support to Buddhism, and by Jitō's day the 46 temples of 623 had multiplied, with some 545 in the Kinai vicinity receiving government support while Fujiwara-kyō alone contained 33. Yet more temples were found in outlying regions, some of them elegant structures indeed. Thus excavation has revealed that a temple in the vicinity of the older Izumo realm included "elaborate frescoed walls and multiple tiled chapels, galleries, towers, and gates as impressive as those at royal and noble establishments in Yamato."[4]

Tenmu promoted Buddhist ceremonies at court and announced restrictions on hunting, fishing, and meat eating. He built temples and ordered monks to pursue the holy work of copying the *Tripitaka* (a huge Chinese compendium of Buddhist texts). He lavished gifts on immigrant monks and promoted especially the reading of sutras that offered protection to rulers, notably the *Konkōmyō-kyō* or Sutra of Golden Light. In the spring of 685 the provinces were informed that

> in every house a Buddhist shrine should be provided, and an image of Buddha with Buddhist scriptures placed there. Worship was to be paid and offerings of food made at these shrines.[5]

At the same time Tenmu saw to it that Shintō affairs were carefully attended, affirming the centrality of the Ise Shrine and its gods in state ritual. He also assured that diverse Chinese-style court ceremonies and customs were properly implemented.

Tenmu's successors continued such practices, both promoting religion and regulating it to assure that it served government interests. Shōmu, however, was the one who most vigorously advanced the cause of religion in political life. A deeply religious man, he saw the terrible suffering of the day as evidence of his inadequacy as ruler, and he strove to cope by being as virtuous as possible. That meant promoting not only diverse secular policies, which he did with great energy, but also religious devotion, Buddhist in particular. As smallpox ravaged the realm during the mid-730s, he ordered scriptural readings at court and in the provinces. He decreed the practice of austerities and Shintō shrine services and eventually called for the construction of more religious structures and images throughout the country.

Then in 740, when Fujiwara no Hirotsugu rebelled in Kyushu, Shōmu reinforced his armies of suppression by ordering seven-foot statues of the bodhisattva Kannon cast and suitable scriptures read in all provinces. His commanding general, upon reaching Kyushu, went to the Hachiman Shrine at Usa to pay his respects, presumably to neutralize any resentment the Kyushu god might feel toward the invading army. And the following spring, after Hirotsugu had been seized and executed, the court conveyed appropriate thanks and gifts to Hachiman. These included Buddhist sutras and, eventually, new shrine buildings that were heavily Buddhist in architectural style.

Shortly after learning of Hirotsugu's death, Shōmu also ordered officials in each province to build, staff, and provision a provincial temple (*kokubunsōji*) and nunnery (*kokubunniji*) where the Sutra of Golden Light was to be expounded. He also reiterated an earlier order that each erect a seven-story pagoda. The accompanying commentary offered insight into Shōmu's understanding of affairs.[6] After apologizing for his incompetence as ruler, he listed his actions in response to the smallpox disaster. Thanks to those, he observed, fine weather and good harvests had followed. But he had remained concerned and ordered the erection of pagodas and the copying of more sutras, as advised by the Sutra of the Four Heavenly Kings (Shitennō). Now, he continued, to assure the eternal flourishing of both the realm and Buddhist teachings, he again called for the erection of pagodas. In addition, he ordered the building of provincial monasteries and nunneries to bring Buddhist teachings close to the people everywhere. His order then specified how these establishments were to be staffed and sustained.

Shōmu's next major religious initiative occurred in conjunction with his great plan for a new capital. Early in 741 he launched palace construction at Kuni. And in the following year he started a second palace project at Shigaraki in the hills some twenty kilometers to the northeast, at a site that distanced him from factional critics in his government while bringing him closer to sources of timber, iron ore, and clay for roof tiles. In the autumn of 743 he ordered the casting of a great Buddha statue there, intending it to become the center of a new state cult.

The image he wanted at Shigaraki was Rushana (Vairocana), the central figure in the Kegon Sutra. That sutra had been translated into Chinese and brought to Japan only a few decades earlier, giving it the virtue of up-to-dateness. Moreover, its teaching was doctrinally appealing because it pictured a great central Rushana surrounded by "the thousand great buddhas and billion small buddhas," all responsive to Rushana's guidance.[7] The sutra informed its readers that they, too, could join this celestial community by accepting its teachings.

One suspects that Shōmu found this sutra and its awesome imagery especially attractive as an ideal representation of the political order he sought, with a *tennō* graciously guiding "the thousand" aristocratic families and, below them, "the billion" ordinary folk. His new system of a central temple and provincial monasteries and nunneries was to be the physical instrument that unified political and spiritual realms. He expressed his hope this way when he announced his decision to build the gigantic bronze statue at Shigaraki:

> Having respectfully succeeded to the throne through no virtue of Our own, out of a constant solicitude for all men We have been ever intent on aiding them to reach the shore of the Buddha-land ... Our fervent desire is that, under the aegis of the Three Treasures [of Buddhism], the benefits of peace may be brought to all in heaven and on earth, even animals and plants sharing in its fruits, for all time to come.
>
> Therefore, ... We take this occasion to proclaim Our great vow of erecting an image of [Rushana] Buddha in gold and copper ... that the entire land may be joined with Us in the fellowship of Buddhism and enjoy in common the advantages which this undertaking affords to the attainment of Buddhahood.[8]

Workmen were assembled and the project commenced. However, the combined tasks of building Kuni and Shigaraki soon proved excessive, so Shōmu halted the work at Kuni. Evidently completion of the religious project had acquired higher priority.

Despite that retrenchment, fiscal conditions worsened. Other problems also intruded, and the Kuni–Shigaraki enterprise grew chaotic. Then, for reasons that we suggest below, in 744–745 the two sites were endangered by outbreaks of raging wildfire. When violent earthquake added further evidence of godly displeasure, the entire venture tottered.

Shōmu did his best. He ordered more sutras read and read more sutras himself. He humored Hachiman and the ghost of Hirotsugu by authorizing family ranks for those notables in Kyushu who lacked them. He prayed for rain when another forest fire erupted, and made Shintō offerings at the tombs of all his imperial ancestors. All came to nought, however, and in the end he and his followers returned to Nara, they with relief, he in defeat. Officialdom then undid most of his policies of preceding years, in the process transferring the great Rushana project to a temple in the city.

In 747 Shōmu returned to his religious undertaking. He ordered that work be accelerated on the provincial monasteries and nunneries, and assigned them more land and cultivators to facilitate the task; within a decade over a third of them had been built. Then early in 749 gold was discovered in the former Emishi territory of Mutsu Province, making feasible the gilding and hence the completion of the relocated Rushana image. A month after receiving this proof that the gods and Buddhas approved his project, Shōmu staged an elaborate state ritual of thanksgiving at the temple, which was designated Tōdaiji from its location due east of the palace. One of the participants was the Shintō priestess from the Usa Shrine in Kyushu, who joined in ceremonies that thanked Hachiman for aiding in the Rushana project, presumably by acquiescing, or perhaps assisting, in the defeat of Hirotsugu nine years earlier. Hachiman was then installed in a new shrine adjacent to Tōdaiji's inner compound (see figure 4.3). There he could serve as eternal protective *kami* of both the temple and the imperial family, in the process binding Kyushu closer to the Kinai leadership.

On that occasion Shōmu also commanded that additional rice fields be awarded to the temples of major families, including the Fujiwara's Kōfukuji. Not long after that he abdicated in favor of his daughter, who ascended the throne as Kōken *tennō*.

Construction at Tōdaiji continued for years, eventuating in a complex of awesome grandeur. Doctrines and images of the Kegon school enjoyed special favor, but the temple's monks were organized into scholarly groups who studied and translated texts in all the major doctrinal traditions of Buddhist thought as then expounded: the "six schools" (Kegon, Hossō, Ritsu, Sanron, Kusha, Jōjitsu) as they are commonly known. Tōdaiji thus became the

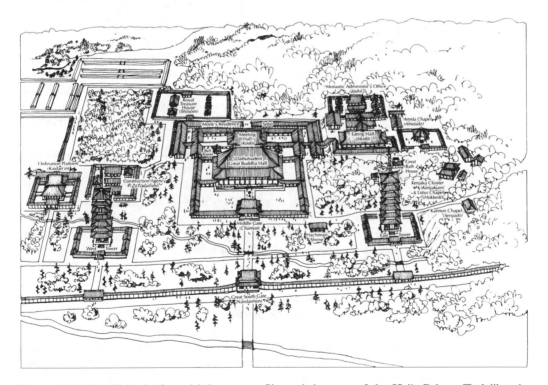

Figure 4.3 Tōdaiji in the late eighth century. Situated due east of the Heijō Palace, Tōdaiji at its height was a grand establishment complete with two pagodas, residence and administration buildings and various ancillary facilities. Its towering central Vairocana image in the "Great Buddha Hall" was protected by Hachiman in his modest shrine adjacent the front right corner of the Buddha Hall's walled enclosure. *Source*: Joan R. Piggott, *The Emergence of Japanese Kingship* (Stanford: SUP, 1997), p. 270.

supreme center of all Buddhist learning, the one place in Japan qualified to train and license monks for the entire realm.

By the time of his death, then, Shōmu had created the instruments of a state church. His Tōdaiji, with its great Rushana Buddha, constituted the centerpiece of a doctrinally grounded religious structure that enveloped the entire realm. Its powers radiated outward through an array of subordinate provincial monasteries and nunneries, all bound to the Tōdaiji by doctrine, regulations, and staffing arrangements, and all supported by sustenance households (*hehito*) that provided tribute goods and labor.

THE RITSURYŌ STATE AT 750

The *ritsuryō* state rose through a convoluted and opportunistic process that involved both political intent and accident. As in other societies, the system that resulted from this process rarely functioned according to the rules, and administrators continually modified them in attempts to improve their efficacy. It is still useful, however, to describe in static terms the state envisioned by creators of the Taihō and Yōrō codes.

THE HIERARCHY OF STATE

Their *ritsuryō* state was an elaborately organized structure that linked the imperial court to the ordinary commoner through a hierarchy of central, provincial, district, and local governmental organs. Those organs, staffed by officials of appropriate pedigree, were intended to assure that the peace was kept and that producers forwarded tribute as stipulated to those running the government.

The head of state, the *tennō*, was chosen by malleable rules from among a small group of the preceding monarch's immediate kin. Once properly enthroned, she or he could claim, as Shōmu did in 743, that "It is We who possess the wealth of the land; it is We who possess all power in the land."[9] This claim to authority was sanctioned by an intricate web of ideas that anchored imperial rule in a godly ancestry and that defined good governance in broad terms of cherishing the gods, Buddhas, ancestors, all living creatures, and the realm itself.

The emperor exercised his (or her) absolute authority – and much less than absolute power – through a government staffed and operated according to a plethora of written regulations. As formulated in the Yōrō code, the central administration consisted of two parts, the *jingikan*, which actually was a minor bureau that handled the many Shintō rituals of state, and the *daijōkan* or Council of State, which oversaw most matters. The *daijōkan* was headed by a small group of officials (Prime Minister [or Chancellor: *daijō daijin*], Ministers of Left and Right, and a few Counselors) who served as the emperor's advisory council. A dozen or so other senior officials provided the administrative linkage between this small ruling group and the eight ministries that constituted the body of central government.

These eight ministries were staffed by some 350 administrators and 6,500 subordinate clerks, technicians, and menial assistants. Another 3,000 people of similar character staffed the Council of State's inspectoral agency, the households of the *tennō*, his consorts, and heir, and the several capital guard and police units. By 750, then, some 10,000 people found employment in the central government at Nara.

Chains of command linked these central organs to the general populace. Metropolitan offices administered Nara city itself, and special offices handled border affairs at Dazaifu and at times in the northeast. The rest of the realm – the four million or more tribute payers resident in the 4,000 or so "townships" (*gō*) that officially comprised the hinterland – was controlled, in principle at least, through the sixty-odd provincial headquarters (*kokufu*) and the 550–600 district offices below them.

A *kokufu* contained the several instruments of secular government: "administrative offices, storehouses, a school, a military garrison, and other facilities."[10] Its staff, which numbered somewhere in the hundreds, depending on the province's population, was managed by a handful of supervisory officials. This staff handled the governor's basic tasks: to propitiate the deities, register the people, nurture them, foster their production, and reward their virtue. The Yōrō Code instructed every governor to

> oversee rice fields and residences, persons of both free and unfree status, settlement of disputes, tribute collection, storehouses, and corvée labor. He is also in charge of troops, weapons, drums, and flutes; post stations and relay horses; beacons, forts, and pastures; checkpoints; all draft animals including those publicly and privately owned; goods abandoned; and Buddhist temple-monasteries and their clergy.[11]

Little lay beyond his purview.

Associated with each *kokufu* as instruments of state religious authority were the personnel of the provincial Buddhist monastery and nunnery and the administrators of provincial Shintō shrines (*sōja*). Much as the Buddhist units served to link provincial religion to the Tōdaiji, so the presence of Shintō units placed local gods in a proper relationship to the imperial gods at Nara, Ise, and elsewhere. They helped resolve any conflicts of practice between local and imperial shrines, incorporated local gods and their festivals into the imperial Shintō pantheon, assigned ranks and ritual offerings to local shrines, and fostered the construction of such shrines where none existed.

Each province was divided into several districts (*kōri*) headed by magistrates, who generally were local magnates and commonly passed their offices on to their heirs. Assisted by kin and servant households that provided administrative and military staff as well as artisans and a labor force, these magistrates oversaw various types of handicraft production and controlled tax collection and forwarding in their district.

It was at the next lower level that the tidy schemes of system builders collided with the untidy reality of the realm. The actual producer population was distributed irregularly in hamlets and isolated houses in accordance with the particulars of geography. A hamlet consisting of 20–30 dwellings with

4–6 occupants apiece may have been typical, but the number and proximity of houses in a locality varied considerably. Insofar as children were raised in their mother's natal household, moreover, nuptial households formed belatedly and natal households tended to be large, consisting of a house head, his (or occasionally her) siblings, their offspring, and other kin and subordinates, perhaps a total of ten to twenty members, who presumably occupied two to four dwellings.

For purposes of taxation and public control, however, *ritsuryō* regulations transcended this irregularity by declaring that a statutory household (*ko*) numbered about twenty people, that fifty such households were to constitute a township, and that about seven townships were to be included in an average district. Presumably each district magistrate had the task of determining how the actual residents of his bailiwick would be fitted into this scheme, and problems in making the fit may have been one reason for occasional modifications in the legislation.

Each statutory household was to be controlled by its head (man or woman), who was responsible for its diverse tribute obligations. Each township was officially under its headman, a local notable, who was responsible for

> supervision of population, planting of agricultural [crops] and mulberries, prevention of wrongdoing, and exaction of taxes and corvée.[12]

Thus were producers to be kept in line and their output funneled upward via district headquarters to their betters in high places. Ideally those goals would be attained peacably, but should that hope not be realized, coercive alternatives were at hand.

The military system that backed up civil officialdom was headed by the Ministry of Military Affairs in Nara. It administered "troop registers, armories, pastures, war-horses, public and private pack animals, boats, fortifications, signal fires, and postal roads," and was charged with overseeing weapons production, intelligence, and troop deployments.[13] Guard forces for the capital consisted of select units composed of lesser nobles and other units composed of peasant troops drawn from provincial battalions. These latter proved of little military value, however, and gradually were displaced by guard forces led by professional military men whom more and more capital aristocrats hired as bodyguards.

The provincial military system was in essence a moderately trained reserve force available for emergency mobilization. In principle local magnates commanded battalions of 600–1,000 men apiece, the troops being conscripted at the rate of about one per statutory household. Each conscript was obligated to appear for periodic drills, to furnish his own provisions, and to arm himself as both archer and swordsman, complete with weapons and, "one straw helmet, one pouch for rice, one water cup, one salt container, one set of leggings, and one pair of straw sandals."[14]

Because of the low productivity of agriculture, however, these obligations proved onerous, particularly when duty took a man out of his hamlet during cropping season, and conscripts often fled rather than serve, even though service won them exemption from other tribute burdens. In consequence provincial conscript forces were smaller and much less effective in practice than planners intended. And that situation reinforced the reliance on horse warfare that had emerged during the fifth century, a reliance reflected in courtly encouragement of horse breeding, training in mounted warfare, and the utilization of local figures experienced in such matters.

STAFFING AND FINANCING THE GOVERNMENT

Officials to staff central and provincial posts were chosen from among those of appropriate aristocratic rank. The Yōrō Code reserved the most senior ranks for members of the imperial family while allotting twenty six lower grades to the aristocracy as a whole. A few favored families, Fujiwara most notably, dominated the highest of these, which gave them nearly exclusive access to top government posts and the generous income that came with them. This income enabled imperial princes and the highest ranking aristocratic households to maintain palatial residence compounds that included many buildings and large support staffs in Nara and, later, Heian.[15] Indeed, a striking characteristic of this regime, one that resembles the present-day, mega-business world, was the great disparity in wealth, status, and power between the handful of senior-office-holding households and the thousands of lesser aristocrats. The heads of these lesser families occupied the lower ranks, which gave them access to lesser offices and sharply less income and opulence. In the hinterland top *kokufu* positions normally were held by middle-rank appointees despatched from Nara, while provincial magnates had access only to subordinate provincial and district posts.

Ideally aristocratic status was hereditary, and in fact very few lesser folk entered the ranks of the elite. Within the aristocracy, however, households and lineages flourished and failed unpredictably, depending on the vagaries of politics, procreation, and pathogens. The fact that some family names, most notably Fujiwara, were held concurrently by several related households obscures the continual ebb and flow of fortune among the favored few. Aristocrats of the day recognized the uncertainties of life, however, and that awareness, together with the intense desire to protect one's position at or near the apex of the tall, slender pyramid of privilege, helped spawn the succession disputes, factional struggles, and other rivalries that constituted so much of elite political history.

Life's uncertainties also shaped land-holding arrangements because those atop the *ritsuryō* pyramid devised the arrangements, and unsurprisingly they did so with their own fiscal interests uppermost in mind. Builders of that pyramid recognized two basic truisms about their fiscal base. First, they realized that while yield from forest, fishery, and mine was valuable, agricultural production was its core. That perception led them to view land in terms of two categories, arable and other, and to focus their attention on the former. Second, they realized that arable land was worthless to themselves unless someone worked it, and that insight led them to regard arable as essentially a tool to be allocated to producers in the same manner as farm tools, residence lots, and seed-rice loans (*suiko*).

Continental examples, which played a key role in shaping *ritsuryō* political structure, also provided guides for organizing the fisc. From the 640s onward, rulers strengthened control of their tribute sources by conducting surveys to locate arable land and censuses to identify the membership of producer households. By the eighth century they had developed an elaborate system of cadastral registers designed to assure the elite a durable, stable income base.

Pertinent regulations specified that the amount of arable to be assigned a producer household depended on the number of men, women, and children it contained, with allotment per capita ranging from about a fifth of a hectare (a half acre) on down, depending on the assignee's gender and age. It was presumed that parcels of that size would enable villagers to sustain themselves while providing rulers with the requisite tribute: an optimal use of land and labor alike, a happy conjunction of benevolent rule and efficient exploitation. To perpetuate the system, rules stipulated that parcels of land should be reassigned periodically as household size changed. Surely the system invited villagers to misrepresent their family numbers – and to keep married daughters at home. But even though regulatory changes of 723 and 743 complicated and slowed the original six-year reallocation procedure, surviving documents suggest that the policy was in fact sustained until about the year 800.

The land itself was recorded in surveys not in terms of actual fields but in areal equivalents. Administrators envisaged the surveyed arable in geometric terms, picturing a checkerboard layout with large squares of approximately 45 hectares divided into thirty-six, city-block-sized squares of about 1.25 hectares apiece. These were divided, in turn, into ten rectangular parcels of equal size, hypothetical fields called *kubunden*, that were to be bounded by footpaths and irrigation ditches.

In fact the *kubunden* in this model did correspond to paddy fields as actually laid out on some flatlands. However, given the need for tabletop-flat fields with good quality topsoil and a watertight layer of subsoil, topography thwarted the model's application in most areas, giving rise instead to irregularly shaped fields of varying size. Because this *kubunden* system was basically a mechanism for applying official producer-acreage-tribute ratios to the land, however, it only needed to exist as statistics in survey documents to fulfill its fiscal purpose.

Cadastral documents thus identified tribute-producing households and the quantities of land, by definition the emperor's land, that had been assigned to them. Once identified, statutory households served as the basic units of fiscal calculation when emperors wished to grant income to their relatives, officials, or religious institutions. For that purpose they were designated "sustenance households" (*hehito*; later *fuko*) and were assigned in township-sized multiples of fifty. In theory they were the emperor's to give or deny as she or he deemed proper. In fact, of course, imperial control of these assets depended on the collaboration of aristocrats, and *ritsuryō* leaders always recognized that the claim to absolute imperial authority required some degree of aristocratic acquiescence. As a result the actual allocation of sustenance households amounted to a continual calculus that involved power relations between the imperial household, princely households, the households of other aristocrats and local magnates, and the temples and shrines affiliated with them.

These fiscal arrangements identified tribute sources and facilitated their allocation to beneficiaries. The actual goods and services that they extracted were diverse and fell into several official tribute categories. In essence, however, villagers provided rice, a variety of other local products – salt, textiles, handicrafts, miscellaneous foodstuffs, and forest products – civilian corvée labor, and military service and supplies.

As a whole these cadastral arrangements linked producers to land with sufficient consistency so that the rulers could still treat people, whether registered as taxable households on imperial land or as "sustenance households" assigned to tribute recipients, as the basic units of fiscal calculation. However, the continual movement of people and the constant forming, fizzuring, and failing of household units made registration extremely difficult and rendered many cadastres obsolete even before their information entered government files. Moreover, as tracts of tillable and well-wooded land became scarce in the Kinai vicinity, land itself acquired intrinsic value, and competition for it intensified, as we note below. These circumstances undermined the new arrangements, leading to modification and eventual abandonment of periodic land redistribution and to other changes in the mechanisms of land control.

As of 750, however, the cultivators of much of Japan's arable produced tribute that found its way to the warehouses of provincial headquarters and the central government in Nara. Some of that income sustained the imperial family and maintained the court and its activities, but much was distributed to aristocrats as office salary and special merit rewards. The tribute from other cultivators, the roughly 15 percent known as sustenance households, went directly to the warehouses of temples, shrines, and aristocratic households, thanks nominally to imperial decrees.[16] Whichever path the tribute followed, however, the goods thus transmitted served to sustain the favored few of the *ritsuryō* order.

THE BROADER CONTEXT

The century or so in which the *ritsuryō* order became established witnessed remarkable changes in the world of the Japanese elite – in terms of their urban environment, routines of political life, higher cultural interests, religious practices, and relations with the wider society and its encompassing ecosystem. The *ritsuryō* order was, however, essentially a system for structuring life among the privileged classes – a pool of thousands in an ocean of millions – and its effects on the broader society and environment were much less pronounced.

Insofar as an impact at this broader level is still visible in the surviving record, it suggests that creation of the *ritsuryō* system generally had unfavorable consequences in terms of both human and biosystem well-being. The evidence seems to tell us that during the eighth century the *ritsuryō* order, given its norms and technology, overloaded the ecosystem's "carrying capacity" in central Japan, to the harsh disadvantage of many. In doing so it made those decades a watershed of sorts, the time when Japan's non-intensive agricultural system passed from a long era of comparatively rapid and sustained growth to an era when growth was appreciably slower and more erratic.

THE HUMAN CONDITION

As a whole the *ritsuryō* system had only a modest impact on the *modus operandi* of the agricultural order that had taken shape during Yayoi–Kofun centuries. In that order most people lived in hamlet-sized communities numbering only a few rather large households. Dwellings commonly were dispersed irregularly about the countryside rather than clustering in larger settlements, as in more recent centuries. Houses were few and scattered because from the inception of cultivation arable and reclaimable land had been plentiful, tillers used little fertilizer, and yield per acre was modest. Paddy soils were nourished by the nutrient load of incoming irrigation water, but dry field soils quickly became exhausted. When fields became depleted, tillers abandoned them for a few years until they regained fertility, which meant that unused and temporarily unusable land was interspersed among active fields. Such untilled areas were of only modest value, mainly producing fodder for horses, which served as cavalry mounts and pack animals.[17] Relatively large areas of land could therefore support only modest numbers of people living in sparsely populated, poorly nucleated settlements.

Rulers, as well as some members of the clergy, most notably the celebrated monk, Gyōki, tried to expand production, especially in the Yamato River Basin. They promoted land clearance, fostered construction of irrigation ponds and systems, produced and distributed farm tools, and diversified the crops grown. However, their success was limited; in the outcome agricultural practice changed very little. In consequence, persistent government attempts to extract more income notwithstanding, the combined yield from basic rice tribute and seed-loan interest seems to have stuck at about 6 percent of total output. One suspects that this inelasticity in the tax base was a major reason for the hierarchy of state being so narrow at its peak, with so very few top families enjoying opulence and relative security while so many aristocrats found life risky and only marginally comfortable. As a corollary, it helps explain why competition for land and status was so intense and even violent.

This does not mean, however, that cultivators were cleverly outfoxing the tax man and thereby living comfortably. Even at the existing tribute rate, one scholar suggests, "the yield from a [peasant] household allotment was not sufficient to meet the basic needs of its members."[18] So villagers had to supplement their income through tenant farming, illicit swidden production, and the pursuit of secondary occupations, whether as foragers or manual laborers. Indeed, so many cultivators tried to escape their legal burdens by leaving home and becoming vagrants that the government repeatedly issued decrees to halt the practice, if only because vagrants were nearly impossible to tax.

Insofar as the *ritsuryō* order did impinge on the lives of villagers, it seems most commonly to have been hurtful. For them the most consequential changes appear to have been twofold: heavier tribute obligations and greater exposure to epidemic disease. These changes were most pronounced in and around the Kinai vicinity, where government control was most firm and the aristocracy, along with its large supporting population of servants, laborers, and provisioners, most permanently resident.

Of the villagers' several tribute obligations, the most onerous seem to have been civilian and military service. The rulers enjoyed a long-standing capacity to mobilize huge numbers of corvée laborers, as the giant *kofun* attest. And their various military campaigns reveal their ability to deploy impressive conscript armies. However, they were unable, or perhaps unconcerned, to give their manpower adequate care, and the harsh conditions of corvée work and military life were a chronic problem. Court and aristocracy resorted to deceptive and coercive measures to obtain and hold their conscripts, while many soldiers and laborers protested and absconded. Others died of disease or malnutrition while on the job or completed their terms of service only to encounter difficulty getting home again. Together with burdensome levies on food production, these service obligations placed many people at risk of malnutrition, whether at home or in crowded, unsanitary military and labor camps.

The public hardship of these decades surely helped foster the type of "social Buddhism" in which Gyōki and other monks and nuns left their monasteries and nunneries to work among Kinai commoners, promoting the construction of "gardens, ponds, medical facilities, harbors, bridges, roads, and resting places for the weary," as well as Buddhist structures of religious import.[19] The success of these itinerants in winning followers troubled rulers and Buddhist leaders, who saw in their performance a corruption of doctrine and a challenge to authority. That concern led in turn to the issuance of more regulations and prohibitions to maintain Buddhist discipline and control the religious community.

Creation of the *ritsuryō* system thus produced hardship and socio-political complications due to the costs of capital-city construction and elite maintenance. Other facets of the new political order led to a medical catastrophe. For centuries, one suspects, contact with the continent had repeatedly brought pathogens to Japan. However, the development of an extensive highway system, with its traveling officials, messengers, tribute transporters, conscript battalions, and corvée laborers en route to and from work sites, helped assure the dissemination of germs widely about the countryside. The level and frequency of dissemination were sufficient, it appears, to transform such communicable diseases as smallpox and measles from local, family tragedies into a deadly social menace, producing widespread and recurrent epidemics but not a sustained general immunity. Much as the stone-citied European society of the fourteenth century offered a favorable environment for the bacterium of bubonic plague, so the hamlet-based *ritsuryō* order evidently provided welcome conditions for select pathogens, most notably the smallpox virus.

Little is known about epidemics before the eighth century because a system for reporting and recording them was not developed until the 690s. For the reigns from Jitō to Genshō, however, there are several references to worrisome epidemics, and after a lull during the 720s came the outbreaks of the mid-730s, which were catastrophic in scale. Caused, perhaps, by an exceptionally virulent form of smallpox, they not only ravaged the aristocracy in Nara but also appear to have decimated the producer populace more generally, especially from the Kinai basin westward, where travelers spread the disease most thoroughly. By one estimate total human losses for the country may have been 25 percent or more.[20]

In following generations the population recovered, but for the next four centuries or so it appears to have grown only modestly, rising from an estimated 5,000,000 around the year 700 to perhaps 5.5 million as of 900 and about 7,000,000 by 1200, with most of the growth occurring outside the Kinai Basin.[21] Moreover, the centuries were marked by recurrent epidemics, less horrendous than those of the 730s but sufficient to cut repeatedly into recent growth as successive generations were born only to be struck down in adulthood because they had not been exposed in youth to smallpox, measles, or other pathogens that would enable them to establish immunity against fatal adult infection.

TRENDS IN THE ECOSYSTEM

By its nature an ecosystem is a wonderfully complex bundle of interacting variables, and any attempt to disaggregate the whole for purposes of analysis yields an oversimplified understanding of internal dynamics and causal relationships. This is all the more true when the evidence offers only tiny glimpses of the whole and when one must discuss it with brevity. Nevertheless, a few observations about environmental context during the *ritsuryō* heyday seem needed.

For the realm as a whole, creation of the *ritsuryō* system had only a modest impact because it failed to alter the existing hamlet-based agricultural order and could not therefore support as grand a social superstructure as its founders may have intended. In Tōhoku, it is true, considerable forest habitat was reduced to arable as Emishi territory was taken over by settlers from elsewhere, mainly the Kantō. But even there the changes yielded a pattern consonant with the long-established biological configuration of other regions: in essence, rice culture on lowlands, dry field tillage on diluvium and the upper reaches of alluvial fans, and patches of swidden scattered through the prevailing woodland of bedrock mountains. Elsewhere in the realm this configuration persisted with only modest incremental changes, which suggests the durability of the existing agricultural order within the larger ecosystem.

For the Kinai vicinity, however, formation of the *ritsuryō* order, and most particularly the creation of a great capital city, led to what seems best characterized as a condition of "ecological overload." That outcome is evidenced by a constellation of developments: more frequent reports of crop failure, famine, and epidemic disease; proliferating reports of wildfire in Kinai woodlands; and intensified elite competition for tribute income and the control of natural resources.

The court and aristocracy did try to supplement their Kinai income by expanding their tribute base elsewhere. Thus, Tōhoku policy in Genmei's day was in large part a drive for more food production. And the quest for arable and its tribute yield may also have underlain Shōmu's repeated expeditions into Emishi territory. However, difficulties of transport and the limits of state power meant that the central elite gained little from Tōhoku, remaining largely dependent on the yield of Kinai and adjoining areas.

For the Kinai Basin, one may suggest, the signs of "overload" were appearing because, in the first instance, most of the area's flat land had been logged off by the 690s, even before the great urban construction projects commenced, which forced woodsmen to harvest steeper and more distant hillsides, including those of Iga and Ōmi. Conversion of Kinai from forested realm into a land of open fields and deforested hills gradually modified the area's hydrological behavior, letting water flow to the sea more rapidly and possibly reducing the area's annual rainfall. Especially as logging and fuel wood gathering exposed soil on more hilly areas, water runoff and erosion accelerated and the problem of alternating flood and drought became more pronounced. In consequence the acreage of paddy that existing irrigation systems could reliably nurture may well have been declining and the frequency of destructive local floods increasing during the very decades when rulers and cultivators were attempting to expand agricultural output to meet the needs of the new *ritsuryō* order and its nascent cities.

Furthermore, the logging of hillsides produced comparatively little reclaimable land. As opportunities for reclamation diminished, released corvée laborers found fewer chances to support themselves as cultivators, and more of them ended up vagrants or dead. Finally, the patches of upland that could be tilled often were of relatively poor quality, and in some cases their use diverted water from other, better, lower-lying fields.

Cumulatively these trends probably increased the proportion of the harvest likely to fail and thus heightened the potential for famine. The problem is suggested by a type of decree issued during periods of drought in 693, 715, and 723. In the 723 version the Council of State encouraged people throughout the country to plant barley and wheat because they are

> unexcelled as sustenance during periods of starvation. For this reason, We allocated government resources and had them planted throughout the realm in the reign of the Empress Jitō. Since that time, We have failed altogether to cultivate the grains and have been afflicted by starvation.[22]

Although dry-field grains yielded a smaller harvest per acre than did paddy, they did not depend on an overburdened irrigation system and were therefore less vulnerable in times of drought.

The sustained wood cutting necessitated by city construction and maintenance also meant that more and more logged-over hillside simply was left to throw up stands of scrub growth, such as dwarf bamboo and red pine, which are highly susceptible to fire. Wildfire began showing up in the chronicles in 703, erupting in areas that had provided timber for earlier building projects. In following decades brush fires became more frequent and more destructive, and during the 740s, as earlier noted, fast-moving blazes in areas logged for the building of Nara ravaged sections of Ōmi and Iga, threatened Kuni and Shigaraki, and contributed to the upset of Shōmu's governance.

City building, forest depletion, and difficulties in Kinai agriculture also led from Jitō's day onward to an intensified elite scramble for control of land. That trend suggests that even though tribute regulations continued to treat producers as the real base of the system, land was actually acquiring more intrinsic value in aristocratic eyes, in part because the trees thereon provided the timber and fuel wood for urban construction and living. Whereas large trees were becoming scarce by Genmei's day, agricultural producers could always be found thanks to population growth and the continual turnover of corvée labor crews, so the latter became less highly prized. Then, however, the epidemics of the 730s reduced the population so abruptly, especially in the Kinai region, that abandoned land became common and people to work it scarce. That shift in the land–labor balance led to new changes in regulations, which were designed to encourage producers to stay put and aristocrats and temples to foster production on lands they controlled.

In following decades the problems of deforestation, wildfire, drought, flooding, and timber scarcity persisted. They altered the biological composition of some woodlands in the Kinai region, led eventually to the long-term dessication of parts of Ōmi, helped thwart construction of new capitals, sustained elite competition for land, and contributed to changes of foodstuffs and other items in the markets of Heian.

In short, it appears that, given the norms and technology of *ritsuryō* governance, its creators were able to establish the level of social superstructure one sees around 750, but beyond that they could not go. Instead, in following centuries leaders struggled simply to maintain what they had. Their best efforts notwithstanding, however, the *ritsuryō* system gradually fell apart – although it lasted far longer than most regimes the world has known. A new, more elaborate polity and urban society became possible only centuries later, during the 1500s, after changes in the hinterland had substantially increased the rural population and rural productivity, enabling the privileged classes to achieve a level of tribute extraction that could support a much more thorough institutional consolidation.

[5]   RITSURYŌ *ADAPTATION AND DECAY (750–1250)*

CHAPTER SYNOPSIS

A POLITICAL NARRATIVE
EMPERORS AND REGENTS
(750–1050)
INSEI AND *BUKE* (1050–1250)

THE ELEMENTS OF STABILITY
CONTEXTUAL FACTORS

ADAPTIVE STRATEGIES

FORCES FOR CHANGE
DIMENSIONS OF CHANGE
RISE OF THE *BUSHI*

With creation of the *ritsuryō* system, demographic trends shifted from growth that was relatively rapid and sustained to a condition of near-stasis. Stasis is not changelessness, of course, and processes of change persisted. To considerable extent, however, they constituted forms of social churning, adjustment, and adaptation in which the basic character and scale of affairs, the distribution of power and privilege, and the informing mentality of society – insofar as one can deduce that – retained a high level of constancy for centuries.

In thinking about the highest levels of political power, it is helpful to conceive of the centuries 750–1250 in terms of four phases. In the first, roughly 750–850, emperors (*tennō*) were dominant, moving the capital to Heian-*kyō* and consolidating imperial rule there. Then, from about 850 to 1050 or so, the chiefs of the most powerful Fujiwara household dominated affairs, followed in about 1050–1180 by a few hardy, retired emperors (*in*) who governed essentially as the most powerful and prestigious landed magnates of the realm. Finally, from about 1180 to 1250, the leaders of a coalition of warrior households (*buke*) centered in the Kantō region suppressed rivals across Japan and working from their Kamakura headquarters kept the peace in the emperor's name. To considerable degree, however, they did so through the attenuated *ritsuryō* arrangements of the day and with the collaboration of select aristocrats who continued to staff the organs of imperial government in Kyoto, as Heian was coming to be called.

This story of changing leadership overlaps other narratives that focus on different aspects of political process. Thus, in military matters, the original *ritsuryō* arrangements were modified over time. The conscription system was abandoned; aristocrats distanced themselves from military tasks, and career military men (*bushi*) assumed more and more responsibility for bandit suppression and peace keeping, in the end riding those tasks to the heights of power. In fiscal matters, the authority to control producers and collect tribute income was transferred bit by bit from government offices to the administrative organs of temples, shrines, aristocratic households (including that of retired emperors), and eventually warrior households. That process slowly undercut the central government's control of the fisc, making it more and more dependent on the support of others. In the end what these several narratives combine to reveal is the broader story of how authority, administrative dominance, coercive power, and the control of landed wealth migrated as time passed, finally coming to rest in the hands of groups that had little reason to preserve the *ritsuryō* distribution of power and privilege.

That process took a half-millennium, however. Surely the fact that the old order finally fell is less remarkable than the fact that it lasted so long. After adumbrating the central political story line so as to identify key figures, arrangements, and events, let us ask what cluster of factors may explain the longevity of the *ritsuryō* regime and after that what constellation of forces led to its disintegration. This approach, as we shall see, points up the conditional quality of history: developments that up to a point helped sustain the old order finally became destructive of it because of the changing way they related to other variables, in the end contributing to the emergence of a new distribution of advantage.

In the end, of course, the *ritsuryō* system did fall apart and new governing arrangements emerged. Several factors – changes in agronomic practice and rural organization, new economic and intellectual influences from the continent, and the appearance of local warriors who rejected aristocratic claims to primacy – combined to overwhelm the old elite. The changes ushered in a long season of political disorder as warriors struggled to control expanding production and the power potential it represented and to avoid defeat at the hands of rivals engaged in the same project. That renewal of competitive state building became visible in Tōhoku near the end of the eleventh century and, as we note in subsequent chapters, it intensified more or less steadily thereafter until completion in the early seventeenth.

A Political Narrative

The story of elite politics can be adumbrated using the four phases mentioned above: rule by emperors, Fujiwara regents (*kanpaku*), retired emperors, and a domineering warrior house.

Emperors and regents (750–1050)

Following Shōmu's death in 756, factional politics in Heijō-*kyō* grew savage. His daughter weathered two tumultuous terms as Kōken and Shōtoku *tennō*, but the factional fighting was not brought under control until the mature and strong-willed Kanmu ascended the throne in 781.

In the manner of his most celebrated predecessors Kanmu viewed the creation of a new capital as a major expression of righteous governance, and he promptly launched a new building project at Nagaoka, just west of where the Katsura, Kamo, and Uji rivers join. Three years later he formally moved into his new palace, but the site proved faulty, mainly because much of it was susceptible to flooding. That condition, together with violent political quarrels and worrisome omens, soon led him to abandon Nagaoka-*kyō* in favor of another site some ten kilometers to the northeast and across the Katsura, a capital he designated Heian-*kyō* and occupied in 794. Although his immediate successor (Heizei, r. 806–809) attempted to return the capital to Nara, the attempt failed, and Heian remained the *ritsuryō* headquarters for centuries. Indeed, simply completing its construction proved impossible, despite Kanmu's unexampled reliance on recycled timber and tile and his exceptionally vigorous measures to commandeer timber stands and labor crews.

The builders did, however, complete the capital proper, the sprawling, rectangular, 160-hectare compound chockablock with government buildings that dominated the north central part of the city (see figure 5.1). Outside of its walls builders erected blocks of aristocratic residences, other blocks of plebeian housing, two large city markets, and the great axial boulevard, Suzaku Ōji, which ran four kilometers southward to the city's main entrance, the Rajō gate (Rajōmon). The grandeur of that boulevard has echoed down through the centuries:

> Light green they shine,
> Dark green they shine,
> Stretching into the distance as far as the eye can see,
> They glitter like jewels.
> Oh, how they glitter – those low-hanging boughs
> Of the willows on Suzaku Ōji.[1]

Rajō gate we know from museum models and movie sets, and the palace's main audience hall (Daigokuden) from a modern replica, the Heian Shrine of present-day Kyoto, built in the 1890s as one in a host of measures to celebrate the new Meiji imperial regime.

Kanmu and his gifted son Saga both proved to be energetic and creative rulers. The construction of Heian was their most visible accomplishment, but they did much more. They promoted Buddhist temple construction and doctrinal exegesis, most influentially that of the Tendai and Shingon traditions, as a way to establish Heian's stature as a center of spiritual truth and religious power superior to Nara with its Tōdaiji, Kōfukuji, and other great temples. They fostered cultural contacts with the continent. They made key changes in domestic administrative procedure to simplify control and improve governing effectiveness. They reformed military organization and procedure. Finally, they deployed armies to drive stubbornly resistant Emishi forces farther northward, eventually stabilizing the frontier in the Morioka vicinity. All in all they enjoyed an uncommon degree of success.

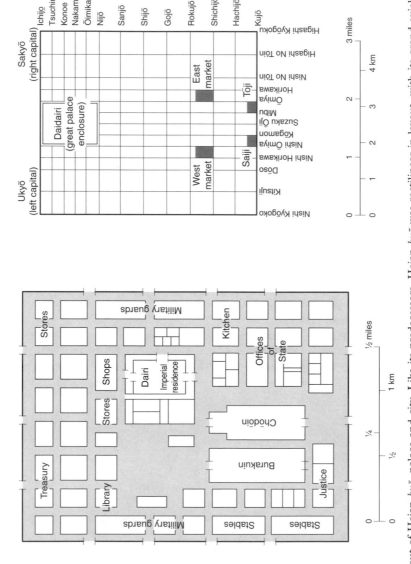

Figure 5.1 Layout of Heian-*kyō*, palace and city. Like its predecessors, Heian-*kyō* was rectilinear in layout, with its grand axial boulevard, Suzaku Ōji, leading from Rajō Gate at the south to the palace enclosure at the city's north end. That palace enclosure, the Daidairi, was crammed with buildings for the officials who handled the diverse aspects of central government operations during early Heian, before fire, disorder, and political change led to their attenuation and dispersal about the city. *Source:* John W. Hall, "Kyoto as Historical Background," in Hall and Jeffrey P. Mass, *Medieval Japan, Essays in Institutional History* (New Haven: YUP, 1974; Stanford: Stanford University Press), pp. 9, 14.

Ironically, however, their very success in making the government easier for a strong man to operate contributed to the disempowerment of their successors and the elevation of senior Fujiwara figures to political pre-eminence. Since the days of Kamatari and his son Fuhito, it will be recalled, Fujiwara chiefs had enjoyed incomparable ties to the imperial family as favored in-laws, advisors, and senior officials, establishing by later Nara a *de facto* imperial-Fujiwara duopoly of power. By the year 850, however, Fuhito's descendants had proliferated into rival clusters of lineages supported by sustenance households, rank and office income, and other sources of wealth that they controlled with varying degrees of completeness and permanence.

One of these Fujiwara lineage clusters, known as the Hokke or Northern House, was particularly well endowed and influential, and in 858 the head of one of its lineages, Fujiwara no Yoshifusa, assumed a *de facto* role as supervisor of the child-emperor Seiwa, who was his grandson. A few years later Yoshifusa was instructed, by himself one suspects, to "carry out the governing of the realm."[2] To that end he assumed the official title of *sesshō* or regent to a child emperor, a position hitherto reserved to imperial family members. Subsequently he passed the title on to his successor, Mototsune, who during the 880s continued handling, and thereby controlling, imperial decrees and other correspondence even after the emperor had come to maturity. In the process he became known by the irregular title *kanpaku*, which thereafter denoted the regent to an adult emperor. For most of the next two centuries his successors, identified by elided title as the Sekkanke (house of *sesshō* and *kanpaku*) Fujiwara, dominated courtly affairs.

A few emperors tried to resist the Sekkanke incursion on their authority by forging alliances with other aristocrats, whether from rival Fujiwara houses or lesser lineages, most famously the celebrated scholar-official Sugawara no Michizane. Michizane's humiliating political defeat at Sekkanke hands produced such bitterness that for centuries thereafter calamities of the day were attributed to his angry spirit. Indeed, that belief prompted nervous Fujiwara leaders to perform ceremonies of pacification and to construct and maintain shrines to honor Michizane's spirit (*tenjinsama*), most notably the Kitano Tenmangū, whose amuletic powers survive in present-day Kyoto.

Such resistance notwithstanding, Sekkanke chiefs repeatedly overcame their challengers. They used their dominance to supply consorts to imperial boys and to ease young emperors into retirement as soon as a Sekkanke-mothered successor was available. One consequence of this strategy was that women ceased to serve as emperors: doubtless these regents realized that it was easier to manipulate a male child than a mature woman, even one's own daughter.

Besides maintaining marital connections, Sekkanke chiefs controlled official appointments, promotions, and rewards, which assured them, even in Yoshifusa's day, a large number of suppliants and collaborators. The celebrated poet Ariwara no Narihira suggested, more bitingly than admiringly perhaps, the reach of Fujiwara (literally "wisteria plain") benevolence:

> Longer than ever before
> Is the wisteria's shadow –
> How many are those

> Who shelter beneath
> Its blossoms.[3]

Sekkanke chiefs also used their power to assign more and more agricultural hamlets to themselves, their allies, followers, and collaborating fanes – meaning temples and shrines. Most importantly, they endowed the Fujiwara ancestral Kōfukuji in Nara, together with its affiliated Kasuga Shrine, with extensive holdings, eventually making it the predominant landholder in Yamato Province and a formidable political force in its own right. Furthermore, Sekkanke governments revised *ritsuryō* statutes so as to grant the administrative organs (*mandokoro*) of aristocratic households more and more legal authority over the hamlets assigned to them. In the process they transformed much of the countryside from imperial tax land into *shōen* (corporate estates or manorial lands) that were largely exempt from government administration and tribute.

Sekkanke leaders reached the apogee of their glory during the eleventh century, when Michinaga and his son Yorimichi dominated affairs. The contemporary historical work *Ōkagami* summed up Michinaga's accomplishments, in the process revealing courtly priorities of the day.

> Michinaga was named *kampaku* in his thirtieth year [996]. After governing as he pleased during the reigns of Emperors Ichijō and Sanjō, he became the present Emperor's *sesshō* when His Majesty ascended the throne at the age of nine. He was then fifty-one. During that same year, he assumed the office of Chancellor, ceding the regency to [his eldest son,] Yorimichi. He took Buddhist vows on the Twenty-First of the Third Month in the third year of Kannin [1019], when he was fifty-four. On the Eighth of the Fifth Month, the Court made him equivalent to the three Empresses in status, with annual ranks and offices, even though he was a monk. He is the grandfather of the Emperor and the Crown Prince, and the father of three Empresses, of the Regent Minister of the Left, of the Palace Minister, and of many Counselors; and he has governed the realm for approximately thirty-one years.[4]

Within this courtly world Michinaga's was a remarkable age, as we note more fully in the next chapter. In particular it was a time of extraordinary literary productivity that was dominated by women, most famously Murasaki Shikibu, author of the sprawling fictional narrative of court life, *Genji monogatari* (Tale of Genji).

Gradually, however, Sekkanke dominance waned. It weakened in part due to internal feuding among Fujiwara lineages but in part due to challenges from other contenders for privilege: temple prelates, ambitious warrior leaders, and rival aristocrats. The most effective rivals, however, were energetic heads of the imperial household itself. As retired emperors, they out-hustled the Fujiwara at converting imperial tax lands into *shōen*, which they then managed through the offices of their retired-emperor organization, the *insei*.

INSEI AND *BUKE* (1050–1250)

Much as Sekkanke figures had parlayed a long history of Fujiwara ties to the imperial household into a hegemonial role after 850, so a series of retired emperors converted the imperial legacy of abdication and oversight, which traced back to the days of Jitō and Genmei, into a century of dominance after 1050. The central narrative is straightforward.

The mature Go-Sanjō exploited mistakes and misfortunes of the venerable regent Yorimichi to become emperor in 1068, and he then moved energetically to reassert imperial authority and trim Sekkanke power. Despite his untimely death five years later, his vigorous twenty-year-old son Shirakawa was able to ascend the throne and control affairs. He adroitly pitted Fujiwara leaders against one another, employed officials of other ancestries, and after retiring in 1086 enlarged his *insei* structure and expanded the number of *shōen* it administered. He undertook major construction projects in Heian and so dominated political life during the early twelfth century that a senior Fujiwara figure declared:

> the grandeur of the abdicated sovereign is equal to that of His Majesty, and at the present moment this abdicated sovereign is sole political master.[5]

Subsequently Shirakawa's son Toba took command, rapidly adding *shōen* to his *insei* holdings and using that fiscal foundation to sustain the splendour of imperial rule until his death. After his death, however, personal conflicts so poisoned the atmosphere in Heian that political life grew violent. The energetic retired emperor Go-Shirakawa lost control, and during the 1180s politics dissolved into all-out civil war, after which retired emperors never regained their pre-eminence.

In an immediate and visible sense this rule by retired emperors constituted a vigorous reassertion of imperial governance, even though the *shōen* mechanism of fiscal control and the dominant role of the *insei* institution itself constituted subversions of *ritsuryō* governing procedure. It reaffirmed the authority of the imperial household and helped perpetuate the existing distribution of power and privilege. Moreover the great construction projects of Shirakawa and Toba produced two of the most elegant mansion layouts in Japan's history, Hosshōji and Toba-dono, while Go-Shirakawa's reconstruction of the original Heian imperial palace during the 1150s restored briefly a monument that had burned and been abandoned generations earlier.

In other, more basic ways, however, *insei* rule witnessed considerable decay in *ritsuryō* governance. Most strikingly, the early-Heian arrangements in northern Tōhoku grew shaky late in the Sekkanke heyday as rival magnates in the region jockeyed for position. In the 1050s warfare erupted, and during the 1080s a breakaway regional regime arose at Hiraizumi, south of present-day Morioka. For a century thereafter that entire region was lost to imperial rule.

Closer to home, *insei* leaders were repeatedly challenged, as Sekkanke chiefs had been, by the armed warrior-monks of major temples, most notably Kōfukuji at Nara and the great Tendai establishments of Enryakuji and Onjōji near Heian. Furthermore, pirate gangs in the Inland Sea, which commonly consisted of local warriors and their henchmen, had been a sporadic source of trouble from Sekkanke times onward. By the 1130s they were such a severe menace, defying provincial authorities and directly threatening

Heian, that the court bypassed its normal officials and placed a professional warrior, leading his own armed followers, in charge of their suppression.

This courtly reliance on professional warriors points to the biggest problem of all: the rise of career military men or *bushi* as key players on the national political scene. For reasons that we explore below, by the mid-twelfth century large numbers of men surnamed Minamoto and Taira (using characters also pronounced Gen and Hei; hence Genpei) held government office, drew income from *shōen*, and commanded bands of armed retainers. Increasingly they functioned as key military figures, being employed by civilian authorities to counter disruptive monastic groups and to suppress pirates and rebels who themselves commonly were *bushi*. More and more, Genpei leaders also provided muscle in quarrels between aristocratic rivals. During the 1150s they played central roles in violent factional clashes at court, and in the outcome the ambitious and willful Taira no Kiyomori emerged as the pre-eminent warrior in the city and the major ally of Go-Shirakawa.

By the 1170s Kiyomori's performance was resembling that of Sekkanke chiefs. His daughter became the consort of the young emperor, Takakura, who was himself sprung from a Taira mother, and in 1178 she gave birth to a boy who ascended the throne two years later as Antoku. By then Kiyomori had garnered high rank and office, assembled a grand array of *shōen*, and at his Rokuhara mansion on the east side of Heian surrounded himself with all the amenities of the privileged life. By 1180, however, his bald ambition, rise to positions unprecedented for a *buke* chief, seizure of lands, and harsh punishment of any who resisted, finally even including Go-Shirakawa himself, had won him many enemies and alienated most old-line aristocrats.

One sorely aggrieved figure was the imperial prince Mochihito, a son of Go-Shirakawa who believed that Kiyomori had denied him the throne. In 1180 he joined a plot to oust the Taira chief, and his call to arms reveals much about both the grievances people had and the rhetoric of political mobilization. Kiyomori and his followers, asserted Mochihito,

> have incited rebellion and have overthrown the nation. They have caused the officials and the people to suffer, seizing and plundering the five inner provinces and the seven circuits. They have confined the ex-sovereign, exiled public officials, and inflicted death and banishment, drowning and imprisonment. They have robbed property and seized lands, usurped and bestowed offices. They have rewarded the unworthy and incriminated the innocent. They have apprehended and confined the prelates of the various temples and imprisoned student monks. They have requisitioned the silks and rice of Mount Hiei to be stored as provisions for a rebellion. They have despoiled the graves of princes and cut off the head of one, defied the emperor and destroyed Buddhist Law in a manner unprecedented in history.

Clearly such heinous behavior deserved punishment, and therefore,

> I, the second son of the ex-sovereign, in search of the ancient principles of Emperor Temmu, and following in the footsteps of Prince Shōtoku, proclaim war against those who would usurp the throne and who would destroy Buddhist Law. We rely not on man's efforts alone but on the assistance of providence as well. If the temporal rulers, the Three [Buddhist] Treasures, and the

native gods assist us in our efforts, all the people everywhere must likewise wish to assist us immediately.[6]

Mochihito's declaration, with its litany of complaints, its invocation of the cultural progenitor Shōtoku and the warrior-emperor Tenmu, and its appeal to gods, Buddhas, and all who have grievances, was distributed to a number of warrior leaders. The most notable recipient was Minamoto no Yoritomo, resident of Izu Peninsula, survivor of an earlier purge, and mature head of the Seiwa Genji, a major Minamoto lineage that claimed descent from Seiwa *tennō*.

Numerous courtly, Buddhist, and *bushi* groups rallied to the insurgent cause, but in fact it fared poorly. Taira troops quickly hunted down and destroyed Mochihito and his supporters, in the process torching Onjōji, Tōdaiji, and Kōfukuji for their involvement. Even as that calamity was engulfing the Kinai, however, Yoritomo in the east was mobilizing forces. Whether he was driven by simple ambition, a desire for revenge, or the conviction that Kiyomori would in any case destroy him because of his position as a senior Minamoto leader is unclear. Whatever moved him, during the next four years he and other *bushi* leaders pursued a complicated series of deployments and battles in campaigns that raged across the realm from Kyushu to Tōhoku, providing grist for the most celebrated war tales in Japanese history. By 1185 Kiyomori's supporters were defeated, and by 1190 Yoritomo had eliminated rivals within his own family, most famously his younger brother Yoshitsune. He had also reduced the handsome political headquarters at Hiraizumi to ashes, in the process nullifying Tōhoku autonomy for another century.

During these years of warfare Yoritomo consolidated his position by securing more income-producing territories for himself, awarding land to his followers, and striking a series of *ad hoc* bargains with the court that delineated lines and areas of authority. What emerged from this process was a sort of dyarchy. Yoritomo's house government at Kamakura actually controlled most of the Kantō and sustained and governed its own followers. Yoritomo also assumed responsibility for keeping the peace throughout the realm and guaranteeing the income rights and most functions of the imperial government, cooperative aristocrats, temples, and shrines.

The court retained, or in some cases regained, its customary authority over imperial tax land and non-*bushi shōen*, including the authority to resolve legal disputes thereon. It also retained its customary appointive powers, though of course with all due attentiveness to Yoritomo's wishes. Yoritomo himself received numerous fine titles from the court, including that of *seiitaishōgun*, which translates grandly as "barbarian-subduing generalissimo." His Kamakura headquarters acquired the unpretentious designation *bakufu* or "tent government," reflecting the fact that the shogunal title had customarily been assigned as a temporary office for the leader of an expedition sent to subdue some rebel or "barbarian" group, most commonly the Emishi.

In following years Yoritomo's own lineage failed to survive the savage personal rivalries of the day, his second and last son being murdered in 1219. Instead, the Hōjō, the natal lineage of his storied wife Masako, provided effective leadership by selecting titular shogun from Kyoto while controlling affairs themselves through a sort of regency (*shikken*) for the shogun. They maintained a branch headquarters in Kyoto at the former Taira mansion, Rokuhara. And they oversaw an array of shogunal vassals (*gokenin*), many of whom were posted about the country, mainly east of Kyoto, on assigned parcels of land. At their posts these men, titled *jitō* or "land steward," had the tasks of keeping the local peace, assuring proper tribute collection, and being available for military deployment as needed.

Court leaders had accepted Yoritomo's arrangements as the least awful of unwelcome choices, but they did not intend to let the bakufu become a permanent ruling center. In particular Go-Toba, a grandson of Go-Shirakawa, resented these *bushi* inroads on imperial authority, and he maneuvered to revive *insei* control of the realm. By 1220 he was on a collision course with Kamakura, and in 1221, after political setbacks disrupted his gradualist strategy, he launched a desperate insurrection, evidently hoping that malcontents would rally to him as they had to Mochihito in 1180. In the event, however, his backers proved inadequate to the task, and after shogunal leaders had crushed the imperial insurgents and exiled Go-Toba to Sado Island, they deepened their control of both the city and western Japan.

During the next several years the Hōjō further strengthened their position, most famously by issuing in 1232 a simple code of judicial principles, the *Goseibai* (or *Jōei*) *shikimoku*, to guide judges in settling legal disputes. By then governance seemed firmly in their hands. Once the Hōjō had secured their own interests, however, they were content to leave much of the old order's distribution of power and privilege in place. They used their muscle mainly to keep other warrior bands under control, and in consequence their policies preserved much of the old imperial order, its *ritsuryō* forms of government, and the elite groups whose interests it had served so well for so long.

Over the course of five centuries, then, *ritsuryō* leadership and its mechanisms of control had slowly changed. Nevertheless, even in its most radically modified form, that of dyarchy, those in control still claimed to be derived from the original duopoly of imperial and Fujiwara households and to be governing as legitimate parts of the established order. As we note more fully below, however, the *bushi* leaders at Kamakura also saw themselves as a group distinct from the old civil elite in Kyoto, their claims to imperial ancestry notwithstanding. And in practice their mode of governance had about as much in common with that of later centuries as earlier. Even as they propped up the old order, moreover, their very capacity to play such a role was a measure of its decrepitude.

THE ELEMENTS OF STABILITY

One can point to several factors that contributed to the durability of Japan's classical elite order. The *ritsuryō* political system itself was designed to that end, of course, but other contextual factors require brief consideration here.

Moreover, a number of adaptive strategies modified or supplemented *ritsuryō* procedures in ways that helped perpetuate the established distribution of power and privilege.

CONTEXTUAL FACTORS

Perhaps the single most important factor sustaining political order throughout the Heian period was the presence of a single voice of authority at the highest level. Also important, however, were a social structure and social values that reinforced the established order and, more broadly, a level of ecological stability – in terms of both domestic economy and foreign relations – that helped preclude the appearance of new, disruptive forces.

Regarding that single voice of authority, Jitō *tennō* and her successors had devised techniques of imperial succession that tempered conflicts of authority at the highest level, and throughout the Heian period violent struggles at the apex of the polity were rare, even though actual control of policy making migrated from emperors to regents and thence to retired emperors before settling ambiguously and insecurely among leaders of court–bakufu dyarchy. That apical stability facilitated the orderly refereeing of disputes and the enforcement of resolutions while minimizing the opportunity for malcontents to play higher authorities off against one another.

In terms of elite social structure, the fluid, polygamous marital arrangements and the close nexus between family rank, office, and wealth linked aristocratic households together in continually changing, opportunistic, patron–client relationships that created interest groups with access to top figures in the polity while delineating clear hierarchical relationships within the groups. These patron–client relationships drew much of the day's discontent into the system, channeling it into normal political maneuver that left intact the basic principles of *ritsuryō* aristocratic bureaucratism. That process helped dampen the divisive effects of political rivalry, which intensified as major households, most notably the imperial and Fujiwara lines, split into competing branches.

Elite social values reinforced the stability. They presumed aristocratic superiority *vis-à-vis* the masses. And among the favored few themselves, they sustained belief in – or at least rhetorical affirmation of – an ascending order of virtue congruent with the hierarchy of status and wealth. That outlook was securely anchored in religious concepts of godly ancestry and karmic influence and in the notion that the *ritsuryō* order was an expression of both the Buddhist cosmos and the holistic "way" (*tao*) of classical Chinese philosophy. Things were as they were because that was how they should be. Those born to high position were so born because they deserved to be, and the lowly as well. When personal conduct indicated otherwise, as it often enough did, that was evidence of individual defect (or unusual gift), a result of karma, perhaps, but not a fault in the system. At the highest level, as Shōmu knew so well, any calamity of nature or man was proof of a ruler's lack of virtue and consequent failure of understanding or action. At lower levels, this outlook deterred the ambitious from usurping the imperial throne, helped sustain the Fujiwara near-monopoly on the few top government offices, and heightened distaste for any, such as Kiyomori, who overreached his proper place.

This religious underpinning of hierarchy was sustained by sturdy institutional arrangements. During early Heian the legacy of Shintō–Buddhist support for the established order was strengthened by the construction of numerous fanes that served first and foremost as guardians of courtly elite and capital city. And it was sustained thereafter by the regular performance of elaborate religious rituals of state that celebrated imperial sanctity and elite virtue and that bound participants to the court by enmeshing them in its pageantry and promising them its protection against the dangers of life. For many key figures, moreover, the links to religion were personal because those who staffed the principal offices of temples and shrines were members of aristocratic families, and some of them moved between secular and sacred office with considerable fluidity, as need and opportunity dictated.

These several factors held the ruling elite together well enough to avoid the most violent internal eruptions. Meanwhile other factors helped preclude, or at least postponed for centuries, the rise of effective external rivals. The social structure as a whole contributed insofar as it drew an unusually clear distinction between the literate, cultured consumers of production and the mass of illiterate producers. The distinctions were hereditary and well documented, and they were manifested in residential arrangements and daily-life routine. In town, where rank, title, status, and function were known, the boundary between class and mass was clearly drawn. In the hinterland, where *hoi polloi* mostly lived, small cadres of village chiefs and district office personnel stood between those below and those above. As a whole these arrangements helped to exclude the unauthorized from participation in political process, thereby denying them means to use it to their own ends.

More basically, the stability of agronomic practice and the consequent absence of notable economic expansion shielded the elite from outside challenge. By minimizing the creation of additional exploitable wealth, that stability severely restricted the power potential that ambitious outsiders could parley into a viable force for change. Such increases in production and such changes in economic arrangements as did occur – and some certainly did – were coopted with considerable effectiveness by the existing elite through adaptive strategies of their own devising, as we note below. As a result, the intermediate groups that did appear, notably local warriors, traders, artisans, and mendicant preachers, were small, scattered, and dependent on patrons. Mostly they were fitted into the existing order. Consequently the established division between elite few and teeming mass showed little change before the twelfth century and only gradually accelerating change after that.

Finally, in foreign affairs these centuries witnessed a striking decline in the level of continental contacts. Immigration had fallen off sharply with the restoration of continental peace during the seventh century, and it never again had a major demographic impact on Japan. Diplomatic tension had also eased, especially during Tenmu's reign. And while renewed turmoil in the Korea–Manchuria border region during the later eighth century did produce a spate of defensive preparations and renewed talk in Nara about "subjugating" Silla, the occasion passed uneventfully. Instead early-Heian continental contacts became cultural and commercial in focus, with embassies going to T'ang to study and bring back learning and material goods.

The boat trip to China was dangerous, however, and only the strongly motivated were willing to risk it. By late in the ninth century voyages had largely been abandoned because the tottering T'ang dynasty had lost its luster and the Heian elite believed they had little more to learn from it. Then, after T'ang did collapse in 907, travel became even more risky, and the several struggling successor regimes appeared to be unworthy usurpers. By the time the Sung dynasty emerged later in the century, it seemed to be but the most recent newcomer, hardly a regime to be compared with the once-illustrious T'ang, which, after all, had antedated Heian, Nara, Tenmu, even Taika, in effect existing since the dawn of history. In consequence, although a low level of overseas contact continued, it was mostly the activity of obscure traders and monks.

So the continent had almost no impact on Japanese affairs from the tenth century into the twelfth. Later, as commerce grew and political and cultural influence began again to impinge, those trends became evident only slowly, especially from the thirteenth century onward. In contrast to the centuries before Nara, that is to say, during the later *ritsuryō* period, the continent provided few of the people, ideas, goods, and equipment that shaped Japan's development. That situation spared the favored few a major disequilibrating factor, thereby abetting the established order's persistence.

Adaptive strategies

In every society those atop the social heap have ample reason to keep things as they are and to espouse rationales that justify doing so. Things keep changing, however, so those above must continually maneuver to hold their footing. During the later *ritsuryō* centuries changes in urban provisioning, in the control of rural production, and in the character and exercise of military and religious power all elicited responses by the ruling elite, who modified regulations and devised new procedures and rationales to assure, as best they could, that those activities continued to serve their interests.

Urban provisioning.   Heian, like Fujiwara-*kyō* and Nara, was laid out in geometric form with two large market areas of some twenty hectares (fifty acres) apiece situated near the city's south end, east and west of the axial Suzaku Ōji. Originally most of the city's artisan production had been overseen by government agencies, and much of the fabricating, processing, and distributing was handled in the two market areas. By the Sekkanke heyday, however, and on through the era of *insei* domination, more and more of that activity was taken over by officials, craftsmen, and workmen affiliated with major fanes and aristocratic households. They generally lived and worked on or near their patron's grounds, and because recurrent fires and other urban problems prompted the well-placed to flee to the suburbs, where they erected temple and mansion establishments of suitable size and elegance, more and more of these work sites were on the city's periphery. Thus the location, organization, and personnel of urban economic activity changed. Nevertheless, the locus of control stayed within the *ritsuryō* elite, who remained the core of the consumer populace.

Provisioning from the hinterland changed similarly. *Ritsuryō* rules intended that the township–district–province hierarchy be the channel for goods and services heading upward by road and waterway to the capital. And to some degree the process worked that way throughout these centuries. Goods came to the city via the tribute system and were stored in government warehouses or in the marketplace. There workers and market officials processed, traded, and allocated them to authorized recipients. From the beginning, however, aristocratic households had done some of their own provisioning, directing household staff to collect goods from sustenance households or other subordinate villagers. They then stored, processed, and distributed those goods from their own warehouses and work areas. During the eighth century temples, too, began handling more of their own provisioning.

As the Heian period advanced, major fanes and aristocratic households, and most visibly the imperial household itself, developed direct links to more and more hinterland providers, bypassing tribute routes and city markets. Thus certain comb makers in Izumi province provided combs to the imperial family, while metal casters in Kawachi furnished it with "bronze lanterns, temple bells, gongs, pots, caldrons and water basins."[7] Lumbermen along the upper Ōi River in Tanba Province came to view themselves as occupants of imperial estates and provisioners to the court. Rice-malt makers in the western suburbs of Kyoto made malt for Kitano Shrine. And sesame-oil processors at the Yodo river port of Ōyamazaki supplied nearby Iwashimizu Hachiman Shrine with lamp oil. As with urban production, however, all this provisioning continued to serve the established elite, these procedural modifications notwithstanding. Only later would these changes translate into real shifts in power.

Controlling agricultural production. In the more richly documented area of agriculture, one sees the same general pattern of change in procedure but persistence of elite control. As centuries passed, land control categories became increasingly bifurcated. More and more agricultural hamlets were legally assigned to fanes and aristocratic households under the rubric *shōen*, and as these "manorial lands" proliferated the remaining imperial tax land came to be known as *kokugaryō* or "provincial dominions." Managerial arrangements on *kokugaryō* gradually changed, however, with operational control devolving into the hands of local officials, much as it was doing on *shōen*. Nevertheless, for both categories of land, controlling authority continued to derive from above. Moreover, in a curious and, one suspects, unintended way, the co-emergence of *shōen* and modified *kokugaryō* created a competitive situation that helped perpetuate local officialdom's dependence on higher authority, thus helping sustain the *ritsuryō* elite's position.

To elaborate that last point, initially, as noted in chapter 4, *ritsuryō* rules envisaged all arable as imperial tax land that was subject to periodic reassignment. Furthermore, such reassignment was to apply to both producers and recipients of tribute in accordance with legal statutes. Almost from the outset, however, those rules began to be modified, and by the ninth century periodic reassignment was largely abandoned at both levels.

After surrendering the right to reassign tillers, land, and tribute, Heian leaders (Sekkanke regents in particular) tried to compensate by strengthening centrally-appointed provincial officials *vis-à-vis* the locally resident provincial, district, and township officials who were their subordinates. These latter people, being local magnates with legal standing, commonly dominated hinterland affairs, and court leaders tried to weaken them by allowing more and more governors-designate to select their own staffs and take them as a preformed ruling group to their assigned provincial headquarters (*kokufu*). Moreover, the court simplified tribute and other regulations on *kokugaryō* to give governors more autonomy of operation. These changes provided appointees with enough expertise, trustworthy manpower, and administrative flexibility to dominate resident officialdom, and by later Heian they were controlling affairs with little oversight from the court – provided they kept the peace and forwarded the stipulated levels of tribute income.

By later Heian, provincial governors had thus gained power at the expense of the court above and local notables below. In effect, a system of tax farming had taken shape on *kokugaryō*. It was, however, a system in which the *kokufu* tax farmer's rapacity and autonomy were constrained by the concurrent proliferation of *shōen*.

To explain, during the eighth century the term *shōen* had referred to parcels of woodland or abandoned fields that the court authorized temples or aristocrats to bring into cultivation. In principle, at least, management of the parcels remained subject to government oversight, and income rights and limits were specified by the court. During early Heian, however, with "vacant" land having become scarce again, temples and shrines, and a bit later aristocrats, began acquiring actively cultivated fields as well. In following centuries that trend accelerated. On a case by case basis, moreover, *shōen* proprietors were able to negotiate more favorable income arrangements and fuller immunity from both official tribute obligations and government oversight. In due course many proprietors acquired total immunity for their *shōen* and even extended those gains to lands they originally held as sustenance household allotments.

This proliferation of *shōen* could restrain the rapaciousness and autonomy of tax farming provincial governors because landholding villagers on *kokugaryō* discovered that if they commended their fields to a *shōen* proprietor, the latter often could by legal maneuver relieve them of tribute obligations. That process removed their fields from provincial tax rolls and enabled them, in return for rental payments, to escape the increased levies that tax farming governors tried to impose. Similarly, local notables and minor aristocratic and monastic landholders found that they could strengthen their tenures and defend their interests against rivals, who commonly worked out of provincial headquarters, by commending their holdings to more powerful figures who could then obtain imperial decrees extending the fiscal and legal immunities of their own *shōen* to the commended holdings.

These several processes shifted so much territory from the status of imperial tax land to that of manorial land that by the late 1100s *shōen* encompassed fully half of Japan's arable. It was a trend that threatened the fiscal bases of *kokugaryō* tax farmers, inducing them to restrain their own tribute demands and to resist acts of commendation by legal protest. To succeed in such protests, however, they had to appeal to their superiors in Heian, and that necessity prodded them to be appropriately solicitous, particularly when forwarding tribute payments.

Provincial governors thus found that despite their administrative autonomy, it behooved them to retain the good will of senior officials in Heian. *Shōen* holders had equally compelling reason to do so because only court documents certifying their *shōen* rights shielded them during lawsuits. In fine, as long as a reasonably clear top authority was present at court, whether emperor, regent, or retired emperor, court leaders were able to use their powers of adjudication, punishment, and reward to play a balancing role that helped keep their increasingly powerful subordinates in check. Until the later twelfth century, they generally prevailed and the tribute kept rolling in.

One other aspect of *shōen* land control contributed to the comparative stability of these centuries: the *shiki*, a legal declaration of estate function. The operation of a *shōen* involved many people, including cultivators, the resident manager, the legal proprietor, and any high-ranking protector he or she might rely on. *Shiki* were the documents that specified the particular functions, the rights and obligations, of these several parties to the *shōen*. Depending on the needs of the case, they identified tenure rights, land boundaries, crops to be grown, other use rights, rents or fees to be paid or received, authority to be exercised, or services to be rendered. Because *shiki* defined these functions with specificity, their value was calculable and they became negotiable items that could be modified as circumstances changed or even transferred among persons or institutions.

Shiki thus introduced a high level of adaptability into land usage. Whereas the *ritsuryō* system had shifted resources about by central fiat, *shōen–shiki* arrangements permitted shifts in accordance with the particular circumstances of those involved in the transaction. One suspects that this process, despite its intricacy and chaotic appearance, responded to shifts of power and fortune more efficiently than did the older *ritsuryō* procedure, thereby helping resolve points of conflict that otherwise could have festered and finally disrupted the established order. Indeed, creative use of the *shiki* mechanism to accommodate the newly triumphant followers of Minamoto no Yoritomo facilitated the restoration of order in the 1190s, enabling the old elite to enjoy several more decades of comparative comfort.

Finally, and in the end most fundamentally, the ambitions of *kokufu* tax farmers and *shōen* proprietors and managers were restrained by the chronic shortage and limited productivity of cultivators. Because of the earlier-noted stability in agronomic practice and the depressive demographic effects of recurrent epidemics, neither group of tribute takers had strong incentive to seize abandoned land for its own sake. And they had considerable reason to avoid alienating the cultivators they did have. These circumstances restrained the impulse to conquer or to exploit rapaciously. Because governors and *shōen* holders also had compelling reason to satisfy the tribute expectations of senior figures in Heian, for centuries they found themselves unable to accumulate enough wealth and power to pose a lethal threat to the city's entrenched elite. Instead they – even the most dangerous of them, the *bushi* or military men – continued for the most part to serve their Heian betters, however reluctantly, and to turn that service to advantage as best they could.

Coping with military change. *Ritsuryō* rules had institutionalized the principle of military command as a facet of political leadership. Senior military command was handled by regular senior officials, who were presumed militarily competent because in their rise through the bureaucratic hierarchy they had served periodically as commanders of imperial guard forces. At the lowest rank, as well, military duty was regarded as but one of a subject's several tribute obligations to the realm. At the provincial level, on the other hand, many field command positions were essentially professional military posts. However, their occupants functioned primarily as training and mobilization cadre; during a campaign they came under the control of senior officials who held command appointments for the duration, whether the campaign be to "subjugate Silla", suppress Emishi "barbarians," or subdue domestic troublemakers.

In practice the conscript army was a source of dissatisfaction among conscripts and commanders alike, being costly and ponderous to deploy and not terribly effective in combat. Almost from the beginning, therefore, commanders tended to improvise, employing experienced fighting men in support of (or in lieu of) conscript troops, most famously in wars on the Emishi frontier, where imperial forces were heavily laced with seasoned warriors from the Kantō. Elsewhere as well, rulers used career fighting men more and more for routine patrol, criminal investigation, pursuit and arrest, and forceful suppression work. The trend was most visible in and around Heian, where a special police agency, the *kebiishi-chō*, was established to oversee such operations. During the Sekkanke heyday, as *shōen* multiplied and provincial governors gained more autonomy, officials of the court and great households alike relied more and more on experienced military men to guard property, punish enemies, and keep the peace. And temple heads developed their own organizations of warrior-monks to protect monastic interests.

For generations the *ritsuryō* elite were able to keep these proliferating warrior forces under control through a combination of material and ideological inducements. Most obviously court leaders, provincial governors, *shōen* proprietors, and temple heads provided them with employment, rewards, and promotions, all of which could be withheld for cause. But more importantly, perhaps, as this professional military arose, its senior commanders retained a considerable sense of identity with the imperial household legacy that lay at the heart of the *ritsuryō* order. As a consequence few were willing overtly to defy imperial authority and many were eager to be seen as acting on its behalf.

The basis for that sense of imperial identity lay in the origin of leading warriors. *Ritsuryō* regulations stipulated that cadet branches of the imperial family were to lose their royal status and perquisites after six generations, being reclassified as autonomous families of modest court rank. In practice many cadet progeny made the break much sooner than required because doing so allowed them to fill government positions too low for royal occupancy. Some of those posts were in the capital; others, in the hinterland, mainly at provincial headquarters. Some were civil in function; others, military.

As a matter of course these déclassé royals received the surnames Taira and Minamoto. However, they and their descendants generally identified themselves not by the broad categories of Taira and Minamoto but in terms of the particular emperor from whom their line derived. Their lineages stemmed from several emperors, but the most well known are those Taira who claimed descent from Kanmu *tennō* (the Kanmu Heishi), epitomized by Kiyomori, and those Minamoto sprung from Seiwa *tennō* (the Seiwa Genji), the lineage of Yoritomo.

During the generations of Sekkanke domination, declassed royal households proliferated, and their members came to be used in much of the day's police work. It was *insei* leaders, however, who used them most extensively in higher office as counterweights to the Fujiwara. Retired emperors were "packing the court," so to say, rebalancing the imperial–Fujiwara duopoly in favor of their own family tree. Indeed, by the 1090s the large number of Minamoto in high office prompted one Fujiwara leader to lament that for them to occupy so many senior posts, "is in truth a rare achievement for another family, and is a great threat to the Fujiwara family."[8] Meanwhile other warrior leaders, both Taira and Minamoto, were receiving imperial commissions to suppress pirates, insurgents, or other troublemakers, who often enough were themselves disgruntled Genpei warriors. Such appointments had the effect of drawing these men into association with the court, reinforcing the patrilineage conceit based on claims of imperial – and hence godly – ancestry.

Nor was that godly connection inconsequential. Whether from convenience or conviction, warrior leaders were careful to invoke the support of *kami* in their undertakings, particularly the dangerous military ones. And they offered thanks when success revealed godly aid. Most famously the Seiwa Genji claimed Hachiman as their patron deity. It was Seiwa *tennō* who established the great Iwashimizu Hachiman Shrine south of Heian, thus bringing to the city the mighty Kyushu deity that Shōmu had installed at Nara a century earlier, after it had, evidently, vouchsafed his military victory over Fujiwara no Hirotsugu and later enabled him to complete his Tōdaiji project. And the Seiwa Genji – Yoritomo, his ancestors, and descendants – were forever after careful to nurture Hachiman's good will at Kamakura and elsewhere with shrines and rituals that preserved awareness of their links to the court and its godly powers and progenitors.

In sum, the mechanisms of reward and advancement, together with their ancestral associations, encouraged generation after generation of senior military families to collaborate with the high born in keeping the peace, to suppress those who would disrupt it, and thereby to help perpetuate for centuries the basic *ritsuryō* distribution of power and privilege.

Religion and the state. The reference to Hachiman highlights another factor in the durability of the classical elite order: the supportive role of religion. It requires comment because major temples such as Kōfukuji, Enryakuji, and Onjōji became in fact powerful, autonomous institutions that repeatedly disrupted the tranquillity of Heian and gradually shifted wealth and power from the court to themselves, clearly complicating the lives of courtly rulers. However, other aspects of institutional religion served to neutralize that effect and reinforce the established order.

The supportive role of Shintō needs little comment because it was so explicit. Court leaders constructed and maintained handsome shrines dedicated to protecting the court and all those associated with it. Innumerable ceremonies of state reiterated the ideology of godly origins and reaffirmed the linkage of all consequential lineages to the imperial pantheon of deities.

The political value of this Shintō support was enhanced by its Buddhist affiliations. By the mid-eleventh century Heian leaders had established in and around the Kinai region a three-tier ranking of twenty-two, well-staffed shrines, each linked to a Buddhist temple and endowed with landed income. Their official function was to conduct rituals and prayers that would shield the realm by protecting the imperial family and its loyal associates. To that end the shrines adopted and developed a number of practices of Taoist, Buddhist, and Confucian origin that gave them an incomparably rich sacred aura. These major shrine complexes were then linked downward via provincial headquarters to thousands of local shrines scattered about the countryside. There, local officials were expected to conduct rituals that would enable the imperial gods to benefit the community, thus giving its members reason to appreciate the imperial solicitude. Moreover, as shrines acquired *shōen*, they despatched officers to oversee the erection in each of a local shrine to house the appropriate *kami* and facilitate the proper performance of ceremony.

Less obviously than Shintō, Buddhist temple organization, for all its disruptive impact at the center, helped perpetuate a social order favoring the established elite. Like shrines, when temples acquired *shōen*, they despatched priests to take up residence and activate a local temple that would help to expedite rent collection while succoring the locals, handling religious ceremonies, and dealing with problems and disputes as they arose, *in toto* helping assure central control of the hinterland. The importance of religious sanction was evident in the many documents surrounding these local disputes: suppliants invoked the same gods and Buddhas, swore the same oaths, and uttered the same imprecations as did the courtly nobility in their legal wrangling. In the outcome the *shōen* of temples, like those of shrines, aristocrats, and even warrior households, continued directly or indirectly to provide a material foundation for the established elite in Heian.

At a historically more visible level, until the mid-thirteenth century the aristocratic leaders of established temples, the Enryakuji most importantly, were able to suppress new religious movements that in various ways challenged the premises of elite supremacy. Most notably the unique merit ascribed to Pure Land (Jōdo) sutras by such reformist prelates as Hōnen and Shinran, challenged the validity of the syncretic religious thought central to *ritsuryō* ideology. In response Enryakuji leaders arranged to have them and others of their persuasion exiled to far corners of Japan and their teachings proscribed, thereby helping reaffirm existing doctrine among the ruling classes well into the thirteenth century. Concurrently, teachings in the Zen canon were being introduced from the continent as autonomous doctrine, which formulation also challenged established religious truth, and proponents of this view, most famously the monks Eisai and Dōgen, also encountered persecution, mainly from Enryakuji prelates. As with Jōdo, that response slowed the spread of sectarian Zen, keeping it out of Kyoto until the later thirteenth century.

FORCES FOR CHANGE

Buttressed by these several factors, the *ritsuryō* elite retained control of their bases of power, albeit by modified means, well into the thirteenth century. By then, however, the regime was riddled with fault lines that had led to a major rupture in the 1180s, then a temporary restoration of order, and during the centuries after 1250 or so a basic restructuring that slowly, violently dismantled the old order, opening the way for creation of a new one.

In broadest terms this restructuring was compelled by a longer-term process of overall social growth and change that gave Japanese society a greatly expanded power potential, which the ambitious tried to turn to advantage. Military men proved to be most well placed for that task, but for generations the attempts by victorious *bushi* to preserve their gains by devising new hegemonic arrangements proved less than satisfactory. Rivals continually challenged those claiming the right to rule and did so with such success that, as chapter 7 recounts, *bushi* engaging in disruptive military action remained central figures in political process until the seventeenth century.

DIMENSIONS OF CHANGE

The change associated with this overall social growth had many facets, some of which began appearing in the eleventh century, although the process as a whole wasn't evident until the later thirteenth. Some change was political: weaker central control and stronger local control. Some related to the rural economy: changes in agronomic technology and practice, fuller use of arable, the appearance of new villages, and heightened inducements (both carrots and sticks) for peasants to settle in larger, permanent villages and produce more goods. Some involved trade: the renewal and expansion of continental trade and other contacts, the growth and spread of domestic commerce, and an increase in the number and organization of traders. And some change was demographic: altered patterns of epidemic disease, overall population growth, and a shift in regional demographic balance. Analyzing satisfactorily the relationship between these several factors is difficult because they played interactive roles in a complex field of action. However, some of their more noteworthy characteristics merit note.

Local control. Further comment on the weakening of central control seems unnecessary, but the strengthening of local control requires note because the way it occurred contributed to other changes. During late Heian, as more and more rural localities were being designated *shōen*, the holders of these new *shōen* faced the task of identifying their property, assessing its productive capacity, and determining who would oversee the collection and forwarding of rent and the maintenance of order. To do so they updated existing data by conducting new cadastral surveys that identified property boundaries and recorded information on acreage, yield, and resident population. This information was then organized to form standard units of account known as *myō*. They put such *myō* under the control of local men of influence, whom they referred to as *myōshu*. The binding contractual document, the *myōshu shiki*, specified the rent that a *myōshu* was to forward in return for the holder's recognition of his perquisites of office, any other land holdings he might claim, and such other aspects of his local standing as seemed appropriate. In the Kinai region *myōshu* tended to be small proprietors whose assigned parcels of land averaged about 2.5 hectares, but in outlying regions, such as Kyushu and the Kantō, a *myōshu* holding might encompass 20 hectares or more.

Myōshu were thus people of local consequence whose status and functions were sanctioned from above. Being resident in the locality, they were well placed to open new land if it was available, discourage absconding by cultivators, recruit people to till vacant land, and improve agronomic practice if better techniques became available – in short, to foster increases in production. Doing so became worthwhile for them once land rents were set, which assured that at least part of any future gains would stay with the locals. Moreover, periods of elite disorder, especially after the 1150s, provided *myōshu* with opportunities to maneuver, and the more successful among them gradually became local magnates whose substantial residence compounds included outbuildings, storehouses, protective fences, in-house servants, and satellite servant households. During times of turmoil these servants could function as fighting men for any *myōshu* who was inclined toward military methods, found he had little choice, or was serving as the retainer of a more powerful warrior leader in the vicinity.

Rural production. As operational control of hinterland areas came into the hands of *myōshu* (or such other influential local figures as resident officials at district or provincial offices) more and more villagers found themselves encouraged or pressured to cultivate land more intensively, put nearby scraps of land to use, double crop in southerly regions, work more upland as dry field and orchard, and keep fields in production season after season. This intensified agronomy spurred the development of new hamlets and an increase in hamlet size. Local leaders welcomed the larger, more productive settlements, as did villagers, for whom greater numbers meant greater security against bandits, marauding pirates, and pillaging military men during the increasingly frequent periods of turmoil.

A number of changes in agronomic technique contributed to the slowly growing rural output. Regular tillage of more land was made possible by greater utilization of fertilizer material, mainly ashes, mulch, and manure. The last was becoming available because cavalry mounts were proliferating and draft animals were being used more widely. Improvements in iron-smelting technique provided more and better farm tools, including the swelling numbers of plows and harrows drawn by horses and cattle, which enabled cultivators to prepare more land for cropping. Irrigation works expanded, and water wheels for lifting stream flow to new paddy fields came into wide-spread use. More and better-adapted varieties of crops were grown. Most notable was a more hardy variety of rice (*daitōmai*), which came from the continent, probably in the later twelfth century, and which improved the yield on inferior plots and during inclement weather. With these changes, output rose and society grew, empowering more people to challenge the established ruling elite's claim to a monopoly of power and privilege.

Continental influence. As the mention of *daitōmai* indicates, one factor contributing to changes in agronomic technique was renewed contact with the continent. High-level continental contacts were all but abandoned in early Heian, as noted above, and during the Sekkanke–*insei* heyday, the Heian elite became remarkably insular. Their understanding of China and their interest in it evolved into a vague and condescending romanticism that was reflected in artistic and literary works, notably the fictional *Hamamatsu Chūnagon monogatari* of ca. 1070 and *Matsura no Miya monogatari* of ca. 1190. These works treated China as a distant, mysterious, and troubled realm whose finest sons were no match for the visiting Japanese hero, whose virtue and bravery earned Chinese admiration, whether grudging or willing, and who saved the day for his hard-pressed hosts.

In fact Sung China was at that time undergoing changes whose effects Japan could not escape. Its agriculture was becoming more productive, its economy much more commercialized, and its overseas trade extensive. Moreover, during the twelfth century its political order started to disintegrate in the face of Jurchen and later Mongol incursions, which were setting the stage for one of Japan's most traumatic encounters with continental politics. The renewed foreign contact produced by these changes in China brought Japan new religious ideas, notably the Zen creed mentioned above, and after 1250 political complications of the first magnitude. During later Heian, however, China's main impact on Japan was economic.

A lively trade developed between Kyushu and China during the twelfth century, and sailing vessels gradually extended their runs eastward, exchanging goods along the Inland Sea and by the thirteenth century venturing as far as Kamakura. It was a diverse trade, mainly in luxury goods. However, a major Japanese export was large timbers, which were hauled from Kyushu to timber-starved China, and a major import was Sung coins. They proved so convenient, despite official objections to their use, that during the 1220s resistance disappeared and their use became widespread. They also added to disorder in the realm, however, because the compactness and marvelous fungibility of coins, compared to most booty, encouraged piracy and banditry. Moreover, coins injected a new source of uncertainty into transactions and made the established elite more dependent on marketmen, who not only understood the mysteries of monetary process but also were in a position to provide, and hence to profit from, the luxury goods that foreign trade was making available.

Domestic trade. For most of the Heian period, as earlier noted, changes in domestic economic arrangements did not undercut elite control of exchange because the favored few remained the main consumers of non-essentials as well as the overseers of much production. By the twelfth century, however, some trends were beginning to undermine that control, one being the emergence of organized groups of artisans and skilled provisioners that became known as *za*.

Many Heian-period artisans functioned, as in the earlier-noted cases of comb makers and metal casters, as house provisioners, directly providing goods and services to fanes, aristocrats, and the imperial house itself. During the twelfth century, with political tensions more acute, Heian in disarray, and provisioning ever more problematic, more and more of these elite institutions licensed specialized *za* to provide such diverse goods as reed mats, cloth, sewing needles, malt, lamp oil, charcoal, firewood, and lumber. The more successful of these provisioning groups expanded their roles as time passed, and when coins came into use, *za* members were optimally placed to exploit them.

Moreover, these *za* gradually acquired an array of new customers thanks to the proliferation of well-to-do local magnates, including *myōshu*, resident officials in district and provincial offices, and local warrior leaders, thereby reducing their dependence on the privileged few of Heian. Then, during the decades around 1200 formation of the Kamakura bakufu, with its country-wide network of subordinate peacekeepers, provided *za* with yet more customers. By the thirteenth century *za* members were peddling in the hinterland, controlling sectors of the market, functioning as money lenders, and lobbying among the favored few to promote their own interests and fight their rivals. And they were doing so with minimal regard for courtly interests or sensibilities.

Demography. Cumulatively the foregoing trends meant that material production was rising; goods, services, and their providers were becoming more diverse, and exchange was growing more extensive. Contact among people across the realm was increasing, and villages were becoming larger, more numerous, and more densely settled. These developments appear to have altered the epidemiological environment, elevating smallpox and measles pathogens to the status of endemic parasites of the human community. As such they gradually became, from the late eleventh century onward, sources of habitual, non-lethal childhood disease rather than recurrent fatal epidemics of adulthood. This change in disease mortality smoothed out demographic trends, reducing the incidence of suddenly depopulated hamlets and abandoned land, and contributing to a renewal of overall population growth.

For generations, however, that growth was slow, erratic, and regionally unbalanced. Much of it occurred in outlying areas, mainly the Kantō, but also Tōhoku and Kyushu, where more land was still reclaimable, where woodland offered more resources, and where the elite capacity to commandeer new production was weaker. Even there, however, population increase was slowed by a series of weather-related crop failures that may be attributable to global climatic perturbations of the day. Most notable were crop failures in western Japan that severely weakened Taira opponents of Yoritomo's eastern insurgency during the early 1180s and, later, crop failures that affected the realm more broadly around 1230 and 1260.

These later crop failures caused severe and widespread starvation, which precipitated social disorder and banditry. Thanks to recent gains in seafaring capability, the banditry extended even to raids on Korea by Japanese pirates (*wakō*). Sailing mostly from Tsushima, and largely beyond government control, these *wakō* seized rice and other goods for consumption and profitable sale back home. Besides stunting population growth, these subsistence calamities thus exposed the inability of dyarchy to cope with crisis, control foreign relations, or keep the peace. They foreshadowed even more traumatic difficulties of that sort during the three decades after 1260.

Periodic demographic setbacks notwithstanding, the overall population did grow slowly, rising from five million or so around 700 to an estimated seven million by 1200, and expanding more rapidly thereafter to perhaps twelve million by 1600. And because this slowly accelerating population growth was regionally imbalanced, it was reducing the relative power of central Japan, the heartland of *ritsuryō* elite dominance, while strengthening the Kantō and helping sustain the breakaway potential of Tōhoku and Kyushu. Changes of the day were thus undermining the geographical basis of the *ritsuryō* order as well as its socioeconomic foundation. And fighting men were the ones most successfully turning these changes to advantage, in the process rising to political prominence.

RISE OF THE *BUSHI*

Clearly the *bushi* "rose" long before the thirteenth century, just as the Fujiwara had risen long before the Sekkanke heyday. Clearly, too, their rise did not destroy the favored position of the *ritsuryō* elite. It did, however, constitute one of the many Heian-period developments that changed the way the classical aristocracy sustained itself. And it helped lay the groundwork for eventual displacement of that aristocracy and its reduction to a symbolic remnant of old elegance whose residual political function was to help legitimize new ruling power.

One facet of the *bushi*'s evolution from a force supportive of imperial–Fujiwara duopoly to one destructive of it was a gradual change in the social composition and character of the warrior population itself. The rising *bushi* of Heian are usefully envisaged as a two-tier populace: a small upper stratum of men with paternal imperial ancestors, and a vastly larger lower stratum commonly sprung from local magnates of one sort or another. Unlike the upper stratum, these lesser *bushi* had little reason to support the favored few. As generations passed, moreover, the distinction between high-born and lesser *bushi* blurred, and changing interests eroded the *bushi* leadership's commitment to the established order.

Already by the 1090s, as earlier noted, the proliferating Minamoto seemed a threat to at least one Fujiwara observer, and from the 1160s onward Kiyomori's incursions on aristocratic privilege severely eroded elite trust in *bushi* behavior. Then Yoritomo's assertion of a permanent ruling function undermined the very basis for aristocratic faith in warriors as obedient subordinates. Unsurprisingly *bushi* leaders repaid the growing aristocratic distrust and disdain with an elevated sense of their own worth. This changing mood was implicit in the emergence of the terms *kuge* and *buke* to distinguish the civil aristocrats of *ritsuryō* tradition from the powerful warrior houses affiliated with the bakufu. As the two came to view one another as separate and dissimilar social groups, moreover, the warriors developed an accompanying rhetoric of self-esteem that increasingly defined *buke* as competent governing houses and *kuge* as cultured dandies of doubtful worth.

This new attitude was evident in the war tales (*gunki monogatari*), an emerging literary genre that recounted – and embroidered as seemed fit – battle heroics of the day. They celebrated bravery, lamented loss, and generally made warriors, their doings, and their values the central matters of concern. The lingering sense that aristocrats were more cultured, elegant, sophisticated, and possibly therefore superior was offset in these tales by assertions of warrior hardiness, integrity, and competence. Around 1240 this subtle transvaluation was nicely expressed in a letter of instruction written to his heir by Hōjō Shigetoki, who was serving in Kyoto as senior representative (*tandai*) of the Kamakura regime.

> [When invited to show your] skill in the polite arts [i.e. dancing, singing, calligraphy, playing instruments, verse-capping etc.], it is best to say that you cannot, because you lack such skill, and to comply only when they insist. Even then, never allow yourself to be puffed up by success, so that you come to angle for applause and expressions of personal popularity. You, a warrior, should, [on the contrary,] excel in the skilful handling of public affairs, in possessing sound judgment, and above all, in mastering the arts of war. What lies beyond these fields is of secondary importance.[9]

Men such as Shigetoki, key figures in the new governing setup, had reason to feel good about their situation and hence to start inverting the *kuge–buke* relationship: whereas *ritsuryō* rules held that career civil officials ought to command military forces when need for them arose, this *bushi* view held that career military men could properly control civil affairs and rule the realm, albeit as loyal protectors of the imperial house.

Even more threatening to the old order were the many other warriors, particularly those of pedestrian ancestry, who had fared less well and who felt alienated not only from the old *ritsuryō* elite but also from its *buke* collaborators in the court–bakufu dyarchy. Yoritomo's victories during the 1180s, after all, were essentially the victories of one assemblage of warriors over rivals, most notably the Taira of Kiyomori but also diverse others situated all the way from Hakata to Hiraizumi. The victors acquired income rights, mainly in the form of *shiki*, many being gained at the expense of vanquished war-riors. Subsequently the peace-keeping tasks of victors often put them at odds not only with the survivors of defeat but also with the many others who found avenues of advancement closed and means of support few. Those policing the peace referred to the many sorts who broke it as *akutō*, "evil bands," and as decades passed, their numbers grew. By the later thirteenth century *akutō* had become a major element in civil disorder, a growing threat to dyarchy and its beneficiaries.

Finally, one particularly noteworthy source of manpower for *akutō* was Kamakura's own retainer force. Those shogunal retainers who had been sta-tioned about the country after the Taira defeat and the later suppression of Go-Toba in 1221 were mainly supported by rents and fees from the lands they supervised. As generations passed, however, their families grew, they split their inheritance among heirs, and household well-being declined. In the end branch families became distant from their main lineages, much as in the imperial and Fujiwara families. When such men requested aid, bakufu leaders tended to respond inadequately, in part because the Hōjō chiefs in Kamakura were more solicitous of their own proliferating kin than of other shogunal retainer families. By the later thirteenth century a considerable number of *bushi* who supposedly were supportive of court–bakufu dyarchy had in fact lost their sense of commitment to Kamakura and were agents available for hire, *akutō*-in-waiting so to speak, should anyone offer them good reason to serve.

By 1250, the *buke* leaders of dyarchy saw themselves not as dutiful ser-vants of an esteemed aristocratic ruling class but as the operators of a politi-cal order that accepted, as one of its tasks, the obligation to assure the perquisites of a bothersome, often feckless, but useful populace of civil aris-tocrats. Within that *bushi* ruling group, however, cohesion was weak and the regime's personnel foundation was eroding badly. In its cobbled-up form as dyarchy, the old *ritsuryō* order and its privileged elite were in parlous condition, while many in the warrior class were primed for further, more radical change.

[6] CLASSICAL HIGHER CULTURE (750–1250)

Perhaps the most impressive and delightful facet of *ritsuryō* society was its higher culture, meaning arts and letters of the literate few. Those who produced them drew on both domestic and continental precedents to create works of striking originality that transcend such familiar genre categories as factual and fictional prose, poetry, painting, or religious exegesis. Some of those works stand today as monuments to human talent, and the values imbedded in them have influenced future generations down to the present. The corpus has given rise to voluminous scholarly study and to intensely held opinion about this higher culture's intrinsic character and worth, its contribution to Japanese ethnic identity, and its standing in global cultural history.

These arts and letters were produced by diverse people. Some creations, particularly paintings, statues, and buildings, were the work of professional artisans. Some, notably official histories and poetic compilations, were produced as assigned tasks by court officials of known skill. A great deal of prose and poetry was composed and compiled by courtly and priestly amateurs, partly as recreation or act of self-expression, but more importantly as means of promoting one's career, countering one's rivals, and advancing family or factional interest. Whatever the provenance of individual works, however, the elite as a whole shared the world outlook and value system they embodied.

This cultural production appeared when political consolidation provided the favored few with enough security, wealth, and time for scholarly, aesthetic, and recreational creativity. It is visible in artifacts dating from the eighth century, works of prose, poetry, and sculpture in particular, and reached full flower some two centuries after the *ritsuryō* order's heyday, during the years of

Sekkanke supremacy. Works of that era, most famously Murasaki Shikibu's *Genji monogatari* (Tale of Genji), have come to epitomize this classical culture, and they had a powerful influence on the arts and letters of later generations.

Subsequently, during the generations of *insei* rule and dyarchy this cultural activity continued to broaden and yield rich new attainments. As the *ritsuryō* order aged, new work increasingly derived from and spoke to a wider, more variegated segment of the population, which gave it more diversity, wider appeal, and greater influence on the broader process of social change. One is struck by the increased volume of cultural production during the *insei*–dyarchy centuries, partly a real increase and partly an increase in the amount that has survived. Even more striking is the centrality of religious concerns to the age, concerns evident in all forms of art – literary, graphic, and performance.

THE BEGINNINGS

Few societies have chosen as difficult a path to literacy as did Japan. The Chinese and Japanese languages are radically dissimilar – in sound, syntax, and means of inflection – but for reasons of historical geography, the Japanese employed a writing system adapted to Chinese to represent their own language. Writing in Japan was done initially by immigrant scribes who wrote Chinese, but during the seventh century a small cadre of Japanese scholar-aristocrats also started reading and writing Chinese, mainly for official purposes but also to study and promote Buddhism. For centuries thereafter official and theological writing was done in the Chinese manner, although it became increasingly hybrid, with Chinese and Japanese words and syntactical elements being combined in various, more-or-less prescribed ways.

Attempts to represent spoken Japanese with Chinese characters (*kanji*) date from Nara or earlier, and by the tenth century a radically new script, *wabun* or "Japanese-style writing," had emerged. Using highly simplified *kanji* (referred to as *kana*) to represent the syllables of Japanese, it permitted rapid and easy expression of the spoken language. Court women in particular, for whom mastery of Chinese was not an esteemed skill, put *wabun* to good use. For male courtiers, however, knowledge of Chinese remained *de rigueur*, even if real mastery was decidedly infrequent, and they continued to write in cumbersome mixed styles that contained many Chinese elements of vocabulary, pronunciation, and syntax.

Those mixed styles kept changing, however, and – to note the matter *en passant* – in following centuries, as foreign contacts waxed and waned, the language greatly expanded its vocabulary. These additions helped it stay abreast of broader social and technological change, but they also added greatly to its aural and syntactical complexity, inviting yet more efforts at reform. In fact the process of developing an efficient, internally consistent system for writing Japanese continued on into the twentieth century.

During the Nara period, in the early years of this long process, creative literary output was meagre compared to accomplishments in government organization, religion, sculpture, and architecture, the meagreness largely due, one suspects, to the difficulty of written expression. Most of what was written was in Chinese: *Nihon shoki* and later histories, gazetteers, myriad regulatory documents, religious tales, and Chinese-style poems (*kanshi*). The *Kojiki*, however, and a few decades later the 4,500 poems of *Man'yōshū*, Japan's first major poetry compilation, were in Japanese, with a Chinese character representing each syllable.

For prose passages this writing style proved exceedingly ponderous, but for Japanese poetry (*waka*) it was manageable thanks to the brevity of most poems. In consequence the rich legacy of early song – songs of love and loss, praise and joy, beauty and reverence – has been preserved. For example, Jomei, monarch during the later years of Soga eminence, is credited with singing the praises of the Asuka vicinity, whose gentle beauty is still visible to the modern sojourner despite encroaching suburban sprawl:

> Countless are the mountains in Yamato,
>   But perfect is the heavenly hill of Kagu;
>   When I climb it and survey my realm,
>   Over the wide plain the smoke-wreaths rise and rise,
>   Over the wide lake the gulls are on the wing;
>   A beautiful land it is, the Land of Yamato![1]

The lake and its gulls may well have been creatures of poetic license, but they do liven, broaden, and beautify the view.

By the time *Man'yōshū* appeared in 759, the Nara elite had developed a rich legacy of temple and palace architecture, religious sculpture, and ritual ware. And almost certainly religious paintings, although so few have survived that they are scarcely known today. Continental customs of elegant courtly dress and protocol were also solidly established, along with orchestral music and formal dance (*gagaku*; *bugaku*), complementing older traditions of flute music, Shintō shrine dance, and sacred ritual.

Within the Buddhist monastic community, meanwhile, a variety of religious practices had developed and spread outward among the populace, in the process starting to weave the indigenous customs of *kami* worship into Japan's version of the richly variegated religious practice that constituted continental East Asian Buddhism. One noteworthy facet of this religious practice was the pursuit of austerities at sacred mountain sites, which in Japan developed into the mountain asceticism later known as Shugendō.

Religious knowledge and practice of the Nara period was notable for its heterogeneity and disorder, and that situation, as noted in chapter 4, spurred aristocratic leaders to clamp down on deviation and insist on proper training and control of the clergy. Buddhist sutras and commentaries were used in training acolytes, while short didactic tales, many of continental origin, became a major tool for instructing lay men and women. Around 822 a large collection of such tales was published as *Nihon ryōiki*, a work written in mixed Sino-Japanese style. It became an influential teaching text for the promotion of both language and religion as well as a precedent for other compilations. These came to constitute a major literary genre, with collections commonly containing both religious and secular tales and serving both didactic and recreational functions. An estimated hundred such compilations were made over the next five centuries, of which nearly fifty survive today in part or in full.

FLOWERING: THE SEKKANKE HEYDAY

By early Heian, higher culture included a rich array of plastic arts, religious texts and practices, official documents and records, grand courtly ceremonies, and handsome collections of poetry. The most celebrated addition to this body of accomplishments during the Sekkanke heyday was the creative courtly literature that came to be defined as diaries (*nikki*) and tales (*monogatari*). Their development was facilitated by the introduction of new forms of Buddhism, Tendai and Shingon, which fostered prose writing and imparted spiritual significance to the life styles and aesthetics of those who created the diaries and tales.

ARISTOCRATIC RELIGION

To help consolidate the authority of their new capital, Emperors Kanmu and Saga labored to center new and superior Buddhist teachings there. The result was the establishment of Tendai doctrine, thanks to the efforts of the prelate Saichō, and Shingon, due primarily to Kūkai. The main headquarters of Tendai was auspiciously situated high on Mt. Hiei, immediately northeast of the capital. With Saga's support, meanwhile, Kūkai established a Shingon monastic retreat at Mt. Kōya in the mountains of Kii province and shortly afterward a headquarters at Tōji – Heian's analogue to Tōdaiji – within the city itself. Heian's ideological supremacy advanced farther when Kūkai began the process of transforming Tōdaiji itself into a center of Shingon teachings. In that process prelates redefined Shōmu's great Rushana Buddha statue as Mahāvairocana, which Shingon texts held to be the most primal and transcendent form of Buddhahood.

Shingon flourished throughout the Heian period, but in the longer run Tendai proved the more influential of the two, with monks from Enryakuji, the Tendai headquarters atop Mt. Hiei, initiating the major sectarian movements of later centuries. In part this unique fecundity reflected Enryakuji's closeness to the elite, which gave it access to talent and opportunity. But in part it is traceable to Tendai's central text, the *Lotus Sutra* (*Hokekyō*), with its richness of folksy parables, encouragement of learning, and support of diverse religious practices: meditation, textual study, good works, and faith. These qualities helped Tendai proponents appeal to a broad range of followers and, as a corollary, adapt to social change.

During high Heian, however, Shingon attracted a greater following among the *ritsuryō* elite. Many of its Esoteric (*mikkyō*; Tantric) teachings were gradually adopted by prelates at Enryakuji and other Tendai temples, and also by

Tōdaiji priests and the clergy at other Nara fanes, most importantly the powerful Fujiwara household temple Kōfukuji and its branches.

Doubtless Kūkai's exceptional mastery of Buddhist theology and his authoritative and compelling writings made him a persuasive teacher within the clerical community. However, the appeal of his teachings to the broader aristocratic populace more likely reflected their elitist character. He described elegantly the levels of spiritual enlightenment that lead one to Buddhahood, showing that Shingon doctrine stood at the apex of religious teachings. He also discussed the practices one must pursue to attain enlightenment, explaining that:

> Since the Esoteric Buddhist teachings are so profound as to defy expression in writing, they are revealed through the medium of painting to those who are yet to be enlightened. The various postures and mudras [depicted in mandalas] are products of the great compassion of the Buddha; the sight of them may well enable one to attain Buddhahood.[2]

To escape the fetters of the reasoning mind, one should thus allow religious art to open one's sensibilities to spiritual awakening. Elegant ceremonies, meditative practices, icons and ornate accessories, and other evocative devices, all aid the religious quest. It was a praxis that helped validate the courtly emphasis on aesthetic mastery, which we discuss below.

Shingon, which spared one the necessity of tedious textual study or the solitary pursuit of faith, was an immensely appealing doctrine for those with the time and wealth to participate in gorgeous ceremonial. Moreover, whereas Tendai doctrine promised enlightenment in due course, perhaps in another incarnation or two, Shingon offered an unqualified promise of enlightenment "in this very existence."[3] Blessed thus with astute leadership, appealing doctrine, and excellent connections, Shingon flourished, making courtly religious practice of the Sekkanke heyday a wonderfully rich, aesthetically gratifying experience.

The predominant theological element in this aristocratic religious practice was Buddhist, but it was interwoven with the ascetic practices of Shugendō, the many rituals and requirements of *kami* worship, and a wide array of practices associated with *yin–yang* dualism: "a magic order that controlled human affairs by an alternation of the universal *yin* (female, dark, cold, passive, earth, water, moon) and *yang* (male, light, active, Heaven, fire, sun)."[4] It also included Taoist ideas on physical health, medical treatment, and self-cultivation in pursuit of the Way of philosophical enlightenment. And it embraced geomancy and astrology, directional and calendrical taboos, and a panoply of other divination techniques for securing favorable outcomes and warding off malevolent spirits and misfortune in general.

All in all the *ritsuryō* elite enjoyed an uncommonly complex and comprehensive spiritual armamentarium. By the Sekkanke heyday, however, the very success with which Tendai and Shingon prelates had developed grand temple organizations and accumulated *shōen* holdings had contributed to intense rivalries among temples and between prelates and secular authorities. In part the rivalries involved issues of prestige and doctrinal conviction, but they stemmed primarily from the institutional expansion itself. Given the near absence of economic growth, such expansion was commonly achieved at the expense of others. During the tenth century these conflicts of interest began escalating into episodes of violence that killed people, damaged temples, destroyed precious treasures, demoralized clerics, and dismayed aristocrats.

In this context of deepening religious distress, more and more monks began finding comfort in teachings of the Amidist sutras. These texts, which had long been a part of the Buddhist canon in Japan, explained the troubled times in theological terms of the approaching "defiled latter age" (*mappō*) when the teachings of Gautama (the historical Buddha, Sakyamuni, or Shaka in Japanese) lie so far in the past that enlightenment is beyond human grasp, no matter the elegance and dedication of one's religious practice. Having defined the problem, the sutras then offered an attractive solution: the Buddha Amida's vow to save all sentient beings regardless of their condition. Even in this latter age one can achieve sure escape from the sorrows of life by placing one's faith in Amida's saving grace, evidencing that faith by devout utterance of the *nenbutsu* (*namu Amida butsu*; "invoking Amida's name"). Tendai priests, with their tradition of broad textual study and eclectic praxis, were particularly receptive to this Amidist message – as one element in a diversified religious practice – and as the Sekkanke heyday passed, Amida worship gained popularity among priests and aristocrats alike. It also began to be promulgated more widely around the countryside by mendicant nuns (*bikuni*) and monks (*hijiri*).

Shingon and Tendai prelates thus contributed centrally to the richness of aristocratic religious practice. They also enriched elite culture more broadly by fostering literacy and helping develop a writing style that could represent spoken Japanese. They contributed to innovations in art and architecture and provided a body of values to be articulated in literary works.

COURTLY ARTS AND LETTERS

The volume and variety of arts and letters produced by the courtly few during the Sekkanke heyday are impressive. When one recalls that this elite numbered only a few thousand, that most members spent most of their time on the humdrum business of government administration and family affairs, that only a fragment of their total creative output survives today, and that most of the celebrated monuments of the day were created during the century or so after about 940, by people who knew each other personally or by word of mouth – with all that in mind, it is difficult not to be awed by their accomplishments.

This cultural production can be examined from many perspectives, but a few broad themes seem to merit emphasis here. First, it revealed and helped justify the declining interest in and knowledge of China. Creative works moved away from Chinese precedents, enriching indigenous traditions to form what in retrospect is termed classical Japanese culture. Second, the scope and excellence of this creative output reflected a pair of strongly held convictions: that all aristocrats worthy of the name will cultivate their aesthetic sensibilities and hone their literary, musical, and other artistic skills; and that in doing so they will settle for nothing short of mastery because anything less would constitute a failing to be concealed on pain of public humiliation. Third, perhaps because of this ideal of broad aesthetic mastery, creative works mingled literary forms and graphic art in ways that quite defy later genre categories even as they delight our senses. Finally, and most strikingly, this ideal of mastery was gender-free. Courtly women made contributions to Heian cultural efflorescence that surpassed those of men, particularly in the literary and sartorial fields, but also in broader terms of the core ideals relating to decorum, deportment, and aesthetic sensibility.

Indigenizing arts and letters. The interest in T'ang higher culture that became so evident in the seventh century persisted through the eighth and peaked during the reign of Kanmu *tennō*, but it declined as the ninth century advanced. The change was implicit in the earlier-noted emergence of *wabun* writing style. It was more overtly evident in the process whereby legal codes originally based heavily on continental precedents were continually modified to accommodate domestic realities. The whole accumulation of these changes was incorporated in the greatest legal compendium of the *ritsuryō* age, the *Engi shiki* of 927, which survives today as our finest source of information on how Heian courtly rule was supposed to function.

In material terms of architecture and urban design, as well, one sees the T'ang model of imperial governance being abandoned. For generations official business had been handled in the buildings of the imperial palace compound, and while emperors and senior aristocrats had built suburban residences, those had served as secondary villas, not as primary residences in which government affairs were ordinarily addressed. By the Sekkanke heyday, however, Heian's whole palace arrangement was in disarray thanks to fire and changing political procedures, and more and more affairs of state were being handled in aristocratic mansions. Increasingly, moreover, those mansions, and Buddhist temples as well, were being built not in firm rectilinear order on the checkerboard flatlands of the city proper, as continental precedent advised, but at sites in the suburbs, irregularly tucked into spots adjoining streams or sheltered by hills. And the buildings themselves were being designed and laid out more informally, as particulars of the site dictated, with little obedience to Chinese architectural canons.

The finest surviving example of Sekkanke-era architecture is the "birdlike" Phoenix Hall (Hōōdō) of the Byōdōin (figure 6.1), an Amida chapel that the redoubtable regent (*kanpaku*) Fujiwara no Yorimichi built in 1053 at his retirement villa in Uji, southeast of Heian. The site was uneven ground adjacent to the Uji River, and Yorimichi situated the Byōdōin's several buildings irregularly as topography dictated. Phoenix Hall itself was so oriented that suppliants in the chapel faced due west to view the large Amida image and, beyond it, Amida's Western Paradise (Jōdo or Pure Land). Turning to the east, they could gaze out across a landscaped reflecting pool to the river beyond, their eye following its curving ascent and disappearance amongst the hills.

Figure 6.1 Phoenix Hall of Byōdōin. This airy structure was built by the venerable regent Fujiwara no Yorimichi in 1053 as an Amida worship hall at his retirement villa in Uji. It exemplifies the creative architecture of high Heian and provided a model for other Amida halls in later Heian. *Source*: Mimi Hall Yiengpruksawan, "The Phoenix Hall at Uji and the Symmetries of Replication," in *Art Bulletin* 77/4 (Dec. 1995): 648.

Yorimichi intended Phoenix Hall's idiosyncratic design as "a three-dimensional representation of the *Visualization Sutra*," an important Amidist text.[5] The Hall consisted of a modest Amida chapel flanked by two long wings resting on high, openly framed pillars and a cental corridor extending to the rear. Its many paintings represented scenes from the *Visualization Sutra*, but they deviated from established religious iconography, being brightly colored panels in which the Amidist imagery was set in scenes strongly influenced by "the Four Seasons (*shiki*) and Famous Places (*meisho*)," an art theme that derived from T'ang courtly antecedents but became central to the Heian court's own secular painting tradition.[6]

At Byōdōin, Yorimichi devoted structures now lost to other aspects of courtly religious practice, notably a hall for the worship of Mahāvairocana. But given that the age of *mappō* was reputed to be commencing, it was Phoenix Hall that proved to have the greatest religious pertinence. Others replicated the Hall in following years, and one suspects that its religious character as much as its aesthetics inspired them to make that choice.

Along with architects, sculptors gradually deviated from the continental precedents of early *ritsuryō* days, and painters likewise modified their style and subjects, as at Yorimichi's Byōdōin. By the Sekkanke heyday painters not only employed continental precedents in new and creative ways but also took inspiration from domestic literary works and the routines of Heian court life itself. More and more they employed innovative perspective, formatting, and color, combining their art with poems or other calligraphy to produce decorative handscrolls, folding screens, and door panels in a distinctive style that came to be known as Yamato-*e*, "Japanese art."

The declining interest in continental precedent was also evident in the handling of history. Official Chinese-style histories in the manner of *Nihon shoki* continued to be compiled through the ninth century, eventually forming a group of six, the *Rikkokushi*, which recorded courtly affairs down to the year 887. During the tenth century, however, repeated imperial orders that the official record be brought up to date proved ineffectual, and the histories that did appear were no longer written in Chinese. Moreover, they deviated strikingly from the older histories in format, focus, and the treatment of documentable fact, being as a result much more lively, revealing, and challenging to interpret.

The most remarkable product of this new approach to history was *Eiga monogatari*, the bulk of which appears to have been written during the 1030s by Akazome Emon, a now-obscure court lady. Writing in *wabun*, Akazome started her narrative where the last official history left off, at the year 887, the accession date of Uda *tennō*. Akazome described the efflorescence of Fujiwara power, focusing her attention on the triumphs of Michinaga. In effect she wrote a biography with explanatory background, but in the process she described court life in unprecedented detail. She focused on courtly "marriages, pregnancies, births, deaths, and rivalries in the Imperial harem," and on "festivals, entertainments, pilgrimages to shrines and temples, religious events, literary occasions, Court ceremonies, and individual triumphs and tragedies."[7] She was thus addressing the issues that concerned her aristocratic peers, not the wider issues of historical process that today's reader might seek to understand. But while her interests may have been no broader than those of *Rikkokushi* compilers, they were different, much more attuned to the times. They brought the lives of court ladies much more fully into view and explained them in terms that made sense to people of the day, rather than in the stylized terms of traditional "praise-and-blame" historiography.

Another, lesser historical work of the Sekkanke heyday merits note because it, too, showed departures from the principles of Chinese historiography. Moreover, it foreshadowed a major new Japanese genre, the *gunki monogatari* or war tale. This was *Shōmonki*, dated 940, author unknown, a work written in Sino-Japanese that recounted the rebellion and destruction of the military man Taira no Masakado. It explained his grievances, reported the suffering his rebellion caused, and narrated the course of events, treating the whole as a cautionary tale and finding in it evidence that the degenerate age of *mappō* was approaching.

The shift away from continental precedents was also evident in poetry. The interest in Chinese verse, which had been particularly apparent during later Nara and Kanmu's day, was substantially displaced by a devotion to Japanese poetry. By then this *waka* had become standardized in format, having thirty-one syllables arranged in 5–7–5–7–7 sequence, the form known today as *tanka*. Its content was also becoming more fixed in terms of word usage, acceptable topics and images, and their placement in the poem. In this more highly disciplined form *waka* was celebrated in a great new imperial anthology, the *Kokinshū* of 905, which is credited to the esteemed poet Ki no Tsurayuki. A plethora of lesser, private poetic collections also reflected this heightened preference for *waka*.

Whereas the triumph of *waka* was essentially the revitalizing and disciplining of an older lyrical tradition that reached back to pre-Soga times, the creative prose writing that emerged during the tenth century was a major new cultural invention. In essence it emerged from the interplay and extension of two literary traditions. One was poetry; the other, the diverse anecdotal tales known collectively today as *setsuwa*.

Poesy led to prose by way of poetic anthologies. The compilers of those anthologies gave overall coherence to their projects by organizing the poems according to one or another set of principles and by inserting headnotes that provided readers with information about a particular poem's provenance or import. Some tenth-century authors in effect expanded the headnotes to create poetry-laced diaries or narratives, such as *Tosa nikki*, which evidently was constructed by Tsurayuki from diary entries he made during a Tosa-to-Heian boat trip in early 935. His *nikki* amounts to a poem-studded, semi-fictionalized, day-by-day narrative of that two-month voyage. Some forty years later a court lady known to us only as the Mother of Michitsuna arranged and annotated her cache of poems and letters to create a narrative autobiography, *Kagerō nikki*, which follows her through twenty-one years of unhappy marriage to a callously neglectful high official.

Other authors were inspired by *setsuwa*, particularly by the tales found in *Nihon ryōiki*, the religious collection of Saga *tennō*'s day. Some writers formed new assemblages of *setsuwa* in much the same manner; thus, in 984 an aristocrat compiled *Sanbōe*, a large, didactic collection of Buddhist tales intended for his daughter's edification. Others used the anecdotal format in new ways, producing more variegated collections of *setsuwa*-like anecdote, opinion, and commentary, and arranging materials chronologically or by some other principle to form longer works. Ultimately this inventiveness gave rise to a genre of miscellany known today as *zuihitsu*.

The most famous miscellany of high Heian is *Makura no sōshi* (The Pillow Book) of Sei Shōnagon. It is a wonderfully imaginative and insightful collection of observations, tart and humorous, on myriad facets of court life and the world she observed. At one point, for example, Shōnagon wrote:

> Small children and babies ought to be plump. So ought provincial governors and others who have gone ahead in the world; for, if they are lean and dessicated, one suspects them of being ill-tempered.[8]

Some authors expanded the *setsuwa* tradition to tell more elaborate tales, arranging them more tightly, inserting poems as seemed apt, and structuring the tales around a central character, real or fictional. The style was most brilliantly realized in Murasaki Shikibu's *Tale of Genji,* but in a sense it was also employed by Akazome in *Eiga monogatari.*

Mastering arts and mingling genres.　The great esteem in which these cultural accomplishments are held today reflects the high value that aristocrats attached to artistic mastery. Regarding poetics, for example, Tsurayuki in his introduction to *Kokinshū* not only defined standards but also spelled out the shortcomings of even the most acclaimed poets. "Archbishop Henjō," he wrote,

> masters style but is deficient in substance … The poetry of Ariwara Narihira tries to express too much content in too few words … Fun'ya no Yasuhide's language is skillful, but his style is inappropriate to his content. His poems are like peddlers tricked out in fancy costumes. The language of the Ujiyama monk Kisen is veiled, leaving us uncertain about his meaning … Ono no Komachi['s] … poetry is moving and lacking in strength. It reminds us of a beautiful woman suffering from an illness. Its weakness is probably due to her sex. The style of Ōtomo Kuronushi's poems is crude. They are like a mountain peasant resting under a flowering tree with a load of firewood on his back.[9]

Not only did a poem have to be properly composed; it must also be properly delivered. Wrote Sei Shōnagon, ca. 1001,

> Once I wrote down in my notebook a poem that had greatly appealed to me. Unfortunately one of the maids saw it and recited the lines clumsily. It really is awful when someone rattles off a poem without any proper feeling.[10]

Doubtless plenty of bad poetry continued to be badly presented, but the threat of public disdain surely spurred better performance, even as it deterred the less polished.

That was true in all areas of creative art. Thus Murasaki recorded in her diary that,

> I remember how in the cool of the evening I used to play the koto [zither] to myself, rather badly; I was always worried lest someone were to hear me and realize that I was just "adding to the sadness of it all." How silly of me, and yet how sad! So now my two kotos, one of thirteen strings and the other of six, stand in a miserable little closet blackened with soot, ready tuned but idle.[11]

Mansion architecture and living arrangements assured that if Murasaki had played, others would have heard. Even today those who shyly make music for their own pleasure in the privacy of their own homes will understand what silenced Shikibu's *koto.*

Dress was as subject to scrutiny as poetry, music, or any other activity. Mastery of sartorial rules was essential, and the ultimate expression of that mastery was knowing how and when to bend the rules. On one occasion Sei Shōnagon described in loving detail how Empress Sadako and her retinue were turned out. She reported that the Empress wore, over a three-layered scarlet dress of beaten silk,

> two plum-red robes, one of heavily embroidered material and the other more lightly worked. "Tell me," she said, "Do you think the plum red really goes well with dark scarlet? I know this isn't the season for plum red, but I can't stand colours like light green."
>
> Unusual though the combination was, Her Majesty looked beautiful. The colour of her clothes went perfectly with her complexion.[12]

Sadako had defied the rules, but being a person of appropriate status and impeccable taste, she could do so successfully.

The empress's performance points up other aspects of this courtly value system. Rank and excellence were presumed to be inextricably linked. It was expected that those of high rank would be the most cultured, the most skillful, such expectations descending rank by rank, with plebeians being regarded as cultural incompetents. Sei Shōnagon again voices the matter with bracing clarity:

> If a servant girl says about someone, "What a delightful gentleman he is!" one immediately looks down on him, whereas if she insulted the person in question it would have the opposite effect. Praise from a servant can also damage a woman's reputation. Besides, people of that class always manage to express themselves badly when they are trying to say something nice.

Upstairs was not about to be confused with downstairs.

More subtly, this aristocratic value system merged the conceptual categories of ethics and aesthetics into an undifferentiated sense of virtue. To be beautiful and to appreciate the canons of beauty – i.e., to master the aesthetic standards of courtly life – was to be good. Aristocrats referred to their own kind as *yoki hito*, "good people," in contrast to the uncultured masses. They saw mastery of aesthetic standards as evidence of spiritual virtue, sign of a good karma, promise of redemption. Mastery of the courtly ideal was, therefore, not only critically important for making one's way through this life with reasonable comfort and security; it also was one's best chance for spiritual ease in the longer term, a perspective that fitted nicely the hermeneutics of Shingon.

Expected to produce and perform at a level commensurate with their high-born status, the *yoki hito* of Heian created works that skillfully mingled artistic forms and functions. Such mingling was pervasive, as seen in the habitual combining of prose and poetry and in the "docu-drama" style of history that purposely combined veracity and verisimilitude, prose and poetry, to tell stories that functioned at once as entertainment, biographical history, and didactic moral text. Rather similarly music and dance functioned as both religious instrument and entertainment at both Shintō and Buddhist ceremonies, much as art and icon did in aristocratic temple-residences.

Perhaps the most noteworthy form of genre mingling was that of writing and painting, particularly as practiced on handscrolls and standing screens. During the Sekkanke heyday it became fashionable to affix appropriate poems to silk screen paintings as decorative art, producing an art form known, depending on the viewer's disciplinary interest, as screen poems (*byōbu-uta*) or poem art (*uta-e*). Later generations, as we note below, developed this linkage of written and graphic expression into the brilliant tradition of the narrative picture scroll (*emakimono*).

Women in the arts.   Cultural mastery was no joking matter, and that was especially so for courtly women. The central role of court women as literary giants in their own day invites further comment because it has occurred so rarely in human history and because it was only one aspect of their aesthetic achievement. Doubtless the reluctance of court men to use *wabun* left an opening for women writers, and doubtless court ladies had the leisure time to engage in composition. But accomplishment requires more than opportunity. The very organization and values of court life equipped women to write and gave them cause to do so. In particular, marital arrangements, with consorts often not resident in their husband's household and with transient liaisons common, served to give these women a rich array of acquaintances, an abundance of personal experience, and a not necessarily reassuring view of human affairs.

In addition, most of these court women were daughters of middling aristocrats, and given the steepness of the aristocratic social hierarchy and the extremely limited space near the top, they had compelling reason to do what they could to advance, or at least sustain, their family circumstances. Service among the high born was one of the few avenues of advancement open to them and, via them, their relatives. So it was important for these women and their kin that they win and retain the favor of emperors, empresses, regents, and the like.

Success in that social enterprise meant outshining other women engaged in the same task, and the key to victory was mastery of the courtly arts, which included poetry writing and an enormous range of other social and aesthetic skills. The importance of such mastery may in turn explain the ubiquity of two associated courtly recreations: competitions and the preparation of lists. In one popular courtly game the challenge to competitors was to identify and complete a famous poem after reading or hearing the first few words. In another, players prepared incense and had to identify one another's ingredients and compare their olfactory merits. Other games required participants to identify the celebrated Chinese antecedents of verbal or visual images.

Listings were myriad. Compilations of poems and collections of *setsuwa* constituted listings. Other lists were assemblages of information by category, and surely none were more varied or numerous than the lists in Shōnagon's *Pillow Book*. Scattered among her anecdotes of courtly life are scores of lists – of things splendid, elegant, exciting, rare, annoying, embarrassing, unsuitable, depressing, hateful, or despicable; of kinds of birds, insects, herbs, trees, flowering plants, festivals, shrines, illnesses, musical instruments, and so on and on. Shōnagon's cleverness was evident in her short list of things that have "a long way to go":

> The first day of a thousand-day abstinence.
> When one starts twisting the cord of a *hampi* jacket.
> When a traveller bound for Michinoku passes Ōsaka Barrier.
> The time a new-born baby will take to become a man.

When one starts reading the Sutra of Supreme Wisdom.
The day when a man starts up the mountain to begin a twelve-year retreat.

Women developed and acquired lists such as this, one suspects, as devices to aid them in the courtly competitions, poetic exchanges, flirtations, and other routines of life that required knowledge.

Once collections of poems and lists of items became available, however, they served as "crib sheets" that raised the level of competition, making mastery more difficult and prompting the invention of new competitive categories. The *Pillow Book* may be our best indicator of how demanding courtly games had become by Shōnagon's day. Considering how unforgiving courtiers were of social lapses, it is difficult to imagine a more clever but rigorous means of inducing people to memorize minutiae or develop the agile wit of clever repartee, qualities invaluable to a woman making her way at court or recording her thoughts for posterity.

During the Sekkanke heyday, court women responded to the demands of their situation by learning and practicing, fretting and coping, in the end achieving a level of mastery such as the world has rarely seen. Equipped with literate skills, richly knowledgeable about their small, aristocratic universe, and under constant pressure to appear at their best, they turned to writing as a means of self-expression, escape, and commentary on their own lives and the lives of those around them.

Which brings us to Murasaki Shikibu and her *Tale of Genji*, the sprawling biography of beautiful, fictional Prince Genji. As Murasaki wrote its many installments over the years, they evidently circulated among her associates at court. They provided entertainment but also functioned, one suspects, as a how-to-be-an-aristocrat instructional text for male courtiers, whether callow beginners just learning their trade or older men who all too often were self-indulgent, insensitive, and unreliable, and on occasion brutish and cruel. Whether or not it was Murasaki's goal to do so, her text in fact provided a model for such men in the impeccable Prince Genji, who matured into every court lady's ideal gentleman – beautiful, polished, generous, unforgetting of his every liaison, and thoughtful to the end.

Whatever the intent of Murasaki or the other women writers of her day, later aristocratic generations found in their works expressions of courtly ideals and guidebooks to proper behavior, behavior that was universally revered even if rarely matched in practice. More broadly yet, these works became key statements of "Japanese taste," continually invoked as standards of aesthetic polish and cultural mastery even to the present day.

Finally, this Sekkanke cultural production gave rise to two semi-mythic figures whose stature as cultural icons came to match Prince Shōtoku's stature as political icon. These two, both faulted by Tsurayuki in his preface to *Kokinshū*, were Ono no Komachi and Ariwara no Narihira, who eventually came to exemplify the cultural ideals of the classical elite.

The obscure Komachi, thought to have been a palace attendant in the mid-800s, became celebrated as a legendary poet and beauty. In this poem she devises a way to meet a lover without provoking gossip.

> Yielding to a love
>> that recognizes no bounds,
> I will go by night –
>> for the world will not censure
>> one who treads the path of dreams.[13]

One wonders: does Komachi slip out to a secret rendezvous while others dream, or safely dream of such a risky joy.

Having lived at the dawn of Sekkanke cultural flowering, and being so utterly unknown save for the few poems credited to her, Komachi was rapidly elevated to the status of classic beauty, passionate poet of impeccable taste, eventually tragic figure emblematic of the vulnerability of court women and, ultimately, celebrated exemplar of Buddhist verity.

Komachi's male equivalent was Ariwara no Narihira, imperial grandson and court official, who is known mainly for a number of poems in *Kokinshū*. In the decades following his death, however, unknown hands gradually fashioned a work called *Ise monogatari*, a sort of "poetic anthology with greatly expanded and fictionalized headnotes," that seems in early form to have been intended as a didactic collection of love poems.[14] In final form, however, it became a semi-orderly, quasi-chronological pseudo-biography of an unnamed "man of old" whose amorous affairs and poetic accomplishments mark him, as he advances through life, as an elegant courtier.

In time *Ise* came to be viewed as the story of Narihira's life because poems by him were central to the story, because the official posts held by the "man of old" were those he held, and because the tale's romantic incidents included those that rumor had already credited to him. The work played a crucial role in creating the enduring image of Narihira as model lover, poet, and aesthete. As a corollary it helped define proper aristocratic poetics and behavior for all later generations. In so doing, like the stories about Komachi and the works of Murasaki and other court ladies, it became basic to later understanding of this courtly culture and the civilization it presumably epitomized.

BROADENING: THE LATER YEARS

By 1050 the Heian elect had created a rich and distinctive body of arts and letters, and during the next two centuries their cultural output remained vigorous. Particularly impressive are works produced during the decades around 1200, when warfare ravaged the capital, ruined the lives of many aristocrats, and humbled most of the others. The old order was in disarray, the well born afflicted as never before by warfare, hardship, and changes that were as unpreventable as they were unwelcome. Perhaps it all bears out the unpleasant truism that creativity springs more from pain than comfort.

As a whole, this cultural production retained basic attributes from the Sekkanke heyday: consciousness of status propriety, emphasis on mastery, the transcending of genre, and the active role of women. Until late in the day, moreover, elite interest in things continental remained minimal.

Other trends also became evident, however. There was greater interpenetration of elite and plebeian culture, particularly in the realm of performance art, where popular traditions of music and dance were adopted for use by the better classes. One also sees, especially in literary works, expressions of regret for a better and more beautiful bygone day. What most stands out, however, is the heightened religiosity evident in literary output, music, dance, and the visual arts. Religion provided intellectual depth to the regret for a bygone day and an explanation for troubles of the nonce.

This is not to claim that society as a whole was more religious than before; one supposes that villagers had always taken their local *kami* and their customary rituals seriously as they confronted the terrors of life and death. Rather, it is to suggest that among the favored few deteriorating conditions were giving greater salience to religious thought, Buddhist in particular, helping it to displace Confucian ideas and infuse most courtly life with strongly Buddhist convictions and concerns. And given the broader changes that were beginning to reshape society (particularly the rise of local power holders, growth in travel and commerce, and expansion of rural production), this heightened religiosity among the elite began to be shared more broadly, reaching beyond Heian and its cultured few to the swelling population of intermediate folk and villagers.

RELIGIOUS TRENDS

The two centuries to 1250 were a time of striking religious dynamism. A major aspect of this dynamism was the enrichment and systemization of religious consociation, particularly in terms of Shintō-Buddhist combination but also in regard to Shugendō. In institutional terms consociation entailed sustained collaboration between select temples and shrines. In doctrine and praxis it involved a "combinatory" or syncretistic strategy that imbricated the deities and customs of collaborating fanes to form a complexly integrated system of religious thought and action.

A second aspect of the dynamism was revitalization of established Buddhist teachings. A third was the appearance of new doctrinal emphases that gave heightened expression to the principle and practice of sectarianism. And a fourth was the diffusion of this polymorphic religious activity much more widely through society.

On syncretism. The elements of late-Heian syncretism were long established in *ritsuryō* religion. In later Heian, however, two concepts were invoked with particular frequency to explain combinative practice. One was the concept of *hōben* or "expedient means," which held that depending on a person's ability and level of religious understanding, differing praxis would best expedite the quest for enlightenment. The other was the concept of *honji suijaku* (*hon-jaku* for short), which held that a phenomenon had both a true nature (*honji*) and one or more manifestations or "traces" (*suijaku*). This proposition was invoked to characterize innumerable associations, in which living or recently deceased individuals were identified as manifestations of some god or

Buddha or glorious forerunner, Prince Shōtoku most commonly. Or a particular *kami* was defined as a trace of a Buddha, or – eventually – a Buddha as trace of a *kami*.

During the *insei*–dyarchy centuries, *hon-jaku* theory was primarily important as rationale for the linking of Shintō and Buddhism. The aristocratic poet and Shingon monk Saigyō expressed it this way:

> Waving the leafy branch
> Of the *sakaki* tree,
> I'll pledge my heart unto the gods,
> For I perceive that
> Gods and Buddhas are all one.[15]

These *hon-jaku* linkages of god and Buddha were specific: Mahāvairocana was a *honji* and the Sun Goddess Amaterasu its *suijaku*; Amida a *honji* and Hachiman its *suijaku*, and so forth. Such linkages then undergirded the shrine–temple complexes that we noted in chapter 5. By late Heian both Tendai and Shingon prelates had developed *hon-jaku* formulations into systems of institutionalized religious practice for their complexes, the Tendai version being known as Sannō Ichijitsu Shintō; the Shingon, as Ryōbū Shintō.

Shugendō also experienced institutional consolidation and the enrichment of doctrine and praxis, developing into an organized and extensive religion. Its professional practitioners, mountain ascetics known as *yamabushi*, adhered to rich bodies of religious practice that incorporated worship of various *kami* and Buddhas at select shrines and temples, as well as rigorous austerities at sacred mountain sites, mainly in the Yoshino vicinity south of the Yamato Basin. Shugendō acquired adherents at court, including such powerful retired emperors as Shirakawa and Go-Toba. And those courtly connections enabled favored *yamabushi* to acquire the landed income necessary to support their places and methods of worship. Indeed, Shugendō leaders acquired so much wealth that they and major temples, notably Kōfukuji, engaged in sporadic warfare for decades as the latter struggled to dominate these rivals and strengthen their control of tribute-bearing land.

In addition to the vitality of these combinative practices, these centuries witnessed heightened intellectual vigor within established Buddhist organizations, both Tendai and Shingon and the older Nara-period fanes. Troubled, one suspects, by the evidence of general social disorder, and spurred by the challenge of dissident theologians who questioned the worth of much contemporary religion, a number of monks prepared new theological works to clarify and reaffirm established doctrine and practice. They restored dilapidated and war-ravaged temples, copied sutras to rebuild monastery libraries, painted didactic scrolls and screens, sculpted new images, revitalized monastic communities, and promoted the combinative doctrines and practices they favored.

On sectarianism. These revivalist efforts by monks at established temples enjoyed considerable success, strengthening the syncretic strategy and helping their temples remain vigorous for several more centuries. It was, however, teachings by some of the dissident monks that laid foundation for the more notable religious developments of the next several centuries, most importantly proponents of Amidism, Zen, and the *Lotus Sutra*.

Whereas Amidist sutras had earlier been treated as simply a portion of the larger Buddhist canon, their later-Heian proponents insisted on the unique excellence of these teachings. Because of Amidism's exceptional simplicity, clarity, and salience, its proponents proved particularly successful at winning followers. Textual exegetes established that the degenerate age of *mappō* commenced in the year 1052 and that Amida's vow was thereafter the only sufficient vehicle for attaining enlightenment, or salvation as it was commonly understood. It followed, therefore, that all other religious practices were useless, or even obstacles to such salvation. Late in the twelfth century, as political turmoil engulfed the realm, the monk Hōnen, who was well schooled in Tendai doctrine, began to teach that only the Amidist *nenbutsu* worked and that other practices should be abjured: *hōben, hon-jaku,* the very notion of syncretism had no merit.

Given their fundamentally heretical character, these *nenbutsu*-only teachings of Hōnen and his disciples, most famously Shinran, soon brought them into conflict with main-line clerics. Most grievously offended were those at Enryakuji and Kōfukuji, whose religious convictions were being repudiated and institutional interests threatened. The scope and intensity of the doctrinal battle was suggested by the nine-count charge of heresy brought against Hōnen by Kōfukuji in 1205. It charged that his teachings slighted other practices, ignored the *kami,* distorted doctrine, hurt the Buddhist order, and threatened the realm "by undermining the teachings of the eight [Buddhist] schools which uphold it."[16] Thanks to these efforts, in 1207 the court exiled Hōnen, Shinran, and others to distant provinces.

Much as Amidist worship had long been one of many Tendai practices, so meditation as propounded in Chinese Ch'an (Zen) writings had been accepted on Mt. Hiei. When contact with China revived during the twelfth century, however, Japanese clerics discovered that in Sung Buddhism, Ch'an as an independent sectarian creed had displaced Tendai as the preferred doctrine. This discovery encouraged certain monks from Enryakuji, the most well known being Eisai and Dōgen, to promote more exclusively Zen practice. Like the exclusive *nenbutsu,* however, these teachings challenged the claims of combinative doctrine, and their proponents soon faced retaliation.

Eisai was forbidden to preach in Kyoto, so in 1199 he traveled east. Finding Kamakura leaders more responsive to his message, he spent his last fifteen years teaching there. He had, however, learned his lesson: to avoid alienating his new patrons, he fitted his Zen into Kamakura's established syncretic arrangements, which included both esoteric rites as propounded on Mt. Hiei and worship of Hachiman in the *hon-jaku* tradition. Meanwhile, Dōgen, preaching in Kyoto and insisting on doctrinal purity, encountered opposition so fierce that he abandoned the city in 1243, retreating to a monastery in the mountains of Echigo.

Even as Dōgen was establishing his heretical Zen religious community in Echigo, Nichiren another Tendai monk, was launching what eventually developed into a third major sectarian movement. Evidently seeing himself as the arch defender of Tendai against the breakaway ideologies of Amidism and Zen, he invoked the *Lotus Sutra*, the central text of Tendai, to justify harsh denunciations of them. In the tradition of Tendai he accepted select esoteric practices and *hon-jaku* reasoning. However, his approach to religion – his insistence on the unique correctness of his own interpretation, his conviction that he must convey it to people of consequence and ultimately to all his countrymen, his belief that the problems of the day were attributable to the pernicious doctrines of his rivals, and his readiness to attack them polemically and to denounce them to the authorities – quickly drew him into dangerous disputes and into a confrontation with officials in Kamakura, where he attempted to promote his views during the 1250s. His performance won him persecution, prosecution, and exile, and the severe isolation of his teachings until well after his death in 1282.

Despite this persecution, the salience and simplicity of these sectarian teachings sustained their appeal, and in following decades priests propagated them in more and more temples. Nevertheless, until the later thirteenth century the defenders of combinative doctrine managed to retain their dominant position in both Kyoto and Kamakura.

As these references to exiled religious communities suggest, religious practices that earlier had been associated with the Heian elite were involving more and more of the realm, with itinerant preachers, pilgrims, recluses, and religious exiles spreading their messages among ever more people. It is worth noting, moreover, that while itinerant monks (*hijiri*) and male recluses (*tonseisha*) were active in this process, and while most of the celebrated figures were men – such as Saigyō, Hōnen, and Dōgen – a considerable portion of the proselytizing force was female.

An important antecedent to this female proselytizing was the venerable northeast Asian tradition of female shamanism. Evident in the *Wajinden* report on Himiko of Wa, it was institutionalized in the role of Shintō shrine priestesses and in the use of shamanesses (*miko*) to intercede for the distressed and dying. This tradition enabled some women to support themselves as healer–proselytizer–entertainers who contacted spirits, told tales, sang, and danced in presentations that ranged, depending on circumstances, from the salvific to the seductive. In the process they disseminated and enriched religious practice of the day, particularly that of a combinative sort. Similarly, mendicant nuns (*bikuni*) traveled about, some on temple fund raising projects (*kanjin*), others as proselytizing entertainers, singing hymns, dancing, and telling didactic tales illustrated by picture cards. They, too, spread doctrines that, while Buddhist at heart, were generally of an eclectic sort appropriate to a variegated audience.

By the mid-thirteenth century Japan thus displayed a remarkably complex religious order. Its central thrust was still combinative, and diversity of practice prevailed. However, internal disputes that reflected both doctrinal disagreements and harsh conflicts of material interest had become recurrent and often violent. Moreover, the field of historically visible religious interaction had broadened substantially. Geographically this religious activity covered much of the realm, and socially it reached well beyond the *ritsuryō* elite to include tens of thousands of lesser warriors, a growing population of artisans, traders, and entertainers, and, in the villages of the realm, at least those more influential householders who handled the affairs of local shrines and temples.

Diverse male and female itinerants and proselytizers thus played key roles in the diffusion of religious thought and practice. In addition, as we note below, the widespread incorporation of religious themes and concerns into the arts and letters of the day constituted another major means of their dissemination.

ARTS AND LETTERS

A sentiment powerfully evident in arts and letters of the *insei*–dyarchy centuries was a growing regret for what the favored few saw as a dying courtly culture. What was being lost, presumably, were standards of excellence and the high value attached to cultural mastery, qualities that ought to be preserved for the edification of future generations.

Key religious views of the day underlay this attitude. The increasingly popular concept of *mappō* encouraged people to regard the past, when Gautama's teachings could still be understood, as a spiritually superior day that unavoidably was being lost. And because of the Shingon view, which aristocrats generally favored, that cultivation of the sensibilities opened the way to religious awakening, the loss of cultural mastery became evidence of declining spiritual potential and diminished prospects for salvation.

Given those views of past time and religious truth, authors and artists of these centuries cherished and lionized the earlier accomplishments of courtly culture and produced works designed to echo and elaborate them. Besides seeking to preserve, evoke, and celebrate the past, however, their works also attempted to explain the present, its calamities in particular but also its achievements. These themes – of religiosity, evocation of the past, and explanation of the present – show up widely in this corpus of literary, performance, and visual art. Nowhere is this more delightfully so than in the narrative picture scrolls (*emakimono*) that were perhaps the most exquisite creation of the age.

Literary arts. Authors continued to employ diverse styles of writing. However, *kanamajiribun*, a style that combined the boldly simplified characters of the *wabun* syllabary (*kana*) with the extensive use of Chinese characters (*kanji*), came to predominate. While less easy to write than *wabun*, it was more capable of refinement and growth. The use of *kanji* permitted adoption of new words, mostly from the continent, without the confusion and ambiguity created by homophones, which otherwise would have become increasingly common as more and more new words entered the language, most of them pronounced in modified forms of monosyllabic Chinese. Consequently *kanamajiribun* empowered Japanese authors to accommodate social and cultural change and still write with nuance and precision, handling even the most complex writing tasks in their own language. Indeed *kanamajiribun* was sufficiently flexible that in modified form it has survived to the present as the written language of Japan.

Thus equipped, authors of these centuries produced a grand array of works, building on past precedents even as they explored new terrain. They defined new priorities and agendas and modified taste and viewpoint, sometimes intentionally, sometimes not. These qualities, as well as the themes of religiosity and concern for the present, were particularly evident in the writings of historians, who made good use of *kanamajiribun*.

Several histories of varying detail and reliability were written, a number of them under the generic name *kagami* or "mirror" (e.g., *Ōkagami*, *Imakagami*), with one or another *kagami* continuing to appear throughout the thirteenth century. War tales became common as incidents of warfare proliferated after 1050. A number of short battle narratives appeared in collections of *setsuwa*, and the fighting of the 1150s and 1180s elicited longer works that provided explanations for the resort to arms and recounted the ensuing struggles, naming combatants of stature and recording their deeds. Not until the fourteenth century, however, as we note in chapter 8, were these war tales embroidered and developed into the grand sagas epitomized by the mature *Heike monogatari*.

The most remarkable historical work of the *insei*–dyarchy centuries was *Gukanshō*. It was a major interpretive essay composed in 1219 by the influential Tendai cleric, Jien, one of the staunchest defenders of the classical order and its syncretic religious tradition. Writing in hopes of restoring imperial authority and the political fortunes of his family, the Kujō branch of Fujiwara, Jien presented the imperial regime's history as a story of decline that was proceeding in accordance with *mappō* doctrine. The decline could be slowed and even reversed, however, by officials sufficiently attentive to the will of the *kami* and as a result properly aware of Buddhist virtue. Focusing most of his attention on the decades after 1156, he argued that only if the current retired emperor Go-Toba followed the sage advice of men such as the Kujō could the divided governance of dyarchy be overcome and the realm properly reconsolidated as of old. As matters worked out, Go-Toba failed to heed him and Jien's restorationist hopes came to nought.

Meanwhile the collecting of *setsuwa* continued apace, the most celebrated compilation being the huge, skillfully organized *Konjaku monogatari-shū* of ca. 1120. Consisting of some 1,200 tales of all sorts, about two-thirds of them Buddhist in content, *Konjaku* provided material for the many smaller collections that appeared during the early thirteenth century, when didactic religious purpose was more overtly expressed. By the 1250s *setsuwa* collections seemed more strongly marked than before by regret for the fading grace of yore.

Court ladies continued to compose poems and write diaries and tales, even though their role in higher culture was declining by the thirteenth century. Perhaps the most revealing work attributed to a woman is *Mumyōzōshi*, evidently compiled ca. 1200–1 by a poet commonly known as the Daughter of Shunzei, who was in fact a niece of the poet Fujiwara no Teika. Using a cleverly structured, conversational format, the author engaged in a lively discussion and critique of literary gems from past centuries. She dwelt particularly on works by women, devoting about a third of her effort to the *Genji*.

Mumyōzōshi gives us unexcelled insight into how readers of the day viewed their literary heritage, and it exemplifies the processes of romanticization and misrepresentation that are endemic to the writing of history. Thus, to look again at our cultural icons Ariwara no Narihira and Ono no Komachi, we are told that *Ise monogatari* is reputed to "describe actual events" and that it "was composed to show the passionate heart of Narihira." As for Komachi, everything about her, "her appearance, character, and behavior – is quite wonderful." Sadly, however, "Her old age was most unhappy. I don't believe anyone has experienced such wretched last years as Komachi."[17] The process of romanticizing Narihira and Komachi continued in following centuries, producing images so much larger than life that even today they can move us to tears of joy and sorrow.

Writers of prose thus displayed an unprecedented level of literary consciousness, but poetry remained the queen of literary arts. The political upheaval of the late twelfth century elicited a remarkable burst of poetic creativity even as it produced a major shift in the character of that verse. The emphasis on subjectivity, decorum, and elevated tone that Ki no Tsurayuki had favored three centuries earlier gave way to a more somber, descriptive poetry that employed colloquial expressions and more irregular syntax. Teika is probably the most famous of several celebrated poets of the day, while *Shinkokinshū* (ca. 1205), which he and others prepared under the guidance of retired emperor Go-Toba as an expression of imperial reassertion, was the most influential of the major new poetry compilations.

The heightened religious content of poetry was evident in the verse by Saigyō quoted above. And *mappō* thought notwithstanding, the belief that cultural mastery had religious import found new proponents. Thus, Teika's father, the poet-official Shunzei, argued explicitly that poetry can "communicate the Buddha's Way." He declared that,

> if as time passes I can come to an understanding of the limitless profundity of the Buddha's Law through an understanding of the profundity of Japanese poetry, I will thereby create the effect of being reborn in paradise and will be able to realize the Bodhisattva's vow to save all living beings.[18]

Centuries earlier Kūkai had proposed that the sight of "the various postures and mudras" of Shingon paintings might bring one to enlightenment; Shunzei found the same potential in *waka*. Others of his day saw comparable spiritual promise in music and dance.

Performance arts.   Music and dance had long combined religious and recreational functions in the forms of court music and dance, shrine dances, and temple liturgies, and during the centuries of *insei* and dyarchy they continued to do so. They also provided avenues for linking the aristocratic few to a plebeian population of entertainers and their art. Two streams of plebeian vocal music became particularly fashionable among the courtly elite. One was folk songs (*saibara*), which were already charming aristocrats in Murasaki's day. The other was *imayō* or "popular songs" – ditties, love songs, and laments – that seem to have sprung from the musical enticements employed by women entertainers who worked the roads and rivers wherever paying customers might be found.

The most famous patron of *imayō* was the retired emperor Go-Shirakawa, who retained the elderly and esteemed *imayō* singer Otomae as tutor. He recorded and annotated her songs, combining that material with relevant anecdotes and information in a manner not unlike collections of poetry, miscellaneous lists, and most particularly *setsuwa*. Like other compilers, he found religious significance in the pieces he gathered, declaring:

> The *imayō* that are popular these days are not intended simply for entertainment. When they are sung with sincerity at shrines or temples, they bring about divine revelations and fulfill our wishes. They obtain for people their desire for official positions, prolong human life, and immediately cure illnesses.[19]

Nor was Go-Shirakawa wrong in finding a religious sensibility in *imayō*. Many were Buddhist in theme, most commonly taking inspiration from the *Lotus sutra*. The overlap of salvific and seductive reflects the absence of a clear line between entertainers who sang the songs for personal income and nuns who sang them for proselytizing and institutional fund raising.

Women danced as well as sang for customers, and during later Heian *shirabyōshi* dancers, women who were in effect "both entertainer and courtesan, the geisha of her day," enjoyed great vogue at court.[20] Dressed in white costume, equipped with a hand-held fan, and supported by the rhythms of drum and cymbal, they provided lively, fetching entertainment as well as moving evocations of religious tales. The pinnacle of *shirabyōshi* favor appears to have been achieved by Kamegiku, beloved of Go-Toba, who, it is said, followed him into exile on Sado Island after his failed revolt of 1221.

Ensemble dance also won court favor. Late in the Sekkanke heyday aristocrats began entertaining themselves with *dengaku* ("field dances"), which evidently were song and dance rituals earlier associated with the planting of rice on shrine or temple lands. Around 1100 the retired emperor Shirakawa became an enthusiastic supporter of *dengaku* performances, and the dance was worked into some court rituals. In following decades, as economic activity intensified, professional performance troupes (*za*) developed *dengaku* into choreographed programs of flute, drum, and vocal music that accompanied dance and served as both entertainment and religious ritual. Depending on the performance site their audiences consisted of aristocrats, *bushi*, temple and shrine personnel, pilgrims, and diverse others.

Similarly, *sarugaku* presentations, which originally were diverse light entertainments but increasingly became performances built around comic mime, became better organized. Major fanes served as patrons, in return for which the troupes performed religious dances and magic to please the gods. Troupes also pleased priest and pilgrim by acting out miraculous tales that highlighted the sponsoring institution's traditions or doctrines. By late Heian troupes of professional *sarugaku* performers were developing dramatic plots and story lines and incorporating *imayō* songs and *shirabyōshi* dances that enhanced their audience appeal. In the process they were laying a foundation for later forms of theatre.

Visual arts. The religious sensibilities of the age were even more fully expressed through the visual arts, which attained unprecedented levels of richness and vitality. Breaking new ground in style and technique, sculpture and painting captured the syncretic and sectarian themes of the day. In doing so they both reflected and shaped religious developments and left distinguished monuments for later generations.

Sculptors continued to produce formulaic Buddhist images for installation in temples and family chapels, but they also broke free of formula to produce other images of striking vigor and diversity. They solved a number of technical problems and gained immense flexibility of design when they adopted the technique of joining smaller pieces of wood together, rather than working with a single log. Most famously Unkei and his colleague Kaikei used the technique to craft remarkably lifelike images of both celebrated Japanese prelates and legendary figures of the Buddhist textual tradition. *Hon-jaku* thought prompted sculptors to create images of various Shintō deities and Buddhist guardian figures, beatific or fearsome as appropriate. One of the most awesome examples is the pair of towering, twenty-six-foot tall Niō guardian deities standing on alert in the great gate tower of the Tōdaiji. Craftsmen working under Unkei and Kaikei installed them in 1203 as reconstruction of the temple neared completion two decades after its destruction at Taira hands.

Religious painting was equally impressive. One exquisite type was the *raigō*, an image based on the increasingly popular Amidist teachings. *Raigō* were joyously bright evocations of Amida and his host descending to receive the believer and escort him – or her – to the Western Paradise, where ultimate enlightenment was assured.

Another popular type of painting, a type that embraced much more of the day's religion, was the mandala (*mandara*), originally a stylized representation of Buddhist doctrine as expressed in a particular sutra. Especially valued by adherents to Shingon, mandala constituted ideal vehicles for expressing the combinative *hon-jaku* thought of the age, with gorgeous paintings being prepared for fanes of all sorts. Some of the most elegant were shrine mandalas, such as that of the Iwashimizu Hachimangū. It celebrated the shrine's deities, festivals, architecture, and landscape, all of which embodied the shrine's sacred powers.

These paintings and sculptures, like shrine dances, *sarugaku* performances, and liturgies themselves, were integral parts of institutional life at temples and shrines. Because of their spiritual powers, they too attracted worshippers and pilgrims, inspiring viewers to make material contributions that helped sustain the fane. As time passed and the old landed order became less stable and the economy more monetized, donations from the faithful, and hence the role of these religious performers and producers, became more and more important to temples and shrines throughout the realm.

The role of creative artist as link between religious institution and parishioner was also evident in the pictorial handscroll or *emakimono*. Working in color or in black and white, the handscroll painter arranged text and illustration so that as one unrolled the scroll from right to left a coherent narrative unfolded. That narrative might illustrate a story from sutra or *setsuwa*, recount the life of a celebrated figure, illustrate the powers and mysteries of the temple or shrine where the scroll was displayed, or provide instruction in proper religious performance. The turmoil and dismay of the Genpei wars and their aftermath were reflected in *emakimono* of the day, such as *Gaki zōshi*, which depicts in polychrome horror the suffering of the damned and diseased. In the less hectic decades that followed, some scrolls celebrated famous religious figures, as does *Saigyō monogatari emaki*, which portrays in idealized terms the pilgrimages of the famous poet-priest Saigyō.

Emakimono were not limited to religious themes, however. Being produced by government offices and individuals as well as by temple and shrine artisans, some of the most well known are secular works. Artists expanded the earlier Heian practice of combining *waka* and painting to produce scrolls that illustrated secular *setsuwa* and longer tales and diaries. The oldest surviving example of a secular scroll (see figure 6.2) is *Genji monogatari emaki*, which dates to about 1120–40 and is thought to have been created by the joint effort of artistic court women and men.[21]

Other secular scrolls illustrated court life, official rituals, and notable events, including warfare. Several *emakimono* versions of war tales were

Figure 6.2 A scene (detail) from *Genji monogatari emaki*; color on paper, twelfth century; artist unknown; Tokugawa Art Museum, Nagoya. Based on Lady Murasaki's classic masterpiece, this scroll painting exemplifies the Yamato-*e* style of art – its view as an angle-shot from above, lush color, flowing hair and garments, fine-line delineation of spatial layout, and stylized representation of faces, round with slit eyes and "rosebud" lips. *Source*: Reproduced courtesy of the Tokugawa Art Museum.

prepared, most famously the *Heiji monogatari emaki*, which illustrated battling of the 1150s. Yet other scrolls celebrated famous historical figures, Prince Shōtoku most commonly. The merging of secular and sacred agendas is nicely evident in the several handscrolls known as *Kitano Tenjin engi*, the earliest version dating to 1219. They honored the early Heian official Sugawara no Michizane, who, as noted in chapter 5, had fallen afoul of the Fujiwara, taken his revenge as an angry spirit, and subsequently been placated by being deified and enshrined at Kitano and other Tenjin shrines about the country. At these shrines the *engi* functioned as totemic images, giving suppliants access to the storied powers of Tenjin.

Emakimono became a major vehicle for the Yamato-*e* painting style with its distinctive "bird's-eye" view of a scene and its use of fine brushwork and stylized representations of face and figure. Like the histories, biographies, and other literary works of the *insei*–dyarchy centuries, moreover, these handscrolls contributed to romanticization of the classical epoch and to the definition of classic virtues. Those definitions in turn shaped the culture of later generations, continuing to influence Japanese values and viewpoints down to the present.

All in all, the centuries from Nara's founding to mid-Kamakura witnessed a remarkable flowering in arts, letters, and religious thought. A formerly nonliterate elite mastered an array of new cultural practices, fitted imported customs to their own, adapted their arts and letters to changing times, and left a rich cultural legacy for future generations. Much would be modified as time passed, but the priorities and ideals embedded in this cultural legacy continued to shape Japanese civilization in the centuries that followed.

This brief tour through Japan's classical higher culture has taken us far from the environmental concerns that prompted this study. Or maybe not so far. In terms of production, distribution, and representation, the tripartite categorization adumbrated in the Introduction, this chapter has dwelt mainly on the representational aspect of the dispersed agricultural society's phase of stasis. The underlying conditions of a steeply stratified system of distribution and a productive base that showed little growth seem to be reflected in – and reinforced by – the elite values and conduct revealed in these courtly arts, letters, and religion. For much of the period this representational activity helped sustain the established elite's routines of behavior and claims to legitimacy.

As the underlying agricultural order began to change, however, and with it the distribution of wealth and power, one sees complementary changes in cultural output, especially during the early thirteenth century. The priorities of new interest groups found more literary, visual, and religious expression, even as entrenched interests fought back, using cultural tools as well as economic, political, and military. Until 1250 or so, the latter held the upper hand despite the fear and dismay they so clearly evinced. That success notwithstanding, however, the forces of change finally broke loose, as Part III will show, with ramifications that ultimately changed Japanese life and culture from paddy field to palace.

Part III

The Age of Intensive Agriculture (1250–1890)

Introduction to Part III

Part III, to evoke again the chronological framework sketched in the Introduction, brings us to the age of intensive agriculture. Following the long eras of early and later forager culture and the millennium and a half of dispersed agriculture, it was the fourth of the five basic phases of Japanese history and lasted until industrial arrangements displaced it in the twentieth century.

The rhythms of the intensive agricultural age in some ways recapitulated those of the non-intensive. In broadest temporal terms, during both ages a relatively lengthy "growth stage" was accompanied by "state-building," or less euphemistically, by a struggle for dominance among groups competing to control society's expanding output. That struggle culminated in the triumph of a faction – imperial–Fujiwara duopolists and their *ritsuryō* order in the first case; the Tokugawa, their allies, and the *bakuhan* system in the second – which then imposed its control across the realm, arranging a system of exploitation that sustained the ruling faction's successor generations. On both occasions the imposition of order was followed within a few decades by a broader shift from growth to a shorter stage of stasis, within which context processes of adaptation and accommodation occurred. These processes gradually modified the procedures of control and eventually the distribution of power, finally producing internal stresses that combined with exogenous influences to precipitate a rupture and open the way for a new historical stage.

These cyclical qualities notwithstanding, history never starts carte blanche and never "repeats" in a tidy fashion: in each new phase there is always something to build on and something to reject. Much as Jōmon foragers had utilized and improved stone-working and hunting techniques of their paleolithic forebears and Yayoi agriculturists used and adapted foraging, housing, and pottery techniques of their predecessors, so intensive agriculturalists – and also today's industrial-age Japanese – built on the legacy of their forerunners.

In the outcome the growth stage of intensive agriculture gave rise to a society and agronomic system that was much larger and more complex than that of earlier centuries. The accompanying political struggle was much greater in scale than that of pre-*ritsuryō* centuries, and the eventual Tokugawa arrangements for distributing wealth and power far more elaborate. The yield extracted from the ecosystem was commensurately larger, and as a corollary, the environmental impact was much greater: whereas the *ritsuryō* order had disrupted and done long-term damage only to the Kinai ecosystem, that of the Tokugawa disrupted it from southern Kyushu to northern Honshu. The increased scale and severity of environmental disruption led, in turn, to remedial efforts that were far more extensive than the few, ineffectual restrictions on forest use decreed by the court during the *ritsuryō* heyday. And finally, at the level of representation, while the arts and letters of these centuries did draw heavily on the classical legacy, they also broadened cultural participation, addressed more diverse agendas, and developed new forms of expression and rich new bodies of thought and imagery.

Examining this history in terms of growth and stasis produces a different chronology from that based on the rise and fall of central regimes. For the age of dispersed agriculturalists, as we have seen, this approach split the Nara period, with the decades of Shōmu *tennō*'s reign constituting the central watershed. For intensive agriculture it places the break nearer 1700 than 1600 and thus seems to disregard one of the most solidly entrenched boundaries in Japanese historiography, that between *chūsei* and *kinsei* or "medieval" and "early modern" history.

That traditional boundary is instructive, however. It marks the shift from an era of endemic warfare and social turmoil to one of disciplined political stability and social order, a shift that was much more pronounced than any comparable one during creation of the *ritsuryō* order. Moreover, whereas the rise of *ritsuryō* arrangements in the early eighth century seems to have produced little more than a temporary spurt of socioeconomic growth, and that limited to the Kinai vicinity, formation of the *bakuhan* system contributed to several decades of sharply accelerated expansion in the size of society, the scale of social activity, and the scope of its environmental impact throughout the realm.

Finally, the growth-and-stasis approach, as used here, breaches yet another procrustean political boundary, that between *kinsei* and *kindai*, "early modern" and "modern" history. One can, certainly, date the rise of Japan's industrial society from the Meiji Restoration, but doing so seems to ascribe to early Meiji society qualities that it did not begin to evince in appreciable degree until decades later. Admittedly this is a small point, but the approach used here treats the Meiji Restoration as a less transformational event than we usually envisage. Instead it highlights the ways in which old political values and orientations as well as older social, economic, cultural, and ecological characteristics persisted, in part due to human choice but in greater part because industrialization did not really get underway and start to have a broad social impact until the 1890s or even later.

On the other hand, formation of the Meiji regime was a sufficiently important watershed in itself – to say nothing of its standing in later ideology – so that early Meiji seems to require treatment independent of later Tokugawa. In that sense it differs from establishment of the Kamakura bakufu, which we have treated, with the term "dyarchy," as an awkward modification of the gradually changing *ritsuryō* order.

This is not to deny similarity in the two developments. Triumph of eastern warriors in the 1180s and of western warriors in the 1860s occurred at moments when long-established power structures were in parlous condition. The Restoration, like the formation of court–bakufu dyarchy, did restore order following a brief burst of political violence. In both cases lesser, even marginal, participants in the established elite order, disgruntled with the way dominant figures were handling affairs, did seize control. They did redistribute power modestly and did modify governing procedure within the established ruling classes. And in the outcome both events did contribute to the passing of an age.

Still and all, during the 1180s Kamakura leaders faced far less radically altered external circumstances than did the insurgents of 1868, and largely as a consequence of that difference they felt far less compulsion to pursue radical changes at home. Then, during the decades immediately following their rise to eminence, they and their successors had to cope with far less rapid external change, and hence far fewer domestic complications, than did Meiji leaders, who faced imperialist traders, politicians, and proselytizers. So rulers at Kamakura were far less inclined to seek yet further change than were those of Meiji, who by 1890 ended up jettisoning almost all the institutional baggage they had inherited from the Tokugawa. Consequently, whereas we were able to fold Kamakura's rise unobtrusively into the narrative of later non-intensive agricultural history, early Meiji receives separate treatment in chapter 12, where it foreshadows the future as much as it reflects the past.

Chronology of Part III

1272	Start of quarrels over imperial succession.
1274, 1281	Failure of two attempts by Mongols to conquer Japan.
ca. 1307	Lady Nijō composes *Towazugatari*.
ca. 1330	Yoshida Kenkō writes *Tsurezuregusa*.
1334	Go-Daigo undertakes Kenmu Restoration.
1338	Ashikaga Takauji establishes Muromachi *bakufu*.
1358	Nijō Yoshimoto compiles *Tsukubashū*, first *renga* anthology.
1370s	Kan'ami's style of *nō* drama wins shogun Yoshimitsu's favor.
1392	Ashikaga Yoshimitsu ends period of divided imperial house (*nanbokuchō*).
1402	Ming emperor awards Yoshimitsu title "King of Japan."
1420s	Start of forceful public demands for debt cancellation.
1441	Akamatsu Mitsusuke murders shogun Yoshinori.
1467	Ōnin War erupts; start of *sengoku* period.
1483	Ashikaga Yoshimasa constructs Ginkakuji.
1480s–1532	Peak of Honganji sectarian power.
1540s	Kanō Motonobu establishes Kanō style of painting.
ca. 1550s	*Wabicha* popular among elite of Sakai, Nara, Kyoto.
1571	Oda Nobunaga annihilates Enryakuji.
1582–92	Toyotomi Hideyoshi pacifies the realm.
1592	Hideyoshi launches attempt to conquer China; fails.
1600	Tokugawa Ieyasu wins at Sekigahara; founds Tokugawa *bakufu*.
1590s–1620s	Nationwide construction boom; Kyoto flourishes.

1630s	Tokugawa Iemitsu regularizes internal and foreign relations.
1670s–80s	Hishikawa Moronobu produces woodblock prints in Edo.
1680s	Ihara Saikaku writes diverse *ukiyo zōshi* in Osaka.
1697	Miyazaki Antei publishes *Nōgyō zensho*.
1688–1703	Genroku period of urban cultural vitality.
ca. 1690s–1720s	Population growth decelerates sharply.
1720s	Tokugawa Yoshimune implements Kyōhō Reform.
1759	Yamagata Daini writes *Ryūshi shinron*.
1780s	Tenmei famine.
1790s	Matsudaira Sadanobu promotes Kansei Reform.
1808	*HMS Phaeton* affair at Nagasaki.
1825	Bakufu orders prompt rejection of all foreign ships.
1830s	Tenpō famine.
ca. 1830s–40s	Printmaker Katsushika Hokusai flourishes.
1842	Japanese leaders learn of Opium War outcome.
1854–58	Unequal treaties imposed on Japan.
1868	Meiji Restoration announced.
1871	Daimyo domains abolished
1877	Satsuma Rebellion crushed.
1880s	Matsukata deflation stabilizes currency.
1889	Meiji Constitution issued.

[7] THE CENTURIES OF DISORDER (1250–1550)

Minamoto no Yoritomo had no desire to destroy the established aristocratic order; quite the contrary, he only wished it to function more satisfactorily, which meant assuring a proper place in it for him and his followers. And in the short run he succeeded handsomely. In the longer run, however, the very trends that had made major political players out of such men as him worked as well for others, and those others grew so numerous and competed so fiercely during the "medieval" period – meaning here the centuries 1250 to 1550 – that they eventually destroyed nearly every vestige of *ritsuryō* arrangements. Once that was done, by the late sixteenth century, power seekers were able, indeed were forced, to devise mechanisms of control that enabled the shrewdest and/or luckiest of their number to overwhelm the others and restore order to the realm.

The processes of change that underlay this political narrative were broad in scope and intertwined. They proceeded, however, with such limited connection to the particulars of elite politics that it makes sense to flesh out the broader story first. Doing so will help clarify the larger issues that lay behind the intricate maneuvers of those struggling to dominate a world that increasingly lay beyond their control, notably the leaders of dyarchy until its collapse and, from the 1330s onward, the chiefs of the Ashikaga *bakufu* (shogunal regime) and their innumerable rivals and insubordinates.

TRENDS IN PRODUCTION AND DISTRIBUTION

Beneath the turmoil that marked political life in medieval Japan lay a number of basic developments. Most fundamental was a broad-ranging increase in society's material production (and, by various measures, productivity), primarily agricultural but also artisanal. That increase made possible overall demographic growth as well as expansion in the historically more visible classes. It also allowed a striking acceleration in the rate at which the output of producers and ecosystem was consumed in warfare and self-indulgence. A second development, also made possible by agronomic change, was the emergence of larger, much more cohesive, and internally directed villages that were capable of engaging in the broader political life of society. Thirdly, changes in the handling of goods and services – commercialization, in a word – helped make this growth in rural output more accessible to society at large, which abetted the growth while broadening its effects. Finally, this growth in agricultural production, together with changes in political and religious life, spurred urbanization, meaning the proliferation of towns across the realm, which fostered the diffusion of power, wealth, and a shared higher culture.

In toto these changes expanded the size and complexity of Japanese society, the array of goods and services available to it, and the level of demand it made on the ecosystem. They also increased dramatically the power potential of society as a whole, dwarfing that of dyarchy's heyday, overwhelming those who tried to rule, and ultimately eradicating almost every vestige of the old order. They also, however, provided the basis for someone – whoever could manage it – to construct a new political order that would be far more powerful than any Japan had ever known before.

AGRICULTURAL INTENSIFICATION

Multivariate processes of interaction, such as those that undid the *ritsuryō* order, never reduce to tidy narratives because they cannot adequately be treated as simple chains of cause and effect. Chapter 5 foreshadowed the matter by examining several of the processes involved in the early stages of agricultural intensification and related social change. By 1250, to continue that inquiry, diseases that had once caused periodic population declines had become mainly illnesses of childhood. As a diarist noted, concerning a smallpox epidemic in 1243:

> From the fifth month, nineteenth day, smallpox spread more and more. This time it is afflicting young children.[1]

Comments about children but not adults dying appeared in later outbreaks, which suggests the disease's endemic character. Although painful to experience, deaths of children lacked the demographic impact of adult mortality because the youngsters were not crucial as producers or reproducers and because they could be replaced within a few years.

Even after these pathogens had lost their demographic punch, crop failure and famine continued to slow population growth into the later thirteenth century. From about then, however, growth accelerated, and by 1600, as noted earlier, the estimated seven million people of 1200 had increased to some twelve million. A portion of that growth enlarged society's intermediate and upper status populations, swelling the numbers competing to control usufruct, which was the basic force driving elite politics. In gross terms, however, demographic growth led mainly to the proliferation of villagers and the emergence of larger, denser settlements. Indeed, of the villages that have existed in more recent centuries, most seem to date from the 1300s or later, and they commonly occupy sites that older records characterize as unsettled or waste land.

More revealing than the appearance of so many new villages was the emergence of larger ones, because their existence meant that fields within walking distance were capable of supporting substantially greater populations than in earlier centuries. People might cluster in villages at behest of a *myōshu* or other local authority figure, or they might do so voluntarily, whether to defend themselves against marauders, to form a religious community, or for other reasons. Whatever the impetus, however, they were able to do so only because the changes in agronomic practice adumbrated in chapter 5 – more regular tillage, more elaborate irrigation and field management, more use of water wheels, iron tools, and fertilizer materials, and more crop diversification – were increasing yields enough to allow such clustering.

A low-technology strategy that proved particularly valuable for increasing output per hectare was field leveling, which assured all plants proper amounts of moisture. In one common method for achieving table-top flatness a farmer would level a parcel of land to form paddy field and spread the surplus soil on an adjacent plot, raising it enough for dry-field cropping. After that he could move soil back and forth between plots as climatic or other considerations advised to optimize field level and usage. It was a labor-intensive procedure that minimized topsoil waste while providing well-bounded, level fields for paddy culture and conveniently placed dry fields for diverse other crops. And it made the swampy flood plains of large rivers more usable even though the rivers themselves remained uncontrolled.

More significantly, perhaps, rice growers pursued riparian work. It was essential because paddy requires water until the rice starts heading out, and in many areas the natural supply of water from streams and springs did not last through the hot, dry months of summer. To address that problem, farmers utilized more water wheels, dammed more brooks to form ponds, and diked and ditched to create more elaborate irrigation systems (see figure 7.1). On broader plains, such as the Yamato Basin, they supplemented permanent dams with shallow holding ponds (*saraike*) that could trap and hold spring and monsoon runoff until needed as supplement for declining streamflow. Water from such ponds was doubly beneficial because it had warmed while standing in the sun, which enabled plants to utilize it more rapidly, and thus to mature faster.

Figure 7.1 A foot-operated water elevator; detail from *Tawara-kasane kōsaku emaki*; color on paper; late sixteenth century; artist unknown; University of Tokyo. This device, which raised water from small streams to adjacent irrigation ditches, was one of the several labor-intensive techniques employed by cultivators to increase the output of their arable land. *Source*: Bradley Smith, *Japan, A History in Art* (NY: Doubleday & Co. Inc., 1964), p. 143.

The use of these improved techniques spread across the country during the centuries to 1550, by which time about a quarter of the paddy land in central and western Japan was being double cropped. Many dry fields, as well, produced two crops a year; some fields grew three. In 1420 an envoy from Korea observed that in the Hyōgo vicinity farmers sow winter crops of barley and wheat,

which they harvest in the early summer of the following year. After that they plant rice seedlings. In the beginning of the fall they cut their rice ... and plant buckwheat, which they cut in early winter [prior to planting the barley and wheat]. They can plant seeds three times in one year on one paddy field because they can make it into paddy by damming the river and letting water in and then make it into a dry field by removing the dam on the river and letting the water out.[2]

The particulars of cultivation differed by region, but with each passing generation disciplined, intensive, and continuous tillage was becoming standard in more and more of the country.

This agronomic regimen enabled individual villagers to sustain their households on a hectare or less of decent arable land, and much of the medieval land reclamation was being undertaken, it appears, by small holders trying to increase their arable to the needed amount. Peasants who had enough fields to sustain themselves tended not to add more, perhaps because their household labor pool would be unable to give them proper attention. As decades passed, that constraint was reinforced in more and more places by scarcity of reclaimable land, limitations of accessible water and fertilizer supplies, and the risk of antagonizing neighbors if one attempted to open more land to tillage. In consequence, as generations passed, producer households with a hectare or so of arable land became increasingly common, in the Kinai region first and elsewhere later.

THE CHANGING VILLAGE

The changes in agronomic technique that made small holdings sustainable also led to changes in village society. Because small-scale farm households were generally able to survive without draft animals, outside help, or other assistance from *myōshu* or other local notables, they were less beholden to the village elite, less obliged to provide labor on request. *Myōshu* coped with their resulting labor shortage by splitting their holdings into household-sized parcels to be operated by neighbors and kin. Particularly in central Japan, where *myōshu* had from the beginning been weakest, as their local power declined, they tended to act less and less like appointees of *shōen* holders or other higher authority and more and more like leaders of self-governing village associations (*sō*) or local religious groups.

Village associations and local religious solidarities formed initially, it appears, to resolve intra-village disputes that higher authority had once settled but no longer could because of disorder among the elite. Even as the external adjudicator was being lost, however, intensifying agronomic practice and the rise of larger villages were making neighborly disputes more numerous and more complex. Mostly the quarrels related to allocation of common-use goods and services: the handling of woodland and waste, which provided fertilizer material; the use of irrigation water, which served more and more households as villages grew and water systems became larger and more complex; or disputes over land boundaries, one's duties and rights as a village resident, or innumerable other aspects of daily life.

Gradually villagers worked out mechanisms for managing community affairs: they developed rules of conduct, specified punishments, handled religious and recreational matters, set village membership fees, defined residence rights and duties, and enforced them. Depending on particulars of local geography, economy and tradition, these affairs might be handled in a quite egalitarian manner, but in most villages the *sō* consisted of heads of cultivating households while kin and other dependants were excluded. Also, it appears, women did not ordinarily participate in *sō* meetings even when they were recognized as land holders and even though they were fully engaged in the village's productive life and sometimes had influential roles as shrine mediums (*miko*) and festival participants.

As the term "residence rights" suggests, villagers increasingly distinguished themselves from outsiders. That trend appears to have reflected a shift from later-Heian ampleness of tillable land, when added hands were recruited and welcomed, to a situation in which, thanks to population growth, nearly all available arable was being worked and ampleness of labor made immigrants unwelcome. Because of that trend an increasingly important function of the *sō* was to keep outsiders out. Moreover, as higher political life became more violent, especially during the fifteenth century, *sō* also became the instruments for defending life and property against neighboring villages, rival religious groups, or marauding outsiders, whether *bushi*, bandits, or enforcers of old *shōen* interests.

By the mid-1400s these village associations were widespread. They took over tribute-collecting functions once performed by *myōshu* and other appointees of higher authority and initiated petitions to – and lawsuits against – *shōen* proprietors and others. Moreover, they provided institutional cores for the rural local-interest organizations known as *tsuchi ikki* ("solidarities of the locale"). *Ikki* protests and demonstrations against tribute takers, money lenders, and others mostly erupted in the Kinai vicinity, originating, as an observer noted in 1430, in "villages that belonged to the powerful nobles, temples, and shrines."[3] Furthermore, as *sō* became more solidly established, they enhanced local autonomy by gradually regularizing mutual cooperative arrangements. Thus in 1494 village leaders from several *sō* in Ise jointly pledged that, "if there is a dispute among us, we shall together come to a decision after examining all sides of the case."[4]

In many instances religion provided an invaluable glue for binding villagers together. The Jōdo Shin (True Pure Land) sect, which was grounded in the Amidist teachings of Shinran, was particularly prominent in this role, but various other religious affiliations also served that function. For the most part, however, it was local shrines with their shrine organizations (*miyaza*) that constituted the matrix of village cohesion. *Sō* meetings commonly were held in shrine precincts, in the very presence of the gods, with members summoned there by beating of the shrine drum, which exposed them to godly ire should they fail to respond. Moreover, disputants continued to invoke the gods and Buddhas in the oaths that sealed both their petitions and their declarations of communal solidarity on matters of mutual concern.

As social disorder intensified, villagers responded by building ever stronger defenses, physical as well as social. By the sixteenth century large numbers of villages in the Kinai region were surrounded by ditches or moats that enabled members to define their village's boundaries and regulate ingress by out-siders. Indeed, in Yamato Province, which was severely wracked by warfare, one scholar has identified 173 moated villages.[5] Commonly the moats were an integral part of the village's irrigation system, but their scale and arrange-ment reveal their political uses. They foreshadowed the role of moats later in the century for protecting urban centers and warrior headquarters.

ENVIRONMENTAL TRENDS

Agricultural intensification thus had effects that reached up the biosystem's "food chain" or "pecking order," yielding a larger human population. Most of the increase was occurring in villages, which were becoming more numer-ous, larger, more complexly organized, and more powerful. However, as we note below, many more people – mainly warriors, merchants, artisans, and clerics – also came to be situated between cultivators and the ruling elite. In addition, intensified cropping permitted greater consumption per capita, at least among the more advantaged sectors of society.

Unsurprisingly, these ramifications of agricultural intensification meant that the increase in crop yields had an impact downward as well as upward. It affected collaborating plants and animals in the human-centered biological community and, below them, the undomesticated biota of the archipelago. In essence, domesticates gained; others lost. Unfortunately for the historian, however, disintegration of the *ritsuryō* order ended the central record keeping that had shed some light on earlier environmental developments, and as a result it is difficult to speak with any certainty about the particulars of inten-sive agricultural society's impact on the medieval ecosystem. Nevertheless, some observations can be made about general and regional effects.

For Japan as a whole – basically meaning Honshu, Shikoku, and Kyushu, but not Hokkaido, which still lay beyond the pale – long-term increase in arable had the obvious consequence of reducing habitat for wild biota while expanding the areas given over to cultivated crops and domesticated animals. Perhaps more importantly, the end of fallowing meant that large tracts of land once used alternately by domesticated and wild growth were given over fully to rice and dry-field crops.

The effects of greatly expanded irrigation activity are very difficult to assess. How extensively the directing of water to paddy use deprived untilled areas of needed soil moisture is hard to say. Perhaps the main consequence of intensified irrigation was greater irregularity of downstream water flow, with streams shrinking more sharply during summer months, which allowed a build-up of stream bed vegetation that could then capture floating debris and contribute to silting, sporadic local flooding, and intensified erosion during seasons of high stream flow.

Domestic plants and animals benefited at the expense of other biota not only through expansion of arable and diversion of water but also through new inroads on non-arable land, woodland in particular. Sustained cul-tivation and double cropping led farmers to cut and collect ever more grass, brush, forest litter, and other material to produce mulch and ashes.

The practice altered natural communities in nearby woodland, and, when the harvester lacked skill or prudence, fostered erosion and reduced biomass production. The use of more and more draft animals and cavalry mounts increased the demand for fodder, which also came from nearby woodland and waste as pasturage or harvested roughage. Moreover, the nutrient yield of manure was then applied as much as possible to arable land, not to the areas from whence it originated.

In the same vein, growth in the human population, especially at higher social levels, combined with a great increase in iron-mongering and other industrial uses of fire to create a much heightened demand for fuel wood and charcoal. The consequent rise in tree cutting, hardwoods in particular, contributed to changes in woodland composition, favoring the spread of hardy red pine and brushy growth. It also facilitated the establishment in select localities of orchards for tea, mulberry, chestnut, and other fruiting trees.

Finally, as arable came to be fully utilized and villagers coped by policing themselves and keeping outsiders out, more and more people resorted to swidden culture. They burned patches of hillside to grow crops in the resulting ash, abandoning the patches in a couple of years after erosion and cropping had destroyed their fertility. The abandoned sites then gradually reforested, commonly with red pine and tropical grasses capable of surviving on deteriorated soils. For Japan as a whole, in short, intensification added substantially to the portion of the archipelago dedicated to members of the human-centered biological community and its parasites while reducing the portion, especially in lowlands and the lower reaches of hillsides, still available to other flora and fauna.

These environmental effects were not spread evenly across the realm, however. As in preceding centuries, human impact was greatest in the Kinai region. The deforestation associated with construction and maintenance of Fujiwara-*kyō*, Nara, and Heian had stripped the region of accessible old growth stands, and little of the new growth was left long enough to reach maturity. Consequently builders had to look elsewhere for large timbers. As centuries advanced, they pressed ever farther afield, reaching into southern Kii, over mountains into Ise, westward along the Inland Sea, and across the straits into Shikoku.

The problem of timber scarcity was acutely expressed around 1200 when the leaders of dyarchy set about rebuilding the Tōdaiji. For the main pillars they had to settle for less-than-ideal trees that were extracted with great difficulty from mediocre stands in far western Honshu and hauled at great cost by sea, river, and land from there to Nara. Smaller timbers came from various places in central and western Japan. For generations after that, builders made do with smaller timbers, which they brought by water from here and there or hauled overland from forests lining river valleys along the northern rim of the Nobi Plain. Thus fifteenth-century reconstruction work on the great Rinzai Zen temples Tōfukuji and Nanzenji consumed thousands of cart loads of timber hauled from the upper Nōbi region to Lake Biwa and then rafted via Uji to Kyoto.

Within the Kinai Basin the corollary problems of dessication and soil deterioration persisted. An unusual indicator was a shift in mushroom growth. Areas around Kyoto that during the *ritsuryō* heyday had still produced *hiratake*, a mushroom that prefers moist, shaded sites, had become so dry by the thirteenth century that they habitually produced *matsutake*, which grows atop the shallow roots of pine trees in dry, comparatively sunlit soil. By the later fifteenth century *hiratake* evidently were found only in protected monastery woodland. Similarly, Kinai areas originally renowned for their fine timber stands were celebrated by later generations for their firewood and charcoal, the products of scrub woodland. And in some localities that were particularly susceptible to dessication, soils gradually deteriorated to where they could not sustain significant vegetation. That outcome contributed to the broader problems of erosion and downstream silting that complicated river use, most notably in the Yodo River estuary. Yodo silting also expanded the delta, leaving Sumiyoshi Shrine stranded ever farther inland even as it created the foundation for much of present-day Osaka.

Elsewhere around the country proliferation of towns and military headquarters and the spread of warfare gave rise to frequent instances of local environmental injury. However, the only region of clearly sustained woodland deterioration seems to have been Izu Peninsula and environs, where the construction and maintenance of Kamakura created unprecedented and continuing demand for timber and fuel wood. Already by the 1250s the city's leaders were troubled by the marketing of undersized (and hence not very useful) timber and by "overpriced" fuel wood. And in following centuries persistent demand for forest products in the Izu region seems to have prevented extensive woodland recovery. By the 1550s the dominant figure in the region, a provincial magnate or *daimyō* (lit. "great name") named Hōjō, who was headquartered at Odawara, was attempting to regulate forest use. He invoked his authority to tax and restrict the activity of woodland users, in part for the income it generated but primarily to assure himself the timber, bamboo, and fuel wood he needed. It was an early instance of a practice that spread rapidly in following decades.

COMMERCIALIZATION

Agricultural intensification thus had consequences that reached "downward" through the human-centered biological community to undomesticated flora and fauna. Its consequences also reached "upward" via cultivators and intermediaries to the political and religious elites, where it fueled greatly expanded social activity. That upward-reaching process was hugely expedited by commercialization, which included the expansion of foreign and domestic trade, monetization of transactions, and development of more elaborate forms of commercial organization.

Continental trade revived during the twelfth century, as noted in chapter 5, and it continued to expand in scale and importance in later centuries. The trade with Korea and China, which contained items transshipped from Southeast Asia, included imports of cotton, silk, and other cloth goods, porcelain, ceramics, lacquerware, books, scrolls, medicines, and foodstuffs. Exports included copper, sulphur, other minerals, folding fans and screens, lacquerware, inkstones, swords, and other weapons. The trade was thus diverse in content, but for the medieval centuries as a whole, the crucial import was coinage because it became the currency of domestic use, save for some counterfeit coins whose generally low quality undercut their commercial credibility. The trade also moved people about, bringing a very modest renewal of immigration, most notably a foreign settlement at Hakata but also a smattering of other trading, refugee, and missionary immigrants. And Japanese went abroad, some of them settling permanently at ports scattered along the continental rim.

The trade involved many sorts of people and varying degrees of officialness and mutuality, with both Japanese and continental figures participating in all its forms. A significant portion of the commerce was accomplished by pirates (wakō), men who bargained with the willing and stole from the others. They did the latter especially during the chaotic decades 1330–80 and 1470–1570 (nanbokuchō and sengoku), when pirate squadrons became multi-ethnic scourges of the East Asian littoral. Some wakō operated with the consent, tacit or active, of daimyo or other authorities; some operated in defiance of them. More peaceful entrepreneurial commerce was pursued by merchants, temple officials, and daimyo, mainly from the fifteenth century onward, as official trade between the Ming Dynasty and Ashikaga bakufu petered out and before sengoku disorder confounded it.

The most visible trade, however, even if not the most important in the long run, was this last, the official trade, the "tally trade" as it was known. In 1402, the Ming emperor authorized the Ashikaga to send periodic official envoys to court to present "tribute" while the accompanying merchants conducted trade as a reward. These tally trade missions, though numbering only seventeen between 1404 and 1549, usually consisted of several vessels outfitted by merchants, temples, and other investors, and they carried large quantities of goods in both directions. Despite their official function in Chinese eyes, however, they in fact were bakufu missions only during the early years, gradually being taken over by daimyo, temples, and merchants as decades advanced. After 1500 the bakufu no longer was a participant, and in 1549 the Ming terminated them because of political turmoil at home and piratical trouble-making along the coast.

By then, however, this continental trade, particularly the coin imports, had helped spur the rise of countrywide domestic commerce and had sharply altered its instruments of denomination as well as its character and personnel. Back in ritsuryō days goods had generally been denominated in terms of cloth or rice and handled as tribute or land rent, but by the sixteenth century most had come to be valued in terms of coinage and moved as trade goods.

As noted in chapter 5, ritsuryō-era provisioning had largely been handled by officials assigned to provincial headquarters, transshipment points, and city markets. Artisans and purveyors had always conducted some exchange outside of these formal channels, and much of the provisioning in later Heian was handled through shōen hierarchies. Then during the thirteenth century, as commerce grew and the ruling classes became more fragmented and fractious, traders who originally had been licensed (as *za*) by *shōen* holders and other authority figures began gaining unprecedented levels of autonomy in their business dealings. As the fourteenth century advanced, they combined in various ways the functions of wholesaler, warehouseman, transporter, money changer, and pawn broker. And they struck bargains of convenience with the stronger power-holders of the moment, notably the Ashikaga but also successful daimyo and flourishing temples.

Partially protected by these patrons, entrepreneurs produced and peddled goods and services more widely, whether at city market, residential compound, temple gate, or on the road. They moved goods along highways by packhorse and backpack and along rivers and coastline by boat, off-loading, storing, processing, and reshipping or selling their wares at more and more places around the realm. By the sixteenth century many autonomous *za* were based in the countryside, nearer sources of supply and farther from warring armies. Some, such as rural merchants from a poorer corner of eastern Ōmi Province, had developed far-reaching peddling routes.

As this commercial activity grew, so too did employment of more menial sorts. The members of socially marginal groups, who in the *ritsuryō* heyday had provided the Heian elite with service in such "unclean" tasks as sweeping, cleaning, or disposing of corpses, found more and more work as ferrymen, leather handlers, metal workers, dyers, fortune tellers, and entertainers. And much as merchants and villagers were organizing themselves into corporate entities such as *za* and *sō* to protect their interests against outsiders, so these groups of plebeian technical specialists gradually formed associations that strove to monopolize their professions and keep outsiders out.

URBANIZATION

Urbanization went hand in hand with commercialization. Its most important aspect was the proliferation of towns throughout the realm. Their populations handled much of the burgeoning commerce, engaged in diverse types of fabrication, and consumed a growing portion of society's output. However, developments in Kyoto also command attention.

Medieval Kyoto. There were noteworthy continuities between early Heian and medieval Kyoto. The political elite, such as it was, still resided there most of the time. And the city remained, even during the grimmest days of political turmoil, the center of Japan's urban culture and economy. Indeed, it retained that centrality until the growth phase of intensive agriculture petered out around the end of the seventeenth century. As economic hub of the realm Kyoto not only received goods from overseas but also from throughout the country. Its artisans sustained the city's reputation as source of the finest domestic silks and handicrafts. And at the lowest social level, as noted above, its pariahs and marginal folk still made their way through life as best they could, dwelling along the river banks, ravines, and waste spaces unwanted by the more well-off and handling the unpleasant jobs that others would not.

By the thirteenth century, however, much had also changed. The old, rectilinear Heian, which was never completed in any case, was long gone, its great imperial palace compound transformed into a ramble of house lots, garden plots, fields, and waste. Much of the world of Murasaki Shikibu, with its mansions and palaces, was also lost, as were the outlying *insei* establishments of the Toba and Shirakawa districts south and east of the city. During the later decades of dyarchy a number of new temples, mostly of the flourishing Zen and Jōdo sects, were erected in and around town, but they tended to be modest in scale. And many burned periodically or were relocated to the city's periphery. Warfare of the mid-fourteenth century repeatedly damaged the city, but during the Ashikaga heyday, ca. 1370–1440, it flourished anew, becoming home to bakufu officialdom and also to many daimyo, their retainers, and a large population of service personnel. Its inhabitants swelled to an estimated 200,000, but the number dropped sharply after eruption of the Ōnin War in 1467, only starting to recoup around 1550.

The city proper lay along the west bank of the Kamo River, with fingers of settlement running outward along the highways (see figure 7.2). Some handsome new villas came to adorn the cityscape, and on the outskirts a substantial array of Buddhist temples, old and new, ringed the city, many situated in foothills east of the Kamo. During the fifteenth century, however, and especially after Ōnin, Kyoto bifurcated into a northern part, Kamigyō, where the rulers clustered, and a southern part, Shimogyō. There the city's bustling merchant and artisan population maintained most of its establishments, along with a growing number of temples of the Hokke (or Lotus) sect, which had sprung from the disciples of Nichiren.

In this changing city setting business flourished during periods of order, and merchants throve. During wartime some profiteered; some disappeared; others muddled through and rebuilt after the fighting and destruction tapered off. In the process survivors acquired a greater role in city governance. By the mid-fifteenth century the neighborhoods of artisans and merchants that clustered around major intersections in Shimogyō were organized into self-administering units (*machi*) under the supervision of their own *za*. Especially after the Ōnin War ruptured the city's control structure around 1470, merchants – notably silk weavers, rice dealers, *sake* brewers, freight warehousemen, and shippers – took over or organized their own *za* and collaborated to regulate markets and manage their *machi*.

By the sixteenth century the urban commoners who filled these neighborhoods, and whom commentators identified generically as *shokunin* or "people of skill," were a wonderfully variegated population that included,

fishmongers, herb sellers, incense and medicine vendors, and peddlers of firewood, charcoal, brooms, footgear, salt, oil, and fresh greens ... carpenters, roof tilers, stone cutters, and plasterers ... armor makers, indigo dyers, wig makers, sword sharpeners, hat lacquerers, comb makers, needle sharpeners, fabric weavers, embroiderers, cord weavers, rosary makers, metal workers, blacksmiths, and religious image makers ... doctors, mediums, soothsayers, and geomancers.[6]

Figure 7.2 The vicissitudes of medieval Kyoto. In this composite figure, the rectilinear outline of Heian, with the Kamo River on its east side, occupies about as much space as the area enclosed in Hideyoshi's *odoi*, the vertically lengthened, irregularly shaped outline. The lightly visible checkerboard area that fills much of the eastern half of Heian denotes medieval Kyoto before the Ōnin War, with its many sake brewers, pawnbrokers, and oil dealers identified by the black dots. The two small, darkened areas linked by a wide dark line are the semi-walled remnants of Kamigyō and Shimogyō during the depths of *sengoku*. *Source*: Mary Elizabeth Berry, *The Culture of Civil War in Kyoto* (Berkeley: UCP, 1994), pp. 65, 67.

The streets swarmed with vendors of all sorts, carters and their animals, diverse religious itinerants, and entertainers to lift the heart and lighten the purse.

A portion of those vendors were women. In Japan, as in other societies needless to say, commoner households got by as best they could, which meant that they utilized their labor resources as effectively as possible. Farm women worked the fields, and as the market economy grew, women participated in the production and sale of goods such as *tōfu*, rice products, and craft items. In addition, as the polygamous patterns of elite society decayed, and as the urban populations of warriors and other middling classes grew, women found a larger, more monetized market for sexual favors, which gave rise to a more regularized prostitution industry.

By then many city folk viewed themselves as residents of particular city blocks. Many owned street properties and were paying taxes on them, rather than renting from ruling-class landlords, as in earlier centuries. They were organizing their blocks for self-defense and by the 1520s were even beginning to fortify them with barricades and eventually earthen walls and moats. As political authority collapsed, Hokke temples provided an alternative structure for regulating town affairs, settling disputes among blocks, and defending neighborhoods against outsiders. In 1536, however, as we note more fully below, the Hokke groups were smashed by rival armies, and thereafter leaders of Kyoto's townsmen (*machishū*) functioned essentially as secular neighborhood administrators, becoming fully subordinated to samurai during the final decades of the century.

Other towns.   For all the trauma it experienced, medieval Kyoto was thus a dynamic and engaging city. However, the broader, more important aspect of urbanization was the proliferation of towns, especially along the Inland Sea and in the Kinai vicinity. In earlier centuries urban centers had included the capital city, secondary administrative headquarters, and a few small settlements at major temples, near the homes of local magnates, or at tribute-transfer points, river landings most commonly. But with growth in agricultural output, population, and trade, commercial nodes proliferated.

Development from "node" to "town" was slow, however. Commercial sites commonly functioned as periodic markets for generations before they became permanently settled. Peddlers who carried the goods they made and sold – "pots, pans, needles, hoes, plows, knives, sesame oil," and other daily-use products of artisans such as woodworkers and potters – displayed their wares near temple entrances or at transshipment points where travelers tarried.[7] During the thirteenth century such peddlers began gathering regularly at predetermined sites, assembling three times monthly at first, but six times monthly by the late fifteenth century. Where the business was lively, more and more settled permanently, creating the need for support personnel, and in due course for some form of town organization to regulate residents and cope with unwelcome outsiders. By 1550 numerous such towns counted hundreds or even thousands of residents. The larger ones numbered 5,000 to 30,000, the greatest being creatures of special circumstances: Hakata was the principal port for the China trade; Sakai, the major eastern terminus for Inland Sea shipping.

Many such towns began in conjunction with monastic *shōen*, and a goodly number remained under the control of major temples into the fifteenth century because the clerics were able, in return for suitable rents and fees, to expedite and protect the marketing efforts of affiliated artisans, merchants, and *za*. As that century passed, however, and especially after the Ōnin War, *shōen* proprietors proved to be of less and less value to townsmen. In place after place the locals took charge. They formed their own governing councils, drafted their own rules, oversaw their local shrine ceremonies, and delineated their town boundaries. They forwarded such tribute to higher authority as their situation required, eventually deployed their own police, and even bargained or battled with outsiders.

In some of these towns the major merchants controlled affairs; in others control was spread more widely among residents. In some instances local temple priests were powerful, in others local warriors were in control. And sometimes power was shared awkwardly by residents and outside figures. But in any case, the upshot was a massive decline in central control of producers and distributors and a rapid growth in the hinterland economy and the towns it provisioned.

House-proud daimyo of these centuries maintained administrative headquarters of their own. Especially after Ōnin, when Kyoto rarely lured daimyo away from their hinterland bases of power, much more expansive baronial towns arose. Centered on the daimyo's luxurious and increasingly well fortified mansion, these towns bustled with samurai who were serviced by resident priests, merchants, artisans, laborers, and entertainers. And in the hinterland around such towns artisans produced more and more goods for the daimyo and his followers. In the process they spurred the rise of local and regional output that competed with that of Kyoto and provided additional income for the lord.

In several ways, then, this medieval urbanization reinforced other aspects of social change, cumulatively weakening the old forces of order and opening the way for political turmoil and reconstruction. Narrating that convoluted story is the burden of the pages that follow.

A POLITICAL NARRATIVE

"Chaos," as currently defined by students of "chaos theory," does have an underlying order, albeit one of sublime complexity. Medieval Japanese politics was chaotic in that sense. The political cohesion of dyarchy, which weakened sharply from the 1260s onward, was lost during the 1330s and disorder came to prevail. It was, however, disorder with a logic: real, identifiable issues were at stake, and the idiosyncratic variables of individual personality, ability, and chance operated within a structured field of interests, orientations, possibilities, and constraints that was ever more fully shaped by the socioeconomic trends discussed above.

Out of this field, in due course, aspirants to power reassembled the political building blocks of wealth, military power, and ideology. The most celebrated attempt, the Kenmu Restoration of Go-Daigo during the 1330s, was premature and died aborning. The first effective attempt, by Ashikaga leaders during the later fourteenth century, was inadequately founded and incomplete. Their polity has been aptly characterized by scholars as a *kenmon* regime, a government of "powerful houses."[8] In essence it was an unstable coalition of the currently privileged: court, *kuge*, great fanes, and higher-status *bushi*. At first the instability persisted because coalition members fought among themselves, but as generations passed, they increasingly had to defend their interests against challenges from lesser segments of society, notably minor provincial warriors (*kokujin*), artisan-merchants, village leaders, and proponents of sectarian religious movements.

Like the *ritsuryō* order the *kenmon* regime was designed to protect established interests, but whereas the former protected a small and relatively undifferentiated elite and operated in an era of very slow change, the latter was trying to accommodate a much larger and more diverse constituency and to cope with rapidly changing times. It fared poorly in the effort, beginning to disintegrate almost as soon as it showed signs of success in the years around 1400. The ensuing disorder of the *sengoku* or "warring states" period, commonly dated 1467–1567, shredded almost all remaining vestiges of the classical system for controlling wealth, power, and ideology. In so doing it undermined the *kenmon* and left the way open for ambitious figures to construct new bases of power. These they employed to challenge one another and to topple their betters in a process nicely expressed as *gekokujō*, "those below overthrowing those above," until finally during the 1590s the victors in this process pacified the entire realm.

THE DECAY OF DYARCHY

Several problems were afflicting court–bakufu dyarchy by 1250. The *kuge* resentment of *buke* persisted, continually abraded by enervating disputes, most commonly over landed income. Such disputes also fueled the rise of factionalism among leaders of both court and bakufu as offspring of senior figures quarreled over titles, income, and inheritance rights. At lower levels, as well, warrior households fizzured as descendants struggled over succession rights. Basically these conflicts arose, it appears, because the consumers of landed usufruct were proliferating faster than the numbers of producers, the hectares they tilled, and the tribute goods they could provide. The situation was exacerbated by the spreading use of money, which added layers of unpredictability to tribute collection and created opportunity for shady maneuvering by collectors. The use of money also facilitated imprudent borrowing, which shortly gave rise to collisions between debtors and creditors.

By 1270 the ruling classes were riddled with cross-cutting tensions, and at that juncture foreign political complications placed the creaking power structure under unprecedented strain. In 1268, as the Mongol armies of Kublai Khan were attempting to conquer Sung China, the Khan despatched a message demanding Japan's submission. Bakufu leaders rejected the demand and ordered men to prepare Kyushu defenses. Kublai reiterated his message and finally, in 1274, after severely weakening the Sung, deployed a seaborne force, reportedly 28,000 Mongol warriors and Korean conscripts, only to have it bloodily repulsed on Kyushu's shores. Despite that setback the Khan warned that he was not yet through with Japan. Kyushu defenders stood on alert for years, and after the Sung collapsed in 1279, the Khan prepared to try again. Two years later he despatched another invading army reported as 140,000 fighters, mostly Chinese, on 4,400 vessels, but dogged resistance and a fortuitous typhoon – the *kamikaze* or "divine wind" of later legend – wrecked the invading force on the beaches and led to the venture's collapse. The frustrated Khan threatened anew and more years of defense work ensued. But after Kublai's death in 1294 Mongol leaders abandoned the scheme.

By then, however, large numbers of warrior households had sacrificed blood, treasure, and years of life to defense of the realm, and the leaders of dyarchy had failed to reward them satisfactorily. Religious institutions, as well, which had been summoned to defend the nation with prayer and material aid, claimed credit for the happy outcome but found little thanks forthcoming. The Hōjō, meanwhile, in their attempt to mobilize defenses, had assigned family members to key command positions and rewarded them commensurately. In the outcome there was ample reason for the disappointed to conclude that the Hōjō had only served themselves in the name of saving the nation. So the Mongol invasions not only cost directly in lives and wealth, but also cost the leadership in terms of good will. And they severely exacerbated many pre-existing rivalries and disputes over land, income, and perquisites of office and status.

In consequence the rootless and lawless proliferated, with *akutō* or "evil bands" becoming a chronic source of banditry and disorder, especially in central Japan where opportunities for plunder were greater. Others among the disgruntled, the desperate, and the determined resorted to piracy, not only marauding along Japanese shores but extending their depredations to the coasts of Korea and eventually China. From the 1220s onward, as noted in chapter 5, Japanese pirates or *wakō* made sporadic raids on Korea during periods of famine, and during the fourteenth century the scale and frequency of attacks escalated, growing into a major and chronic problem for coastal regions throughout East Asia.

Even as lawlessness was increasing in central Japan and on the high seas, the old problem of regionalism was reappearing. By the fourteenth century much of Tōhoku and Kyushu was again slipping into the hands of local leaders whom neither Kamakura nor Kyoto could control. And across the heartland religious proselytizers were actively promoting sectarian doctrines that fostered creation of local religious groups united in their faith and defiant of the combinative principles that the established elite had long used to help sustain its links to the hinterland residents of *shōen* and *kokugaryō*. The most widespread sectarian movement was grounded in Amidist doctrine, but the somewhat newer Hokke sect also grew rapidly during the fourteenth century.

Finally, at the center of authority an untenable situation had developed. Following the death of retired emperor Go-Saga in 1272, his two sons fell to quarreling over the matter of imperial succession, behind which lay the substantive issue of who would control the imperial family's resources. The disputants asked Hōjō leaders in Kamakura to settle the matter, but having just survived a fratricidal quarrel of their own, leaders there simply tried to hush the issue lest it undermine their efforts to mobilize support against the Mongols. To that end they procrastinated, later on making *ad hoc* decisions about imperial succession, in the process gradually establishing the principle that succession to the imperial throne should alternate between descendants of Go-Saga's two sons. That policy, if it can be called one, sufficed to avoid rupture during the decades of Mongol danger. But in the longer run it pleased no one and helped poison the political atmosphere in both Kyoto and Kamakura.

It was Go-Daigo, a great grandson of Go-Saga via one of the rival lines, who finally and effectively defied the Hōjō handling of imperial succession. His intention was to restore ruling power to the imperial family, but his effort served only to destroy the remnants of court–bakufu dyarchy and precipitate decades of violence and disorder.

RUPTURE

Go-Daigo was one of the most able, dedicated, and ruthless politicians in Japanese history. Well schooled in the principles of imperial governance and beholden to no faction save his own, he maneuvered ceaselessly during the 1320s to build a power base among the many whom the Hōjō had alienated. He urged courtiers to study the principles of Confucian governance and filled the vestigial offices of imperial government with supportive *kuge*. He cultivated the good will of major fanes, including the Zen temples favored by shogunal authorities, and nurtured ties to disaffected *bushi*. When the bakufu moved to throttle his schemes in 1331, he fled Kyoto, was captured, and the next spring was exiled to the Oki Islands in the Sea of Japan.

During Go-Daigo's exile, other dissidents continued to resist, men whose names subsequently were emblazoned across Japanese history as glorious imperial loyalists. They included the heroic warrior Kusunoki Masashige and the scholarly advisor Kitabatake Chikafusa. During 1333 Go-Daigo escaped Oki, and men rallied to his cause, most famously Ashikaga Takauji, a senior bakufu commander whom the Hōjō had despatched to crush him but who decided instead to seize the moment. He overran the Hōjō bastion in Kyoto and become the ruling protector of a presumably obedient emperor.

Matters worked out poorly. Go-Daigo obeyed no one, and over the next few years he pressed ahead with his Kenmu Restoration, energetically pursuing the myriad tasks of restoring a ruling imperial house in Kyoto. Takauji meanwhile pursued a parallel project, building a shogunal regime of his own in the Muromachi section of town. And various other warriors pursued military ventures of their own, which aligned them with or against Hōjō survivors, Go-Daigo, or Takauji as seemed most advantageous at the moment. During 1336 the jockeying got out of hand and the realm slipped into nearly uninterrupted warfare. At one point Takauji and his army were driven westward to Kyushu, but they returned shortly and seized the partially destroyed city, after which Go-Daigo, having lost Kusunoki and many other supporters in battle, fled south into the Yoshino Mountains. There he and his successors maintained a rump "southern court," while the Ashikaga in Kyoto installed puppet emperors in a "northern court." Claiming to govern in the latter's name, Ashikaga leaders then attempted to project their power outward across the realm, with some success placing kinsmen (*ichimon*) in charge of provincial affairs, only to find them little more reliable than the unaffiliated magnates (*tozama*) who continued to control other areas.

In a story laced with melancholy and black humor – but also with much that reveals the changing times – two imperial courts, the *nanbokuchō*, existed for half a century. They provided rallying points for military men seeking to improve their positions in life by battling others, burning Kyoto, obtaining rewards, seizing land, and shifting sides as seemed meet. In the process the battlers gradually disrupted older land-holding arrangements and discredited the pretensions of "authority." Furthermore, the new shogunal regime at Muromachi was from the outset riven by internal conflicts that led to internecine violence. And even though both Muromachi and Yoshino tried to project their control across Tōhoku, Kantō, and Kyushu, their successes were mixed at best.

By the 1360s the Ashikaga had generally gained the upper hand, save in Kyushu. There a mixed bag of regional barons, local warriors, and *wakō* pirate chiefs held sway under the banner of Yoshino's Prince Kanenaga. In 1370 China's Ming rulers, newly triumphant over the Mongols and hoping to suppress the *wakō*, despatched a mission to establish a properly Sino-centric tributary relationship with Japan. Kanenaga met the mission in Kyushu and after some tergiversation agreed to an arrangement that designated him "King of Japan" – much as Himiko had been designated "Queen of Wa" more than a millennium earlier – making him the focus and beneficiary of Ming interest.

Muromachi leaders thus found that an imperial prince affiliated with the derelict Yoshino regime seemed poised to receive Chinese backing. The Mongols had recently proven that large armadas could reach Japan from the continent, and any observer versed in *Nihon shoki* and *Shoku Nihongi* could recall the names Tsukushi no Iwai and Fujiwara no Hirotsugu, whose challenges to Kinai authority had also been linked to continental affairs. To thwart the emerging Kanenaga–Ming linkage, Muromachi leaders despatched one of their best generals, Imagawa Ryōshun, to conquer Kyushu, suppress the pirates, and by that act of good will shift the Ming connection to Kyoto. Moving skillfully for the most part, Ryōshun succeeded in his task, enabling the Ashikaga to establish ties to China that led to lucrative trade. In the process he destroyed the Yoshino regime's last significant base of support and thwarted the newest expression of Kyushu secessionism.

One striking aspect of these violent decades was the pervasiveness of breakdown in social order. At the highest level, warriors repeatedly betrayed their contempt for the courtly elite. Kō no Moronao, a key retainer of the Ashikaga and a man given to candor, put it this way:

> What is the use of a King? ... And why should we bow to him? If for some reason a King is needed, let us have one made of wood or metal, and let all the live kings be banished.[9]

Among warriors themselves, opportunism was rampant and side-switching a way of life. In Kyoto satirists jeered at the crudity of the *arrivé*, even as battlers torched buildings with utter indifference to treasures lost. In the hinterland the struggle for control of land reached down to local warriors who characterized themselves as *kokujin*, "provincials," to distinguish themselves from those feckless "outsiders" whose only claim to authority was some silly patent given them by a fellow claiming to be shogun. Lower still, at the level of hamlets, rival armed groups from neighboring villages battled, pillaged, and burned when law suits and petitions to higher authority failed to resolve their grievances acceptably.

Perhaps because of this pervasive disorder, those struggling for supremacy wrapped themselves in ideological pretensions with unsurpassed gusto. The rhetoric of imperial loyalism was one expression of this quest for acceptance by power grabbers, its most intellectually elegant expression being *Jinnō shōtōki*, an imperial chronology qua ideology that Kitabatake Chikafusa wrote around 1340, while assisting in a fruitless effort to restore imperial control of Tōhoku.

Another dimension of this ideological combat was the pious invocation of gods, heroes, and great events from the past. Godly powers were continually invoked and sacred alliances sought. Most notably, in the manner of Shōmu's *kokubunji* and pagodas, Takauji tried to set up a countrywide system of Zen temples (Ankokuji), along with pagodas (Rishōtō) to be built in Tendai and Shingon temples. He also erected the grand Zen monastery Tenryūji to pacify the spirit of the deceased Go-Daigo and tried to make it the liturgical center of the regime he was putting in place, much as Shōmu had done with Tōdaiji. In the same spirit, provincial magnates celebrated ancestral links to the gods, supported fanes, solicited godly good will, and touted their reverence for gods, Buddhas, and the imperial house.

Meanwhile, at a more overtly practical level, bakufu leaders were striking bargains in a piecemeal manner with the regional and local warrior chiefs whose collaboration they needed to stabilize affairs. By the 1370s a general pattern had emerged in which Ashikaga leaders allowed the greatest of these provincial magnates, who increasingly were known as daimyo, to administer the territories they controlled in return for their readiness to support the Ashikaga against others. By then this *kenmon* regime – a shogun–daimyo dyarchy, so to say – was establishing dominance in central Japan and projecting its power westward into Kyushu.

THE *KENMON* REGIME

The pivotal figure in the *kenmon* regime's emergence was Hosokawa Yoriyuki, a daimyo ally of the Ashikaga. Holding the title of *kanrei* during the 1370s, he served as regent to the youthful shogun Yoshimitsu, rather as Hōjō chiefs had been regents to shogun at Kamakura, and Sekkanke Fujiwara, regents to emperors in Heian. Whereas those earlier regents had headed houses that collaborated with their nominal superiors in forms of duopoly, however, Yoriyuki functioned more broadly as a powerful voice for daimyo interests in Ashikaga councils, assuring that as the new regime consolidated its position, the concerns of regional magnates were properly heeded.

Yoriyuki also recognized, however, that daimyo security was enhanced by a bakufu strong enough to help them suppress aggressive rivals and unruly subordinates and elegant enough to overawe the residual *ritsuryō* elite. So he supported Yoshimitsu's moves to elevate the bakufu's stature. Most visibly, in 1378 he oversaw construction near the north end of Muromachi Street of a handsome new shogunal residence, Hana no Gosho, whose grandeur thoroughly impressed the court, courtiers, and monastic leaders. Yoriyuki wished them to be impressed because they still controlled considerable land and their continual clamor for restitution of estates seized by daimyo and lesser warriors in the hinterland required diplomatic handling. The handling had to be diplomatic because just as daimyo benefited from shogunal support, so the shogun benefited from the good will of court and major fanes, who provided political legitimation as well as spiritual and material aid. So it was important that the shogun appear kingly, virtuous, and appropriately solicitous of the aggrieved as he made decisions that in fact accommodated most daimyo claims.

By the 1390s Yoshimitsu had emerged as an energetic leader in his own right. He used the military might of collaborating daimyo to pound others into submission, thereby establishing solid bakufu control throughout Honshu west of the Chūbu highlands. In 1392 he induced the impoverished Yoshino pretender to return to Kyoto on the promise – broken, in the end – that in due course his heir would become emperor. Three years later Yoshimitsu's improved circumstances enabled him to order Imagawa Ryōshun, who had become the *de facto* ruler of Kyushu, to return to Kyoto and thence to a diminished role in Suruga. He also improved the bakufu fisc and administration, nurtured valuable monastic ties, spurred further rebuilding in Kyoto, and developed a lively official trade with China.

Yoshimitsu had, in short, managed to pull together all the key parts of his *kenmon* ruling coalition. His one major failure was in reasserting Kyoto's control in the east: the Kantō and Tōhoku regions came under the sway of Ashikaga leaders at Kamakura, and the most Yoshimitsu could secure was a live-and-let-live entente, with Kyoto controlling the realm west of Hakone and Kamakura the area to its east.

The creators of the Ashikaga regime appropriated much office and procedural nomenclature from the earlier Kamakura bakufu, but in fact the regime was very different in administrative, military, and fiscal terms. Whereas vassals of the Kamakura shogun had administered the realm in awkward collaboration with imperial officials and the appointees of *shōen* proprietors, most of the Ashikaga realm lay partially or wholly under daimyo control while the bakufu's own retainers administered only a very small portion, and court and fanes controlled sharply diminished areas through their *shōen* arrangements. Whereas Kamakura's fighting men were commanded by shogunal retainers who, originally at least, had strong ties to bakufu leaders, most Muromachi-era fighting men were commanded by daimyo who were essentially shogunal allies of convenience, despite their nominal subordination. And whereas Kamakura was financed almost entirely with revenue stemming from the land, the Muromachi bakufu was funded by a miscellany of domestic and foreign trade and business tariffs, modest fees assessed on landholders in the emperor's name, and other fees levied on fanes in what amounted to routinized bribes and sales of church office and rank. Only a small amount of bakufu income came from Ashikaga lands.

In essence, then, Yoshimitsu's bakufu at its zenith was an opportunistically funded element in a coalition regime that controlled central and western Japan. Thanks to overall growth of population, production, and mobilized military might, however, total political power in the archipelago was far greater than ever before. And while the center may have had effective control of a smaller portion of that total, Yoshimitsu was keenly aware that his power had not been equaled in Japan in a long, long time and that he was awesomely powerful when compared to the penurious emperor. He was also aware that the recently risen Ming, like other Chinese dynasties, did not prop up emperors from former regimes, and his handling of numerous ceremonial matters suggests quite strongly that he was toying with the idea of elevating one of his own sons to the imperial purple. Such a move, should it occur, would presumably terminate the existing imperial patriline in a way that Fujiwara and Taira marrying of daughters to imperial heirs had never threatened to do. It would give rise instead to an Ashikaga imperial lineage.

By 1401 Yoshimitsu had, for all practical purposes, absorbed what little authority remained to the throne. That year a well-placed priestly observer noted that the shogun managed all court rituals and appointments and that:

> The emperor only writes down the names proposed to him on a small piece of paper. He is totally out of touch on those appointments made below the ministerial level.[10]

And a year later the Ming emperor acknowledged Yoshimitsu's stature by assigning him Prince Kanenaga's briefly held title, "King of Japan." As matters worked out, the Ashikaga chief's untimely death six years later precluded the actual elevation of his son to imperial status, but the evidence does suggest that, however weak Ashikaga rule may seem from afar, when viewed from the angle of the old elite, it was of unprecedented absoluteness.

Nevertheless, almost as soon as Yoshimitsu died, the new *kenmon* order started unraveling. His successors backed away from his inroads on imperial prerogatives and, in an erratic fashion, reduced bakufu trade and diplomatic links to Ming, at considerable cost to the fisc. The first major problem, however, was deteriorating relations between the Kyoto and Kamakura wings of the Ashikaga family, with resultant plotting and in 1416 re-eruption of savage conflict in the Kantō. In the course of that warfare, which went on sporadically for years, rival leaders in the Kantō recruited supporters from among the region's *kokujin* by rewarding them with parcels of *shōen*. In the process they denied landed income to a number of major fanes and other Kyoto interests, thereby striking at the very heart of the *kenmon* coalition and complicating relations between aggrieved groups and the bakufu.

The bakufu was further weakened during the 1420s by inept leadership that culminated in an enervating succession dispute. The bakufu's advisory daimyo finally resolved the quarrel in 1428 by selecting Yoshinori, a son of Yoshimitsu who had been serving as abbot of Enryakuji and chief prelate of the Tendai sect. An energetic man like his father, Yoshinori was in essence the right man at the wrong time. He was mature, well schooled, experienced in running a complex organization, strong willed, and uncompromising. And he was clear in his objective of restoring shogunal power and glory to the level of his father's day.

From the outset, however, Yoshinori was plagued by intractable problems. In the tumultuous Kantō, *shōen* proprietors were rapidly losing their income and authority to daimyo, *kokujin*, and other local interests. And west of the Chūbu highlands, in the Muromachi heartland, an essentially similar process was at work. There, however, the challenge to *kenmon* interests took more convoluted forms because the economy was more highly commercialized. Groups of merchants, guildsmen, and villagers increasingly organized themselves and lobbied and maneuvered in the political arena, playing segments of the *kenmon* coalition off against one another and even taking on the bakufu itself. In the process they won diverse economic and political concessions that cumulatively undercut the positions of fanes, courtiers, and others of the old elite.

Thus challenged from below, the *kenmon* – bakufu, daimyo, and major temples and shrines most notably – quarreled more and more heatedly. Moreover, whereas Yoshimitsu had proven adept at exploiting to his own advantage the less acute tensions of his day, Yoshinori, who was more abrasive in manipulating the more deeply divided and distrustful *kenmon*, only succeeded in making a bad situation worse. His attempts to stabilize the Kantō were of only passing success, some short-term gains notwithstanding. In the Kinai region he was unable to stop sporadic eruptions by major fanes, notably Kōfukuji and Enryakuji, as they tried to recover former *shōen* rights. Nor could he stop warriors who seized land, some of them doing so in the name of a disgruntled southern pretender to the throne. To the west, daimyo in far western Honshu and Kyushu were quite out of control, battling one another and seizing *shōen* with ever more abandon, thus adding to the tension among the elite in Kyoto.

As of 1441, in short, Yoshinori had little to show for twelve years of energetic governance, and his forcefulness had given him many enemies. One of them, the daimyo Akamatsu Mitsusuke, took it upon himself to murder the shogun at a garden party, conveniently providing other daimyo with ample excuse to attack him, force his suicide, and distribute his lands among themselves. Other, lesser figures seized the moment to advance their demands by taking the entire city of Kyoto hostage, thereby obtaining policy changes they had sought for at least two decades.

To elaborate, by the 1420s coalitions of *kokujin*, commercial producers, and other village members were forming alliances to create local organizations that came to be identified as *tsuchi ikki*, the earlier-noted "solidarities of the locale." Most commonly their grievances centered on indebtedness to urban money lenders, some of whom were merchants but mostly temple administrators. The bakufu customarily supported creditors' calls for repayment, doing so as quid pro quo for tribute income and other assistance, and through the 1430s the bakufu was able to resist demands by *ikki* protestors for debt cancellations and reductions (*tokusei*: "acts of virtuous rule").

However, in 1441, within weeks of Yoshinori's murder, and while daimyo forces were out cannibalizing the Akamatsu domain, a major protest erupted. The demonstrating groups, who reportedly numbered many thousands, streamed into town, ringing the city with camps. They seized such major temples and shrines as Tōji and Kitano Tenmangū, raided the city center daily, shut down markets, and halted city provisioning until the bakufu conceded by issuing a series of debt cancellation decrees. With certain exceptions these restored land or other property to "its original owner." And whereas titled creditors could retain any property they had held for over twenty years, "commoners" received no such protection.[11]

Shogunal leaders had learned their lesson, and in following years they repeatedly yielded to demands for *tokusei* decrees. That accommodation undercut their good will among money lenders, but the bakufu partially replaced that source of income with bribes from those demanding *tokusei*.

One reason the bakufu was so weak after 1441 was that Yoshinori's death left it in the hands of two successive youthful shogun, the second being Yoshimasa, who shortly came under the control of the ambitious young daimyo Hosokawa Katsumoto. As *kanrei*, Katsumoto dominated affairs – insofar as anyone did – during the 1450s and sixties.

By then the bakufu had been reduced to little more than a city administration. As of the mid-1450s its police were even having difficulty controlling robbers in town, while its greatest efforts were devoted to scrounging for income. Its administrators issued a plethora of regulations on monetary matters: loans, pawns, debts, coinage, interest rates, etc. They erected toll barriers, and they tried to extract more fees from merchants, guildsmen, and prelates. They invoked vestigial authority to raise funds for repairing the emperor's palace, Ise Shrine, and Tōdaiji. They tried to enhance the yield of their China and Ryukyus trade, and Yoshimasa even solicited assistance from Korea to repair major monasteries, including the Zen temples Kenninji and Tenryūji and the venerable Yakushiji in Nara.

These frenetic efforts sufficed to pay Yoshimasa's expenses, even enabling him in 1483 to construct a new retirement villa, today's Ginkakuji. By situating it in the Higashiyama hills about as far east of the emperor's palace as Yoshimitsu's Kitayama villa (today's Kinkakuji) lay to its west, Yoshimasa gave medieval Kyoto a sadly attenuated version of the east–west, Tōdaiji–Saidaiji symmetry that had characterized Nara about 700 years earlier and the Tōji–Saiji symmetry that Kanmu *tennō* had envisioned for Heian. Beyond the city, however, daimyo and *kokujin* held sway, quite indifferent to bakufu policy or the tribute claims of *shōen* holders, whose income base was rapidly disappearing, just as it had in the Kantō a few decades earlier.

By the 1460s, then, the *kenmon* regime was already in a state of deep disarray: court and courtiers were but parlous remnants; *shōen*-holding fanes were becoming more impoverished and desperate; the bakufu was unsafe in its own city and had almost no control over daimyo; major daimyo domains were riven by factions and threatened by lesser warriors; diverse other social groups were becoming well enough organized to use coercive force on their own behalf. A condition of perfect political *laissez faire* seemed at hand.

ŌNIN AND BEYOND

During 1467 warfare erupted in downtown Kamigyō between daimyo armies that had been assembled as bargaining chips in a disputed shogunal succession. The political haggling got out of hand, tempers frayed, and violence erupted. Battling in narrow streets, enclosed courtyards, and garden spaces, and in and amongst buildings, the combatants quickly resorted to fire and pillage to deny the enemy shelter, acquire material for defensive fortifications, and clear space for archery duels and foot assaults. One after another, mansions, palaces, and temples, as well as lesser residences, storefronts, and warehouses were sacked and burned. Over the next few years combat engulfed Shimogyō and the city's several suburbs, prompting the elite to flee for safety and leaving lesser folk to face gangs of robbers, food shortages, and epidemics while residents in nearby areas mobilized their own defense forces to repel marauding samurai.

By 1477 the city was largely destroyed. The symbols of central authority were a shambles, the key figures in the war's outbreak dead, and the armies gone back to the countryside where they continued battling for control of the land. This shift in the locus of warfare reflected the fact that when daimyo took their armies to Kyoto, their domains became unstable. Local warriors, whether neighbors or subordinates, would exploit the opportunity for aggrandizement, seizing territory and shifting productive resources to their own use, thereby laying the foundation for *gekokujō*.

As that last phrase suggests, the Ōnin War, as this ten-year battle over Kyoto and its symbols of authority is generally known, was in broad terms little more than an occasion when the ongoing countrywide struggle for control of landed output intensified. In essence it furthered the reorganization of control mechanisms and the redistribution of power and wealth.

For Kyotoites, however, the war was a catastrophe. And for court and *kuge* it was decisive. It destroyed most of the city's treasures and much of its wealth, spurred many key figures to flee, and so thoroughly impoverished the *kuge* as a whole that they nearly disappeared from history. During the turmoil die-hard supporters of the southern court made their last futile attempt to reclaim the throne. And the imperial household itself, having lost its *shōen* and finding that it could no longer depend on support from shogun or daimyo, ended up too poor to maintain a palace or even pay the costs of enthronement, retirement, or any other ritual of state.

Because there was no longer any advantage in being a retired emperor and because no one had any reason to manipulate the imperial position, in the century after Ōnin emperors did not retire. During the 122 years from 1464 to 1586 four insignificant figures held the title of emperor until death. Longevity in imperial office, far from being a sign of strength, had become a sign of inconsequence. The imperial plight was suggested in 1500 by a comment of Hosokawa Masamoto, son of Katsumoto and a dictatorial *kanrei* who happened momentarily to control Kyoto. When asked to provide funds so that a new emperor could be enthroned, he opined, in the spirit of Kō no Moronao:

> Even if the enthronement ceremonies are held, one who is not in substance a king will not be regarded as a king.[12]

So he refused to pay. No one else offered, and two decades passed before a proper enthronement ceremony was finally executed. Even then the funds appeared only because the shogun of the moment was desperately – and ineffectually – trying to buy enough good will to avoid being ejected from the city by a daimyo.

As that last comment suggests, the Ōnin War left the bakufu itself nearly as inconsequent as the court. It lost control of most sources of income and was nearly powerless to maintain order in its own capital city. As one distraught *kuge* complained in 1484, after a nearby pawnshop was plundered and the neighborhood consumed by the resulting fire:

> In a world without a *kanrei*, without a Board of Retainers, without a city magistrate, without a police chief, without any inquiry into or investigation of crime, we have such calamities all about us. It is unbearable.[13]

In fact all those bakufu posts were occupied, but to no avail.

In the absence of bakufu effectiveness, city administration was gradually taken over by resident merchants and artisan groups. A few members of the Ashikaga family continued to scrap over the shogunal title, and daimyo opportunistically supported, opposed, or – most commonly – ignored the contenders, whether those contenders be in Kyoto, fleeing it, or trying to return, as they repeatedly did. But in the larger view, none of that really amounted to much.

In this story of *kenmon* disarray, the most visible part was the ceaseless march and counter-march of a few major daimyo fecklessly maneuvering and battling for control of the empty symbols of authority. The names and particulars are eminently forgettable, but the effects of the turmoil on Kyoto merit note. The capital shrank to the dimensions of a slender, bifurcated town, a mere shadow of its classical self (see figure 7.2), with many former city blocks returning to tillage, others going to brushy waste. In 1526 a traveling poet came swinging down toward the city from its eastern entryway, which offered a panoramic view of the Kamo Plain. As the scene opened out before him, he noted:

> looking over Kyoto, at the homes of high and low alike, I saw but one building where once there had been ten. The dwellings of the common people are given over to farming. The palace is a tangle of summer grasses. It is too much for words.

Renewed fighting during the next few years only made matters worse.

Finally, the list of *kenmon* losers after Ōnin included most of the great fanes, major Buddhist temples most notably. Prior to that war the most venerable of them, such as Enryakuji, Kōfukuji, Tōdaiji, and Tōji, had held on to many of their *shōen* in regions west of the Kantō despite the recurrent disorder and warrior incursions. But after Ōnin, they rapidly lost their tribute sources, which led in turn to bitter internal factionalism and violence and the physical decay of their grand temple complexes. Moreover the city's great Zen temples, such as Tenryūji, Shōkokuji, and Nanzenji, which were of much more recent provenance and flourished mainly thanks to their shogunal connection, faded with it, their glorious structures lost to urban conflagration, decay, and disassembly and their income to turmoil and warrior expropriation. Even major Shintō shrines, such as Ise, Kitano Tenmangū, and Iwashimizu Hachimangū, found their fiscal bases collapsing, and they decayed amidst internal bickering and external indifference.

Even as the religious wing of the *kenmon* disintegrated, however, new religious forces moved into the political arena. In previous decades disarray among the powerful had given sectarian groups, the Shinshū (or Jōdo Shin sect) and Hokkeshū (or Lotus sect) most notably, both reason and opportunity to organize local congregations that could defend their own interests and support higher-ranking sectarian leaders. After Ōnin this activity accelerated, and by the sixteenth century the Honganji branch of Shinshū had developed into a well organized and powerful force in the Kinai region, while a coalition of Hokke temples emerged as the dominant force in Kyoto, mainly Shimogyō, with allies in the towns of Nara and Sakai. With power came interests to promote and the ability to do so, and the sects willy nilly became participants in the military politics of the day.

Most notably, around 1480 Rennyo, the man who developed Honganji into the dominant branch of Shinshū, built a grand headquarters temple at Yamashina, the mountain-girt cul-de-sac directly east of Kyoto, from whence he commanded his increasingly well-organized followers. The Yamashina Honganji consisted of several buildings and decorative gardens that sprawled across fifteen acres and were surrounded by walls, huge gates, and a moat. A town quickly sprang up around it, and workers dug a moat around that too, heaping up the soil to form an additional earthen defense. The town, which was completely under Honganji legal and fiscal control, serviced both temple residents and pilgrims, thereby helping sustain links between central temple and hinterland faithful.

Rennyo's successors maintained Honganji dynamism and gradually extended their sway to embrace Shinshū congregations from Hokuriku to Kii. In doing so they not only overwhelmed other Shinshū branches but also collided with Hokke congregations and became involved in daimyo politics. That trend peaked in the 1520s, with Honganji armies battling all over central Japan. The sect's very vigor, however, gave rise to hostile coalitions, counter-attacks, and in 1532 utter destruction of the Yamashina Honganji. After that catastrophe, Honganji leaders regrouped, anchoring their movement in another fortified bastion, Ishiyama, in the swamps of the Yodo River estuary. There they trimmed their sails and negotiated settlements with major daimyo. In the outcome they left the warfare to daimyo while they focused on more peaceful forms of proselytizing and institution building, in the process laying a base for what later became the city of Osaka.

Meanwhile destruction of the Yamashina Honganji had strengthened the hand of the Hokkeshū, which administered Kyoto with near autonomy. In 1536, however, leaders of the Enryakuji, who found the Hokke temples cutting into their urban sources of income, allied themselves with a daimyo in Ōmi to storm the city and torch it. According to one observer:

> They set fire to the twenty-one temples of the Hokke sectarians and, beyond this, all of southern Kyoto. More than half of northern Kyoto has also burned. They have attacked and killed Nichiren adherents and various others. I do not know the number of the dead. I think it is about three thousand.

Following that calamity, Hokke leaders, like those of Honganji, withdrew from military politics. Instead they concentrated on administering their own temples and neighborhoods and ceded the unpleasant political high ground to daimyo and would-be daimyo.

The most important political narrative of *sengoku*, however, was a less visible story then unfolding in the countryside. It was the story of local warriors building more solid bases of power on the wreckage of the old *shōen–kokugaryō* order, establishing much more complete domination over the people and output of the land they claimed to control and much more effective control of the fighting men they commanded. Step by step they extended their sway into adjacent areas, slowly building larger domains – mini-states in effect – until the most successful of them were strong enough to battle for the highest symbols of power and authority without being undercut by rebellious subordinates. That, however, is the story of the rise of the "early modern" or *kinsei* state, and it is told in chapter 9.

Suffice to note here that by 1550 three centuries or so of socioeconomic growth had completely flummoxed the *kenmon* elite and dissolved the *ritsuryō* order. The elements of a new and more powerful order were already beginning to take shape, but they caught the attention of very few observers. Far more common was awareness of how much had been lost, especially in terms of higher cultural complishments.

[8] *MEDIEVAL HIGHER CULTURE (1250–1550)*

By 1550, as chapter 7 suggested, three centuries of medieval change had destroyed nearly all remnants of the *ritsuryō* order, in the process ruining the arrangements of the *kenmon* elite and laying groundwork for a new order. The economic growth and social change that underlay these political developments also shaped the character and content of cultural production. At the most basic level, as the population was growing and society becoming more complex, arts and letters also increased in volume and variety: more temples, mansions, gardens, paintings, poems, songs, dramas, tales, and get-togethers for worship, tea-drinking, versifying, and appreciation of cultural artifacts.

As intermediate social strata expanded, the distinction between elite and commoner culture blurred and the extent of identifiable cultural sharing grew. The proliferation of towns carried both the production and consumption of literate culture beyond Kyoto to ever more of the realm. Commercialization fostered entrepreneurial cultural output – the production and marketing of arts, letters, and performance as a means of livelihood – and a decline in the importance of aristocratic "amateurs" as cultural creators. Furthermore, the renewal of continental contacts, trade in particular, led to renewed continental influence on arts and letters. Finally, at all social levels, whether among the ruling *kenmon* or at the level of village associations (*sō*), cultural life became more overtly participatory, as in poem linking, tea drinking, communal dancing, or congregational religious services.

Just as the foundation of intensive agriculture was the pre-existing agronomic order, however, and just as *kenmon* rule grew out of the *ritsuryō* order by way of dyarchy, so the cultural life of these centuries owed much to its classical parentage. Most obviously, arts and letters in their particularity – poetry, tales, painting, architecture, the performance arts – all stemmed from classical precedents and in greater or lesser degree reflected that ancestry. In the same vein, although text-based religion became much more fully the religion of the general population, it sprang from the aristocratic religious tradition and continued to show the powerful legacy of syncretism as well as the counter-tendency toward sectarianism.

More narrowly, at the level of "*kenmon* culture," as the arts and letters of the ruling classes can be labeled, participants aspired to the excellence so central to classical *kuge* culture. And they did so despite major obstacles: impoverishment of the courtly elite, the unschooled quality of so many samurai, and the bawdlerization demanded by the marketplace. While the quality of certain arts, notably *waka*, scroll paintings (*emakimono*), and sculpture, declined noticeably, the old ideal of cultural mastery was affirmed in other arts: interior decoration, garden design, ink-line painting, linked verse, *nō* drama, and ceremonial tea drinking. That affirmation of excellence helped sustain the association of aesthetics with ethics: masterful participation, it was held, could be a religious experience. And in the outcome it gave rise to some of the most highly esteemed hallmarks of Japanese civilization.

The role of women in this cultural life is less easy to characterize. Whereas court ladies of the Heian period had been pre-eminent literary figures, particularly in terms of creative prose writing, that role disappeared by about 1350. In less visible ways, however, women continued to shape arts and letters. They appear to have been major figures in the development of certain war tales, the enrichment of performance art, and the spread of Buddhism. And in conjunction with that last role, the "problem" of women and salvation became an important topic in religious discourse.

The several themes foreshadowed here do not, of course, appear in all aspects of this cultural history. But they show up time and again in *kenmon* culture. And they are evident as well in those facets of cultural production, most particularly tale-telling and participation in text-based religions, that were being shared most widely through society.

KENMON *CULTURE*

Elite culture of the medieval centuries displayed the several qualities adumbrated above. It sprang from an elite that was much more varied socially than that of the *ritsuryō* era, including *kuge* remnants, clerics, particularly those of the Rinzai branch of Zen, ambitious *bushi*, strategically placed merchants, and professional entertainers and aesthetes. It also diffused widely through the realm thanks to the proliferation of trading towns and regional baronial headquarters (notably Hakata and Yamaguchi in the west, Nara and Sakai in central Japan, Kamakura and Odawara in the east) and the cultural diaspora caused by the warfare that prompted those who could do so to flee

Kyoto, settle elsewhere, and support themselves by teaching and entertaining the locals.

LOSSES AND GAINS

This *kenmon* culture only gradually displaced the *kuge* culture of later *ritsuryō* centuries, and some who saw the old world decaying lamented the change. One of the most celebrated works of the age, *Tsurezuregusa*, written around 1330 by the high-born Shintō priest Yoshida Kenkō, is a miscellany (*zuihitsu*) in the style of Sei Shōnagon's *Pillow Book*. Like that work it is replete with anecdotes, observations, and gossip, but it is less biting in its wit and contains more didactic entries and meditative reflections. It also is marked by much nostalgia for past elegance and fallen times. "When I sit down in quiet meditation," he wrote, "the one emotion hardest to fight against is a longing in all things for the past."[1]

Perhaps the single most noteworthy cultural loss was the literary output of court women. The impoverishment of court and courtiers gradually undermined the polygamous arrangements of classical *kuge* society, reducing the numbers of household underlings and prompting even senior court houses to employ their women in secretarial functions once handled by males. By the fifteenth century court women had thus become, so to say, more "useful" cogs in much smaller wheels. Nor did the women of warrior households replace them as literary lions because they functioned more fully as "wives," living in their husband's house and providing valued services that occupied their time while restricting their range of experience and their opportunity for literary expression.

As far as is known today, "the last journal written by a court lady in the medieval period" appeared in 1349.[2] The last truly celebrated work in the tradition of courtly female prose was *Towazugatari*, composed in about 1307 by a certain Lady Nijō. It recounts with verve, insight, and imagination thirty-six years of her complicated life at court as she struggled to manage her men, control her romantic impulses, and nurture her religious sensibilities. Reflecting the increased geographical mobility of the day, an unusually large portion of the book is devoted to recounting Nijō's experiences traveling the length of central Japan, in the course of which she reveals an appreciation of lesser folk that was remarkable in aristocratic works and that surely bespeaks the changing character of Kyoto's high society.

Even *waka* composition, the most treasured literary activity of the classical age, which had been so revitalized by Fujiwara no Teika and others during the early years of dyarchy, lost its vitality despite a continued outpouring of 31-syllable poems. In about 1450 Shōtetsu, who was a monk at the great Rinzai temple Tōfukuji, a disciple of the poet/politician Imagawa Ryōshun, and the most celebrated poet of his time, said this of the day's leading *waka* poetic groups:

> Both factions are tiresome. I myself have no respect for those degenerate houses. I study only the essence of Shunzei and Teika.[3]

In place of *waka*, however, linked-verse forms were developing, as we note below, and these in due course acquired many of *waka*'s qualities.

Meanwhile, the rising classes of warriors, merchants, and entrepreneurial providers of arts and letters were developing their own cultural polish. Around 1250 the senior bakufu official Hōjō Shigetoki admonished his descendants to acquire an adequate education.

> Although you do not read them yourself, you should have an educated person recite and expound sutras and didactic writings for you. We have but limited natural understanding, and if we do not listen to such works, we remain narrow-minded and without wisdom.[4]

Succeeding generations of *bushi* leaders continued to promote learning and cultural mastery, in the process giving merchants and cultural entrepreneurs reason to cultivate their own talents, the better to deal with *kenmon* figures.

By 1400 the gentrification of *bushi* leaders enabled them and their religious and artistic associates to dominate Kyoto's elite culture. To look briefly at the most consequential example, the Ashikaga shogun Yoshimitsu was well schooled, having studied original Confucian texts such as *Analects* and *Mencius* under the guidance of hereditary court scholars and the Rinzai monk Gidō. Gidō was also well versed in the newer Sung interpretations of Confucianism and instructed the shogun on both them and Ch'an (Zen) doctrine, which prompted him to establish a major new Rinzai temple, Shōkokuji, adjacent to his grand Hana no Gosho mansion. As Yoshimitsu matured, he also acquired an interest in *sarugaku* performance and Chinese poetry. Indeed, he patronized the former with such commitment, as we note below, that Kan'ami and Zeami, two playwrights whom he favored, were able to refine and discipline it into the *nō* drama. At Hana no Gosho, and later at his Kitayama retirement mansion with its Kinkakuji pavilion, Yoshimitsu promoted music, dance, and poetry sessions, along with other refined pastimes, doing so for both pleasure and political profit.

The renewal of continental contacts, which had begun in late Heian, was particularly evident in elite cultural output. It was clearly visible in architecture, landscape design, and painting, as we note more fully below, and also in the *kenmon* enthusiasm for collecting and displaying continental bric-a-brac, or *karamono* as such items were known. Sectarian Zen Buddhism was introduced from China in the early Kamakura period, and the Rinzai branch remained particularly close to its Chinese roots. It did so in part because a number of immigrant prelates held high positions in the *gozan* (as the several senior monasteries of the Rinzai temple hierarchy were known collectively), and in part because *kenmon* culture had a strong Sinophilic element that *gozan* priests helped perpetuate through their continuing commercial and cultural contacts with the continent.

Less visible than *karamono* or the *gozan* but of more enduring consequence for later generations was revitalized Chinese influence on the language, both in written and spoken form. Renewed continental contact introduced a large number of new characters (*kanji*) to the Japanese language, and with things

Chinese being fashionable, writers willingly employed them in their *kana-majiribun* prose. In consequence the written language became more heavily laced with Chinese characters. Their use kept it abreast of changing technologies and gave it added conceptual richness, which, had the *kanji* all been reduced to the *kana* syllabary form of *wabun*, would have introduced more homophones and hence more ambiguity of meaning to the written page.

Less helpfully, because the spoken Chinese language varied regionally and was continually changing, the renewal of continental contacts brought the introduction of different Chinese pronunciations, which were modified to form stylish new Japanized Chinese pronunciations (known as *on* readings), mainly for use in compound words that consisted of two or more *kanji*. The new *on* readings were used not only with newly introduced *kanji*, however, but also in some compound usages of *kanji* introduced centuries earlier, during the *ritsuryō* heyday. In consequence the spoken language became more complex than ever, with speakers having to know not only the long-standing domestic pronunciation of a word (the *kun* reading) but also the one, two, or more Chinese-like pronunciations that were appropriate to specific *kanji* compounds. Even today, for an egregious example, the honorific prefix written as 御 is pronounced *go, o, on, mi*, or in rare instances *gyo*, depending on the specific usage.

In short, the medieval changes in language constituted a mixed blessing. They did, however, illustrate the depth of the renewed continental influence. That depth, together with the ideal of cultural mastery and the finding of religious merit in such mastery, was evident in the most celebrated facets of *kenmon* culture: painting, linked-verse poetry, the *sarugaku nō* drama, and tea ceremony. Perhaps the greatest expression of these qualities, however, lay in the architecture and ornamental gardens of the age.

ARCHITECTURE AND GARDEN DESIGN

In terminological shorthand, during the medieval period the *shinden* style of elite residential construction gave way to the *shoin* style, which acquired its finished form during the sixteenth century. The change involved several architectural modifications. In its original, full-blown form a classical *shinden* residence consisted of a sprawling set of single-story pavilions linked by corridors to form a U-shaped complex that opened southward onto a many-acred garden with central pond, island, bridges, and pleasure boating (see figure 8.1). This *ritsuryō*-era mansion was limited, however, to the merest handful of families. Lesser households settled for more modest versions, and by later Heian almost no one could maintain the full three-sided arrangement. Later yet, as *kuge* grew still poorer, they made do with even more attenuated circumstances, including rental housing, while *kenmon arrivé* took over old mansion grounds with their surviving *shinden* layout and construction, and rebuilt to taste.

As *bushi* rulers acquired *kuge* mansions and built new ones, they distinguished much more clearly than had the Heian elite between "private" household living space and "public" space, designating those rooms where they conducted official business as *kaisho* or "meeting places." Whereas *shinden*

Figure 8.1 *Shinden*-style architecture. A reconstruction of the Higashi Sanjō Palace by Mr. Mori Osamu. The spacious elegance of the Heian-period mansions of the high aristocracy is seen here in this view of the main buildings and the sprawling garden to their south. The expansiveness contrasts with the compactly designed layout of medieval *shoin*-style structures and gardens. *Source*: Osamu Mori, *Typical Japanese Gardens* (Tokyo: Shibata Publishing Co. Ltd., 1962), p. 19, plate 8.

rooms had been board floored, with only raised sleeping areas softened by matting, *kaisho* came to be fully floored with *tatami* mats. These mats, which measured about 1 × 2 meters in surface and 5 cm in thickness, and which were made of compressed rushes (*igusa*) that gave them a spongy but firm consistency, allowed comfortable, easily re-arrangeable seating. The use of translucent paper-covered sliding doors (*shōji*) along exterior walls and movable, opaque, paper wall panels (*fusuma*) between rooms permitted easy changes in enclosure size and interior lighting, and as much privacy or exposure to adjoining gardens as one desired. The adjacent garden areas, moreover, were designed to function in conjunction with the meeting rooms.

These basic changes in *kaisho* room design were further refined with the adoption of window styles and other features of Ch'an monastic origin and the installation of display shelves for exhibiting *karamono*. Rooms so designed provided venues where socially diverse groups of differing sizes could gather for various purposes: "flower-arranging and vase competitions, *sarugaku* and *nō* performances, tea-guessing, the monthly Chinese and Japanese linked-verse meetings, moon-, flower-, and snow-viewing parties, and even on occasion for Buddhist ceremonies."[5] They could do this, moreover, without presupposing set status relationships or unwarranted intimacy and without risking unintended male–female encounters of the sort that so often had seemed to complicate Heian elite life.

Then during the sixteenth century, in conjunction with the rise of *wabicha*-style ceremonial tea drinking, which is discussed below, these several features of interior design were combined in a fairly standardized form that came to epitomize the *shoin* style of residential architecture. It became normative during the Edo period and survives today as stereotypically "Japanese" construction: ideally a *tatami*-floored room with *shōji*, *fusuma*, and a set of peripheral display areas that consist of a decorative alcove (*tokonoma*), an alcove with built-in, split-level shelving (*chigaidana*), and a writing alcove (*tsuke shoin*) that faces outward through *shōji* (see figure 8.2).

These interior changes went hand in hand with changes in garden design that also accommodated the modified social relations and aesthetics of

Figure 8.2 Mature *shoin*-style architecture. As this idealized rendition of the mature *shoin* style indicates, the liberal use of *tatami* mats, plaster walls, paper panels on doors and windows, and slender woodwork throughout produced light, airy structures that demanded relatively little of the forest but much of the artisan class. *Source*: John Whitney Hall & Takeshi Toyoda, eds., *Japan in the Muromachi Age* (Berkeley: UCP, 1977), p. 239.

kenmon culture. In place of the spacious, sunlit, pond-centered gardens of Heian appeared wooded walking gardens and small, carefully designed viewing gardens. They combined stone, sand, vegetation, and water in highly disciplined arrangements that were informed with spiritual implications and intended to foster religious sensibilities. Partly inspired by Ch'an precedents, some of the early Muromachi gardens included Sung-period elements, notably high arched bridges, boathouses, two-story buildings, and tea pavilions, replacing the expansive gentility of Heian gardens with the more ostentatious, dynamic spirit of the newly triumphant *bushi*. The later, poorer, more chastened *kenmon* figures of post-Ōnin decades, however, settled for more modest and subdued garden ornamentation.

In sum the new residence and garden arrangements facilitated the socially diverse, participatory culture of *karamono* viewing, linked verse, tea ceremony, and other performance arts. They also accommodated and helped disseminate the newer continental influences, encouraged efforts toward cultural mastery, and gave physical expression to the linkage of aesthetics and religion. As the elite dispersed about the realm, they carried these building practices with them, and by 1550 *shoin*-style architecture and garden design were well established as the preferred style of those who pretended to cultural accomplishment.

Besides fitting the elite society of its day, this architecture accommodated changes in Japan's forests, agriculture, and work force. The *shoin*-style construction coped with the diminished condition of central Japan's woodland by employing smaller framing timbers and roof supports. It used lightweight, paper-covered sliding doors in place of heavy interior walls and wooden shutters. And it replaced high-quality wooden flooring with low-grade underflooring concealed by *tatami* mats. The paper was available from the secondary forest stands that arose after old growth was logged off, and *igusa* for *tatami* became plentiful thanks to the irrigation work that increased the amount of controllable swamp-like arable land.

The new garden style also responded to other environmental changes. It made do with less space, thereby accommodating the growth in population and urban density. The use of sand and stone in lieu of running water responded to the reduced streamflow of summer, when irrigation systems were steering more and more water into rice paddies. And finally, the intensified labor requirements and heightened technical demands of this construction were met by the larger, more diversely skilled population of commoners who, thanks to commercialization, could more easily be employed as paid labor.

A number of Japan's most celebrated monuments to building and garden design date from this era, including Yoshimitsu's Kinkakuji and Yoshimasa's Ginkakuji. But perhaps the most instructive example is the Daisen-in, a residential sub-temple situated in the sprawling compound of the Daitokuji, another of Kyoto's *gozan* temples. Built early in the sixteenth century, the Daisen-in is constructed in *shoin* style with its chambers opening directly on a set of diminutive dry landscape (*kare sansui*) gardens that embody the aesthetic principles of the era's garden design.

In Daisen-in the observer, seated on *tatami* and looking northeastward onto a rectangular garden space of about four by sixteen meters, begins his spiritual journey from the left. Imaginary water tumbles down a falls of two vertical stones, then races noisely over the pebbles and ledges of a narrow mountain stream, on under a stone bridge to a lowland river. There a stone "boat" carries the engaged observer southward along the broadening, quieting stream of raked gravel, past stone and shrub vistas, and thence, in the adjacent garden on the building's south side, to a tranquil sea of limitless gravel interrupted only by two conical mounds and swirling lines of gravel. Then, with the two cones and most of the sand eddies left behind, the observer turns his gaze westward in the direction of Amida's paradise, reaching the pure tranquillity of a completely linear gravel garden.[6]

In short, whereas the sprawling *shinden* mansion with its expansive garden had been a legitimate expression of the character and clout of *ritsuryō* rulers, the gradual attenuation of that style, its replacement with the exuberant and eclectic style of the Ashikaga heyday, and the scaling down of later *kenmon* architectural pretensions fairly reflected the subsequent vicissitudes of the central elite. Its members clung to what they had, however, making a virtue of adversity by defining modesty of scale, simplicity of design, and absence of ornamentation as aesthetically desirable and spiritually beneficial.

In consequence, as we note later, when a newly powerful elite emerged in the late 1500s – an elite that could commandeer great timbers from afar, build to its heart's content, and channel all the water it wanted into ornamental ponds – it still embraced this attenuated *kenmon* architectural style as proof of its own cultural sophistication. The result, for a time, was an awkward mixing of pseudo-humble taste and bombastic display. In following decades, however, as these new rulers stabilized society, they elevated the architecturally humble, disciplined the ostentatious, and in the outcome fixed the heritage of *shoin*-style architecture as a whole and of the tea hut in particular. In the process they ended the line of architectural evolution that had marked earlier centuries.

PAINTING AND POETRY

Shoin-style rooms provided ideal venues for gatherings of the privileged. And gather they did, with great frequency, to eat, drink, talk, and – what mainly interests us here – to view paintings, compose poetry, observe or participate in drama presentations, and share in ceremonial tea drinking. Of these four arts, painting and poetry were more fully derivative and drama and ceremonial tea more fully creations of the age.

Medieval painting drew heavily on older precedents and principles, in particular the later Heian legacies of Yamato-*e*, *emakimono*, and the religious art of *mandara* and *raigō* painting. In addition, the renewal of continental contact brought to Japan the ink-line (*sumi-e* or *suiboku*) style of Sung-Yüan painting.

To note sculpture briefly, its torpor stood in sharp contrast to the vitality of painting. The burst of early-Kamakura dynamism associated with the names Unkei and Kaikei gave way to a long period when sculpture entailed little more than the replication of Amida triads and other standard temple images. One suspects that the frequency of conflagrations discouraged sculpture, prompting patrons and artists alike to invest their time and resources in the creation of more portable forms of art. Indeed, one could argue that masks of the *nō* drama, with their powerful and subtly expressive evocations of youthful beauty, femininity, agedness, and demonic energy, were the sculptural masterpieces of the age.

Painting, in contrast to sculpture, enjoyed an era of incomparable vigor, displaying in particular the religiosity of the age and the syncretism it embodied. Gorgeous *mandara* representations of temples, shrines, and doctrinal teachings gave particularly rich expression to the combinative ideal. Amidist images were central to much medieval art, notably in the *raigō* images of Amida descending to receive the departed and the triads that depicted Amida flanked by two celestial associates. *Emakimono*, arguably the most glorious art of the age (and the most portable), also portrayed Amidst holy men, as in the celebrated *Ippen Shōnin eden*, a scroll completed in 1299 by the obscure monk, En'i. Even in the *Eden*, however, the combinative legacy was evident, with the artist depicting Ippen visiting Shintō shrines and being aided in his quest for enlightenment by the gods of Kumano.

Other *emakimono* recorded the stories found in Buddhist sutras, especially the *Lotus*, and also the traditions of particular temples and shrines. After victory over the Mongols validated the claim that *kami* were Japan's protectors, a number of the finest *emakimono*, such as the *Kasuga Gongen genki* of 1309, were prepared to memorialize the godly power of shrines associated with Buddhist temples. In the narrative that accompanied its illustrations of Kasuga legends and traditions the *Genki* made explicit the theological imbrication of Buddhist and Shintō elements, revealing the underlying principles of *honji suijaku* and *hōben*. It explained that, because the Shintō ideal of purity

> is itself the Pure Land, our own Kami are the Buddhas. How could the Shrine not be the Pure Land? Jōruri and Vulture Peak are present within the shrine fence ... surely that is why the Venerable Myōe revered the Mountain as Vulture Peak, and why He [the shrine deity] told Lord Toshimori that it is the path to enlightenment ... [Indeed,] the guidance He gives each kind of being, according to that being's own needs and mind, passes all understanding.[7]

Such is the incomparable virtue of the Kasuga deity, then, that it cherishes and can save all creatures. Hence, presumably, in any quest for guidance and help one need seek no farther than Kasuga and its affiliated Kōfukuji.

Secular classics also were memorialized in *emakimono*, with artists producing new handscrolls of *Ise monogatari*, the *Pillow Book*, and other celebrated works. To help assure fidelity of reproduction, *kenmon* leaders continued to appoint professional artists to the court painter's office (*edokoro*), which dated from the *ritsuryō* era. And officials and artists fostered the preparation of artists' manuals, which provided guidance for painters of both secular and religious *emakimono*, with iconographic drawings constituting visual models and written instructions explaining how specific scenes were to be depicted.

This concern for "correct" visual celebration of past glories reflected the times. For prelates, works of art promoted and embellished the sacred claims of their fanes and doctrines. For *kuge*, scrolls of the *Genji, Ise*, and other classical masterpieces, and of court rituals and the legends of imperial shrines, served to authenticate their claims to privileged standing. For *bushi*, *emakimono* enabled them to display their appreciation of the classics, which helped legitimize their claims to the privileges of power. The production of hand scrolls was also encouraged by their use in competitive display. Given the severity of status ambiguities among the elite, exhibits of paintings, vases, and diverse other *karamono* in the *kaisho* of one's mansion became important means of demonstrating one's cultural mastery, wealth, or influence and hence one's right to high esteem.

More broadly, as suggested above, the fact of widespread disorder and destruction may have combined with the notion of *mappō* to inspire the *kenmon* as a whole to preserve in the portable *emakimono* form self-explanatory images of the sacred powers and past cultural glories that ought to be cherished. Even if the wish to preserve an endangered legacy did not underlie the vigor of handscroll production, however, the effect was the same: these stunning *emakimono* are today our single best source of imagery for envisioning the world that was lost to the ravages of medieval turmoil.

Like all attempts to "preserve" the past, this effort was at best a severely qualified success. It was compromised by repeated losses, of course, but also by the cumulative effect of minor errors in depiction. Moreover, with the elite becoming ever more impoverished, the effort suffered from declining quality and fidelity of reproduction as less well-trained artists painted more hurriedly to sell more works. Finally, stylistic changes altered images, as the received Yamato-*e* style was modified by the appropriation of elements from Sung-Yüan painting (*kanga* or "Chinese-style" art).

The most important Sung-Yüan contribution was ink-line painting. It was from the outset linked to religion and favored by *kenmon* leaders, but successive generations of entrepreneurial painters spread it through the realm. Most notably, during the Ashikaga heyday a lineage of artists situated at Yoshimitsu's Shōkokuji produced masterful paintings, both polychrome and monochrome, in the Sung-Yüan manner. The most famous of these artists are Josetsu, who flourished in the years of the two shogun Yoshimitsu and his successor, his disciple Shūbun, who spanned the next few decades, and Sesshū, who flourished after the Ōnin war. Sesshū, the best documented of the three, fled Kyoto after the outbreak of war in 1467. He studied in China at the expense of the powerful western daimyo, Ōuchi Masahiro and spent much of his remaining life in the comfort and safety of Ōuchi headquarters at Yamaguchi. There he painted, taught, and reputedly designed landscape gardens.

By the *sengoku* period these artistic traditions of Yamato-*e* and ink-line painting were well established in *kenmon* culture. The Yamato-*e* style was most self-consciously sustained by artists of the Tosa lineage, who served in the court painter's office, while *sumi-e* flourished in temples. Both styles were employed more eclectically by artists working as entrepreneurs out of their own ateliers. In particular the artist Kanō Motonobu, who painted screens, scrolls, fans, and other objects for shogun, courtiers, prelates, and merchants, mastered the main styles of his day and during the 1540s established the Kanō style, as it is known. He did so by combining the most fashionable elements of Yamato-*e* and *kanga* in works that proved highly popular among his clientele.

In the outcome Motonobu and his successors produced a thoroughly indigenized Chinese style of art in which "*Kanga* themes and techniques, especially brushwork derived from ink landscape painting, were synthesized with compositional features derived from *yamato-e* screen and wall painting."[8] This elegant style, with its strong brushwork, bold designs, and bright colors, proved so satisfying to those who could afford it that the powerful figures who pacified the realm in the decades around 1600 employed it to decorate their gargantuan castles and mansions. Subsequently Kanō-style painters became entrenched as official artists to the Tokugawa regime.

Turning to poetry, the queen of classical arts, as early as the Nara period poets had enjoyed recreational verse-capping, and by late Heian two forms of the verbal sport were being enjoyed by the courtly elite and monastic communities. In one form, called *wakan renku*, poets alternated stanzas of Chinese and Japanese verse; in the other, *renga*, they added more and more stanzas to 31-syllable *waka*. With renewal of continental relations and the establishment of Zen temples, *wakan renku* gained great popularity, particularly among Zen monks who also revived interest in Chinese poetry itself (*kanshi*). Concurrently the poets who were revitalizing *waka*, such as Fujiwara no Teika and his father, Shunzei, were beginning to treat *renga* as a serious poetic form. In the process they established its basic principles of prosody: that each verse should be complete in itself; that the many conventional themes of *waka* tradition should appear in the course of the whole poem; that no particular theme should be repeated often or overwhelm the others; and that within these constraints variety and ingenuity were to be valued.

During the Ashikaga heyday *renga* acquired great popularity, displacing *wakan renku* as the ruling elite's favorite type of linked verse. By then learned treatises on both types had appeared, and the courtier Nijō Yoshimoto had emerged as the first distinguished *renga* poet. At court behest, he compiled *Tsukubashū* (1357), the first imperial anthology of *renga*, and fifteen years later he completed *Ōan shinshiki*, a rulebook for *renga* composition. Later generations of poets added more and more rules, in the outcome transforming recreational versifying into a rigorously disciplined poetic form in which the hundred-stanza verse (*hyakuin*) was considered standard.

In its poetic principles *renga* was strongly shaped by *waka*, embracing its compositional categories and sequences, its standards of decorum, and its heavy use of allusion. And much as some *waka* poets, such as Saigyō, invested their versifying with religious meaning, so some *renga* masters treated theirs as a "Way" and, in the case of the celebrated poet Shinkei, regarded it as a Buddhist discipline. Much as *waka* had provided the compositional basis for Heian-period travel diaries, moreover, so *renga* appeared in travel diaries of these centuries, most famously the diaries of the revered poet Sōgi. Sōgi rose from obscurity to a position in the *gozan* monastery, Shōkokuji, where his poetic mastery, appealing personality, and shrewd political sense gave him entrée to inner circles of the power elite. Thanks to those connections he was able to travel as far afield as Kyushu and the Kantō despite the turmoil of the day. And on his journeys he joined people of consequence in versifying parties, in the process contributing to the diffusion of *kenmon* culture.

NŌ AND *CHANOYŪ*

Rather in the manner of *renga*, dramatic performance provided both an avenue of social advance for talented people of modest origins and an occasion for the socially mixed elite to mingle in their *kaisho*. Much as *renga* grew out of the *ritsuryō* poetic legacy, moreover, the stories told in these performances, forerunners of the *nō* theatre, were drawn from a variety of older sources. These included courtly *monogatari*, war tales, didactic tales found in the Buddhist canon, and tales taken from the sprawling, eclectic collections of *setsuwa*.

The music and dance elements in this performance art were essentially of plebeian origins. In their performances *sarugaku* and *dengaku* troupes (*za*) utilized dance styles that stemmed from the *shirabyōshi* dance tradition mentioned in chapter 6 and from *kusemai*, a lively recitative dance style that became popular during the fourteenth century. The troupes honed their skills as story-telling, musical dance performers by hiring out to entertain military men at their headquarters and the priestly residents of fanes. They also helped priestly patrons raise funds for temples and shrines by providing pilgrims and donors with didactic entertainment.

By *nanbokuchō* times entrepreneurial troupes of *dengaku* and *sarugaku* entertainers were making careers out of their performance art, enriching their repertoires and techniques as they competed for patronage. During the Ashikaga heyday the competition was intense, but in the end it was the plays and professional commentary of two *sarugaku nō* actor/playwrights that survived as the foundational elements of the mature *nō* drama. These were the works of Kan'ami and his son Zeami, whose troupe, the Kanze-za, was originally based in Nara, where it enjoyed the patronage of Kasuga Shrine.

From the 1370s onward Kan'ami and Zeami won the favor of Yoshimitsu by skillfully adopting the performance styles he preferred. They succeeded despite the status prejudices of surviving *kuge*, one of whom said of the likes of Kanze-za and of young Yoshimitsu's fondness for the lad, Zeami,

> *Sarugaku* like this is the occupation of beggars, and such favor for a *sarugaku* player indicates disorder in the nation.[9]

By diligently mastering *kenmon* tastes, however, Zeami neutralized that prejudice, prompting Nijō Yoshimoto, who served as his mentor, to say of his poetic skills, "This is no ordinary talent."[10]

For the rest of his life Zeami labored to retain the good will of his betters, modifying his style as taste changed. Most notably, whereas the Kanze-za had originally favored boisterous, lively productions, as Zeami matured he found Yoshimitsu wanting more refined plays that focused on the psychology of their characters rather than the story line and that treated this psychological exploration in aesthetically pleasing, emotionally moving terms. Modifying his style to satisfy his patron, Zeami invoked the term *yūgen*, which in earlier *waka* poetics had denoted "subtle mystery," to express the "elegant and graceful beauty" he wished his plays to embody.

Aware, however, that the continued success of his troupe depended on pleasing many tastes, Zeami produced plays that appealed to the various segments of his audience, plays about warriors, prelates, aristocrats, and lesser folk. Religious themes were common, as were warrior heroes and their agony, while other plays explored the complications and hardships of ordinary family life and love affairs. The *Heike monogatari* (of which more below) inspired many warrior plays. The *Genji* and other Heian classics provided themes, sensibilities, images, and poems for the literate elite to savor. Ono no Komachi, the early Heian poet and tragic beauty, starred in several plays. And for comic relief, *kyōgen*, or brief farces and parodies, were inserted in long, serious programs.

In his treatises on theatre, Zeami wrote at length about the art of acting, the structure of a play, the arrangement of a program, and the categories of drama that merit presentation. But he also stressed the necessity of pleasing one's audience, even when that meant compromising artistic ideals:

> Enthusiastic response on the part of the general public is the mark of both initial and continuing success in the art of a *nō* troupe. Therefore, if you perform only in an extremely advanced style you cannot be appreciated by a broad audience ... [But if] you can take into account the need to please even unsophisticated audiences, then you will continue to prosper.[11]

Zeami's treatises, together with those of his successors, guided the Kanze-za thereafter, and his pragmatism surely contributed to its success. It was, however, his aesthetics that endured in the mature *nō* drama, and during the Edo period his dramaturgical principles became established as the norm.

In the meantime the Kanze-za and other performance troupes continued to pursue patrons, enrich their repertoires, and bring their dramas to more and more audiences in the baronial headquarters and trading towns that proliferated as centuries passed. In the process they spread *kenmon* culture and aesthetics among rising hinterland warriors and merchants, much as *renga* poets were doing at the same time.

Ceremonial tea drinking is the last of the elite accomplishments to command our attention. In the manner of linked-verse composing, it acquired a strongly participatory character, providing occasion for members of the *kenmon* to associate with one another. It also evolved into an art that demanded mastery by its participants and came to be invested with religious meaning. Like *nō* and *renga*, finally, it was in due course practiced widely about the realm. To an exceptional degree, however, it became associated with merchants, under whose aegis it developed into the disciplined *wabicha* or "poverty tea" style that was perpetuated thereafter, becoming what we know today as *chanoyū*, "the tea ceremony." For those merchants the virtue of *wabicha* was that it provided opportunity to hobnob with their betters without the need for sustained schooling, religious erudition, or an elegant pedigree. It enabled them to acquire valuable possessions and to parade their material treasures and cultural refinement where it mattered while maintaining a suitable appearance of modesty.

To backtrack briefly, the pulverized tea (*matcha*) of *chanoyū* was consumed in T'ang China or even earlier and was used for a time in *ritsuryō* Japan. With the renewal of continental contacts in late Heian, *matcha* drinking was reintroduced along with Zen Buddhism. By Go-Daigo's day it was well established as a connoisseur's beverage, at least within Rinzai temples, with "tea-guessing" – identifying a tea's provenance – a cheerful priestly pastime. By Yoshimitsu's heyday ceremonial tea drinking had become a part of the elegant but more disciplined Kitayama cultural style.

In a typical instance the host of a *kenmon* tea gathering assembled his *kuge*, *buke*, and priestly guests in his *kaisho*, providing them a sumptuous repast while displaying his paintings and other treasures, mostly *karamono*. He then took them to a handsomely appointed chamber that offered a pleasing view of the mansion's landscaped garden, and there he offered them tea and sweets. Attendants prepared the tea in a separate room and brought it to the guests for leisurely consumption. This expansive mode of ceremonial tea drinking remained fashionable among the powerful for nearly a century, until devastation caused by the Ōnin War and subsequent endemic battling destroyed the urban security that had permitted such indulgence.

As *sengoku* warfare and turmoil pulverized *kenmon* privilege, this prideful form of tea drinking gave way to the style known as *wabicha*. A few people would gather in a small, sparely appointed room – ideally a four-and-a-half mat *shoin*-style hut, approximately 3×3 meters, with a low entryway and thatched roof – to take tea and a simple meal. The host prepared and served the tea, using low-fired pottery pieces, other utensils of plain design, and minimal ceremony.

Merchants of Shimogyō and Sakai were key participants in this emerging *wabicha* practice of the sixteenth century. These were flourishing decades for Sakai, which provided safe haven for refugees from Kyoto even while serving as entrepôt for foreign trade and provisioning site for daimyo. Those same daimyo, however, could menace merchants, so the latter had compelling reason to deal tactfully with them, and the *wabicha* sessions conducted by tea masters facilitated the potentially awkward negotiations between merchants and the mighty. By the mid-sixteenth century there may have been, "several hundred regular practitioners" of tea ceremony in Sakai, Nara, and Kyoto.[12] And the most celebrated tea masters of the day, including Sen Rikyū, were men of Sakai.

For these men *wabicha* provided a venue for social contacts of great political and commercial value. Because the tea house itself was a small and simple structure, moreover, it put little capital at risk of urban holocaust or armed expropriation, while the tea utensils, which acquired great prestige and material value, were easily portable. Indeed, the utensils, rather than the tea or the process of consuming it, appear to have been the main interest of these teamen. For merchant and pauperized Kyotoite alike tea utensils constituted a valuable and relatively secure investment in an age when both fixed property and income rights were highly vulnerable. And for power brokers, such utensils were as useful in bargaining or boasting as were paintings or other treasures. As with all collectibles, however, their value depended on the presence of shared criteria of excellence and a desire to acquire by those who could afford to do so. Consequently the continual promotion of tea utensils through their display and celebration in *wabicha* sessions was important to tea master and power broker alike. Good culture was good business, as many a modern-day merchant can attest.

RELIGIOUS DEVELOPMENTS

The general direction of medieval religious developments was foreshadowed in the changes of late Heian. As noted in chapter 6, prelates trained at Enryakuji, the great Tendai headquarters on Mt. Hiei, played a uniquely influential role in promoting the sectarian movements of later centuries, including the major sects of Zen, Jōdo (Amidism), and Hokke (Lotus). In a broader sense, as well, the classical religious legacy shaped developments after 1250.

To elaborate, the deep religiosity of later Heian persisted during these centuries of disorder and disorienting social change. It informed *kenmon* culture, as noted above, and influenced politics and society more broadly, with ever larger numbers of people becoming engaged in this religious life. That engagement reflected not the rise of an autochthonous religious movement originating among the rural masses, however. Rather, it was at heart a process of spiritual mobilization by itinerant proselytizers, most of whom derived from more favored strata of society and who brought to the general populace doctrines formerly propounded among the elite.

Very clearly, however, the success of these itinerants depended on their skill in linking their message to the pre-existing agendas and local religious customs of those among whom they worked. In consequence the religious movements that flourished were those that most successfully drew on the diverse doctrinal, organizational, and material resources of class, mass, and, most importantly perhaps, burgeoning intermediate groups: merchants, artisans, entertainers, lesser *bushi*, village leaders, and the itinerants themselves. As the new sectarian movements developed, therefore, they retained much of the combinative character that had so marked classical religion.

Indeed, one of the most noteworthy characteristics of medieval religious life was the persistent interplay of syncretic and sectarian tendencies. Individual clerics promoted particular doctrines and practices and developed institutions for which they claimed a special efficacy and importance, thus fostering sectarianism. But their religious principles and practices often were elaborate and overlapping, which meant that most were in greater or lesser degree combinative in content.

THE PERSISTENCE OF SYNCRETISM

Until around 1250, as noted in chapter 6, the older religious centers, with their elaborate practices, systems of branch temples, and ties to the rulers, continued to dominate the religious scene in Kyoto, Kamakura, and much of the hinterland, especially in central Japan. In later centuries they continued to survive as major, if declining, forces in Japanese politico-religious life. In particular, the Kōfukuji–Kasuga complex at Nara remained the dominant power in Yamato Province until after Ōnin, while the Enryakuji continued deploying thousands of warrior monks from its scores of temple residences on Mt. Hiei.

In terms of theology, prelates in these established temples adhered to their elegant heritage of religious thought and practice, and their intellectual influence penetrated the new movements. Thus, Mujū Ichien, trained at a Rinzai Zen monastery but broadly schooled in Tendai cosmopolitanism, expressed the ideal of *hōben* or "expedient means" in 1300 when he wrote:

> There is not just one method for entering the Way, the causes and conditions for enlightenment being many. Once a person understands their general significance, he will see that the purport of the various teachings does not vary. And when he puts them into practice, he will find that the goal of the myriad religious exercises is the same.[13]

Elsewhere he claimed, in the spirit of *honji-suijaku* thought, that for people of Japan *kami* are the most valuable manifestations of the Buddha nature and hence deserve special reverence.

Shugendō adepts (*yamabushi*) also preserved their combinative legacy. During these medieval centuries large numbers of them settled in villages and established temples to minister to their neighbors, employing a rich mix of indigenous and continental magic, nostrums, and godly powers. Even where *yamabushi* were not active, a grand panoply of deities continued to be invoked at the local level: Jizō, Kannon, Maitreya, Amida, and myriad local *kami*. As the economy commercialized, moreover, those involved in it relied more and more on customary gods of good fortune, notably Daikoku, Ebisu, and Bishamon.

Perhaps the most interesting articulation of combinative thought occurred within the Shintō priestly community. Two instances must suffice. In Ise two adjacent shrines, the Watarai and Kōtei ("imperial") shrines, were long associated with the *ritsuryō* elite. When political disorder reduced their income from *shōen* during the thirteenth century, forcing their staffs to retrench and seek alternative sources of wealth, Watarai priests tried to enhance their attractiveness to potential patrons and donors by propounding doctrinal arguments demonstrating their special ties to the imperial house and founding gods, and hence their great religious efficacy. Those claims elicited protests from priests of the Kōtei Shrine, and as the dispute advanced, the

Watarai priests developed a substantial body of doctrine. They drew support from diverse religious sources as seemed helpful and employed *hon-jaku* reasoning to argue that their own particular *kami* were the basic guardians of Buddhism and the state. The resulting corpus, known as Watarai Shintō, influenced religious thought during the fourteenth century, and though it declined thereafter, it continued to provoke scholarly debate down to the present.

In the second instance, some generations later – when Watarai Shintō was in eclipse and after Ōnin warfare had destroyed Yoshida Shrine (which stood across the Kamo River from Kamigyō) – the shrine's hereditary priestly leader, Yoshida (Urabe) Kanetomo undertook to rebuild the shrine. He aspired to make it the center of a unified imperial Shintō creed that would restore peace and order to the realm. As part of that ambitious project he composed a doctrinal tract in which he employed religious thought with grand eclecticism and creativity to explain the sacred meaning of shrine practice and to make clear that *kami* were the *honji* and Buddhas their *suijaku*. He attributed to Prince Shōtoku the declaration that,

> Japan produced the seed, China produced the branches and leaves, India produced the flowers and fruit ... Buddhism and Confucianism are only secondary products of Shintō.[14]

The inclusive character of Kanetomo's argumentation made it attractive as an alternative to divisive sectarianism, and two centuries later, as Tokugawa rulers tried to manage doctrinal quarrels within the intelligentsia, they elevated Yuiitsu Shintō, as his teachings had come to be known, to the status of authoritative doctrine for all but the greatest shrines of the realm.

NEW SECTARIAN MOVEMENTS

In Shintō and Shugendō, combinative thought was thus made central to sectarian development. In other sectarian movements syncretism survived despite priestly attempts to promulgate exclusivistic doctrines. It did so because those proselytizers who were flexible and who incorporated local religious custom into their teachings won far more followers than did those who refused. This outcome was particularly evident in Sōtō Zen and the most durable portions of the Amidist movement. And the Rinzai branch of Zen was not only combinative but, for all its newness, seems in almost all respects to have had more in common with *ritsuryō* Buddhism than with the other religious movements of its own day.

To note Rinzai briefly, like Kegon and Tendai/Shingon in earlier centuries, it was essentially a religion of the elite, the disciplined few, the rulers. Rinzai monks enjoyed the favor of Kamakura leaders during dyarchy's heyday and retained their religious primacy among the Ashikaga. In consequence they were able to develop an elaborate system of main urban temples, the *gozan*, which included the earlier-mentioned Tenryūji, Nanzenji, and Shōkokuji, and which was sustained by a large array of branch temples, extensive income-producing lands, the China trade, and the patronage of bakufu and daimyo. An important part of Rinzai's appeal to the elite was its doctrinal cosmopolitanism and aesthetic sensitivity. Its central practice of meditation was enveloped in a gorgeous symbology that embraced the routines of daily life, images of buddhas, bodhisattvas, arhats, and other sages, and the paintings, architecture, and gardens that were central to *kenmon* culture.

Rinzai flourished as long as the *kenmon* did, but the Ōnin War ravaged its central monasteries, and the bakufu's decay eroded its fiscal base. By way of contrast the Sōtō branch of Zen, which derived from Dōgen, had a very different experience, one much more akin to that of the Jōdo and Hokke sects. Unlike Rinzai, these movements built from below. Proselytizers established their foundation in the general populace by forming local congregations, and they propounded relatively simple doctrines that involved minimal ritual clutter and expense and that offered spiritual solace in return for faith, whether faith in Amida, the *Lotus Sutra*, or one's own spiritual capability.

To spread their message, proponents of these creeds employed various techniques. Priests and nuns sang, danced, told didactic tales, displayed religious art, and distributed talismans. They conveyed their teachings in simple, understandable sermons, songs, and messages. They affirmed the values of customary morality and invoked or devised rationales to accommodate local religious practices. To retain parishioners, they encouraged regular devotional practices, and they attended to daily-life needs associated with birth, death, illness, and misfortune. They developed sites and rites that celebrated their sect's holy founder, and they maintained or distributed lineage charts or other devices that assured parishioners of their priest's credentials and of their own direct connection to the saving power of their sect.

All three sects experienced a more-or-less difficult transition from first exposition to full fruition. The disciples of all the great founders (Dōgen, Nichiren, Hōnen, and Shinran) fell to quarreling and developed competing movements that tended to fragment by region. Not until the fourteenth century did successor generations gradually sort matters out, some falling by the way while others hit on strategies of recruitment and institution building that enabled them to spread their movement widely across the countryside. Those who did succeed were notable for providing ongoing spiritual service to their followers while accommodating their diverse religious predilections and for being attentive to institutional organization and the maintenance of doctrinal coherence within their priesthood. These general points are evident in the histories of the Sōtō, Hokke, and Jōdo sects.

Sōtō and Hokke. To take Sōtō first, it was the most stable sectarian movement of the period and also the most innocuous in terms of visible politics. After Dōgen's death in 1253, his disciples broadened his religious praxis and gradually spread their teachings, particularly in Hokuriku and Kyushu, winning the good will of local warriors and other figures of local consequence. Sōtō priests not only displayed superior doctrinal knowledge, offering their patrons and followers the most up-to-date teachings, but also respected and solicited the good will of local *kami*. They retained the Buddhas of those local chapels they took over, worked miracles, and conducted lush public ceremonies with mystical formulae, scriptural chanting, and energetic prayers for good weather, crops, health, or fortune, all accompanied by special gongs and music. They conducted funeral ceremonies that assured salvation to the deceased and arranged mass ordinations to initiate into the sect the followers of local warriors or the members of families, villages, or workers' guilds.

Thus nurturing supporters and embracing Buddhist divinities and Japanese *kami* alike, the sect won the allegiance of regional barons, local warriors, and diverse villagers and townsmen. These included landed peasants, river boatmen, servant women, and "sake brewers, dyers, metalworkers, carpenters, actors, shrine celebrants, yamabushi, and young boys."[15] By 1550 Sōtō priests maintained some 15,000 temples scattered from northern Honshu to southern Kyushu.

Nichiren, revered as founder of the Hokke Sect (Hokkeshū), ran afoul the Kamakura bakufu, as noted in chapter 6, and spent his last years training disciples deep in the mountains southwest of Mt. Fuji. In his teachings he treated esoteric Buddhist practices as "expedient means" for bringing one to the ultimate truth of the *Lotus Sutra* (Hokekyō), and he affirmed a *hon-jaku* linkage between Buddha and *kami*. He also asserted, however, that the powers of the *kami* would fail unless the truth of the *Lotus* were accepted, an acceptance that the faithful were to express through devout recitation of the mantra, *namu myōhō rengekyō*.

Nichiren's successors, who weathered decades of harsh disputation with one another, developed no central headquarters, forming instead small, scattered congregations, mostly in the Kantō and its borderlands. During the Muromachi period their teachings spread westward, slowly giving rise to communities of the faithful in central Japan, most notably in Nara, Sakai, and Shimogyō. Indeed, one record of the 1470s claimed that "over half of Kyoto is made up of Hokke adherents."[16] Even some *kuge* were joining the faith. As mentioned in chapter 7, these Hokke temples became centers of urban leadership. After a costly period of participation in *sengoku* military politics they revived, and during the later 1500s came to include many of the age's most successful artisans and merchants.

Amidism. It was Amidist or Jōdo (Pure Land) sectarians, who had the most visible impact on political history. Jōdo also was the most complex in its development. From the outset it was linked to the old elite, and it always retained that connection, even as it developed into a religion of the masses. The complications of combinative doctrine and praxis that stemmed from that elite legacy contributed to the rise of diverse, conflicting lines of Amidist theology, and these became embedded in rival priestly lineages and institutional blocs. Some of those lineages were closely associated with the Kyoto elite, while others were regionally centered or broadly rural in focus. Factions proliferated, alignments kept shifting, and doctrinal infighting persisted. Within this general picture, however, one can identify a sequence of pre-eminent Amidist movements, those of the Ji, Bukkōji, and Honganji subsects.

Initially the Ji Sect (Jishū) of Ippen was the most successful Amidist movement. He and his disciples followed Hōnen's Jōdo teachings, and their energetic itinerancy created throughout central Japan a rural following devoted to the belief that sincere invocation of the *nenbutsu* (the mantra *namu Amida butsu*) would assure one's rebirth in paradise. By the Muromachi heyday, ca. 1400, Jishū counted some 2,000 small congregations, most of them situated in the Kantō–Chūbu region.

By then, however, Shinshū, the movement based on Shinran's Jōdo Shin (True Pure Land) variant of Hōnen's teachings, had developed a dynamic center at Bukkōji, a large temple in the foothills east of the Kamo River. It was supported mainly by contributions from the faithful in rural congregations, which its priests created and nurtured by diligent proselytizing, distribution of talismans, and ceremonial use of religious icons and imagery that were as gorgeous as they were eclectic. Temple leaders reinforced the movement's internal coherence and dynamism by issuing regulations and by threats of excommunication and eternal suffering for any who backslid. As they developed their following, they drew people away from the Jishū and other groups. In 1413, one awed observer wrote:

> at the Bukkōji temple in Shibutani, with its salvation registers and portrait lineages, people are as dense as clouds or fog. This is altogether astonishing to behold.[17]

Bukkōji was so successful in fact that it thoroughly overshadowed the nearby Honganji temple, even though the latter claimed to represent the spiritual line directly descended from Shinran and to be guardian of his tomb.

A half century later, however, Rennyo became head of the Honganji, and he proved to be one of the most able, energetic, and shrewd clerical politicians in Japanese history. To attract followers to a simple doctrine of faith in the *nenbutsu*'s redemptive power, Rennyo employed several strategies. He exploited his connections to the *kenmon* elite, utilized some of the techniques that worked so well for Bukkōji, fostered congregational singing of hymns, and distributed pastoral letters (*ofumi*) that he wrote in easily understandable, colloquial Japanese.

His ministry won so many converts, however, and as a corollary so many enemies, that he moved to minimize conflicts over doctrine. He admonished his followers not to slander other Buddhist practices, even as they held to the primacy of *nenbutsu* invocation, and not to "belittle the various *kami*, buddhas, and bodhisattvas."[18] Regarding the *kami*, he assured followers that it was acceptable for a trusting Amidist to have "faith in them all without relying on them individually because the *kami* are encompassed in [the Buddha]."[19]

Rennyo's combination of political skill, organizational attentiveness, and doctrinal flexibility proved effective. Adherents to other Amidist sects switched their allegiance to his, and in 1481, while ensconced in his grand Yamashina Honganji, Rennyo accepted the once-mighty Bukkōji as a subordinate temple. As years passed, the Honganji's following kept growing, and his successors strengthened their control by adopting, in the Bukkōji manner, the power to excommunicate and punish. Excommunication was a powerful tool because it reduced a person to the state of a homeless outsider in this world and denied him or her redemption in the afterlife. As the son of one excommunicant lamented:

> None who is excommunicated escapes hell. What is more, in this life he is shunned by mankind and dies of starvation. It is indeed retribution that embraces the two existences.[20]

By the mid-sixteenth century Honganji leaders had so meshed religious doctrine and practice with social, political, and economic considerations as to make their organization the single most powerful religious force in central Japan.

The "Woman Question".   One element in Honganji success was its policy toward the question of women and salvation. Like the world's other major religious traditions, Buddhism in practice was male dominated and highly sexist in creed and conduct. Buddhist texts, however, contain diverse and mutually inconsistent views on women. Many declare them physically and psychologically inferior to men and therefore incapable of attaining enlightenment. Others circumvent that conclusion, many by accepting the principle of a gendered reality but working around it. Thus, some declare that women can indeed become nuns, provided they learn specified rules as taught by monks and always obey those monks: women "should not scold or be angry with or admonish a monk," and even if a hundred years old, "shall perform the correct duties to a monk."[21]

A widely accepted formulation that applies to women in general holds that if they live virtuous or faithful lives, they can hope to be reborn as males in paradise, from whence the attaining of enlightenment is assured. Yet other texts completely bypass the male–female distinction by asserting the nonduality of truth and hence the unreality of gender characteristics. In this view non-dual, ungendered Buddha-nature abides in all things, so femaleness cannot incur special disabilities or obstruct the quest for enlightenment.

The Buddhist texts of *ritsuryō* Japan contained this rich array of ideas, but most were disregarded. Temples were male domains, and men controlled the nunneries that provided court women with places to pursue spiritual renewal and to escape, temporarily or permanently, the tensions of court life. The changing circumstances of later Heian fostered a rebalancing of emphases, however, and by later Kamakura, religious views more congenial to women were coming to enjoy greater favor.

The driving force behind this shift in attitude was, one suspects, the sectarian competition that led proselytizers to recruit followers widely and energetically. Whatever the motive, however, several lines of textual argumentation facilitated the reorientation. Most compellingly, perhaps, the central idea of *mappō* – that in the "defiled latter age" no one, male or female, could truly grasp Buddhist teachings through self-effort – undercut the doctrinal advantage of men, encouraging proponents of Amidist and Hokke teachings to make faith the key to salvation for men and women alike.

Amidist teachings, particularly those of Shinran and his successors, seem quickly to have attracted women. In part perhaps this was because Amida's close associate, the compassionate bodhisattva Kannon was commonly envisioned in feminine terms and was presented as one who could transform his/her sex with ease. More centrally, priestly followers of Shinran replaced monastic discipline with quotidian married life, raising children and thus willy nilly introducing women and household concerns into the heart of temple life, rather as aristocratic women had once lived in the thick of Heian court life.

Moreover, Jōdo Shin teachings addressed the overriding religious concern of women by declaring that like a man, a woman, "even as woman, will be ushered into Pure Land if she chants [the *nenbutsu*]."[22] With enlightenment thus assured thanks to Amida's grace, it presumably became a moot point whether the woman was transformed into a man in the Pure Land before becoming a buddha. At least the evidence of Jōdo Shin temple registers, where names signify a person's link to the Pure Land, suggest such an attitude: women's names are common in them, in some cases outnumbering those of men.

Nichiren, too, addressed the issue of gender, devoting considerable effort to fostering religiosity among women. He declared that they should place their faith in the *Lotus* because it – and only it among all the sutras – contained assurances that women could attain enlightenment. Leaders of the Sōtō and Rinzai sects also developed doctrinal interpretations more favorable to women. Thus the fifteenth-century Rinzai prelate Ikkyū Sōjun declared:

> with the buddhas enfeoffed in the heart, all wishes and hopes are fulfilled and the body, be it male or female, becomes a worthy vessel for easy buddhahood.[23]

Sōtō formulations, as well as many popular *setsuwa*, continued to affirm the notion that women labor under special disabilities. However, instead of serving simply to legitimate the dismissal of women as being beyond redemption, the idea seemed mostly to justify extra effort to help them overcome their "hindrances" and achieve salvation.

Under these more favorable circumstances a few women acquired historically visible religious roles, most notably, perhaps, the thirteenth-century nun Mugai Nyodai, who headed the system of Rinzai convents that paralleled the *gozan* monastic organization. Hers, however, seems to have been an anomalous experience. The more consequential outcome was that women, who in *ritsuryō* days had been restricted to positions on the margins of text-based religion as cloistered nuns, Shintō priestesses, shamans, and *bikuni* itinerants, became legitimate participants in the communal life of local temples. Sōtō temples gave careful attention to women in their funerals, which were a central concern in Sōtō doctrine, and in the Amidist and Hokke sects, women joined in religious services, becoming a major element in congregations all across the realm.

VOCAL LITERATURE

The arts and letters that constitute *kenmon* culture were essentially works by and for the favored few. Although the medieval elite was much larger and more diverse than that of the *ritsuryō* era, it was still a very small segment of the total population. And that was the case even when one includes merchant participants and the entertainers and artists themselves, of whom so many, such as Kan'ami and Sōgi, rose from obscure origins. The text-based religion of these centuries spoke to a much wider audience, but it did not do so through the literate discourse of priestly commentary, which reached only those who could read and write. Rather, the spread of religious instruction beyond the literate few was largely achieved by the art of oral presentation, as part of a broader, much more eclectic vocal literature that was spread by story tellers, both men and women.

These tale tellers, who arguably were the most significant element in medieval cultural life, were a varied entrepreneurial group, ranging from professional entertainers to devout proselytizers. As generations passed, the stories they told became more elaborate; the techniques of their delivery, more complex. In addition, one can discern a trend in which, as time passed, the purpose of narration came more and more to be entertainment rather than proselytism. Generally, however, even the entertainment conveyed a religious message, however attenuated.

These changes paralleled changes in the audience. During the Heian period anecdotes (*setsuwa*) were told mainly to acolytes in temples, to shrine visitors, most of whom were high-born, and to *kuge* men and women in their mansions or retirement residences. Collections of *setsuwa* commonly served "as source books for priests to use in preparing services and sermons."[24] By late Heian itinerants were becoming more active in the hinterland, soliciting funds and proselytizing among the locally powerful. And by the Ashikaga heyday tale tellers were plying their stories among a highly diverse population along highways, in village shrines, at the many small temples that had been erected about the countryside, at major temples and shrines, and in the homes of warriors, merchants, and the *kenmon* in Kyoto.

THE TECHNIQUES OF TALE TELLING

To reach this diverse and dispersed audience, tale tellers employed several techniques that combined story with acting, dance, picture, and music. The story-and-acting combination, as earlier noted, developed via *sarugaku* skits into the *nō* theatrical tradition. The story-and-dance combination was favored by numerous itinerant nuns (*bikuni*) and monks (*hijiri*), most famously Ippen and his Jishū disciples. In their technique of religious proselytizing, known as *nenbutsu odori*, proponents of Jishū chanted the *nenbutsu* while joyfully dancing in celebration of Amida's saving grace.

More well known – and probably more common, if only because it was physically less taxing – was the tale-telling art that combined story and picture. Women, known as Kumano *bikuni*, as well as men, the *etoki hōshi* or "picture-explaining" priests, used this technique, working with pictures that illustrated the stories they were narrating. Kumano *bikuni* spoke mostly to women, addressing them in the houses of *kuge*, *bushi*, local notables, and eventually merchants, and they talked to pilgrims at temples, shrines, crossroads, and other gathering places. They drew their stories from *setsuwa* anecdotes, longer narratives, and war tales (*gunki monogatari*), gradually enriching them with episodes about women. They also developed their own confessional stories and distributed copies of tales whose religious efficacy they guaranteed.

The Kumano *bikuni* narrated her story in a more or less rhythmic, chanting manner. As she spoke, she pointed out details in the picture version of the incident being related, using a feather tipped pointer that would neither wear out the picture nor risk insulting any deity portrayed therein. Initially these *bikuni* used handscrolls, but by the Ashikaga heyday they commonly employed booklets of pictures (Nara *ehon*), although the two formats were interchanged, with tellers cutting up scrolls to form booklets or pasting booklet pages together to make scrolls.

Other narrators (*sekkyō bushi*, *goze*, and *biwa hōshi*) combined story and music, relying primarily on vocal skills to hold an audience. *Sekkyō bushi* began as narrators of sutras or other religious texts, beating a bamboo whisk (*sasara*) for rhythm or emphasis as they spoke. By the fourteenth century they had moved beyond temple and courtly elite to work more widely about the realm, essentially as entertainers. They drew on the same broad range of literary sources as Kumano *bikuni*, enriched them to enhance their audience appeal, and wrote down the expanded versions to form "prompt books" that fellow *sekkyō bushi* could use. By the Ashikaga heyday a century later, *sekkyō bushi* texts were being written in colloquial Japanese. They commonly told of a hero who, though born into a high-ranking household thanks to prayer, was cruelly thrust into hard times, took revenge upon his malefactors, and in the end became, or was revealed to be, a divinity.

A similar sort of narrator was the blind woman chanter known as *goze*, who accompanied herself on a drum. In the tradition of the sightless shaman, whose blindness enhanced her capacity to contact the invisible spirit world, the *goze* told her stories as an observer of the scene being described. Conveying this narrative stance through voice and drum, the skillful *goze* drew her listeners into her story, thrilling, terrifying, or teaching them as her story dictated. Like other story tellers, *goze* drew their narratives from diverse sources, enriched them, and thus added to the corpus of widely-shared vocal literature.

Much as *goze* derived credibility from the tradition of shamanism, blind, lute-playing priests (*biwa hōshi*) were empowered by the long-standing notions that blindness connoted a special religious sensibility and that lute music could appease troubled spirits. Because of their sacred powers *biwa hōshi* performed exorcisms, chanted over the dead on battlefields, and entertained troops in camp and urban folk in city streets. By the mid-fourteenth century they were entertainers more than priests, and they were organized in guilds and pursued their trade about the countryside. As generations passed, they added to their repertoire, still doing so even as the *kenmon* regime was tottering to its end.

THE CONTENTS OF TALES

Story tellers thus employed several techniques to attract and retain their audiences. In terms of content, religious concerns predominated, but changes of treatment reflected the changing times. Whereas religious tales of earlier centuries had dwelt on the spiritual quest of monks and nuns, by the Ashikaga heyday characters were more plebeian. Commonly they were itinerants, whether men who traveled to sacred sites such as Mt. Kōya in Kii, or women who visited Zenkōji in the depths of Shinano or such other temples as were open to them. There they shared stories of their experiences: their loves and losses, crimes and confessions, suffering and salvation.

These religious tales reflected the doctrinal diversity and syncretism of the age. Some focused on deities of place, such as Kumano and Kasuga *gongen*, others on deities of doctrine, such as Kannon, Amida, or Maitreya. Incidents commonly revealed that some person or divinity was the *suijaku* of some particular *honji*, or they illustrated the expedient means (*hōben*) that divinities employed to lead benighted souls to salvation. And even tales whose central theme was the secular success of the hero or heroine generally ended by attributing the happy outcome to godly beneficence or the hero's essential character (*honji*) as a divinity.

Even in the few tales that are not overtly religious in theme or tone, moral agendas usually appear. And in the corpus as a whole it frequently is women who are being instructed. Stories dwell on the "depravity" of a woman, jealousy in many instances, often to celebrate the woman's success in mastering her "feminine" weaknesses, thereby attaining or enabling others to attain salvation. Their inherent weaknesses notwithstanding, women have faith. Miracles do happen, and declarations of religious attainment are made. Thus, in a cluster of late Muromachi tales in which seven nuns recount their personal experiences, one relates how she went to join her warrior husband on his campaign in Kyushu, only to find him slain, which outcome led to her tonsure and seventeen years of "continuous pilgrimage throughout the provinces." To console her, an elderly nun replied:

> Truly, as the Buddha said, a woman's terrible fate is to bear the burden of the Five Obstacles and Three Subjugations...However, because the Buddha devises ways to save even women, he appeared as your husband. In that guise he has saved you [because his death led you to pursue your salvation with such earnestness. In consequence, surely, your] relatives, from your great-grandparents down through to your great-grandchildren, will be reborn in paradise.[25]

By such expedient means does Buddha devise ways to save women, and, yes, through women to save others.

Women were so central to this vocal literature because so many tale tellers and audience members were female. The growth in intermediate social strata increased the number of women who had discretionary income and time, and warfare and turmoil of the age produced widespread hardship among them. The result was a large population of female consumers who could afford to hear tale tellers and who knew the sorrows and yearning for redemption of which they spoke.

By the Ashikaga heyday a rich vocal literature had been recorded and was being shared by story tellers. The brief *setsuwa*-type tales had been embellished, and they were supplemented by several hundred longer stories of twenty to forty pages apiece (now identified generically as *otogi zōshi*). Most remarkably, perhaps, tale tellers took episodes from war tales, embellished them, and in the process transformed more-or-less straightforward battlefield reports into complex tales full of human feelings and moral lessons. The most celebrated of these war tales recounted the Genpei wars of the 1180s, with *Heike monogatari* and *Soga monogatari* being the ones most commonly drawn upon by medieval story tellers.

In telling these war tales, raconteurs deleted dates, rearranged material, reworked the prose style, and added details and anecdotes, greatly enhancing dramatic quality at the expense of historicity. Both male and female raconteurs participated in the process, but scholars note that women seem to have been especially important in developing the *Heike* and *Soga* narratives.

A century and a half of reworking the *Heike* added incidents to illustrate religious and moral themes, to celebrate heroes, to honor victims, often women, and to appease angry ghosts. In its finished form the *Heike*'s thousand or so characters move through myriad situations, some of them wrenching as lives are ruined, hearts broken, dreams lost, risks taken, dangers overcome or not, triumphs scored only to be found hollow, and Buddhist lessons learned. And *Soga monogatari*, originally a story of conflict among men close to Yoritomo, was adorned and adapted by generations of blind women chanters until its focus had been shifted to the women whose lives were thrown into turmoil by manly machinations. In mature form, both tales were replete with stories of warriors' wives, widows, and courtesans, of their complicated relationships, their suffering and service, and their deeds of religious and secular dedication.

In the outcome these medieval tale tellers had enriched the content of Japan's literary heritage. They had extended its appeal downward to embrace a far wider spectrum of society and broadened it to give much fuller representation to the female half of humankind. They constituted a bridge of sorts between the aristocratic literary women of high Heian and the broadly based women authors of the present day.

Agricultural intensification, the proliferation of larger villages, the growth of travel and trade, and the expansion of intermediate social strata were thus accompanied by the multiplication of story tellers of many sorts. Drawing on the literary heritage of the classical age, they enriched it and shared it with the general public. In so doing they gave the general populace a historically visible, shared culture of legends, myths, heroes, religious ideas, and behavioral norms, thereby laying a substantial foundation for the widely shared "national" culture of Japan that emerged in subsequent centuries.

Establishing the Bakuhan
Order (1550–1700)

During the century or so after 1550 Japan experienced a political transformation. A state of endemic warfare, *sengoku* or "warring states," gave way to one of durable peace, *taihei*, "the great peace" as celebrants styled it. In the process society acquired a structure as clearly articulated and permanent – in theory at least – as that of the *ritsuryō* heyday, a structure known today as the *bakuhan taisei* or "power structure of bakufu and daimyo domains."

A Political Narrative

By 1550 most of the old *shōen* system was gone, and the realm was largely controlled by battling local and regional lords and their retainers. Political reconsolidation began when the more successful of these local rulers started expanding the territories they were able to control effectively. During the 1570s one of their number, Oda Nobunaga, succeeded in establishing hegemony over central Japan, dominating the region's daimyo and residual *kenmon* and steering its material production to his own use. Following Nobunaga's murder in 1582, his lieutenant Toyotomi Hideyoshi defeated rivals and extended his control over the rest of the country. After Hideyoshi died in 1598, his erstwhile collaborator Tokugawa Ieyasu overcame an assemblage of rivals, and he and his successors stabilized the realm under their own hegemonial control. As they consolidated power, their *bakuhan* regime acquired a degree of institutional articulation and ideological legitimation that approached the *ritsuryō* ideal in its elaborateness if not its architectonic elegance. The speed with which Japan traveled from endemic disorder to enforced discipline is suggested by the fact that the three key figures, Nobunaga, Hideyoshi, and Ieyasu, were not spokesmen for three successive generations but, rather, all men of the same era, the youngest born only eight years after the eldest.

CONSOLIDATING DAIMYO DOMAINS

Medieval socioeconomic growth overwhelmed the Muromachi-era *kenmon*, who allowed the power potential of the expanding, more densely settled, and more productive hinterland population to fall into the hands of local figures, most notably the magnates commonly referred to as *kokujin* or "provincials." These men combined in varying ways military skill, local social control, religious zeal, and landed and commercial wealth to create a plethora of small-scale, competing political units all across the countryside, and as the sixteenth century advanced, some among them devised mechanisms that harnessed more and more of this burgeoning power potential. As that occurred, the age of disorder rapidly gave way to one of unprecedented discipline.

When the harnessing did commence, then, it did so not as a top–down process of conquest but as a bottom–up political tightening that grew from local to regional and finally countrywide scope. Because the reconsolidation began locally with individual leaders confronting immediate problems, it entailed a wide array of governing techniques that yielded varying degrees of consistency and success. However, since all these leaders were maneuvering within the context of post-Ōnin turmoil, a number of widely shared characteristics are identifiable. In a sentence these newly risen lords, whom scholars commonly call *sengoku* daimyo, devised organizational arrangements to control other *kokujin*, village production, and commerce, and they adumbrated rationales of supremacy to justify their domination.

To elaborate, whereas medieval daimyo had lived or spent much time in Kyoto and delegated authority over their domainal affairs to subordinates, *sengoku* daimyo responded to the heightened level of local disorder by staying more or less permanently in the areas they controlled. They encouraged, and eventually required, their retainers to settle at their headquarters rather then in villages with their own followers. And gradually they corrolated the service demands they made on those retainers with the amount of arable land they awarded them, which gave lords greater knowledge of their own military capability and their retainers' bases of power. Finally, they issued and enforced sterner codes of conduct to guide their followers, essentially to prevent them from placing their own family or communal interests ahead of their lord's.

Even as *sengoku* lords were tightening control over their retainers, they were eliminating rival lines of authority in the areas they sought to dominate. Because no central power could prevent their doing so, they repudiated the surviving fiscal or proprietary claims that medieval *kenmon*, great temples most notably, still made to parcels of land and productive villages. They assigned income and authority in some areas to their retainers while keeping other areas under their own administrators. They reorganized taxation, making it simpler, more thorough, and more fully payable to their own treasuries. And they forbade other local figures, including their own retainers, to levy taxes or exact corvée labor without lordly authorization. Finally, as lords resurveyed parcels of land to resolve disputes and clarify yields, they discovered numerous unregistered fields, which they added to their tax rolls, thereby expanding their income substantially.

The yield from land was, however, only part of a lord's tribute base. The *kenmon* had long derived tribute from trade, and *sengoku* lords pursued it as well. They exacted it from such diverse sources as pawnbrokers, *sake* brewers, river and highway users, and occupants of warehouses and street frontage. They encouraged merchants and artisans to settle in their headquarters towns and produce goods or oversee mercantile activity on their behalf by offering them special tax concessions and marketing privileges, as well as title and status. And they imposed taxes on products being exported to the domains of other lords.

Besides improving their control of existing production, lords fostered the expansion of taxable output. Many promoted reclamation projects to expand agricultural production; others fostered output of local specialties, such as lacquer, dyestuffs, or hemp, or encouraged shipping at ports under their control. Those who learned of mines on their domains, such as lords in Iwami and Tajima provinces, recruited miners to exploit them.

The tightening of tax collection and expansion of taxable output yielded substantial increases in tribute income. However, the measures also brought lords into sharper confrontation with villagers, and the latter responded with tax strikes, acts of absconding, and sometimes armed resistance, most commonly in the form of Shinshū sectarian activism. Lest religious dissent escalate out of control, some lords tried to forestall it. Thus the Takeda of Kai stipulated in a clause of their 1547 code that,

> The Pure Land Sect and the Nichiren Band are not permitted to engage in religious controversy within the borders of our domain. If there are people who encourage such controversies, both the priests and their parishioners will be punished.[1]

The relatively large and well organized villages of the day posed a sufficient threat, however, so that lords also tried to conciliate them. They modified corvée burdens and tax levies to secure compliance, in the process discovering the limits of their own power and the forms of compromise essential to political success.

In more elegant efforts to make acceptable the demands they were placing on retainers and producers, *sengoku* daimyo advanced arguments about their right to rule. Because they were usurping the customary perquisites of higher authority figures, they could not easily wrap themselves in the purple of tradition and instead invoked other rationales of authority. One of the most influential was the bald fact of success itself, which some lords presented as evidence that they possessed the virtue necessary to govern properly. In his code of 1526, the Imagawa lord in Suruga Province asserted his right to rule the domain, even without shogunal authorization, by declaring:

> The basis for rule over the *kuni* is not attained by being appointed *shugo* [provincial overlords] by the shogun. Control [of the *kokka*] is achieved when the daimyo, by his own efforts, brings peace to the *kokka* by establishing the laws of the *kuni*.[2]

In referring to the people and territories they controlled as *kokka*, leaders such as Imagawa conflated the older *ritsuryō* province (*kuni* or *koku*) and the venerable lineage group (*ie*, *ke*, *ka*), seeming to imply that in their rule they embodied the legacies of both imperial and household authority.

Sengoku lords were spurred to consolidate power by the turmoil of the times, which continually threatened them. Their primary strategy was to increase the size of their armies – to engage in an arms race – and their measures to control retainers and producers were means to that end. The military consequences were striking: armies grew dramatically. Whereas, for example, the obscure *kokujin* known to history as Hōjō Sōun conquered Izu Peninsula with an estimated 300 warrriors in 1491, a century later his descendant Hōjō Ujinao deployed some 50,000 in a futile effort to defend his gigantic Odawara Castle against an attacking army of some 200,000.

There were changes in the techniques of battle, as well as its scale. With lords staying on their domains and more fighting becoming local, defensive warfare gained importance, leading to vast amounts of fortress construction. More basically, warfare experienced another long-term shift in the balance between elite and mass combat. Some 1,100 years earlier, it will be recalled, horse warfare had displaced foot soldiery as the heart of offense, until *ritsuryō* rulers turned to conscript armies. In later Heian *buke* leaders reaffirmed the primacy of horse-mounted professional warriors, but during *sengoku* warfare was again transformed from an elite career for small numbers of expensively equipped samurai into a plebeian business handled by masses of simply armed men led by a cadre of samurai officers and supported by large crews of corvée labor. Foot solders displaced mounted samurai as the decisive combat force, and heavy armor, swords, and bows were partially displaced by light armor, pikes, and halberds, and from the 1560s by matchlocks. (Subsequently, to note the matter *en passant*, this new primacy of the mass army was concealed for 250 years by the absence of large-scale warfare, but it was reaffirmed during the 1860s and persisted through the early decades of industrialism, until late twentieth-century technology again transformed warfare into an elite, professional enterprise.)

During *sengoku* more and more lords secured the manpower they needed for building and battling by mobilizing and controlling their retainers and also by specifying the numbers of troops each was to provide, with pikemen becoming the predominant type. As force size mushroomed, however, logistical needs also grew apace and provisioning became a major military concern. So lords enticed merchant provisioners into service and put village leaders on notice of their military corvée obligations. To an unprecedented degree warfare had been transformed from an elite affair fought amidst a scarcely involved general populace into an enterprise that mobilized the realm, directing its energies into the conjoined tasks of killing and conquest.

By the final decades of the sixteenth century, the old *shōen* system and medieval *kenmon* were largely gone, and most of the minor lordly holdings had been absorbed by more successful neighbors, a handful of *sengoku* daimyo who were maneuvering and battling to preserve and advance their positions. As of 1570 they included such notable figures as the Hōjō at Odawara, Imagawa and Tokugawa in the Tōkai region, Takeda and Uesugi to their north, Oda in the Owari–Kinai region, Chōsokabe on Shikoku, Mōri in western Honshu, and Ōtomo and Shimazu in Kyushu.

PACIFYING THE REALM: NOBUNAGA AND HIDEYOSHI

Oda Nobunaga, the son of a struggling *kokujin* in Owari Province, defeated rival heirs and in 1560 took charge of his family's fate. Seven years of warfare and conquest then enabled him to relocate his headquarters northward to a castle astride the Nakasendō, where he gained the attention of power brokers in Kyoto. A year later he marched into the city at imperial behest and installed Ashikaga Yoshiaki as titular shogun. By the time of his death in 1582 he controlled central Japan from west of Himeji to the highlands of Kai, having extended his sway by battling fiercely, maneuvering shrewdly, and adhering singlemindedly to his goal of pacifying the realm and thus assuring his own security and glory.

In an action that revealed his sense of historical place, in 1567 Nobunaga gave the name Gifu-jō to his new bastion on the Nakasendō, thereby evoking the career of the Chinese general who founded the Chou dynasty by conquest some twenty-five centuries earlier. Moreover, from about this time he adopted as his signature motto the phrase *tenka fubu*, "Rule the Realm by Force." He claimed that the realm (*tenka*) "is the common property of all men," as Chou-dynasty precedents asserted, not the property of some hereditary ruling line, and that his task was to govern it properly.[3] Accordingly, his writ transcended that of a mere shogun, who spoke only for a private interest. In 1570, as tensions between him and Yoshiaki grew, he sent the shogun a five-clause notice in which he declared:

> Because the affairs of the realm [*tenka*] have in fact been entrusted to Nobunaga, he is free to act as he wills towards anyone without having to obtain the shogun's consent.[4]

In the spirit of *tenka fubu*, he demanded complete loyalty from his followers and submission by his enemies, and he punished harshly any who defied him. Unsurprisingly, given his governing style and principles, his success generated resistance far beyond the shogunate, producing an *ad hoc* coalition of *kenmon* remnants, daimyo, and Honganji sectarian forces that battled him off and on for the rest of his life.

In this long-running contest Nobunaga employed warfare, intimidation, warning, hectoring, and rewarding to divide, isolate, and overwhelm his opponents. In 1569, to illustrate his diplomatic style, he reprimanded the Shingon clerics at Mt. Kōya for consorting with his enemies:

> Your groups of mountain priests have allied themselves with the enemy. Time and again you have taken part in military compaigns, and you have even constructed fortresses. You also confiscated Uchi county. Your behavior is outrageous. You are to vacate your position as quickly as possible, and to return what you seized. Otherwise you will be punished forthwith.

In fact he then directed his military energies elsewhere, but other opponents found his sword as sharp as his word.

To note some of the most significant developments in Nobunaga's career, he aided a portion of the residual *kenmon* by providing material assistance to the court and its closest *kuge* and clerics, but in return he demanded their cooperation. And he obeyed the occasional imperial instruction only when doing so seemed advantageous. In 1571, after the prelates of Mt. Hiei responded to his seizure of some Enryakuji lands by allying with his enemies, he destroyed the temple's great assemblage of buildings and treasures and slaughtered its population of men, women, and children as a horrific warning to others in the city. Two years later he effectively ended the shogunate by driving Yoshiaki out of Kyoto after the imprudent shogun began conniving against him.

Nobunaga continually battled other daimyo, but his single most intractable opponent was the Ishiyama Honganji, whose earlier militance had revived in the face of his harsh demands. Honganji followers were spread across central Japan, which enabled the temple's leaders to collaborate actively with daimyo on all sides of Nobunaga, thereby giving greater coherence and durability to the coalition of forces that tried unsuccessfully to prevent his rise to supremacy. Indeed, the difficulties posed by Honganji supporters prompted him to send one of his ablest generals, Shibata Katsuie, to Echizen to establish control of Shinshū forces there, and later to station another of his best, Toyotomi Hideyoshi, near the northern end of Lake Biwa, where he could control the local population and interdict Honganji-Hokuriku contact. And in 1576 it led him to place a son in charge of Gifu while he relocated his own headquarters to a hillock overlooking the eastern shore of Lake Biwa, where he could control not only lake traffic but also the Nakasendō to the east and its northern fork to Hokuriku. There, in the heart of Honganji territory, he launched the construction of a gigantic and splendiferous new castle, Azuchi-jō. By 1582 it was surrounded by a bustling town of some 5,000 residents.

As a battle commander Nobunaga was known for his audacious use of surprise, the severe demands he made on his men, and his exceptional readiness to apply new technology. Most famously, he was one of the first daimyo to use firearms effectively. But in addition, in 1575, when he found himself unable to subdue Ishiyama Honganji because it could be resupplied from ships in the Yodo estuary, he ordered construction of his own navy, equipping five new vessels with cannon and armor plating. With those armored vessels in the van, his flotilla destroyed a large resupply fleet that Shinshū adherents sent to the fortress in 1578, and it subsequently repulsed a major armada that Mōri despatched to relieve the bastion. After that, Ishiyama was isolated and its collapse became a matter of time.

Even as he struggled with Ishiyama and strove to expand his realm with one military campaign after another, Nobunaga also took steps to tighten control of his domain and its tribute resources. He weakened local magnates by ordering innumerable small fortifications torn down. Although he did not actually deploy land surveyors to measure agricultural land as his successors would, he did demand that *shōen* proprietors and others possessing tax registers and records of arable acreage submit the information to him for examination and spot checking. Doing so helped him know who controlled how much income and thus what he could reasonably expect from them as support or threat. Moreover, he used the receipt of that information as occasion to affirm the income rights of proprietors, thereby establishing the legal fiction that they held those rights not through some hoary historical grant but thanks directly to him.

To generate commercial income, he attracted merchants to his domain by abolishing numerous highway tariff barriers that the medieval *kenmon* had maintained. And he induced them to settle in his castle towns at Gifu and later Azuchi by offering tax concessions and other advantages. He confirmed or abolished guilds (*za*) in accordance with their utility to himself. He closed down the trading towns located at temples that opposed him and imposed tribute levies on others. Finally, to ensure proper tribute collection, he stationed his own appointees at key ports such as Sakai, Kusatsu, and Ōtsu.

By the summer of 1582 the great Ishiyama Honganji had fallen. Nobunaga had extended his control into Kii Province, and his men were busy preparing an invasion of Shikoku. To the east he and his allies, notably Tokugawa Ieyasu, had secured much of Suruga, Kai, and Shinano. To the north Shibata dominated the Echizen vicinity. To the west Hideyoshi, who had been redeployed to Himeji in 1577 after Nobunaga's move to Azuchi, was pushing the Mōri back toward far western Honshu. Another senior vassal, Akechi Mitsuhide, had just been ordered to open another front against Mōri by pressing westward along the Sea of Japan coast beyond Tajima. Feeling ill-used of late, however, Akechi marched back to Kyoto instead, much as Ashikaga Takauji had done in 1333 when he turned against the Hōjō, and in a swift attack caught Nobunaga poorly protected in one of Shimogyō's larger Hokke temples. There he destroyed him.

When death ended Nobunaga's twenty years of hard-won gains, he was still expanding his realm, and there is every reason to believe that his triumphs would have continued for some time had he not been betrayed by Akechi. But he was betrayed, and Hideyoshi became the beneficiary of his accomplishments.

Hideyoshi the conqueror. Whereas Nobunaga (as well as Ieyasu) was born of recognizably *kokujin*-like ancestry, Hideyoshi rose from the obscure ranks of sometime foot soldiers produced by the changing world of warfare. By 1582, however, years of skillful service to Nobunaga had transformed him into one

Figure 9.1 *Toyotomi Hideyoshi gazō*; color on silk; dated 1598; artist unknown; Kōdaiji, Kyoto. Despite his obscure parentage and want of cultural polish, Hideyoshi's exceptional skills as politician and military man compelled even the most disdainful of daimyo to accept his supremacy and accommodate his wishes. *Source*: Bradley Smith, *Japan, A History in Art* (New York: Doubleday & Co. Inc., 1964), p. 170.

of the Oda house's most able and valued generals. His reaction to news of Nobunaga's death demonstrated his prowess: with stunning alacrity he broke off his battle with Mōri, negotiated an advantageous armistice, and then rushed back to Kyoto where he destroyed Akechi and seized the city, doing so before Ieyasu or anyone else could act. In following weeks he consolidated his control of the Kinai region and most Oda vassals, and in 1583 he destroyed Shibata Katsuie when he raised a challenge. For months Ieyasu maneuvered in search of a strong *point d'appui*. But he found none despite two bloody, large-scale skirmishes and finally decided he must accept Hideyoshi's leadership.

At one point in these maneuvers two armed temple groups from Kii (the monks of Negoroji, a Shingon bastion that looked out over the Ki River valley, and the supporters of Saiga, a Shinshū fortress situated on a coastal promontory near the river's mouth) tried to reassert their independence by battling Hideyoshi alongside Ieyasu's forces. Their misstep gave him pretext to consolidate his control of Kii while making them examples for other restless clerics: in the spring of 1585 his armies destroyed their sprawling establishments almost as thoroughly as Nobunaga had ruined Hieizan. Prelates at Kōya and elsewhere got the message, and by that summer Hideyoshi was securely in control of Nobunaga's old realm and busily preparing to expand it. Collaborating with the Mōri, he implemented Nobunaga's disrupted conquest of Shikoku, and within weeks of its launching sent other armies into Hokuriku to fill the vacuum left by Shibata's destruction and to project his own influence farther up the coast.

Meanwhile the Shimazu of southern Kyushu had launched offensive operations designed to give themselves control of the island, thereby raising again the hoary threat of Kyushu secessionism. Lest they become overly strong, Hideyoshi invited their submission, and when they spurned him, he struck an alliance with those whom the Shimazu threatened. Early in 1587 he sailed to Kyushu with a huge army and within two months forced Shimazu's submission and withdrawal to a shrunken domain headquartered at Kagoshima near the island's southern extremity.

Once Hideyoshi had focused on Kyushu, he discovered other issues that demanded attention. Portuguese Jesuit missionaries had arrived in Kyushu some forty years earlier as one aspect of the Iberian elite's global pursuit of luxury goods and glory. As of 1587 they and their followers were still only a minor presence in the Kinai region, but they constituted a large and growing force in Kyushu. Pursuing their proselytizing activity aggressively, and creating tensions and enemies in the process, the missionaries claimed upwards of 200,000 converts, including a number of major daimyo and lesser warriors. Moreover they controlled a fortified Nagasaki as well as other settlements. Seeing in this situation an analogue to the Honganji operation that had troubled Nobunaga for so long, Hideyoshi affirmed Japan's combinative religious legacy, declaring that "Japan is the Land of the Gods," and asserting that the general populace was free to choose the faith it wished.[5] He seized Nagasaki, ordered the missionaries to leave Japan promptly, denounced converts for attacking shrines and temples, and implied that he would confiscate the lands of any lord who allowed such conduct or who forced retainers or residents of his domain to convert.

The missionaries must go, he said, but traders were welcome to stay. He tried to keep foreign trade separate from the missionary issue because, having established a solid presence in Kyushu, he wished to turn the commerce to advantage. He appears to have begun engaging in overseas trading ventures at this time, and in subsequent years he issued sailing permits to a number of merchants for trade at ports throughout east and southeast Asia. The trade, however, continued to be obstructed by piracy, so after pacifying Kyushu he ordered daimyo to investigate all seafarers in their domains and suppress all piratical activity – or face confiscation of their domains.

Shortly after ordering the Jesuits to depart, Hideyoshi returned to a triumphal reception and boisterous celebration in Kyoto. The questions of piracy and proselytizing that had loomed so large while he was in Kyushu receded, still unresolved, and other issues came to the fore, most notably that of the other breakaway region, the east. In the spring of 1588 he invited the Hōjō of Odawara to submit, but they demurred. Two years of fitful diplomacy failed, so in the spring of 1590 he and Ieyasu planted a huge army around Odawara Castle while an armada blockaded it by sea, and that summer the starving Hōjō capitulated. Odawara's fall strengthened Hideyoshi's hand in the east, but only through a combination of forceful diplomacy and helpful meddling in an inter-domain boundary dispute did he finally induce the vigorous, young Date Masamune of Sendai to accept his authority in the early days of 1591. And that summer a *kokujin* rebellion south of Sendai so alarmed Hideyoshi that he ordered his heir Hidetsugu, together with Ieyasu, to lead a coalition of major lords in its suppression.

By the autumn of 1591 the threat of Tōhoku secession was past, the region effectively subordinated to Kinai rulers for the first time in more than 250 years. Hideyoshi stood astride an orderly realm, its daimyo all subservient to his will. Like others, he had risen to power by using carrot and stick as circumstances dictated, but he balanced them somewhat differently than had his predecessor. Nobunaga, battling in the easily accessible and politically fragmented arena of central Japan, had felt compelled to simplify its unstable hodgepodge of jurisdictions by ousting recalcitrant claimants, absolutizing his authority in areas seized, placing his own vassals in charge of designated districts, and then moving them about as his domain grew and his strategic needs changed.

As the beneficiary of Nobunaga's labors, Hideyoshi was able to concentrate on Japan's outer zones, which were under the more stable and consolidated control of a few major, regional barons. He lacked vassal forces sufficient to conquer and displace them all and was, in any case, well aware that a powerful vassal was in essence an enemy awaiting the chance to act. So he preferred dividing to destroying. He found it expedient to reduce overly powerful rivals, such as Mōri and Shimazu, to manageable size, but to leave them in charge of shrunken domains – provided, of course, that they acknowledged his suzerainty and acted accordingly. He then used the acquired lands to enfeoff vassals and reward deserving allies. Consequently the realm he controlled in 1592 consisted of a large central region under the control of his own senior retainers (*fudai*), while most of the rest of the country was administered by erstwhile rival daimyo (*tozama*), each with his own headquarters, governing apparatus, army, and resource base.

Hideyoshi as governor.   Bargaining and battering daimyo into submission was only one aspect, albeit the most dramatic, of Hideyoshi's techniques for pacifying the realm. He also employed several other strategies. Like other lords of the day, he pursued measures to steer agricultural and commercial resources to his own use. He labored to embed the new ruling elite of Toyotomi daimyo in the legitimizing bosom of *kenmon* authority. In addition he took steps, commonly in response to circumstances of the moment, to demilitarize most of the populace while regulating those men who retained military functions, whether of the most menial or magisterial sort. These matters merit attention because they became basic elements in Japan's governance for the next three centuries.

One policy that contributed to all these outcomes was land surveying. Initially Hideyoshi, like Nobunaga, followed the existing practice, called *sashidashi*, of collecting documents on landholding and income and recording the data for his own use. In 1582 he ordered such a survey for the environs of Kyoto (Yamashiro Province), where courtiers and fanes – temples and shrines – still held many estates, and he used the resulting information when confirming and rearranging income rights as part of his effort to cultivate elite good will. Subsequently, as he extended his sway, he ordered daimyo to prepare land registers and inform him of the results. By the mid-1590s the registers for central Japan, the area he controlled most directly, were recording, at least partly on the basis of actual measurement, field size and putative crop yield (*kokudaka*). Thus an order of 1594 instructed his surveyors to

> measure wet and dry fields and residence [plots] using a rod of 6 *shaku* 3 *sun* [to equal 1 *ken*], and [calculating] the *tan* at 5 by 60 *ken* or 300 *bu*.[6]

Other clauses in his instructions to surveyors specified in terms of rice volume (*koku*) the putative yield ratios of "superior, medium, and inferior" fields and required use of the *kyō-masu*, a standard-sized measuring box, for determining the yield. The order called for assessment and registration not only of paddy and dry fields but also "mountain, wild, and riverbed fields," and, where appropriate, "sites damaged by drought or flood." To assure proper tax assessment and payment, the name of the liable landholder was recorded for each parcel, and surveyors were required to initial their work and villagers to retain copies of the document.

Some daimyo adopted Hideyoshi's survey method; others used their own, with varying degrees of completeness and reliance on *sashidashi* technique. On the whole, however, by the time of Hideyoshi's death, actual measurement was rapidly becoming normal and Japan's rulers were achieving an unprecedented level of knowledge and control over the realm's agricultural production.

Rulers used their cadastral information for several purposes, most obviously to steer tax yields into their warehouses. But in addition it enabled them to allocate resources at rates of their own choosing, as when Hideyoshi awarded specified amounts of taxable production to medieval *kenmon* survivors, lesser fanes, collaborating daimyo, or others. Because he required daimyo to report their survey results to him, the cadastres helped him know the size of daimyo resource bases and hence their general military potential, whether as menace or deployable force. In listing land-tax payers by name, moreover, the surveys also helped identify people as cultivators, placing them in a category distinguishable from warriors, thereby limiting the social consequences of the emergent mass armies.

The agricultural production that land surveys identified remained Hideyoshi's primary fiscal base, but he also developed commercial income. He moved farther than Nobunaga in abolishing residual *kenmon* transit and guild taxes so as to spur merchant activity in the areas he controlled, notably Kyoto. He placed major bullion mines under direct control, and he took modest steps to enlarge the coin supply and bring order to a chaotic coinage by minting copper, silver, and gold coins of reasonably standard weight and fineness. In addition, he engaged in overseas trade, as noted above, and imposed on daimyo onerous levies for goods and services.

An important function of Hideyoshi's wealth was to buy courtly good will, that being one facet of his full-throttle quest for aristocratic acceptance and social legitimation. Utterly lacking in ancestral credentials, and a latecomer to the arts who compensated by going to excess, he honored the court and its associates with fulsome expressions of esteem and prudent awards of land, gifts, and material rehabilitation. The rehabilitation was necessary because well into the 1580s or later court penury was everywhere evident, even in the palace itself. According to the Jesuit interpreter João Rodrigues:

> The palaces of the king and *kuge* were miserable structures of old pine wood ... The exterior appearance of the *kuge* was extremely miserable and poor. The old walls surrounding the royal palace were ... in complete disrepair and utterly deserted. Anyone who so wished could enter the courtyard right up to the royal palace without anybody stopping him.[7]

Besides refurbishing the emperor's palace, Hideyoshi rebuilt mansions, temples, and shrines. He also treated court and courtiers to splendid entertainments. Like Nobunaga he presented himself as spokesman, ruler, even embodiment of the *tenka* or realm. But more than his predecessor he explicitly linked the realm's well-being to the virtue of the imperial throne, insisting, for example, that he punished lords such as Shimazu because they were guilty of disregarding the imperial will, not his own.

Hideyoshi also massaged his genealogy to upgrade his ancestry, and he accepted fine titles for himself, his relatives, and his daimyo. In the process he rose through the ritual court positions that had long been customary for senior *bushi*, and in 1585, while preparing to subdue Shikoku, he acquired the title of *kanpaku*, the first *bushi* to occupy that once-mighty Fujiwara regency. One of his aides tried to make the appointment less offensive to the high-born by explaining how Hideyoshi came to originate in the obscurity of Owari despite his unacknowledged imperial paternity. "Indeed, if he were not of royal blood, how then could he have attained such greatness!"[8]

Hideyoshi's wish to anchor his regime in the imperial legacy was also revealed in his construction work. He built his several headquarters with an appreciation for grand historical precedents: his Osaka Castle was situated at the former Naniwa, where Shōmu and several other early emperors had maintained palaces; his palatial Jurakutei residence was erected on the site of the original Heian imperial palace; Fushimi Castle was located at Kanmu's burial site. Like others, he decorated his decrees with references to Chinese precedents. And in early 1591, perhaps to make Kyoto resemble a Chinese imperial city – or perhaps simply to make palatable the removal of several, smaller, *sengoku*-era urban fortifications – he had a moated, ten-gated, twenty-two kilometer earthern rampart, the *odoi*, thrown up around the city.

While laboring to ensconce himself in the highest echelon of society, Hideyoshi also worked to control the military capability of society as a whole. His attempt to demilitarize the general population had several facets. Within Kyoto the relocation of temples to peripheral areas, the destruction of the numerous moats and earthen walls that had protected neighborhoods, and their replacement with the city-girdling *odoi* reunited Kamigyō and Shimogyō and facilitated his control of a resurgent imperial capital. In the hinterland he continued Nobunaga's policy of ordering fortresses torn down, which undercut the defensive capacity of many provincial warriors. And in what may be his most celebrated edict, during the summer of 1588, while he was inviting the Hōjō to submit and pushing ahead with construction plans to glorify Kyoto and himself, he decreed that

> farmers of the various provinces are strictly forbidden to possess long swords, short swords, bows, spears, muskets, or any other form of weapon.

Lords and vassals are to collect such weapons, he declared, and forward them to Kyoto. And there, to assure that the weapons not be wasted,

> they shall be [melted down and] used as rivets and clamps in the forthcoming construction of the Great Buddha. This will be an act by which the farmers will be saved in this life, needless to say, and in the life to come.

He averred that the order would be, "the foundation of the safety of the country and the happiness of all people." And while it was admittedly an unprecedented act in Japan, in China the legendary ruler Yao "pacified the realm and [then] used precious swords and sharp blades as farming tools."[9] An afterword directed to officials, however, observed that while the swords are to be collected "for the ostensible purpose" of building the Buddha image, "truthfully, this is a measure specifically adopted to prevent occurrence of peasant uprisings (*ikki*)."[10] From this shrewdly calculated measure would arise a grand new Buddha image for the Hōkōji, a central temple emblematic of the newly reconstituted realm, evidence that Hideyoshi's governance was on a par with even that of Shōmu, creator of Tōdaiji's Rushana Buddha.

Three years later, while his heir Hidetsugu and ally Ieyasu were leading Tōhoku daimyo in the suppression of rebellious samurai, Hideyoshi furthered demilitarization by trying to isolate defeated and dissident warriors from the general populace. He decreed that villages and neighborhoods were not to give shelter to any fighting man who sought to settle there as farmer or townsman and that no one was to employ a fighting man who had left his lord without approval. Also, to prevent farmers from leaving their villages – which would tempt those who remained to let newcomers cultivate the idle land and meet its tax obligation – Hideyoshi also forbade any farmer to leave his fields in pursuit of trade or wage labor. The punishment for negligence in these matters was to be severe.

His interest in distinguishing fighting from non-fighting men and in keeping agriculturalists settled productively was reflected in another decree that appeared a few months later. At the time he was preparing to invade China by way of Korea, and he needed to know what manpower resources would be available. So he ordered a census of the realm, instructing daimyo

> to register, by village, the number of houses and the number of persons – men and women, old and young.

He added that they should register, "the military men as military men, the farmers as farmers, and the townsmen as townsmen."[11]

By recording who lived where, identifying who worked which land, and requiring that all except registered warriors surrender their arms, the implementation of these several decrees went far toward demilitarizing the general populace. Hideyoshi also took steps to control those who still carried arms. At lower levels, he promoted distinctions between men of full samurai status and ordinary foot solders. He separated them by rank, stipend, and weaponry. Sumptuary regulations also distinguished them from one another in residence facilities, ceremonial privileges, dress, food, hair style, and other amenities.

At the daimyo level, his knowledge and control of landed income was a key managerial device. He also placed great demands on the lords, most notably military levies (*gun'yaku*) but also requisitions of men and matériel for his monumental construction projects. These demands repeatedly tested daimyo reliability even while turning their wealth and power to his own advantage. At critical junctures he required lords to send family hostages to his headquarters and swear oaths of loyalty to his cause on pain of godly punishment. He also required that they themselves pay visits to his headquarters and share in his public life. Those who served him well he showered with tokens of esteem and rewards of substance, but for those who failed him there was loss of status, income, or life.

Hideyoshi in decline. By 1592 Hideyoshi and his collaborators had combined war, diplomacy, and administrative enforcement to create an orderly realm.

He had powerful reason for wanting it to remain orderly because his attention was beginning to focus on a project that would strip away much of his military support and leave him vulnerable to troublemakers, should they choose to act. This project was his grand plan to conquer the known world, the first and worst of the miscues that were to sour his final years. What inspired the scheme is unknown, whether tales from *Kojiki* or *Nihon shoki*, late Heian stories of Japanese heroes romping through China, legends of the Mongol conquest, reports of current unrest in Manchuria, the fact of Iberians come from afar, or simply ambition seeking yet another outlet. The heart of the matter, however, may be just as he assured the Korean king, Yi Sŏnjo, in 1590: "My wish is nothing other than that my name be known throughout the three countries [of Japan, China, and India]."[12]

As early as 1587, after reporting to his wife the happy news of Shimazu's submission, he had added:

I have sent fast ships in order to urge even Korea to pay homage to the Emperor of Japan, stating that, if it does not, I shall conquer it next year. I shall take even China in hand, and have control of it during my lifetime; since [China] has become disdainful [of Japan], the work will be the more exhausting.[13]

Domestic tasks stayed his hand for the nonce, but late in 1590, while negotiating some pirate problems with the Yi court, he explained that he intended to "enter" China

to spread the customs of our country to the four hundred and more provinces of that nation, and to establish there the government of our imperial city even unto all the ages.[14]

Because the Yi were in contact with him, he added, "you need have no anxiety." In fact, however, Sŏnjo had ample reason for anxiety because with China just across the Yalu River he clearly could not grant Hideyoshi's armies safe passage.

A year later, after Tōhoku had again become quiet, Hideyoshi ordered his generals to ready their forces for conquest of the uncooperative Yi. And he began his own preparations, erecting a major forward command post on a Kyushu promontory that jutted out toward Korea. The following summer he launched his cross-channel operation, but within months his army's initial successes gave way to stalemate. Korean guerrilla resistance stiffened in the face of ferocious samurai savagery. Cannon-equipped, armor-plated ships under the command of Yi Sun-sin gradually stymied his resupply efforts. And finally a reinforced Chinese army drove the invaders back southward. These reverses of 1593 produced an armistice and set in motion long drawn out Sino-Japanese negotiations that ultimately collapsed in acrimony in 1596, leading an angrily frustrated Hideyoshi to renew the warfare, to no advantage, the following spring.

Even as the armies of his daimyo pursued their bloody venture in southern Korea, Hideyoshi pressed on with domestic matters, including tighter cadastral surveys, construction projects, entertainments, and rewards and punishments. And late in 1596 he dealt with a messy dispute involving recently arrived Franciscan missionaries from Spain by ordering six of them executed, along with twenty converts. As with the Jesuits nine years earlier, however, he then let the matter rest, hoping, perhaps, that the "lesson" would suffice, and permitting Iberian traders and missionaries to continue their operations.

By then, however, his situation was clearly deteriorating. His enthusiasm for the China venture was long gone; his health was declining. Even nature seemed bent on humbling him when a powerful earthquake destroyed his great Hōkōji and wrecked Fushimi Castle. Worst of all, the prospects for a stable Toyotomi succession, never good, grew faint.

Regarding the succession, Hideyoshi proved not very fecund, one of the greatest failings a dynast must fear. His beloved consort Yodogimi bore a son, his presumably, in 1589, but the child died two years later. So despite misgivings he adopted and named as heir his mature, battle-tested, but reputedly vicious nephew Hidetsugu. In 1593, while Hideyoshi was directing continental operations from his base in Kyushu, Yodogimi delivered another son, which prompted the delighted dynast to return permanently to Kyoto. Not too surprisingly, Hidetsugu, who had children of his own, was unable to agree with Hideyoshi on how to fit the infant Hideyori into the Toyotomi future. In the late summer of 1595, even as the expeditionary force in Korea was rotting from inaction and internal discord, Hideyoshi cut the Gordian knot of succession by ordering his nephew to commit suicide, slaughtering his retainers, women, and children, and eradicating all traces of the glorious Jurakutei, where Hidetsugu had lived. The two-year-old Hideyori then became heir.

Recognizing that years must pass before the child could actually control affairs, within a month of Hidetsugu's death Hideyoshi tried to prepare for his own demise by drawing his most powerful allies together as a senior advisory council for the Toyotomi regime. In addition he placed a group of lesser retainers who had long served him as administrators in more regular charge of routine affairs of his domain. Unsurprisingly, however, when Hideyoshi did die three years later, last-minute oaths of loyalty carried little weight and the lords collaborated only long enough to withdraw their bogged-down armies from Korea. Then, with their forces again intact and battle-tested troops available, they fell to quarreling, setting the stage for a new struggle to dominate.

It had taken Nobunaga twenty years to hammer rivals in central Japan into submission. Building on that foundation, Hideyoshi had skillfully employed armed conquest, intimidation, and cooptation to master the rest of the realm in less than ten. Besides extending his control outward over daimyo, moreover, he had consolidated it among the residual *kenmon* and projected it downward into the general population through rules and regulations about commerce, land holding, weapons possession, and rights of residence and employment. But whereas Nobunaga had died while his star was still rising and future triumphs seemed certain, Hideyoshi advanced from triumph to disarray. Most disastrously, he had, in effect, combined state power with the legacy of the *wakō* in an ill-fated attempt to extend his sway onto the continent and then had cruelly mismanaged an unhappy succession situation.

That his death was followed by renewed struggle for supremacy is not surprising. What is surprising is that in the autumn of 1600 the issue of supremacy was settled clearly and permanently after only one major battle-field confrontation, at Sekigahara northeast of Kyoto, and several ancillary skirmishes elsewhere around the country. Tokugawa Ieyasu and his support-ers emerged from that episode as victors and inheritors of the Toyotomi political order. At the time, of course, no one knew that the settlement was permanent, and years of military preparation and watchful waiting ensued, but as things turned out, daimyo forces did not battle one another again until the 1860s.

ROUTINIZING THE REALM: THE TOKUGAWA

As the founder of a long-lived regime, Ieyasu's reputation has been bur-nished by generations of glorifiers. Clearly he was a skillful politician who enjoyed uncommonly good fortune and exploited advantages with excep-tional success. His main achievements, however, can be reduced to two, one purposeful, the other derivative. First, he kept order and continued the basic thrust of Hideyoshi's administrative and political policies long enough to pass on to his mature and prudent son Hidetada a realm that was partially habituated to the rhythms of peace and dominated by elite *bushi* and their emerging "early modern" (*kinsei*) political order, the *bakuhan taisei*. Second, he headquartered his regime at Edo, his castle town since the Hōjō defeat in 1590, rather than at Kyoto, and that choice had the eventual effect of shift-ing the center of Japanese society from Kinai to the Kantō region.

Even in those matters, however, it is not easy to distinguish Ieyasu's achievements from those of his successors, notably Hidetada and the third shogun, Iemitsu. In particular, Iemitsu did much of the administrative regu-larizing that gave the *bakuhan* regime durability. And the shift in geographi-cal center was more a result of Hidetada's caution than Ieyasu's intent. Moreover, the shift became permanent only because the Tokugawa managed to perpetuate their rule for so long.

Domestic political process. After winning at Sekigahara in 1600, Ieyasu used his superiority to extend his domain westward from the Kantō, establishing control over central Japan and coercing and cajoling daimyo into accepting his suzerainty. In following months and years he elaborated regulations to clarify the relationship between himself, fellow daimyo, the courtly and reli-gious elite, and other social groups. He pursued Hideyoshi-like policies to promote land surveying, commercial expansion, mining, and other forms of resource exploitation. And he enjoyed exceptional success where Hideyoshi had faltered most hurtfully, siring sixteen children, most of whom lived long enough to serve as reserve heirs, founders of cadet families, and candidates for marriage and adoption into other households of consequence.

Regarding the Toyotomi lineage itself, Ieyasu labored for years to habitu-ate young Hideyori to a subordinate place in the Tokugawa firmament as a daimyo ensconced at his father's great Osaka Castle. In 1615, however, after vast numbers of *rōnin* (masterless samurai) flocked to the castle in hopes of redoing the settlement of 1600, Ieyasu reluctantly but ruthlessly used force to destroy Hideyori and the Toyotomi legacy and to eradicate the *rōnin*. That sanguinary outcome deprived would-be challengers of a convenient rallying symbol and consolidated Tokugawa control of the Kinai region.

Ieyasu pursued these various policies, however, without actually settling the issue of a political center for his regime. Instead he traveled the Tōkaidō, dividing his time between Kyoto and Edo, both of which appealed to him. At Kyoto, where he governed from Hideyoshi's rebuilt Fushimi Castle, he could oversee the court, supervise Hideyori, and maintain his role as benevolent guarantor of the social and cultural legacy represented by the old elite. On the other hand, the Tokugawa domain was still centered in the Kantō and Edo; and the Kamakura legacy of Minamoto no Yoritomo, which seems to have been Ieyasu's model for governing, was situated in the east. So he dithered. For several years he commuted regularly between Fushimi and Edo, both before and after taking the shogunal title in 1603. And in 1607, two years after retiring in favor of Hidetada, he straddled the issue by settling at his great new Sunpu Castle, located midway between the two.

After Ieyasu's death in 1616, Hidetada stayed at Edo, whose castle and urban facilities he kept expanding. The daimyo, who previously had paid irregular, semi-hostage visits to Ieyasu at Fushimi, Sunpu, or Edo as seemed most advantageous, established visitation mansions in Edo. By the 1620s the city and its bakufu had become Japan's *de facto* political center, which enabled Hidetada to tear down Fushimi Castle, leaving the small Nijō Castle as the main symbol of bakufu presence in Kyoto, a latter-day analogue of Rokuhara. During the 1630s his heir and successor, Iemitsu, further consolidated Edo's position by regularizing daimyo visitation arrangements in the *sankin kōtai* system of "alternate attendance." As formalized then, most daimyo were required to spend alternate years in Edo, during which time they made some three or four ritual appearances before the shogun. They moved to and from their castle towns on set schedules and with retinues of vassals whose number and equipment were proportional to the official *kokudaka* of the lord's domain. Daimyo wives and heirs, meanwhile, lived in Edo as comfortable but permanent hostages in their properly staffed and appropriately spacious mansions.

With those changes, Edo acquired a huge and stable population of samurai consumers whose tax income enabled the city to support a large and diversified provisioning population of commoners. Their activities in turn extended the city's growth for another century or more. In the outcome those trends transformed a regional castle town into the world's largest city with over a million inhabitants and a dominant role in Japan's economic, social, and cultural development.

The *sankin kōtai* arrangements that underlay Edo's rise were but one facet of the bakufu's broader strategy for managing daimyo. Although early Tokugawa leaders recognized the advantages of leaving daimyo strong enough to keep order in their own domains, they also saw the need for keeping them under control. To that end they developed regulations and investigatory organs to guide and oversee daimyo conduct. They also required lords to assist in Tokugawa castle, city, and ceremonial construction. They moved them about, rewarding and punishing as seemed meet, mainly by awarding and expropriating arable land. They ranked and categorized the daimyo with care, using the standard categories of vassal (*fudai*) and outside (*tozama*) lord, and creating in addition a number of Tokugawa collateral (*shinpan*) daimyo with substantial domains of their own. The most powerful of these collaterals were placed at strategically important sites, notably in districts around Kyoto that had been particularly subject to Shinshū unrest: Owari (Nagoya), Kii (Wakayama), and Echizen (Fukui). To secure that region yet further, Ieyasu placed his most powerful *fudai* lord at Hikone in Ōmi, where he erected a major castle to dominate the area much as nearby Azuchi had once done for Nobunaga.

Foreign relations. Besides ordering domestic affairs, early Tokugawa leaders moved to control foreign relations, and there, too, Ieyasu followed Hideyoshi's lead – except in the project of conquering China. Most importantly, he repaired Korean–Japanese relations by accepting the agile mediation of the lord of Tsushima, who managed to restore the cross-channel trade that sustained his domain's fisc. Thereafter the governments in Edo and Seoul maintained a formal diplomatic relationship whose official nature was purposefully left ambiguous, enabling both regimes to view it favorably, which permitted intermediary merchants and officials to carry on the trade that was the settlement's chief *raison d'être*.

Ieyasu's dealings with the Kingdom of the Ryukyus proved less benign. To backtrack briefly, Ryukyu islanders had exchanged goods with Kyushu, Taiwan, and mainland Asia since prehistoric times, and, as noted in chapter 4, delegates from the northern Ryukyus made "tribute" visits to Kinai headquarters of the early *ritsuryō* regime. In subsequent centuries Ryukyuan maritime trade deepened, especially with Sung China, and during the late twelfth century the political disorder that marked the decline of Sung and the collapse of Heian rippled through the islands. Regional hegemons arose, battled for advantage, and pursued trade. In 1372, after Ming armies had ousted the Mongols from China, the Ming awarded official tributary status to the strongest of these Ryukyuan regimes, much as they did to Ashikaga Yoshimitsu a few years later.

By 1429 this Ryukyuan Kingdom, headquartered in Shuri Castle at Naha on Okinawa, had consolidated its control over much of the island chain, maintaining trading relationships and a vague northern boundary with the Shimazu family, which dominated southern Kyushu and extended its influence into the northernmost Ryukyus. During the next two centuries Ryukyuan Kings oversaw a lively commerce in which a combination of private traders and official tribute missions sustained the monarchy and its headquarters town and trading-port population, in the process making Okinawa a major entrepôt for trade all along the Asian littoral. By the late 1500s, however, *wakō* piracy, Ming decline, Portuguese trading activity, and Hideyoshi's Korean ventures were severely disrupting Ryukyuan commerce.

After 1600, even as the newly triumphant Ieyasu worked to consolidate Tokugawa hegemony at home, he moved to rebuild trading contacts all across the board. Whereas Hideyoshi had thwarted the Shimazu family's expansionist ambitions in Kyushu during the 1580s, in 1609 Ieyasu accepted their lightning conquest of the Ryukyus and seizure of Shuri Castle, probably seeing it as a means to revive trade to and via Okinawa as well as a way to place the Shimazu in his debt at no cost to himself. How heavily Shimazu's yoke rested on the shoulders of Ryukyuan commoners is unclear, but for the remainder of the Edo period successive Ryukyuan rulers occupied an unwelcome but ambiguous position, subordinate to the Shimazu of Satsuma and quasi-vassal of the Tokugawa even while they maintained tributary status *vis-à-vis* the Ming and later the Ch'ing. Under these political arrangements Okinawa resumed its role as entrepôt in the region's commercial life.

On the matter of Europeans, Ieyasu, like Hideyoshi, dithered. He wanted to continue trading, but he was troubled by occasional political complications and wished to discourage Iberian missionary activity. In the end he settled for sporadic, half-hearted measures of repression.

To elaborate that last point, by the autumn of 1613, both Dutch and English merchants had trading posts in Japan, and they provided Ieyasu with alternative connections to Southeast Asia and beyond. By then, too, a cluster of domestic issues was roiling the political waters, and when rumors of sedition among Ieyasu's key vassals linked the suspects to a recent and very messy scandal involving some Christian converts and members of his own household, Ieyasu resolved to end the Iberian presence in Japan and limit his European dealings to the Dutch and English. Like Hideyoshi in 1596, he proscribed Christianity and ordered missionaries expelled and churches demolished, doing so on the several grounds, as an advisor put it, that the Iberians had come to Japan not simply to trade,

> but also hoping to spread their evil doctrine without permission, to confound true religion, change the political order of the realm, and make it their own.[15]

As with Hideyoshi, however, other problems soon distracted Ieyasu and at his death the issue was still unresolved, enabling Iberian traders and missionaries to continue their work.

In this matter, as in so many others, Hidetada tried to sustain his father's policy. During the 1620s he enforced the 1613 proscription with sufficient energy that by 1630 most missionaries had departed. Most churches were torn down, and most converts were forced to recant or had been exiled from their home villages. Perhaps four to five thousand were executed, martyrs to their faith. A minor tragedy by industrial-age standards, it was the most horrific pogrom in Japanese history.

During the 1630s Iemitsu found himself facing a tangle of foreign complications that involved unruly European, Japanese, and other Asian traders as well as a burgeoning Manchu assault on Korea and Ming China. To manage these problems, he forbade Japanese to go abroad, tightened restrictions on Portuguese in Japan, and legislated firmer control of trade procedures and missionary activity. Then in 1637 crop failure, famine, and local political abuse precipitated a major rebellion on Shimabara Peninsula in Kyushu. The assemblage of 25,000 commoner and *rōnin* insurgents employed Christian religious banners and rhetoric to sustain themselves, much as Shinshū and Hokke adherents had used their religious devices a century earlier, and for a time they badly embarrassed the ineffectual government forces sent to crush them. In retaliation Iemitsu ordered all remaining Iberian connections severed and all surviving Christian communities suppressed.

By 1640 the Iberians were gone and domestic Christianity was driven underground. The English, unable to turn a profit, had departed some years earlier, so Dutch traders housed on Dejima Islet in Nagasaki harbor were the sole surviving European connection. Foreign trade continued to flourish, however, not only through the Dutch, but with Korea via Tsushima and with China via the Ryukyus, Nagasaki, and other Kyushu ports. That trade was sustained through the turmoil of the 1680s when the Manchus completed their conquest of China, not declining substantially until the eighteenth century.

Finally, on the northern frontier was the least visible, probably least consequential of the Tokugawa external trade frontiers. To backtrack briefly again, the disorder that had characterized fifteenth-century Kantō and Tōhoku had spilled across the porous ethnic border between Japanese and Emishi, the latter increasingly referred to as Ainu. For decades Ainu leaders were able to repel the intruders, but during the sixteenth century successive generations of a branch family of the Takeda warrior house built ties to the local populace, took the name Kakizaki, and ensconced themselves in a small bastion near the southern end of Oshima Peninsula on today's Hokkaido. From there they gradually extended their control and tribute demands to cover Ainu in adjacent regions. During the late 1580s, the second-generation lord, Kakizaki Yoshihiro, accepted Hideyoshi's suzerainty, and in 1599 he changed his name to Matsumae and aligned with Ieyasu. In return for those judicious moves he was awarded authority over the marine-products trade and other fiscal resources of an ill-defined northerly realm identified as Ezo.

During Iemitsu's reign the Matsumae territory on Oshima, later known as Wajinchi or "the Japanese area," was more clearly delineated, and processes of local exploitation, abuse, and decimation by disease gradually cleared it of resident Ainu. The rest of Hokkaido and adjacent areas of Sakhalin and the Kurils remained thinly settled by the multiplicity of small Ainu communities, but there too the introduction of smallpox and other epidemic diseases devastated villages, starting a demographic slide that reduced the Ainu population from an estimated 40,000 or more to some 15,000 by the mid-nineteenth century. The Ainu decline was exacerbated by their loss of economic autonomy to the lord of Matsumae, who licensed his retainers (and subsequently select merchants from Ōmi and Osaka) to trade all along the Hokkaido coastline, treating that commerce in the Sinocentric manner as a tribute–gift exchange between civilized and barbarian peoples.

Unsurprisingly the Ainu resented Matsumae's tribute levies and his restrictions on their own trading activity, which grew more onerous as decades passed. Cross-cutting tensions between traders, Wajin settlers, and local

Ainu groups led to a series of clashes, and by the 1660s an Ainu leader, Shakushain, had emerged as the dominant figure among Ainu in the Hidaka region east of Oshima Peninsula. In 1669 he led an armed rebellion, and three years passed before the badly shaken Matsumae leaders were able to crush the insurrection and reassert control over their maritime domain. They did prevail, however, and much as Satsuma's conquest of the Okinawan kingdom projected Japanese control southward along the Ryukyus, Matsumae armed force thus extended it into the unexplored reaches beyond Oshima Peninsula, establishing trade arrangements that would grow and change for the rest of the Edo period.

Ideology of rule. During these decades when the new rulers were working out domestic and foreign relationships, there also emerged a complex, semi-rationalized, largely Confucian ideology of rule that served to justify Tokugawa dominance and, more broadly, hereditary *bushi* privilege. This dogma was the cumulative creation of scholars, not the work of the early shogun themselves, who were far more managerial than ideological in orientation. Thus, Ieyasu's main desires, in terms of legitimation, seem to have been to establish his credentials, however dubious, as a descendant of the Seiwa Genji, to accumulate the titles appropriate to a shogun, and to pass them on to Hidetada. In addition, he ordered publication of celebrated historical and learned treatises, both Chinese and Japanese, doing so presumably to guide the conduct of people of consequence and also, one suspects, to demonstrate his own virtue as ruler. Otherwise, he concentrated on practicalities: maintaining his network of personal alliances with major lords, sustaining his military capacity, checkmating rivals, and resolving issues as they arose.

Hidetada and Iemitsu lacked Ieyasu's collegial connections to other barons and relied more heavily on routine, and, in Iemitsu's case, on intimidation and discipline. Iemitsu also invested much effort in glorifying his grandfather and sacralizing the regime, most famously by constructing the grand Tōshōgū memorial shrine at Nikkō, in the hills north of Edo. It was not until Tsunayoshi, the fifth shogun (r. 1680–1709), that one finds a dedicated ideologue who aspired to rule as a true Confucian monarch. By then, however, intellectuals had already delineated that monarchical ideal, and Tsunayoshi was more its product than its promoter.

It was these intellectuals, the scholarly associates of shogun and other *bushi* leaders, who applied themselves to the task of legitimizing the new order at a more theoretical level. Besides fleshing out a presentable genealogy for the Tokugawa, they employed the legacy of *honji suijaku* thought to declare Ieyasu a manifestation of Buddhist and Shintō deities. Their greatest contribution to the new order, however, was their unprecedented appropriation of Confucian thought to legitimize the social structure as a whole. Two examples must suffice.

Hayashi Razan, a lapsed Zen monk, Confucian pedagogue, and sometime scholar/scribe for the Tokugawa, justified *bushi* rule this way:

> Heaven is above and earth is below ... in everything there is an order separating those who are above and those who are below ... [and] we cannot allow

disorder in the relations between the ruler and the subject...The separation into four classes of samurai, farmers, artisans and merchants...is part of the principles of heaven and is the Way which was taught by the Sage (Confucius).[16]

Yamaga Sokō, a samurai scholar whose writings were seminal to what became identified as *bushidō*, "the Way of the Warrior," explained that the farmer, artisan, or merchant was too busy at his occupation to master the Way. The samurai, on the other hand,

> is one who does not cultivate, does not manufacture, and does not engage in trade, but it cannot be that he has no function at all as a samurai...The business of the samurai consists in reflecting on his own station in life, in discharging loyal service to his master...and, with due consideration of his own position, in devoting himself to duty above all...[He] confines himself to practicing this Way...[and] upholds proper moral principles in the land [by punishing any who transgress against them].[17]

Bushi thus were to rule, to rule rightly, and not to be questioned by others. And the existing political system was the structure through which their virtuous rule was to be exercised.

By the late seventeenth century generations of attentive governance had given Japan a level of institutional integration and ideologically legitimized political order that surpassed anything in its history. It was an order as well fitted to its intensive agricultural base as the *ritsuryō* order had been to its foundation of dispersed agriculturalists. And the principal beneficiaries of this settlement, the high-ranking *bushi* and their closest collaborators, whether located in Kyoto, Edo, or any of a hundred other castle towns, enjoyed a level of comfort that earlier generations of rulers had rarely equalled.

THE BAKUHAN *SYSTEM AT 1700*

The century and a half to 1700, as preceding pages have shown, was an era of striking political change. Much as the political process to about 750 CE yielded the stabilized *ritsuryō* political order that we were able to describe in static terms in chapter 4, this period of post-*sengoku* reconsolidation gave Japan its second era of sustained political stability. The boundaries of the realm and the basic lineaments of the *bakuhan* polity can be described quite concisely. However, the broader society, which was both more visible and more complex than that of the *ritsuryō* order, invites fuller scrutiny.

BOUNDARIES

By the 1680s Japan's leaders had defined more clearly than ever before the realm's outer boundaries of area, associations, and ideas. In areal terms Japan proper was bounded by the sea, of course, but at its southern extremity the Ryukuan Kingdom stood in the awkwardly defined subordinate status noted above. And in the far north the daimyo of Matsumae held authority over an ill-defined Ezo, which as a practical matter meant essentially the Oshima Peninsula and trading posts scattered along the coast of Hokkaido.

Tokugawa leaders had clarified their foreign associations in a series of discrete actions that peaked in the 1630s but continued into the 1680s. In the outcome they maintained diplomatic relations with Korea, Holland, and the Ryukyus, but not with China, other European states, or the Ainu of Ezo. And they forbade Japanese to go abroad. Regarding trade, they established that Satsuma had authority to trade with China through the Ryukyus, that Tsushima would handle Japan's trade with Korea, and that Matsumae would control all trade with the people of Ezo. In Nagasaki some 2,000 Chinese in their walled compound and a handful of Dutchmen on nearby Dejima Islet were allowed to continue trading under the supervision of local bakufu officials at the magistrate's office (*bugyōsho*). The monetary value of this foreign trade was officially fixed, but in fact the Ezo trade lay beyond bakufu purview while that in the Ryukyus and Tsushima was only partially controlled. And elsewhere along the coast illicit trade occurred from time to time. Finally, inessential fraternizing with foreigners was discouraged, particularly in Nagasaki where officials of the *bugyōsho* oversaw the city and its residents.

In part this policy on fraternizing related to the regulation of trade, but in greater part it related to the control of ideas. The military men who had restored political order were eclectic and use-oriented in their doctrinal preferences. Reflecting the religious heritage of earlier centuries, they generally accepted the established amalgam of Shintō, Buddhism, and other continental thought and frowned on dogmatists who insisted on the unique correctness of their own views. And they utterly distrusted such dogmatists when they seemed to pose a political threat, whether due to daimyo support, popular favor, or foreign association.

This attitude had been most harshly evidenced in the crushing of Shinshū political activists during the years of Nobunaga and Hideyoshi, but Hokke followers also were forced into submission. After the 1580s, however, only occasional measures were taken to suppress homegrown dogmas, notably the Fujufuse subsect of Hokke. The main focus of the rulers' doctrinal concern became the Christianity introduced by Iberian missionaries. Linked from the beginning to Iberian state power, weapons imports, and daimyo politics, and in its popular aspect reminiscent of Shinshū communalism and Fujufuse dogmatism, Christian missionary activity provoked the slowly escalated retaliation noted above. By 1670 the last visible remnants of the creed had disappeared. Missionaries stayed away thereafter, and indigenous Kirishitan practice survived as a secret faith found only in small, poor, isolated communities, mostly in southwest Kyushu.

With exclusivistic doctrine tabooed, what remained within the boundaries of acceptable thought was the combinative legacy that had long been the mainstream of religious doctrine. Within those boundaries, however, a vibrant philosophical discourse developed that changed substantially the emphasis of thought. Among intellectuals, at least, the corpus of Confucian ideas rather than Buddhist dialectics became the grist of debate and the core philosophical ground for explaining social organization and process.

THE POLITY

Early Tokugawa shogun, as noted above, were very attentive to major daimyo, cultivating and coercing with care. They were so attentive because those lords and their lieutenants exercised nearly as much autonomy as they had under Hideyoshi. Daimyo retained their own armies, administrative organs, tax arrangements, rule-making authority, defensible headquarters, and defined domanial borders. As the seventeenth century advanced, however, daimyo modified more and more of their local arrangements to accord with shogunal practice, and by century's end they were well acclimated to the routines of stability. Together with the bakufu, they gave Japan an orderly system of control, the *bakuhan taisei*, which in its totality blanketed the realm with a shared political culture. Although lacking the elegantly centralized character of *ritsuryō* theory, the *bakuhan* system was in fact a more firmly consolidated political order than any in Japan's history.

At the heart of *bakuhan* political power, as of *ritsuryō* power, was control of the land and the producers who worked it. Whereas *ritsuryō* rulers had been able to maintain only a very slender pyramid of privilege on the basis of a tribute rate of roughly 6 percent, however, *bakuhan* leaders sustained a much larger and fatter pyramid thanks to overall population growth and the increased productivity of intensive agriculture, which allowed a skimming of perhaps 25–35 percent of the yield as tribute.

Most of the realm was controlled by daimyo, although the bakufu and its lesser vassals (*hatamoto* and *gokenin*) held a quarter of the whole. Other groups held small portions (see table 9.1, a calculation for around 1700). Celebrated fanes and the courtly few had not been forgotten, but they clearly survived only as token elements in a fiscal scene dominated by shogun, daimyo, and their major vassals.

By the 1690s there were some 240 daimyo in all, including about 105 *tozama*, 115 *fudai*, and 20 *shinpan*. Only a handful held large domains; most had minor holdings of 10,000 to 50,000 *koku* in estimated yield, numbers that correspond roughly to a domain's total population. Many of these minor

Table 9.1 Early modern land control

Category	Total *Kokudaka*
Tozama daimyo	9,834,700 *koku*
Fudai and *shinpan* daimyo	9,325,300 *koku*
Bakufu domain	4,213,171 *koku*
Hatamoto and *gokenin* lands	2,606,545 *koku*
Temple and shrine lands	316,230 *koku*
Imperial family lands	141,151 *koku*

Source: John Whitney Hall, *Government and Local Power in Japan* (Princeton: PUP, 1966), p. 343.

domains were branches of other daimyo houses, and a majority were too small even to maintain a castle. Of the ten largest domains, eight were held by *tozama* lords, including Maeda of Kaga with 1,022,700 *koku* and Shimazu of Satsuma with 729,000. The Mōri of Chōshū had 369,000 while the largest *shinpan* lord, headquartered in a great castle at Nagoya, had 619,000 *koku*. No *fudai* daimyo had a major domain; by far the greatest of their number was the Ii family at Hikone (350,000 *koku*) in charge of former Shinshū territory. Most *fudai* domains were very modest in size (well under 100,000 *koku* apiece) which helped assure that their lords, as the bakufu's senior officialdom, would not neglect bakufu interests *vis-à-vis* major lords, who, in the event of political disorder, would pose a danger to lesser neighbors.

Whereas major daimyo were richly landed, the courtly and religious elites retained very modest territories. And even those holdings were subject to bakufu oversight. In addition elaborate regulations governed the behavior of court, *kuge*, and prelates. Certain key rules discouraged daimyo from associating with the court and forbade the court to make any unilateral grants of rank or title to daimyo. In their entirety the rules sought to habituate courtiers and clerics to an orderly, culturally uplifting, and safely apolitical life in Kyoto or at their temples and shrines.

In the *bakuhan taisei* as a whole personnel policy limited government office to a lord's retainers, and office level was linked to a vassal's hereditary rank. Thus the shogun's senior vassals, the *fudai* daimyo, provided the bakufu's senior administrators. Lesser shogunal retainers, the *hatamoto* and *gokenin*, staffed lower offices and the plethora of minor attendant and guard posts. In daimyo domains, similarly, the few senior offices were reserved for vassals holding high hereditary ranks and stipends while the many middling and minor positions were held by retainers of commensurately lower standing. Much as bakufu rules guided daimyo and lesser shogunal retainers, moreover, so daimyo rules guided the lives of their retainers. And by 1700 these rules were highly articulated, defining proper housing, dress, and daily routine as well as weaponry and duties. In a sense the steeply hierarchical, hereditarily ranked, bureaucratic system of the *ritsuryō* order had been replicated a hundred times over.

The bakufu's structure of command exemplified the system. In it a group of four or five high-ranking shogunal retainers, the senior councillors (*rōjū*), who were moderately enfeoffed (30,000–100,000 *koku*) *fudai* daimyo in their own right, jointly controlled overall government operations while officials of *hatamoto* rank (under 10,000 *koku*) occupied most of the subordinate administrative posts. The staff at a central finance office (*kanjōsho*) oversaw district intendants (*daikan*) who managed the bakufu domain, mainly to ascertain that village headmen (commonly called *shōya*) and their subordinates kept the peace and forwarded tribute as stipulated by law. In Edo and other bakufu towns, city magistrates (*machi bugyō*) oversaw neighborhood chiefs who kept urban order and provided such services and special contributions as higher authority might demand. Other bakufu offices exercised oversight of temples and shrines, rivers, highways, ports, forests, mines, mints, warehouses, government construction and repair agencies, armories, fire-fighting organizations, and a host of lesser matters. Similar but proportionally smaller arrangements existed in daimyo domains, giving the realm as a whole a highly decentralized but generally standardized system of administration.

SOCIAL STRUCTURE

Within the boundaries and the political framework adumbrated above, Japan's reconsolidated social order took shape. Scholarly ideologues, such as Hayashi Razan and Yamazaki Ansai, drew on Confucian theory to characterize it as a hereditary four-status order consisting – in descending socio-ethical rank – of warrior-rulers, peasants, artisans, and merchants (*shinōkōshō*). The functions of the four, which are implicit in their labels, were seen as symbiotic, separate but mutually beneficial, presumably enabling the groups to form a larger, interdependent whole that would constitute a stable and virtuous society.

This view of society as an organic whole consisting of four parts was reflected in official rhetoric of the day, but in fact the *shinōkōshō* model represents very poorly the society that emerged from *sengoku*. It creates a misleading sense of hierarchical relationships, implies clear divisions where only vague ones existed, obscures economic disparities, and omits important segments of society. A different model, an elitist one that links Tokugawa society to the medieval model of *kenmon* and "others" – with the others constituting almost the entire population – may portray things somewhat more satisfactorily.

The Kinsei Elite. Like the medieval *kenmon* the seventeenth-century elite operated a government of "powerful houses" that constituted a coalition (to repeat earlier phrasing) "of the currently privileged: court, *kuge*, great fanes, and higher-status *bushi*," along with affiliated merchants and literati. Indeed, one could almost characterize them as *kinsei kenmon*. But there were important differences, too. Most obviously they were more securely settled than the Muromachi *kenmon*. And more importantly the new coalition reflected a further shifting of power within the elite: from the *kuge*-dominated *ritsuryō* order, to the uncomfortably balanced system of Kamakura dyarchy, thence via the Ashikaga order with warriors unstably in control, to the firmly entrenched ruling *bushi* elite of the Edo period.

The dominant segment of this realigned ruling elite, then, was high-status *bushi*, meaning the households of shogun, daimyo and their senior retainers. By the 1640s they were settled into routines in which daimyo and their families adhered to the rules of *sankin kōtai*, while senior retainers and their families lived in their lord's castle town or at Edo, as directed by the lord.

The surviving *kuge*, who had lived in and out of *sengoku* Kyoto as conditions permitted, had reassembled in the city by Ieyasu's heyday. There they were housed in a newly built, densely settled, walled compound (today's Kyoto *goen*) that also contained palaces for the emperor and his heir (today's *gosho* and *sentō gosho*). They abided, most of the time, by rules of conduct that originated in Edo and that were enforced by bakufu officials resident in Kyoto. The most powerful of these officials was the Kyoto magistrate (*shoshidai*), a senior bakufu official whose tasks were to assure the court's dutiful tranquillity and to address such problems as might arise. Rather similarly, prelates of the great old fanes, most notably the surviving shrine–temple complexes and the rebuilt Rinzai *gozan*, but also priests of Sōtō and the rehabilitated Shinshū and Hokke sects, were granted stipends of varying largesse and allowed to maintain their religious facilities and practices – as long as they did not run afoul of *bushi* law and its enforcers.

The members of this *kinsei* elite did their best to preserve their predecessors' cultural legacy: elegant buildings, landscaped gardens, courtly ritual, Kanō and Tosa-style art, poetry, *nō* drama, and tea ceremony. To do so, however, required wealth and expertise, and while tribute income enabled high-status *bushi* to afford experts and finery, the court and *kuge* had to cultivate patrons assiduously. As a consequence select merchants, most of whom lived in Kyoto and constituted successors to the Sakai–Shimogyō merchants with their *wabicha* taste, helped sustain elite culture by collaborating with the courtly few as patrons of esteemed painters, poets, scholars, and artisans. They thus found a place for themselves on the margin of high society.

The official others. Below these several thousand people was the general population. Most of its members fell within the *shinōkōshō* categories, but they can be examined more fruitfully in tripartite terms of warriors, townsmen, and villagers. That in fact is the way the ruling *bushi* perceived them, as indicated by the lines of governing authority they articulated. Warriors, being seen as a caste apart, were controlled by their lords through designated chains of command. Artisans and merchants, being perceived as townsmen, were overseen by neighborhood chiefs who answered to officials appointed by the lord of the castle town. Peasants, being defined as village dwellers, were supervised by village officials who were subject to regional overseers, appointees of the lord who in turn were subordinate to higher officials in his castle town. Separate chains of command thus linked rulers to their retainers, urban commoners, and rural folk.

Within this structure of control the most visible segment of this non-elite population was the two million or so members of lesser warrior families, whose household heads were formally identified as retainers of upper-class *bushi*. The shogun had some 17,000 retainers, and the 250-odd daimyo had scores of thousands, while senior vassals of daimyo and higher ranking *hatamoto* had scores of thousands more, to total some 400,000 samurai. Most of these retainers lived with their families in modest or even penurious homes in their lord's headquarters town, but a few resided in the hinterland, a few lived near their lord's visitation residence in Edo, and many stayed in barracks while accompanying their lords during alternate years in Edo.

All samurai held hereditary stipends and titles, and they performed functions that ranged from a few, well-paid, and important administrative jobs to an overwhelming majority of ill-paid, inconsequential, and routine tasks. These latter jobs were handled by men who eased the tedium of life by pursuing study, self-cultivation, and rowdyism and cushioned their poverty through by-employment as farmers, teachers, artisans, and petty tradesmen. Despite the variety in their circumstances, all were situated, not always firmly, in military chains of command controlled by high-ranking *bushi*. Their wives, busy operating a household and maintaining neighborhood life, cultivated select arts and, depending on personal taste, stole moments to enjoy the escapist literature and other entertainments that appeared in towns across the realm.

At the heart of the urban economy were merchants and artisans, almost all of whom lay outside the governing establishment. Initially a few merchants had enjoyed close ties to the political elite as official provisioners, but as the seventeenth century advanced, even those few were excluded from participation in privileged society. Instead merchants learned how to function in an entrepreneurial climate, and despite their formal standing at the bottom of ideology's socio-ethical hierarchy (the *shō* of *shinōkōshō*), as a group they in fact became the segment of society that controlled the greatest amount of discretionary wealth after senior *bushi* themselves. They remained subject to neighborhood and town officials where they resided, but commonly successful merchants were themselves the neighborhood officials, and those who had dealings with higher figures were able to bypass town authorities when doing so served their interests.

Also crucial to the economy, but much less successful at garnering household wealth, were artisans, skilled professionals who mostly lived in the major cities (Kyoto, Osaka, Edo) and castle towns. Although a few acquired weighty patrons, which enabled them to participate in elite culture, most stood far from the favored few. The commercial and craft guilds (*za*) that medieval artisans had earlier developed to manage marketing had been dissolved by the new rulers, and during the seventeenth century most artisans operated as independent professionals, producing and selling their own goods or working for merchants, clerics, daimyo, bakufu, or other employers as opportunity arose. They were subject to the same neighborhood officials and rules as were the merchants among whom they lived.

Finally, occupying the rest of the seventeenth-century realm, the villages of the hinterland, was the peasantry, the highly touted *nō* of the *shinōkōshō* order. A diverse group, they constituted roughly 80 percent of the entire population. Some were wealthy landholders, a few well schooled, while many more were illiterate but modestly secure, small-scale cultivators. Most villagers were poorly housed, being maintained as subordinate members of large households (*ie*) or as indentured farm laborers. They lived in villages overseen by *ie* heads, who served as village officials and linked the village to higher domain authorities, who were the collectors of taxes, organizers of corvée labor, and enforcers of the peace.

Most women were farm wives, mothers, and daughters, and most worked at the family business, running the household and assisting in crop production. Urban women, mostly members of merchant and artisan households, were similarly occupied with the family enterprise. Some were literate and read materials that came their way; most were not and filled their leisure moments with other activities, including prayer and other religious performance, neighborhood life, and participation in the numerous holiday routines of the year.

Regardless of a seventeenth-century person's status in the *shinōkōshō* categorization, the main determinant of "quality of life" was wealth. Well-to-do samurai, merchants, and village leaders lived comfortable lives indeed, with servants, schooling, leisure, and luxury possessions. Those in all categories who enjoyed middling incomes lived lives of modest comfort, while the poor, whether samurai, shopkeeper, craftsman, or villager, struggled to get by with wretched housing, poor nutrition, scraps of well-worn possessions, and chronic uncertainty about the future.

The miscellaneous others. Important groups also fell outside the *shinōkōshō* categories. One was the thousands of lesser clerics who staffed temples and shrines throughout the country. Most were married, and many were essentially villagers who sustained their families by tilling land, taking time to handle their religious tasks as needed. In their priestly roles they (initially those on bakufu lands and later those elsewhere as well) fell under the authority of the bakufu's superintendents of shrines and temples (*jisha bugyō*). The task of superintendents was to oversee the fanes, to assure their orderly operation and innocence of tabooed practice, and to resolve any serious problems that might involve them.

Vastly more numerous than minor clerics were shophands and household servants, many being young men and women, who worked in the homes and businesses of all who could afford them. They were an appreciable portion of the urban populace: in Edo, by one estimate, servants of samurai households alone constituted about 10 percent of the city population. The tasks of shophands and servants were diverse, and their conditions varied, depending on the wealth and personality of their employers. Authorities regarded them as primarily the responsibility of their employer, as this bakufu regulation of 1655 suggests:

> In suits between townsmen and their servants, those who submit complaints and go to trial do not understand the proprieties of the master and servant relationship. When the servant is at fault, he will be imprisoned. Furthermore the complaint is a matter to be entrusted to the master's discretion.[18]

In practice the rhythms of shophand and servant life commonly kept participants linked to both their natal and employer households. However, professional employment agencies arranged many placements and bore some responsibility for performance, particularly of employees who came into town from the countryside.

Another important group was day laborers. They constituted a significant portion of town populations, although they commonly were poor villagers who eked out a livelihood by working away from home (*dekasegi*), mostly hauling people and things or handling other manual tasks. They tended to live in dingy tenements in the shabby parts of town, as this comment on a seventeenth-century Osaka slum indicates:

> One does not see independent travellers there, but homeless beggars who have fallen into bankruptcy, or day laborers who leave the city daily [to work], or

porters and laborers who work in rice-polishing mills, sake breweries, and oil-squeezing shops.

Rulers preferred to regard laborers as temporarily relocated villagers who remained under the jurisdiction of their village elders. However, some workers stayed away from their villages for long periods, becoming enrolled in labor gangs controlled by bosses who arranged work for them, and the bakufu treated those bosses as the legally responsible figures, as in this edict of 1653:

> people working as day-laborers must receive a license from the day-laborers' chiefs. Anyone employing persons without such a license will be fined. This is a criminal offense.

Other day laborers came from the populations of hereditary pariahs (*eta* or *kawata*) and non-hereditary, punitive outcasts (*hinin*). Found mainly in the Kyoto vicinity or elsewhere in central Japan, these pariahs generally lived in their own communities, pursued their own professions, and were subject to their own leaders.

On the edge of this pariah population were the entertainers: singers, dancers, actors, story tellers, trick artists of various sorts, and denizens of the licensed quarters, such as Shimabara in Kyoto or Yoshiwara in Edo. These were bordello areas, the centers of a lively world of mainly heterosexual entertaiment, and they had their own organization and chain of command under city authorities. Prostitution was sanctioned only in these quarters – although an illicit skin trade persisted elsewhere – and there the business developed a social hierarchy and procedural decorum whose elaborateness reflected the practices of society at large. Bordello society differed from the world outside in one way, however: although most prostitutes were there from necessity and lived hard and ill-rewarded lives, a young woman of uncommon gifts could aspire to ascend the formal hierarchy of courtesans, enjoying within her profession a degree of formal social mobility and associated economic gain that none on the outside could expect for themselves.

From the first, rulers treated prostitution as a problem of social management, their concerns nicely reflected in the original regulations that accompanied Yoshiwara's establishment in 1617:

1 No establishment [for prostitutes] shall be permitted to operate outside the licensed quarter. Regardless of the origin of requests, courtesans shall not be sent out for prostitution beyond the walls of the quarter.
2 No bordello client shall be permitted to stay longer than a day and a night.
3 Courtesans shall not wear luxurious clothing embroidered or appliquéd in gold and silver. They shall wear simple blue cotton clothes wherever they are.
4 The buildings in the pleasure quarter shall not be sumptuous, and they shall conform to the Edo architectural style.
5 Anyone of unknown origin or strange behavior found wandering within the quarter shall give his address regardless of his class – whether he is a

samurai or of the merchant class. If still under suspicion, he shall be reported immediately to the district police.[19]

Later, posted regulations reiterated, ineffectually, the proscription on such business outside the quarter and declared that:

> Apart from doctors, no one is permitted to ride [horse or carriage or palanquin] inside the Yoshiwara gate. Also, spears and long swords shall not be brought inside the gate.

In much the same spirit rulers strove to regulate the popular *kabuki* theatre and other forms of recreation and entertainment.

In sum, then, the society that had taken shape during the *post-sengoku* century was far more complex than the simple *shinōkōshō* image projected by Confucian theorists. The rulers who had restored a stable, *kenmon*-like central elite and adopted an ideology of rule to legitimize their privileged position accommodated this *de facto* social complexity by developing structures of control and exploitation that reflected the reality of their day. Those pragmatic adjustments enabled them to sustain the essentials of public peace and hence their own privileges well into the nineteenth century.

[10] THE AGE OF GROWTH (1590–1700)

CHAPTER SYNOPSIS

DIMENSIONS OF EXPANSION
  DEMOGRAPHICS
  TRANSPORTATION AND TRADE
  TECHNOLOGY AND COMMERCIAL
  ORGANIZATION

KYOTO REVIVED

PHYSICAL RECONSTRUCTION
CULTURAL BLOSSOMING

ENRICHING A COMMON HIGHER CULTURE
  THE RISE OF KAMIGATA CULTURE
  TO EDO AND BEYOND

The political transformation of the decades around 1600 was accompanied by striking socioeconomic growth and cultural development, and those processes were cybernetically linked to the political change. On one hand the coming of peace spurred the initial burst of growth and development. On the other, the resulting increase in output sustained the peace by providing enough gainful employment and personal satisfaction so that most of the demobilized troops and the many who were denied their dreams of glory were willing to make do with the choices that peacetime offered. In consequence the realm enjoyed more than a century of vigorous growth and change.

There were several dimensions to this overall expansion, but its most vibrant manifestation was Kyoto, which experienced a century of economic and cultural dynamism. Despite the eastward migration of political control, that dynamism sustained the city's role as Japan's cultural center into the eighteenth century. The cultural ramifications of socioeconomic expansion reached well beyond Kyoto, however, embracing other towns and cities and, to some degree, the populace as a whole. In the process they enriched the common higher culture that had begun to appear during medieval centuries.

DIMENSIONS OF EXPANSION

Several aspects of expansion command attention. Most noteworthy were population growth, improvements in transportation and trade, and advances in material technology and commercial organization.

DEMOGRAPHICS

Perhaps the most striking expression of this century's socioeconomic expansion was population growth, with an estimated ten to twelve million in the later sixteenth century approaching thirty million by 1700. Almost all of that increase was among the producer populace because the size of the *kinsei* elite was fixed by regulation and fiscal restraint. And most of the growth occurred in the hinterland, where established villages grew larger and a plethora of new satellite villages (*shinden*) were spun off by them. Some of the additional people settled in urban centers, however, and those grew in size as daimyo assembled retainers in their castle towns and commoners moved in to service them. As the seventeenth century aged, most castle towns ceased to grow and some shrank, but highway, port, trading, and production towns continued expanding to handle the commercial activity that provisioned urban residents and affluent hinterlanders.

Several developments contributed to this growth in production and population. Initially the key factor was restoration of peace. It eliminated an immense amount of waste and fostered purposeful efforts to expand output. By the unspeakable standards of the twentieth century, *sengoku* warfare may not seem very wasteful, but it was when compared to earlier times of disorder because the fighting was so chronic and its scale so great. To an unprecedented extent, crops were burned and ruined and fields idled. Fortifications were repeatedly erected and destroyed. Buildings and settlements of all sorts were burned, built, and burned again. Foodstuffs and other matériel were wasted by armies plundering, fleeing, and struggling to survive. And an incalculable amount of productive labor time was lost to wasted effort, war making, and corvée labor demands that had little enduring value and which violated the productive rhythms of village life.

Peace ended most of that waste. Even the corvée labor that rulers continued to commandeer so freely was put to more productive use and increasingly scheduled to accommodate the cropping cycle. Moreover, those rulers fostered diverse sorts of production, and while their purposes were narrowly fiscal, the effects were more broadly economic. Not only rulers, but villagers and townsmen too, being more confident that their labors would bear fruit, directed their energies to reclaiming land, fabricating goods, and fostering commerce. Their confidence sprang not only from the halt in fighting but also from particulars of the land settlement: the surveys that assured rulers of their tribute income also clarified use rights among producers, reducing their vulnerability to arbitrary expropriation of yield and strengthening their security of tenure on the land itself.

Basic to the demographic growth, of course, was expanded food production. It was achieved by a striking increase in acreage under tillage and in the proportion of that acreage devoted to paddy culture. Many of the *shinden* that villagers established were byproducts of uncelebrated land reclamation efforts in which villagers cleared and leveled patches of woodland and waste to form arable fields. They did so with simple tools and much labor, a few square meters at a time. Other, much grander projects were undertaken by government, mainly to convert dry fields to paddy culture, with both daimyo and bakufu officials organizing major efforts to lessen river flooding and channel the flowing water into fields previously out of reach. By one set of figures, paddy acreage grew as follows:[1]

Date	Area in Paddy
Around 1450	946,000 *chō*
Around 1600	1,635,000 *chō*
Around 1720	2,970,000 *chō*

Thanks to careful land surveys and enforcement of the peace, rulers were able to convert the yield from this expanded arable into commensurately greater tribute income, but a greater residue also remained to support a larger population of rural producers.

TRANSPORTATION AND TRADE

The need to convey tribute from countryside to castle town helped spur improvements in transportation facilities. Much effort went into highway work, with the Tokugawa establishing regulations for the operation and maintenance of major roads all the way from Kyushu to the far north. The most important highway, the Tōkaidō, linked Kyoto to Edo, and the Englishman John Saris, visiting Japan in 1613, wrote of it:

> The way for the most part is wonderfull even, and where it meeteth with Mountains passage is cut through. This way is … for the most part sandie and gravell: it is divided into leagues and at every leagues end are two small hills, viz. on either side of the way one, and upon every one of them a faire Pine-tree trimmed round in fashion of an Arbor. These markes are placed upon the way to the end, that the Hacknie men, and those which let out Horses to hire, should not make men pay more than their due, which is about three pense a league. The Roade is exceedingly travelled, full of people.[2]

One reason the highways bustled was that bakufu rules forbade tariff barriers or other unauthorized hindrances to travel. Thus a decree of 1617 specified that, "Roads, post-horses, boats and bridges shall be used freely, without interruption."[3]

The tree-topped highway markers that Saris noted also informed travelers how far they were from Edo, while other roadside guideposts, stone lanterns, and rest facilities enhanced highway convenience. The main roads generally were about four to seven meters in width, and they were maintained by nearby villages, which were supposed to follow guidelines such as the following, issued by the bakufu in 1612:

1　Areas worn down by the weight of traffic, on both major and minor roads, should be filled in with either sand or stones to give them a hard surface, and water should be drained off into ditches dug on both sides of the road. Muddy sections should be treated in the same manner.
2　Grass on the road embankments must not be removed.

3   In all areas, whether under shogunal or private control, bridges… in poor condition must be repaired by the authority of an intendant or his deputies.

Inspectors periodically investigated the highways, and in general the roads appear to have been maintained in satisfactory condition, though mountain stretches commonly were treacherous and secondary roads inferior.

Other transport facilities also improved. Governments and entrepreneurs erected wharves and warehouses, dredged canals, cleared rivers of obstructions, and constructed cargo vessels to carry goods and passengers along the Inland Sea. Harbors proliferated, and by the 1670s, coastal shipping routes encircled Honshu, linking all regions of the realm to Osaka and Edo.

Improvements in transportation aided the movement not only of foodstuffs but of myriad other goods. Mining was fostered by daimyo and shogun seeking iron for military and other uses, and gold, silver, and copper for coinage and industrial purposes. Logging continued at an unprecedented pace to sustain the countrywide building of monuments to the powerful – castles, palaces, mansions, temples, and shrines (see figure 10.1) – and the associated construction of ships, commercial facilities, and ordinary housing. Indeed, the need to extract timber from ever more inaccessible sites was a primary factor promoting river dredging and clearance.

Part of the bullion that rulers obtained from their mines they minted into coins, which enabled them to replace the existing hodgepodge, mostly

Figure 10.1   Himeji Castle. The immense investment of labor and resources in construction of monumental projects such as this during the decades around 1600 spurred economic growth throughout the country. And the absence of renewed warfare thereafter left some of the monuments intact to serve as movie settings today. *Source*: Reproduced courtesy of Morton S. Schmorleitz.

imported, with a more orderly currency. Ieyasu was particularly influential in this regard, establishing mints that produced gold and silver coins of such fineness and consistency that they became standards against which subsequent Tokugawa mintings were routinely measured. Besides rationalizing the coinage, rulers standardized commercial measures, most notably Hideyoshi's volumetric *kyō-masu* for measuring rice and the linear measure, *ken*, which was gradually fixed during the seventeenth century at six *shaku* (1.82 meters), giving greater consistency to wood products and carpentry.

TECHNOLOGY AND COMMERCIAL ORGANIZATION

Embedded in many of these changes were technological improvements that helped workmen overcome obstacles to resource exploitation. Some of the improvements were domestic inventions; others were imports, mostly from Korea and China. Most importantly, perhaps, the formation of paddy fields on flood plains of larger rivers required dikes, dams, and sluices capable of controlling rivers whose stream flow fluctuated sharply. The Chinese had long experience with major riparian projects, and their techniques began to be applied: closer study of hydraulics; more flexible dike layouts that could handle surging water levels safely; sturdy bamboo baskets filled with rock, linked together, and held in place by poles to form dikes that could withstand stream flow; and the consolidation of dike surfaces with rock facings, grass plantings, and shrubs.

Miners also adopted new techniques. As they consumed placer deposits and more accessible veins, they began tunneling, ventilating, and draining to obtain ore from deeper underground. They adopted Chinese smelting and refining techniques that extracted metals from lower-grade ores, and they used more powerful bellows to produce higher quality pig iron for superior tools and weapons. In timber extraction, processing, and utilization, technological improvements facilitated not only the harvesting of less accessible stands but also the construction of sturdier, more defensible fortresses and larger, more seaworthy ships.

The development of more elaborate commercial arrangements also facilitated socioeconomic expansion. Initially large-scale construction and commercial projects had been handled by merchant-administrators in the employ of domanial leaders. From the 1620s onward, however, both bakufu and daimyo reduced their commercial involvement as they routinized tribute collection, completed construction projects, and placed overseas trade in non-Japanese hands. More and more of the urban provisioning and repair was assumed by merchant houses (*ton'ya*) that replaced their official duties with entrepreneurial ventures, elaborating their business organizations, procedures, and principles as needed.

To stabilize markets and facilitate cooperation, groups of merchant houses formed trade associations (*nakama, kumiai*) that regulated market access, prices, and product quality. They divided up the market by commodity and locality and worked out fields of specialization as purchasing agents, shippers, wholesalers, jobbers, and financiers. By late in the century there were some 380 *ton'ya* in Osaka alone and large numbers in other cities as well. The country as a whole had a highly articulated system of merchants operating an elaborately integrated commercial economy that moved goods all about the realm, by land and sea, transcending domanial boundaries, overcoming the complexities and inadequacies of the trimetal monetary system, and offsetting disruptive swings in supply and demand.

Besides organizing the larger structure of commerce, *ton'ya* heads developed elaborate internal arrangements, establishing branch offices, clerks, managers, and personnel training systems to perpetuate essential knowledge and dependable performance. Some also drafted codes of conduct that were admonitory in the manner of daimyo codes. As an early example of the genre, one financier prepared a long, rambling statement of 1610 in which he admonished his house members that:

> Those with even a small fortune must remember that their duty in life is to devote themselves to their house and to its business. They must not become careless, for should they buy what they want, do as they please, and, in general, live sumptuously, they will soon spend that fortune.[4]

Particulars of such codes varied with the business and the age, but the ideals of frugality, diligence, and risk-avoidance were universal.

In short, the general populace was able to use the arrangements and priorities of the new order to achieve substantial changes in agronomic technique, transport, industrial technology, and commercial organization. Those changes enabled them to exploit much more fully the potential of intensive agriculture, resulting in unprecedented growth for society as a whole. And nowhere was this dynamism more evident than in Kyoto.

KYOTO REVIVED

Social growth during this century-plus of reconsolidation was basically a continuation, albeit at a sharply accelerated pace, of the general expansion that agricultural intensification had spurred during preceding centuries, as discussed in chapter 7. The *sengoku* period had constituted, in effect, a destructive interregnum that eliminated residual obstacles to change, permitting pre-established trends to revive and speed up. In particular, Kyoto, which had blossomed during the Ashikaga heyday and shriveled during *sengoku*, reclaimed its role as the dynamic heart of Japan's culture, society, and commercial economy. The point merits emphasizing because the shift of political control to Edo has tended to conceal Kyoto's renewed prominence and vitality. Indeed, by comparison, Edo remained a crude cultural backwater well into the eighteenth century, a Sparta, so to say, to Kyoto's Athens.

PHYSICAL RECONSTRUCTION

Throughout the *sengoku* century Kyotoites had repeatedly struggled to rebuild, and pockets of wealth and comfort survived the turmoil. After

Nobunaga stabilized the Kinai region, the city's recovery began in earnest, even though the court itself remained impoverished for another generation. As early as 1565 the Jesuit Luis Frois could write of Kyoto, evidently as it stretched southward from the emperor's palace into Shimogyō:

> we went along some long streets, very straight and level, all of which are closed by gates at night...All of these streets are occupied by merchants and crafts-men who weave and embroider damask and other silks, and make golden fans and all the other things used in this country. In the middle of these streets is a temple of Amida which is the most frequented in all the city. An enormous crowd of people comes to give alms and pray to the idol all day long, but espe-cially in the afternoon when the shops have been closed and the people are free.[5]

During the next several decades, ceaseless construction gave the city an opulence that probably surpassed even the days of Ashikaga glory. The cele-brated projects of Hideyoshi and Ieyasu are most well known, including the former's general reorganization of the city and the latter's work on the imper-ial palace and Nijō Castle. In addition a number of other lords contributed to the city's revival, and many temples and shrines were rebuilt and new ones added. More importantly, an immense amount of simpler construction by commoners produced business establishments and dwellings for most of the city's residents. At its peak in the mid-seventeenth century, the city came to number some 400,000, the growth filling in vacant areas between Kamigyō and Shimogyō and sprawling laterally well beyond Hideyoshi's *odoi*. It pushed fingers of settlement westward into Saga, and eastward into lowlands and foothills across the Kamo River all the way from Shirakawa down to Fushimi.

Describing the city of Ieyasu's heyday at considerable length, João Rodrigues wrote:

> in each of its broad streets is to be found water from excellent springs and streams which run along the middle. The streets are swept and sprinkled with water twice a day and are thus kept very clean and fresh, for every man looks after the part in front of his own house...The houses facing the streets are usually shops, offices and workshops of different crafts; the people have their living quarters and rooms for guests inside. Some streets are very long and wide, and on either side have cov-ered passage ways, along which the people walk to avoid the rain or the sun or to look in the shops; in these streets they sell rolls of cloth and silk for the whole king-dom...There is in Miyako [Kyoto] a register of more than 5,000 looms which weave various silks and almost all are to be found in one ward.

Rodrigues went on to extol the character of the citizens and the beauty of the surrounding countryside. And he reported that,

> along the roads leading into the city there are gated wooden enclosures in which are held continuous performances of drama, comedies, farces and plays which recount ancient stories with certain songs and tunes accompanied by musical instruments, and these provide much recreation for the Japanese. The gates are always kept closed and the people who enter pay a certain sum, and the actors earn their living with the money thus collected because a goodly number of people attend each performance.

Moreover,

> The city is provided with abundant provisions, such as much game, mountain birds, various kinds of fresh fish from rivers and lakes, and sea fish, especially in the winter … There are many different kinds of vegetables and fruit according to the season and these are brought in at dawn from the nearby places and farms and sold in markets of two hundred or more people. In addition to the markets where every kind of food is sold, men walk through the streets selling their wares … All over the city there is an enormous number of inns and taverns which provide food for people from outside, and there are also many public baths where a man blows a horn and invites people to the baths, for the Japanese are very fond of having a bath.

Kyoto, as these reports suggest, was notable less for its elegant upper-class establishments, though they were there, than for its quotidian bustle. A similar image was conveyed by the many *Rakuchū rakugai zū* ("Scenes in and out of Kyoto"), large-scale paintings of the city that highlighted famous places and celebrated urban activities of the decades before and during pacification.

CULTURAL BLOSSOMING

The city's renewed vitality stemmed from a blending of past and present that no other town, no pretentious "little Kyoto" and certainly no newly risen garrison town in the eastern marches of the Kantō, could hope to match. That blend is nicely exemplified by the Saga *bon*, new editions of such celebrated classics as *Ise monogatari*, *Hōjōki*, and *Shinkokinshū*, that were produced by a publishing venture of Ieyasu's day. These new editions linked Kyoto to its past through their content, of course, but also through their very provenance because they were produced in Saga, an area rich with courtly associations from early Heian onward and close by the Tenryūji with its legacy of Ashikaga and Rinzai cultural attainments. Saga publishing evinced the medieval *kenmon* tradition in that it celebrated *kuge* accomplishments and was sponsored by a senior *bushi*, namely Ieyasu, executed by a gifted artist from a Kyoto artisan family, Hon'ami Kōetsu, and financed and expedited by a wealthy and culturally ambitious merchant, Suminokura Soan, a close confidant of Ieyasu.

Even as those Saga *bon* echoed the city's past, they also spoke of its present insofar as the roles of Suminokura and Ieyasu reflected the outcome of recent struggles for supremacy. Moreover, Suminokura's wealth was linked to his trading ventures in Southeast Asia and to his role as a major provisioner of lumber for Kyoto's reconstruction. Those commercial enterprises led him to base his business operations – and consequently his printing press – on the Katsura River, where he constructed wharf, beaching, and storage facilities near the Tenryūji. Further reflecting the new foreign connections, Saga books were printed with moveable type, which technology came from two overseas sources: a Korean-style moveable type introduced to Japan during Hideyoshi's invasion of the peninsula, and a European-style press brought by the Jesuits. Finally, Saga *bon* were produced with meticulous care, displaying a standard of technical excellence in publishing that was much higher than that of recent centuries and that reflected the standards Ieyasu displayed in his minting of currency and drafting of behavioral regulations.

Within a few decades woodblock printing replaced the moveable-type press, probably because of its greater cost-effectiveness in marketing to a population with wide interests and greatly varying degrees of literacy. However, Kyoto remained the center of publishing, with some seventy two publishers active there in the year 1702 alone. They put out scholarly works in Chinese, classics of Japanese literature, Buddhist texts, moral treatises, poetry compilations, works of art, and instructional texts on arts, crafts, and military and other skills; as well as theatrical texts, commentaries, and advertisements. There were simply written popular works (*kana zōshi*) of history, mystery, and fiction, commonly with a didactic twist, as well as travel guides, inelegant picture books, broadsheets of myriad sorts, and some of the world's most hilarious pornographic art.

One reason Kyoto could sustain such variegated publishing was that during the seventeenth century there emerged in the city a cultural ideal of gentlemanly accomplishments, *yūgei*, that transcended class and was shared by everyone with pretensions to cultural polish. According to one observer at the time, many kinds of cultural activities are appropriate for the gentleman,

> and so medicine, poetry, the tea ceremony, music, the hand drum, the nō dance, etiquette, the appreciation of craft work, arithmetic and calculation are all included, not to mention literary composition, reading and writing... It is well to master at least one of these.[6]

In these arts Kyoto produced many of the era's most celebrated masters.

Thanks in some degree to that cosmopolitan cultural ideal, the city continued to derive dynamism from the interplay of its heterogeneous population. This populace included a reinvigorated courtly elite, revitalized priestly communities, and resident samurai from scores of daimyo domains as well as the large administrative staff of the bakufu's city offices. To varying degrees these people interacted with a much expanded merchant community, an assortment of writers, artists, intellectuals, and other cultural producers, and the large urban population of artisans, laborers, entertainers, and pariah communities.

As in the Ashikaga heyday, the city stood on two fiscal legs, tribute and commercial income. However, the latter was more important than ever before. The former, tribute income, came from several sources: the 450,000 *koku* of land assigned to court, *kuge*, temples, and shrines; the gifts and contributions they frequently received from bakufu, daimyo, and lesser samurai; and the daily expenditures of the many *bushi* garrisoned in town. Commercial income was generated by the many goods and services that Kyotoites provided the larger society. In monetary terms high-grade silk goods produced by weavers in Kamigyō's Nishijin neighborhood were most important, with some 7,000 two-person looms and innumerable smaller, single-operator looms generating a flood of material by late in the century.

Indeed, according to one estimate the spinning, weaving, and dyeing work of Nishijin involved upwards of 100,000 people.[7]

An array of other city artisans, as least as varied as that of the sixteenth century noted in chapter 7, produced luxury items, craft goods, and basic commodities. During the 1690s Engelbert Kaempfer, visiting from Dejima, observed of Kyoto that it is

> the great magazine of all Japanese manufactures and commodities, and the chief mercantile town in the Empire. There is scarce a house in this large capital, where there is not something made or sold. Here they refine copper, coin money, print books, weave the richest stuffs with gold and silver flowers. The best and scarcest dies, the most artful carvings, all sorts of musical Instruments, pictures, japan'd cabinets, all sorts of things wrought in gold and other metals, particularly in steel, as the best temper'd blades, and other arms are made here in the utmost perfection, as are also the richest dresses, and after the best fashion, all sorts of toys, puppets, moving their heads of themselves, and numberless other things, too many to be mention'd.[8]

Services also were important. In 1685 the city was, by one count, home to

> 51 doctors [of various specialties]..., 41 men of letters, including poets and specialists of Chinese classics; 16 experts on painting and calligraphy; and 125 masters of the tea ceremony, flower arrangement, the noh theater, and the board games *go* and *shōgi*.[9]

Kyoto thus teemed with teachers of diverse sorts, whose presence lured students from around the realm.

The city dominated literary production as well. It had from its beginning been the center of *waka* poetry and later the principal home of *renga*. During the seventeenth century the Kyoto poet Matsunaga Teitoku played a seminal role in transforming the frivolous 17-syllable *haikai* verse form into serious poetry, arguing on the venerable grounds of "expedient means" (*hōben*), that:

> It should not be despised as a vulgar pastime. In these Latter Days of the Buddhist Law its virtue is broader even than that of the *waka*.[10]

By late in the century some 739 teachers of *haikai* were said to be active in Kyoto.

Also the country's most influential Confucian scholars, such as Matsunaga Sekigo (Teitoku's son), Yamazaki Ansai, and Itō Jinsai, operated schools there. Concurrently the city's intellectuals and aesthetes led a new burst of "neo-classicism," re-examining Shintō, reviving courtly rituals, studying classical literature, and producing new editions of famous works. The most celebrated artists were there, including Tawaraya Sōtatsu and Ogata Kōrin, as well as Hon'ami Kōetsu and most of the Kanō masters. They participated in the classical revival, producing new editions of classic *emakimono*, while also creating elegant new works that reflected the grand pretensions of their patrons.

Finally, even as Kyotoites celebrated their classical and medieval legacies, they were playing a seminal role in stimulating new currents of popular entertainment. These, which we note more fully below, included not only *haikai* but also puppet theatre (*ningyō jōruri*), *kabuki* drama, and "floating world" art and narrative literature (*ukiyo-e* and *ukiyo zōshi*). Kyoto folk mastered these arts, but ultimately the city did not dominate the new cultural arenas as it did those of the classical revival. Rather, in them one sees most clearly the process wherein the common higher culture that had begun to appear before *sengoku* was enriched and diffused yet further through the realm.

ENRICHING A COMMON HIGHER CULTURE

The builders of the *bakuhan* polity had labored to reaffirm the separateness of class and mass, and the appearance of widely shared arts and letters did not undo their handiwork. It did, however, obfuscate that separateness, whether defined in social terms of patrician and pleb or in geographical terms of center and periphery. At the center it produced a redefinition, with the venerable "Kyoto culture" being transformed into "Kamigata culture," meaning arts and letters of the Kyoto–Osaka region, a term commonly used to juxtapose Kamigata's reputed cultural sophistication against the boorishness of "the Kantō," meaning Edo. More broadly the diffusion of arts and letters provided a cultural level of commonality to Japanese life that paralleled the political and economic commonality resulting from political reconsolidation and socioeconomic expansion.

THE RISE OF KAMIGATA CULTURE

The port of Sakai had earlier emerged as a vital center of commerce and culture, as evidenced in the China trade and the rise of *wabicha* tea ceremony, but Sakai and Kyoto, being well separated geographically, were always regarded as distinct and dissimilar entities. During the seventeenth century the former Ishiyama Honganji temple town evolved by way of Hideyoshi's Osaka castle town into a major entrepôt that thoroughly overshadowed Sakai and was much more closely linked to Kyoto by politics and location. The city processed rice and other tribute goods that daimyo shipped from western Japan to cover the costs of their *sankin kōtai* travel and their residences, warehouses, and offices in Edo, Osaka, and Kyoto. And it handled a vast amount of other commerce, including considerable production of its own, thereby creating a wealthy merchant class serviced by a large population of lesser folk. By the latter half of the seventeenth century it was emerging as a rival of Kyoto. It siphoned off business and population and by 1700 numbered 350,000 people or more.

As it grew wealthy, Osaka became a source of patronage for creative people, particularly those catering to merchants and less affluent commoners. Most famously Ihara Saikaku, who drew on the medieval tradition of short tales (*otogi zōshi*) to create the *ukiyo zōshi* genre of piquant prose fiction, was originally an Osaka *haikai* poet. During the early 1680s he discovered a lucrative market for a series of salacious prose tales written in easily readable *kana*, and from the late eighties until his death in 1693 he followed those successes with diverse tales about daily life that for all their lightness of tone were moving and insightful evocations of the absurdity and hardship found in ordinary existence.

To suggest the tone of Saikaku's later works, in *Seken munezan'yō*, a collection of tales he prepared in 1691, he sought to portray the difficulties people face at year's end, when all debts are supposed to be settled.[11] In one tale he described the rhythms of a well-ordered life this way:

> One should of course strive to be ever alert from the age of twenty-five, the peak of youth; make his fortune around thirty-five, the prime of manhood; consolidate his house and put his son and heir in charge at fifty, the age of discretion; and go into carefree retirement at sixty, … and spend the rest of his life making pilgrimages to temples, if only for the sake of appearances.

In practice, however, Saikaku saw few people of any age or class who could handle their affairs so skillfully by half. Rather, they made installment purchases through the year and, unable to pay their year-end debts, resorted to every imaginable ruse to secure cash or evade the collector. One method among poor tenement dwellers was to pawn:

> One of the families pawned an old paper umbrella, a cotton gin, and a teakettle, and managed to get by on the 1 momme of silver which these three items brought. In the house next door, the mother took off the sash she was wearing and in its place put on a cord of twisted paper. She pawned this sash along with a man's cotton hood, [several other items] … and a hanging Buddhist altar with an assortment of fittings.

The penny-pinching people of Sakai got by more shrewdly:

> they cover the front of their shops with latticework to give them the appearance of a shop that has been closed up … They replace the shingles a few at a time before damage is done to the roof; they put stones under pillars [just] before they rot; they install copper rain gutters on the eaves only after years of bargain hunting … They entertain with the tea ceremony [because] it doesn't involve much of an outlay at all since they have utensils that have been in the family for generations.

Then, having thus told how the affluent of Sakai cope, he went on to describe the conniving by the poor as they struggled to survive into the New Year.

From Osaka the *ukiyo zōshi* genre spread quickly to authors in Kyoto, most notably the well-to-do shopkeeper turned satirist, Ejima Kiseki. At about the same time Chikamatsu Monzaemon, a Kyoto librettist for *kabuki* and puppet theatre, was shifting his attention from Kyoto to Osaka, moving there in 1705. By then this sort of cultural intermingling had established the image of the two cities as parts of a single cultural realm, Kamigata.

Chikamatsu is celebrated as the first and greatest of playwrights for *kabuki* and puppet theatre, but his triumph was made possible by generations of prior theatrical development. As noted in chapter 8, popular traditions of music, dance, mime, and narrative tale had been incorporated during the Ashikaga heyday to form the *sarugaku nō* drama, which was then elevated to the status of an elite art. Plebeian traditions of music and dance persisted, however, commonly in conjunction with stories and skits narrated by itinerant tale tellers, some using puppets for animation. Both men and women worked as tale tellers, traveling widely and serving secular and sacred purposes as the situation dictated.

In Kyoto puppeteers were able to perform on shrine grounds or other open spots, while dry strips of riverbed along the Kamo River provided other entertainers with a convenient place to put on live shows for audiences lining the river bank. By Ieyasu's heyday, as Rodrigues noted, enclosures for entrepreneurial performers stood along roads leading into the city. In those days live shows by women actors functioned largely as a prelude to prostitution, but by mid-century the stage and skin trades had been more or less separated, and *kabuki* developed into more serious theatre, as puppet drama had already done.

The main fare of both theatres was lively period pieces (*jidaimono*) that mostly derived from the long-popular war tales, but stories of ghostly mystery and religious miracles also furnished popular dramas. By century's end contemporary domestic dramas of love and loss among common city folk (*sewamono*) were emerging as the most powerful works and, in Kamigata, the most popular. In Edo, too, *sewamono* gradually acquired favor, but battle stories remained particularly popular with its large samurai population.

To Edo and beyond

As a recently risen garrison town, early seventeenth-century Edo was rough-hewn, predominantly male, and culturally undeveloped. However, because it had deep political links to Kamigata and because its shogunal and daimyo treasuries gave it control of so much discretionary income, it could not remain a backwater indefinitely. From early in the century its higher-status *bushi* aspired to cultural elegance, building gorgeous mansions, employing Kanō artists to decorate them, laying out grand landscape gardens, constructing *nō* stages, practicing *wabicha*-style tea ceremony, studying *waka*, hiring Confucian scholars to teach their sons, and arranging for their daughters to master the domestic arts of proper households. Lesser samurai, meanwhile, began learning the literate skills of peace, and as the century advanced and the city grew like topsy, publishers set up shop in Edo and the commoner arts of Kamigata became established there. These included the puppet and *kabuki* theatres, *ukiyo zōshi*, and by the 1670s *haikai* poetry, this last when Matsuo Bashō and his mentor, the Kyoto poet and disciple of Teitoku, Kitamura Kigin, went east to seek their fortunes.

In the area of popular *ukiyo* art, Edo's very backwardness enabled it to play a seminal role. In Kyoto *ukiyo-e* had developed as a style of painting, an iconoclastic style that deviated in subject and technique from the Kanō and Tosa traditions. In Edo, however, the buying public for such art was mainly lesser samurai who preferred cheap woodblock prints to pricey paintings. Particularly they welcomed prints that portrayed actors and beauties, urban life, and the arts of love. From the 1660s onward prints of this sort gained popularity in the city, with voluptuous images by the Edo artisan Hishikawa Moronobu acquiring particular fame during the 1670s and eighties. By the eighteenth century the Edo manner in print-making was sweeping Kamigata, even as *ukiyo zōshi*, *kabuki*, and *haikai* became solidly established at the heart of Edo cultural life.

Nor did the diffusion of Kamigata arts and letters end at Edo. As earlier noted, a few medieval daimyo had created "little Kyotos," much as eleventh-century magnates in Tōhoku had created Hiraizumi. And medieval trade and the *sengoku* diaspora of *kuge* to Sakai and elsewhere added further to hinterland acquisition of elite cultural traditions. After the realm was pacified, daimyo and lesser samurai continued the tradition of introducing Kyoto taste to their castle towns. They created elegant mansions and landscaped gardens, recruited scholars, artisans, and experts in diverse arts, and promoted taste and learning among relatives and retainers alike.

Concurrently cultural diffusion through the hinterland was proceeding at more plebeian levels. The simpler works of city publishers, written in *kana* and increasingly illustrated with woodblock prints, found their way into towns throughout the realm. Kumano *bikuni* and *etoki hōshi*, the religious itinerants of earlier centuries, continued to ply their trades as well, still employing *mandara* that portrayed the sufferings of the damned, the miracles of particular temples or shrines, or other religious imagery.

Itinerants also continued entertaining their audiences with stories and skits that were less explicitly religious in intent or content. War tales based on the recent battles of pacification do not seem to have gained wide popularity, in part, one suspects, because the faceless, nameless hordes of mass combat are not easily amenable to lionization. More importantly, perhaps, many losers were still around, and shogun and daimyo in their pursuit of stability discouraged unwonted heroics, their celebration, and the accompanying perpetuation of old resentments. Older war tales, however, continued to be reworked and retold, whether as stage production or as monologue with musical accompaniment. In particular, tale tellers found that *Soga monogatari*, with its central theme of filial piety, its heroine Tora-gozen, and its richness of domestic sensibility, enjoyed much popularity.

The enrichment and wide diffusion of a common culture was reflected in travel diaries and guidebooks. The earlier-noted *Rakuchū rakugai zū*, which constituted stylized visual guides to Kyoto ca. 1550–1600, were followed by narrative guides such as *Kyō warabe* by Nakagawa Kiun, published posthumously in 1658. Scores of entrepreneurial guidebooks followed, informing readers not only of the wondrous and salacious joys of Kyoto, but also of Osaka and Edo. When Asai Ryōi drafted his *Tōkaidō meishoki* in 1660 as a guide to famous places on the Tōkaidō, he drew heavily on *Kyō warabe* to characterize spots in Edo. By doing so he infused Edo's "famous places" with Kyoto's panache. Later guides to the city borrowed, in turn, from the earlier ones, thereby perpetuating legends and heightening the sense of Edo's antiquity even as they updated particulars to stay abreast of current notorieties.

The wish to embed the present in a celebrated past reached well beyond efforts to discover the qualities of Kyoto in Edo. Matsuo Bashō, although associated with the newly fashionable *haikai* style of poetry, also exemplified the persistence of literary tradition and the broadening of cultural participation. The travel diary, as noted in preceding chapters, was a well-established literary genre, initially covering short distances, such as Tosa to Heian. Even well into the Ashikaga period, traveling poets such as Sōgi had regarded the Shirakawa barrier on the Kantō's northern edge as the northeastern terminus of the proper literary journey. Bashō extended the genre. His most celebrated work, one of several travel sketches he composed, was *Oku no Hosomichi*, a poem-studded narrative of a trip he made from Edo to northern Tōhoku and then back via the Sea of Japan littoral to Ōgaki, where illness stopped him from continuing on south to Ise.

In the tradition of the travel diary, Bashō evoked history and habitat by mentioning places celebrated for their beauty or associated with famous people and events.[12] Bidding farewell to the "faint shadow of Mount Fuji and the cherry blossoms of Ueno" as he left Edo, he headed north, climbing Mount Nikkō, which, he tells us, received its name from Kūkai. He traverses the exotic highlands of Nasu, visits numerous famous shrines and temples, and claims, implausibly, to view a willow tree celebrated in a poem by Saigyō. He comes "at last to the barrier-gate of Shirakawa," with its rich poetic legacy, and later stands weeping before the "ruined house of the brave warrior Satō," who was associated with Yoshitsune's tragic death in 1189.

As he traveled he kept encountering poets, and they joined him in impromptu composition parties. He visited "the ancient site of the Taga castle" with its echoes of Emishi wars, and later Matsushima, which he found as beautiful as any Chinese scene. Finally he reached Hiraizumi, with its remnants of the northern Fujiwara and its memories of Yoshitsune's violent end. Gently summoning those Genpei ghosts, he wrote:

> The summer grasses,
> all that remains
> of the warriors' dreams.[13]

Heading westward, he visited a temple reputedly founded by the celebrated Heian monk Ennin, stopped at the Shugendō center on Mt. Haguro, which he linked to the *Engi shiki*, and pressed on through desolate, mountainous regions until he reached Kanazawa, with yet more Genpei memories. He visited Eiheiji, the Sōtō Zen temple of Dōgen, and some days later reached Ōgaki.

Like earlier travel diaries, *Oku no Hosomichi* was thus crammed with historical associations that were shared knowledge among the culturally engaged. His journey reminds us of how much easier travel had become, and the fact that he met fellow poets and joined them in versifying, even in the deepest hinterland, reveals how thoroughly the poetic tradition that first found rich historical expression among the courtly elite had become a society-wide avocation that provided a solid cultural bond even between strangers.

In its diffusion this central culture was not, of course, being etched on a blank slate. Local cultural traditions existed everywhere, and as Kamigata arts and letters were introduced, processes of interplay and adaptation went on throughout the country. In consequence regional distinctions persisted everywhere. Indeed, local handicrafts, foods, folklore, festivals, folk songs and dances, as well as dialects and dress lasted on into the twentieth century. These distinctive qualities persisted, however, within the context of shared cultural norms that facilitated discourse and dealings among people throughout the realm, thereby contributing to the spread of commerce and learning and to the formation and maintenance of a common political culture.

[11] STASIS AND DECAY (1700–1850)

The term "Tokugawa period" is mischievous in its effect because it encourages us to treat the period 1600–1867 as a single unit, albeit one that experienced gradual change as time passed, and to end it abruptly at the Meiji Restoration of 1868. In terms of formal political structure and process, the images of commencement, continuity and terminus are valid indeed. In a broader sense, however, the years around 1700 brought Japan more fundamental change than did those around 1600, and "post-Tokugawa" characteristics did not really come to pervade society until the 1890s or even later.

The years around 1700 witnessed the end of four centuries or more of sustained socioeconomic growth that Japan had experienced as intensive agriculture spread across the realm. During the early 1700s Japan entered a difficult period of stasis that persisted for a century and a half until the exogenous force of European imperialism ruptured the established political order. Nineteenth-century European imperialism, which was itself driven primarily by the carrot and stick of early industrial empowerment and western Europe's ecological limitations, undid the Tokugawa political order – along with many others – by depriving it of the stable and non-threatening geopolitical context in which it had operated. The European intrusion also brought in its wake, however, the rudiments of an alternative to intensive agriculture; namely, industrialization, with its fossil-fuel foundation and its technological and social ramifications.

From the 1860s onward, Japanese leaders and an ever-growing portion of the general populace redirected their energies to the task of developing their own industrializing order. Several aspects of their situation, including changes that Japan underwent during its era of later-Tokugawa stasis, enhanced their capacity to utilize the rudimentary industrial practices then developing in Europe. Not until the 1890s, however, did that process begin to alter substantially the rhythms of life in Japan or the role of Japan in the world. That outcome as it unfurled during the twentieth century is addressed in Part IV.

Here, in chapters 11 and 12, we must review the evidence of intensive agriculture's limits, examine the political, social, and cultural ramifications of this change in circumstances, and adumbrate the process of political disintegration and reorientation that came with the imperialist intrusion of the nineteenth century. As in all matters ecological, one is dealing with complex interactions, and all attempts to disaggregate the whole yield arbitrary oversimplifications. Nevertheless, orderly exegesis requires such disaggregation.

PRIMARY PRODUCTION: TRENDS AND RAMIFICATIONS

Several developments of the eighteenth century revealed that the Japanese were exploiting their existing resource base to the full, given the technology, social structure, and values of the day. The picture of stasis is suggested by basic census figures, particularly when one compares them to the estimated 12,000,000 of 1600 and roughly 100,000,000 of 1966:[1]

Year	Population
1721	26,065,425
1780	26,010,600
1846	26,907,625

Even the best modern censuses are imperfect, and these figures all omit about 5,000,000 members and servants of samurai and courtly households, plus an unknown number of young children in all classes. Nevertheless, they reveal general stability, which continued through the 1860s, with a much more complete census of 1872 recording a total population of 33,110,796.

The same general picture of stability is reflected in figures on rice-producing acreage:[2]

Date	Acreage of Paddy
Around 1600	1,635,000 *chō*
Around 1720	2,970,000 *chō*
1874	3,050,000 *chō*

Clearly the era of rapid expansion in irrigable acreage had ended by 1720.

As these figures suggest, Japan after 1700 or so was a society experiencing basic stability. It was by no means, however, an unchanging society. Rather, it was engaged in wrestling with the ecological and social consequences of its contextual limits. Those limits and the attempts to deal with them are evident in terms of mining and forestry, the use of arable land and irrigation water, the utilization of human labor, attempts to expand the realm, and the proliferation of mechanisms for rationing.

MINES AND FORESTS

Doubtless food supply was the basic factor shaping overall Tokugawa demographics, but other resources also played key roles. Mining output was important in several ways.

Iron and copper production met a variety of needs, with copper output being sustained well into the eighteenth century, while iron continued to meet society's needs into the nineteenth. Even iron was scarce, however. When in 1860 the young samurai Fukuzawa Yukichi visited San Francisco on the first official Japanese mission to America, he was most struck not by the new gadgetry so pridefully displayed by his hosts, but by the fact that

> there seemed to be an enormous waste of iron everywhere. In garbage piles, on the sea shores – everywhere – I found lying old oil tins, empty cans, and broken tools. This was remarkable to us, for in [Edo], after a fire, there would appear a swarm of people looking for nails in the ashes.[3]

Until the middle of the eighteenth century copper was so available that rulers promoted it as a substitute for precious metals in coinage. By the nineteenth, however, ore production was dropping as veins played out and shafts exceeded the capability of existing drainage and ventilation techniques. With mine output declining and demand increasing, the quest for copper led some daimyo to seize temple bells and other copper items to obtain metal for use in cannon manufacture. Even then scarcity of metals restrained severely the production of cannon for coastal defense.

For gold and silver scarcity arose sooner and was more complex in its effects. During the years of Hideyoshi and Ieyasu Japanese prospectors discovered more mines, and miners adopted techniques that enabled them to obtain unprecedented quantities of bullion, particularly silver. Indeed, for a few years around 1600 Japan was the world's greatest silver producer. By the 1620s, however, gold production had peaked, and in following decades the output of both gold and silver declined rapidly. By the 1660s the "problem" of precious metal scarcity was provoking political debate, reshaping foreign policy priorities, and ending the minting of coins by daimyo. By the 1690s gold and silver mines were so depleted that bullion scarcity was determining both foreign commercial and domestic monetary policies.

In terms of foreign trade, scarcity spurred restrictions on metal exports as well as attempts at product replacement. The bakufu urged traders to discover or devise new items for export and to develop domestic industries that could obviate imported goods, silk most notably, but also ginseng and others. The efforts at export substitution proved inadequate, however, and during the eighteenth century foreign trade declined appreciably, that with Korea all but ending by the 1750s.

Domestically, bullion was used for industrial purposes, gift giving, and specie, and scarcity affected all these areas. It spurred sumptuary decrees restricting the use and display of precious metals and led to punishment of offenders. The effects on monetary use were particularly visible. Besides prompting daimyo to stop minting in the 1660s, coinage scarcity spurred the bakufu to remint and devalue its coins from the 1690s onward. Meanwhile paper currencies, promissory notes, and other negotiables began to proliferate in lieu of specie. During the eighteenth century bullion scarcity led to the use of copper coinage in place of silver and from the 1760s onward to experimentation with iron coins and the development of "gold" coins made of silver alloy. The result of this scramble to provide negotiables for a sprawling, nationwide marketplace was the creation of a monetary system that was remarkably complex and unwieldy but which accommodated society's needs as long as Japan had minimal contact with foreign monetary systems.

Although trees, unlike ore, are a renewable resource, the history of timber production was roughly comparable to that of mines – until the nineteenth century. *Sengoku* warfare and rebuilding consumed many trees, and the vast building projects of the half century after 1580 or so stripped Japan of most of its accessible timber stands. By the 1660s timber shortages were complicating urban construction, compromising architectural standards, and generating tighter restrictions on wood use. By then deforestation was producing flooding and other downstream damage severe enough to elicit government responses. And competition for the shrinking forest yield was generating conflicts among woodland exploiters.

Affairs continued to worsen: in 1690 the bakufu used a lame excuse to oust a daimyo from Hida Province, thereby acquiring the last well-forested region in Honshu. And in 1704 leaders of Tosa domain, which a century earlier had been a major provider of timber, notified Edo that,

> We no longer have any large trees, so there are no wide boards available of the sort we have provided in the past.[4]

Most tellingly, perhaps, by the eighteenth century the demand for both woodland and arable was provoking a chronic tug-of-war between those who wished to open more areas to tillage and those who wished to reforest marginal plots to control landslides, erosion, and flooding, and to assure supplies of timber, fuel wood, and green fertilizer material.

Unsurprisingly these trends elicited responses. In chapter 7 we noted attempts by daimyo to regulate forest use from about 1550 onward. During the seventeenth century an elaborate "negative regimen" of rules to restrict forest use and ration forest products spread across the realm. During the eighteenth it began to be supplemented by a "positive regimen" of policies designed to encourage regenerative forestry, meaning tree planting and nurturing. Inherently difficult, costly, and risk-laden, actual reforesting projects developed only slowly. By late in the century, however, changes in land-use arrangements together with the spread of technical know-how made widespread reforesting feasible, and during the nineteenth century the yield from plantation stands gradually rose. Whereas revitalized exploitation of mines awaited the introduction after 1860 of industrial techniques developed in Europe, Japanese foresters thus were able to adopt and adapt East Asian forestry techniques to achieve a basic restructuring of forest growth that revived timber production. Not until late in the twentieth century did the limits of that strategy become apparent, as we note later.

ARABLE LAND AND IRRIGATION WATER

After 1720 or so the acreage devoted to paddy culture increased very little, as indicated above. And the persistent conflicts about shifting marginal plots into tillage or woodland suggest that total arable acreage also increased very little. What had happened, in effect, was that the realm as a whole had completed the growth cycle characteristic of an intensively cultivated village. Around 1720 Tanaka Kyūgu, a village headman from near Edo, who rose to become a bakufu civil official, summarized the cycle this way:

> As to the origin of villages, one or two families usually settle where the land is good, and fields are brought under the plow surrounding the dwellings of the settlers. Gradually a village forms; new houses are built among the existing ones, new fields are opened up, and land previously neglected, such as valley bottoms and marsh, is filled in, ditches and embankments are built and new fields are developed until not an inch of land is left.[5]

Nevertheless, Japan's total agricultural output (food plus non-food) did continue to expand, making the trajectory of later-Edo agriculture different from that of both bullion mines and forests.

To elaborate, the long-term trend for precious-metal mines was sharp expansion and contraction during the early seventeenth century and, for want of further technical change, a continuing decline thereafter. In timber production the explosive growth and sharp decline of the seventeenth century and continuing decline of the eighteenth gave way during the nineteenth to a slow recovery made possible by the spread of plantation forestry. On arable land one sees a dramatic expansion of tilled acreage and hence of output during the seventeenth century, followed, possibly after a period of modest decline, by a slow increase in yield that seems to have continued through the rest of the Edo period. That expansion was made possible not by the adoption of striking new agronomic techniques but by rigorous application of the elements of intensification that had, as noted in chapter 7, first become visible centuries earlier.

Most particulars of this agronomic change are familiar. Cultivators were more careful in the many steps of cropping: preparing soil for planting, selecting and preparing seeds to plant, warming irrigation water and regulating its flow, fertilizing, weeding, and cultivating fields, controlling insects, taking in the harvest, and storing the yield. More farmers double- and even triple-cropped. And they fitted crops to field conditions more carefully. They used marginal lands more wisely, as for growing mulberry, tea, or fruit trees. And they produced in response to market opportunities, most notably by making tobacco and cotton major crops in the Nōbi–Kinai region. Indeed, by the early nineteenth century an observer could declare that,

> in recent times so many districts have developed their own special products that it is impossible to list them all. Products which did not exist at all fifty or a hundred years ago have now begun to be produced in large quantities by various domains.[6]

Thus only a portion of the total agronomic gain was in food, most was in other goods, but all generated income for villagers, particularly for the more well-to-do.

Finally, cultivators benefited from a few changes in machinery that improved labor efficiency, partially offsetting the increased demand for labor created by other aspects of agronomic change. These included the adoption of a long-tined hoe that facilitated deeper cultivation, specialized sickles, a multi-toothed threshing frame, winnowing fans to speed harvesting work, and larger looms for weaving silk and cotton cloth.

Behind these elements of intensification lay three basic trends that seem to have proceeded about as far as they could, given the social and technical context of the day. The three were maximal use of horticultural know-how, irrigation water, and fertilizer materials.

A rich literature on horticultural techniques, the so-called *jikatasho* or farm manuals, developed during the eighteenth and nineteenth centuries, being produced by government officials, scholars, and village leaders. Comprehensive in coverage and meticulous in detail, the best of them sought to optimize farm operations to benefit the producing families. Most notably Miyazaki Antei, whose encyclopedic *Nōgyō zensho* of 1697 was a seminal work in the genre, explained his basic concern this way:

> In no class of society are rich men so few and poor men so many as among the peasantry. Unless they lay up stores of money and grain, they run the very great risk of dying of starvation in bad years. Peasants should always bear this in mind, being humble in their persons and practising economy.[7]

By the nineteenth century an array of treatises offered peasants guidance on all facets of their lives as cultivators, landholders, villagers, and family members. How fully they followed the advice is unclear, but works of the genre were at least known and admired throughout the realm.

As for irrigation water, despite increased crop specialization and orchardry, rice remained the predominant crop, in part because governments encouraged it and in part because rice provided a much greater caloric yield per tilled acre than did any other crop. This reliance on paddy culture meant, however, that water resources came to be fully utilized, and during the eighteenth century shortages and disputes over use rights became chronic. The quest for water also led governments and villages to exploit major rivers, and by the later eighteenth century the tasks of maintaining complex irrigation systems and controlling large rivers constituted immense, inescapable burdens that were required of society simply to preserve existing levels of paddy output.

Whereas irrigation water was essential for paddy culture, fertilizer was necessary for intensive tillage of all sorts. And while the spread of irrigation meant essentially a fuller elaboration and refinement of existing techniques, in fertilizer use one sees significantly more innovative developments. In earlier centuries fertilizing had initially entailed gathering litter, burning it to produce ash, and stirring the ash into the soil – in effect, a regularized form of slash-and-burn cultivation. Gradually, however, ash had been supplemented by mulch, meaning rotted rather than incinerated litter, and by dung where available. The great seventeenth-century increase in arable acreage created so much new demand for green fertilizer, however, even as it reduced the source of supply, that farmers began seeking substitutes.

Especially in villages around the cities, where woodland was less extensive and served other purposes, and where nutrient-gobbling crops such as tobacco and cotton came to be most prevalent, the demand for fertilizer grew intense. In response diverse forms of organic waste, notably industrial byproducts from soy, *sake*, and vegetable oil production as well as nightsoil (human bodily waste), came to be utilized. The fertilizer demand was so great, however, that by the later eighteenth century competition for this biowaste had become fierce, theft a problem, and cost a severe burden to the cultivator. Indeed, fertilizer costs were so high, becoming the single greatest expense a farmer faced, that the production and distribution of fishmeal became economically feasible. By the nineteenth century the expansion of coastal fisheries had made fishmeal a major fertilizer for cultivators in many areas.

The interplay of population pressure, government policy, and scarcity of land, water, and fertilizer is nicely illustrated by developments in the vicinity of modern-day Kodaira, a bakufu-controlled area of the Kantō a few kilometers west of Edo.[8] During the 1650s the bakufu allowed Ogawa Kurobei, an entrepreneur from a nearby town, to recruit settlers to open about five square kilometers of the area to cultivation as a *shinden*, a new settlement, Ogawa-*mura* as it came to be called. The area lacked water for paddy culture because of its topography and the need to assure Edo's water supply, so the villagers grew dry crops, using ample fertilizer to compensate for poor soil. Within a decade or so the area authorized for reclamation was all in tillage, and by about 1700 the *shinden* population was large enough so that village leaders petitioned to open more of the adjacent woodland. For twenty years Edo authorities rejected the petitions because the areas in question grew grass and brush that nearby villagers customarily used to fertilize their poor soil. During the 1720s, however, the shogun Yoshimune (r. 1716–45), who hoped to ease bakufu fiscal problems by increasing agricultural output, reversed standing policy and allowed roughly a doubling of arable acreage in the Ogawa-*mura* vicinity as part of a broad-ranging program to bring more of the Kantō into farm production. During the next several years the land was converted to tillage, along with many nearby areas. However, those measures only increased the demand for fertilizer material while eliminating sources, thereby fostering the shift to commercial fertilizer and to the cash cropping and wage work required to generate money to pay for it.

LABOR

As hinted by the above comments on maintenance of irrigation systems and river works and on the scramble for fertilizer materials, the later-Edo economy exploited as best it could not only its mines, woodlands, arable, and water, but also its labor resources. Indeed, the maximizing of labor potential – inducing villagers to work more hours of more days, to work harder, and to work smarter – may have been the single most important factor in sustaining agricultural output and the broader society that depended on it after 1720 or so.

The issue merits attention because on one hand this society for some reason(s) and in some manner stabilized its overall size after 1720, yet at the same time it continued to find the additional labor required by the increasing riparian and road work, the highly labor-intensive agricultural regimen that was taking shape, and the expanded commercial sector of the economy that rode atop rural output. In essence, it appears, the very process that was central to demographic stabilization elicited the additional labor effort. Specifically, in their struggle to survive under straitened ecological circumstances, small-scale agricultural households, which constituted most of the population, adopted rhythms of life and work that trimmed their reproductive output while increasing their labor input. In the outcome these changes met society's heightened demand for labor while halting its demographic growth.

Small-scale farm households, "microfarmers" so to say, did not suddenly appear in the eighteenth century, of course. In chapter 7 we noted that during the medieval centuries small-scale holdings began to proliferate as the *shōen* system with its local land-holding overseers (*myōshu*) disintegrated, doing so in the Kinai first and elsewhere later. Doubtless political disorder continually created larger-scale, land-based units as vigorous heads of rural households reclaimed or seized land and organized their kinsmen and dependants into local defense forces. And the surge of land reclamation that came with pacification around 1600 enabled other landholders to acquire larger holdings that they worked with kin and non-kin help.

With that pacification, however, large-scale farm households began losing much of their *raison d'être*. Local leaders no longer had need for large numbers of subordinates for military support or even as a basis for favored local status since land and status rights were affirmed by government documentation. Moreover, the rapid seventeenth-century growth of arable land and population, together with gains in productivity (per agricultural worker and per tilled hectare), which were mainly due to increased paddy culture, enabled many holders to divide their fields among offspring as occasion dictated.

Then, necessity reinforced feasibility. Declines in mining and construction-related work reduced rural job opportunities, and when reclaimable land and irrigation water started becoming scarce later in the century, heads of large households found it increasingly difficult to keep relatives and non-kin dependants gainfully employed. More and more of them addressed the problem by cutting such people loose. They gave them petty parcels of land complete with tax obligations, and they reduced or ended the service owed them by their former dependants in return for reduction or termination of their own obligation to care for the lowly in times of need. Doubtless many ex-dependants welcomed the chance to have their own fields and thus become their own bosses, only discovering after the fact whether the results were gratifying.

By the early eighteenth century, with land and water scarce, such property division gradually ceased to occur. Villages generally consisted of a large number of small holders plus a handful of well-to-do households with substantial holdings and roles as village leaders. The small holders worked small parcels of a hectare or less that were more-or-less sufficient – under favorable circumstances and if well managed – to support a nuclear household, meaning a couple, two children or so, and perhaps a set of grandparents. As generations passed, residual ties between these microfarmers and neighboring large-holder/village leaders decayed, a process that further shredded the village "safety net" that large households had once provided their weaker members.

However, the fact that microfarmers held land placed pressure on them – pressure from government, village leaders, neighbors, and themselves – to remain in the village, continue producing crops, meet their portion of the village's tax obligation, and thus sustain their families and their status as bona fide peasants (*onbyakushō*). For, however meagre the material worth of status as *onbyakushō*, it did assure one a "place," the foundation of a life and persona. And it situated one solidly above a mere landless villager, laborer, migrant, or pariah (*eta*), much as the most inadequately stipended samurai was a clear socio-ethical cut above a mere commoner, however well-to-do. So small holders had compelling reason to stay put, work hard, and beget an heir to continue the farm's operation.

These changed circumstances spurred microfarmers to minimize inessential expenses and maximize the yield of their land, embracing horticultural techniques advocated by authors of *jikatasho*. Very few of the new techniques were labor savers, however. Indeed, most required labor intensification. Family members provided the labor, but given the small acreage involved, a small family sufficed. Extra progeny, especially during their early years, constituted a burden that seemed unlikely ever to pay for itself and, more immediately, a hindrance to the efficiency of others, especially the wife. Given the high child mortality rates of the day, the trick of raising a healthy heir without having to raise many other children was not an easy one to pull off, and not a few households foundered on the challenge.

The adoption of agronomic improvements thus led small holders to invest more time in their farm work and in the by-employments that generated cash to pay for fertilizer and other necessities. The poorly paid corvée work of riparian and road maintenance consumed an appreciable and growing part of their work year. In the time left over they could engage in *dekasegi*, traveling to take the comparatively well paid but insecure wage work that by the nineteenth century was appearing more widely, replacing jobs earlier lost as the seventeenth century had aged.

Government policy encouraged the rise of these new jobs because governments taxed non-food output inefficiently, which gave villagers incentive to supplement or replace food production with diverse other marketable crops and goods. As that rural production grew, much of it at the expense of urban handicraft and industrial output, it created work opportunities not only for the producers themselves but also for those willing to leave home for wage work.

With husbands away for longer periods while other family members ran the microfarm, pregnancy rates and probably infant-survival rates declined. More young adults remained single, often working as unwed adult helpers in natal households. More couples married later, and they generally had children less frequently. In addition, more households, particularly the poor and especially during hard times, used abortion and infanticide to control family size, trying thereby to maximize the chance that the children they did rear would survive to adulthood. And they supplemented these techniques with adoption, taking in or giving away a child as exigency dictated, in the process preserving adoption as a normal mechanism of lineage perpetuation. By the mid-eighteenth century, it appears, a new set of reproductive norms had become established.[9]

The demographic impact of those norms was reinforced by other changes of the day. As travelers proliferated and cities became more densely settled during the later seventeenth century, epidemics of contagious disease, small-pox in particular, became more frequent and severe. And while the resulting adult mortality was low, child and infant deaths were common. After 1700 crop failure and famine also became more frequent and severe, producing death and malnutrition. By sporadically reducing fecundity and causing more deaths, these trends produced short-term local and regional population declines that contributed to long-term demographic stabilization.

The families of eighteenth-century small holders thus seem to have combined reproductive restraint with long hours of work to get by as best they could. The less gifted and those hit by crop failure, epidemic, or other calamity fell on hard times, borrowing, mortgaging their land, commonly ending up as tenants or landless laborers. The difficulties and dangers notwithstanding, however, microfarming families evidently considered the long hours of attentive work worthwhile, presumably because they offered the best chance of retaining *onbyakushō* status and avoiding the alternatives. Many, indeed most microfarmers pieced together durable lives, holding some land of their own, renting fields from some neighbors, and leasing fields to yet others. In the process they created intricate patterns of property holding that tended to blur status distinctions and obfuscate the lines between large and small holders, thereby imbricating themselves yet more deeply in the fabric of village life.

For some small holders, moreover, entrepreneurial farming brought rich rewards. From around 1700 onward measures that increased the yield on a given field usually did not result in increased taxes because officials so rarely resurveyed villages and recalibrated tax rates. The cultivator who managed to open more fields or increase the yield on those he already had thus gained a comparative edge that enabled him to "aid" hard-pressed, less successful neighbors, commonly by lending money, taking crops or fields as surety, and in time acquiring *de facto* possession of the fields as a landlord. Gradually the skillful landlord could guide his tenants in boosting the output of their lands, keeping the enhanced yield in the village, and mostly in his own pockets.

Over time these trends generated differential tax rates, as noted by Takemoto Ryūhei, a scholar in Okayama domain. Around 1810, while discussing the causes of rural poverty and depopulation, he observed that:

> Fields belonging to wealthy peasants bear a relatively light land tax, and they are consequently profitable. There are, however, usually but one or two such holders in a group of ten villages. As to the number of families that can live without borrowing, there are no more than ten in a hundred. The remainder are all poor. The fields of the latter pay a very heavy land tax without exception. On the other hand, the lands of wealthy peasants though yielding heavily are lightly taxed; hence they yield a surplus.[10]

By the nineteenth century, it appears, villages were becoming widely characterized by the presence of a very few landlord households, a modest number of small, autonomous landholders, and a large and growing number of partial or full tenant farmers who might be away from home working for extended periods.

In sum, the loss of exploitable resources and breakup of larger households seem to have created a large rural population of microfarming families. Except during times of crop failure, most were able to cope with their stabilized environmental context by exercising habits of frugality and caution, laboring long hours, working as skillfully as they could, and controlling their family size by other means when illness and infrequent pregnancies failed to suffice. Some flourished, becoming wealthy and influential; many more did not, ending up as tenants, semi-tenants, or landless laborers. But as a whole their strategy for coping with straitened circumstances caused them inadvertently to play the central role in stabilizing Japan's population size and sustaining agricultural and commercial production.

EXPANDING THE REALM

The later-Edo populace not only maximized the yield of its existing resource base; it also pressed that base outward on land, on sea, and through time. The most fruitful extension was in fisheries development, which enabled Tokugawa society to exploit offshore nutrient resources as food and fertilizer, thereby moving beyond the terrestrial limits that their rulers imposed. The emergence of a market for maritime catch processed in bulk as fish-meal fertilizer spurred the development of large-scale net fishing all along the coast. And it proved particularly effective on the western shore of Hokkaido. There the Pacific herring (*Chupea pallasii*) made annual spawning runs from the Sea of Okhotsk southward to Wajinchi, domain of the Matsumae daimyo on Oshima Peninsula. During the spring run, we are told,

> the first shoals [of herring] approached the shore, their arrival heralded by flocks of sea gulls and gams of whales. During a large run the sea turned white

and sticky from milt; the beach was littered with eggs, milt, and the bodies of fish washed up onto shore; and the water was so crowded with herring that a pole could almost stand unsupported.[11]

These vast schools were present only briefly, however, so the harvest had to be fast, which gave large nets their exceptional value. The herring were processed locally and the meal then shipped southward via the Sea of Japan to the Kinai region, where it played a significant role in sustaining the yield of cotton, tobacco, and other crops.

Much more modest in their effects were entrepreneurial attempts to exploit terrestrial Ezo, whose forests, soil, and subsurface resources were extensive and nearly virginal. Substantial quantities of seaweed and other marine goods from the region were brought into the economy along with fish meal, but political restraints, enforced mainly by Matsumae domain, thwarted nearly all agricultural development beyond Wajinchi. Placer mining had removed gold from some Hokkaido streams during the 1600s, and bear, deer, and freshwater fish catches depleted wildlife stocks – at severe cost to resident Ainu – but the region's timber appears to have remained nearly untouched.[12]

The potentially most profound expansion of the realm was temporal rather than geographical: the beginnings of ground-coal use, which marked the start of Japan's departure from total dependence on recently produced biosystem energy to partial dependence on the eons-old energy of fossil fuel. Much as in the British Isles, where people began using peat for fuel when wood no longer sufficed, mined ground coal when the peat became inadequate, and eventually developed steam-powered pumps to eject water from deep coal seams after shallow ones were exhausted, so in eighteenth-century Japan, where peat was unavailable, scarcity of fuel wood led to the use of ground-coal, mainly in the production of seasalt along the Inland Sea, but also for sugar processing and pottery firing. By the late eighteenth century the pollution produced by mine runoff and coal smoke was generating local opposition to coal mining and burning and eliciting periodic attempts to stop the practices. During the nineteenth century, however, regional fuel wood scarcities persisted and coal use slowly grew, foreshadowing the industrial age that lay in Japan's near future.

RATIONING

On balance the efforts to expand the realm were, save for fisheries, of minimal consequence. Perennial, heroic efforts by the households of microfarmers trying to preserve themselves maximized the yield from the existing resource base, but scarcities persisted throughout the later Edo period. This situation was reflected in the development of a rationing system, perhaps the most elaborate in human history, which constituted a major societal adaptation to the limits of an essentially fixed resource base.

Crop failure, famine, poverty, and market forces played their obvious roles as rationing mechanisms. Other, less obvious mechanisms appeared in the form of unlegislated, customary practice, consciously enforced local rules, and governmental regulations.

Regarding customary practice, private household codes and farm manuals proliferated during the eighteenth and nineteenth centuries, and their emphasis on frugality, diligence, and self-discipline encouraged the rationing of goods, time, and energy. The pervasive acceptance of abortion and infanticide constituted the rationing of life itself. Governments and moralists denounced infanticide mightily, and the extent of the practice is debatable, but even among poorer samurai, who faced the fact that only one son could inherit a family stipend, the practice was used to control family size. In 1788, during the devastating Tenmei famine, the comfortably ensconced Confucian scholar Nakai Chikuzan complained thusly, in the course of discussing infanticide among samurai:

> Most [samurai] families do not take the trouble to bring up any except the first-born. If any family chooses to bring up two or three children, it is held up to ridicule by others. This is simply outrageous.[13]

How much such expressions of outrage, or the government edicts that shared it, deterred the practice of infanticide is unclear; they certainly did not stop it.

More broadly, one could argue that resource constraints underlay an array of frugal practices of daily life. These included the use of fuel-efficient cooking and heating devices, styles of home construction and furnishing that minimized wood usage, clothing designs that avoided fabric waste, diligent recycling of waste products, and consumption of meats that diverted no arable land to pasturage, including "bear, wild boar, deer, rabbit, badger, monkey, pheasant, duck, dove, and other birds," and more chicken as wild game grew scarce in the later Edo period.[14]

Locally, communities developed diverse rationing techniques for coping with resource limitations. The scarcity of arable, together with the fact that villages were communally responsible for tax payments, gave residents a shared interest in assuring that all available land and all able villagers were productively employed. One practice that helped accomplish this end in many places was periodic redistribution of fields among households, a measure that helped assure each household a necessary minimum of good land.

Water, too, came to be rationed. During the later Edo period, as irrigation water came to be fully utilized and water disputes (*mizu mondai*) proliferated, villages across the realm developed rules to regulate its use. They specified the size of water-intake gates, the fields that could be flooded, the days, hours, and sequence in which particular villagers could draw water, the mechanics of enforcement, and the specifics of punishment for infractions. Despite such attentiveness, however, *mizu mondai* remained a chronic source of disputation within and between villages.

The adoption of such communal regulatory practices was facilitated by a long-established approach to "property." From *ritsuryō* times onward, property rights were understood as specified rights of use that carried explicit reciprocal obligations. The concept was elaborately developed in documents (*shiki*) of the *shōen* system, wherein specified persons (names, rather, that could pass from person to person) enjoyed particular rights of income, use, or position in return for providing specified goods or services. Through such documents several people could acquire specific, limited use rights on a given piece of land or other property. When the *shōen* system disintegrated, use rights found expression as *yaku*, specific rights and obligations that were documented, socially sanctioned, and justiciable. Besides acquiring specified rights to irrigation water, villagers held rights to arable land that, for example, could allow one household to grow the main summer crop and another to raise a winter crop on the same plot of land.

The most complicated systems of multiple-use rights related to woodland because its biotic diversity gave it so many potential uses. As woodland grew scarce in villages throughout the realm, elaborate rules developed that allowed specific households to extract set amounts of fodder, fertilizer material, fuel wood, or other goods from particular sites at specified times, in designated sequences, or with particular tools or techniques. This multiple-use system of rationing helped villagers maximize the yield from their resources and restrain abuses by the village wealthy and wanton while distributing the usufruct in a manner that helped sustain the productive capacity of the village as a whole.

Finally, governments too developed rules to cope with scarcity, most pervasively through sumptuary regulations. Originally the bakufu issued a few to give outward expression to *shinōkōshō* status distinctions by stipulating restrictions on residence style and scale, clothing, ornaments, and conduct. As scarcities became more pronounced late in the seventeenth century, however, sumptuary regulations multiplied like topsy. Legitimized by being embedded in the status order, they strove to regulate consumption of all manner of forest products, foodstuffs, metals, clothing, and myriad other items, thereby allocating scarce resources to status groups in proportions acceptable to the rulers. Even labor time became an object of attention as decrees sought to discourage recreation, inessential travel, and other "unproductive" uses of time.

Assessing the effectiveness of these diverse forms of rationing is impossible. However, the established order did survive the harrowing decades of adaptation that moved the larger society from an era of growth to one of stasis, and one can only speculate about the costs and benefits of alternative outcomes. What is clear is that the shift from growth to stasis was not easy: the signs of distress were many, showing up widely in political and cultural developments of the later Edo period.

CULTURAL AND POLITICAL TRENDS

In any setting, needless to say, cultural and political trends are the products of many variables. During the later Edo period, however, difficulties stemming from resource scarcity seem to have been the most influential domestic variables at work, and their effects were evident in the arenas of bakufu and daimyo politics above, village and town politics below, and at intersections of the two. Those difficulties also weighed heavily on intellectual life, fostering new and conflictive attitudes and lines of thought that helped legitimize demands for remediation and change.

Unsurprisingly, these broader ecological issues bore least directly on the realm of aesthetics and entertainment, where arts and letters spoke primarily for and to the beneficiaries of the established order. Even there, however, ramifications of scarcity were indirectly apparent, most notably in the decline of seventeenth-century elite culture, the associated decline of Kyoto and Kamigata cultural dominance, and perhaps, too, in the tone and quality of the cultural production that became dominant, namely that addressed to lesser warriors and commoners.

THE DISPLACEMENT OF KYOTO AND ITS CULTURE

The century following Nobunaga's seizure of Kyoto had been good for the city, as noted in chapter 10. It flourished as never before, experiencing a revival of elite culture that lasted into the late seventeenth century. By then the city had helped shape the gentlemanly ideal of *yūgei*, and it played a central role in the rise of the dynamic, more plebeian, and far more popular Kamigata *ukiyo* or "floating world" culture, the urban culture that spread to larger towns throughout the realm and that is now associated with the Genroku period, 1688–1704.

By Genroku, however, Kyoto was well past its prime, although its decline was concealed by the city's association with Osaka, which was still growing. Kyoto was, after all, at heart a political city, and both directly and indirectly political vicissitudes shaped its destiny. During the decades to about 1630, as rulers increased their income and shifted to peacetime lifestyles, they spent lavishly, and wealth flowed into the city. As forests crashed and buildings rose, Kyoto blossomed. Tax wealth also flowed into the city indirectly when officially chartered lumbermen and other merchants spread their wealth about. They and the artists whom they supported produced the Saga books, as noted earlier, and created, at Takagamine overlooking the city, an artist colony that catered to the city's mixed elite of court, *kuge*, senior *bushi*, and wealthy merchants.

As government income stabilized and treasuries emptied, however, shogun and daimyo cut back their expenditures in Kyoto, disengaging from much of its provisioning. As forests became depleted and the construction boom petered out, merchants as a whole and lumbermen in particular found life increasingly precarious, and as a result their support for cultural production shriveled. By the 1680s the Takagamine colony and its affiliated higher culture were in steep decline. By the 1730s Kyoto city officials faced a struggle simply persuading lumbermen to maintain Shijō Bridge, which was essential to the annual Gion festival procession.

The decline in bullion mining also damaged Kyoto in the decades around 1700. Silver exports had paid for silk yarn imports that supplied the booming Nishijin weaving trade, the city's largest industry, but as the bakufu cut back silver exports, silk imports declined, hurting the weavers. And when during the early eighteenth century rulers tried to reduce bullion exports even further by fostering import substitution, a silk yarn industry developed in the hinterland, which gave rise to rural weaving that competed with, undersold, and gradually squeezed Nishijin out of nearly all but the highest-quality segment of the market.

The effects of these several developments on Kyoto's size seem unclear. As of 1878, however, the city reported a population of some 230,000. That number, which probably reflects a significant decline in the preceding decade or so, is far below the estimated 350,000 of around 1700. Insofar as Osaka's early vitality helped sustain Kyoto into the eighteenth century, moreover, its later economic and demographic contraction also weakened the old capital. Osaka's population, which reportedly peaked at about a half-million before the mid-eighteenth century, dropped to some 375,000 or so by 1801 and 317,000 in 1854 as ruralization of industry eroded its commercial foundation.[15]

The forces that were undermining Kyoto's vibrancy also undercut upper-class *bushi* culture in castle towns across the country. The construction of elegant mansions and gardens, the presentation of *nō* drama and tea ceremony, and the established forms of *waka*, Kanō art, and other accomplishments – all were faltering by the late seventeenth century as fiscal constraints made themselves felt. By the eighteenth, elite culture was essentially defunct everywhere. Two of its last noteworthy expressions were the gorgeous art of Ogata Kōrin and the graceful walking garden Rikugien. Built on the northern outskirts of Edo in 1695 for the mansion of Yanagisawa Yoshiyasu, favorite advisor to the shogun Tsunayoshi, about half of Rikugien survives today as one of Tokyo's most lovely garden-parks.

The spread of ukiyo culture. Some of the wealth that no longer reached Kyoto enriched Edo instead – *vide* Rikugien. As the routines of senior *bushi* life became settled after the 1630s, however, their aesthetic activities in Edo also grew routine, and the expanding city's creative energies came to center in the large population of lesser warriors and commoners. It was most visible, as mentioned in chapter 10, in *ukiyo-e* print-making but also in Edo's appropriation of Kamigata *kabuki* theatre and *haikai* poetry. After 1700 the city emerged as the creative center of these arts, generally steering them in a more plebeian direction. *Haikai* composition there became a popular recreational activity notorious for its poetic shallowness. By the late eighteenth century the city's *kabuki* drama, armed with fantastic scripts, elaborate stages, and doting audiences, had developed into dazzling visual spectacle that overwhelmed the puppet theatre, nearly eliminating it as a rival enterprise. *Ukiyo-e* prints, meanwhile, evolved from monochromes into lush polychromes that treated a wide range of subjects in formats of varying shape and size and at prices for all pocketbooks.

The *ukiyo-zōshi* fiction of Saikaku and Kiseki, with its strong connection to the Kamigata region, was displaced in Edo by other literary genres that emerged in the later eighteenth century. These soon gained wide popularity, in part because they employed a more fully colloquial language. During the early nineteenth century the new literature, commonly known as *gesaku*, acquired unprecedented richness of style and subject matter, with works ranging from short picture books to long, multi-volume narratives, and from simple entertaining tales to complex plots larded with moral pretension.

This art, drama, and literary production was only a part – if the more elegant part – of Edo's rich culture of popular entertainment and edification. During the seventeenth century, when Edo had been a heavily male society, a culture of bisexual entertainment had flourished, but from the mid-1700s onward the city's female population rose, perhaps as hardship prompted hard-pressed rural families to send daughters to work there, and as that trend advanced, male prostitution declined. A richly diverse plebeian culture survived, however, its texture and variety nicely captured in this description from around 1865 of the scene during a carnival in a downtown square near some tea houses and a theatre. The writer mentions

> the "Three Sisters" female kabuki, peep shows ... beggar's opera ... raconteurs, archery booths, barbershops, massage healers, and around them peddlers of toys, loquat leaf broth, chilled water ... confectionery, chilled and solidified agar-agar jelly, *sushi* ... tempura, dumplings, stuffed Inari fritters, fried eel livers, insects, lanterns, as well as wandering masseurs and Shinnai balladeers, peddlers of all sorts, blowgun booths ... fortune-sellers ... vendors of "streetwalker" noodles, drunks, quarrels, pests.[16]

Refined culture it was not, but affordable for nearly everyone. And "everyone" in Edo meant, during the eighteenth and nineteenth centuries, well over a million people, roughly half of them in samurai households and half commoners. Of the latter, one study suggests, "between one-third and one-half were home renters, day laborers and other unskilled workers, [and the] poor," many of them immigrants and transients from the countryside.[17]

The *haikai* of Edo were known for their glibness, but by 1700, as noted in chapter 10, *haikai* composition was also gaining popularity outside the cities. During later Edo serious *haikai* versifying spread across the realm; organizations of amateur poets arose among the more financially comfortable, and several additional names, such as Ema Saikō and Kobayashi Issa, joined Japan's long roster of celebrated poets.

By the nineteenth century *kabuki*, *ukiyo-e*, and popular fiction were also reaching well beyond the city and its daily life, doing so in two senses. In a literal geographical sense the arts were spreading widely through the countryside as performers and peddlers traveled farther and as more fortunate villagers acquired the resources and education necessary to enjoy them. In content, as well, stories and plays reached beyond quotidian city life and interests. By drawing from and adding to older genres, authors and playwrights developed widely popular tales of miracle and mystery, exotic foreign lands, and hazy historical epochs. Print makers similarly added new subjects, most famously portrayals of life and scenery beyond the city limits, as in the well-known landscape prints of Katsushika Hokusai and Andō Hiroshige.

Finally, one must note that although Kyoto had fallen on hard times, the city was never forgotten, and during the nineteenth century it acquired a new, derivative panache, thanks largely to people who had at most only marginal contacts with it and its old elite. The eclipse of Kyoto and its higher culture had undermined the authority of old norms, making new approaches to courtly culture possible. The trend was most evident in *kokugaku* or "nativist" learning, in which, as we note below, scholars with few or no links to the Kyoto elite reworked elements of the imperial legacy, particularly its literary and Shintō traditions, to give that legacy a renewed and deeper salience to their own day. Long-standing restraints on *waka* composition also eroded, and poets across the country used the venerable form with unprecedented freedom, giving it a vitality and pertinence it had lacked for centuries. During the nineteenth century this renewed interest in the imperial legacy acquired a strongly political cast as foreign intruders presented the Tokugawa regime with unmanageable new problems, prompting observers to look for alternative political leadership, which some discerned in the long-defunct tradition of imperial rule.

SIGNS OF STRESS: INTELLECTUAL

Later-Edo difficulties found particularly overt expression in doctrines expounded by scholars and commentators of diverse sorts. Some of the writings were vigorous polemics noisily critical of current conditions. Others were social tracts that sought to enhance well-being and ease discontent with the established order by improving human behavior and attitudes. Yet others were philosophical exegeses that sought to mend society by overcoming perceived inadequacies of sanctioned doctrine. Commonly, however, the meliorist writings contained an unintentionally subversive potential because they provided grounds for questioning one or another aspect of official ideology and arrangements. At a more plebeian level there flourished a less visible body of poorly articulated ideas and attitudes that encouraged followers to place their trust in powers lying beyond the established rulership.

In scholarly writings as a whole, as is usually the case, intellectuals were mainly addressing doctrinal quarrels and philosophical agendas that had a life of their own and only modest operative relevance to the substantive issues of the day. Moreover, when they did address issues and propose remedies, even the most iconoclastic critics rarely called for major change. In part, no doubt, this was so because of the personal risk such advocacy would entail, but in greater part it was so because they generally defined problems as failures of a specific leadership rather than as systemic defects. Much as the modern believer in limitless linear expansion explains the destructive effects of sustained growth as failures of particular, short-term policies, so Tokugawa-era believers in a perfectable order explained discrepancies between theory and fact in terms of discrete policy failures.

These writings and advocacies do nevertheless suggest a widespread mood of skepticism and growing disaffection. That mood was most vividly expressed in the violent protests of the age, as we note below. However, later in the nineteenth century, when circumstances prepared politically consequential figures to welcome anti-establishment ideas, these diverse exegeses helped them to deny the legitimacy of Tokugawa supremacy and even hereditary *bushi* rule, and to propose alternatives.

Polemicists.   Whereas seventeenth-century scholars had been engaged mainly in explaining why Tokugawa *bushi* had the right to rule, eighteenth-century essayists were much more eclectic in agenda and skeptical in perspective. Even proponents of the established order seemed more defensive, more hostile toward perceived enemies of the regime, and more critical of presumably ineffectual officials or policies. Ogyū Sorai, arguably the most influential thinker of the century, was a vigorous Confucian defender of the Tokugawa order and *bushi* supremacy. Although much of his effort was given over to harsh academic disputation with other Confucians, he also wrote on matters political, criticizing official malfeasance that weakened the system, attacking merchants and commerce for impoverishing everyone else, and calling for energetic disciplinary measures to reaffirm proper status relationships, restore the proper allocation of resources, and curtail the extravagance that he saw as the cause of scarcity. His political ideas, which resembled policies of the dynamic shogun Yoshimune, resonated with samurai in general, and in following decades Sorai's disciples spread his teachings to castle towns all across the country, giving rise to intense and enduring doctrinal conflict between supporters and critics of his ideas.

Other writers were as vigorously polemical as Sorai, but none as influential. Three of the most iconoclastic were also three of the least consequential in their own day, but they merit note as exemplars of both the range and limits of the century's thought. One was the young Osaka merchant scholar Tominaga Nakamoto; one, the Tōhoku physician Andō Shōeki; and the third, Yamagata Daini, an erstwhile bakufu policeman who became a teacher.

In a series of iconoclastic essays Tominaga repudiated the verities of the day, dismissing the scholarly writings of Sorai and Itō Jinsai as nothing more than intellectual one-up-manship. He laid bare the inconsistencies of Buddhist writings and asserted that none constituted Gautama's teachings. Shintō teachings, too, were merely scholarly creations and not to be taken literally. Having slashed the intellectual foundations out from under all established Truth, however, Tominaga was left with only quotidian morality as a guide to life:

> As to the way of truth, the way which should be practised in present-day Japan, it is simply to perform our evident duty in everything, to give priority to the tasks of the day, to maintain an upright heart and correct conduct, to be restrained in speech and bearing, and, if we have parents, to serve and honour them well.[18]

And these principles of morality, his essay's internal commentator noted, were found in the three creeds themselves.

Andō Shōeki was even more iconoclastic in rhetoric and reformist in message. Born in a village on the upper reaches of the Yoneshiro River in Akita domain, and well schooled in Sōtō Zen Buddhism, he developed a vigorous, holistic interpretation of existence that basically reflected his Zen discipline but employed the well established East Asian concepts of intrinsic vitalism, numerology, symbiotic pairs and their balancing, historical devolution, and rectification of the universe through rectification of one's own understanding.

Andō compared human society unfavorably with that of other creatures and found the root of human corruption in the false teachings of celebrated thinkers.

> The sages appeared in the world and established the five laws and taught false talking, thieved Heaven's Way and the world. Shakyamuni appeared and taught false talking and "skillful means," set himself above all others and greedily ate their donations. Laozi...Zhuangzi...Writers of medical texts...Prince Shōtoku...All of them made falsehoods their teaching. This is the reason that the entire world is full of false talking and false actions.[19]

He spelled out the social havoc wrought by this falsity – exploitative governance, economic inequalities, crop failure, famine, uprisings, suppression – and pointed to the Dutch and Ainu as human societies dedicated to the simple virtues of egalitarianism and productive work. For Japan, however, the restoration of virtuous order must await the coming of the Right Man, through whom

> it will be possible to finally realize the World of the Living Truth, free from thievery, revolt, delusion, and lust.

In the end Andō's world of virtue, grounded in "the inherent Way of Truth," was hardly more accessible than that of Maitreya (Miroku), Buddha of the future, who, it was popularly believed, would someday establish a virtuous, transcendent realm.

A much more expressly political polemic was *Ryūshi shinron*, drafted in 1759 by Yamagata Daini.[20] To sample a few passages, Yamagata let his readers know at the outset that in the 1180s power fell into the hands of "eastern barbarians" and that subsequently the Ashikaga "waxed impudent toward the throne despite their lowly title of "general-in-chief." Things only worsened after that, and today the men who are daimyo

> assume the airs of military commanders and issue arbitrary decrees unauthorized by recorded precedent. Even cooks and clerks, who never wield arms, presume to be warriors and oppress the people.

He addressed the hoary problem of the emperor–shogun relationship, which reappeared from time to time in Edo-period treatises, acknowledging that some people are troubled and ask, "Which side should we follow?" He belabored the issue at some length, quoting a nativist critic who declared that there really is no problem because of the "beautiful Japanese custom, without parallel anywhere," in which, "The shogun adheres to subject status even though he holds sway over all the realm." Yamagata rejected that view, however, insisting on the need to eliminate the Edo–Kyoto "duality" and "revive a unified power."

At the heart of Daini's complaint stood officialdom. He implied that at present, "No one with virtue has high rank. No one with talent holds office." And he stated explicitly that:

> Men in office today cannot devise policies or create ideas on their own. They adhere to the customs of bygone eras without a thought to validity, saying, "That's how it's always been."

He went on at great length lacerating corrupt, incompetent officialdom, criticizing even Yoshimune's rule, and holding government to blame for the rural misery of the "later ages," which he contrasted with antiquity:

> Farmers work infertile fields for months on end. After wrenching a crop from the thin soil, they must battle tax officers who demand sixty to seventy percent of the harvest plus corvée and taxes in kind. Some farmers work rich lands that leave a surplus for personal use – until officials demand further exactions. Those surcharges, plus corvée duty, lead farmers to destitution and death. But what do officials care? Whether soils are rich or poor, whether harvests are good or bad, farmers shiver and starve; and, ultimately, they give up farming. At the end of their rope, some seek ill-gotten gain in superfluous mercantile activities. Others beg for food, die in ditches, or turn to felony. Tillers become scarce and fields turn to wasteland ... Those good at selling grow rich; those good at farming go hungry. How different from the canons of the former sages!

In such decadent times, officials, long corrupted by sycophancy and gift giving, and utterly ignorant of rural poverty, live out their lives in the capital, where palaces and mansions line the streets, securely protected by high walls.

> State ministers live here, and court nobles serve here. With robes that blur like curtains flowing in the wind, endless processions of mounted retainers and four-horse chariots traverse the avenues. Entertainers line up row on row: actors, buffoons, dancing girls ... Here residents offer no tribute and hawkers pay no duties. Marketplaces are bedecked to look like Persia.

But out in the countryside, farmers exhaust themselves and all goes to ruin, and when the foe attacks, none will have the ability to repel him. Nor will subjects rally round their ruler, for his abuses will have alienated them and they will gladly let him perish.

Daini's imagery was highly drawn, literary in great part, and the analysis imperfect. But his indignation was crystal clear. Yet his proposals for fixing the mess were anything but radical, hardly more demanding than Tominaga's platitudes. He was as dedicated to a firmly disciplined, properly run, four-status society as Ogyū Sorai. Essentially he wanted the ruler to rule effectively and virtuously and "to believe in the Way," for then able officials "will come forth to serve him [and] ... troubles in the realm would then cease." Unhappily for Daini, however, his case became entangled in other problems of the day. In that situation the tone of his polemic helped secure his downfall on grounds that he had seemed to foster revolt, had recklessly

discussed the defenses of a shogunal castle, and had denigrated bakufu treatment of the court, thereby showing "extreme disrespect and the utmost inso-
lence" toward authority. "Hence you are sentenced to death."

The intensity of conflicting opinion and the prevalence of discontent are
suggested not only by this rhetoric of disbelief and alienation – and more
acutely by the violence of protest and retaliation that we note further on –
but also by the many efforts to ameliorate the discontent, solve problems,
and reconcile discordant ideas. Proponents of several lines of thought
engaged in these efforts, their messages growing, in both content and mode
of dissemination, out of established traditions.

Subversive meliorists. Advocates of diverse teachings used the methods of
dissemination long employed by proselytizing entertainers. The rise of a
countrywide landlord class of money-lending entrepreneurs and the movement of commercial production into the hinterland during the later Edo
period spread discretionary wealth widely about the countryside and fostered
more travel activity. These conditions enabled proponents of Shinshū and
other Buddhist creeds, Shintō, Confucianism, and other doctrines to travel
and teach widely, in the process spreading a shared culture even as they
advanced particular doctrinal agendas.

In content some of this religious advocacy was of a doctrinaire sort, but given
the government hostility toward divisive thought, most embraced the age-old
combinative strategy for reconciling discordant views and easing tensions, as in
the teachings of the widely popular Hosoi Heishū, the well-schooled son of a
landlord. Three other combinative lines of thought that merit brief note were
Setchūgaku, Hōtoku, and, most importantly, Sekimon Shingaku.

Setchūgaku, or "eclecticism," is attributed to Inoue Kinga, a physician's
son. It served mainly to muffle the noisy doctrinal quarrels of Ogyū Sorai's
followers and their Confucian rivals by finding merit in both viewpoints, an
approach the bakufu welcomed and fostered among its retainers. A half
century later, Ninomiya Sontoku, a village headman who served the lord of
Odawara and later the bakufu, addressed the heightened problems of rural
hardship and conflict by directing the rehabilitation of damaged lands and
villages and by promoting a doctrine he called Hōtoku. It was a creed that
applied to rural life and work much of the logic of diligence, gratitude, and
religious syncretism that Sekimon Shingaku directed to townsfolk.

Turning to Sekimon Shingaku, it antedates both Setchūgaku and Hōtoku,
and it merits fuller attention than they because during the Edo period it had
appreciably broader influence. Initially propagated by Ishida Baigan during
the early 1700s, it appeared at a time when followers of Sorai and other
bushi polemicists were denouncing merchants as exploitative parasites and
when, as we note below, poorer townsmen were physically trashing their
business establishments (*uchi kowashi*). Facing these provocations, merchants had reason to welcome an ideology that might ease the harassment
and justify their existence, and Shingaku did just that.

Baigan's central concept of *shingaku* ("heart learning"; mental discipline
that brings one's individual mind into accord with the universal Way) was

found in several Confucian and Buddhist teachings of the day, but he drew most heavily on Zen Buddhism and the Ch'eng-chu school of Confucian interpretation that derived from Sung China. With one's mind in tune with the universal, he argued, a person will live a righteous life, engage in honest trade, and make a fair profit.[21] After all, Baigan reasoned,

> The merchant's profit from sale is like the samurai's stipend. No profit from sale would be like the samurai serving without a stipend.

And a reasonable profit from trade is justified because,

> If there were no trade, the buyer would have nothing to buy and the seller could not sell... and all the people would suffer.

Thus the merchant is as essential to the realm as the samurai, peasant, or artisan.

By the late eighteenth century Shingaku teachers were going on extended lecture tours around the country. The most successful fitted their presentations to their audience, as shown by this comment of 1835 by a celebrated Shingaku preacher:

> Shingaku talks on the Way were not created for the sake of intellectuals... Therefore, I simplify my language a great deal, give examples, or tell humorous stories; I draw on whatever is close to the principle, whether Shinto, Buddhism, or anything at all... I just speak this way in order to be easily understood.[22]

A model, surely, for the teacher seeking large enrollments.

Far more than Hosoi and most other proponents of ameliorative thought, Sekimon Shingaku went beyond the traditions of itinerant preachers and doctrinal eclecticism. Baigan's most influential disciple was Teshima Toan, the son of a Kyoto merchant. Under the guidance of Toan and his followers, Shingaku developed an elaborate system of centrally controlled teachers and schools, with programs of instruction aimed specifically at women and children as well as adult males. These schools, which were operating at over 180 locations by the 1860s, became the centers of a shared religious faith. And that faith in turn shaped conduct because Toan taught that a true grasp of one's "original mind" was confirmed in moral behavior.

The bakufu approved Shingaku ideas and, especially during its final century, encouraged Shingaku proponents to open new schools around the country. It did so because the moral behavior advocated by Toan endorsed official Tokugawa Confucian virtues. As Toan wrote in 1780:

> The original mind is simply revering those above and having compassion for those below, completely fulfilling loyalty and rightness in regard to one's lord and retainers, being filial and caring toward one's father and mother, getting along well between husband and wife, having good relations between elder and younger, considering one's servants as one's children and generously bestowing true love on them, and diligently working at one's heaven-allotted trade – nothing more than this.

That Edo welcomed such views is unsurprising. By discouraging doctrinal conflict, encouraging productive, peaceful lives, and fostering prudence, these teachings supported the established order.

Indeed, in 1784, after one of his disciples blundered into a dispute with some Confucianists that led to Shingaku's proscription in a daimyo domain, Toan admonished his disciples that when they tried to set up meeting houses for preaching,

> You must be sure to consider seriously whether it would cause any problem with the government authorities.

In the same spirit, it was said of Toan, that

> Whenever he passed in front of a government proclamation notice, he would always take down his umbrella, bow deeply, and refrain from using his walking stick.

He was similarly respectful of shrines and temples and adhered to important rituals of reverence for Confucius. And his argumentation sought to find the universals underlying different creeds, as when he observed that

> the two teachings, Confucianism and Buddhism, differ greatly in their respective methods of teaching and guiding [people], but the point at which they ultimately arrive is a single principle.

In an age of tension and inter-group conflict, Sekimon Shingaku surely helped keep the peace.

At the same time, however, much as Tominaga's arguments, despite the blandness of his remedies, challenged religious authority fiercely, Shingaku's conciliatory doctrines and praxis had the subversive effect of challenging the socio-ethical tenets underlying *shinōkōshō* stratification and hereditary *bushi* supremacy. By encouraging townsmen to live lives of virtue and pursue their businesses diligently, and by characterizing such devotion as the repaying of a debt of gratitude that they owed their parents and the powers that gave them life, Shingaku raised merchant life to the level of a calling, much as seventeenth-century *bushidō* had done for sedentary samurai. This elevating of moral worth helped make the lives of urban commoners more gratifying and mutually beneficial and justified merchant careers in the face of the growing *bushi* criticism above and poorer-class resentment below. And by implication, at least, Shingaku asserted not only the moral and social worth of people in all walks of life but also their capacity for self-direction.

Other intellectual trends, as well, provided grounds for challenging the established order. One such trend stemmed from the venerable conundrum of how to relate the Japanese legacy to the continental; another, from the Confucian theme of "practicality" or *jitsugaku*.

To elaborate the former, the question of how best to relate and evaluate domestic and continental ideas, influence, and practice was a hoary chestnut, evident in the *Nihon shoki* and many later writings. The basis for scholarly exegesis lay in imported texts and translations of continental writings, which were legion, and in the accumulated corpus of Japan's long literary tradition and medieval writings on Shintō, the court, and related matters. During the seventeenth century Yamazaki Ansai and others labored to work this material into coherent doctrines, Ansai in particular aspiring to formulate a definitive and comprehensive creed based on his understanding of both indigenous and continental learning. In the teaching known as Suika Shintō he employed elaborate argumentation to assert that "throughout the whole universe there is only One Principle," and Shintō and Confucianism are simply its Japanese and Chinese expressions.[23]

For all its elegance, however, Ansai's effort did not settle the matter, any more than a bakufu decision of 1665 to sanction only those Shintō priests trained at Yoshida Shrine in Kyoto ended debate about Shintō tenets. From the late seventeenth century onward *kokugaku* ("nativist") scholars reinvigorated study of the Japanese legacy in attempts to establish its religious, literary, and broader socio-ethical merits, clarify the Japanese–continental cultural relationship, and identify ways of dealing with contemporary problems of governance and public well-being. They studied indigenous texts, mainly such classics as *Kojiki*, *Man'yōshū*, *Kokinshū*, and *Ise* and *Genji monogatari*, and they debated fine points with great intensity. In the process they developed elaborate arguments about the special character of Japan because of its godly origins and about the value to rulers of studying these texts because they reveal the "native" Japanese spirit with its distinctive virtues and thus offer clues on how to govern most effectively.

In neither word nor deed did nativist scholars of the eighteenth century present themselves as hostile to the established order; indeed, most had ties to the bakufu or daimyo. However, in rejecting Confucianism in particular and "Chinese" influence in general as alien and corrupting, these *kokugaku* arguments ran counter to favored integrative doctrines such as Setchūgaku, Shingaku, and Suika Shintō. And by challenging the idea that the regime's preferred creeds offered a proper and sufficient foundation for ruling or even understanding society, the writings added another basis for questioning the *bakuhan* system's claim to legitimacy. During the nineteenth century, when ambient Europeans came to be perceived as a menace, these writings provided ammunition for critics of the regime, who denounced it for failing to control the "barbarian" threat to the sacred realm of the emperor.

Turning briefly to the theme of *jitsugaku*, from late in the seventeenth century, as the era of growth faded, concern with practicality began to acquire prominence among writers addressing problems of governance, merchant affairs, and rural life. Ogyū Sorai and his followers espoused practicality to justify changes in government policy. The codes of merchant houses stressed practical performance. And merchant scholars celebrated the practical skills of businessmen. Indeed, as the eighteenth century advanced, they asserted more and more that the merchants' mastery of money and markets gave them a special capacity to handle affairs. Contemporaneously the *jikatasho* of Miyazaki Antei and later agronomic writers dwelt at length on practical policies for village life and farm work. As the eighteenth century advanced, scholars looked yet farther afield for practical solutions, with some gaining access via Nagasaki to *rangaku* ("Dutch learning"). Mainly *rangaku* meant European writings on medicine, art, and astronomy – and during the nineteenth century military technology – all of which were valued for their "practical" qualities.

Incrementally these diverse new bodies of knowledge and interpretation facilitated the questioning of Tokugawa doctrinal certitudes. And in the background, the capacity of ideas to influence affairs was abetted by the spread of schooling, which particularly characterized the later Edo period. At first it was schools for samurai that proliferated, private academies in the major cities initially and after the mid-eighteenth century domain schools that appeared in castle towns across the realm. Schools for commoners – and for mixed classes – also began appearing, initially in the cities and by the late eighteenth century in rural areas. The spread of schooling fostered basic literacy, especially among males. And among the more well-to-do of both town and countryside, it led to more advanced learning in philosophy, literature, history, and diverse practical arts.

By the 1790s the energetic bakufu leader Matsudaira Sadanobu saw in this spread of diversified learning and literacy, and particularly in the continual bickering of Confucianists, a disruptive influence on affairs. To control the problem, he delineated acceptable learning for Tokugawa vassals, fostering Ch'eng-Chu Confucianism in particular, and promoted this authorized schooling both in and out of Edo. He also enforced punitive measures to discipline writers of more plebeian sorts. On balance, however, his efforts scarcely narrowed the range of articulate thought, and they missed entirely the burgeoning body of inarticulate secessionist opinion.

Plebeian secessionists.   Poorly articulated attitudes among the general populace require attention because not all grievances of consequence find eloquent voice. The sense of grievance varies with time and place, it is true – even hunger may be perceived as normal and not a reason for protest – but the heightened hardship of the later Edo period was not generally regarded as merely one of life's givens. To the contrary, it was widely viewed as unacceptable, and the populace advanced an array of explanations for that assessment and for their resulting conduct.

One of the most durable grounds for demanding redress was the contention that the "honorable peasant" (*onbyakushō*) has an inherent right to live and work productively. That proposition sprang directly from Confucian doctrine that the regime had embraced, and it encouraged villagers to present petitions to the rulers with the presumption that legitimate grievances would be heard and meliorative action taken. During the eighteenth and nineteenth centuries, however, when abuse and suffering seemed more common and aid less forthcoming, more and more villagers turned to other powers for assistance and, when matters went well, directed their expressions of gratitude elsewhere.

Savior figures acquired much importance, some deriving from celebrated heroes or mythical figures, some from established godly traditions, and some from new or transformed deities. The term *daimyōjin* came to identify a wide range of benevolent figures, some understood to be the spirits of virtuous officials, others heroic peasant leaders who had died or been executed for some brave deed such as presenting a village grievance too aggressively. When villagers organized mass protests and invoked the rhetoric of *yonaoshi* or "world renewal," they commonly envisioned a particular *daimyōjin* as the protective power supporting their calls for a world of rejuvenated virtue and justice. By the mid-nineteenth century the rectifying power in some cases was the *namazu*, the mighty subterranean catfish who expressed his anger at injustice by shaking his tail and causing earthquakes.

Other savior figures also flourished. The long-revered Maitreya acquired new importance, most notably in Fujikō, a religious movement of the eighteenth-century Kantō. Fujikō followers turned to Maitreya, enshrined at a holy site on Mt. Fuji, for aid when in need and to express gratitude when blessed. Far greater numbers of people from all over the country made major shrines, notably Ise, the goals of pilgrimages undertaken to seek godly help or to give thanks for good fortune enjoyed by self, household, or village. And others turned to new or transfigured savior deities. Three new religious movements in particular – Kurozumikyō, Konkōkyō, and Tenrikyō – arose during the first half of the nineteenth century as a result of the acute personal suffering and religious experiences of three poor villagers, two women and a man. Each of the three felt compelled to spread the message of the deity's healing power and compassion, and despite the hostility of officialdom and established clerics, all found receptive audiences, mainly among the rural poor.

With the rulers providing less and less relief for the needy, more and more people were thus turning to other remedial and redemptive powers, which they elicited through their own forceful actions. Pilgrimages and other measures undertaken as expressions of gratitude for unusual good fortune also revealed the unprecedented readiness of commoners to act on their own, even in defiance of higher authority. That readiness was particularly evident in *eejanaika* ("ain't it grand!") incidents in which commoners, often poor townsmen, celebrated, usually in connection with a good harvest or other boon, the appearance of religious amulets that sanctioned raucous public drinking, dancing, and singing. On occasion revelers barged into the houses of usurers or other resented figures, demanding food, drink, or other signs of respect and engaging in acts of insoucient disdain. In the process they defied codes of propriety and stood status relationships on their head.

In narrow political terms this body of scholarly and popular thought does not demonstrate that irresistible public revolt was in the making. It suggests, rather, that if the Tokugawa regime were threatened by other forces, few would voluntarily rally to its aid and that if it fell, few would lament its passing. Viewed in broader social terms, this thought reveals that the later-Edo period of difficulty had spawned ideas and disseminated information that equipped the general public to address the problems of life with numerous practical skills, a wide range of perspectives, and a greater confidence in their own initiatives than ever before.

SIGNS OF STRESS: POLITICAL

After about 1700 political agendas at both government and village levels changed noticeably as the ramifications of scarcity made themselves felt. During the seventeenth century, as noted in chapter 10, bakufu leaders had busied themselves arranging daimyo, courtly, clerical, and foreign affairs, building monuments, and regularizing warrior life. They worked out administrative organization and procedure, improved fiscal operations, and dealt with sporadic disorders, most of which involved warriors. Daimyo agendas were essentially the same, save for affairs of court and foreigner.

During the eighteenth century the predominant issues for bakufu and daimyo alike related to the fisc, which faced chronic dearth, and to public unrest, which stemmed from material distress and social resentment. And that public unrest, which had appeared only sporadically during the 1600s, grew ever more pronounced, involving more complex alignments of friend and foe and becoming larger in scale, more frequent, and more violent. These trends continued during the nineteenth century, being supplemented by a new era of foreign complications, as we note in chapter 12.

Government-level politics. Tsunayoshi (r. 1680–1709), the Tokugawa regime's most earnestly Confucian shogun, strove to make ideological considerations central to his rule, but in fact fiscal issues prevailed. Because of his interest in conserving bullion and generating income, his administration's most lasting policies related to foreign trade, which he curtailed, and the currency, which he debased. In the short term his currency devaluation complicated political life, throwing the city of Edo into turmoil by triggering price fluctuations that hurt commoner and samurai alike; in the longer term his actions ushered in an era when fiscal problems dominated politics.

The next shogun of consequence, Yoshimune, was, arguably, the most energetic and imaginative of the dynasty, despite the severe neglect he has suffered in English-language studies. The diversity of his initiatives notwithstanding, however, nearly all his policies were in one way or another responses to the problems of resource scarcity, fiscal inadequacy, and their consequences. Indeed, he acquired the sobriquet *kome shōgun*, "rice shogun" because of his single-minded attention to such matters.

This focus on fiscal issues was evident thereafter in both bakufu and daimyo governance. Problems of currency, tax income, and price instability dominated agendas everywhere, causing political alignments and factional battles to be defined largely in terms of fiscal policy. And little wonder. As income stagnated and treasury reserves disappeared during the later seventeenth century, attempts by *bushi* leaders to handle their governing tasks while maintaining comfortable habits of life spawned endemic government borrowing. The resulting need to meet debt payments, as well as emergency outlays required by the fires, famines, and other misfortunes that became more frequent in the later Edo period, compelled exchequers to find the necessary funds in a timely manner. The single largest regular expense for both bakufu and daimyo being the stipends of retainers, more and more lords dealt with their fiscal shortfall by repeatedly "borrowing" from those retainers, in the process permanently reducing their stipends. Retainers in turn coped with those reductions by borrowing, taking by-employments, dismissing servants, limiting family size, and otherwise trimming expenses as best they could.

One general response to fiscal stress, then, was for rulers to pass the cost downward to lesser *bushi*, who in turn passed it on to their servants and out into the general community. However, because higher and lower warriors were linked by vertical chains of command, which enabled aggrieved samurai to lobby for redress through their superiors, that pattern of response helped assure that disagreements over fiscal policy became central to factional politics within governments all across the realm.

Other fiscal policies generated other types of political conflict. Domain governments tried to generate income by tapping into the commercial economy, monopolizing, licensing, and otherwise taxing diverse types of production. Most aspired to have the products sold outside their domains as a way to spur money imports, even as they tried to prevent currency outflows by discouraging non-specie imports. The perceived linkages between domain finance, commercial production, and resource limitations are nicely illustrated by this fragment of an 1813 manual on silk culture:

> The immediate benefit which silk farming brings to society is that it enables unused land along river banks, in the mountains and by the edge of the sea to be planted with mulberries, and silk spinning and weaving to flourish. Needless to say, when the products of the region are exported to other areas, the domain will become rich and its people prosperous. This is called "enriching the country" ... It is a natural consequence that states which sell their produce to other domains, and so bring in gold and silver, should become rich, while the people of countries with little produce, which thus allow gold and silver to flow out of their lands, become poor. By increasing the production of commodities one enhances the flow of precious metals into the country while suppressing their outflow.[24]

By the nineteenth century, unsurprisingly, these "mercantilist" policies were provoking inter-domain disputes and even conflicts with the bakufu.

The bakufu itself added to the tensions. Its leaders attempted to protect its treasury and cope with public unrest by exploiting commerce, controlling the money supply, managing large rivers, regulating highway corvée and maintenance, and countering the escalating peasant protest. But in diverse ways these policies threatened domain interests and infringed more and more on long-sanctioned daimyo prerogatives. By the mid-nineteenth century, in short, the capacity of rulers to deal with broader issues, whether domestic or foreign, was severely compromised by tensions and distrust between high and low warriors, between and within domanial ruling groups, and between domains and the bakufu. And these tensions and distrust had arisen primarily as a consequence of chronic fiscal problems and the underlying issue of resource scarcities.

Village-level politics. In the years around 1700 political agendas changed at the village level as much as at higher levels. During the preceding century village governance had dealt with problems relating to growth and branching (*shinden*), increases in village size, output, and activity, and government involvement in land surveys, tax collection, and other administrative matters. And when villagers had grievances to bring to their rulers, they mostly did so peaceably, with village officials lodging petitions in approved fashion.

From the late seventeenth century onward, however, large rural households decayed and microfarming became more universal. Local leaders found themselves gradually transformed into enemies of their poorer neighbors, who increasingly bypassed them when lodging complaints, presenting lawsuits, organizing mass protests, and engaging in violent retribution. Whereas seventeenth-century grievances had commonly related to a village's total tax burden, moreover, later ones dwelt more on charges of corruption by village officials, burdensome corvée duties, or inequitable allocation of tax obligations or of use rights in woodland and irrigation systems; that is to say, on what small holders perceived as injustices in the rationing system. Other issues included food scarcities and price jumps, which particularly threatened those not engaged in food production or more completely subject to vagaries of the marketplace.

Because of these changes in the content of grievances, villagers more and more targeted their plaints, suits, protests, and violence at wealthy neighbors – landlords, usurers, small businessmen – who often enough were the village's own officials, rather than at higher government authorities. The graphs in figure 11.1 reveal main aspects of later Tokugawa village unrest: the growing number and magnitude of commoner disputes and protests, the powerful

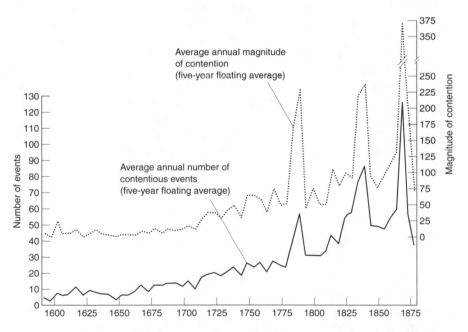

Figure 11.1 Trends in popular unrest, 1590–1880. The generally tranquil seventeenth century gave way during the eighteenth to disorder that intensified in both frequency and magnitude, erupting most dramatically in conjunction with periods of crop failure and public hardship during the 1780s, 1830s, and late 1860s. *Source*: James W. White, *Ikki, Social Conflict and Political Protest in Early Modern Japan* (Ithaca: Cornell University Press, 1995), p. 128.

influence of the Tenmei and Tenpō crop failures and famines, and the turmoil surrounding the Meiji Restoration.

The straitened circumstances of the eighteenth century also complicated the lives of the most disadvantaged groups, the pariah communities (*eta, hinin*), whose social ancestors have appeared on rare occasion in preceding chapters. During *sengoku*, daimyo had recruited groups of pariahs to their castle towns to perform diverse menial tasks, notably as leather workers (*kawata*) and as handlers of animal and human corpses, which the warriors produced in abundance. Then, as peace returned and castle towns expanded, pariah communities were gradually relocated to the margins of towns or to sites where they formed their own villages, mostly in central Japan. Both rulers and commoners took note of their presence, but evidently the relationship of pariah to commoner was not seen as a "problem."

During the eighteenth century, however, conflicts between the two proliferated. So did legislation that sought to protect the self-esteem and material interests of "regular" villagers by elaborating symbols of status difference and enforcing separation of both residence and function. As the century advanced, socioeconomic distinctions between pariah and ordinary folk became more pronounced and rationales to justify them more elaborate. Domains issued rules on the subject, and by the 1780s those rules were being reflected in bakufu regulations that expressed concern over reports of pariahs, "mingling incognito with peasants or townspeople at inns, eateries, drinking establishments, etc."[25]

The tension between pariah and non-pariah villagers was exacerbated by their dissimilar demographic trends. As noted above, during later Edo the rhythms of small holders' lives produced families of very modest size. Because of employment patterns among pariahs, however, they did not face the same procreative constraints. Couples had more sustained contact, and extra children provided extra hands to perform the menial and hereditary professional tasks that sustained their households. In consequence the pariah population continued to grow all through later Edo, which tended to alter power relationships between adjoining villages and posed threats of economic competition. Indeed, in 1834, during the Tenpō famine, the bakufu, using the term *kawata* for pariahs, declared:

> the number of *kawata* is increasing disproportionately in relation to that of the peasants. Someday this will become a source of problems. Henceforward only one male per household can take a bride. The other children must marry out. We will try to decrease the population one by one. Permission to marry must be secured from the appropriate officials.

Eighteenth- and nineteenth-century rulers continually fretted about the scarcity of cultivators, but in Edo's eyes *kawata* were consumers rather than producers of food and so needed to have their numbers reduced. Whereas government could try to send urban commoners back to their home villages, thereby turning them back into food producers, pariahs could not be so simply managed, so biological contraction was decreed, to no real effect.

Within cities and towns, meanwhile, several trends – hardship and unpredictability caused by government monetary manipulation, losses of income and employment due to *bushi* retrenchment and the ruralizing of production, and irregular food shortages and price gyrations caused by crop failure – led to unprecedented trouble. From the 1720s onward, there occurred sporadic incidents of urban smashing, or *uchi kowashi*, most of them directed against merchants accused of usury, price gouging, or grain hoarding. Not since the decades around 1500, when sectarians battled one another and when nearby villagers periodically besieged Kyoto money-lenders, had disorder among commoners been so pronounced. By the mid-nineteenth century the rhetoric of "world renewal" or *yonaoshi* was being invoked ever more frequently to legitimize these assaults on privilege.

In both town and country, that is to say, the stresses of the day were finding expression as confrontation between monied and poor commoners, the more and less favored. This was particularly so in the more commercialized areas, notably the Kyoto–Osaka–Edo vicinities, where price gyrations most threatened poorer folk. In areas where commerce was less developed and survival chronically difficult, notably Tōhoku with its more frequent crop shortfalls, later Tokugawa villagers still tended to direct their ire and dismay mainly against the rulers.

Where villagers did direct their protests at the rulers, their petitions, demands, and disturbances elicited diverse carrots and sticks. In Kanazawa, castle town of Kaga domain, for example, from the 1720s onward, and especially after the 1790s, the daimyo sponsored frequent city festivals, *bonshōgatsu*, to celebrate occasions of lordly good fortune, displaying the benevolence of his rule in hopes of cultivating good will among the townsmen.[26] Also from the 1720s onward, the bakufu and large numbers of daimyo began placing petition boxes in their castle towns so that commoners, lesser samurai, and others could make suggestions, report abuses, or vent their discontent. Thus a particularly irate unemployed samurai of Tosa domain informed his lord in 1761 that:

> Your officials are faithless and the way of your government is unjust!…
> Certainly you do not know of the officials' machinations, but the hatred of all
> of the people focuses on the single person of your lordship.[27]

More commonly the messages complained about specific problems, such as corruption or abuse by a certain local official, or disputes over tax obligations or resource allocations, or else they made suggestions for changes in particular policies. Sometimes the suggestions did lead to change, but perhaps the main value of the boxes was as an expression of lordly righteousness that facilitated the venting of frustration.

More visible, and probably more common, than such moves to defuse trouble was the increasingly frequent use of police action to quiet outbursts of discontent. By the nineteenth century these outbursts were involving thousands of people and could last for days before subsiding. They did subside, however, partly because of their own internal rhythms and partly in response to the carrot-and-stick strategies of authority. Nevertheless the large incidents left a residue of ill will seasoned with tales of heroism and suffering, and this slowly accumulating legacy of defiance helped sustain later protests, enriching the dynamics of conflict during the later Edo period and contributing to its growing scale and intensity.

[12] CRISIS AND REDIRECTION (1800–1890)

The Tokugawa regime, or *bakuhan taisei*, was structurally decentralized, its cohesiveness a result primarily of shared interests and a common political culture among upper-class *bushi*: shogun, daimyo, and their senior advisors and household members. Rules, routine, and their enforcement maintained stable relationships among these figures and between them and the rest of society.

These arrangements worked well during most of the seventeenth century, when warfare's cessation and sustained domestic growth provided enough security, comfort, and career prospects for enough people to offset the loss of opportunity that came with political stabilization. The arrangements worked far less well after the era of growth had passed, when all sectors of society were forced to adapt to more straitened circumstances. And predictably the less favored bore the heavier burden. Yet the regime and its encompassing social order survived despite famine, hardship, riot, embitterment, infighting, and alienation that found one or another expression at most levels of society.

During the nineteenth century, however, that situation changed, and from about 1860 onward the people of Japan were propelled willy nilly toward an age of industrialism. The great new variable that precipitated this change was a drastic alteration in global context: the rise of incipient industrial imperialism in the form of British, French, Russian, and American explorers, adventurers, whalers, traders, missionaries, and politico-military empire builders.

FOREIGN COMPLICATIONS

For over half a century the foreigners were unable to impose their will on *bakuhan* leaders because they brought to bear insufficient firepower and commitment: they were simply too busy elsewhere. In 1853, however, requests gave way to demands, and the Tokugawa, lacking the military means to refuse them, agreed to the treaties that foreigners wanted. The resulting changes in Japan's relationship to the outside world placed the established regime in an untenable position. In short order its military and political inadequacy became apparent to domestic observers, and within twenty years challengers had swept the old political structure aside and begun to lay the foundations for a new era.

EARLY ALARUMS

The Dutch had long protected their special position at Nagasaki by using weapons and wiles to thwart the occasional efforts of other Europeans to reach Japan. However, during the Napoleonic Wars Holland was linked to France, which gave the British reason and excuse to seize Dutch vessels and imperial outposts, thereby rupturing Dutch domination of Euro-Asian trade. After Napoleon's defeat in 1814, the British emerged as the pre-eminent European maritime presence in East Asian waters.

Long before that, even as Czars had battled to expand their empire westward and southward, Russian adventurers, empire builders, and traders gradually worked their way eastward across Siberia. From the 1730s onward occasional explorer-traders sailed the seas around Japan, at times approaching the coast in search of provisions, information, and clandestine trade. During the 1780s these Russian appearances began eliciting worried comments from Japanese students of foreign affairs, and in the autumn of 1808 Japan experienced its first panic of the new era in foreign relations. That occurred when *HMS Phaeton*, a major British warship then cruising Asian waters in search of Napoleonic prey, entered Nagasaki harbor, with crew and cannon deployed for action, to obtain water and other provisions. At the time Edo was responding to a series of armed attacks and demands for trade by a Russian raider in the Ezo region, and the situation seemed particularly threatening because it came as a pincer thrust from two directions by a real or potential alliance of major foreign powers.

As matters worked out, the panic in Nagasaki, Edo, and Ezo soon passed, and the incidents were resolved with only modest difficulty: a few villages sacked and burned, vessels destroyed, goods stolen, a number of people slain, defense forces humiliated, some officials disgraced, and two suicides. However, the episode established a new sense among the observant that Tokugawa Japan was exposed as never before to foreign danger.

Napoleon's defeat and the resulting peace treaties in Europe restored the pre-war Dutch status at Nagasaki, and in following years British merchantmen appeared off Japan only occasionally. With the Russians losing interest in Ezo at about the same time, matters seemed to have quieted down.

During the 1820s, however, a new complication appeared: whalers. By then European and American harpooners, in their quest for oil to fuel the lamps of nascent industrial society, had so depleted desirable cetacean stock in the Atlantic that they had moved into the Pacific. There they found the killing particularly good in the northerly seas east of Japan. Their activity periodically brought whaling crews to shore as shipwrecks or as seekers of provisions or safe haven, and in 1824 a pair of incidents, near Mito and south of Kyushu, revived with particular acuteness officialdom's concern over coastal vulnerability. The incident near Mito helped define the "problem" of foreign ships in alarmist terms because officials of the prestigious Mito domain, operating from the perspective of their own Confucian nativist thought (*Mitogaku*), viewed the affair in terms of the longstanding treatment of Christianity as a proscribed subversive force. In their eyes the whalers constituted the vanguard of a trend that could undermine the Tokugawa order and must, therefore, be thwarted at the outset. The Kyushu incident was more immediately worrisome because it involved an armed clash between Satsuma samurai and the foreigners and thus brought the risk of naval retaliation.

Those two minor incidents brought to completion a reorientation in bakufu foreign policy that had begun in the 1790s as Edo leaders tried to find diplomatic ways of deflecting the Russian advance. Seventeenth-century policy, it will be recalled, had forbidden Japanese to go beyond Ezo, the Ryukyus, or Korea, forbidden Portuguese to land in Japan, tabooed Christianity, and restricted Dutch and Chinese residents to specified locations. Subsequently a few stray vessels had been turned away on an *ad hoc* basis, but no general policy on other foreigners was ever articulated. Not until the years around 1800 did bakufu leaders, gradually and with hesitation, develop a general policy of rejecting requests for trade. They instructed foreign vessels to go to Nagasaki, directed daimyo to repel (*uchi harai*) or impound any vessel that insisted on conducting its business elsewhere, and subsequently modified that last directive to allow essential provisioning. Then the incidents of 1824 prodded leaders in Edo to clarify policy by firming it up in hopes of avoiding further armed clashes and forestalling any subversive proselytizing. An edict of 1825 noted the problems of recent years, reminded readers of the proscription on Christianity, and declared:

> Henceforth, whenever a foreign ship is sighted approaching any point on our coast, all persons on hand should fire on and drive it off.[1]

And the firing was to be done without hesitation (*ninennaku*). It was a policy position of unprecedented firmness. That it was not prudently enforceable did not become apparent for well over a decade, however, in part because few foreign vessels approached and in part because daimyo managed on a few occasions to procrastinate long enough to avoid taking action.

Then in 1842 bakufu leaders learned the outcome of the Opium War, in which combined British and French forces had forced the Chinese to capitulate. A Dutch report of the situation warned that the British fleet was preparing to present undisclosed demands to Edo. The news was alarming because throughout the Edo period China, even when under Manchu (Ch'ing) rule, had been viewed as an Asian power of incomparable strength. If the Europeans could defeat China, what chance did Japan have? As Tokugawa Nariaki, lord of Mito and the most dynamic and influential political figure of the day, had put it as recently as 1839:

> Say what you will, the Ch'ing Empire is a great power; so the [Western] barbarians will not undertake any attack on it lightly...Russia most probably will decide to invade Japan first and then go about conquering China. This is a fearful, hateful situation.[2]

With the Ch'ing down, Japan was fully exposed, so the Dutch report precipitated heated discussion within the bakufu and in short order a revised policy:

> In 1825 it was ordered that foreign vessels should be driven away without hesitation. However...in the event that foreigners, through storm-damage or shipwreck, come seeking food, fuel, or water, the shogun does not consider it a fitting response to other nations that they should be driven away indiscriminately without due knowledge of the circumstances.[3]

That softening of official policy reduced the risk of violent confrontation, and while the British fleet did not in fact visit Edo in 1842, during the next decade a number of foreign vessels did arrive and present requests for trade or other concessions without precipitating gunfire.

Most notably, in 1846, shortly after young Abe Masahiro became the bakufu's leading official, French warships under the command of Admiral Jean-Baptiste Cecille visited the Ryukyus and asked to open trade relations. A nearly concurrent request for trade by an American naval commander in Edo Bay presented Abe with a "two-front" challenge reminiscent of earlier episodes. His response was to reject the American request, which struck directly at the Tokugawa heartland, while side-stepping Cecille's by delegating responsibility to Shimazu Narioki, the daimyo of Satsuma, in keeping with Satsuma's fuzzy but longstanding suzerainty in the Ryukyus. Mindful of the 1824 incident involving Satsuma samurai, however, he instructed Narioki to handle the matter peacefully, even if that meant agreeing to French trade in the Ryukyus. As he explained in a purposefully vague letter to Nariaki of Mito:

> Affairs in the Ryukyus have been entrusted to Shimazu Narioki, and in this present matter he is exercising the greatest wisdom in handling affairs. In fact, the shogun directly instructed him to preserve the *kokutai*, to exercise restraint and adaptability, and in no case to leave seeds of future trouble.[4]

Cecille, however, missed his chance by failing to follow up his initiative, and the rest of the decade passed uneventfully.

Out of the political infighting that accompanied these foreign scares of the 1840s, a policy consensus of sorts emerged: in principle bakufu leaders wished to restore the *uchi harai* policy of 1825, but doing so must await the construction of sufficient coastal defenses. The necessary resources of money and metal were scarce, however, and despite much noisy resolve, little actual defense strengthening occurred – which was just as well because the defense work was based on known weaponry, and the technological changes that were just then beginning to transform European and American war-making capability would have rendered any such defense work a waste of time, effort, and matériel.

As of 1853, then, *bakuhan* leaders had a flexible policy in place, but their hearts still lay with the policy of *uchi harai* and preservation of the political order in which it was embedded. The barbarian was at the gate, and the rulers' task was to defend the *kokutai* – civilization itself – against that threat.

CRISIS AND RUPTURE

It was fitting, surely, that Japan was thrust onto the path toward fossil-fuel based industrialism by the commander of a partially steam-powered squadron whose objective was to secure, by whatever means necessary, coal supplies and coaling stations for steamships moving between California and China (see figure 12.1). Doubtless it was also fitting that while pursuing that goal the commander laid claim to the Bonin Islands and aspired to secure other territories for his government.

Foreign policy upended. The "General Convention of Peace and Amity" which this commander, the American Commodore Matthew C. Perry, signed with bakufu negotiators in the spring of 1854, opened the two ports of Shimoda and Hakodate to foreign vessels in need of provisions or safe haven. It assured safe treatment of shipwrecked sailors and granted the Americans a priori any concessions that other governments might obtain in future ("most-favored-nation" treatment). It also authorized the opening of a consular office at a later date, although disagreement subsequently arose on whether its opening required the consent of both parties or only one. Perry's Convention was quickly followed by comparable treaties with Britain and Russia.

In 1857–8, after British and French authorities renewed their war against the Ch'ing, foreign negotiators in Japan, the American Consul-General Townsend Harris most effectively, used threats of British naval power and the prospect of a coerced opium trade to extract from the bakufu a much broader "Treaty of Amity and Commerce" that prohibited opium imports but allowed other trade. The Treaty called for appointment of diplomatic and consular agents in Edo and three additional trading ports, expanded the travel privileges of Americans in Japan, and permitted them to practice their religion. It gave them immunity from Japanese law ("extraterritoriality") and guaranteed that tariff levels on the trade would be no higher than those any other government might subsequently negotiate.[5] Europeans quickly secured similar concessions, and during the 1860s additional pressure led to Edo's acquiescence in more foreign demands, step by step erasing remnants of the restrictive foreign policy that gradually had emerged during the centuries of Tokugawa rule.

Figure 12.1 A warship in Commodore Perry's squadron; detail from *Perii torai ezu hari-maze byōbu*; color on paper, six-fold; 1854; artist unknown; University of Tokyo. The massive firepower projecting from the opened gunports together with Perry's readiness to employ it were the key factors inducing bakufu leaders to accept Perry's proposal for a "convention of peace and amity." *Source*: Bradley Smith, *Japan, A History in Art* (New York: Doubleday & Co. Inc., 1964), p. 170.

Dimensions of crisis. Initially Commodore Perry's demands had provoked intense policy debate among the ruling *bushi* and bakufu diplomats, but within months a consensus emerged that in effect applied the 1840s Abe-Nariaki formulation on *uchi harai* to the new situation: acquiesce of necessity until defenses have been adequately prepared and then, presumably, restore the *status quo ante*. For a while that posture elicited general support, including measures of defense work and rearmament, but the further concessions of 1857–8 discredited it. The rulers' cohesion abruptly disintegrated and political life rapidly spun out of control. Charges of personal incompetenence, demands for changes in leadership, and punitive retaliation caused ever more bitterness, eventuating in assassination plots and counterplots.

By 1860 policy debates had broken out of the normal framework of factional politics and were drawing new groups and more coercive techniques of persuasion into the political arena. Rivals tried to buttress their positions by soliciting imperial support, but the court's involvement served only to complicate matters. It forced political combatants to control not only the shogun but also the emperor, and a whole cluster of considerations historical and structural made the court a volatile and contentious force that was driven mainly by its own internal agendas.

Even more destructive of orderly process was the eruption of uncontrolled activism by lesser *bushi* and others, known collectively as *shishi* or "activists." Motivated by a mix of considerations personal and professional, by 1860 *shishi* were beginning to participate in affairs as best they could, escalating the tension and the stakes by resorting to sporadic violence and assassination attempts against the officials they held culpable and the foreigners they happened to encounter. Drawing strength from nativist rhetoric of the sort found in *Mitogaku* and *kokugaku*, they invoked calls to "revere the emperor and expel the barbarian" (*sonnō jōi*). They hoped that by mobilizing enough support they could force leaders to repudiate their diplomatic concessions and oust the foreigners, or at least negotiate more acceptable treaties. A contemporary admirer of one such *shishi* said of him: "His character is direct; he is a good patriot, fearless in the cause of justice." In that spirit, our informant continues, in early 1861 the *shishi* and his fellows assassinated Henry Heusken, the young Dutch interpreter of Townsend Harris, "with the intention of sweeping Edo clean, once and for all, of all the Barbarians of the five countries who had legations there."[6]

During the early 1860s this *shishi* activism changed the basic character of political conflict. Whereas *bushi* leaders had previously been locked in increasingly bitter struggle because of the disruptive implications of the new treaty arrangements, by 1864 three years of harsh infighting, policy chaos, repeated diplomatic crises, and escalating domestic violence had persuaded them that *shishi* actions were more threatening to their interests than the foreign presence. The rulers' sense of alarm is suggested by this comment of a high-ranking court noble, who characterized *shishi* as

> a mob of vagabonds, wholesalers in loyalism. They live from day to day claiming to serve the emperor, gradually infecting more and more people.[7]

Leaders of the bakufu and domains generally agreed with that assessment, and across the realm daimyo cracked down on errant retainers. Meanwhile the court punished outspoken young *kuge*, and bakufu leaders and their allies coopted some *shishi* and crushed others, most horrifically insurgents in Mito domain.

By early 1865 *bushi* discipline had generally been reaffirmed, but by then an array of other factors was confounding attempts to restore order more broadly.

For the bakufu in particular, but also for domain officialdom, the confusion and reversals of policy were severely demoralizing. Moreover, the recurrent run-ins with foreigners generated chronic concern and repeated crises. Most notable were a Russian effort to seize Tsushima in 1862; British preparations to bombard Edo in 1863 and their implementation of an assault on Satsuma shortly thereafter; a joint foreign bombardment of Chōshū in 1864; and the deployment to Osaka Bay in 1865 of an allied armada bearing an invasion force that was prepared to march on Kyoto if necessary to extract further concessions directly from the court. Also troubling were contemporary reports of renewed Russian advances in Ezo and, more immediately, continual quarrels over particulars of trade and treaty stipulations.

Meanwhile *bakuhan* leaders were gaining greater awareness of the new weapons technology then developing in Europe and America, notably breech loaders, rifled gun barrels, repeating arms, steamships, and armored vessels. As they learned, they began to reorganize their own armed forces, compelling samurai to abandon cherished martial traditions, adopt "vulgar" new forms of weaponry and warfare, and accept the presence of commoner soldiers. All these measures served further to undermine samurai support for leaders and their institutions even as they destabilized the existing *bakuhan* balance of military power and opened the way for a domestic arms race.

However, it was the fiscal ramifications of the imperialist intrusion that had the deepest and most wide-ranging effects. Foreign pressure spurred *bakuhan* leaders to spend unprecedented sums on military training and deployment, and on weapons purchase, production, and placement, to say nothing of the extortionate indemnities that foreigners demanded for diverse slights and injuries. To make funds available for defense work, the bakufu in 1862 agreed to daimyo demands for the "temporary relaxation" – the end in fact – of the *sankin kōtai* hostage system that had maintained the vitality of Edo and helped keep daimyo under control for over two centuries. Bakufu and domain leaders also squeezed income sources, produced money, borrowed, cut samurai stipends, eliminated jobs, and reduced various perquisites.

More broadly, direct contact with the bullion-based maritime monetary system generated alarming outflows of specie and threw domestic currency arrangements into turmoil. And foreign commerce started rearranging domestic trade flows, of silk in particular, which damaged interests in some places, Kyoto most notably, while creating dramatic but disorderly new opportunities elsewhere.

Strategies for coping.   With the arrangements of elite *bushi* supremacy falling apart and the world of the warrior class as a whole being turned upside down, the search for a new political order began. The searchers in effect mined Japan's political legacy for solutions and when those proved insufficient turned elsewhere. One obvious element in a new order, nearly everyone agreed, was the imperial court. Its salience as an expression of ethnic identity and as a rallying point for the concerned was grounded in a millennium of history, most gloriously that of the *ritsuryō* age. The legacy of courtly rule had been preserved in the revitalized Kyoto of the 1600s and highlighted by recent nativist writings. Moreover the need for strong central leadership of the sort implicit in that legacy was brutally revealed by the imperialist intrusion, which had demonstrated so clearly the *bakuhan* order's utter incapacity to cope with its changing global context.

The imperial court was one element in a new order, but no more than that. Repeated feeble attempts from 1863 onward to give it a central role failed for numerous reasons, and reformers had to look elsewhere. Leaders tried to construct elite coalitions under the rubric *kōbugattai*, "union of court and *bushi*," but these medieval-like coalitions repeatedly foundered on personal and institutional rivalries, policy differences, and structural inadequacies. Neither the *ritsuryō* imperial model nor that of the Ashikaga *kenmon* seemed to work.

A third historical model, the *sengoku* model of the daimyo domain, was available, and it came into play following the one major reversal of the earlier-noted 1864–5 crackdown on insurgent *bushi* and their allies. To explain, samurai from Chōshū domain had been important participants in the *sonnō jōi* activism of the early sixties. However, their attempt in 1864 to force policy changes by seizing the court militarily had been repulsed, producing instead a *kōbugattai*-like decision by senior figures in the court, bakufu, and major domains to punish them. Late that year this coalition's military expedition against Chōshū pressured the domain's leaders to cashier those officials implicated in the Kyoto assault and to suppress their militant followers. A few months later, however, after the expeditionary force had withdrawn, the Chōshū insurgents revolted against their domain's leaders, seized control of the government, and began reorganizing it to form a more effective military instrument for challenging Edo's control of court and country. Bakufu leaders thus found themselves pitted against one of the realm's most powerful daimyo domains, and while the precipitating issue had been foreign policy, the contest had acquired a life of its own.

Even the armed expedition against Chōshū (which court leaders had demanded, certain daimyo had strongly favored, and the bakufu had half-heartedly sponsored) had been opposed by other *kuge* and daimyo and by many lesser *bushi*. When in the spring of 1865 bakufu leaders responded to the insurgents' seizure of Chōshū by ordering a second expedition, the opposition was far more widespread despite hesitant imperial support for the venture. Almost no lesser courtiers approved; some key daimyo lobbied strongly against it, and most domains avoided commitment. Those factors plus others repeatedly delayed the new expedition's implementation, which gave Satsuma officials enough time to reverse their earlier policy and forge an alliance with Chōshū leaders. In it they agreed to help restore Chōshū to the court's good graces and to come to Chōshū's assistance should the war against Edo go badly. By the early days of 1866 politics had thus devolved into a *sengoku*-like interdomanial contest for supremacy that pitted two major domains in the west – the "Sat-Chō" alliance – against the bakufu and a handful of supporting domains, Aizu most famously. As in *sengoku*-era contests, both sides treated the court as a legitimizing symbol to be seized and used as seemed convenient.

That autumn the long-delayed second expedition against Chōshū commenced, but within weeks Chōshū forces repulsed the bakufu army and the venture was abandoned, resulting in an east–west stalemate. With that outcome matters grew eerily calm as exhausted combatants and leaders regrouped and for months puzzled over what to do next. At that juncture, with indigenous political models seemingly exhausted, foreign models began to receive serious attention.

An obvious source of new ideas was the foreign powers themselves. From 1860 onward Japanese diplomatic missions had been going abroad, and scholars and officials within Japan had begun establishing much more contact with *rangaku* experts and even with resident foreigners, who provided instruction on diverse matters European and American. It was one thing to learn about the esoteric political arrangements of alien societies, however, and quite another to find their pertinence to one's own situation. A key pathway for doing so lay in the hoary East Asian distinction between *hōken* (decentralized or "feudal") and *gunken* (centralized or "prefectural") political systems.

To elaborate, during the 1720s Ogyū Sorai had explained that the Tokugawa system was of the *hōken* type, as contrasted with the centralized *gunken* system of the T'ang, Sung, and Ming dynasties. In a *hōken* state, he wrote,

> the realm is divided up among lords, and the Son of Heaven rarely governs directly. Vassals of these lords have stipends and hold their fiefs from generation to generation. Although some worthy individuals are hired, social status is fixed: knights are always knights and lords are always lords; for this reason, people's minds are settled and society is calm. Laws and regulations are rudimentary at best, and the people are governed by means of feelings of gratitude and obligation, with priority given to instilling a sense of shame.[8]

In a *gunken* system, he continued, status is not hereditary, fiefs do not exist, and officials serve as imperial appointees for designated periods. Such arrangements, he implied, foster shortsightedness among officials and selfish ambition in general, and he insisted that they were entirely inappropriate for the present age.

As knowledge of the centralized states of Europe was acquired during the 1860s, it began feeding into discussions of political reform, helping to transvalue the *hōken* and *gunken* models. Late in 1865, for example, the foreigners' threat to march on Kyoto precipitated harsh criticism of the current bakufu leadership, as when one knowledgeable critic from Kyushu denounced senior Tokugawa officials for proposing to

> rely on the foreigners, abolish the emperor and the daimyo, establish a prefectural (*gunken*) system, make the shogun presiding executive (*daitōryō*) of the realm (*tenka*) and base government office on talent.[9]

Such ideas were indeed gaining favor among shogunal advisors, and the culpable officials were relieved of office and confined. The ideas, however, did not die. To the contrary, belief that the *hōken* system was obsolete and that some sort of *gunken* arrangement was required came to prevail. It shaped the political conflict of the next few years and expedited the radical institutional restructuring that subsequently carried Japan into the industrial age.

During the quiet year that followed Chōshū's success in 1866, the main aspects of political life were two: an arms race as the rivals prepared for a rematch, and intense and convoluted maneuvering that involved those rivals, other senior figures, and foreigners. Bakufu leaders pursued radical internal reforms to modernize their armed forces and reorganize their political structure along the lines of a centralized, European-style regime. In the process they forged closer links to French merchants and diplomats even as they proceeded reluctantly to implement more treaty provisions, notably the opening of Hyōgo (in present-day Kobe) to trade. Meanwhile Sat-Chō leaders busily purchased weapons, trained troops, and deepened their ties to British merchants and diplomats while adhering to the *sonnō jōi* rhetoric of the day because it elicited *bushi* support and embarrassed bakufu leaders.

Other lords, aware that they lacked the power to counter either a revitalized, unification-oriented bakufu or a conquest-oriented Sat-Chō leadership, and fearful that the escalating rivalry would open the way to major imperialist inroads into Japan, tried to mediate a settlement on the basis of conservative *kōbugattai* ideas. By the end of 1867, however, the mediation efforts had sputtered out and Sat-Chō forces were ready to act. In the first days of 1868 deployments led to fighting and in four days of hard battle near Kyoto the insurgents prevailed, driving the bakufu remnants back to Edo. There the shogun capitulated, after which forces under Sat-Chō control slowly subdued the holdouts, smashing Aizu domain in the northeast most savagely. By the summer of 1869 the country was under a new leadership.

Meanwhile the rhetoric of *sonnō jōi* had encouraged acts of violence against resident foreigners, and that development forced the newly victorious Sat-Chō leaders to appease the foreigners by repudiating their propaganda and punishing some of their own supporters. It was one of the first of several hard lessons they would receive as they transformed themselves from victorious insurgents into operatives of a regime.

At a broader public level, the whole political upheaval of the 1860s was mainly a source of confusion and irritation. The long-developing alienation from established leadership had been intensified by the sharp political deterioration and socioeconomic disruption that accompanied foreign trade, the arms race, and political violence. Severe inflation and then crop failures in 1865–6 generated widespread hardship and unrest and further disgust with those in power. The abstract notion of restoring imperial rule appears to have been welcomed by many, but none of the contestants for power elicited any real public enthusiasm. Nothing they said or did really spoke to the concerns or aspirations of commoners, and insofar as public comment was forthcoming, it generally was of the "pox on both your houses" sort. The more observant recognized that affairs had taken on a *sengoku*-like character of domains contesting for supremacy. They could see that the imperial court was merely a tool for both sides and that there was no reason to expect the new tax collectors to be an improvement on the old. During the months of Sat-Chō conquest, insurgent leaders bought a measure of public acquiescence by promising substantial tax reductions, but their subsequent failure to abide by the promises only served to reconfirm general skepticism about the victors.

Local identities, however, did matter. Many commoners in Satsuma and Chōshū took pride in the accomplishments of their lords' armies, and a number of non-*bushi* and marginal folk participated in the enterprise. People in Edo were disgusted with bakufu failure but resented the Sat-Chō seizure of "their" city. As Edo castle was being turned over to the victors in the spring of 1868, the following bit of doggeral was being circulated, along with satirical woodblock prints that mocked feckless rulers and loutish warriors on all sides:

> Are we afraid of being called an enemy of the Court? NO!
> Is there a way to escape humble submission? NO!
> Does the emperor know anything? NO!
> Is honor due to the pseudo-princes? NO!
> [items omitted]
> Has Edo ever known greater misery? NO!
> Does wisdom exist among our leaders? NO!
> Does righteousness exist between high and low? NO![10]

Commoners, it appears, were under few illusions about what they could expect to get from any changes among the elite.

REDIRECTION: TOWARD INDUSTRIALISM

In an immediate sense the Meiji Restoration was a *sengoku*-like routing of one warrior clique by another: Sekigahara revisited, one might say. In the months and years following their battlefield triumph, moreover, Sat-Chō leaders pursued policies and dealt with problems in ways that remind one of the early Tokugawa decades: in the way they appeased powerful figures, suppressed lesser malcontents, articulated governing institutions, pursued legitimizing actions and arguments, designed and implemented fiscal and economic policies, and resolved periodic internal power struggles. In the outcome they, like the early Tokugawa, muddled through. By 1875 they had drawn the basic sinews of power to themselves, and by 1890 they had created a new *gunken* system for a new ruling elite. Although its nomenclature and ritual institutional arrangements were heavily influenced by European nobiliary and bureaucratic precedents, its essential character derived from the indigenous political legacy with its flexible combination of hereditary status and real power.

During the early twentieth century, as we note in Part IV, the new Meiji elite's position decayed, and as that happened, power devolved into the hands of other, lesser figures. Mostly these were men more closely linked to the core elements of industrial state power, notably senior figures in military and civil bureaucratic organs and industrial combines and the political-party spokesmen for propertied interests. The established Sat-Chō leaders and their collaborators strove to draw these people into the existing elite order, granting them honors, titles, and material rewards. However, that effort proved only partially successful, essentially because the scale, complexity, and continual flux of industrial society, even in the early decades of its "growth stage," repeatedly thwarted attempts by the favored few to stabilize the distribution of power and privilege.

Contextual variables. Both the use of European precedents and the eventual weakening of the new Meiji elite reflected the fact that in one crucial way the Sat-Chō victors faced a situation very unlike that of the early Tokugawa. Whereas the latter had confronted non-industrial foreigners whose influence they were able to restrict to a level of their own choosing, the new leaders faced, as had those they vanquished in 1868, industrializing powers whose demands they could not safely refuse. To flourish, therefore, they had to promote the reconfiguration of their own society so it could counter those foreign demands. Under the rubric *fukoku kyōhei* ("rich country, strong army") early Meiji leaders launched programs of political consolidation, mass mobilization, military strengthening, economic development, and resource exploitation that began transforming Japan into an industrial society of the sort that western Europe and North America were also in process of becoming.

Their capacity to do so was in part, no doubt, a matter of random good luck. In part it reflected Japan's geopolitical situation, especially the fact that European and American pressures were more fully focused on other societies, China most particularly, and were at critical moments directed elsewhere. But in part it stemmed from good policy choices. And in part it reflected characteristics of Japanese society that had developed over preceding centuries, especially the later Edo period.

To elaborate that last point, at the highest level the earlier-noted presence of the imperial institution as a well entrenched expression of ethnic identity – and one that could be portrayed as innocent of association with the discredited Tokugawa – provided the new rulers with a powerful legitimizing tool that they used to great and continuing advantage for mobilizing support, repelling rivals, and justifying burdensome demands. At a lower level the presence of a countrywide samurai class that was not only needful of employment but also literate and schooled in the ideal of dutiful service on behalf of higher authority surely facilitated the recruitment of competent and reliable administrators for all sorts of civil and military tasks.

More broadly, the fact that most productive resources, arable land in particular, were in the hands of users, rather than the hands of an urban ruling class or rural plantation elite, reduced the need for a major redistribution of control, with all the risk and turmoil such a process would have entailed. In a related matter, widespread familiarity with intensive agriculture, handicraft production, and commercial practices enabled the general populace to exploit opportunities that arose after old restraints on trade and land use disappeared during the 1870s. In the same vein, a labor force that was familiar with disciplined work routines and accustomed to working away from home and for wages on a long-term basis surely facilitated the establishment of factory-style work places. And finally, the existence of a stable demographic order meant that gains in output were not immediately consumed by a burgeoning population of children and could, instead, be channeled into investment or other uses.

The process of exploiting these several characteristics of their situation and society to redirect social energy into enriching and strengthening the country began even before the Tokugawa fell. Early Meiji leaders accelerated the trend sharply, but not until the 1890s or later did the earmarks of industrialism become the dominant characteristics of Japanese society. Until then the rhythms of life, the material culture, and the social norms of most people continued to reflect their Tokugawa ancestry. Thereafter, by contrast, one sees in Japan's foreign relations, domestic political life, economy, and culture qualities that generally have more in common with later decades than earlier ones.

POLITICAL CHANGE

Broadly speaking the process of political change that Japan underwent between 1868 and 1890 moved through two phases. During the 1870s the new rulers disestablished the old: they tore down the remaining elements of *bakuhan* political structure a piece at a time, tried various new organizational arrangements, and survived a series of violent and non-violent challenges to their power and policy. During the eighties they devised the new: they developed stable governing regulations and structures for their incipient industrial order, signaling the completion of that process in 1889 by having the emperor formally announce the Meiji Constitution, a document that adumbrated the basic principles and organization of a regime that was intended to be as permanent as the *bakuhan taisei* it replaced.

Disestablishing the old. From the outset the new leaders claimed to be acting at the behest of the youthful Meiji emperor. Most of them being samurai of only middling rank, however, they had no interest in trying to govern from Kyoto, with its burden of ritual and courtly status consciousness. For a moment they considered making Osaka their new capital but by the summer of 1868 regarded Edo as the better site. In a choice that reminds one of the early *ritsuryō* interest in multiple capitals and a mobile court, they changed Edo's name to Tokyo, "Eastern Capital," and a few months later the emperor visited the city. In due course he and most *kuge* reluctantly moved there from Kyoto, transforming the former shogunal castle into an imperial palace while daimyo mansions and *bushi* residences became housing and office space for the new officialdom.

By the end of 1868 the Sat-Chō conquerors had overcome the last military resistance in daimyo domains of the northeast, and by the following summer a final group of Tokugawa loyalists, who had tried to form a breakaway regime in Hokkaido, had capitulated. In place of the fallen regime the new rulers initially attempted to resurrect a *ritsuryō*-like central government, but as months and years passed, they kept modifying its arrangements. In considerable part they did so as a way of consolidating power in fewer hands but also to reduce costs and improve governing effectiveness. By 1880 they were abandoning the *ritsuryō* model in favor of a cabinet setup patterned on European precedents.

As Sat-Chō-controlled armies had overrun the country in 1868, they seized Tokugawa territories but left most daimyo in charge of their own domains. During 1869, however, the victors began expanding their domanial foundation beyond Tokugawa lands, formally completing the process in 1871. That summer the Tokyo government, backed by its own 8,000-man imperial guard force, ordered all domain armies dissolved and claimed domain tax income as its own. It formally abolished all daimyo authority, buying lordly acquiescence by granting liberal pensions, and it replaced the domains with districts and prefectures (*gun* and *ken*), developing regulations and hierarchies of officials to administer them. The 250 or so former daimyo and 150 or so *kuge* were then pressed to settle permanently in Tokyo, becoming analogues to the comfortable "alternate attendance" hostages of Tokugawa rule.

During 1873 Tokyo leaders projected their control down to the village level by asserting the right to tax production and extract military service from commoners throughout the realm. They issued new land tax regulations and commenced a nationwide cadastral survey that identified all land holders. The survey also assessed the value of their holdings, which were declared freely alienable, and set tax rates in monetary terms based, indirectly, on the land's ascribed market value. They also issued a military conscription law that declared all 20-year-old men subject to three years of active service and four of reserve duty, although they in fact needed – and could afford to recruit, train, and support – only a small fraction of those eligible. By these measures they claimed two of the key prerogatives common to early industrialized states: the right to demand military service and material support from all adult male subjects.

By 1873 Meiji rulers had thus stripped samurai of their lords, domanial identities, and distinctive social function as warriors. Over the next three years the government step by step reduced their hereditary income and discouraged their adherence to customary dress codes, and in 1876 forbade the public wearing of swords and commuted all samurai stipends – meagerly. Unsurprisingly, samurai throughout the country were embittered by these developments, their anger scarcely assuaged by the hollow title of *shizoku* ("gentry") that they were given to distinguish them from commoners (*heimin*). And most embittered were those *bushi* whose own domain leaders had overthrown the old regime and carried out the hated changes: was this what they had marched, fought, and bled for?

While thus pushing through major structural reforms, the new leaders also tried to erect a legitimizing ideology of rule that would reinforce imperial authority and counter the doctrinal appeal of Christianity, which they saw as undergirding European state power. In the summer of 1869, as Restoration warfare was ending and court and courtiers were moving east, the new rulers transferred to Tokyo the Shōkonsha, a small Kyoto shrine dedicated to those who had reputedly died on the court's behalf during the preceding decade. Three years later the shrine was given a grand new main building, and subordinate Shōkonsha were established throughout the country to assuage the spirits of the fallen and thereby assure the realm's tranquillity, in the process projecting outward the regime's religious charisma. Those measures call to mind the *ritsuryō*-period Tōdaiji-Kokubunji setup of Emperor Shōmu and the later Tenryūji-Ankokuji arrangement of Ashikaga Takauji.

Whereas these older expressions of benevolent governance had been primarily Buddhist, however, the new expression was self-consciously Shintō. At a broader level, as well, Meiji leaders worked with diverse Shintō priests and *kokugaku* proponents to mount a frontal assault on the centuries-old legacy of combinative religion, moving to absorb Shugendō into Shintō and erase all Buddhist elements from Shintō shrines.

They defined Shintō as the imperial household's religion and pressed their semi-hostage population of ex-*kuge* and ex-daimyo to subscribe to it as part of a new aristocratic culture. They also developed a national system for ranking major shrines (54 of them in 1879), which were to receive government support, and the multitude of small shrines (176,722 in 1879), which depended on local funding.[11] They then tried to use this "purified" system of government-supported shrines and priests, together with an organization of teachers and training programs, to promulgate an essentially secular "Great Teaching" that would encourage proper civic behavior and respect for gods, emperor, and nation, thereby creating dutiful tax payers and obedient subjects. By 1876, however, the effort was foundering in internal conflict, public ridicule, and official indifference, and over the next few years it petered out.

Even as that attempt to promote a new state ideology was launched and limped into oblivion, quarrels erupted among government leaders over other specific policies, in particular a scheme to invade Korea, nominally to avenge an insult. That dispute led some of those leaders, most notably the Satsuma samurai Saigō Takamori, a key figure in the Sat-Chō military triumph, to leave the government in protest. The combination of discontented would-be leaders and embittered ex-samurai led to a series of scattered but violent outbursts that culminated in the Satsuma Rebellion of 1876–7, a major rising that for several weeks seemed about to topple the new regime. In the end, however, forces of the Tokyo government, bolstered by men from Aizu and other localities who seized the opportunity to wreak revenge on their erstwhile conquerors, managed to prevail. The rebels' defeat near Kumamoto and Saigō's consequent suicide in the autumn of 1877, rather like the fall of Osaka castle and the suicide of Hideyori in 1615, marked the end of attempts by disgruntled fighting men to alter the new regime's policy through armed resistance.

In place of rebellion, dissident figures turned to political organizing, and a host of small political groups formed. Initially they drew their support from declassed *bushi*, but by the late 1870s from more and more landlords, village leaders, and urban property owners who were displeased with tax policy specifically and, more generally, with the deepening penetration of central authority into local and regional affairs. These critics of the government, most famously the Tosa samurai Itagaki Taisuke and the Saga samurai Ōkuma Shigenobu, linked a European-style rhetoric about "freedom and peoples' rights" (*jiyū minken*) to policy positions that attracted the backing of property holders. The linkage of avant garde moral high ground and material interest enabled them to build political movements that demanded creation of legislative organs and their staffing through elections held at local, prefectural, and national levels.

The government responded to this political agitation, and to the aggressively combative journalism that accompanied it, by drafting libel and slander laws, deploying police, making arrests, obstructing gatherings, and otherwise discouraging critics. It employed carrots as well as sticks, however, taking steps to honor those who rendered loyal service. In the summer of 1879 Tokyo reaffirmed its appreciation for those who had died so that the Meiji triumph could be realized, by changing the name of Shōkonsha to Yasukuni Shrine. The emperor explained the new name to the deceased in this way:

> With a loyal and honest heart you have passed away, not worrying about your homes, not minding your own lives. Founded on these great and highly heroic deeds, Our Great Empire is to rule as a peaceful land (*yasukuni*); so We renamed [this shrine] Yasukuni-*jinja*...and made it an Imperial Shrine of Special Status. We vow to make sacrifices of paper and silk and of laudatory congratulations, and, from now on forever, to worship and admire you.[12]

The renamed shrine then developed an array of ritual events to memorialize the fallen and affirm imperial attentiveness to them. Through Yasukuni, moreover, the imperial gratitude was extended to the fallen who had been enshrined at the branch Shōkonsha scattered throughout the realm.

Leaders such as the Satsuma samurai Ōkubo Toshimichi and the Chōshū samurai Itō Hirobumi recognized, however, that somehow the growing opposition must be coopted lest the regime gradually lose its base of public acquiescence. So they began exploring ways to use legislatures and electoral systems as mechanisms to broaden the regime's popularity and better project its wishes into the public arena. Ōkubo was assassinated before he could contribute much to the process, but during the 1880s Itō took the lead in developing structures of government that would consolidate the regime's position while improving its links to society at large.

Devising the new. By 1882 the new government had outlasted its most dangerous critics and was in the hands of a small and stable ruling elite. From around 1885 to 1912, in the words of one scholar,

> an oligarchy of some ten men comprised the inner circle for advising the emperor on the composition of the government and on foreign policy. These men were the creators of modern political institutions, not their creatures.[13]

As with rulers everywhere, of course, their decisions were shaped by the forces about them, the context within which they worked.

Fiscal considerations were important. The costs of overcoming insurgent samurai and coping with other problems of the seventies had severely overburdened the treasury, precipitating a sharp erosion in the value of money and threatening the government with financial disaster. To rectify the situation, another Satsuma samurai, Matsukata Masayoshi, took charge of the Finance Ministry and initiated a rigorous policy of retrenchment. He disposed of pilot factories that the government had erected, slashed other government spending, hiked taxes, and overhauled the banking system to establish firm government control of the money supply. By the later 1880s his measures had halted the inflation, at considerable cost to poorer farmers. With the government placed on a firm fiscal footing, Itō pressed ahead with the creation of permanent governing institutions, building from the center outward.

By then Japan's leaders were much more well versed in European matters. Many had gone abroad on embassies and study tours, and the government had actively hired foreign advisors and employees to help in the development of new governing and educational institutions and new commercial and industrial ventures. Indeed, by 1875 some 520 foreign employees, mostly European, already worked for the government while hundreds more were taking private service, mainly as engineers and educators. Their numbers remained large into the 1890s. For Itō and the others who were developing government organs during the later 1880s, these foreign experts were a valuable source of detailed information on legal codes, monetary policies, and the particulars of bureaucratic organization as well as the larger rituals and rationales that shaped and legitimized European practice.

Itō and his colleagues attached great importance to the matter of a rationale for their regime. The imperial institution had been a core element in the Sat-Chō conquerors' initial claims to legitimacy, and during the seventies and early eighties they despatched the emperor widely about the realm to build public support. Itō undertook to consolidate the court's doctrinal and fiscal bases and to make Tokyo Japan's sole and permanent imperial capital, much as Heian had served despite the earlier ideal of multiple capitals and a mobile court. Leaders aimed to make the emperor an authority figure who would stand securely above the ruck of politics while having legal appointive power over all senior officials and high esteem among *hoi polloi*. As part of that project, and in the spirit of the failed 1870s effort to promote a "Great Teaching," the government rejuvenated the imperial family's Shintō shrines, along with its Shintō rituals, and added new shrines to enrich the imperial legacy. *In toto* these became key expressions of the emperor's sacred origins, Japan's unique status as land of the gods, and godly sanction for the new government.

To assure the emperor's permanent fiscal independence, Meiji leaders ordered that vast regions of woodland once controlled by shogun and daimyo be assigned in perpetuity to the imperial household. And within the household they established administrative organs to oversee the land and use its harvest as a source of enduring courtly income. They also began endowing the household with a rich investment portfolio in banking and other industrial ventures and placed those assets under household management.

In 1885 Itō began drawing the threads of institutional consolidation together. He established an Imperial Household Ministry as a self-perpetuating organ to handle the emperor's affairs. Then he flanked it with a newly created hereditary Peerage (*kazoku*) of some 500 names, mainly ex-*kuge* and ex-daimyo. A few years earlier, in 1876, the logic behind creation of such a Peerage had been nicely expressed by Kido Takayoshi, one of Itō's Chōshū colleagues, in a letter to an ally:

> The creation of titles of peerage is an indispensable device for fortifying the position of the Imperial House…We have both been concerned about the recent tendency of all classes to slip unknowingly into the spirit of republicanism. If nothing is done about it now, the situation will become irremediable.[14]

The samurai unrest that particularly alarmed Kido soon passed, but his interest in assuring order endured.

With these core elements of a permanent new social elite in place, Itō fleshed out the rest of his new *gunken* system. He drafted regulations for a new body of cabinet ministers under a prime minister and below them ministries that were to function according to new civil service regulations. Through these ministries the regime would extend its control into the countryside via refurbished regional and local administrative organs. Experts drew up codes of civil, criminal, and commercial law, as well as regulations for general staffs of the army and navy. As desired by the military reformer Yamagata Aritomo of Chōshū, the chiefs of staff, like the prime minister were made direct appointees of the emperor and thus, Itō hoped, insulated against political factionalism and bound to the interests of emperor and nation. The government established an imperial university in Tokyo to train future personnel for the new administrative organs, and in 1888 Itō created a Privy Council, its members selected by the cabinet, to serve as senior advisors to the emperor and his ministers.

These several moves provided the imperial household with a secure financial basis, a durable administrative structure, a lofty sociopolitical position, and an elegant ideological foundation. In 1889 Meiji leaders strengthened it's cultural role by establishing an Imperial Household Museum to hold and preserve its collection of masterpieces of Japanese arts and letters, thereby making it – and hence the regime that it headed – an important guardian of the nation's cultural legacy. As a further boost to imperial prestige they erected a handsome new palace befitting a modern monarch in the shogun's former castle. They gradually cleared the flat area directly to its east, which had once been crammed with official housing, transforming it into a great reviewing ground where subjects could assemble to express devotion to their sovereign lord. And by then, the former imperial grounds and imperial tombs in Kyoto were being tidied up for permanent preservation.

Meanwhile Itō had completed the drafting of a Constitution, obtained Privy Council approval of his handiwork, and in early 1889 had the emperor promulgate it amidst grand pomp and ceremony. This Meiji Constitution situated sovereignty in the imperial person, adumbrated the rights and duties of emperor and subject and the functions of main government bodies, and established a bicameral legislative body, the Diet. The Diet's upper house was to consist of men selected from the new hereditary Peerage, supplemented by men of special distinction who held titles as imperially appointed, life-term Peers. Members for the lower house were to be chosen by a small, propertied electorate that initially numbered some 450,000 voters. The Diet had authority to enact legislation during its annual three-month sessions, and it could reject the new government budget proposal. If it did so, however, the previous year's budget would apply in its stead. Through these arrangements Itō hoped to provide clear lines of communication between rulers and ruled and engage political activists and local elites in the governing process while assuring that government leaders could pursue their policies without becoming hostage to fickle opinion and unwelcome political pressure.

By 1890, then, Itō and his colleagues had put in place the elements of a regime that linked emperor to people more elaborately than ever in Japan's history. And that October the emperor issued an Imperial Rescript on Education, a document that expressed the social ideals Meiji leaders hoped would ensure their new order's durability.

> Know ye, Our subjects:
> Our Imperial Ancestors have founded Our Empire on a basis broad and ever-lasting, and have deeply and firmly implanted virtue; Our subjects ever united in loyalty and filial piety have from generation to generation illustrated the beauty thereof. This is the glory of the fundamental character of Our Empire, and herein also lies the source of Our education.
> Ye, Our subjects, be filial to your parents, affectionate to your brothers and sisters; as husbands and wives be harmonious, as friends true; bear yourselves in modesty and moderation; extend your benevolence to all; pursue learning and cultivate arts, and thereby develop intellectual faculties and perfect moral powers; furthermore, advance public good and promote common interests; always respect the Constitution and observe the laws; should emergency arise, offer yourselves courageously to the State; and thus guard and maintain the prosperity of Our Imperial Throne coeval with heaven and earth. So shall ye not only be Our good and faithful subjects, but render illustrious the best traditions of your forefathers.
> The Way here set forth is indeed the teaching bequeathed by Our Imperial Ancestors, to be observed alike by Their Descendants and the subjects, infallible for all ages and true in all places. It is Our wish to lay it to heart in all reverence, in common with you, Our subjects, that we may all attain to the same virtue.[15]

Solidly grounded in the Confucian and nativist thought of the Tokugawa era, the Rescript sought to mobilize public support for the new order and counter the divisive tendencies that change seemed continually to generate.

SOCIAL AND CULTURAL CHANGE

In terms of political structure the early Meiji decades clearly witnessed dramatic changes. As the Rescript on Education suggests, however, new departures were less striking in the realm of political ideals. In social and cultural terms, as well, change was less pronounced, and for the populace as a whole one is inclined to emphasize continuity of behavior and values rather than change. Particularly in villages, where most people still lived, older norms of workaday routine persisted. In some areas daughters went off to work in new textile mills; some sons were called up for military service; and a few souls boldly left for Tokyo and tomorrow. More and more villagers raised silkworms, and more became tenants, commonly because of inability to pay taxes, and particularly during the years of Matsukata deflation. However, the techniques of agriculture changed only incrementally and in familiar ways. The principal forms and objects of rural protest were nearly unchanged. Even the 1870s government efforts to separate Shintō and Buddhism had only superficial effects on the religious practice of most people. And the broader changes in government, economy, and foreign relations mostly appeared as modest new perturbations in a world where diet, dress, speech, and the rhythms and expectations of daily life retained most of their later Tokugawa character.

Certain cultural trends do merit attention, however, primarily because of their implications for the future. One was changes in education; another, rearrangement of the status hierarchy; and a third, heightened disparity between elite and mass culture.

On education. Much as early Meiji leaders promoted politico-economic change by invoking rhetoric about "rich country, strong army," so they advocated social and cultural change under the slogan "civilization and enlightenment" (*bunmei kaika*). By that they meant, somewhat imprecisely, the understanding, emulation, or adaptation of desirable European socio-cultural attributes. Their orientation was foreshadowed by the Charter Oath of April 1868, a five-clause, wartime propaganda document issued in the name of the young Meiji emperor while Sat-Chō armies were overrunning the Kantō region. The Oath outlined general goals of the new regime, declaring that "evil customs of the past shall be broken off," and that "knowledge shall be sought throughout the world so as to strengthen the foundations of imperial rule."[16]

For centuries a growing portion of the general populace had been acquiring basic literacy while the size of the cultured elite had also gradually expanded. During early Edo literacy became normal, although certainly not universal, among samurai. In later Edo basic literacy became established among both the rural well-to-do and the urban business classes, while the most wealthy commoners gave their sons advanced schooling in philosophy, arts, and letters. As a benchmark figure, scholars suggest that by the mid-nineteenth century some 40 percent of boys and 15 percent of girls were being schooled outside the home, most commonly in reading, practical skills, and morals.

Meiji policy built on that foundation. In 1871 the fledgling government established a Ministry of Education and began drafting plans for a national system of schooling that would reach from elementary to university levels.

Implementation was slow because the collaboration of local elites had to be secured, funds located, schools constructed, teachers trained, textbooks prepared, and families induced to send off to school children who otherwise could be gainfully employed. By 1890, however, the basic system of public education from primary to advanced was established, together with a number of private schools. Official enrollments at the mandatory, four-year, elementary level ranged, depending on the prefecture, from about 40 percent to 55 percent of the eligible populace, and for the country as a whole upwards of 35 percent of school-age girls and 70 percent of boys.

The government's goals in this educational effort were twofold. First, as leaders both in and out of government became aware of the organizational and technological developments then beginning to transform Europe and America, they recognized the need for their own populace to master the knowledge and skills required by those developments. Second, whereas Tokugawa rulers had desired a populace that was dutiful and proficient in its tasks but passively obedient to authority, Meiji leaders wanted a public that would be positively supportive of their undertakings. To that end they wished a public firmly conscious of its politico-ethnic identity as loyal subjects of the emperor, but given the government's origins as a Sat-Chō conquest regime whose triumph had laid up much regional bitterness, most especially in Tōhoku, winning countrywide support was not easy.

Initially educational policy emphasized the former goal, the need to learn about European civilization, which led not only to the introduction of diverse new subjects of study but also to new approaches to schooling and learning. During the seventies and early eighties the emerging community of professional educators emphasized questions of instructional method, speaking only secondarily about the larger purpose of schooling. They charged that Edo-period pedagogy had ignored the psychology of child development and merely involved rote memorization, "pouring in" the material to be learned. In modern-day schooling, they argued, pupils should learn by active mental engagement with their world, so as to "develop their abilities and gain the knowledge they will need to take up employment in the future," as one educator put it.[17]

By the eighties, however, the initial enthusiasm for foreign ways was cooling while the traumas of samurai revolt, peasant protest, and political assassination and confrontation were producing a greater concern with the promotion of social order and public support for the regime. Increasingly that concern influenced education, and questions about instructional method became more clearly subordinated to the issue of educational purpose. By the 1890s that purpose was being defined in terms of responsibility to society and commitment to the well-being of emperor and nation, as evidenced in the Rescript on Education.

On the status hierarchy. As the new rulers stabilized affairs and sorted out priorities, they concluded that in place of the Tokugawa status structure, a European-like social order should be established, with a small, hereditary aristocracy and its collaborating "men of affairs" governing a population of commoners stripped of most hereditary distinctions. The Confucian principle of a four-caste society was abandoned. The new, elaborately stratified Peerage was linked to the throne through elegant, highly status-sensitive rituals, and the children of Peers were given their own court-sponsored school, Gakushūin, where they received training appropriate to their position in life. Ex-samurai had to make do with their essentially hollow rank of *shizoku*, though disproportionate numbers of them were able to make careers staffing military and police organizations.

The rest of the mainstream population – the farmers, artisans, and merchants of the old order – were lumped together as commoners, *heimin*. At the bottom of the social heap, the hereditary pariah status (*eta*) of Tokugawa society was, as a step toward standardizing control of land and people, formally abolished, thus eliminating, in name at least, "a national shame in foreign eyes" and "a flaw in the imperial rule."[18] And far to the north, in newly-renamed Hokkaido, the Ainu, who hitherto had been clearly distinguished from "Wajin," were also defined as *heimin*. However, other official documents still recorded the Ainu's earlier status as "natives" (*dōjin*), much as family registers of former pariahs preserved information on their ancestry.

The position of women also was to change, to be brought more in line with that of "advanced" societies. The "evil customs" of teeth blackening and eyebrow shaving were discouraged, but long hair, so favored by the better classes of Europe, was encouraged. In 1870 concubines were freed of their disabilities, acquiring rights equal to those of wives. And two years later prostitutes were freed from legal servitude, although the law was in fact not enforced. These moves, as subsequent chapters show, were but the beginning of a complex story of discussion and agitation over many facets of "woman's place" in society as rulers, observers, and growing numbers of women weighed in with opinions about what constituted proper gender relations and women's roles in an "enlightened" society.

On elite and mass culture. Even as an integrated, nationwide education system and a reconfigured status order were starting to produce – rulers hoped – a useful, diligent, patriotic, and cohesive populace, other cultural developments were having the contrary effect of exacerbating urban–rural, rich–poor, elite–commoner differences that to considerable extent were perceived as "Tokyo vs. the rest of us." Edo, as earlier noted, had developed into a metropolitan giant by the 1700s, becoming the cultural as well as the political hub of Tokugawa society. During later Tokugawa, however, the far-reaching diffusion of learning and popular urban arts and letters had gradually deepened the shared culture of the entire realm.

During Meiji that trend reversed and the "center/periphery" disparity intensified again. Not only was political power much more fully centralized than before and the favored few more completely settled in Tokyo, but the new, "progressive" cultural initiatives almost always began there, thanks to the government's purposeful advocacy of "civilization and enlightenment." And many of these initiatives penetrated the hinterland only slowly, if at all.

One of the earliest and most famous expressions of this Tokyo-centrism was Meirokusha, the "Meiji-Six Society," a group of some thirty intellectual activists that included most of the celebrated thinkers of the day. During 1874–5 they published *Meiroku zasshi*, a woodblock-printed journal of "progressive" essays and opinion pieces on topics of the day as well as translations of European writings. At 3,000 copies per issue, it was one of the largest circulating publications of its day, but save for some copies of later issues that were distributed in Osaka, it went to readers in Tokyo.

Several factors slowed dissemination of the new cultural products, including cost, language barriers (both social and geographic), residual distrust of the Sat-Chō conquerors, and the simple inertia of "custom." Furthermore, hinterlanders, local elites in particular, had their own pride of place, their own legacy of cultural practice that they preferred and that they used as the basis from which to pursue their own forms of cultural and social change. During these decades they started their own local newspapers and produced their own poets and pundits, in the process minimizing the appeal and impact of influences emanating from Tokyo. Only gradually, and mostly after 1890, as leaders in Tokyo despatched school teachers about the realm, as military service exposed more young men to new experiences and nationalist indoctrination, and as economic development rearranged the flow of goods and people, did the new Tokyo culture begin to make real inroads elsewhere.

In Tokyo, however, and especially during the 1870s, proponents of "progress" fostered the notion that Japan's own cultural legacy was anachronistic and socially hurtful and that Japan's future well-being required people to master European knowledge and ways of thinking. The senior official Ōkubo Toshimichi, referring to the states of western Europe, declared that:

> at present all the countries in the world are directing all their efforts toward propagating teachings of "civilization and enlightenment," and they lack for nothing. Hence we must imitate them in these respects.[19]

Others agreed, a notable voice in the campaign being the minor Kyushu samurai Fukuzawa Yukichi, who as a career educator, man of letters, and member of the Meirokusha became a celebrated proponent of *bunmei kaika*.

In that spirit Meiji leaders hired the earlier-noted foreign teachers and experts, encouraged study abroad, and promoted the learning of foreign languages and translation of European books. They accepted the introduction of such cultural elements as contemporary European food, dress, art, architecture, music, dance, drama, literature, philosophy, and science. Most of this activity transpired in Tokyo, however; little penetrated the hinterland until long afterward.

Associated with this flurry of interest in European culture was an indigenizing literature that drew on both domestic and imported ideals of ambition, diligence, and practicality (*jitsugaku*) to spur the young toward education and advancement in life. With unprecedented opportunities available, sons of the well placed and well-to-do imbibed the new learning, pursued their opportunities, and oftimes went on to lives of comfort and fulfillment, mostly in Tokyo. Inevitably, perhaps, the disparities in knowledge and differences in perspective that emerged between those who reaped the benefits of change and those who did not provoked invidious comparison between the favored few, who most eagerly adopted foreign pretensions, and the general populace, which held to time-tested custom and looked askance at the curious goings-on of the avant garde.

The early 1880s witnessed some of Tokyo's most frivolous excesses of dress and deportment – ballroom dancing, hoop skirts, top hats, and the like – and some of the most extreme ideas. These included replacing Chinese characters with the Roman alphabet, abandoning Japanese in favor of English, Christianizing, and inter-marrying with Caucasians to produce a stronger population. By the later eighties, however, the "frontier" age of discovery and opportunity was fading as new social structures became established and the new Meiji aristocracy entrenched, and as fear and awe of the foreign powers waned.

The tide of educational opinion turned, and the undiscriminating embrace of foreign culture began to ebb. More and more scholars and aesthetes affirmed the value of indigenous traditions and the desirability of adapting older values and practices to the changing times. In 1891 Miyake Setsurei, a broadly schooled journalist, reconciled Japanese ethnicity and the ideal of cosmopolitanism in this way:

> To exert oneself on behalf of one's country is to work on behalf of the world. Promoting the special nature of a people contributes to the evolution of mankind. Defense of the homeland and love of mankind are not at all contradictory.[20]

It was a view that resonated nicely not only with the Social Darwinism that was modish but also with *laissez faire* economic thought, even if not necessarily with the long-term requirements of a globally-based industrial order.

By then the period of uncritical fascination with things European was well past, even in Tokyo. However, the more basic problems of growing disparities in wealth, prospects, and world outlook, which were distancing the educated, urban, upper classes from the laboring masses, particularly villagers, continued to worsen. Sustained by economic development and overall change, this trend was to persist as a source of social tension and distrust well into the twentieth century.

On the other hand, whereas the seventeenth-century gap between upper-class culture and that of ordinary villagers was perpetuated by hereditary status differences and immense socioeconomic distance, the newly emerging cultural gap in Meiji Japan was gradually bridged by processes that continually drew a few rural folk into the new urban world of Tokyo. The experience equipped some of them to bring cosmoplitan perspectives back to the hinterland for sharing, thereby helping to sustain social cohesion and foster creation of a populace more receptive to change and positively supportive of the new regime. Ultimately such people played a crucial role in the rise of Japan's industrial order.

Illustrative of those who bridged the gap between Meiji upper crust and rural masses was Ikegami Chinpei.[21] His career exemplified many aspects of the day, and we shall, therefore, encounter him again in later chapters. Suffice here to note that Chinpei's life started somewhat inauspiciously but then took a path of its own. Born in 1862 to a well-established land-owning family in a village east of Okayama, five years later he was given to the household of a maternal relative situated in a village south of Tsuyama. Preparing the lad to be heir, his adoptive family, one of several Ikegami households in the vicinity, sent him to teachers in nearby villages where he received a proper Tokugawa-style education, learning to read and write, practicing calligraphy, and studying both Chinese and Japanese poetry.

Chinpei proved to be an unusually able lad, but stubborn, and in 1877 he was again given away, this time to a nearby family, the Sasaki, who expected him to take over the family's medical practice. Sent to a nearby teacher to study Chinese thought and medicine, Chinpei soon displeased him by showing no interest in his tasks, preferring instead to spend time with friends, talking politics and public affairs. In 1879 the teacher sent him home, informing Sasaki that the young man would never make a doctor. Sasaki, however, was determined that he would and in 1882 bundled him off to Tokyo to enroll in medical school. Chinpei did enroll as directed, but eventually he transferred to the study of law, doing so without informing Sasaki.

By 1890 Chinpei had acquired a degree in law from Tokyo School of Law (Tokyo *hōritsu gakkō*; renamed Hōsei University in 1903), reputedly the first person from his district (*gun*) to receive an advanced Meiji-style education in Tokyo. He had also gained a considerable familiarity with the political scene, acquiring, on the one hand, a distaste for the contemporary excesses of chic exoticism and for the Sat-Chō "clique" domination of government (*hanbatsu seiji*). On the other hand, he had developed sympathy for the policies of the Kaishintō, a political party in which his fellow Okayama native, Inukai Tsuyoshi, had played a founding role in 1882.

Chinpei had also developed an interest in promoting the self-government, economic development, and *bunmei kaika* of his home district, seeing in that process, one suspects, a way to build his own reputation as a person of consequence, a progressive man of the times. And that, as we note subsequently, is what he spent the rest of his life doing, in the process helping to hold mass and class together, contributing to Japan's industrialization, and abetting the new regime.

RENEWAL OF GROWTH

During the early Meiji decades Japanese society entered a new era of socioeconomic growth that foreshadowed its industrial future. The rate of growth was slow, certainly, but by the 1890s a sustained trajectory was clearly evident, a trajectory that would continue for a century despite a devastating setback during the 1940s.

The most basic aspect of early Meiji growth was expansion of agricultural production, which permitted both population growth and the deployment of more social resources to other tasks. That expansion was facilitated by the Meiji regime's structural changes, particularly in taxation and land-use rights, but also by developments in commerce, transportation, and industry, which increased market opportunities for rural producers. Most famously, sustained growth in overseas sales of silk spread cash income through the hinterland, enabling many farmers to invest more in their other farming operations.

Tidy statistical analysis of early Meiji economic development is impossible because basic figures are unavailable or unreliable. However, a careful scholarly estimate has suggested that during the decades to 1890 farmers brought about 100,000 additional *chō* (a *chō*=0.99 hectares; 2.45 acres) into paddy tillage while adding another 80,000 *chō* of dry fields. Over half of the latter was in Hokkaido, which although too cold for widespread rice culture was being newly opened to pasturage, orchardry, and other forms of agricultural use.[22] Farmers also increased the output of their fields by better use of fertilizer, seed, and tillage techniques, as long advocated by authors of *jikatasho*. Moreover, the development of new transportation capabilities, together with improvements in distribution and storage that accompanied dissolution of the old domanial rice-tax system, reduced losses between producer and consumer. One result of these undramatic changes in agriculture was that Japan, which began exporting food during the 1860s, remained a net exporter into the 1890s. And that modest surplus existed despite an overall growth in population from about 34 million in 1872 to 40 million in 1890.

Within this broader context the most notable facets of early Meiji growth were in mining, communication and transportation infrastructure, foreign trade and production for it, and the appearance of diverse new factories that anticipated the industrial plant of later decades.

Mining – of copper, iron, coal, and other materials – received much attention, the yield being seen as basic to so much else: government income, currency, export goods, industrial production, and machines themselves. The Meiji finance official Inoue Kaoru observed in 1873 that mines

> ought to be considered the country's most important industry and ought to produce large profits … [but they] in fact are unable to produce enough for the manufacture of coins.[23]

Accordingly he advised the government to acquire mines and promote their technical improvement, and in following years mine development did in fact become an important part of Meiji policy. Foreign advisers were hired to assist in the task, and technical schools were established to train mining and metallurgical engineers. Operators of larger mines introduced the use of steam-driven pumps to eject water, forced-air systems for ventilation, blasting powder to loosen ore, and winches to transport and lift it to the surface. Japanese entrepreneurs were encouraged to cooperate with government, and later they took over most of the mining operations.

Gradually progress was made. Coal mining, which had begun to expand during the eighteenth century in response to scarcities of fuel wood and which was yielding upwards of 150,000 metric tons annually during the 1820s, nearly tripled production to some 400,000 tons by the 1860s, much of it to fuel foreign steamships. It then expanded another sixfold to about 2,600,000 tons by 1890.[24] Copper mining, which had reached a Tokugawa peak annual output of some 5,200 tons in 1685 and declined thereafter to about 1,000 tons by 1860, expanded in following decades, especially after 1888, reaching a level of some 29,400 tons by 1900. Similarly, gold, silver, sulphur, and lead mining expanded. And in iron mines European and American techniques of mining and processing slowly replaced indigenous methods, which enabled annual iron production to rise to some 28,900 tons by 1900. These gains notwithstanding, the construction of industrial infrastructure proceeded so rapidly that mine output scarcely kept pace. By the 1890s it was beginning to lag, imports started to grow, and that trend accelerated thereafter.

Telegraph and postal facilities were set up during the 1870s and eighties, and by 1895 telegraph lines spanned 4,000 miles. Meanwhile a number of entrepreneurial investors hired foreign experts to help them build short railroads near major cities, and by 1895 their railway ventures, together with some by the government, had been linked together to create over 2,000 miles of railroad. One line ran from Aomori in the north to Kobe on the Inland Sea while another crossed the mountains from Tokyo to Naoetsu on the Sea of Japan, improving dramatically the efficiency of long-distance travel and transport. Within cities the *jinrikisha* ("rickshaw") provided a similar benefit, replacing the labor-intensive palanquin and facilitating swift travel through narrow city streets. An early Meiji invention, by 1878 some 110,000 were in use in Japan and others abroad.[25]

Railways expedited not only the domestic movement of goods and people but also the transport of overseas trade goods to and from ports. During the 1860s it was foreign vessels, mainly British, that carried the goods abroad. From the 1870s onward, however, entrepreneurs and government officials cooperated – not always easily – to create Japanese shipping companies, most famously the Mitsubishi line of the Tosa samurai Iwasaki Yatarō. These companies gradually reasserted Japanese control over coastal shipping and established overseas lines to Hong Kong and elsewhere. By 1893 Japanese vessels constituted 14 percent of those entering Japanese ports from abroad, with a rising percentage being steamers and a slowly growing portion of these the creations of Japanese shipyards.

The total volume and value of foreign trade grew substantially during these decades, although it remained a minor item in the overall economy. Imports included steel, ships, and machinery for military and industrial uses, sugar, cotton fabrics, and by the later 1880s swelling quantities of raw cotton. The predominant exports were tea, silk thread, marine products, rice, coal, copper, and miscellaneous handicraft goods such as ceramics. Of these exports, silk thread was the most important, its volume roughly quadrupling between 1868 and the early 1890s, by then constituting 42 percent of total exports.

On balance Japan's foreign trade in 1890 was still that of a non-industrial society, in effect a "colonial" economy, mainly providing raw materials to the somewhat more industrialized states of Europe while receiving manufactured goods from them. However, that character was destined to change. One reason for the change was that by the 1890s the population was reaching a size that required all of Japan's domestic food output and more. Another reason was that the railways, steamships, and domestic factories that were being established were developing a great enough need for copper and coal to preclude their sustained export and to create instead a need for raw material imports and manufactured exports sufficient to pay for them. Thus, total coal output grew less than fourfold during the decade 1884–94 while factory use of coal increased sixfold, figures that only hinted at the disparity to come.

As of 1890 large-scale enterprises were still few. They included those established by the government during the 1870s: arsenals, shipyards, and bullion mines, as well as the Tomioka silk-reeling works and other pilot plants for cement, glass, and woolens. They also included a handful of entrepreneurial ventures, most notably the Osaka Spinning Mill of the early 1880s with its 10,000 spindles. That mill was one of several enterprises promoted by Shibusawa Eiichi, an uncommonly gifted and energetic landlord-entrepreneur from the Kantō. In the main, however, small shops continued to handle industrial production, silk-reeling in particular but also ceramics, matches, metal goods, and handicraft products in general. In innumerable small ways these shops enhanced their output through innovations and adaptations that were encouraged by individual entrepreneurs, trade organizations, and local, prefectural, and central government organs seeking more and better-quality products for export and domestic sale.

Cumulatively this growing agricultural and industrial output helped keep Japan's foreign accounts in balance while providing the government with income for its policies of *fukoku kyōhei* and *bunmei kaika*. And not accidentally it assured comfortable lives for the new rulers and the flourishing classes of bureaucrats, entrepreneurs, and landlords. Together with the era's programs of institutional reform and cultural reorientation, it laid the foundation for the much more dramatic phase of industrial growth and imperial expansion that was to begin during the 1890s.

PART IV

The Age of Industrialism:
Early Decades (1890–present)

Introduction to Part IV

To reiterate our overall chronological framework, industrialization has constituted for the Japanese, as for much of humankind, the second fundamental transformation in their history. The first changed a foraging system into the human-centered biological community of agricultural society. The second has entailed one basic new departure, one key corollary, and myriad secondary changes.

In the basic new departure of industrialization, a society that hitherto has been sustained by current output of the biosystem gives way to one that depends on a combination of current biological output and the yield from ancient biomass (coal, oil, and gas). The latter provides immense quantities of fuel for conversion to energy, as well as myriad plastics and other chemicals, and it can do so at a pace vastly exceeding that of current biological production. As a key corollary, a society that essentially has lived off the biological yield of the territory it occupies is transformed into one that depends for its basic functioning (rather than just for elite consumption, as in earlier times) on materials obtained from widely scattered sources – in effect a global resource base – and paid for by the export of goods and services, and/or by coercive effort. The secondary changes of industrialization are innumerable, including radical technological change and new patterns of political organization, ideology, and conflict. They also include establishment of a low-grade mass literacy, broadened socio-political consciousness, lengthened life spans, astounding population growth, urbanization, sharply heightened material consumption, and new forms of material and expressive culture.

In addition, to pick up a theme adumbrated in the Introduction, industrialization has led to a stunning increase in space monopolization by humankind. That trend is obvious in the many forms of "urban sprawl," some of whose malign effects on the broader biosystem are immediately apparent. But equally important are "packing" and "stacking," the fitting of more and more people into given spaces and the widespread adoption of multi-story structures – for housing, work, play, and travel. Because the humans of industrial society have so many needs and wants that cannot be satisfied by activity within their packed and stacked slots, these trends multiply the load on other areas, escalating society's need to monopolize such residual spaces as still support other biota.

Japan has been one of the world's first societies to industrialize, along with parts of Europe and North America. And while the process in each case has been idiosyncratic, all have been similar in the essentials. One can, nonetheless, identify two particularly noteworthy ways in which Japan's industrialization has been distinctive: in the conceptual framework in which participants and commentators have viewed it and, somewhat less clearly, in its timing and temporal rhythm.

Regarding conceptual framework. Japan's industrialization has persistently been envisaged in terms of "Westernization" or "modernization," concepts that generally are employed in simple, overlapping dyads. The former concept, as foreshadowed in the Introduction, juxtaposes an ill-defined ecumene called the West against something else variously identified as Japan, the East, or the Orient. The latter contrasts a newer socioeconomic condition, the "modern," against an older condition variously labeled pre-modern, under-developed, traditional, backward, or feudal.

Although these constructions bear the earmarks of "in-group/out-group" or "we–they" reductionism, they have not precluded insightful analysis, as many fine studies attest. But they have served to distance Japan's experience from that of its fellow industrializing societies.

Doubtless this conceptual framework was produced by the conditions under which Japan's industrialization commenced, namely the imperialist intrusion treated in chapter 12. When at home, Europeans (and their descendants living in America, Australia, and elsewhere) may habitually sort themselves out along religious, political, linguistic, and class or status lines, regarding one another with all the forms of contempt, envy, distrust, and hatred that such lines of division commonly encourage. When thinking about or dealing with "non-Westerners," however, those same Europeans commonly close ranks, utilizing what they perceive as their shared identity or interests to present a "racial" united front that they have legitimized in terms of a presumably superior cultural community usually labeled Western civilization.

Nineteenth-century Japanese observers, whether encountering Europeans in Asia or during visits to Europe, were at first poorly equipped to distinguish among them. The many commonalities of material culture and creed produced by centuries of interaction among the language groups of Europe were much more obvious than the enduring differences and tensions. Consequently those observers found it entirely reasonable to accept the dyadic West/other image of cultural relations. Doing so, however, raised another question: was that "other" merely Japan or was it some broader community, "Oriental" or whatever. That question entangled the new problem of Europe/Japan relations in the older, Edo-period Japan/China cultural dyad that nativists (*koku-gakusha*) had highlighted, giving new complexity to Japan's relationship to its continental neighbors, who might now just as plausibly be viewed as "us fellow Asians" as "them," whether Chinese, Koreans, or whomever.

Once established, the Westernization and modernization dyads assured that issues of ethnic identity and global social position would remain central to commentary (both Japanese and foreign) about Japan's recent history. In the process they have tended to obscure the more basic ways in which that history has been part and parcel of the broader experience of industrializing humankind and its changing role in the global biosystem.

On timing and temporal rhythm. Just as the earlier shift from forager culture to an agricultural order (as well as the intermediate shifts from early to later forager, from dispersed to intensive agriculture, and the inter-stage shifts from growth to stasis) occurred slowly, so industrial society in Japan has taken shape gradually. Selecting the process's starting point is, therefore, a fairly arbitrary exercise. If fossil-fuel usage per se is our key determinant, after all, one could argue that the first signs of industrial society appeared in the eighteenth century, a "proto-industrialization" so to say. However, if we focus on the larger picture – the use of fossil fuel for the express purpose of producing and operating industrial gadgetry, together with Japan's participation in a globalizing order of industrial societies, and its implementation of such domestic change as those activities seemed to require – then the Meiji Restoration of 1868 makes a reasonable starting point. That was the moment when a predominant wish to revitalize older arrangements began yielding subtly, reluctantly, tentatively to a commitment, however hazy, to a future that was very unlike the past.

The Restoration is, with good reason, commonly treated as the starting point for "modern" Japan. However, as earlier suggested, the foreshadowings of an industrial future notwithstanding, until the 1890s Japanese society as a whole continued to move to the rhythms of life that had taken shape in preceding centuries, and only after that time did new influences begin to transform society as a whole.

By the 1890s, however, the basic structure and ideology of Japan's industrial order were in place, along with foundational elements of its new economy. And during that decade Japan began to manifest an industrial society's dependence on external sources of raw material – metals, raw cotton, and food initially, other goods later – and began to flesh out its basic strategies for global resource acquisition and future development. Moreover, it started to display the social and cultural attributes of an industrial society. It seems reasonable, therefore, to pick the 1890s as a point of departure.

Subsequently industrial growth accelerated and Japan, like other industrializing societies, became ever more deeply bound to the world beyond its borders. By the 1920s the ramifications of industrialization were shaping lives throughout the realm. In later decades, even as the overall population continued its historically unprecedented rate of growth, the numbers of farming families and the role of agriculture in Japanese life declined. As that occurred, urban cultural norms diffused through society and the rhythms of agricultural life gradually transmogrified from the basic determinant of human experience into elements of retrospective ideology, nostalgia, and urban romanticism.

That basic trend has continued down to the present. One can, however, identify moments of shift within this larger story of continuing process. From the 1890s to about 1914 the recently created Meiji ruling elite retained its essential coherence and control. It scored a series of diplomatic triumphs abroad while sustaining a program of accelerating industrial development at home. With the eruption of World War I, however, the global context changed, and after 1914 exogenous factors combined with the effects of accelerated domestic growth and change to undermine elite cohesion, generate socioeconomic disorder, and foster heightened internal political tensions. These trends eventuated in increasingly reckless foreign adventurism and the cataclysmic defeat of 1945.

In a broad sense the mid-century years of war, defeat, regression, and reconstruction constituted but a brief disruption in the history of Japan's industrialization. Certainly prewar-to-postwar continuities cannot be ignored. At a strategic level, however, the defeat of 1945 produced an exceptionally sharp break in basic policy toward resource acquisition, and the new strategy, which has lasted into the 1990s, has had profound consequences for the nation.

To elaborate, as a whole the developers of Japanese industrialism have from the outset employed pretty much the same portfolio of politico-military, economic, and ideological strategies to advance their purposes as have their fellows elsewhere. However, the rhythm of their employment has been rather more sharply punctuated. Meiji leaders initially adopted what appeared to be the basic strategy of their day for attaining strategic security, market access, and essential resources – that of empire building. As decades passed, the creation of autarchic empire became increasingly the preferred strategy of those in power, especially during the 1930s. However, in 1945 that strategy ended abruptly, giving way within a decade to one that employed wealth to gain access to global resources by negotiating advantageous exchanges of goods and services. That shift in strategy was accompanied by noteworthy changes in domestic social and political organization and ideology, and those new arrangements sufficed to give the Japanese people decades of unparalleled peace and prosperity. Shōwa Genroku they termed it, in memory of the reputedly flourishing years around 1690.

Consequently 1945, even more than 1914, constituted a major breaking point in the still-brief but rich history of industrial Japan. Various difficulties notwithstanding, the dynamism of Shōwa Genroku persisted until about 1990, when a cluster of developments seemed to introduce a new and less gratifying period of history, that of the present day, a time when the larger historical issues of growth and stasis again catch our attention. This rhythm, with its punctuations at 1914 and 1945, is reflected in the chapters that follow.

By their natures industrialism and genuine national independence seem ultimately to be incompatible. The very processes of learning, social mobilization, and technological and institutional change that are embedded in the rise of industrial society initially enabled nation-states to appear and then to flourish for a time. But the associated patterns of global material interdependence, human mobility, and broadened consciousness erode the capacity of nation states to stand alone. If, in the end, industrial society does prove to be sustainable, one suspects that Japan's autonomy, like that of other nation states, will shrivel, yielding to other modes of social integration and delineation.

For the foreseeable future, however, it appears that anachronistic national loyalties will continue to prop up the ruling groups and industrial elites of nation states. As a happy corollary for old academics like myself, the writing of national histories may not yet be an antiquarian indulgence or a mere exercise in nostalgia.

Chronology of Part IV

1890	First general election.
1893	Kitasato Shibasaburō establishes Institute for Infectious Diseases.
1894–5	Sino-Japanese War.
1897	Peak of Ashio mine pollution incident.
1899	First Yamaha piano manufactured.
1904–5	Russo-Japanese War.
1907	Labor disturbance at Ashio mine.
1910	*Shirakaba* literary magazine debutes; government annexes Korea; founds Military Reservist Association.
1911	Government establishes Factory Act; creates Special Higher Police; conducts Great Treason Trial. Nishida Kitarō publishes *Zen no Kenkyū*; Hiratsuka Raichō founds *Seitō*.
1912	Meiji *tennō* dies.
1913	Taishō Political Crisis; Takarazuka Revue established.
1914	Natsume Sōseki publishes *Kokoro*.
1914–18	World War I.
1915	Twenty-One Demands presented to Chinese government.
1918	Countrywide food riots.
1919	Kita Ikki drafts *Nihon kaizō hōan taikō*.
1921	Yamakawa Kikue and others found Sekirankai.
1922	Washington Conference to settle Asia-Pacific issues; *burakumin* form National Levelers' Society.
1923	Great Kantō earthquake.
1924	Katō Kōmei forms majority-party cabinet.
1925	Peace Preservation Law and Male Suffrage Act passed; Tsukiji Little Theatre opens.
1926	Yanagi Sōetsu and others found Japanese Folk Craft Association.
1928	Countrywide roundup of leftists.
1929	Great Depression commences, ravaging world silk market; Tanizaki Jun'ichirō publishes *Tade kuu mushi*.
1930	Tōyō Muslin factory strike.
1931–3	Kwantung Army conquers Manchuria.
1932	Assassination of Prime Minister Inukai Tsuyoshi.
1935	Japan Romantic School established.
1936	Coup attempted on February 26 by rebellious young officers.
1937	Marco Polo Bridge Incident.
1939	Russo-Japanese warfare at Nomonhan.
1941	Japanese naval forces attack Pearl Harbor.
1945	World War II ends; Supreme Commander for the Allied Powers establishes Occupation control of Japan.

1947	Shōwa Constitution comes into effect; Dazai Osamu publishes *Shayō*.
1949	SCAP purges leftists.
1950	Korean War erupts.
1950s	Reforestation proceeds briskly.
1952	Occupation ends; Kurosawa Akira produces the film *Ikiru*.
1954	Animated film *Godzilla* appears; Yoshihara Jirō founds experimental art group Gutai Bijutsu Kyōkai.
1955	Conservative factions coalesce in Liberal Democratic Party.
1956	Mishima Yukio publishes *Kinkakuji*.
1959	Hijikata Tatsumi founds Ankoku Butō theatrical troupe.
1960	Treaty revision crisis; Miike coal mine strike.
1960s	Economic boom; cinema industry declines.
later 1960s	Industrial pollution issues proliferate.
1968–9	Turmoil in universities.
1972	Tokyo regains administrative control of Okinawa; Japan Foundation established.
1973	First "oil shock."
1970s	Nuclear power plant construction flourishes.
1974	University of Tsukuba opens.
1980s	"Bubble economy" creates labor shortage.
later 1980s	Large influx of foreign workers.
1989	Shōwa *tennō* dies; Imamura Shōhei produces film *Kuroi Ame*.
1990	Sustained economic recession commences.

[13] *EARLY IMPERIAL TRIUMPH (1890–1914)*

CHAPTER SYNOPSIS

DOMESTIC POLITICAL PROCESS
MACROPOLITICS
ON LOCAL LEADERSHIP

BECOMING AN IMPERIAL POWER
BEGINNINGS

FIRST FRUITS

DOMESTIC GROWTH
DEMOGRAPHICS
INDUSTRIAL GROWTH

The history of twentieth-century Japan has been shaped primarily by domestic economic growth, with all its sociocultural ramifications, and by the external process of arranging access to the necessary global resource base. Those developments have been inextricably entwined, and from the outset acute observers realized this, even while differing in the particulars of their understanding. In 1903, for example, as Japan was protesting the Russian military presence in southern Manchuria, Kanai En, a professor of political economy at Tokyo Imperial University, expressed the predominant view of his day when he wrote that,

> the two most critical responsibilities of the modern nation are foreign policy and social policy. By foreign policy I mean establishing ideal relations with the powers and achieving an imperialist policy of sending migrants overseas. Social policy basically plans conciliation of all social classes at home and thereby attempts to bring about a perfect unity of the entire nation ... Social policy must go together with imperialism.[1]

Doubtless Kanai's "ideal relations" abroad were to be ideal from Tokyo's perspective, and emigration would ease "overpopulation" at home while establishing Japanese control of territories abroad, in the manner of the European diaspora of recent centuries. Kanai hoped that measures of domestic conciliation would obviate both the threat of "socialism" and the political dangers inherent in sustained intersocietal contacts and the hardship that came with industrial development.

Until around 1914 both the domestic process of growth and the external process of establishing Japan's global position proceeded comparatively smoothly, in part because the recently articulated, European-dominated, imperialist order in East Asia provided a relatively stable context. By its nature such an order (with its outside ruling elite whose capacity to control and exploit indigenous populations was based almost entirely on coercion and the collaboration of hired "natives") had an unpromising future, especially among intensive agricultural societies with the rich political legacy of East Asia. Nonetheless, only when the Ch'ing dynasty fell in 1911 was the order's future placed in jeopardy. And not until Europe's coercive power was crippled and its credibility compromised by World War I did the imperialist order begin to crumble. Thereafter, as we note in later chapters, global political conditions grew more and more disorderly, and as Japan became more deeply enmeshed in the global economy, that disorder reverberated through domestic life, exacerbating stresses that were being produced by the accelerating change at home.

Even as industrialization was generating political complications, it was also having ramifications that affected all levels of society, cultural production, and the ecosystem. Population growth, urbanization, increased mobility, heightened socioeconomic differentiation, widespread schooling, and technological change gave rise to new forms and levels of social conflict and environmental damage as well as new means for expressing new cultural agendas, and these are treated in chapter 14.

DOMESTIC POLITICAL PROCESS

During the 1890s Japan's leaders implemented the electoral process called for by the Meiji Constitution. They also continued promoting industrial development and took their first decisive steps to arrange foreign relations in a manner acceptable to themselves. At the national level these undertakings by the new ruling elite – meaning court and nobility, senior officialdom, major industrialists, and political party leaders – involved jockeying among interest groups that used their wealth and connections as best they could to advance their agendas.

No matter how the jockeying worked out, however, the programs of reform and development required cooperation from below even as they produced more and more social dislocation and discontent. Consequently government success depended on the support of local leaders who could promote the desired local change while damping down any resulting tensions sufficiently to preserve the regime's fiscal and military foundation.

MACROPOLITICS

Itō Hirobumi and the other founders of the Meiji constitutional order had, as noted in chapter 12, designed a governing system that located national sovereignty in the emperor, secured the imperial household's fisc against public meddling, buttressed the household with a hereditary Peerage and a Privy Council of wise elders, and made senior civil and military figures imperial appointees. They also established a bicameral Diet and prefectural and local government organs so as to link this ruling oligarchy to the general public through official channels. Those channels included a voting franchise that was carefully restricted to "qualified" voters, meaning monied males. The founders hoped that these arrangements, as well as others, would assure social order, government stability, policy soundness, and active public support for their regime.

It was not the intention of Meiji leaders that just any ambitious fellow be able to gain control of the state. Even before 1890, however, political outsiders had employed diverse forms of bait and bullying to acquire a say in national affairs. A technique favored by some figures on the margins of power had been the formation of pressure groups – political parties – to promote the agendas of their supporters, mainly ex-samurai, businessmen, and landlords. Commonly the party leaders justified their claim to a say in affairs by employing a rhetoric of "popular rights" (*jiyū minken*), by denouncing current governing arrangements as "Sat-Chō clique government" (*hanbatsu seiji*), and by attacking specific policies of those in control. In 1890, when the government implemented an election to determine membership in the constitutionally authorized lower house of the Diet, that political *modus operandi* prevailed.

In the election's outcome two political parties, the Jiyūtō and Kaishintō, emerged as dominant forces, together winning more than 170 of the 300 house seats, and during the next four years political battle essentially pitted their leaders against the cabinet. The Diet majority repeatedly obstructed government measures in attempts to obtain concessions of power while successive cabinet leaders responded by trying to bribe, bargain, bully, and beggar party leaders into submission. The rhetorical combat of these years included much talk about national dignity and foreign relations, and in 1894 when, as we note more fully below, the government resorted to war to displace Ch'ing political influence in Korea, cabinet and Diet closed ranks to cooperate for the moment in the name of national unity. That collaboration continued through the war and the gratifying peace agreement that Itō subsequently negotiated at Shimonoseki.

A month later, however, in April 1895, Germany, Russia, and France denounced a segment of the treaty, forcing Japan to surrender spoils of war, and Jiyūtō leaders used that moment of government humiliation and weakness to negotiate a political entente in which Itō and his colleagues agreed to collaborate with them in forming a new cabinet. This party-oligarch alliance proved so satisfying to participants that other Diet members coalesced around the Kaishintō to form a rival alliance with Matsukata Masayoshi and in 1899 with Yamagata Aritomo, the Chōshū samurai who played a central role in the creation of Japan's modern army. They then challenged the supremacy of Itō's party, which after 1900 was called the Seiyūkai.

As a result of these changes, a pattern of governing became established in which oligarchs, their bureaucratic underlings, Diet party leaders, and their financial backers collaborated – not always easily – to recruit followers, engage in electoral contests, form governments, enact legislation, and implement policy. For over a decade governing alliances of this sort formed and reformed, with the prime ministership being held alternately by Katsura Tarō, acting as a strong-willed lieutenant of Yamagata, and Saionji Kinmochi, the much less willful lieutenant of Itō Hirobumi.

Itō's faction was strongly anchored in the Seiyūkai, but Katsura had better ties to the Meiji leadership as a whole, and he held the prime ministership for most of the decade 1901–11. By the eve of World War I, however, broadened public schooling, the spread of popular journalism, and the socioeconomic ramifications of industrialization had given rise to public unrest, vigorous lobbying efforts, and mass demonstrations, both peaceful and violent. Political combatants attempted to exploit this discontent to embarrass, frighten, and intimidate their rivals. It was a trend that threatened to open the political process to a much larger and more fractious populace than Meiji leaders really wanted or intended.

Near the end of 1912 that trend culminated in a noisy national political contest known hyperbolically as the Taishō Political Crisis (Taishō *seihen*). In that contest Katsura attempted to form his own party and oust the Seiyūkai from power as a way to resecure oligarchal control and reaffirm a Constitutional principle of "transcendental cabinets" (*chōzen naikaku*), meaning cabinets responsible to the emperor and above the tawdry fray of partisan politics. Katsura's opponents, most famously the politicians Inukai Tsuyoshi of Okayama and Ozaki Yukio of Kanagawa, threw their support to the Seiyūkai and, amidst widespread agitation against "clique government" and fiery rhetoric about defending the Constitution, enabled the reinforced Seiyūkai to prevail.

By 1914, then, the political process was proving far more tumultuous than Meiji builders had wanted. It did, nevertheless, link local politics to those at the center more smoothly and securely than Tokugawa arrangements had ever done. For all its clumsiness, it furnished a tolerably civil forum for the expression of a modest range of political views. And by giving a legitimate voice to interest-group politics that had deep roots in society at large, it provided mechanisms to accommodate shifting balances of power within the realm.

ON LOCAL LEADERSHIP

The linkage of national to local politics was important because the readiness of local leaders to cooperate was essential to any national undertaking. That was especially true given the persistent rhetoric about "Sat-Chō clique government," which continually reminded listeners that the Meiji rulers got where they were through military triumph and implied that they were primarily committed to perpetuating their power and privileges as a conquest regime.

Quite apart from the need to allay doubts about the rulers' motives, the government's agendas of "strengthening" and "enlightening" (*fukoku kyōhei*; *bunmei kaika*) required local collaborators because they involved the pursuit of agricultural improvement, industrial and commercial development, administrative reorganization, construction of roads, railroads, schools, harbors, and other facilities, and – here's the worst rub – policies of tax collection and disbursement to accomplish those tasks. Political parties became the principal channels through which individuals and local groups could present grievances or participate in the government's ventures. And they provided the means to align local plans and ambitions with the broader policies of national leaders, which were implemented through bureaucratic hierarchies that reached down to the local level.

The role of local leaders in national affairs is nicely evidenced in the career of Ikegami Chinpei, the handsome, energetic, young man from Okayama who in 1890 received a degree in law, rather than medicine as his adoptive family, the Sasaki, had intended.[2] After Chinpei's return to his home village that year, a disgruntled Sasaki sent him back to the Ikegami household, and in 1894, aged 32, Chinpei succeeded to the headship there. By then he had already launched his political career, forming discussion groups with neighbors and advocating local road construction and other improvements. By 1899 he had acquired a sufficient following to be elected village head.

From then until his illness and death in 1920 Chinpei's performance epitomized that of local leaders throughout Japan. His local connections and activities were closely tied to his involvement in prefectural and national politics, in the course of which he spent much of his own family fortune, as well as his wife's. From 1898 onward he served as a local stalwart in Inukai Tsuyoshi's famous Okayama political machine (*jiban* or bailiwick), obtaining as *quid pro quo* both prefectural and national government support for many of his local projects. As an Inukai loyalist he helped dislodge the Seiyūkai from control of northeast Okayama Prefecture (formerly Mimasaka Province), and in 1913 he kept his district loyal to Inukai during the Taishō Political Crisis.

The crisis split Inukai's party down the middle. Inukai himself, as noted above, threw in his lot with his old rivals in the Seiyūkai, doing so in hopes of drawing enough of its members into his own party to elevate himself to the prime ministership. However, about half of his party's Diet members – including Chinpei's most powerful patron, the wealthy Okayama businessman Sakamoto Kin'ya – collaborated with Katsura against the Seiyūkai. In the outcome Katsura lost, but Inukai's hopes for the prime ministership also went unrealized. He did, however, retain his position in Okayama, and Chinpei, though severely embarrassed by the sudden reversals, was able to continue pursuing his local projects with support from above.

Local and national connections were essential to Chinpei's efforts. However, his engaging personality and his skill at keeping goals of community and national improvement in clear view when promoting policy helped him acquire a reputation as one who could inspire men, smooth disagreements, elicit cooperation, and get things done. He also succeeded because he could exploit his advantages of education and experience in Tokyo as well as his large family base in the Ikegami clan of Kume District. Even his childhood training in calligraphy and Chinese and Japanese poetry served him well, with his published poems giving him stature as a properly cultured man.

Exploiting his talents and connections, Chinpei held numerous offices. He was elected village chief six times, got elected to village, district, and prefectural assemblies, and chaired or participated in local and prefectural committees that promoted the construction of schools, medical and relief facilities, and village offices. He headed local branches of national organizations, including the Red Cross, and pursued measures to help the elderly. On occasion he led investigating committees to other provinces and cities to observe progressive agricultural, industrial, and administrative policies – and doubtless to enjoy the sights and reward his supporters.

Chinpei put exceptional effort into agricultural improvement, promoting riparian work and silk marketing. He encouraged forest development, road and railroad construction, telephone and telegraph installation, local electrification, and the establishment of a local post office and bank. Perhaps his most celebrated achievement occurred during the period 1903–5 when he led his district's participation in a prefectural program of paddy-field rationalization and agronomic development. The program expanded paddy acreage, increased yield per household, and enabled his district to make a large, special contribution of rice to troops engaged in the Russo-Japanese war. His efforts proved so successful that when Hiroshima and Fukuoka prefectures undertook similar programs a few years later, they invited him to take charge. He declined, however, preferring to concentrate on his own district. There he continued to play his role as one of the thousands of local leaders who fostered change all across the archipelago, linking center to periphery and helping Japan sustain its transformation into an industrial society.

BECOMING AN IMPERIAL POWER

Even as the Chinpeis of the realm were promoting the domestic elements of Japan's industrial order, other leaders were pursuing the requisite global resource base. The process by which Japan gained access to that resource base was not, of course, a grand, foresighted plan that sprang fully articulated from an objective appreciation of the intrinsic requirements of industrial society. For Japan, as for other industrializing societies, after all, those requirements have developed slowly, and their particulars have continually changed with industrialism's advance. The fact that access to distant resources has become essential to society's basic functioning, and is not merely the indulgence of elite desires as in earlier ages, has only gradually become obvious. So a host of secondary considerations – diplomatic rivalry, personal ambition, entrepreneurial profit-mongering, elite pursuit of luxury, religious and other ideological zealotry – all played a part in the process of early industrial empire building.

For Japan the process of resource acquisition entailed the opportunistic initiatives that are common to industrialization. They fall into two basic categories: entrepreneurial ventures and politico-military undertakings, with much interplay between the two. In gross monetary terms the former have constituted by far the larger portion of Japan's overseas commercial activity throughout its modern history. Prior to 1945, however, the latter, empire building, was the socially more visible and ideologically more esteemed portion, as the earlier quotation from Kanai En suggests. Furthermore, empire building gained more and more relative importance as decades passed, emerging during the 1930s as the goal of national foreign policy and the preferred method for securing resources.

BEGINNINGS

The politico-military process of empire building evolved primarily out of ventures originally intended to deal with new, exacerbated versions of an old question with a long, sporadic, and multi-layered history: the question of Japan's relationship to Korea. Starting before the Tokugawa fell, Japan's leaders, as they became familiar with European conceptions of state sovereignty and territorial jurisdiction, addressed boundary issues close to home, claiming full political authority over the Bonin and Ryukyu island chains to the south and the large island of Hokkaido, so named in 1869, to the north. Early Meiji leaders reaffirmed those claims, deploying police and administrative cadres to consolidate Japanese control over indigenous populations. And Ryukyuan and Chinese protests notwithstanding, they dissolved the Ryukyuan Kingdom, which Satsuma had left semi-intact, much as they dissolved daimyo domains.

In the case of Hokkaido they also began almost immediately to promote settlement and land reclamation by ex-samurai and others. Aware of the long and troubled Ainu-Wajin (Japanese) relationship and of the earlier concern with Russian penetration of Ezo, Meiji leaders sought to retain Ainu good will as they secured their control of Hokkaido. In 1869 they admonished those charged with developing the island to

> make efforts to spread welfare, education and morals with kindness. With the gradual immigration of mainlanders, make sincere efforts to encourage harmony with the natives and a prosperous livelihood.[3]

In practice, however, Hokkaido's development proceeded with little more regard for the interests or sensibilities of the resident Ainu population than Anglophone immigrants to other lands displayed toward the indigenes they overran. Raw numbers suggest the story: even as the Ainu population of Hokkaido, battered by poverty, disease, and demoralization, hovered in the range of 18,000, the Wajin population leaped from an estimated 60,000 in 1850 to 111,000 in 1873 and 1,800,000 by 1913.

Korea lay beyond those localities as the next noteworthy area of geopolitical concern. As earlier chapters noted, the Korean Peninsula has been important to Japanese civilization since prehistoric days, initially as a source of people and know-how and later as an avenue of access to continental culture and commerce more broadly. On such occasions as the Mongol invasions and later the Manchu conquest of China, however, it has also been perceived as a source of political danger. From the mid-nineteenth century onward this sense of the peninula as source of danger gained renewed prominence, initially in the 1860s because of French actions there. By the 1880s the focus of concern was revitalized Ch'ing influence in the Yi dynastic regime; and during the 1890s, the expansion of Russian activity throughout northeast Asia.

By then, moreover, this strategic issue of a perceived foreign threat had been supplemented with other considerations. One was Japan's growing continental economic involvement. Korea was becoming a market for cotton goods and sundries and a source of rice and soybeans, while also beginning to look like a crucial rail link to the continent beyond. Indeed, by 1894, the gaining of treaty rights to develop mines and build railroads and telegraph lines had emerged as a key strategic goal of policy makers in Tokyo. More importantly, perhaps, the question of policy toward Korea had become enmeshed in the broader agenda of asserting Japanese dignity and interests *vis-à-vis* the imperialist powers as a whole.

This broader agenda was understood in several ways. Many of Japan's leaders, viewing the global international order as a geopolitical expression of the West/other or modern/pre-modern cultural dyad, envisaged a two-tier system of "civilized" states whose vigor and technological capability enabled them to establish empires, on the one hand, and "primitive" societies that became their colonies, on the other. They aimed to place their own country within the former group.

Other observers enfolded the issue in a broader ideological construct that drew on both European Social Darwinist notions of "survival of the fittest" and indigenous notions of Japan's unique godly origins to assert that Japan must and can strengthen itself to avoid being overrun by other nations. Some pundits contended that this task required Japan to repudiate its discredited "Asiatic" heritage, but others tied the task of self-strengthening to the concept of an Oriental ethno-cultural ecumene. They argued that the Japanese must lead their fellow Asians in the creation of a dynamic, modern Asia capable of repelling the Europeans, preserving itself, and extending its classic cultural virtues, minus its vices, into the future.

One step toward attaining this cluster of goals was revision of the late Tokugawa treaties, whose unequal stipulations constituted one of the clearest signs that Japan stood within the primitive colonial category and was at risk of being overrun, a Darwinian loser. From the early days of their rule Meiji leaders attempted to renegotiate those treaties, but foreign governments continually rebuffed them. Not until the summer of 1894, even as Sino-Japanese relations were sliding toward war, did Meiji programs of internal reform and national strengthening, together with changes in the global balance of power, induce the British, and subsequently others, to renegotiate the treaties on the basis of legal equality as defined by "civilized" states.

A second method for elevating Japan into the charmed circle of "the Powers" was for its leaders to play the two awkwardly associated roles embedded in imperialist policy, those of empire builder and civilized enlightener of backward folk. Even without the older strategic issue of the peninsula as source of foreign danger, Korea's very proximity made it a prime candidate for inclusion in any such imperialist enterprise. From the 1870s onward the question of how to implement such a policy – i.e., matters of timing, particulars of procedure, and forms of cooperation or control to be established – became for Japan's policy makers and pundits a topic of periodically intense debate. During the eighties Japan's political and economic activity on the peninsula began to grow briskly, and by the nineties the Korean issue had acquired considerable urgency because of the heightened Chinese and Russian activity in the region, greater turmoil among Koreans themselves, and the growing importance of Japan's trade there.

As the situation in Korea grew more disorderly, Tokyo leaders faced increasingly harsh domestic criticism from opportunistic party leaders in the Diet and jingoistic elements in the press who were supporting Korean reformers and attacking Yi and Ch'ing leaders as enemies of "progress." Thus Tokutomi Sohō, publisher of the *Kokumin shinbun*, advocated the use of force because,

> For Korea to be independent, Korea must be educated, Korea must be reformed. Freedom, hope, and progress must be instilled in Korea.

Three weeks later he reiterated his call for action,

> to build the foundation for national expansion in the Far East, ... to be recognized by the world as an expansive Japan, ... to take her place alongside the other great expansionist powers in the world.[4]

Pressed by conditions abroad and critics at home, Itō's cabinet concluded in 1894 that it must exert greater pressure to reverse the erosion of Japanese influence in Korea. It must end Ch'ing dominance there, expand economic opportunities, and steer Korea in the direction of Meiji-like reforms and closer cooperation with Japan.

FIRST FRUITS

Whereas early Meiji leaders had rejected proposals to use military force in Korea in 1873, lest they fail and suffer grievously, and had dithered indecisively during the eighties, in the summer of 1894 Itō's advisors believed their military preparations would suffice for war not merely with the Yi but even with the Ch'ing. Their calculations proved correct, to the surprise of many observers, and the resulting victories silenced their domestic critics. Furthermore, victory brought Japan the first of it colonial possessions, Taiwan, as well as a large indemnity that not only paid for the war but also facilitated investment in further military strengthening and industrial development.

With Ch'ing influence eliminated from Korea, Japanese trade and investment advanced, most notably when a syndicate under Shibusawa Eiichi launched construction of a railroad line from Pusan to Seoul that led subsequently to other railroad projects. On Taiwan, meanwhile, a military government was established. Most local resistance was overcome in comparatively short order, and the processes of organization, development, and exploitation were initiated.

In other ways, however, Tokyo found the outcome of victory less gratifying. In the treaty settlement at Shimonoseki, Ch'ing diplomats had ceded control of the Liaotung Peninsula, the site of excellent harbors and a major gateway to Manchuria. However France, Germany, and Russia, for reasons of European diplomacy, jointly demanded that Tokyo re-cede Liaotung. That action deeply embarrassed Japan's leaders, as earlier noted, and laid up bitterness that was doubled in 1898 when the Czarist regime took Liaotung for itself. Worse yet, victory over the Ch'ing failed to enhance the Korean court's receptiveness to Tokyo's advice, and in following years, even as Japanese firms and settlers pressed ahead with investment in and exploitation of the peninsula, the Japanese government found itself becoming more deeply mired in Korean politics, with Russia as its major rival.

In 1900 the Boxer Rebellion in China gave Japan and Russia occasion to collaborate, deploying large military forces to northern China and Manchuria. After the Rebellion's suppression, however, Russian troops held fast to their bases in Manchuria, a decision that Tokyo found unacceptable. Prime Minister Katsura fretted that if Russia retained Manchuria, its advance "will inevitably extend into Korea and will not end until there is no room left for us."[5]

Diplomacy, however, failed to dislodge the Russians. Indeed, in 1903 they began expanding their military and economic presence adjacent to and within Korea. In 1904, with chauvinist rhetoric again flourishing in the press, with the risk of third-power aid to Russia obviated by a newly negotiated Anglo-Japanese Alliance, and believing that an armed effort might suffice thanks to a decade of intensive military strengthening, leaders in Tokyo again resorted to war. Again – but just barely – they prevailed. In the Portsmouth Treaty, a settlement made possible by the two combatants' exhaustion, Japan acquired Karafuto (the southern half of Sakhalin Island) along with Czarist recognition of Japanese primacy in Korea and the cession of all Russian treaty rights and interests in southern Manchuria. These included the Liaotung Peninsula and a new railroad (the South Manchurian) with its substantial right-of-way and associated mining concessions.

By the standards of the day Tokyo's accomplishment was impressive: more territorial gains, an internationally accepted, hegemonial role in Korea, opportunity to develop southern Manchuria, and victory over an imperialist rival that placed beyond doubt Japan's status as a "Great Power." Moreover, the way to China had been cleared of a major obstacle. That was important because by then leaders in Tokyo saw China as the most promising market for exports to pay for the imports of machinery and materials that would enable Japan to maintain its role among the Powers and advance its presumed task of Asian leadership.

On its face the government's gamble had paid off handsomely; something akin to Kanai En's "ideal relations with the powers" had been attained. However, the cost in blood and treasure had been fearsome. Casualties were appalling; wartime tax and price hikes had caused hardship and angered many. Moreover, government promises and chauvinistic media propaganda had created untenable public expectations, so the terms of settlement, most notably the absence of an indemnity, were greeted with disappointment and outrage. Despite triumphal parades and official hoopla, press denunciations and public displeasure persisted, culminating in September 1905 in a massive flurry of destructive, anti-government rioting by the common people of Tokyo, and subsequently elsewhere about the country, the first instance of mass demonstrations fueled by issues of foreign policy.

Nor was the outcome on the continent fully satisfactory. In Korea Japanese negotiators imposed a protectorate arrangement on the Yi monarchy, but widespread public resentment and stubborn armed resistance to the new rulers persisted. Over the next few years Japan's frustrated leaders step by step abolished the monarchy and its army, took over police and judicial functions, suppressed the resistance, and in 1910 formally annexed the country. The international community acquiesced in these developments, American leaders agreeing to Japan's free hand in Korea in return for their own free hand in the Philippines; the British, trading Korea for India. Resistance within Korea continued, however, being met with harsh military rule that only stiffened the defiance as years passed.

In terms of empire as resource base, meanwhile, military victory brought one solution to the emerging problem, in California particularly, of foreign hostility toward emigrants from Japan. Already by the 1890s officials and observers were talking about the desirability of establishing emigrant populations to ease "overpopulation" at home while creating economically and strategically useful settlements abroad: to "transplant our people abroad and erect a bulwark for our state," as one pundit put it in 1891.[6]

Korea was seen as serving that purpose. In 1904 the government in Tokyo declared that Japanese should move to Korea to engage in agriculture because if that were done,

> we will acquire an immigration colony for our excess population on the one hand, and on the other will be able to augment our insufficient supplies of foodstuffs.[7]

The following year brought new acquisitions, and in 1909 Foreign Minister Komura Jutarō noted that,

> as a result of the Russo-Japanese War the status of the empire has changed and the area under its administration has grown larger; we should avoid scattering our people in the foreign countries where they are lost. It has become necessary that as far as possible we should direct our people to one area and avail ourselves of their collective strength.

He, like Kanai, evidently envisaged these emigrants continuing to identify themselves with Japan, much as Europeans and their descendants abroad have continued to define themselves in terms of the "Western" racial/cultural ecumene.

In practice, as table 13.1 indicates, Korea's population of Japanese settlers, like that of Taiwan, kept growing as immigrants filled the posts of colonial government, developed and worked in industrial and commercial enterprises,

Table 13.1 Japanese residing overseas, 1890–1920

	1890	1900	1910	1920
Korea	7,245	15,829	171,543	347,850
Taiwan	n/a	37,954	98,048	166,621
Hawaii	12,675	57,486	70,764	112,221
China*	864	3,243	36,529	212,651
Americas**	2,077	35,847	38,641	177,706
(Vladivostok, Karafuto, and Australia omitted)				
Total	23,327	156,276	449,227	1,116,639

Notes:
  *Mostly Manchuria, including Kwantung.
**Mostly USA.
Source: Figures derived from Peter Duus, *The Abacus and the Sword, The Japanese Penetration of Korea, 1895–1910* (Berkeley: UCP, 1995), p. 290.

and acquired control of farm land. In the process they expanded the export of foodstuffs and raw materials to Japan and the import of finished goods to the colonies.

In Manchuria, meanwhile, Japanese economic involvement grew apace. Using the South Manchurian Railway as a base, investors and empire builders founded a government corporation with entrepreneurial support that rapidly improved the railroad's tracks and equipment and promoted exploration, research, mining, manufacturing, and commercial ventures. Whereas Japan had, by one estimate, about $1,000,000 of investment on the continent in 1901, by 1913 the sum stood at about $220,000,000, most of it in Manchuria, the result of military victory. And trade with Manchuria (the export of Japanese manufactured goods and the import of coking coal, iron ore, raw cotton, and foodstuffs) grew rapidly, facilitating faster population growth and industrial expansion at home.

Insofar as empire building was a sign of industrial modernity, late Meiji Japan was clearly moving from the status of "primitive" to "advanced" society. Trends in overall foreign trade reinforced this image. Before 1890, as noted in chapter 12, manufactured imports had been far more essential to Japan than raw material imports. After that date, the continuing heavy dependence on raw silk exports (for which America was the chief market, taking a full quarter of the volume shipped) was still suggestive of a "colonial" or "underdeveloped" economy, but otherwise Japan's foreign trade had lost most of its colonial character by 1914. Copper and low-grade coal exports were being offset by other copper and coal imports. Food imports were growing rapidly, even as exports declined. Tea was no longer a significant export, being replaced by cotton goods and diverse manufactures. And raw cotton for the country's booming textile industry had become the major import, along with diverse other raw materials, plus steel and machinery for use in the proliferating shops and factories.

This growth and change in trade was accompanied by changes in the merchant fleet. Before 1890 ships of foreign registry had handled nearly all overseas trade while Japanese vessels concentrated on the coasting business and some China trade. The two foreign wars sharply expanded the fleet's size and modernity, however, with the number of steamships rising ninefold from 169 in 1894 to 1,514 in 1913. These vessels plied the sea between Japan, the colonies, and China, and they also reached ports in Europe, while shippers established regular lines to Southeast Asia and across the Pacific. Whereas Japanese bottoms had handled only about 8 percent of the country's foreign trade in 1893, they carried some 50 percent in 1913.

By 1914 Japan had thus made significant strides in the expansion of its resource base. However, empire building as means to that end was, in trade terms, still more promise for the future than performance in the present. The main source of manufactured imports was still Europe, Britain in particular for steamships, railway rolling stock, and other machinery. And the single most important export market was the United States, with its demand for silk. As of 1913 Taiwan and Korea were taking less than 13 percent of Japan's exports and providing less than 9 percent of imports. On the other hand, their share had been nearly nil twenty years earlier. And as we note in later chapters, it was destined to grow disproportionately in following decades, along with that of other colonial areas and the quasi-colonial regions of Manchuria and northeast China.

That trade trajectory notwithstanding, empire building was proving difficult, mainly due to indigenous resistance in Korea. It led to Itō's assassination by an angry Korean in 1909, and it tended to draw the government ever deeper into enterprises that were not necessarily to its liking. A bit sooner than the leaders of their sister Powers, Japan's rulers would discover that empire provided an unsatisfactory resource base. Until 1914, however, the larger imperialist order held together, and within it Japan had successfully transposed itself from the category of backward colonial society to that of advanced imperial Power. And rice and other materials from the colonies were already contributing significantly to the accelerating growth and industrial development of Japan proper.

DOMESTIC GROWTH

Meanwhile domestic affairs also evidenced Japan's march into industrialism. An array of demographic trends and agricultural developments revealed it, as did factory production and commerce.

DEMOGRAPHICS

From the 1870s onward one sees clear signs of a renewed population growth that signaled the end of later Tokugawa demographic stability. The trend accelerated as years passed (see figure 13.1), with the country's population reaching some 52 million by 1915, roughly 20 million above the stable level of the later Edo period. And at that point it had only begun its industrial-age surge. The growth was due to an increase in births, reduced childhood

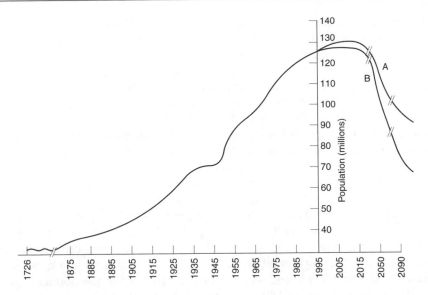

Figure 13.1 Industrial Japan: population trend and projection. Japan commenced its industrial-age population explosion by growing slowly in the 1870s. It traced upward during the twentieth century, save for the mid-1940s, and began to show signs of leveling off near century's end, which may possibly lead to population decline a few decades hence. (Estimate A from 1995; estimate B from 1998.) *Source: Nihon tōkei nenkan* (Japan Statistical Yearbook) (Tokyo: Statistics Bureau, Management and Coordination Agency, annual), *1996*, pp. 31–3; *1999*, pp. 31–3.

mortality, and lengthened life spans, with the occasional massive loss to modern military carnage being outweighed (except during 1943–5) by reduced losses to famine, malnutrition, and disease (except tuberculosis).

This demographic growth was made possible by gains in food production, with rice output increasing roughly in tandem with total population to reach some 51 million *koku* around the period 1910–14. Insofar as basic caloric intake per capita rose, however, it could do so thanks mainly to imports, with rice in the vicinity of 3 million *koku* entering the country annually during the years before World War I. India and Southeast Asia provided considerable quantities, but Taiwan and Korea were becoming the principal sources by 1914.

The gains in domestic food output were due in part to expansion of arable acreage, most notably in Hokkaido. That island, whose stunning population growth we noted above, was still viewed as frontier territory, and immigration, logging, land clearance, and mining activities continued apace. They advanced the early Meiji policy of displacing Ainu culture and transforming the island into a full-fledged part of the realm, while agricultural development there contributed substantially to the overall growth in farm output. According to one analysis Hokkaido's acreage of dry fields increased some sixteen-fold between 1890 and 1920 (from 45,000 to 740,000 *chō*). And by growing the more cold-resistant strains of rice that had been developed in recent decades, farmers were able to expand its paddy field acreage forty-fold (from 2,000 to 83,000 *chō*).

Of longer-term consequence than the opening of Hokkaido were country-wide improvements in agronomic technique, spurred by local improvers such as Ikegami Chinpei. Reorganization of paddy fields, modest improvements in use of seed, land, storage, etc., and greater use of fertilizer slowly increased the productivity of cultivators. As in early Meiji, however, what most buoyed the rural economy was continuing expansion in silk production and export. The 11.5 million pounds of raw silk produced in 1894 swelled to 31 million by 1914, providing enough thread and fabric to constitute about a third of the nation's exports while generating income that farmers could plow back into their other productive efforts.

Agricultural expansion permitted the population growth, but the enlarged work force had its most striking demographic impact on urban centers and the industrial sector. The portion of the population living and working in cities and towns grew rapidly, with Tokyo numbering some two million by 1903 and Osaka nearly a million, roughly triple its size a half-century earlier. More broadly, the population living in cities of 50,000 or more doubled between 1888 and 1913, and whereas only 16 percent of the populace lived in towns of over 10,000 in 1893, 28 percent did by 1913.

Cities and towns could experience this growth because nearly all of the country's swelling work force was going into non-agricultural jobs, most of which were found in town. In consequence the portion of domestic output that came from agriculture declined, by one estimate dropping from 45 percent in 1885 to about 32 percent in 1914, a trend that would continue for the rest of the century (see figure 19.1, p. 471). Industry, commerce, and their myriad ancillary jobs in government and social service were displacing agriculture as the heart of the economy.

INDUSTRIAL GROWTH

Large-scale industrial production, which the government had tried to foster during the 1870s, was by the 1890s mainly in the hands of entrepreneurs, the most successful of whom developed their enterprises into wide-ranging combines, the *zaibatsu*. Illustrative of these entrepreneurs was Chinpei's patron, Sakamoto Kin'ya, the son of an Okayama samurai who was schooled in law in Tokyo and returned to Okayama in 1889. There he joined others in forming a local political movement, established a newspaper (the *Chūgoku minpō*), and ventured into industry. He erected a spinning mill, developed a coal mine, took over and expanded the output of a copper mine, and in 1907 established a foundry, in the process emerging a major industrial figure in the Okayama vicinity.

In the meantime his political career advanced and he rose via prefectural politics to become a Diet member aligned with Inukai Tsuyoshi. In 1906 he freed up time for political activity by hiring Chinpei as overseer of his industrial empire. Chinpei held the position for four years, resigning when Kin'ya became embroiled in a financial scandal, some three years before he and Inukai went their separate ways during the Taishō Political Crisis. Sakamoto survived that reverse, and his enterprises passed on to his sons a few years later.

On a grander scale, a far more celebrated – or reviled – example of Meiji entrepreneurship was Furukawa Ichibē, the son of a headman and beancurd maker from a village near Kyoto. Moving into the city's silk trade in late Tokugawa, he became a skilled businessman. Around the time of the Restoration he went east, got into Yokohama silk exports, and established in Tokyo a technically advanced silk mill that proved profitable. In 1874 he began acquiring a string of productive ore mines, and within two decades was operating one gold, eight silver, and twelve copper mines. He also acquired some influential Meiji political friends, including Shibusawa Eiichi. With their help he obtained his most valuable asset in 1877: control, and eventually full ownership, of the Ashio copper mine in the mountains of Tochigi Prefecture north of Tokyo.

During the eighties Furukawa consolidated, modernized, and rapidly expanded his mining and smelting operations at Ashio (see table 13.2), enabling the mine to produce some 40 percent of the country's total copper output during the 1890s. In the process he turned it into a cash cow that he milked with enough diligence to transform himself into one of the realm's richest and most influential men.

As we note in chapter 14, the rapid expansion of Ashio's output produced Japan's first pollution disaster and a dramatic eruption of labor conflict. Nevertheless, Furukawa was able to parlay his profits from Ashio into the development of an industrial empire, public esteem, and high imperial honors. After he died in 1903, one of his political allies, the future prime minister Hara Kei, served for a time as unofficial manager of the mine, much as Chinpei served Sakamoto. Later others continued Ashio's operation, preserving the mine's role as a major source of the copper exports that helped pay for the imports required by industrialization.

Men such as Sakamoto and Furukawa were instrumental in developing all sorts of commercial, manufacturing, and mining enterprises. Coal production deserves particular note because it provided Japan with the fossil-fuel energy boost essential to industrialization. Output grew rapidly during these decades, spurred by export sales and expansion in steel and other heavy industrial production, along with increasing railroad use, textile output, and urban population growth. Domestic reserves were still available, mostly in Kyushu and Hokkaido, and coal output rose from about 5 million metric tons in 1895 to 21 million in 1913, with low-grade bituminous exports still

Table 13.2 Ashio copper production, 1877–1917

1877	77	1891	12,705
1881	290	1897	13,650
1883	1,089	1917	21,000
1885	6,886		

Note: Figures in thousand *kin*; 1 *kin* = 1.32 lbs.
Source: F. G. Notehelfer, "Japan's First Pollution Incident," *The Journal of Japanese Studies* 1/2 (Spring 1975): 354–6, 360–1.

offsetting the swelling imports of anthracite and coking coal. Some of the coal energy was made available via conversion into electricity, but hydroelectric power plants began replacing coal-fired generators after 1910, foreshadowing their later proliferation.

Along with large-scale ventures, smaller-sized industries also continued to multiply, remaining an important element in the total economy. Most notable were the widepread rural silk spinning operations. However, myriad other small shops arose as people acquired industrial skills and set up their own firms, and as artisans continued to produce much of what people utilized in their daily lives.

Most industrial production, both large and small scale, lay in entrepreneurial hands, but the government did assert a leadership role in areas of strategic interest. As noted earlier, it pressed ahead vigorously with military strengthening after the Liaotung humiliation, developing its arsenals and naval yards into the country's largest industrial operations and giving them the capacity by 1904 to produce high-grade ships and armaments. As part of its drive for military self-sufficiency the government used a portion of the Shimonoseki indemnity to finance construction of Japan's first major steel mill, the Yahata works in northern Kyushu, which it situated convenient to coal mines and port facilities. Not only could Yahata produce iron and steel for military needs but also for railway track, rolling stock, and the myriad machines and other iron goods of the civilian economy. By 1914 the plant was producing upwards of a half million tons of pig iron and steel annually, meeting about a third of the country's total needs in each category.

Transportation also came to be viewed as a strategic concern. Most of the early Meiji railroad construction had been pursued by private interests, as noted in chapter 12, and by 1901 a trunk line, partially private, ran from Aomori via Tokyo to Shimonoseki. By the time of the Russo-Japanese War, however, the government recognized the strategic value of a well-coordinated national system of railways, and to assure such coordination it nationalized nearly all 5,000 miles of rail line in 1906. In later years it continued laying track to fill out a more integrated network, and one goal of the political maneuvering by local leaders such as Chinpei was to secure the local benefits of such construction.

By 1914 Japan had established many of the basic political and economic elements of an industrial order. Designed to preserve the realm from foreign danger and to secure the interests of its creators and their collaborators, that order accomplished its main tasks estimably well. Its effects on the broader society, however, were more ambiguous, as the following chapter notes.

[14] EARLY IMPERIAL SOCIETY AND CULTURE (1890–1914)

CHAPTER SYNOPSIS

SOCIAL ISSUES
    ENVIRONMENTAL POLLUTION
    INDUSTRIAL LABOR
    THE AGRARIAN ISSUE
    ACTIVIST WOMEN
    YOUNG GENTLEMEN
    SOCIALIST INTELLECTUALS

ARTICULATE CULTURE
    THE FIELD OF DISCOURSE
    THE MECHANICS OF CULTURAL
    PRODUCTION
    LEARNING NEW AND OLD
    ARTS AND LETTERS

The quarter century to 1914 was a heady time to be alive in Japan. Life was changing fast; new and unimagined possibilities seemed to be opening up; national triumphs could make the heart leap. And these trends, all grounded in politico-economic developments, were evident in arts and letters of the day. But not all was going well, not everyone benefited. For many life was hard and disappointment their reward. And even as older problems were being resolved, new ones were appearing on the horizon, foreshadowing more troublous years to come.

SOCIAL ISSUES

These decades of economic growth witnessed the emergence of social problems commonly associated with industrialism. They included its two paradigmatic markers, namely, destructive environmental pollution and industrial labor grievances, as well as problems of social dislocation and disorientation that sprang from the commingling of new difficulties and opportunities. These latter included a diffuse concern about the fate of rural folk and rural life, an emerging feminist interest in women's rights and roles, discontent among the ambitious young who sensed that life's prospects were narrowing, and the appearance of an intelligentsia versed in the radical thought then blossoming in Europe. There also appeared, as we shall note in chapter 16, the beginnings of a protest movement by those of pariah (*eta*) background against the persistent discrimination they faced.

ENVIRONMENTAL POLLUTION

Environmental pollution was a very minor issue during the later Edo period, having been associated mainly with the mining and burning of coal, but it became pronounced during Meiji as mining and manufacturing expanded. Japan's first major incident of industrial pollution, which occurred downstream from Furukawa Ichibē's Ashio copper mine, merits attention because it furnished a signature announcement of industrialism's arrival, epitomizing the pollution, resource depletion, and "bio-health" issues that have become endemic in our own time. It displayed the usual patterns of these issues: industry–government collusion, sacrifice of the vulnerable in the name of the greater good or some other fine principle, disregard of the future for the convenience of the present, belated and minimally adequate responses, lasting aftereffects, transience of public concern, and the consequent certitude of further incidents.

The pit heads, processing plants, and lodgings of the Ashio mine were situated in a narrow, dendritic valley whose main river, the Watarase, debouched onto the densely populated Kantō agricultural plain about a hundred kilometers northwest of Tokyo. Furukawa's energetic introduction of new mining and processing technology and his discovery of major new veins of ore facilitated a massive expansion in the mine's copper output, as noted in chapter 13. That expansion led to a sharply increased need for mine timbers, railway ties, building lumber, and especially fuel for smelting, which stripped surrounding hillsides of timber and poured sulfuric acid into the air, devastating the residual vegetation.

The resultant denuding of surrounding mountainsides combined with the dumping of tailings into and along the Watarase to produce flooding and poisonous runoff on an unprecedented scale. Already by 1880 mine effluent was poisoning the river, and throughout the decade the situation worsened. In 1891 a belated scientific analysis established that arsenic, various heavy metals, and especially copper sulfate were spreading downstream along the Watarase and Tone rivers and flooding into nearby fields and villages. They had already destroyed the riverine fishing industry and ruined over 1,500 hectares of arable, and were producing poverty, illness, and death.

The most outspoken critic of the Ashio operation was Tanaka Shōzō, a village headman's son, who rose via Tochigi prefectural politics to become a Diet member in 1890. Known for his unkempt appearance, noisy assertiveness, and stubborn forcefulness, in 1891 the freshman legislator demanded in the Diet that the mining at Ashio be halted.

> The poisonous effluent ... has been allowed to inflict heavy losses and hardship each year since 1888 ... With fields being poisoned, drinking water contaminated, and even the trees and grasses lining the dykes being threatened, no one can tell what disastrous consequences the future may hold.[1]

Few of his colleagues listened, however, and Furukawa and his allies insisted that the mine's value to the policy of *fukoku kyōhei* justified any slight damage it might be causing. The government continued to turn a blind eye despite the new and compelling scientific evidence, declaring in 1892 that the mining operation was not "injurious to the public interest."[2] The government view was nicely expressed by an editorial in the *Tokyo Nichi Nichi Shinbun*:

> Suppose for the sake of argument that copper effluent were responsible for the damage to farmland on either side of the Watarase – the public benefits that accrue to the country from the Ashio mine far outweigh any losses suffered in the affected areas. The damage can in any case be adequately taken care of by compensation.[3]

The situation continued to worsen as deforestation produced ever more severe flooding. In 1896 surging waters killed over 300 and inundated some 13,000 households in 88 villages, reaching from the upper Watarase to the outskirts of Tokyo. And they increased the polluted farmland thirty-fold to an estimated 47,000 hectares. The devastation having reached such a scale, aggrieved villagers finally mobilized in sufficient numbers to catch Tokyo's attention, thousands organizing in protest, battling police, and marching on the capital. With both peasants and poisons bearing down on them, the city's intelligentsia at last became alarmed enough to visit the region and see what was happening. When they did, a broad coalition of voices called for remedial action, a coalition that included such diverse journalists as the Christian Uchimura Kanzō, socialist Kōtoku Shūsui, and nationalist Miyake Setsurei, along with members of the House of Peers.

With the imperial capital itself seeming threatened and the intelligentsia beginning to protest, a few key politicians, including Ōkuma Shigenobu, also took note and the government finally moved into action. In 1898 it spelled out in detail what steps Furukawa must take to end the menace, and it set clear deadlines for completion of the task. The repair work – construction of holding ponds for effluent and changes in ore processing procedure to lower the metal and acid content of runoff and reduce the smelter's forest-killing air pollution – was a decade late and minimally adequate, but it did set the stage for a slow recovery of the Watarase flood plain.

Within a few years the river's level of toxicity began falling, but many years were to pass before reforestation eased the flooding and before the river beds were scoured of poisonous residue. Reflecting this continuing state of affairs, in 1900 Shōzō lamented in his diary:

> Our people's loyalty to their Emperor has no parallel throughout the world. But our rulers use this loyalty, as they use the whole polity of the nation – to serve their own power, and to hold down the ordinary folk... The Restoration was carried out in the Emperor's name; but now evil subjects block the Way, and that Name is misused. Indeed, they use it now to *destroy* our nation, to *kill* our people.

Two years later, as though to give expression to Shōzō's fears, the government decided on a plan to deal with the persistent flooding by sacrificing three villages just above the confluence of the Watarase and Tone rivers. It proposed to tear them down and convert their land into seasonal flood plain to absorb the raging flood waters, thereby protecting Tokyo. In the end the authorities settled for the destruction of only one village, the badly poisoned Yanaka, whose people were given modest compensation, forcibly relocated, and prevented from returning to their ancestral lands.

The Watarase region was not, of course, the only locality being polluted by dramatically expanded mining, the spread of factory production, and construction projects that were rearranging the face of the land. It was, however, the only area of environmental devastation that acquired national visibility during later Meiji, and its painful experience foreshadowed comparable problems of more recent decades.

INDUSTRIAL LABOR

Much more widespread than protests against pollution were movements against unsatisfactory industrial wages, harsh working and living conditions, and exploitative employers. Most industrial labor worked in factories, but the importance that Japan's leaders attached to mining gave underground workers unprecedented social importance.

Mining was particularly grim work. The coal industry developed from an Edo-period tradition of spare-time mining by rural households in coal-bearing districts of Kyushu. During Meiji, mine expansion meant primarily increasing the numbers of families at work, with husband loosening coal at the mine face, wife filling her basket and dragging it to the mine's mouth or, as the mine deepened, to a wheeled tub that she hauled out when it was full, with any children assisting as best they could. The heavy demand for coal – and also for metal ore – spurred rapid expansion of mine production, forcing miners to dig deeper and deeper. As they did, however, the work became more difficult and dangerous, producing from the 1880s onward more frequent accidents, sporadic riots and resistance, and acts of suppression by employers and police.

The technological changes that permitted deeper mining also changed workplace relationships in ways that heightened tensions even as they facilitated labor organizing and protest. In essence the profitability of older, small-scale "mom-and-pop" mining operations, with their elements of entrepreneurial independence and craftsman-like skills, gradually declined as technology increased the labor output in larger mines, reducing the small-scale miners to grinding poverty and driving many out of business. In those larger mines, however, the older practice by mine owners of using labor recruiter-supervisors to provide and control the workers was gradually undermined by new mining techniques that created larger mine shafts and permitted bulk ore removal by larger work crews under direct control of mine officials. So mine owners reduced the fees they paid the supervisors, and the latter passed their losses on to the workers by reducing the quality of the lodging and meals they provided. In 1897 a journalist described mine lodgings at Ashio this way:

> the buildings are constructed out of rough wooden planks. In their extreme filthiness they compare unfavorably to the worst of Tokyo slum dwellings...They have neither ceiling nor floor; crude straw mats are laid on the bare ground around open hearths. Only in the sleeping area are a few wooden boards laid down to guard against the damp. On top of these are placed wooden draining boards and over these in turn are laid thin straw mats, never *tatami*. No ceiling, no *tatami*, no furniture; a constant accumulation of rubbish, filthy eating utensils, and bedding that gives off a dull sheen, so covered is it with soot and dirt.[4]

In following years the condition of lodgings at Ashio – and elsewhere – may well have worsened.

These trends in mining embittered workers and supervisors, whose individual skills were no longer valued and whose pay and status dropped accordingly. They also encouraged new-style organizers to promote labor unions and socialist strategies of reform, which prompted mine owners to retaliate. Out of such conditions emerged a rash of work stoppages, acts of sabotage, and countermoves by management and political authorities.

One of the most dramatic labor protests occurred at the Ashio pits in 1907. There the costs of dealing with pollution had led management in 1897 to freeze miners' wages, and workers in the pits suffered the most because concurrent changes in mining technology were slowly eliminating their older status as autonomously skilled professionals. Subsequently market fluctuations associated with the Russo-Japanese War led to further retrenchment that precipitated demands for improved wages and working conditions. When the demands were not met, miners launched a violent protest that quickly boiled out of the mine to involve other poor workers in Ashio town proper. In the resulting turmoil rioters destroyed many of the mine's facilities, including sixty-five buildings lost to flames, which led to police and army intervention. The Furukawa cash cow had been devastated.

In the outcome over 600 people were arrested and scores punished. The mine's owners instituted a mass layoff, followed by selective rehiring to exclude union activists. As they rebuilt, they also established tighter direct control of the work force and closer police surveillance of workers and "agitators" alike. And as palliative gestures they made belated wage increases and remedied some other grievances.

On the surface of the land, meanwhile, the burgeoning textile industry was heavily staffed by the teenage daughters of hard-pressed rural families, the girls commonly being lured to mill work by recruiters who misrepresented both wage arrangements and workplace conditions. One angry young silk worker wrote in 1888:

> Silk thread manufacturers, using contracts as a shield, treat us abominably. They think we are like slaves, like dirt. We think the silk-thread bosses are vipers, are our bitter enemies.[5]

As factory lighting was installed during the eighties, thread mills became notorious for their long hours and use of child labor. One elderly woman, recalling her years as a girl in the silk mills during the nineties, wrote:

> In the lamplit factory we worked from morning darkness to about ten o'clock at night. By the time we had finished work we could hardly stand on our feet.

Unsurprisingly the workers protested occasionally and absconded frequently, the majority breaking contract and fleeing their jobs within six months of recruitment. They did so, moreover, despite "barbed wire, high walls, guarantee deposits, and company regulations," and despite the hardship that doing so might cause their families, whose ability to repay debts often depended on daughterly income.[6]

In heavy industries, such as foundries and shipyards, where jobs were dirty, deafening, and dangerous, production became more mechanized and more complexly structured and shopfloor procedures more specialized, repetitive, and disciplined. These trends fed the discontent of workingmen resentful of managerial disdain and still unreconciled to the tedium of factory life and the status disparities of large organizations. As a machinist put it in 1898:

> a worker is someone who travels broadly, enters factories here and there, accumulates greater skills and, overcoming adversity, finally becomes a worker deserving of the name.[7]

This ideal of a free-living man dedicated to broad mastery of his craft fitted poorly the employer's ideal of a diligent, obedient, narrowly specialized worker.

Starting in the 1890s, dissatisfaction with industrial working conditions, together with growing knowledge of the laborite and socialist ideas and movements that European industrialism was in the process of spawning, began to yield agitation for labor legislation, attempts at union and party organization, and a considerable body of articulate political commentary. These efforts led, in turn, to more police regulations and measures of suppression, and to worried government inquiries into the conditions that were provoking discontent and possibly even fostering politically disruptive radicalism. One influential government official warned in 1896:

> If the state does not take some slight role in employer–employee relations there will be no way to protect the interests of the employed, and as a result there will be increasing cases of social illness, disturbance, and struggle…If we leave things as they are today, we will see a process producing extreme social illness much like that which befell England at the beginning of this century.

Industrialists, who opposed government "meddling" in "their" businesses, countered with a rhetoric that opposed factory legislation on grounds of the need to compete with "the West" and, as a consequence, to minimize production costs, mainly by keeping wages down. Doing so will not harm workers, they argued, because Japan does not suffer from the destructive sort of employer–employee relationship found in Europe and America. There, averred the Nagoya Chamber of Commerce, the relationship is generally "nothing more than an exchange of labor and money." By way of contrast, as the Tokyo Chamber put it, in Japan,

> relations between employers and employees are just like those within a family ... [being] enveloped in a mist of affectionate feelings.[8]

Few workers saw things quite that way. And in 1898 Kanai En, the earlier-noted academic, attacked the industrialist position head-on, contending that although Japanese employers might indeed be less exploitative than Western ones,

> while the treatment may not be cruel it is far from good. The individual relations which existed between master and servant in the past no longer obtain. With the coming of factory organization such as we see today there is an estrangement between managers and workers.[9]

Consequently, he concluded, new arrangements are necessary and will become moreso in future.

As Kanai forewarned, labor unrest kept intensifying, and by 1910 it prompted the government, in defiance of manufacturers' objections, to draft a set of factory laws. This Factory Act, which was enacted in 1911 to become operative in 1916, set at twelve the minimum employment age and also at twelve (with some qualifications favorable to employers) the maximum daily work hours for women and children.

Industrialists continued to talk about Japan's "beautiful custom of master–servant relations firmly based on a spirit of sacrifice and compassion."[10] However, lest workers be unpersuaded, they also sounded patriotic calls to diligence. Thus in 1911 textile makers admonished young women in the silk industry to serve the country by working hard.

> If you do not work thus [but instead] stay idly at home, the country of Japan will become poorer and poorer. Therefore, work with all your might for the country's sake, enabling Japan to become the greatest country in the world.[11]

And work they did, but not solely for the nation's glory and not always happily.

THE AGRARIAN ISSUE

Both the Ashio pollution affair and the nervousness about growing labor discontent fed into a much broader cluster of concerns that included diverse, diffuse worries about rural decay and a sense of heightened domestic injustice. This agenda gained much of its emotional depth, one suspects, from its placement in the underlying dyadic East/West perspective. Industrial society being seen as quintessentially "Western," the agricultural society that was being displaced became the repository of ethnic identity. Its passing seemed to entail the loss of Japaneseness itself.

Many commentators posed the problem in more immediate terms, however, and as time passed they advanced various explanations for the day's social troubles. Observers attributed them to the evils of landlordism (whereas 30 percent of arable land was worked by tenants in 1868, 45 percent was by 1913), callous government, the heavier taxes required for creation, maintenance, and use of modern military forces, the appearance of an industrial labor force, the introduction of socialist thought, Japan's deepening entanglement after 1890 in global monetary fluctuations, and the corrupting lure of "the city."

The heart of the "city" problem, of course, was the earlier-noted urbanization that came with industrialism, which was rapidly shifting society's center of gravity: a society 80 percent resident in villages in 1870 was, after all, 80 percent urban a mere century later. As city populations grew, so did incidents of unrest as city folk protested increases in local taxes, streetcar fares, and other daily expenses, as well as issues of broader import.

Reaction to rural decline and urban unrest began to appear in the 1890s, and it became particularly vigorous after the Russo-Japanese War. Diverse people – landlords and local officials such as Ikegami Chinpei, intellectuals with rural attachments, city residents whose careers tied them to agriculture, and the many Diet members such as Tanaka Shōzō with rural constituencies – began in diverse ways to celebrate rustic virtues and evoke idyllic images of farm and forest. These "agrarianists" (*nōhon shugisha*) contrasted village life with the corrupting influence of the city, insisting that villages (their better members, anyway) were the bedrock of Shintō, the anchor of Japan's allegedly distinctive family system, and the fountainhead of Japanese civilization; or at least the backbone of the modern military.

In 1897, with the Ashio disaster at its height, the prominent agrarianist Yokoi Tokiyoshi put the issue this way. With rural areas rapidly falling behind cities in economic and cultural terms, he declared:

> the pitiful farmers will gradually be oppressed by the urban rich, becoming sacrifices to their interests and growing weaker and more impoverished year by year ... The vitality of the nation will thus be sapped, our national power will be exhausted, and in the end there will be no way to rescue it.[12]

Some years later, as Yokoi saw the specter of socialism stalking the land, he asked:

> What can be done? We can only depend upon the peasants. The city will forever be a factory of revolution, while the country will always be the protector of the social order.[13]

Villagers might be sacrificed to industrial pollution, but neither government official nor agrarianist ideologue was about to surrender them to dangerous thought. To "revitalize" rural society, replace "backward" customs with ones more useful to the nation, and counter the mushrooming urban economy by fostering agricultural production and rural industry, agrarianists created numerous private and government organizations and promoted more elaborate ties between local and central government agencies.

Most notably, perhaps, the Home Ministry presented as a model for villagers Ninomiya Sontoku, the later-Edo village leader who had rehabilitated villages and promoted his own Hōtoku teachings of diligence and frugality. Building on informal, local Hōtoku groups already found in many Meiji-era villages, mainly in the Kantō, officials urged village leaders to organize formal Hōtoku Associations (Hōtokukai) complete with statues of Ninomiya. The purpose of these Associations was to sponsor speakers, organize other community activities, and inspire rural youth to be diligent yet content in their lives and to abjure the negativism of "decadent" city youth. The Home Ministry also promoted youth groups (*seinendan*) to safeguard the virtue and vigor of the young, and by 1913 nearly 30,000 were reportedly in existence. Agricultural cooperatives also proliferated, with some 11,000 of them embracing about 90 percent of rural localities by 1914. Finally, the government gave encouragement to those women who were promoting local branches of the Patriotic Women's Society (*Aikoku fujinkai*), an organization intended to strengthen the ties between village and armed service by providing assistance to soldiers, sailors and their families.

Officials in Tokyo were able to implement such plans because of their links, via political parties and administrative chains of command, to local leaders throughout the country. Thus, when national leaders established the countrywide Military Reservist Association (*zaigō gunjinkai*) in 1910, Chinpei headed the local chapter in his corner of Okayama prefecture. At one time or another he also headed the village youth group and the local branch of the Patriotic Women's Society. And in 1919 he established Hōtokukai branches in the hamlets of his consolidated Kami Village. To a degree that Tokugawa leaders could scarcely have imagined, center and periphery worked together, for better or worse, and the bogeyman of agrarian unrest was kept at bay.

ACTIVIST WOMEN

In Japan, as elsewhere, industrialization generated pollution, gave rise to urban labor problems, complicated rural life, and in due course radically diminished village influence on society at large. At the same time, however, it was broadening the general public's intellectual vistas, creating new career alternatives, and to an unprecedented degree institutionalizing the separation of household and work place. These trends affected women as well as men, and as a result questions about their roles and rights began to acquire greater visibility than in the past, foreshadowing an even more heightened presence in later years.

When architects of the Meiji state undertook to define social and political roles in the years around 1890, it will be recalled, they utilized principles and practices of both indigenous and alien provenance to forge a centralized, paternalistic regime that would, they hoped, build a rich and strong Japan, a "modern" society, a Great Power. How best to situate women in this new order was a question that evoked much comment. Some men and women advocated expanded roles for women, especially during the 1870s when everything seemed in flux. Kishida Toshiko, the daughter of an established Kyoto merchant, was well versed in progressive European thought, and she became one of the day's most eloquent proponents of women's rights. She spoke widely and effectively on behalf of education and opportunity for women, declaring in 1883, at age twenty:

> Equality, independence, respect, and a monogamous relationship are the hall-marks of relationships between men and women in a civilized society.[14]

A handful of men echoed this view, but as national affairs stabilized during the later 1880s, a counter-argument came to prevail, one that reflected the growing separateness of home and work place and that was grounded in both foreign and domestic precedents. It defined woman's proper role as that of responsible operative of the household, dedicated homemaker, "good wife; wise mother" (*ryōsai kenbo*).

In 1899, when the Education Ministry was prodding prefectural authorities to establish more high schools for women, a Ministry official explained the government's reasoning this way:

> Since the family is the root of the nation, it is the vocation of women who become housewives to be good wives and wise mothers, and girls' high schools are necessary to provide appropriate education enabling girls from middle- and upper-middle-class families to carry out this vocation.

Viewing the proper role of women in these terms, Meiji leaders encouraged them to pursue appropriate education. They also argued, however, that women should be excluded from politics lest such involvement endanger their morals, conduce to social disorder, and compromise their role as wife and mother. Accordingly Article 5 of the Police Security Regulations of 1890, reaffirmed in 1900, barred women from joining political organizations, participating in political meetings, voting, or standing for office.

This official posture failed to satisfy the growing number of women who wished to pursue other careers or expand their range of life choices. Nor did it address social issues that affected women in general, notably concubinage, prostitution, and male drunkenness, but also harsh conditions of the working poor, such as those in the textile mills. Indeed, the situation of the working poor seems to have been as far beyond the mental horizon of the Meiji elite as of elites elsewhere.

Worst of all, perhaps, were the lives of the earlier-mentioned women coal miners. Recalled one observer:

> The life of the female coal-miner was appalling. Returning black and grimy from a day's work in the pits with their husbands, they immediately had to start preparing meals. In those days there were no nursery facilities, so infants were placed in the care of others. Mothers returned from the mines to nurse their babies. Men would return from their work to bathe and sit back and relax, displaying their tattoos and drinking sake. This was the accepted behaviour of these lowly people, and no man would be found helping with what were designated as women's tasks. If a woman so much as protested, she would be beaten.[15]

These women miners generally were mature and married. Younger, single rural girls commonly took jobs in the textile mills and as domestic servants, while poor urban women and girls held a wide range of jobs: as "low-grade factory workers, used paper and junk collectors, ... peddlers, paper-makers, ... fishmongers, and vegetable-sellers," working as day laborers, and engaging in "cart-pushing and itinerant tea-picking."

These working poor were nearly as invisible to activist women as they were to male leaders. Even among the women of privilege, moreover, differing needs, priorities, and interests led to the pursuit of differing agendas. In consequence it was exceedingly difficult for activists to form a united front and promote a shared program for change in women's circumstances.

One of those who confronted most thoughtfully the dilemma of a fragmented female populace was Fukuda Hideko of Okayama samurai ancestry. An admirer of Kishida, she spent some years as radical political activist and prison inmate before settling down to a life devoted to teaching and feminist-socialist activism. In 1907 Fukuda established a magazine, *Sekai Fujin* (Women of the World), as a vehicle of feminist-socialist thought and information. In the editorial that launched her new venture, she declared,

> as far as women are concerned, virtually everything is coercive and oppressive, making it imperative that we women rise up and forcefully develop our own social movement.[16]

Recognizing with particular clarity the social basis of the divisions that prevented women from developing a united front, she frequently pointed out that women labored under both gender and class discrimination. For that reason, she argued in another essay the same year, women should support socialism:

> While socialism prevents the exploitation of workers by the capitalist class, it also stops the arrogance of the male class against women. It gets rid of the rich and poor classes, and removes sexual discrimination.[17]

In hopes of appealing to the broadest spectrum of women, Fukuda chose as a major goal of *Sekai Fujin* the repeal of the above-noted Article 5. But even that focus failed to elicit a unified women's movement. Harassed by authorities and unsympathetic to the sorts of paternalistic governmental measures that many less fortunate women welcomed, Fukuda was unable to build a broad movement. A few years later the women's movement drifted into desuetude in the wake of a plot to assassinate the emperor (noted below), in which the young and angry journalist-turned-anarchist Kanno Suga became deeply involved at the price of her life.

Not all women activists were so firmly opposed to the established order. A number of them founded schools for women where they instructed students in values and subjects that could accommodate the "good wife; wise mother" vision even while promoting a broader sense of women's possibilities (see figure 14.1). Most famously, in 1901 Tsuda Ume founded the Women's English School (Joshi Eigaku Juku), the later Tsuda Women's University. She urged her students not only to be ladylike but also to pursue practical

Figure 14.1 Biology students at Japan Women's University. Founded in 1901 and attended by daughters of more well-to-do families, the school illustrates the linkages between the Edo-period ideal of useful learning, the new schooling techniques of the day, and the broadening intellectual horizons that have encouraged women activists of industrial-age Japan. *Source*: Sharon L. Sievers, *Flowers in Salt, The Beginnings of Feminist Consciousness in Modern Japan* (Stanford: SUP, 1983), at p. 66.

schooling in marketable skills. As she observed in a speech of 1915, "Economic independence is the one thing that can save a woman from an unsuitable or distasteful marriage urged on her by relatives."[18] Educators such as she gave encouragement to the growing number of young women who pursued the study of medicine, training them to be licensed as nurses and after 1912 as doctors. And even larger numbers were trained as school teachers, especially for women's schools.

Among noted women of the day, the one who enjoyed the most success was Okumura Ioko, daughter of a Buddhist priest in Kyushu. An energetic participant in Restoration politics, she became a firm supporter of Meiji continental expansion, traveled about Northeast Asia, and in 1901 established the Patriotic Women's Society. Its main functions were to assist troops departing for war, aid those families of soldiers that were experiencing hardship, and console the bereaved. Because Okumura's organization so clearly contributed to government policy, she quickly won the backing of leaders and her organization grew with striking rapidity, counting 465,000 members by 1905 and a million or more by World War I, with branches in villages throughout the realm.

YOUNG GENTLEMEN

As the burgeoning growth of Okumura's Society suggests, the Home Ministry and other organs of late Meiji governance welcomed active public support and were enjoying considerable success in obtaining it. Nevertheless, as preceding pages have also indicated, the overall situation, with the new political order being consolidated even as socioeconomic change was accelerating, was producing a growing number of discontented women, industrial workers, and villagers. Even within the ranks of upwardly mobile young men of relatively favored birth – who were second only to the titled nobility as beneficiaries of the new regime – discontents were becoming more pronounced. And those discontents mattered despite student powerlessness because they contributed to the political radicalism of later years.

To elaborate, during early Meiji young men of fortunate birth, namely sons of samurai, landlords, and merchants, could aspire to grand careers if they worked hard and obtained the right education. By the 1890s, however, with the new political structure in place, the new social elite established, and admission to the best universities less and less likely because of a rapidly expanding applicant pool, career prospects seemed dimmer. Properly schooled job applicants were proliferating more rapidly than desirable positions, and salary levels were failing to keep abreast of rising costs of living. Even within government, although low-ranking positions kept multiplying (from some 15,000 in 1887 to 100,000 in 1909), higher positions did not keep pace. Facing these diminished prospects, students found less satisfaction or purpose in schooling. Doubtless the writer Kunikida Doppo spoke for many a student in 1902: "School teachers! I despise them. Sitting around like fat toads blinking their eyes after having just missed a mosquito."

Much as early-Tokugawa samurai had been forced to abandon the grand dreams of *sengoku* and settle for petty hereditary positions, late-Meiji youth of good background found themselves looking forward to lives of tedium or worse. Accordingly youth magazines stressed the need for young men to be ever diligent and to avoid imprudent behavior so as to gain access to the few university openings that could still lead one to the desired career of government official.

By the early 1900s, the spread of schooling and literacy had created a broader readership for commentators. With competition for admission to advanced schooling much greater and official careers looking less and less promising, more essayists pointed to the world of business as the venue where the diligent could still overcome obstacles, acquire great wealth, enhance the commonweal, and reap the rewards of public esteem.

Even there, however, jobs might be scarce, as a didactic writer noted in 1906:

> Recently, in our country there are many with a middle-school education who cannot enter banks or companies or who cannot enter higher school and are thus wandering without a goal.[19]

Such people, the essayist admonished, must redouble their efforts, take such work as they can find, and prepare for a more self-reliant future. Or, as others advised, they should cultivate useful connections and master the social graces that make one more employable. Yet others saw the answer in emigration. With domestic avenues of advance so few, one should seek one's fortune elsewhere. "Go! Go abroad! Abroad! Go!," exhorted one writer in 1911.[20] Korea, in particular, was the place to go. As another advocate saw it:

> In Korea one can carry on some kind of independent enterprise with oneself as master, freely able to employ Koreans at low wages and tell them what to do.

And young men did respond.

For example, Ikegami Chinpei, having given his eldest son away to head another family, prepared his second son Taizō as his successor by sending him to the nearby agricultural higher school to learn the skills necessary for a progressive village leader. Young Taizō, however, as stubborn as his father, had other dreams. Unable to go on to a satisfactory university, he "lit out for the territories," going to Korea, taking a job with a bank in Seoul, and spending about two years on the peninsula as a land surveyor. With his father's decline and death, he returned home, arranged to sell enough of the farm so he could enroll at Meiji University and build his mother a house in Tokyo, and after graduation went on to a career as reporter and editor at the Asahi newspaper.

For other youth facing the discouraging prospects of late Meiji, none of the nostrums of perseverance, personal ambition, or grand national purpose seemed compelling, and the heady optimism of early Meiji students gave way to a questioning of life's purpose and value. As Iwanami Shigeo, founder of the Iwanami publishing firm, later recalled:

> It was an age of introspection and despair that focused on such questions as "what is human nature?" and "where did I come from?" and "where am I going?"[21]

The mood prompted a rhetoric of despair and a rash of suicides that elicited government condemnation. Increasingly as the 1900s advanced, authorities advised students to lower their ambitions: humdrum paper pushing rather than heroic empire building seemed to lie ahead. It was a prospect that could hardly cheer young men maturing in the backwash of one of Japan's most dynamic ages.

SOCIALIST INTELLECTUALS

One factor that spurred officials and pundits to counsel lowered expectations for the young, to favor movements such as Okumura's Patriotic Women's Society, and to attempt to outflank or suppress the efforts of feminists, labor unionists, and other critics of the newly established Meiji order was their awareness of the growing attention intellectuals were giving to social problems and tensions of the day. During the 1890s some observers began to think about society's problems in terms of the recently articulated Marxist and other socialist analyses that they encountered through study abroad and the discussion of imported texts. In 1901 a group in Tokyo formed the Social Democratic Party, declaring as their goal:

> to abolish the gap between rich and poor and secure a victory for pacificism in the world by means of genuine socialism and democracy.[22]

The government responded to the group's manifesto by promptly seizing all copies of the document and ordering the party disbanded.

That response notwithstanding, the handful of intellectuals who comprised this initial socialist movement continued their peaceful proselytizing over the next several years, and in early 1906 the government allowed them to form a new political party. During 1906–7, however, after wartime boom and patriotic zeal had given way to industrial slump and political anger, the country was racked by strikes and labor disputes involving both mine and surface workers. That turmoil, together with socialist editorializing (and especially socialist criticism of government action in suppressing the labor protest at Ashio), led to the new party's disbandment. By then Kōtoku Shūsui, a journalist, socialist party participant, and critic of the Ashio mine operation, was also denouncing the harsh government policy in Korea. He called for more radical revolutionary action at home, even as he and others were having run-ins with the police. Moreover, some of his associates were mounting a rhetorical attack on the imperial institution itself.

These developments led government leaders to see the socialists as a dangerous threat to their new constitutional order. Declared Prime Minister Katsura Tarō in 1908:

> Although socialists at the moment are said to constitute little more than a thin thread of smoke, if we overlook this thread of smoke, it will someday develop the force of a wildfire, and then it would be too late for anything but regrets.[23]

Therefore, he argued, their meetings and publications must be controlled and their growth stymied. The government cracked down, using tight surveillence, jailings, suppression of the socialist press, and severe constraints on speakers.

Nevertheless, underground socialist activity continued. In the spring of 1910 authorities discovered a plot to mount a bomb attack against the emperor, presumably as part of an attempt at violent revolution that was inspired by recent anarchist actions in Russia. Viewed by the government and press as an utterly heinous crime – and as an opportunity to squelch socialism – that incident led to the arrest, trial, and eventual conviction and execution of Kōtoku, along with Kanno and ten others, on the charge of high treason.

The government took other steps, as well, to forestall dissident activity. It moved to consolidate its control of Korea by replacing the existing Korean administration with a Japanese governor-generalship. At home it established a special police force, the Tokubetsu Kōtō Keisatsu (Tokkō or Special Higher Police), to watch for "dangerous thought." And, as noted above, it gave formal approval to the creation of a locally-based, nationwide army reserve system. That reserve, its leaders hoped, would assure that the army's ideals of imperial loyalism, durable social order, and diligent national service came to pervade community life, thereby eliminating the threats of sedition, selfishness, and sloth.

The government employed carrots as well as sticks, most notably the aforementioned Factory Act of 1911. With those acts of repression and concession the socialist movement became inactive, not reviving until the Russian Revolution brought it a new surge of hope.

Social conflict in later Meiji can thus be examined in terms of such categories as agrarianists, socialists, and their government critics. Doing so, however, risks concealing the elements they shared. Their differences were less about what they saw as being wrong with society than about their vision of the preferred future and the interests this future would most fully serve. Socialists agreed with agrarianists that greed, selfishness, and vulgar ambition were causes of society's problems and evils to be eradicated. Thus Kōtoku lamented in 1899 that since the Restoration, "national virtues had been supplanted by a vicious struggle for monetary gain."[24] And Kōtoku's Christian sympathizer, Uchimura Kanzō, denounced the continuing Ashio mine problem with an attack on Furukawa's inordinate wealth:

> Must tens of thousands starve, that one man may strut in glory? Is "the survival of the strongest" really the "Way of Man"? Is this what the new civilization means? Was it for this that Imperial Rule was restored?[25]

Moreover, socialists and at least some officials agreed on what gave rise to the new, radical thought. In 1910 government leaders pointed with disapproval at the growing demands of common people, which eventuate in

> what is called socialism. Its immediate causes are the extreme division between rich and poor and the marked changes in ethics that accompany modern culture.[26]

The radical agrarianist and advocate of tenant reform Yokota Hideo would have agreed. As he wrote in 1914:

> severe class conflict is occurring in our agricultural world, and as a result the time has come when socialism has swiftly arisen and spread to shake the very foundation of our two-thousand-year-old state ... We are on the verge of a fearful national crisis.[27]

While disagreeing on the desirability of socialism, all could agree on the evils of moral decay and acute economic disparities. Whereas agrarianists sought to address the issues by reaffirming rural virtues and vitality, however, socialists proposed to eradicate the economic inequalities directly. And government leaders defined the problem as a need "to preserve order and stability" through proper moral schooling and measures of public relief.[28]

The triumphs of later Meiji notwithstanding, society clearly was torn by multiple concerns and conflicts. Nevertheless, on balance, and especially when compared to the immediately following decades, the process of socio-economic growth and change to 1914 seems more notable for its orderliness than its turmoil.

In the realm of cultural production, as well, these years were a time of growth and diversification. They were marked by accomplishments and complications of the moment, by signs of nostalgia for a lost past, and by developments that foreshadowed a later day.

ARTICULATE CULTURE

During the quarter century 1890–1914, two basic characteristics of articulate culture stand out. First, "national-level" cultural production, as distinct from the poetry and other output of local elites in the hinterland, was to a striking degree a creature of Tokyo, with its political power, publishing industry, educational predominance, and foreign presence. In consequence of its insular provenance, much of this cultural output bore earmarks of an "in-group" activity, characterized by familiarity, factions, and coterie publications that reflected school affiliations and had only a limited, albeit growing, impact beyond itself.

Second, as foreshadowed above, participants in this cultural activity mostly developed their agendas in terms of an ill-defined and reductionist East/West dyad. Edo-period pundits, as earlier noted, had battled over the relative merits of Chinese and Japanese cultural legacies, with rivals hurling charges of Sinophilia and chauvinist provincialism at one another. Functionally, however, the most influential position was an essentially pragmatic inclination to utilize or enjoy those domestic or continental principles and practices in arts and letters that seemed most satisfactory. It was a posture that conformed to the notion of *jitsugaku*, or "practical learning," and it reflected the older legacy of combinative religious thought.

During Meiji, commentators reassessed "China," but the burning issues of ethno-cultural identity and worth were resituated in the East/West dyad, with discussants hotly debating the relative merits for Japan of indigenous and European cultural norms and practice. And while in actuality considerable pragmatic selectivity was again evident, the debate over principle was wider, more intense, and more convoluted than that of the Edo period.

THE FIELD OF DISCOURSE

Until the 1860s, Tokugawa-era observers had insisted almost universally that the established order and the culture it vouchsafed should, for all their warts, be safeguarded against the barbarizing influences coming from Europe. In conjunction with the Restoration, however, there occurred a transvaluation, as noted in chapter 12, in which many activists and articulate observers repudiated the old order, in whole or in part, and embraced the alien as they understood it. During the eighties, however, as the Meiji winners entrenched themselves and fostered an ideology to legitimize their rule, intellectuals began to challenge that repudiation of the old, initiating debate over the

relationship of Japanese legacy and new alien influence. The resulting arguments were at least as contentious as the earlier Tokugawa ones about
"China," in part because the core rhetorical categories of "Japan" and "the
West" embraced so many disparate, ill-defined elements and could therefore
mean so many things, and in part because the underlying issue of intersocietal imbalance in power and privilege was so acute, evident, and invidious.

As the 1890s advanced, and especially following treaty revision and victory
over the Ch'ing, a consensus of sorts emerged. It held, on the basis of
achievements at home and abroad, that Japan had indeed meshed indigenous
and alien in a manner enabling it to function effectively in the world.
Fukuzawa Yukichi, long a champion of "Westernization," put it this way
after the military victory of 1895:

> One can scarcely enumerate all of our civilized undertakings since the
> Restoration – the abolition of feudalism, the lowering of class barriers, revision
> of our laws, promotion of education, railroads, electricity, postal service, print-
> ing, and on and on. Yet among all these enterprises, the one thing none of us
> Western scholars ever expected, thirty or forty years ago, was the establishment
> of Japan's imperial prestige in a great war ... When I think of our marvelous for-
> tune, I feel as though in a dream and can only weep tears of joy.[29]

The Triple Intervention over Liaotung temporarily stilled the euphoria, and
voices of dissatisfaction continued to be heard, as we note below, but for
many observers the Anglo-Japanese alliance of 1902 and victory over Czarist
forces in 1905 confirmed the national accomplishment. For them Japan was
well and truly a "modern nation." Moreover, as the Imperial Rescript on
Education had made clear in 1890, it was its own nation, with its own constitution, and its own *kokutai*, which, whatever the term meant, "served to
identify the nation and separate 'them' from 'us.'"[30]

Political consolidation at home and military–diplomatic triumph abroad
did not, however, resolve all problems. Rather, they contributed to new ones
even as they settled some of the old, and that process spurred much
commentary by the intelligentsia.

In terms of foreign relations, a dilemma was built into the later Meiji
national self-image, a dilemma that echoed the older debate about "China."
As foreshadowed in the Introduction to Part IV, it boiled down to the issue
of whether Japan's role in the world was to be based on the country's unique
historical legacy and modern accomplishments, or whether policy should be
based on a broader "truth," namely, that Japan was part of a wider East
Asian or "Oriental" ecumene, be that cultural, racial, or geopolitical in character. Did Japan's policy toward other Asian societies, that is to say, properly
flow from a narrower assessment of self interest? Or did Japan, as the only
Asian Great Power, have a broader obligation to help its fellow Asians stop
the exploitation by that rival cultural/racial ecumene, the "West?"

Pundits argued the issue vigorously, their views being influenced by new
access to China. From the 1860s onward more and more Japanese travelers
discovered and reported to their countrymen that contemporary China was
not at all the glorious "China" of earlier academic imagery. Facing this new

awareness, commentators gradually redefined "China" in one way or another, with some pundits contending that Japan could become a fully "modern" society only by distancing itself from the decadent and doomed "Asia" that China represented. By late Meiji, however, the view that was coming to predominate regarded China as a fellow Asian society that, whatever its faults, must be "modernized" – whether willingly or by force – so that Asians together could resist the predatory "Western" threat. In practice, unsurprisingly, the dynamics of state power and interest tended to determine actual policy, while learned rhetoric mainly provided ideological cover for the policies chosen, with the result that governmental self interest tended to be served in the name of the greater East Asian good.

In terms of the more basic issue of indigenous vs. European culture, by the 1890s a range of positions had emerged, extending from those who remained dedicated to the newly imported to those who sought to "preserve" or recapture facets of the past. Between the extremes stood those who tried in a syncretist, *jitsugaku*-like manner to mesh indigenous and foreign so as to produce a new and ethnically gratifying wave of cultural creativity that would, as some saw it, constitute Japan's contribution to global civilization. In 1892 the student and future novelist Natsume Sōseki characterized the dilemma of native vs. foreign this way:

> Unless we totally discard everything old and adopt the new, it will be difficult to attain equality with Western countries. [But, he fretted, to do so would] soon weaken the vital spirit we have inherited from our ancestors [and leave us] cripples.[31]

A decade later, in 1901, the brash, young literary critic Masamune Hakuchō seemed to feel that affairs had worked out just so. In a tone reflecting the discontent of so many young gentlemen, he took his countrymen to task for failing to measure up to his romantically bookish image of "the Elizabethan Age or Periclean Greece":

> Look at our country today!...How extremely prosaic everything is – our speech, our literary compositions, our apparel, everything down to the last detail of our behavior! No ideals can be detected in *our* people. I wonder if there is even enough intellectual activity to stir the small number of intellectuals? Religious movements, Japanism – the whole picture is depressing.[32]

The dilemma that this particular foreign intrusion presented to the ethnically conscious was hardly unique, but the intelligentsia of few societies have sensed it more acutely. The tasks of indigenizing the alien, preserving the treasured, and making Japan's mark on a wider world were projects that would continue to engage Hakuchō and Sōseki's countrymen down to the present.

THE MECHANICS OF CULTURAL PRODUCTION

Even as the Meiji cultural agenda acquired this complexity, trends in education, publishing, and language usage were facilitating its pursuit throughout the realm. Education was crucial, swelling the number who could create as well as those who could enjoy the fruits of creative effort. At the primary-school level, by 1906 95 percent of school-age children were reportedly in attendance, up from about 50 percent in 1890, and the following year compulsory schooling was extended, with little public complaint, from four years to six. By then, moreover, patriotic school-day rituals were in practice, and standardized, government-approved texts were being used in most of the country for instruction in ethics, history, language, and geography. Intermediate levels of public schooling also had expanded, enrolling over 150,000, while other students pursued technical training in locally-sponsored, intermediate programs promoted by people such as Chinpei. And at the advanced level the three early-Meiji universities in Tokyo (Keiō, Waseda, and Tokyo Imperial) and the private Dōshisha in Kyoto were supplemented by other private universities and by regional Imperial universities in Kyoto (1897), Sendai (1907), and Fukuoka (1910). As noted earlier, however, at neither intermediate nor advanced level was expansion keeping pace with the growing public demand for further education.

The world of publishing also grew, providing print material not only for the expanding school system but also for the broadening adult readership that the system was producing. Edo-period woodblock print technology had been supplemented during the 1860s by the reintroduction of moveable-type presses, and during the next several decades publishers employed both technologies in the production of a continually growing number of newspapers, magazines, and books.

Early Meiji newspapers had enjoyed official favor because they served as valued organs for disseminating news and views approved by Meiji reformers. By the eighties, however, journalists were more critical of authority, finding a broader base of support among the day's proliferating political activists and the growing population of literate city commoners. By 1890 well over 400 periodicals, mostly small, local publications of tenuous durability, were in circulation despite government restrictions and harassment.

From about that time newspapermen began using telegraphs and telephones to speed news reporting. They added illustrations and photographs to their papers and during the nineties imported more up-to-date printing presses that permitted larger and speedier press runs. The larger papers also broadened coverage as they extended their readership beyond the main cities and as they pursued a more diverse clientele, hiring a few women writers to enhance their appeal to women readers. Most of all, however, they employed more and more "gimmicks, stunts, and promotion schemes" to build circulation and entice advertisers.[33]

And circulation did grow, dramatically spiked by coverage of the wars with China and Russia. By 1914 the several largest papers had daily circulations ranging from 100,000 to 350,000. Small-scale newspapers and periodicals also continued to proliferate, coming to number some 2,000 by 1914. By then the means to produce good-quality, European-style bound volumes also were in place, and records indicate that Japan was second only to Germany in its rate of book production, publishing over 27,000 titles a year.

During these years the use of colloquial Japanese in most publishing became established. Early Meiji reformers had urged the simplification of written Japanese and its grounding in the spoken language, but as of 1890 journalists, littérateurs, and academic authors were still using the diverse Chinese and Japanese literary forms of the Edo period. During the nineties, however, and especially during the war with China, debate about language reform and the desire of writers to reach a broad readership led more and more of them to write in the colloquial. Given the richness of Japan's regional dialects, this desire led many in the provinces to employ local usages in their publications, but because of Tokyo's socio-political pre-eminence, the Tokyo dialect emerged during late Meiji as "standard" (*hyōjun*) Japanese.

By 1914 Japan had acquired, in its school system and publishing world, a unified language, meaning a standard spoken form that was to serve also as the written language. That outcome was not everywhere welcomed: Kyotoites found their style of speech, once associated with the city's cultural supremacy, being reduced to a quaint localism. And many elsewhere found that their use of local dialects – which in fact persisted long into the post-1945 period – marked them as provincial and ill-cultured in the eyes of those whose Tokyo dialect had been elevated to the status of "proper Japanese." But it did mean that written and spoken forms coincided and that teachers, writers, and others had norms to guide their use of language throughout the realm, regardless of their origins, status, or position.

LEARNING NEW AND OLD

At the heart of the continuing dedication to imported learning lay the study of science and technology, fields of knowledge that were newly developing in conjunction with the rise of industrial society in Europe. These fields became and remained central to the advanced education and research that government in particular encouraged. During the 1870s and eighties the Meiji regime established institutes for the study of such technical subjects as agriculture, forestry, geology, hydrography, hygiene, and meteorology, and during the late 1880s, it enlarged and updated programs of physics, chemistry, engineering, and medicine at the newly consolidated Tokyo Imperial University. Also, during the eighties initial attempts to develop schools of medicine, engineering, and science were made at Keiō, Waseda, and Dōshisha. These last attempts did not flourish, however, and it was not until the 1890s that the new fields of study really acquired self-sustaining momentum.

During the nineties foreign advisors who had introduced the new disciplines and bodies of information departed one by one and Japanese scholars took over the programs of instruction and research. European medicine, which had been a major element in Edo-period *rangaku*, continued to be the subject most actively promoted by government and most widely taught, but as the decade advanced, expansion of scientific facilities proceeded on a much broadened basis.

Reflecting medicine's pre-eminent stature, in 1893 the celebrated bacteriologist Kitasato Shibasaburō established an Institute for Infectious Diseases that developed within a decade into "a world-class laboratory" whose distinction in the development of therapies against cholera, tetanus, and diphtheria enabled it to export diphtheria serum to Europe and America.[34] Other programs proved less illustrious, but during these years a network of agricultural experiment stations was established and in 1900 an Industrial Experiment Laboratory to promote applied research in chemistry. Finally, the government responded to social needs and to industrial demands for trained personnel by establishing schools of medicine, engineering, and science at the newly opened, regional imperial universities.

Indigenous expertise in some technical areas, notably agriculture, forestry, and medicine, continued to dominate actual practice. However, this expertise was mostly passed on by word of mouth, observation, and the study of established texts. New developments in these fields were based almost entirely on imported learning.

At the other pole of the alien/indigenous dyad, those who labored to preserve or recapture facets of the past did so for several reasons. For a number of notables, it was a way to celebrate their own past triumphs or justify past failures, sometimes in the name of admonishing the young. For others, retrospection constituted nostalgia for times past and races run, evoking and preserving memories and enjoying them as something precious but apart. For yet others it was an attempt to preserve a record of the past before it dissolved into illegible fragments of paper or an attempt to perpetuate cultural attributes that they regarded as important to the future of Japan and even humankind.

These diverse sentiments were evident from the nineties onward in an outpouring of reminiscences and in the launching of major projects of historical compilation and preservation. Thus, people associated with the defunct Tokugawa regime produced a journal, *Kyūbakufu*, in which they reminisced about events, described old customs, and lauded people of former note. That they dared do so and that the government permitted it suggest how fully the agendas and animosities of the 1860s had in fact faded, the continuing rhetoric about Sat-Chō domination notwithstanding. Lengthy reminiscences by leaders of the fallen, such as the last shogun, and by Restoration heroes and captains of Meiji progress, including Fukuzawa Yukichi and Shibusawa Eiichi, appeared in profusion. People once affiliated with such daimyo domains as Aizu, Chōshū, Echizen, and Mito began to arrange compendia of documents that recorded the roles of their domains in the Restoration. The greatest of these historiographical projects commenced in 1911, as the Meiji emperor was nearing his life's end, when an imperial edict ordered that throughout the realm all records of the years 1846–73 that might be pertinent to the Restoration be assembled, copied, and prepared for publication. The project continued for two decades and yielded one of the world's greatest collations of documents, *Dai Nihon ishin shiryō kōhon*, a compilation arranged chronologically in the manner of classic documentary collections and filling 4,180 *kan*, or Chinese-style volumes. It is now available on microfilm and is made accessible by a published table of contents that fills ten large volumes.

Nor was the Meiji government's interest in the past limited to its own glorious founding. With its imperial anchor and its newly refurbished elite, it could not be indifferent to Japan's cultural legacy. Even as it was founding universities to introduce and promote the new scientific learning, it moved to shore up that legacy. In 1889 it founded the Tokyo School of Fine Arts (Tokyo Bijutsu Gakkō; today's Tokyo Geijutsu Daigaku) to revitalize "Japanese" arts and, as noted in chapter 12, established the Imperial Household Museum to preserve artifacts. The following year it allowed a small, aristocratic school devoted to the study of *kokutai* to expand into Kokugakuin University specifically to promote the study of Japanese arts and letters and train priests for the recently "purified" shrines of State Shintō. In following years other universities, as well, established programs, institutes, and journals to promote indigenous studies. And in 1909 a grand new hall was constructed for the presentation of *sumō* wrestling contests, thus assuring that a sport of hoary ancestry would flourish in the new age. In the outcome *sumō* has survived to the twenty-first century as the "Japanese" sport par excellence.

Viewed more broadly, these extremes of interest in the foreign and the native constituted the outer margins of the combinative "middle ground" occupied by most of the intelligentsia. That middle ground fitted the times, an age when cities were an unkempt architectural hodgepodge of Edo-period structures standing cheek by jowl with new brick factories and their smoke-belching chimneys; when narrow streets were starting to be draped in electric wires; and when packhorses and porters coexisted with streetcars and railroad trains, oil lamps mingled with gas lights, and *hakama*, *kimono*, and *geta* shared space with silk hat, frock coat, and leather shoe. Music, art, and literature added to the eclectic din, with late-Edo genres persisting and being modified even as European forms were introduced and reworked, both purposely and unwittingly, to accommodate domestic tastes and techniques. As the poet Kitahara Hakushū expressed it in a poem of 1910:

> A *nocturne* in gold and blue,
> A duet in spring and summer,
> In young Tokyo the songs of Edo,
> Shadows and light in my heart.[35]

ARTS AND LETTERS

The interplay of indigenous and alien was evident in the styles, subjects, and sensibilities of religious thought, creative literature, drama, art, and music.

Religion. In the realm of philosophy, one of the most elegant intellectual syntheses of indigenous and alien epistemologies was that of Nishida Kitarō. Schooled in contemporary European philosophy, notably the works of Kant and Hegel, and in science (which in his view provided no adequate grounding for knowledge), Nishida turned during the late 1890s to the pursuit of Zen Buddhism. His intense engagement with Zen, and the broader reading

in religion and philosophy that surrounded it, yielded in 1911 a major interpretive work, *Zen no kenkyū* (A Study of Good). In it Nishida developed the
thesis that Zen embodied, as did other mystical religious traditions, the universal principles of faith and intuitive, non-dual apprehension that constitute
the keys to grasping reality in it entirety.

Perhaps Nishida's work is best seen as one philosophical expression of a
broader, late-Meiji process of reconciliation among indigenous and alien religious legacies. Early Meiji developments – the assault on Buddhism and
Shugendō, the contemporaneous advances scored by Christianity thanks to
diplomatic pressure and the broader elite fascination with things European,
and the moves to establish Shintō as a "non-religious" basis of imperial
authority – had laid a foundation for bitter religious disputes. These grew
heated in the 1890s when the celebration of national accomplishments and
evocation of indigenous virtues enabled proponents of Buddhism to seek
rehabilitation and critics of Christianity to denounce it as intrinsically subversive. Advocates of Shintō, meanwhile, seized the moment to lobby – unsuccessfully – for government recognition of Shintō as the official state religion.

By 1914, however, much of the religious debate had subsided. Buddhism
had generally regained recognition as a legitimate part of social life. The fifty-
four government-supported Shintō shrines of 1879 had grown to about one
hundred, but these were defined as non-religious instruments of state ritual.
Shugendō, as well as several idiosyncratic religious movements (the so-called
New Religions or *shin shūkyō*) that had arisen during the preceding century,
were in process of being fitted, not always comfortably, into the established
religious order. And Christianity had begun to acquire legitimacy as an indigenized creed, most notably through the Mukyōkai movement of Uchimura
Kanzō, which was not missionary-dominated and which by 1910 was gaining
followers among the educated elite of Tokyo.

Literature and drama.   During early Meiji the enthusiasm for *bunmei kaika*
had led to translation of diverse European writings, including works of
Shakespeare and other literary figures. However, creative writing, story telling,
and drama mostly continued to follow Edo-period precedents. Even in later
Meiji *kabuki* flourished, *nō* was preserved, and established forms of poetry
continued to appear. Some writers composed prose works consciously modeled on the *ukiyo zōshi* of Saikaku while others nurtured the oral-literature
tradition of story tellers. Some, such as Izumi Kyōka, found inspiration in literary traditions of mystery, demonic powers, and fantastic imagery. Others,
such as the elderly San'yūtei Enchō, followed the *gesaku* style of employing
everyday speech in narratives written for popular consumption.

Even in established genres, however, changes appeared. In *kabuki*, for
example, the actor Ichikawa Danjūrō modified his facial makeup and his
stage diction and movements to make them more "realistic." And during the
1880s he presented new, more contemporary plays, but to no great acclaim
despite his towering professional stature. More successful was the poet
Masaoka Shiki, who sought along with others to revitalize Japan's main traditions of verse. They criticized the conservatism of Meiji court poets and

during the 1890s used *haiku, tanka* (a Meiji term for the 31-syllable *waka*), and *kanshi* more creatively to express their own individualism, freedom, and romantic sensibilities.

By then, however, the main thrust of both poetry and drama lay in the direction of utilizing European precedents, especially as known from the works of nineteenth-century English writers. New styles of poetry (*shintaishi*) supplemented the older forms, and new types of drama supplemented and partially displaced established ones.

One new theatrical form, *shinpa*, began in Osaka in the late eighties, it appears, as amateur productions using daily-life speech in plays inspired by contemporary events. *Shinpa* proved popular, spread to Tokyo, and during the nineties was partially taken over by *kabuki* actors who introduced their own styles of presentation, giving the genre an idiosyncratic character more notable for its popularity than its dramaturgical coherence. In the years after 1905, *shinpa* gave way to *shingeki*, a much more disciplined theatre modeled on European precedents. Unlike *nō* and *kabuki*, *shingeki* cast women in female roles, and it was used for the presentation of foreign plays, most famously those of the Norwegian dramatist Henrik Ibsen.

In the field of prose fiction, during the later 1880s a group of young Tokyo littérateurs began trying to portray ordinary lives by employing colloquial language and European notions of plot, character, and authorial viewpoint. Such works as *Ukigumo* (Drifting Cloud, 1887–9) by Futabatei Shimei and *Gan* (The Wild Goose, 1890) by Mori Ōgai foreshadowed a remarkable burst of literary production. During the nineties young men (and a few women), who were schooled in the new literature and pursuing literary careers, mounted sharp attacks on the late-Tokugawa *gesaku* tradition of popular fiction. They denounced the *gesaku* notion of literary invention as frivolous, arguing instead for "serious" literature marked by "sincerity," whether as evidenced by "candid" confession, "truthful" portrayal of emotion or sensibilities, treatment of serious "problems," or the cultivation of a polished and elegant style.

Meanwhile a plethora of short-lived, small-circulation coterie magazines (*dōjin zasshi*) began to appear, providing writers with vehicles for presenting their works and opinions. Literary cliques arose around the magazines, some cliques becoming known as proponents of Romanticism or Naturalism, others constituting clusters of idiosyncratic writers united mainly by shared enrollment at schools such as Tokyo Imperial and Waseda universities.

Of these literary coteries, two deserve particular note: the proponents of "Naturalism" (*shizen shugi*) and the writers associated with *Shirakaba*, a literary magazine. In 1893 the influential Naturalist author Kunikida Doppo noted in his diary that his aim "as a man of letters and poet" was "to describe with my pen all that my independent soul has been able to learn, observe, and feel."[36] By 1914 the Naturalist school was past its peak, but it had established precedents for a quasi-autobiographical type of confessional prose that came to be known after 1920 as the "I Novel" (*shishōsetsu* or, more formally, *watakushi shōsetsu*). The writer of an I Novel sought to distance himself from the putatively frivolous legacy of *gesaku* fiction and demonstrate literary seriousness by conveying, in the spirit of Doppo, a sense of authorial sincerity or authenticity. Commonly the author did so through seemingly candid presentation of the narrator's role in, and views regarding, some incident, usually private and sordid, that polite society in its customary "hypocrisy" would deem unfit for public display.

Less influential, perhaps, but socially more visible than Naturalist authors was the group of writers who in 1910 established the coterie magazine *Shirakaba* (White Birches). Consisting of self-confident sons of the privileged who were schooled at Gakushūin, the elitist Peers School, the group was diverse in interests but generally rejected the unpleasant "realism" of the Naturalists. *Shirakaba* authors aimed instead to cultivate a refined literary humanism that was inspired by such authors as Tolstoy, grounded in the aesthetics of European art, and celebratory of the goodness of the human spirit. Reflecting that broader artistic interest (as well as Japan's own grand tradition of trans-genre cultural production), *Shirakaba* reached beyond literature to become a vehicle for discussion and display of works by such European artists as Rodin and Renoir.

Whereas the Naturalists purported to find the stuff of art in real experience sincerely reported, *Shirakaba* writers saw a more complicated connection between art and life. Shiga Naoya, the most celebrated of their number, declared early in his career that:

> I want to write about everyday life and by doing so to improve it. I shall develop into a better person, and my creative writing shall be a by-product of that development.[37]

Reflecting that ideal, Shiga's best known works – notably *An'ya kōro* (A Dark Night's Passing), which he started writing in 1912 but began serializing only in 1921 – have a strong autobiographical quality. However, they are firmly shaped by an authorial will to produce artistic fiction and not merely to "report" on sordid reality. And they are marked by a spare and evocative style that distinguishes them from the verbal self-indulgence of many Naturalist works. Because of their stylistic elegance, Shiga's works, *An'ya kōro* in particular, contributed greatly to reshaping the Naturalist autobiographical style into the more disciplined I Novel genre that flourished in later decades.

During these formative years of modern Japanese literary culture, a number of works appeared that survive today as esteemed examples of the new Japanese fiction. These include the semi-factual works of historical fiction in which Mori Ōgai explored past values and virtues, short stories by Nagai Kafū that constituted elegaic evocations of the past, and some of the works by Naturalist authors. Of these, a noteworthy example is *Hakai* (Broken Commandment, 1906), by Shimazaki Tōson, which portrayed the harshness of life faced by pariahs (*eta*, or *burakumin* as they came to be designated) in mountainous central Japan. And *Futon* (The Quilt, 1907), by Tayama Katai, set a major precedent for the later I Novel. Most celebrated among these pre-World War I works were the pychological novels, notably *Kokoro* (1914), of

Natsume Sōseki, an author who defies assignment to any literary pigeonhole because of his felicity with diverse old and new prose and poetic styles. Sōseki's later works, with their deep sense of loneliness and human isolation, fitted nicely the sterotypical young intellectual's earlier-noted mood of "introspection and despair."

Other arts. The interplay of indigenous and alien sensibilities was very evident in the work of aesthetes versed in painting, tea ceremony, music, and other arts, some of whom helped preserve the venerable ideal of the cultural polymath. Most famously, Okakura Tenshin, who headed the Tokyo School of Fine Arts during the years 1890–6, fostered interest in the legacy of Japanese art, tea, calligraphy, book-binding, and other cultural accomplishments. When abroad he labored to enhance Japan's international stature by proclaiming the uniqueness and unique excellence of Japan's aesthetic legacy; while at home he encouraged artists to draw on both imported and domestic artistic traditions to forge a distinctively Japanese art for the new age.

In the field of painting more narrowly, *rangaku* artists of the Edo period had long since introduced elements of European style and technique to Japan. During Meiji the most striking import was oil painting, which in its materials and aesthetic possibilities was quite unlike the water colors employed in Japan's own rich legacy of Yamato-*e*, Kanō and Tosa art, *ukiyo-e*, and Buddhist and Chinese-style painting. Indeed, the distinction seemed so clear that Meiji-era art circles made it the basis for one of the most rigid expressions of the West/Japan dyad. They designated oil painting, whatever its style, as *yōga* ("Western painting"), while all styles of Japanese watercolors were lumped together as *nihonga* ("Japanese painting"). Artists were then encouraged to identify the distinctive qualities of *yōga* and *nihonga* and to combine them to form a vital new art that would be both "Japanese" and "modern." However, because the two categories embraced a rich diversity of artistic styles and ideals and because both were in continual flux and subject to the changes fostered by developments in industrial technology, values, and organization, artists and art critics quickly discovered that their craft invited endless experimentation and reinterpretation but very little certitude of evaluative criteria. The result was – and has remained – a rich, variegated artistic output laced with continuing and intense judgemental disagreement.

Other plastic arts followed much the same pattern. Perhaps the most successful linking of "Japanese" and "modern" was in the field of print-making. There the Edo-period wood-block technique provided, with stylistic modifications, an effective vehicle for representing contemporary affairs, most famously in the works of Kobayashi Kiyochika, particularly his prints of warfare in the Sino-Japanese and Russo-Japanese wars. In sculpture European techniques and styles were studied from the 1870s onward, with the works of Auguste Rodin acquiring great éclat by late Meiji. Some sculptors combined elements of indigenous and foreign design, but "realism" was favored. That preference, which served to elevate the reputation of such sculptors as Unkei, who had produced lifelike images centuries earlier, spurred the Buddhist sculptor Takamura Kōun to study European-style metal casting and from the 1890s onward to produce giant-sized images of national heroes, including Saigō Takamori and the medieval loyalist Kusunoki Masashige. Finally, architecture was even more fully influenced by European precedents. In a manner that reminds one of the role of Chinese mortise-and-tenon construction during the seventh century, brick and stone construction and its associated European decorative styles became the norm in urban public construction while the established forms of wood–plaster–tile construction prevailed in most residential work.

In the field of music, indigenous song continued to prevail among the public at large, but new musical genres gained high visibility. The rich pre-Meiji legacy – *gagaku* Court music, Buddhist chant, musical accompaniment for *nō* and *kabuki* drama, folk song and dance, the mendicant's flute, the story teller's lute, and the seductive song of tea house and bordello – was supplemented with marches and church music during the 1860s and children's music in the eighties. Foreign military forces brought the sounds of fife, drum, and bugle; missionaries, those of organ and choir. The provenance of children's music was more convoluted and instructive.

During the 1870s young Izawa Shūji studied in the United States, where he discovered that educators viewed school music as good for the health and diction of children. When he sought to promote the idea back in Japan, he found that issues of educational reform were being argued in dyadic West/Japan terms, so he advocated school music on the ground that it would promote the development of a "suitable music for our country," a music that would combine the "European and oriental." During the eighties, when the emergent Meiji elite came to regard education as a way to produce a diligent, supportive population, Izawa and other proponents of school music presented it as conducive to "proper moral education," a discipline that would enhance patriotism and "the spirit of reverence for the Emperor."[38] By the nineties music was accepted as a proper subject for public schools, and by late Meiji musicians were employing both domestic and foreign melodies as well as new tonal patterns that echoed both musical legacies.

By then marching bands were sending troops off to war, school music was widely taught, school choirs were proliferating, and college students were producing European operas. Musical instruments of European design were being manufactured (the first harmonium in 1887; the first Yamaha piano in 1899), and the European system of musical notation was in use. Song books with Japanese librettos set to European and American as well as Japanese tunes were common, the newest ones written in the colloquial tongue and largely free of stilted literary archaisms. Moreover, Japanese composers were beginning to produce their own "modern" works, such as the well-known *Kojō no tsuki* (Moon over the Ruined Castle) by Taki Rentarō. In the process these composers integrated Japanese and European musical styles and sensibilities in ways that foreshadowed the richness of Japan's present-day musical culture.

By World War I, then, the many aspects of domestic and foreign development revealed Japan's major strides into industrialism. And in the course of taking those strides, Japanese society had enjoyed considerable success in indigenizing the new influx of foreign thought and practice. How well post-Meiji society could sustain that process remained to be seen.

[15] LATER IMPERIAL POLITICS AND ECONOMY (1914–1945)

CHAPTER SYNOPSIS

THE POLITICS OF DISORDER
POLITICAL PROCESS
POLITICAL DISCOURSE

DOMESTIC GROWTH
DEMOGRAPHICS
FLUCTUATIONS AND IMBALANCES
GROWING IMPORT DEPENDENCY

The decades of industrialization prior to 1914 were hardly free of social tension, as chapter 14 has shown. However, basic order was maintained at home, foreign policies did work out, the domestic power structure remained intact, and the trajectory of socioeconomic growth was sustained. This relatively orderly situation was greatly facilitated by the fact that during those decades Japanese society was able to meet enough of its growing raw material needs – food, fossil fuels, other subsurface yield – from domestic sources so that industrialization could proceed without leaders feeling compelled to adopt unsustainable measures to secure the needed resource base. Rather, they found that existing international trade arrangements, together with the imperialist order that Europeans had created and maintained in East Asia, met their current needs or could be modified enough to do so.

Already by 1914, however, the domestic resource base was looking less and less adequate, and the accelerating growth of following years made the question of how to secure essential materials an ever more pressing one. The issue was severely complicated by the disintegration of the existing East Asian imperialist order, and World War I was the key event in that process because it crippled the European capacity to preserve it. Hence we treat 1914 as the watershed year that ushered in an age of escalating disorder.

At the time, however, 1912 far more than 1914 seemed the great watershed. The death of Meiji *tennō* that year was wrenching for many of his subjects, especially the beneficiaries of recent change, who felt that an era had ended, their link to the great age of the Restoration been severed, and themselves cast adrift in a trackless world. The emperor was mourned throughout the realm in elaborate ceremonies that employed both indigenous and foreign precedents. As an enduring sign of his extraordinary historical significance the deceased was interred in Kyoto amidst the ghostly remains of Hideyoshi's great Fushimi Castle, overlooking the Uji River and adjacent to the burial site of Kanmu, illustrious founder of Heian. He was given a gigantic hemispheric tomb set in a grand precinct whose scale puts one more in mind of the great tombs of the pre-Buddhist *kofun* era than the modest burial sites of Kanmu's 70 other successors.

Despite the intensity of feeling, the elegance of funeral ritual, and the grandeur of interment, however, Meiji's death changed things very little. In 1914, by contrast, when the governments of Europe allowed ethnic hatreds, rigidities of military technology, and political bungling to lead them into the most sanguinary and devastating fratricidal conflict in an age of unprecedented military destructiveness, their actions had major effects on Japan, even though the war was in fact fought half a world away and its outbreak seemed initially of little concern to most Japanese.

In reality the war mattered a lot. By crippling the European capacity to shape affairs in East and Southeast Asia, it created new geopolitical uncertainties and opportunities. It enabled the Japanese government to augment its imperial holdings, and insofar as it paved the way for the Leninist triumph in Russia and the emergence of the United States as a major global force, it altered the politics of Northeast Asia and the Pacific. The war also offered Japan's generals military lessons, most notably in the use of tanks, airplanes, and colonial manpower. By creating a large European market for wartime exports and an opportunity for vigorous commercial penetration of erstwhile colonial and semi-colonial territories, moreover, it facilitated striking advances in Japan's industrialization. In short, the war ended the era of a relatively stable East Asian context, ushered in one of much greater instability, and deepened Japanese involvement in that new era.

Within this changed geopolitical context, to foreshadow chapters 15–17, Japan experienced a quarter century of striking domestic development. Socioeconomic growth and change were broad and deep, giving rise to more complex domestic tensions and more strained, ultimately disastrous foreign relationships. Political thought and action reflected and addressed – to uncertain effect – the problems of the day. Rhetoricians gave complex, even tortured expression to the perdurable discourse on "East and West" and "China and Japan," and in the process they ultimately contributed to the military catastrophe of 1945.

In the realm of representation more broadly, as education and literate culture became more nearly universal, cultural production grew more varied in both content and form. It built on precedents of the recent past while addressing the diverse literary, philosophical, and artistic agendas engaging the global intelligentsia of the day. It employed the new media, notably radio and film, that technological change was creating, and it began to reverse the Meiji-era trend that separated an avant garde, elitist Tokyo from a culturally "backward" countryside.

THE POLITICS OF DISORDER

By the late 1930s, as we note below, the Japanese government was busily interposing itself in a broad range of domestic social and economic matters. That busyness did not necessarily constitute effective action, however: much legislation proved a dead letter in practice. Indeed, for most of the post-1914 period, one is struck by the modesty of governmental effectiveness in domestic affairs, in contrast to early Meiji, when government initiative was central to so much socioeconomic change. Much as the decisive role of government in the formative years of Tokugawa rule gave way to a later phase when government scrambled ineffectually to guide and exploit, so in post-Meiji Japan government played an increasingly marginal and erratic role in shaping social, economic, and cultural developments, its best efforts notwithstanding. Even in foreign affairs its role was inconsistent and indecisive, the continental initiatives of the Kwantung Army (the large garrison force in Manchuria) being the most vigorous, most consistent in purpose – and ultimately most calamitous.

POLITICAL PROCESS

To pick up the political narrative again, founders of the Meiji Constitutional order had attempted to assure permanent political order by insulating central leadership from the fickle masses and wantonly ambitious. Their ideal of a government leadership chosen by and loyal to the emperor and standing above partisan politics acquired the rubric "transcendental cabinets" (*chōzen naikaku*). Political outsiders, on the other hand, advanced the counter-model of a cabinet formed by the majority party in the Diet and thus, by implication, subject to the will of the propertied, male electorate. During the 1890s their maneuvers produced a series of tactical political alliances, most importantly one centered on what became the Seiyūkai political party. By collaborating with senior statesmen, military figures, bureaucrats, and industrialists, Seiyūkai leaders dominated electoral politics for years. The party not only survived Katsura Tarō's attempt to reaffirm oligarchal hegemony in the Taishō Political Crisis (Taishō *seihen*) of 1913, but emerged stronger than ever.

The whole *seihen* episode proved so disruptive, however, that for a decade thereafter, during the diplomatic and economic turmoil of World War I and its aftermath, *ad hoc* coalitions of oligarchs, bureaucrats, senior military officers, and politicians were content to jockey cautiously for power, invoking the rhetoric of transcendental and party cabinets as seemed advantageous but not pressing the issue to resolution. Despite their caution, however, leaders were repeatedly embarrassed and discredited by economic disorder and diplomatic miscues, and the public discontent that grew out of those conditions galvanized demands for more political rights, economic reform and relief, and even revolutionary change.

While the central leadership wrestled with increasingly thorny problems, local leaders pressed on with their various enterprises. In Okayama Ikegami Chinpei spent the years of World War I busy as village head, active member of the Provincial Assembly, and participant in the political party affairs of

Inukai Tsuyoshi. As adumbrated in chapter 13, he was active in numerous committees and projects, doing more at the provincial level than in earlier years, and by war's end his supporters were starting to discuss his standing for election to the national Diet.

In the autumn of 1919, however, Chinpei sickened, and a year later he died from encephalitis, aged 58. Neighbors remembered him for his many efforts, including his key role in addressing his locality's version of one of the era's most widespread and intractable problems, that of local administrative consolidation. In particular they recalled his role in 1915 in masterminding a four-day bargaining session that resolved eight years of conflict between two adjacent villages, enabling them to merge as Kami Village, combine their hamlet Shintō shrines, and consolidate their resources to build a new school and other facilities. Similarly he helped reorganize Okayama's Kume District, thereby facilitating broader local cooperation and economic efficiency despite the pain of erasing long-established local identities and arrangements.

Illustrative of the links that bound local politics to national, at Chinpei's death, over 600 people came for the elaborate funeral ceremony, including national figures in Inukai's party. A year later he was honored with a memorial biography, and in 1934 a bronze statue of him was unveiled in Kami Village, a local analogue to the statues of Ninomiya Sontoku that were then being erected in so many other villages. The statue stood there until taken for use as scrap metal during the desperate last stages of the Pacific War. Given Chinpei's view of the infrangible links between local and national affairs, he probably would have approved that use.

By the time of his death most of the early Meiji political heroes were gone, the last of them disappearing with the deaths of Ōkuma Shigenobu and Yamagata Aritomo in 1922 and Matsukata Masayoshi two years later. Even as the old guard was passing and "lesser men" tried to fill their shoes, the din of political agitation was growing louder, its rhetoric taking inspiration from Bolshevik victory, Wilsonian idealism, and the failure of German authoritarianism.

Of the many problems, self-inflicted and otherwise, that plagued Japan's rulers and fueled the political rhetoric of these years, probably the food riots of summer 1918 were most noteworthy, in part because they reinforced contemporary protests over unemployment, housing, and other issues. The riots, which grew out of sharp wartime inflation, went on for two months, with 526 incidents that evidently involved millions of people being reported from fishing and agricultural villages, mining towns, and cities all across the country. The rioters ransacked food stores and *sake* shops, making off with some 70 percent of store stocks in Kobe, for example. And in the manner of Edo-period *uchi kowashi*, sometimes they went on from ransacking to smashing. As one rioting dockworker in Kobe shouted to his fellows:

Rice is expensive because the evil rice dealers boost the price. Rents are high because of the likes of the Heishinkan (property rental agency). We should wipe them out.[1]

The crowd agreed and proceeded to trash the Heishinkan.

With images of the Russian Revolution in some officials' minds, authorities moved to save the day. They deployed 100,000 troops, arrested over 8,000 people, and convicted and punished some 5,000 on one or another charge. And in the course of suppression they killed thirty and wounded scores. Local leaders and merchants tended to respond differently. Being more aware of people's needs – and more vulnerable to the crowd's wrath – they commonly collected rice and other goods for distribution to the needy and took other measures to ease the hardship. After the event central authorities also took remedial actions, changing policies on food imports, commodity trading, police procedures, labor relations, and social welfare.

The 1920s. Within this context of growing public turbulence, leaders of the established political parties (the Seiyūkai and Kenseikai most notably) and their allies in journalism and academia invoked the ideals of Wilsonian democracy, the threat of Soviet radicalism, and the fear of social upheaval to advance their own quest for power. Their efforts were aided by the writings of influential political thinkers, most famously Minobe Tatsukichi and Yoshino Sakuzō, whose philological fine tuning helped justify Diet supremacy despite the Meiji Constitution's explicit declaration of Imperial sovereignty. The widespread demand that government follow "the trends of the times" eventuated in a factional realignment, and in June 1924 Katō Kōmei, head of the Kenseikai (renamed Minseitō three years later), formed a majority-party cabinet.

Katō's government inherited myriad problems: labor unrest, tenant-farmer disputes, union activism, growing labor and intellectual interest in radical socialism, feminist and pariah (*burakumin*) agitation, student activism, the establishment of a Communist party, and the immense difficulties posed by the Kantō earthquake of 1923, which had devastated much of the Tokyo–Yokohama vicinity. He also faced the military aftereffects of the Siberian Expedition and Washington Conference, which are discussed in chapter 17. In the face of these issues, Katō adopted what amounted to a carrot and stick strategy. To ease tax burdens and rein in obstreperous military men, he reduced armed service budgets, manpower, and unit strength despite bitter objections from the officer corps. He also trimmed the civilian budget. He promoted measures to aid tenant farmers and pursued, with only limited success, legislation aimed at reducing worker grievances. And most famously, less than a decade after Britain and Germany passed similar legislation, he enacted a law establishing nominally universal male suffrage.[2] The electorate had grown slowly in preceding decades as the property requirement was lowered and more households met it, but this newest change roughly tripled eligible voters to upwards of thirteen million.

The principal stick to balance these carrots was the Peace Preservation Law of 1925, which Katō enacted a few days before the suffrage bill. The law's passage culminated several years of effort by senior government officials to develop strong anti-subversive legislation. As one supportive Diet member saw it, that law would not infringe upon free speech itself, but

> when thought becomes involved in creating organizations, agitation, and meetings, then, for the first time it will be punished.[3]

The law criminalized participation in, instigation of, or assistance to any scheme undertaken "for the purpose of changing the national polity (*kokutai*) or of denying the private property system," and it specified prison terms for such offenses.[4]

Katō's policies had several goals. By lowering taxes and meliorating social conditions, he hoped to ease hardship and reduce the appeal of radicalism. He extended electoral participation so as to enhance the legitimacy of party-based cabinets, thereby broadening public engagement in the established order, forestalling social upheaval, and strengthening the Meiji Constitutional system as a whole. And through the Peace Preservation Law he defined more clearly the limits of acceptable dissent and the core values of the state, facilitating judicial action against proponents of tabooed change.

For the next few years Katō and his successors were able to retain enough support so that Minseitō and Seiyūkai party cabinets followed one another fairly smoothly, and successive administrations dealt with developments at home and abroad in a reasonably orderly manner. The restrictive function of the 1925 settlement was revealed in the spring of 1928, a few weeks after the first national election held on the basis of the male suffrage legislation. On March 15 the government launched a mass roundup of "Communists," in which simultaneous raids on more than 120 locations were made to seize evidence that would permit successful prosecution of the detained. By year's end police had arrested over 3,400 people, raising the total to 8,368 the following year, in the process overloading the courts and producing "the biggest event in Japan's judicial history." The massive arrests and jailings were spurred on by Prime Minister Tanaka Giichi and others who advocated, "absolutely no mercy for the traitors who tried to change the *kokutai*."[5] That roundup, together with the heightened surveillance that followed it, succeeded in breaking the back of radical political activism.

The 1930s.   Even as this domestic crackdown was in progress, its long-term efficacy was being nullified by the intersecting issues of Asian geopolitical change, world depression, and accelerating socioeconomic change at home. By heightening public hardship, fear, and tension, these issues were beginning to undermine public order and unleash new political forces, ushering in a decade of turbulence. Especially during 1930–2 a cluster of factors – job layoffs, labor unrest, rural misery, plots and assassinations, military scheming and insubordination, alarming/exhilarating news from Manchuria, and charges and counter-charges of corruption and abuse by politicians and others – fueled public resentment, disgust, excitement, and alienation and spurred angry calls for corrective action of one sort or another.

By then several small groups of military officers and civilians were taking just such action, discussing and implementing assassination plots and other measures to rectify affairs at home and abroad. In one of the most ambitious plots, in 1932 a group of naval officers and civilians, including followers of the articulate agrarianist Tachibana Kōsaburō, attempted a *coup d'état*, their venture bolstered by the tacit support of a few army officers. On May 15 they assassinated the aged Prime Minister Inukai Tsuyoshi, attacked other targets, including major party and *zaibatsu* offices, issued a revolutionary manifesto to the "farmers, workers, and all the people," and hoped that War Minister Araki Sadao would declare a national emergency and seize power. Araki refused, however, and the insurgents were captured and tried. At the trial one young officer defended his actions by declaring that:

> We are neither rightists nor leftists. We oppose communism, but we also reject fascism. What we stand for is a restoration-revolution (*ishin no kakumei*), which would establish direct Imperial rule.[6]

Many observers were alarmed by the violence, but many others applauded the young officers for their patriotic devotion, finding more to praise in their motives than to condemn in their methods.

In the incident's aftermath the army high command negated the principle of party-based cabinets by refusing to designate anyone army minister and thus thwarting attempts of civilian politicians to form any new governments except with their consent. From then until mid-1940 successive cabinets were headed by senior admirals or Peers whom military leaders deemed acceptable. Cooperating with supportive Diet members and career ministry officials, these cabinets carried on contentious diplomatic negotiations, worked out arrangements with the semi-autonomous Kwantung Army and other organs of continental empire, implemented policies of military strengthening, dealt with radical activists at home, and enacted bills relating to the economy and social order. As the decade advanced, this legislation authorized more and more government intervention to control "dangerous" thought, enhance production, and improve labor–management relations. By decade's end ideas and policies modeled on those of Nazi Germany were gaining considerable éclat.

The most dramatic political event of these years was another attempted *coup d'état*, that of February 26, 1936. The incident merits note mainly because it revealed how deeply riven was the military, no more able to speak with a single voice than were the heads of political parties, agencies of civil government, or *zaibatsu*. Military factionalism, already present in the Sat-Chō conquest of 1868, was institutionalized in the form of army–navy rivalry and in tensions among officers trained in different military schools and assigned to different commands. It was sustained by differing doctrinal convictions and strategic assessments. And it was repeatedly manifested in disputes over military policy abroad, in Manchuria most notably, and in plans for optimizing military preparedness at home.

During the 1930s these disputes became more harsh as the stakes grew, eventuating in 1935 in the murder of the powerful General Nagata Tetsuzan by a field-grade subordinate who regarded the general's factional allies and relatively cautious policies as traitorous. This unprecedented rupture in command control prompted army leaders to tighten discipline over radical junior officers, but in February 1936 a group of the latter, who were stationed in Tokyo, retaliated by launching a military coup. They deployed their 1,400 troops from barracks near the Imperial Palace, hunted down and murdered a few senior government officials, missed others, seized police headquarters and other key sites, and encircled but failed to penetrate the palace grounds.

In their manifesto the insurgents denounced "the senior statesmen, the military clique, the bureaucrats, and the politicians" whose heinous policies "have encroached upon the authority of the Emperor, caused utmost misery to the people, and brought humiliation by foreign powers upon our country."[7] To rectify the situation, they demanded specific personnel changes in the army, a more forceful policy abroad, and unspecified changes in the government to achieve a "Restoration" of genuine imperial rule. They then presented these demands for a "Shōwa Restoration" to the War Minister and awaited their implementation.

Within the palace, meanwhile, the emperor was outraged, and he demanded that the mutineers, as he characterized them, be suppressed. After two days of confusion, uncertainty, and maneuver, army and navy forces of suppression assembled and the insurgency collapsed. Senior officers then punished the mutineers, tightened control of the officer corps, and suppressed much of the radical plotting and rhetoric that had flourished in preceding years.

In the outcome, military discipline was reaffirmed and military control of the government tightened. The substantive issues of foreign policy were not thereby simplified, however, and starting in the summer of 1937, leaders made one decision after another that led Japan deeper and deeper into the morass of a continental war. It was a contest they proved unable to win but were unwilling to settle by acknowledging defeat. Instead, they became locked in a war of attrition and, as we note in chapter 17, during 1940–1 started looking for ways to expand their war with the Chinese Nationalist Government of Chiang Kai-shek in hopes of isolating him and ending the deadlock by forcing his capitulation.

POLITICAL DISCOURSE

The political discourse of these years was as tortured as the political process. Rhetoricians both in and out of government advanced forceful arguments on behalf of one or another policy or principle, but a viable consensus never emerged.

Government leaders tried to cope with the rising tide of dissent by tightening legal control and using that control to reintegrate deviants into approved society. "Thought police" (*Tokubetsu kōtō keisatsu*) and subsequently military police (*Kenpeitai*) grew more numerous, gained broader authority, and became more vigilant in their surveillance of "thought criminals." And the Home and Justice Ministries developed extensive programs of "suspended charges" and "protective supervision" to immobilize with minimal legal fuss those accused or convicted of holding ideas contrary to the *kokutai*. As a police textbook explained in 1930, whereas a murderer may kill a few people, "and there it ends, thought criminals endanger the life of the entire nation."[8] Policy focused, therefore, on encouraging the rehabilitation or conversion (*tenkō*) of the deviant, "to lead them," in the words of the Minister of Justice in 1937, "to a realization and voluntary acknowledgement of their offense. Simultaneously it prepares them for a return to active and grateful service to society." Further to encourage such conversion of the wayward, the unrepentent were to be punished harshly.

Civil officials were not the only ones disturbed by the welter of conflicting ideas and interests that characterized the day. With intensifying stridency, diverse critics challenged the Yoshino-Minobe arguments on behalf of electoral authority and political pluralism. Thus, in 1935, as attacks on Minobe were reaching their peak, a group of army reservists put the matter bluntly while burning some of his writings:

> A non-Japanese, blasphemous, Europe-worshipping ideology which ignores our three-thousand-year-old tradition and ideals is rife. This liberalism which threatens to turn us into Western barbarians is basic to Minobe's beliefs.[9]

This sort of patriotic rhetoric, which spoke directly to ethnic sensibilities and claimed to transcend all "selfish" interests, industrial and party-political most especially, proved widely appealing.

Civilian politicians tried to capitalize on the rhetoric by employing more moderate versions themselves. Few listeners found politicians' claims to the mantle of public virtue compelling, however, because by the thirties party leaders had established a long record of opportunistic, self-promoting conduct that was public knowledge thanks to their own efforts at mutual vilification. Far more compelling to many observers were claims by military officers that they were the true defenders of emperor and nation. There was, after all, much precedent for this view.

The military's mission.   The Tokugawa political order, lest we forget, had not conceptualized government in terms of a civil–military dichotomy. Indeed, the proposition that senior government figures properly handled both civil and military command traced back to the *ritsuryō* era and earlier, and Tokugawa-era doctrine held that only samurai could effectively master both the civil and military arts (*bunbu*). The Meiji founders, likewise, presumed that ex-samurai could properly handle all affairs of state. As decades advanced, however, military and civilian aspects of rule were sorted out, and separate hierarchies of office and arenas of responsibility were established, limiting Japanese military officers to a much more circumscribed realm of responsibility.

That restricted institutional role notwithstanding, the informing ideals of the modern military remained expansive, as reflected in the 1882 Imperial Precepts to Soldiers and Sailors, which stood thereafter as founding principles for the armed services. In that document the Meiji Emperor admonished his troops to be diligent and dedicated, brave in war, prudent in peace, simple in taste, and sincere in behavior. But first and foremost, they should loyally serve the emperor:

> Soldiers and Sailors, We are your supreme Commander-in-Chief. Our relations with you will be most intimate when We rely upon you as Our limbs and you look up to Us as your head. Whether We are able to guard the Empire, and so prove Ourself worthy of Heaven's blessings and repay the benevolence of Our Ancestors, depends upon the faithful discharge of your duties as soldiers and sailors... If you all do your duty, and being one with Us in spirit do your utmost for the protection of the state, Our people will long enjoy the blessings of peace, and the might and dignity of Our Empire will shine in the world.[10]

The well-being of all – the people, the realm, the emperor himself – depended on dedicated performance by the armed forces. How could a mere civilian bear such responsibilities or be so essential?

Yamagata Aritomo, revered as founder of the modern military, was unshakably convinced of the army's centrality to Japan's well-being. And General Tanaka Giichi, his loyal supporter, key proponent of the Military Reservist Association, and architect of the 1928 crackdown on radicals, shared that conviction. Tanaka's interest in the military reserve was grounded in his understanding of industrial-age warfare. As he put it in 1915:

> The outcome of future wars will not be determined by the strongest army, but by the strongest populace. A strong populace is one which has physical strength and spiritual health, one which is richly imbued with loyalty and patriotism, and one which respects cooperation, rules, and discipline.[11]

Military training instills such virtues, he held, and the reserves spread them among the general populace even as they spread respect for the armed forces.

This public respect for the armed forces was essential, in turn, because of the army's political importance. In 1924 Tanaka warned of the evil inherent in "dangerous ideas spread by socialists," such as had occurred recently in Italy, and declared that, "The main force in saving the Japanese people from this kind of national crisis is the army and the reservist association."

This military legacy and outlook, together with the high command's institutional location, enabled military officers to see themselves as the surest and most sincere guardians of emperor and nation. Others, however, claimed equal concern for the fate of the realm, and during the 1920s and 1930s nationalist rhetoric flourished.

Patriotic gore. The threads of patriotic verbiage can be traced well back in history, through the declamations of late Tokugawa activists (*shishi*) and ideologues such as Aizawa Seishisai, and even back to Nichiren's thirteenth-century denunciation of bakufu unpreparedness for a Mongol invasion. Rhetoricians of the twenties and thirties, civilian as well as military, invoked these precedents and more as they pressed their arguments for rectification at home and action abroad, whether that be undertaken to counter radicalism, stop exploitation by the privileged, or free Japan – indeed, all of Asia – from the yoke of "Western" cultural and political domination.

To elaborate, in 1919, with much of Europe still in ruin and Japan facing resistance in China and Korea as well as disorder at home, a handful of Tokyo intellectuals formed a discussion group, the Yūzonsha, and issued a founding manifesto in which they declared that,

> because we really believe in the Japanese nation's destiny to be the great apostle of mankind's war of liberation we want to begin with the liberation of Japan itself.[12]

Their efforts at political action proved inconsequential, but Kita Ikki, a participant in the group, became through his writing one of the age's most influential proponents of forceful rectification. A "frail, one-eyed visionary, clad in a Chinese robe," Kita gave particularly effective expression to the idea of a radical reformist program grounded in the virtue of Japan's military forces.[13]

In a work authored in 1919, and published in 1923 as *Nihon kaizō hōan taikō* (Outline Plan for the Reorganization of Japan), Kita the polemicist and political dabbler advocated a revolutionary *coup d'état*.[14] Citing the precedents of Napoleon and the Bolsheviks, he called for dissolution of the Diet, suspension of the Constitution, proclamation of martial law to suppress resistance by "the aristocratic and wealthy classes," and formation of a ruling Council of Advisors that would govern through the Military Reservist Association. The Association's members, he argued, epitomize the best of Japan, possessing

> a perfect popular core of patriotism and good sense. And they are the healthy working classes of the state, the great majority of them being farmers or workers [in origin].

While foreign precedents might help Kita legitimize a coup, foreign influences were not welcome; thus he warned that the English language poisoned the Japanese mind and should be replaced with Esperanto.

Once cleansed of foreign impurities, he wrote, a revitalized Japan was destined to triumph in the cataclysm of nation-states at war, going on to build a "great revolutionary empire." Appropriating images with grand panache, Kita envisaged the glorious future in these terms:

> After destroying England [in Asia] and restoring Turkey, after making India independent and China autonomous, the Rising Sun Flag of Japan shall offer the light of that sun to all mankind. The second coming of Christ, prophesied in every country on earth, actually signifies the scripture and sword of Japan [as a new] Mohammed.

During the twenties Kita himself mostly pursued a quiet, apolitical life of teaching, but his *Outline Plan* enjoyed considerable popularity among discontented intellectuals and young military officers.

Other radicals were more active. A number of people were inspired by the writings of the agrarianist Gondō Seikei, particularly his denunciations of bureaucracy, *zaibatsu*, military leaders, absentee landlords, and political parties. In their stead he advocated "self-rule" by ordinary folk as the sole means of developing both a better homeland and sufficient agricultural colonies for Japan's surplus population.

The younger and more action-oriented agrarianist Tachibana Kōzaburō echoed the popular themes of Japan's unique virtue and destiny.[15] As he put it during the early thirties, "We must sweep clean the dominance of modern Western materialistic civilization and return to the surviving essence of the founding of the country." Radical change is necessary because:

> The world of national politics is being poisoned by mammon and the gang of corrupt industrialists who sit in the top seats. The corrosion of local politics by dissolute landlords and the sons of liquor dealers must not be overlooked.

Once Japan's house is in order, he argued in another essay,

> we will have the strength to mobilize our peerless army and navy for the world revolution … to pulverize American power in the Pacific, sweep away the influence of the Chinese military clique … liberate India from England, make Russia realize her mistakes … and rouse the Germans.

Much, clearly, had to be done, and the task had to start with reconstruction at home.

As matters worked out, however, the domestic forces opposed to radical change – the industrial, bureaucratic, military, and political party interests that had taken shape over preceding decades – proved strong enough to thwart all but the most modest reform at home. The most consequential changes effected by the proponents of radical reform occurred abroad, where patiotic rhetoric helped legitimize resort to brute force.

Empires of the mind. The writings of pundits such as Kita and Gondō spoke viscerally and directly about "East and West," "Japan and Asia," reaching and inspiring a reasonably broad audience. More scholarly rhetoricians employed essentially the same dyadic forms in more esoteric writings addressed to smaller, more elite audiences.

As Japan's political and economic involvement in China deepened during these decades, the older ethno-cultural dyad of China/Japan became more tortured. At universities and research centers located in Japan, the empire, Manchuria, and China, Japanese Sinologists, supported mainly by government funding, vigorously promoted the study of Chinese and other East Asian history, culture, society, and geography. As decades passed, however, the research findings (most substantially those of the South Manchurian Railway's research bureau, which employed some 2,000 personnel by the late 1930s) were directed more and more to government use. And while many of the Sinologists were privately uneasy with their government's escalating use of armed force, most had from the beginning favored "progressive" reform in China and saw Japan as having a helpful role in that process.

Thus in 1924 the celebrated Sinologist Naitō Konan, who was dismayed by China's failure to "modernize" and irritated by the anti-Japanese sentiment then surging through the country, argued, on the basis of a reductive culturalist view of Chinese history, that

> if Japan were to form one nation politically with China, even if the center of culture moved to Japan and even if Japan became active in China socially and politically, the Chinese people should not look on this as an extremely odd phenomenon.[16]

During the 1930s, with Sino-Japanese tensions rising higher than ever, more and more Sinologists came, on diverse grounds, to favor a stronger Japanese role on the continent. Thus Tachibana Shiraki, a scholarly pundit working in China and Manchuria who viewed matters in much the same light as the domestic agrarianist Tachibana Kōsaburō, called for a strong Japanese role in developing a new Manchurian state that would be linked directly to village cooperatives so as to eliminate "social exploitation by landlords and merchants prospering on unearned incomes."[17]

As that phrasing suggests, some of these Sinologists were inspired by Marxist concepts fully as much as they were by indigenous agrarianist notions, and tension and disagreement between them and political authorities were common. By 1940, however, dissenting views had largely been silenced, and most articulate opinion, like that of pundits and academics in general, served to legitimize government foreign policy.

Commentary grounded in the broader East/West dyad revealed similar shifts in function and assessment. Especially during the later 1930s the academic participants in that discourse became more closely associated with policy makers. Most notably a group of cultural theorists at the University of Kyoto developed geopolitical analyses that served to support naval strategic thinking, while another assemblage of intellectuals formed the Shōwa Kenkyūkai as a "brain trust" whose views helped Prime Minister Konoe Fumimaro develop rationales for the pursuit of forceful policies at home and abroad.

As these developments suggest, intellectual assessments of "East" and "West" reflected the growing tension between Japan and the Powers. The overt praise for matters "Western" that was common in the years immediately after World War I gave way to more frequent denunciation as Japan's relations with the outside world deteriorated, with academics producing a literature that was ever more critical of things Western, or "modern" as they increasingly characterized them. In their writings they drew freely from both European and Asian intellectual traditions to develop new interpretive stances, much as Nishida Kitarō had done in his *Zen no kenkyū* of 1911.

In 1939 Kamei Katsuichirō, a former Marxist who during the thirties threw his support to things "Japanese" and "Asian," posed the problem this way:

> while the Black Ships that represented the material might of the West have left, a hundred years later the Black Ships of thought are still threatening us.[18]

In his view the actions of Japanese soldiers abroad were destroying an unacceptable cultural status quo. In place of the rejected "West," he and other authors advanced arguments to demonstrate Japanese or Asian cultural superiority and/or Japan's key role in the creation of a new and preferable cultural order. That order, whether envisioned as embracing Japan, Asia, or the entire world, would "overcome the modern," i.e., displace existing industrial values and arrangements, which they labeled variously as Western, capitalist, materialist, utilitarian, or whatever.

Some scholars tried to justify the new order in terms of one or another rationalistic scheme, as did the political scientist Rōyama Masamichi, one of Konoe's advisors. In 1941 he declared that:

> I for one have been making efforts to construct a regionalistic globalism, based on geographical analysis, such that it may provide a foundation for our continental policy, as it has developed in the most recent decade from the outbreak of the Manchurian Incident through the China conflict.[19]

Much more commonly pundits asserted that the new order had its philosophical roots in the "East," whether meaning traditions such as Buddhism, the virtue of the Imperial lineage, or a present-day rationality, holism, or humanism that these academics presented as deriving from the Asian legacy.

Thus Nishitani Keiji, a student of Nishida and an active participant in the group of Kyoto intellectuals associated with naval strategists, developed an elaborate argument in which he called for the "overcoming of modernity," having defined modernity in 1942 as, "the age in which the foundations for an integrated worldview have broken down." Ousting the West from Asia was part of the task, certainly, but another part was the rebuilding of Japan, "to make the nation into a single organism" in which the individual would freely submit himself to the communal interest, realizing true freedom therein.[20]

In the end, of course, the actions of fighting men, fired by patriotic gore, compelled by superiors, and sustained by industrial production, determined the fate of Imperial Japan. Because the outcome proved so contrary to the ones envisioned by these academics, their musings quickly dropped from view, the written texts surviving today as embarrassments for some, but as precedents for reformist rhetoric by others, and as reminders for all of how marginal tendentious theorizing can be to the outcomes of life.

DOMESTIC GROWTH

During the 1930s Japan's military commanders were able to pursue major foreign wars and contemplate even more grandiose enterprises only because their country's domestic economy had grown rapidly since the triumphs of late Meiji. That story of growth is in part a tale of demographic continuities, but temporal fluctuations, sectoral imbalances, and growing import dependencies also merit note.

DEMOGRAPHICS

The demographic story is one of continuing rapid population growth, with the 51 million of 1914 exceeding 70 million by 1940, augmented by nearly a million Korean immigrants, voluntary and forced. An ever larger portion of this population was urban, with large cities in particular expanding to absorb the added numbers, most of whom originated in villages. Whereas 28 percent of the populace had occupied towns and cities of 10,000 or more in 1913, by 1940 29 percent dwelt in cities of 100,000 or more. And Tokyo, which at a million-plus had been the world's largest city during the early eighteenth-century, exceeded two million by 1905 and grew to some 6.7 million by 1935, rivaling the recently developed behemoths, London and New York. This urban growth did not, however, significantly draw down the rural population, which held at some 5.5 million farm families through 1945.

The demographic increase was nationwide but particularly striking in Hokkaido, which was rapidly being transformed from frontier region into integral part of the realm. The island's industrial urbanization rapidly overwhelmed the remnants of Ainu society, keeping the Ainu population static in size and disadvantaged and demoralized in condition. Meanwhile the Wajin population continued its Meiji-era growth, rising from 1,800,000 in 1913 to about 3,300,000 by 1940, due mainly to emigration from Honshu. Cities and towns grew apace, the island's three major cities topping 100,000 during these years: the port of Hakodate by 1915, the prefectural capital of Sapporo in 1920, and the industrial port of Muroran in 1940. Other smaller centers also contributed to the island's rapid transformation, as did the development of Karafuto's mines and oil fields, and its settlement with some 200,000 immigrants by 1940.

Japan's large-scale manufacturing industries employed only a small portion of the swelling city population, relying instead on machinery for much of their growth. As in other industrializing societies, most of the urban employment gains were in myriad, generally low-wage, service, satellite, and small-scale industries. Nevertheless the scale of technological change was so great that urban centers did become markedly more industrial in character.

As in the Edo period, urban Japan was concentrated along the Tokyo-to-Shimonoseki axis with its rich port facilities and productive hinterland valleys. But small centers were also scattered widely across the rest of the realm. Whereas geopolitics had determined the siting of many Edo-period castle towns, twentieth-century urbanism was heavily shaped by the location of industrial raw materials and transportation facilities. The presence of rapidly descending streams throughout the country encouraged widespread development of small hydroelectric plants after 1914, and scattered mineral deposits fostered the siting of mines, factories, and satellite towns at many places from Kyushu to Karafuto.

The key variable, however, was harbors. All along the shoreline ports expanded, primarily because coasting vessels carried much of the burgeoning domestic bulk cargo and secondarily because all overseas cargo passed through them. Exemplifying the modern, port-centered urban site was the

Kawasaki vicinity on Tokyo's southern edge, which began acquiring its present-day, globally-oriented, industrial character during the 1920s thanks to its convenience for waterborne transport and overseas trade. In the words of a 1950s report:

> Between 1915 and 1919, Asahi Glass, Asano Shipyard, and Asano Steel were built. In Kawasaki, the Ajinomoto Co., Daiichi (formerly Asano) Cement, and Japan Electric Wire (Nippon Densen) were founded. Nippon Kōkan built a blast furnace, and Tokyo Electric combined with G.E. of America to build Mazuda Lightbulb (the present-day Toshiba-Horikawa plant). Yokohama Sugar evolved into Meiji Seika, a bakery of western-style cakes and sweets, while Columbia of Japan, Japan Truss Concrete, and Fuji Electric (broken off from the Furukawa group in a joint venture with Siemens) both developed.[21]

Comparable manufacturing complexes sprang up during these years on the northeast side of Tokyo, near Osaka, and at other coastal cities, in the process playing a key role in the growth and urbanization of Japan's population.

FLUCTUATIONS AND IMBALANCES

As with population and urbanism, so for the economy as a whole the primary story is one of continuing growth. Foreign trade grew in scale and diversity but gradually changed in composition and geography, becoming more industrial in character and more Asia/empire-centered. The domestic economy grew commensurately, but two characteristics of that growth command particular attention: its sectoral imbalance and its temporal irregularity. The rate of growth varied by sector, depending mainly on trends in labor productivity, with heavy industry scoring the greatest gains and agriculture the least. In temporal terms, economic growth fluctuated between rapid and slow, between "boom" and "bust," doing so more and more because of global factors beyond Japanese control.

Temporal fluctuations. The growing intensity of boom and bust is striking. Whereas early Meiji economic fluctuations had been mainly consequences of domestic policy – notably the 1870s inflationary spiral and 1880s Matsukata deflation – in following decades Japan, like other industrializing societies, became ever more subject to the vagaries of poorly regulated global commerce, with external political and economic developments and related domestic moves becoming the deeply entangled determinants of economic flux. World War I spurred explosive growth in the production and export of Japanese goods to Europe and European colonies, and with that boom came improved wages and urban living conditions, as evidenced in reduced levels of indigency and working wives and slightly increased family size.[22]

Soon, however, the wartime eruption of activity produced steep inflation and an untenably favorable balance of payments, and it was followed in 1920 by an abrupt collapse as export markets were lost again. Then political and diplomatic developments in China, along with global agricultural recession and higher tariffs that governments (including Tokyo) unilaterally imposed, complicated trade for several years, further hurting domestic economic interests. Most grievously, declining silk prices, difficulties in the China cotton trade, and continuing government support for rice imports drove the real income of farm families down by about a third during the later 1920s.

The destructive effects of global economic mismanagement became most painfully evident with the world depression that began in 1929. It hammered rural silk producers most harshly but also generated widespread urban unemployment, wage cuts, work speed-ups, and harsher living conditions. The problem was compounded by the ill-timed decision of Prime Minister Hamaguchi Osachi to return to the gold standard in January 1930. A later cabinet repudiated that measure at the end of 1931, shortly after London took the same step, and during 1932 the resulting sharp fall in the yen's exchange value facilitated a trade revival by 1934. That revival was strengthened by substantial gains in industrial efficiency as businesses laid off workers, tightened shop discipline, and installed new machines and production techniques.

Concurrently, government policies of civil pump priming and expansion of military expenditures spurred recovery. After 1936, with continental conflict the central issue in state policy, military-dominated government programs of industrial expansion in Japan, the colonies, and the Manchurian vicinity produced a spurt of industrial growth. That spurt brought only modest social benefits, however, because it was accompanied by an unprecedented shift of resources and effort to capital investment and warfare at the expense of the general public's standard of living.

Sectoral imbalances. The most dramatic growth of the decades after 1914 occurred in heavy industry: metallurgical, chemical, and electrical. Domestic steel production increased 18-fold between 1913 and 1936, coming to exceed 4.5 million tons annually. That expansion reduced dependence on foreign-made steel from about 70 percent of total consumption in 1913 to 30 percent in the late 1920s. However, escalating demand for steel during the thirties stayed abreast of increases in domestic, colonial, and Manchurian production, leaving Japan in chronic need of imports. Pig and scrap iron imports also remained essential, continuing to exceed 50 percent of domestic requirements. Much of the iron and steel, along with diverse other imported metals, was used to produce machinery, and by the mid-1920s domestic production of railway rolling stock, electrical machinery, ships, and other heavy equipment was reducing dependence on imports. By the later 1930s, most types of machines could be fabricated at home, although demand for them was so great that importation continued, most notably of motor vehicles and technically complex machinery.

The chemical industry, practically non-existent before World War I, grew thereafter, producing commercial fertilizer, much of it from imported raw materials, along with dyestuffs and the diverse chemicals used in industrial processes. Especially during the 1930s chemical output grew, rising from a net product of 357 million yen in 1930 to a net of 911 million in 1936, as business and government leaders pressed ahead in their drive to establish a more broadly based, autarchic industrial plant. With the production of chemicals came environmental pollution, but it did not erupt into major political scandal until after World War II, as we note in a later chapter.

The electrical industry also grew rapidly, in terms of both the manufacture of electrical motors and equipment and the production and distribution of electricity. Electric generating capacity, both hydro-powered and coal-fired, increased more than sixfold between 1919 and 1937, mainly to service industry, and by 1935 the country was so thoroughly electrified that 89 percent of Japanese homes had access to current, compared to 85 percent in Germany, 68 percent in the US, and 44 percent in Britain. Most households could afford only a light bulb or two, but had their income levels been higher, the power lines would have been there for use.

One reason heavy industry could grow so rapidly was the presence of an entrepreneurial leadership that was both interested in and capable of financing and operationalizing major, new ventures. The entrepreneurs who had collaborated with government leaders to launch Meiji-era economic development, the likes of Shibusawa, Furukawa, and Sakamoto, continued to expand their enterprises. By the 1920s some ten to twenty large-scale industrial combines had developed, the so-called *zaibatsu*, of which four (Mitsui, Mitsubishi, Sumitomo, and Yasuda) were the greatest. Using their political connections, capital resources, and mercantile know-how, and exploiting the legal space provided by government regulations that they helped shape, the *zaibatsu* absorbed diverse lesser banks and businesses, thereby rapidly moving into a broad array of commercial arenas. By their heyday in the late twenties they were among the world's largest, most diversified, and most tightly controlled entrepreneurial institutions. The chart of the Mitsui industrial empire as it existed in 1945 (figure 15.1) suggests how combined stockholding by family, main company, and satellite companies, together with interlocking directorates and collaborative operations, enabled a few firms to dominate entrepreneurial life all across the economy.

In striking contrast to this story of rapid and sustained industrial expansion was the situation in the rural sector. Gross agricultural output did expand, most notably in raw silk production, which tripled between 1913 and 1929, holding steady thereafter at about 50,000 tons per year. Intensified tillage, in particular the use of commercial fertilizer, which roughly tripled between 1912 and 1939, also bolstered farm yields. And rural labor productivity was enhanced by greater use of power-driven equipment, with electric motors and gasoline engines for farm work increasing over a hundred-fold in two decades (from 2,500 in 1920 to nearly 300,000 in 1939). As a result of these trends, farmers achieved notable gains in output of wheat, fruit, vegetables, and meat, types of produce that appealed to the slowly diversifying urban diet.

These gains in output notwithstanding, agriculture's role in the economy continued to shrink. Whereas farming had accounted for 32 percent of total domestic output in 1914, by 1940 it had declined to 19 percent. Moreover, increases in output did not translate into rural prosperity. With costs up and sale prices down, farm income stagnated. Farm household numbers stabilized, and arable acreage ceased to expand after World War I, with

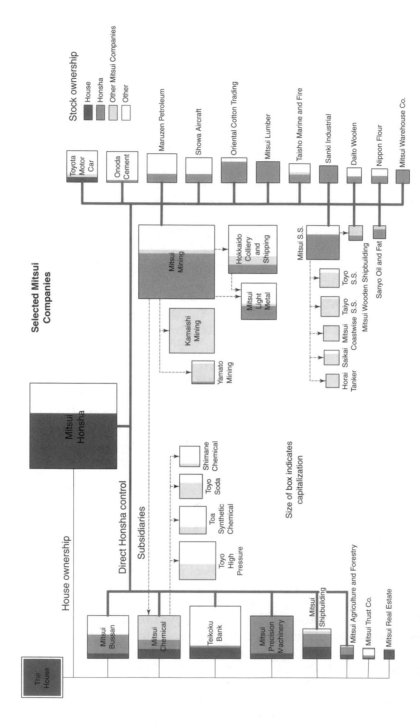

Figure 15.1 The Mitsui industrial empire. At its height in the 1930s–40s, the Mitsui *zaibatsu* consisted of a broad assemblage of enterprises that the Mitsui house proper controlled through a complex set of legal arrangements and personal connections. *Source:* William W. Lockwood, *The Economic Development of Japan, Growth and Structural Change, 1868–1938* (Princeton: PUP, 1954), pp. 218–19; originally adopted from US Department of State, *Report of the Mission on Japanese Combines*, part 1, Washington, 1946, following p. 122. Data are as of September 30, 1945.

tenants continuing to till about 46 percent of the total. Production of rice, the principal crop, grew very little, in part no doubt because government measures to hold down urban rice prices depressed sale prices on the farm, encouraging farmers to concentrate where feasible on alternative crops such as those noted above.

GROWING IMPORT DEPENDENCY

Domestic food production was also failing to stay abreast of population growth. By the 1930s the colonies were providing more than 15 percent of the foodstuffs required domestically, with Korea and Taiwan furnishing about a third of the rice available on the retail market. From Korea alone rice imports grew from 17,000 tons in 1910 to 400,000 in 1919 and 1,500,000 by the mid-1930s. This dramatic increase was partly achieved by expansion in peninsular rice production, but partly by more complete expropriation: whereas about 12 percent of Korean rice output was exported in 1915, over 50 percent left the colony by the early thirties. The drain was offset in part by transfer of sorghum from Manchuria to Korea and in part by the migration of impoverished Koreans to Japan and Manchuria.

Other areas of the economy also revealed the deepening linkages between domestic and offshore production. The demand for terrestrial food imports was held down by a major expansion in fisheries output. Before World War I fishing had been a small-scale, coastal enterprise, but technological improvements yielded no appreciable gain in the coastal catch because at two million metric tons per year those fisheries were already being maximally exploited. Rather, they were supplemented by large-scale pelagic operations, including the use of cannery ships with satellite catcher boats. By 1938 pelagic fishing had grown from nil to 38 percent of the total catch, and although cannery boats prepared goods for export, over 90 percent of the total maritime harvest was consumed at home. In addition, the yield from Japan's own fishing fleet was supplemented by that of foreign vessels, with total imports of fish products exceeding the exports.

Other primary production also grew, but it too failed to keep pace with the rise in domestic industrial demand, which increased the economy's dependence on imports. In terms of wood products, Japan has always been, and still is, an extensively forested realm, but even during the later Edo period forest yield had scarcely met public demand. By late Meiji improvements in transportation were making more and more of Japan's interior woodland accessible to loggers. And sawmills and other new technology were enabling them to produce lumber at a much faster rate than ever before. In addition Hokkaido provided a major new source of timber and pulp. Demand grew so rapidly, however, that despite energetic programs of reforestation and stand management timber exports shriveled, giving way to imports during the 1920s. By the 1930s about 70 percent of total need was met by wood from Hokkaido and other domestic sources, while nearly 20 percent came from intensive felling on Karafuto and over 10 percent from other colonies and foreign countries.

The trend was even more evident in copper and coal, two major exports of the Meiji era. Copper production, which in 1913 totaled 66,500 metric tons and permitted some 40,000 tons of net exports, rose by 1936 to 78,000 tons. But by then the shrunken exports of 12,400 tons were thoroughly overshadowed by imports of 53,300.

In coal mining the trade reversal was less dramatic but equally permanent. Annual coal output rose from 21 million metric tons in 1913 to 33 million in the late twenties and 40 million by 1936, thanks largely to mechanization of the industry. However, total demand grew faster than output, and most of the domestic coal was of inadequate quality for coking, so anthracite and much coking coal had to be imported, mainly from Korea and Manchuria. Before World War I coal exports, largely to China, had far surpassed imports, the peak export year being 1913 when one-sixth of production went abroad. Thereafter, however, exports dwindled, and during the 1920s imports regularly exceeded them, with most of the residual, low-grade exports going to Korea by 1930.

Several developments slowed the growing dependence on coal imports. Electric motors rapidly replaced steam engines in factories and on some railways after 1914. And with the development of hydroelectric plants, more and more electricity production shifted to water power. By 1936 hydropower provided 75 percent of the total electricity consumed, with coal-fired turbines mostly being held on standby for use during periods of low water. Improvements in mechanical efficiency also helped: between 1914 and 1932 coal-fired turbines tripled their electricity output relative to coal consumed; between 1914 and the mid-1920s railroad locomotives and steel plants achieved 75 percent gains in efficiency. Nevertheless, the scale of industrial expansion was so great that coal use continued to increase and the need for high-grade imports to rise with it.

By the 1930s, moreover, internal combustion engines had become substantial energy users. The 3,856 motor vehicles registered in 1917 grew to 128,735 by 1937, while airplanes, oil-fueled ships, tanks, and other military vehicles also proliferated. To operate this burgeoning fleet, domestic oil deposits were located and developed, together with natural gas, mainly along the Sea of Japan from Noto Peninsula northward to Karafuto. Demand, however, vastly exceeded domestic yield. As of 1932, about 80 percent of the petroleum consumed was imported, and of the so-called domestic production, nearly 40 percent came from Karafuto.

The domestic economy thus continued to grow, most rapidly in its industrial sector. And despite efforts at rationalization and energy efficiency it became more deeply entangled in the global economy and more fully dependent on imported fossil fuels and other raw materials. These trends involved both entrepreneurial exchange and empire building, and while the former strategy remained more important in monetary terms, the latter became the favored one, in part because the increasing instability of international trade severely complicated domestic affairs and encouraged leaders to seek more controllable access to foreign resources and markets. So even though empire building encountered more and more difficulties and laid up horrendous costs for the future, it continued to make headway in both economic and spatial terms, as we note more fully in chapter 17.

In sum, Japan's economy expanded dramatically during the decades to 1940 despite the temporal gyrations and sectoral imbalances. And that expansion yielded real gains in material standard of living, at least for the more favored classes. Accompanying those gains, however, were greater apparent disparities of wealth, sharper swings in fortune, and a heightened sense of economic vulnerability. These trends, as we note in the next chapter, spurred the proliferation of labor unions, industrial strikes, and protests by tenant-farmers, as well as industrial and government counter-measures to quel unrest and cushion hardship. And they helped shape cultural production of the age.

[16] LATER IMPERIAL SOCIETY AND CULTURE (1914–1945)

CHAPTER SYNOPSIS

SOCIAL ISSUES
THE POPULATION ISSUE
ACTIVIST WOMEN
MINORITIES AND STUDENTS
RURAL PROBLEMS
URBAN LABOR

ARTICULATE CULTURE
CREATIVE LITERATURE
THEATRE AND FILM
MUSIC AND ART

The Japan of 1940 was a much larger, much more complex, and much more industrialized society than that of 1914. It was also far more deeply and uncomfortably enmeshed in global politico-economic life. The processes of change that yielded these outcomes were all evident in the social agendas and cultural output of these decades.

SOCIAL ISSUES

Many of the domestic trends that had appeared before 1914 accelerated in following years, but the magnitude of their impact varied considerably. Radical political thought, which previously had functioned as a minor external irritant for those running the government, acquired a more substantial role, as noted in chapter 15, influencing the political analysis of rulers and pundits alike. Industrial pollution, on the other hand, did not produce another *cause célèbre* on the scale of the Ashio mine until after the Pacific War, even though the amount of pollution itself kept increasing as industrialization advanced.

The issue of "surplus population," mentioned only rarely before 1914, acquired a prominent place in social polemics. Moreover, it was linked to some of the other vexing issues of the day. These included intensified activism by women, members of the *burakumin* community, and immigrant Koreans. They also included heightened ethnic consciousness among Ainu, greater anger among (and political engagement by) upwardly mobile young men, increased hardship and protest among rural folk, and growing activism within the industrial working class, all of which elicited counter-measures, both rhetorical and operative, from government and employers.

THE POPULATION ISSUE

Reflecting the fact of unprecedented demographic increase, "overpopulation" became an issue as never before. Observers associated the social problems of the twenties and thirties – rural hardship and a growing dependence on food imports; larger numbers of people seeking education, jobs, and housing; the persistence of low wages, poor working conditions, and underemployment – with that unprecedented growth. The perceived solutions were birth control, economic growth, and emigration. In actuality the rapid economic expansion of the post-1890 decades was absorbing the increased numbers, even if not to everyone's satisfaction, but the intensified international disorder of the twenties and thirties undermined confidence in that strategy and spurred discussion of alternatives.

A small movement to control unwanted births was promoted after 1920 by socially active Japanese women, notably the well-born social critic Ishimoto Shizue. Her interest in birth control was triggered during World War I by an unpleasantly close encounter with women coal miners and their children in Kyushu, which led her to promote knowledge and practice of reproductive control. Society's leaders discouraged the notion, however, contending that such a policy would eventually threaten the labor supply and reduce Japan's strength vis-à-vis the other Powers. They persistently obstructed Ishimoto's efforts and at the end of 1937 closed her recently opened clinic in Tokyo.

Whereas birth control carried innuendos of social weakness, emigration had all the éclat of the successful and up-to-date. It was, after all, a policy that demonstrated a society's Darwinian virility. Furthermore, it was fully legitimized by the European diaspora, which had during recent centuries employed cunning, force, and disease to wrest entire continents from the grasp of forager and non-intensive agricultural populations in the Americas and elsewhere.

Already by late Meiji, as noted in chapter 13, pundits were linking an emerging belief in Japan's "surplus population" with the notion that an empire settled by Japanese would both demonstrate and enhance the nation's position as a Great Power. From the mid-nineteenth century onward Hokkaido had functioned, mainly at government behest, as a frontier emigrant region, and during later Meiji other nearby areas, Korea in particular, began to be viewed similarly. Proponents invoked the themes of too many mouths, too little food, and the need to develop a Japanese-populated empire to justify the establishment of emigrant communities there and elsewhere.

In practice, Hawaii and California became major destinations for contract-labor emigrants by later Meiji, followed soon by migration to Taiwan, Korea, Karafuto, the Manchurian vicinity, and, especially after World War I, Micronesia. Anti-Japanese legislation in the United States closed one promising avenue of emigration, in the process reinforcing the growing sense that Japan's future lay in an East Asian empire that would ultimately become home to Japan's extra progeny. Diverse groups continued to promote emigration during the 1920s, and the polemical uses of the idea were evident in an essay that Colonel Hashimoto Kingorō drafted in the mid-1930s:

> there are only three ways left to Japan to escape from the pressure of surplus population ... namely emigration, advance into world markets, and expansion of territory. The first door, emigration, has been barred to us by the anti-Japanese immigration policies of other countries. The second door, advance into world markets, is being pushed shut by tariff barrriers and the abrogation of commercial treaties ... It is quite natural that Japan should rush upon the last remaining door.[1]

For the likes of Hashimoto the notion of "surplus population" constituted little more than political fodder: he disregarded birth control as an option, and his own government not only opposed it but also was a dedicated participant in the trade and tariff wars he denounced.

Such cynicism notwithstanding, the issue of "overpopulation" was one that could elicit public attention because for hard-pressed parents, unwanted births were a harsh household reality that evoked frightening images of a grim Tokugawa past while threatening their hopes for a decent future. For some emigration seemed to offer an answer that was promising even if not ideal, and people did emigrate, mostly in search of better lives. By the later 1930s two million or so resided in Manchuria and the colonies (roughly 750,000 in Manchuria, 700,000 in Korea, 300,000 on Taiwan, 200,000 on Karafuto, and 60,000 in Micronesia) while nearly another million lived elsewhere abroad. Although the total was far fewer than empire builders wanted, and insignificantly few when compared, for example, to emigrant British populations scattered about the world, it was still a substantial measure of the difficulties facing poorer people in Japan.

ACTIVIST WOMEN

At the household level the problem of "overpopulation" was most painfully a woman's, and the inability of Ishimoto Shizue and her allies to gain support for practical methods of birth control helped perpetuate the problem and validate the growing demand by women for a broadened menu of rights and reforms. Article 5 of the Police Security Regulations of 1890, it will be recalled, had forbidden women to participate in political life, and activists' efforts to change that situation had failed in following years.

Government hostility clearly was one factor undercutting those efforts, but another was divisions within the women's movement. Thus the magazine *Seitō* (Blue Stocking), which was founded in 1911 by Hiratsuka Raichō as a venue for discussing issues of concern to women, soon emerged as a vehicle for literary women. It also gave expression to feminist political thought more broadly, however, especially after the editorship was assumed in 1915 by Itō Noe, gifted writer and fiery advocate of women's rights. More cautious women reformers, fearful that radical rhetoric of the sort espoused by *Seitō* would foster government hostility toward their own more moderate programs of female education and advancement, criticized the more extreme voices. The educator Tsuda Ume asserted of *Seitō* members that, "their doctrines are lawless, & their teachings immoral." *Seitō* positions are inappropriate, she contended, because the women of Japan, "above all, work in quiet places, in quiet ways, but nonetheless they attain their ends."[2] Criticism of this sort did not deter Itō, but a combination of overwork and government harassment did. Her magazine was already running afoul of government censors by 1915, and a year later the exhausted Itō ceased publishing.

In 1917 the articulate Yamada Waka, who had a much keener awareness of human vulnerability to economic exploitation than did many of her socially comfortable colleagues, described the women's movement, somewhat too simply, in terms of two branches:

> One branch asserts that motherhood is a woman's heaven-ordained occupation, that a woman's world is the family, and that for a woman to leave the family and compete with men degrades the woman and damages the family. The other branch argues that women are human beings deserving all the rights and privileges accorded men as well as the freedom to participate equally with men in life.[3]

The former group, which included Waka, promoted the idea that the vital role for women lay in homemaking and that they deserved government support in the task. The latter, arguing for fuller independence and most forcefully represented by the remarkably talented and hardy poet-activist Yosano Akiko, rejected such claims on government as demeaning. Both branches, however, and other women who fell between them, were addressing essentially "middle-class" concerns; neither was really confronting the problems faced by women in the mines, the textile trades, or the miscellaneous jobs of the urban poor.

These divisions and limitations notwithstanding, feminist activism continued, sustained by the swelling numbers of women enrolled in higher levels of education despite their exclusion from male institutions of learning, and by the appreciable and rapidly growing numbers of women who were moving into the "white collar" work force, mainly as teachers, nurses, and office staff. Thus, by the mid-twenties about a third of all elementary teachers were women. And the 14,000 women nurses of 1914 numbered 42,000 a decade later.

Following the Bolshevik revolution socialist thought gained great popularity among both men and women, laborers as well as intellectuals. That development spurred the creation of several new women's organizations, notably Sekirankai (Red Wave Society), which a group of radical young women established in 1921 with the advice of Yamakawa Kikue. Yamakawa's manifesto for the organization proclaimed Sekirankai's goal:

> to destroy the capitalist society and build a socialist society. The capitalist society turns us into slaves at home and oppresses us as wage slaves outside the home. It turns many of our sisters into prostitutes. Its imperialistic ambitions

rob us of our beloved fathers, children, sweethearts, and brothers and turn them into cannon fodder… [and] for the sake of its greedy profiteers, [it] crushes and sacrifices our youth, health…, even our lives.[4]

Such views were winning greater popularity because, as one commentator noted, the recession of the twenties threatened even women of the better classes, whether through loss of their own jobs or those of male family members. As a result,

women, who, until now, moved on after girls' schools to flower arranging and sewing and who did not know the taste of poverty, are suddenly facing the storms of life.[5]

In these circumstances more fortunate women gained a new appreciation of the textile worker's view of affairs. And that appreciation gave credibility to Yamakawa's persistent contention that, "the fundamental solution lies only in a revolution in the economic system that brought about women's problems."[6]

This growing radicalization, together with the concurrent global vogue for Wilsonian democracy, prodded the government to mollify its female critics by promoting a moderate reformist agenda, much of it legitimized by reference to "the trends of the times." This interplay of radical pressure and official concessiveness revitalized debate about Meiji concepts of the household, the role of women in society, and their political rights, and led in 1922 to government revision of its police regulations. The new version allowed women to organize and participate in political meetings, but not to vote, hold office, or belong to the political organizations of men.

In the aftermath of the Kantō earthquake of 1923, in which Korean residents were brutalized, radical movements were also harshly suppressed. Itō Noe died at police hands, along with her socialist lover. And young Kaneko Fumiko, a recent convert to anarchism, was arrested with her Korean lover, jailed, eventually convicted, and sentenced to life imprisonment, which she cut short in 1926 by hanging herself in her cell. By then Sekirankai had been dissolved, but other organizations, including the Fusen Kakutoku Dōmei (League for Women's Suffrage) had been established in conjunction with the male suffrage movement as a more moderate force to press for women's right to vote.

Furthermore, government displeasure notwithstanding, ever more women were writing about, and participating in, professional organizations, labor union activities, and strikes. Thus in 1926 the leaders of one radical women's group issued a recruiting statement in which they solicited new members with this ringing declaration.

Who was it who decided that women are weak? We are not at all weak! The only reason for our [seeming] weakness is that we have been shut up at home and relegated to the edges of society, and this has dispersed our strength. When all women stand up together in opposition to the discriminatory social and economic treatment [we have received] in this country, no one will be able to call us weak! That's right! When all women arise in solidarity, that is when our strength will be radiant, that is when a new age for women will be born.[7]

The rhetorical vigor notwithstanding, however, within a few years this group, along with the left-wing organization of which it was a part, was suppressed by police action.

Even as activists experienced ups and downs, women were carving out larger and more durable niches in the world of entertainment. Their Edo-period role as courtesan in the licensed quarter, whether as the most elegant and expensively maintained high-class courtesan or the humblest tea-house geisha, and their ancillary role as street walker and prostitute in the many unlicensed brothels of the day, came under attack during Meiji from an opportunistic alliance of foreigners, "Westernizers," Christian reformers, public health officials, and articulate women. While those career options, pathetic as they too often were, lost social legitimacy, new entertainment venues were developing.

One was the theatre. In late Meiji women regained access to the stage, mainly in *shingeki* productions, and in following years other new types of variety shows began to appear, notably "all-girl revues," of which the most famous, successful, and socially influential was the Takarazuka Revue. Started in 1913 in the town of Takarazuka, just north-west of Osaka, by a Kansai railroad magnate looking for an entertainment device to improve the profitability of his rail line and spa, the Revue's productions of song, skit, and dance quickly blossomed into major attractions. After 1920 the Revue derived performers from its own new, well disciplined training school of drama, and it flourished, acquiring a new 3,000-seat, hometown theatre in 1924 and a decade later a grand second theatre in the heart of Tokyo.

From 1917 onward other entrepreneurs launched rival all-female revues, mostly in Tokyo, and during the twenties women found more and more roles in their productions, which took inspiration from Japan's own theatrical legacy as well as that of Europe and America. The gorgeous, melodramatic productions, grand-scale song and dance, and performances by highly skilled, seductively androgynous stars drew large and loyal audiences packed with adoring girls and women. Besides offering admired jobs and careers to many women, the productions gave their audiences a respite from the tedium of reality and, in one scholar's wonderfully apt phrase, "a chance to dream of other lives in other worlds."[8]

At least as important in establishing women as publicly visible and widely admired entertainers was the film industry, which blossomed during the twenties in significant part because women replaced male actors in female roles. Famous actors and actresses enhanced the reputations of film makers, who promoted their business by putting their stars on display in variety shows that interspersed snippets of film with song, dance, and live drama. By the late twenties a culture of movie stars had taken shape, and during the thirties successful actresses continued to gain fame and following, their diverse film roles broadening the urban movie-going public's image of women's character and lives.

Under these circumstances it became possible for gifted actresses to move about as never before, as in the case of the talented and energetic Yamaguchi Yoshiko. Born and raised in Manchuria, she began her acting career in the late thirties when the government was prodding film companies to produce "Asian brotherhood" films. Much film shooting was done on location on the continent and at handsome new studio facilities in Manchuria. Yamaguchi, using the stage name Li Hsian-lan and playing roles of beautiful, needy Chinese maidens, starred in several such films, most famously *Shina no yoru* (China Night, 1940). The heroic Japanese naval officer of *China Night* saves Yamaguchi, the beautiful Chinese war orphan, from abuse. Love blossoms, after which the couple goes on to one of three happy or tragic endings, depending on whether the film was being shown to Japanese, Chinese, or Southeast Asian audiences.

As early as the 1920s the increasingly public nature of urban women, particularly their new visibility in the world of entertainment, was reflected in the creation of a largely male-invented caricature, the *moga* or "modern girl." The *moga* was a polyvalent image that for some men revealed the decadence and immorality of "liberated" women, for others their threat to society's health, and for others their seductive appeal as sluts of a better sort. For some women, such as Yamakawa Kikue, the image revealed bourgeois degeneracy; for others, such as Hiratsuka, the *moga* was, potentially at least, a "fashion slave" to men. Other women, however, and some men, found in the image figures who had escaped the "old morals" of the household woman and felt free to deal with life "as their convictions move them."[9]

Magazines for young women, which had proliferated from late Meiji onward, projected an optimistic view of women's prospects.[10] They addressed the many topics that interested their readers, providing a range of appealing materials, as in this summary of contents of a popular 1920s magazine for girls:

> serialized novels, poems, fairy tales, historical tales, detective stories, articles on etiquette, stories praising successful and famous people, humorous accounts, Western arts and fashions.

Contributors encouraged their young readers to persevere, much as other magazines admonished young men. Wrote the author Miyake Yasuko in an article in a 1924 issue of *Shōjo kurabu* (Girls' Club):

> The era in which the girl simply obeys others without exercising her own judgement is gone. You have reached the time when it is considered best to take action based on what you think is right, after consulting with your superior and obtaining advice.

Be tactful but be your own woman. It was, one might suggest, a linking of the upper-class tradition of social sensitivity with the lower-class tradition of doing what needs to be done.

In the political sphere, however, not much changed. The modified restrictions of 1922 did not lead women to further gains at the national level. Once the radical branch of the feminist movement was brought to heel by censorship, surveillance, and police violence, the government saw little to fear in the more moderate lobbying for suffrage. Indeed, more and more politicians and government officials saw some form of suffrage as a right women should have or as a device to elicit women's support for the government and its vision of social betterment. Or at the very least, support for women's suffrage looked like a way to forestall radical feminism. Reflecting that shift in attitudes, during the later twenties a number of bills to allow women a fuller franchise were proposed, and some were sent up for a Diet vote. However, the last such proposal before the Pacific War was killed in the House of Peers in 1931. It was in other legislative areas, notably those of labor law and social policy, that women found their situation modestly improved by government action – not, that is to say, as women per se, but as workers or homemakers.

MINORITIES AND STUDENTS

Much as women sought to improve their condition through political action but disagreed on the relative merits of reformist and revolutionary strategies, several other social groups also began – in varying degree – to evince greater discontent with the social arrangements of the day. *Burakumin*, Koreans, Ainu, and students merit brief notice.

Burakumin. The *de facto* pariah populace of *burakumin* became more active during the 1920s. From later Meiji onward, the persistence of widespread popular discrimination against them had troubled some government officials, who saw in the situation potential for political trouble as well as a real loss of productive resources for the realm. Doubtless their concern was heightened by the first signs of sustained *burakumin* political activism, which appeared from the 1890s onward. In 1913 the Home Ministry helped *burakumin* leaders form a national organization to foster self-improvement and assist in resolving disputes between pariahs and others. However, the benefits were modest, and both the inflation of World War I and the recession that followed it bore heavily on *burakumin* communities, heightening the risk of trouble.

Like some young women, many *burakumin* drew encouragement from the post-1917 global revival of radical thought. In 1922 militant local movements coalesced in the Zenkoku Suiheisha, or National Levelers' Society. Its demands for complete emancipation, economic and occupational freedom, and human dignity for *burakumin* – which legally had been theirs since 1871 – reflected the degree to which their problems were centered not in government policy but in public prejudice, which, we may add, the government did little to overcome. Thus in their organizing declaration, Suiheisha founders identified the center of their problem as the public ridicule they had long suffered and their willingness to tolerate it. "The time has come for the victims of discrimination to hurl back labels of derision ... We must never again insult our ancestors and profane our humanity by slavish words and cowardly acts."[11]

Supported largely by women and young people, Suiheisha branches proliferated, coming to number 703 by 1925. However, strategy disputes among radicals weakened Suiheisha cohesion, and the government moved to neutralize the organization by expanding its own support for older, conciliatory, self-help *burakumin* groups. It also provided pariah communities with token assistance along with heightened police surveillance and control. During the 1930s *burakumin* activists continued to fight back against popular discrimination, but by then the movement had lost much of its impact in the political arena. And in the late thirties, *burakumin* organizations, like labor, feminist, and other groups, mostly threw their support to the government once it was embroiled in a sustained foreign war.

Koreans. More worrisome to rulers than *burakumin* were immigrant Koreans, whose numbers mushroomed during the 1920s and thirties. Huge numbers of Koreans traveled to and from the islands, lured to Japan by reports of manual labor opportunities in mills, mines, and construction projects, and driven out of Korea by rural hardship as a rapidly growing population tried to survive on an agricultural economy that more and more was being managed to meet Japan's domestic food needs.

Those Koreans resident in Japan at any given moment (roughly 1,000 in 1910, 10,000 in 1917, 300,000 in 1930, over a million by 1940, and thanks in part to massive labor conscription, two million by war's end) were mostly crowded into boarding houses and factory housing in mining towns and on the outskirts of major cities. About half of them were illiterate, and most were desperately poor and unaccustomed to urban life. Widespread opinion in Japan held that they were dirty, lazy, quick to anger, and untrustworthy, but also uninterested in union organization or political issues and willing to do foul jobs for meagre pay.

Korean students, by contrast, were viewed as dangerous, the moreso because their numbers also were growing, the 481 of 1915 surpassing 8,000 in 1930, by one account, and reaching 29,000 in 1942. Officialdom recognized that most of them supported the national resistance movements in Korea and that a few had ties to Japanese radical groups. They feared that Korean students and Japanese labor organizers might together succeed in mobilizing the huge immigrant laboring population, thereby threatening domestic order and even Japan's control of Korea.

Those fears, which some panicky or irresponsible officials fanned in the hours after the Kantō earthquake of 1923, greatly contributed to the outburst of vigilantism that within days left an unknown number of Koreans – anywhere from 400 to 6,000 or so – dead. They also prompted officials to seek ways of reducing tension between Koreans and Japanese. Thus a report of 1933 advised that,

the government should educate Koreans in Japan with assimilation policies as the base, try to improve their living conditions and make them pursue their duties as the emperor's subjects. Meanwhile the government should enlighten Japanese to deepen their understanding of Koreans, promote mutual friendships between Japanese and Koreans and lead Koreans to assimilate themselves into Japanese society of their own accord.[12]

As with "uplift" and "assimilation" policies of other conquest regimes, it was a strategy of doubtful promise.

Ainu. The "problem" of *burakumin* and even moreso of resident Koreans was of considerable concern to Japan's rulers. The Ainu were, by comparison, a small and distant concern. Two centuries of sustained interplay between Ainu and the Wajin of Matsumae had by 1850 drawn most Ainu into some degree of engagement with Wajin-controlled fisheries work and trade, which modified the Ainu economy, culture, community health, and life style, disadvantageously for the most part. The Meiji regime's vigorous development of Hokkaido sharply accelerated those trends, and by 1914 little was left of "traditional" Ainu culture or economy. By the 1920s about half of all employed Ainu were poor tenant farmers working land they had acquired in the preceding decade or two, and most of the others worked as laborers in a variety of Wajin-owned enterprises, while a substantial number survived on welfare.

Officials involved in Hokkaido's development, and those concerned with public order and welfare regarded the Ainu as a "dying race," even more destined than Koreans to be assimilated, to become "Japanese" in biological, cultural, and economic terms. Welfare and education policies reflected that perception, but the efficacy of programs was continually compromised by the prejudice and discriminatory conduct that Ainu encountered from many of their Wajin neighbors and workplace associates. Further complicating the assimilation policy were the modesty of resources that government devoted to its programs and Tokyo's greater commitment to Hokkaido's development, even at Ainu expense.

Nor was that government policy entirely welcomed by the Ainu themselves. Many did accept the concept of assimilation and agreed that better education was a key strategy. But some objected to official policies that sought to replace their language with Japanese or that prohibited symbolic traditions such as tattooing and the use of ear-rings. Some objected to the way Ainu culture was treated as a quaint entertainment for tourists or as an artifact for museum display. Others resented the way European and Japanese scholars, spurred by racial theories of the day, tested and measured them to determine their proper anthropometric pigeonhole. Many saw persistent Wajin prejudice and discrimination as basic problems, and others focused on such issues as alcoholism and demoralization among the Ainu themselves, arguing that self-help rather than government help was needed.

By the 1920s small numbers of educated Ainu were beginning to record and celebrate facets of Ainu culture, including songs, legends, and customs, while others found their concerns addressed by the radical thought of the decade. Unsurprisingly these latter, like labor, minority, and female activists elsewhere in Japan, became objects of police attention. In 1930, in a policy comparable to that used with *burakumin*, government officials in Hokkaido collaborated with assimilation-oriented Ainu leaders to establish and fund the Ainu Kyōkai, an association designed to promote Ainu well being in accord with government aims. In 1931 one contributor to the Association's newsletter characterized the Ainu predicament this way:

> Our social existence weakens day by day… [and we are treated like animals.] Moreover, whether we are mistaken for antiques and preserved as anthropological specimens, or have our blood sampled, the fact that we have become research materials for scholars is unbearable for a human being with the slightest degree of personality. Of course, because there are those of us who turn themselves into exhibits to make a living, I cannot very well blame them.[13]

As the decade advanced, the Association addressed issues of welfare and education, made some progress in moving Ainu children into mainstream schooling, and saw more young Ainu go on to advanced education. But the problems of prejudice, poverty, and demoralization persisted, even as wartime social pressure swallowed dissent in the name of the great national crusade.

Male students. Whereas *burakumin*, Koreans, and Ainu were among the emperor's most disadvantaged subjects, young men of "middle class" and finer origins were among his most favored. Yet they too shared in the growing discontent of the day. One problem was that the late Meiji perception of diminished prospects persisted. The school system continued to expand at all levels, and university enrollments, which numbered 9,695 in 1915, grew explosively during the years immediately after World War I, hitting 69,603 in 1930 and 81,999 in 1940.

The expansion was unable to keep up with demand, however, and worse yet, the swelling numbers of graduates discovered that because of postwar recession and then global depression, the employment rate for college graduates was gradually declining and good jobs were few and uncertain.[14] As a student-oriented newspaper put it in 1930:

> Having spent some seventeen years of preparation all the way from grade school through the university and about to enter the "real world," the graduate finds a situation of reckless over-supply and stands on the brink of joblessness, his status of "Bachelor of Arts" having little value.

Unsurprisingly, dissatisfaction with schooling and dismay at grim job prospects made students receptive to the new lines of reformist thought that appeared in the wake of World War I, and the result was an unprecedented level of student activism.

Student groups were notably idealistic, being influenced by radical thought, "left" and "right." Mainly, however, they were socialist, as in the case of Shinjinkai, the "New Man Society" that was founded by law students at Tokyo Imperial University in 1920. For most of the twenties Shinjinkai and other student organizations promoted study and reading groups to disseminate their opinions, tried awkwardly to cooperate with labor unions and radical political groups, and sparred with nationalistic student groups that rose to counter them. From 1928 onward, however, government measures of suppression gradually ended most of the open activism, driving remnants underground. As the Education Minister declared that summer, such an outcome would enable universities to:

> establish appropriate means of guidance, and eliminate the slightest opportunity for the interference of outside temptations. Thus can we nurture healthy, responsible citizens and assure the effectiveness of education.

Doubtless many a parent, teacher, and school administrator, as well as government official, shared his pious hope.

RURAL PROBLEMS

Students, for all their youthful energy and articulateness, proved a minor nuisance to government because of their limited success in building links to other discontented groups, of which rural folk and urban workers were the most politically consequential. Regarding those rural folk, their difficulties during the 1920s sprang in significant part from the shift in government policy away from support of rice prices to efforts at rice-price reduction, which reflected the declining role of rural interests in Japan's political life.

To elaborate, during World War I business leaders, who were trying to counter workers' demands for wage increases, lobbied for abolition of tariffs on food imports as a way to lower grocery prices, and the rice riots of 1918 forced the government's hand. By then the voice of rural landlords in the Diet had weakened considerably as more members came to represent urban constituencies, and following that riotous reminder of the urban public's capacity to wreak havoc on targets of choice, government policy shifted. The resulting measures to control rice prices and promote imports from the colonies depressed farm income during the twenties.

Declines in silk prices and cotton mill wages aggravated the situation, and during the early thirties the Great Depression ravaged the countryside, the damage scarcely mitigated by belated modifications in rice policy. Rural demands for relief multiplied, and organized groups of petitioners descended on Tokyo. "Left-wing" rhetoric flourished in village newspapers, and worried authorities moved to control the situation by intensifying police surveillance and promoting programs of assistance as well as the government-led cooperative movement. Conditions improved during the later thirties, but only modestly: gains due to the industrial boom were offset by military service that took away able-bodied young men. And wartime price controls, fertilizer scarcity, and other complications hindered producer efforts until black markets shifted more of the burden onto city folk.

A longer-term change that was fostering rural tension was the rise of absentee landlordism. Especially in the Kinai region, where other career options were most available, ever more landlords moved out of farming and away from their home villages, but most of them retained ownership of the property they leased out to tenants. In the process they commonly lost interest in maintaining the personal connections or practicing the *noblesse oblige* that had sustained their local prestige and eased village distress in earlier generations. Then the hardships of the 1920s spurred tenant farmers to unionize and demand rent reductions while encouraging yet more landlords (fully three-fourths of whom owned less than one *chō* of land in 1940) to shift discretionary wealth into urban investment.

During the twenties these several factors combined to produce widespread unrest, with tenant disputes growing like topsy, the 85 of 1917 becoming 2,751 in 1926. The number of conflicts increased yet further during the thirties, reaching 6,824 in 1935. Whereas disputes of the twenties had mostly been initiated by groups of tenants demanding rent reductions in more urbanized central Japan, however, during the thirties most incidents occurred in the less urban Tōhoku region. And commonly they were initiated by hard-pressed petty landlords who lacked alternatives to farming and who were seeking to raise rent or oust renters but were being thwarted by desperate tenants who refused to vacate their premises.

Other trends also reveal the worsening plight of the countryside, especially during the depression years. One was an increased rate of emigration. Two others, which merit further comment, were the spread of tuberculosis and the booming trade in rural young women, who were being sold into prostitution by desperate parents.

The rate of tuberculosis infection grew from the Meiji era onward, largely due to the creation of urban work and residence arrangements – crowded, dark, dusty, and ill-ventilated – that favored reproduction and dissemination of the human tubercle bacillus. Most especially the dormitory and factory environments of cotton mills proved ideal sites for the infection of young women, a segment of humankind particularly vulnerable to the bacillus. When they became sick, they commonly were dismissed, whereupon they returned home or went elsewhere, spreading the disease to others.

Nor were official countermeasures effective. Government agencies for public health were focused on other communicable diseases, notably smallpox and cholera, and authorities hoped that Kitasato Shibasaburō's research would shortly produce an anti-TB vaccine. Moreover, many doctors and the general public held to an older view that "consumption" was a hereditary disease and something to be hidden. From about 1910, however, some measures were taken to reduce workplace causes of disease, to establish hospitals, diagnostic clinics, and other treatment centers, to educate the public on the relevant issues of nutrition and housing, and to contain the disease by resort to sanatoria and quarantine.

Those efforts notwithstanding, workplaces and housing remained crowded, and young women in particular continued to sicken and carry the disease elsewhere from textile plants. During the twenties, even as tuberculosis death rates in other industrial societies were rapidly declining, the rate in Japan held at around 200 per 100,000 population, as figure 16.1 indicates. Subsequently, in the later thirties, when military leaders saw TB as a menace to their troop strength, trials of an effective French vaccine began. However,

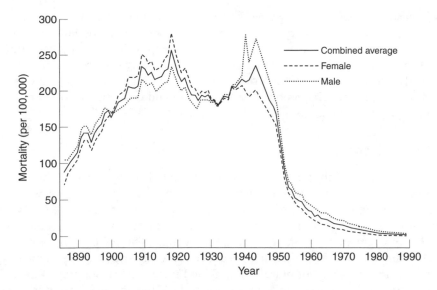

Figure 16.1 Tuberculosis mortality, 1886–1990. The tuberculosis epidemic that plagued Imperial Japan peaked between the two World Wars and was not brought under control until the 1950s, when anti-biotics and closer medical attention became available and housing and labor conditions that favored the tubercle bacillus were modified. *Source*: William Johnston, *The Modern Epidemic, A History of Tuberculosis in Japan* (Cambridge, MA: HUP, 1995), p. 39.

wartime conditions prevented its general utilization and created a state of deteriorating public health, which set the stage for a pandemic that ravaged the country during the catastrophic forties. Indeed, not until the 1950s was the disease finally brought under control thanks to improved public health and the use of powerful anti-biotics, notably streptomycin.

Young women were particularly vulnerable to the tubercle bacillus, and they were even more completely singled out by the prostitution industry, which fed off rural hardship. In the words of a Tokyo investigative reporter describing one Tōhoku family's situation in 1934:

> The father did not sell his daughter willingly. But the family had no rice to eat because of the crop failure. On top of that his wife was pregnant and was afflicted with beriberi, and the moneylenders pestered him every day … So he finally sold his daughter.[15]

Reports such as this troubled authorities, being seen as evidence of government failure, social disintegration, or even as forewarnings of revolutionary upheaval.

Military leaders had reason to be troubled. Many officers and men themselves came from rural homes or from urban families with connections to villages, giving them personal knowledge of and concern about rural suffering. Moreover, troubles at home tended to disrupt the effectiveness of recruits, undercutting army morale and threatening the devotion of troops to emperor and nation. Also, commanders wanted strong, healthy troops, but roughly half of all recruits failed to pass their physical examinations. Although the failure rate was some 5–10 percent higher among urban youth than rural, the folk wisdom enshrined in agrarianist rhetoric envisioned sturdy farm boys as the army's backbone, and rural poverty stood out as an obvious cause of their unhealthiness. Because so many officers shared the view that the urban wealthy were to blame for much of this woe, village distress contributed directly and bitingly to military discontent with civilian leaders and the business elite. It helped shape policy in Manchuria and contributed to the rash of domestic plots and assassinations that marked the 1930s.

URBAN LABOR

Linked to the mainly rural problems of unwanted births, poverty, hardship, unrest, and emigration were the urban problems of low wages, poor working conditions, and labor disputes. From the 1890s until the late 1930s, when wartime pressures exacerbated matters, there was, it appears, a modest but real improvement in working conditions overall. The gains were not equitably distributed, however, in part because disparities were appearing between the situations of more highly skilled male workers employed in such heavy industries as iron works and shipbuilding and the less skilled workers who filled most jobs.

Working conditions. After 1914 skilled workers were in short supply because of the extreme rapidity with which the industrial sector grew, and because neither industry nor government developed labor-training programs sufficient to the day. These workers could – and frequently did – change jobs, whether to advance their technical skills, get better pay, or simply escape a disagreeable workplace. By doing so, however, they left bosses with a scarcity of adequately trained workers, which prompted firms to offer better wages, performance incentives, and fringe benefits in hopes of holding employees for longer periods. In addition, employers gradually articulated work rules that improved shop discipline and efficiency, and while workers commonly resented them, the rules enhanced the productivity of new machinery as it was introduced, enabling companies to provide the better employment packages that helped to hold workers. The capacity to pay more also helped employers minimize or resolve the strikes and other labor actions that proliferated during periods of sharp consumer inflation, such as 1917–20, or job layoffs, such as 1929–31. In short, skilled workers in heavy industry achieved gains in productivity per capita that they were able to translate into better compensation.

Scattered all through the urban economy, meanwhile, were less skilled employees whose wage levels were set, essentially, by reference to the principal alternative job market, which was farm work. For the mainly rural young women who continued to staff the textile industry and who constituted even as late as 1930 over 50 percent of the total factory work force, meagre wages and harsh conditions persisted, only marginally improved by government regulations. That situation sustained rapid employee turnover, which led factory operators to recruit and train replacements continually, thus helping perpetuate low worker productivity and the unhappy conditions that low output seemed to justify. Presumably these operators eschewed the heavy-industry strategy of using better wages and conditions to hold workers because they were much more export-oriented, faced greater overseas competition, and so felt compelled to keep wages, their main cost, as low as possible.

Unskilled men filled many more sorts of jobs than did women, but mines, which remained the most notorious of industrial sites, employed both. Legislation of the 1920s that prohibited underground female labor reduced sharply the number working in the shafts (66,396 in 1920; 4,841 in 1936), and by then the labor-contractor system of supervision was gone. Nevertheless, government regulation and technical advance did little to benefit those who continued to mine. Indeed, work conditions worsened as shafts went deeper and seams grew thinner, becoming hotter and more subject to sudden flooding and collapse. The plight of coal miners was compounded by the fact that Manchuria contained large deposits of coal that could be extracted by strip mining, which was far less costly (as long as its devastating environmental effects were disregarded). Imports from the immense open-pit mine at Fushun served to depress the market value of domestic coal, pressuring domestic mine operators to exploit their labor all the more ruthlessly.

Mine conditions became so grim that during the 1930s Korean immigrants became a major source of mine labor and, as years passed, an ever more harshly driven, forced-labor component. When war escalated late in the decade, the demand for coal increased and in 1939 women returned to the pits. By late in the war they constituted nearly a fifth of the mine force and Koreans nearly a third, but by then mine machinery had deteriorated badly and output per worker had declined sharply (from 200 tons per miner in the mid-thirties to 126 by 1944), with at least commensurate decline in the miners' living conditions.

For most unskilled labor, life was less brutal, but it was still a matter of bad housing, poor food, inadequate health care, and crude entertainments. And it involved great insecurity due to the growing impact of global economic and political disorder. These conditions fostered more vigorous attempts at remedy through organization, protest, and reform, and those efforts acquired a more strident political character as industrialism advanced and more combative forms of socialism and nationalism emerged.

Through the 1920s. Even in the wildly booming economy of World War I benefits were so ill-distributed that labor activism flourished. Union membership rose despite fierce employer resistance and government harassment, with the 3,000 members of ca. 1910 growing ten-fold to 30,000 by 1919. Moreover, industrial strikes proliferated: in 1914 there were 50 with 7,904 participants; in 1919, 497 with 63,137 strikers. These trends prompted politicians and pundits alike to fret about labor's dangerous potential. In 1920 one Diet member, conscious of the linkage between domestic and foreign affairs, warned:

> if postwar international rivalries are characterized as a form of economic or industrial competition, those nations that best resolve the problems between labour and capital will be in the most advantageous position.[16]

Timely preventive reform and intervention would head off "socialism" while enhancing industrial efficiency and hence Japan's international competitiveness. Official discomfort with blatant abuse of children and attempts to qualify for admission to the recently formed International Labor Organization, which was promoting minimum labor standards, reinforced government interest in such a strategy.

During the twenties these concerns prodded officials, especially those in the Home Ministry, to re-examine and update the labor legislation of 1910. Despite bitter internal disagreements, that process slowly yielded a series of acts and revisions of law that attempted to reduce labor-contract abuses, facilitate job-hunting, and foster conciliation of disputes over property, rents, and employment conditions. They also provided modest health and accident benefits, reduced the working hours of women and children, and raised the minimum work age to fourteen.

This factory legislation, such as it was, emerged despite opposition from factory owners, especially the big industrialists. Some tycoons, including Shibusawa Eiichi, were by then arguing that the "beautiful custom of master–servant relations" was no longer adequate and that both labor legislation and a system for orderly labor-management bargaining were necessary. But powerful businessmen in general still resisted unionization and factory legislation, lobbying heavily against them through their employer associations, most notably the Japan Industrial Club (*Nihon kōgyō kurabu*). They asserted that European-style labor relations would not be appropriate for Japan and that their introduction would, contrary to intent, undermine the "beautiful tradition" and curse Japan with the social turmoil and radicalism that was allegedly plaguing Europe.

Upbeat rhetoric failed to compensate for downbeat wages and workplace conditions, however, and workers, unsurprisingly, disputed their bosses' view of affairs. Labor troubles persisted, with job actions proliferating and young women in the spinning industry continuing to flee the mills long before their contracts expired.

Reflecting the increasingly radical thought of the day, more and more workers viewed themselves as members of an exploited class, and they saw unionizing and strikes as proper responses to their predicament. During the sharp industrial recession of 1920–1, one worker declared in a labor periodical:

> I do not believe that vainly shouting violent slogans, distributing so-called propaganda leaflets, and fighting with the police in the streets is the way to bring on the new society. We must storm the citadel of capitalism openly and honestly, brandishing steel, increase our supporters, and strengthen their unity.[17]

Less pugnaciously a metal worker wrote in 1924:

> We are human beings, upright producers, and as humans have various rights. Yet capitalism still treats us as machines, as commodities, especially through the contract and incentive-pay systems ... We have to work like crazy to supplement the low base pay and take home a sufficient income. Then our high output levels are made the new standard, and the unit price is lowered.[18]

To him neither compassion nor love was evident in work speed-ups and pay rates unilaterally set.

The Great Depression intensified labor unrest and radical thought, and in Japan, as in Europe and North America, it spurred more vigorous government attempts to improve the economic climate. When the Hamaguchi government in 1929 tried to head off political trouble by enacting labor legislation to legitimize moderate unionism, an official proponent of the measure warned businessmen that:

> We have entered the era of universal [male] suffrage elections. From now on, the proletarian parties will steadily gain in strength. [We should, therefore] effect a moderate union law while the proletarian parties have yet to make major gains.[19]

In the end, however, business interests, less fearful of red menace than red ink, mobilized their resources and succeeded in thwarting the union bill.

The 1930s. Denied legal redress, workers pursued their interests in other ways. One of the most famous job actions, one in a series of textile strikes during 1930, occurred when women (and a few men) workers at the Tōyō Muslin factory in Tokyo went on strike to protest job layoffs, wage cuts, and wretched working conditions. For two months the women fiercely held their own in the face of harassment by company and government alike, deriving inspiration from socialist rhetoric and the sympathy of other labor unions and women's organizations. As a pamphlet by one proletarian women's group put it, midway through the strike:

> In order to protect first of all their own livelihood, and, by extension, to stem the raging tide of rationalizations which threatens our one million sisters throughout the country, the 3,000 sisters at Tōyō Muslin have been united in strike action for 26 days.
>
> We of the Proletarian Women's League give our unqualified support to this struggle, in order to fulfil our duty to our class, and to defend all proletarian women against starvation.[20]

Ultimately, however, the strikers could not prevail against a management that retained government sympathy while being buffeted by global depression, and their effort ended in failure.

During the thirties the concept of industrial interest-group bargaining lost favor, and the ideal of "harmony" came to prevail, at least at a rhetorical level. Government officials had promoted the ideal of industrial harmony throughout the twenties, and after 1928 that effort intensified as foreign entanglements deepened and domestic tensions and hardships rose. A senior bureaucrat warned in 1932 that social strife was becoming widespread:

> between large firms and small, between financial markets and industrial concerns, between cities and villages, between department stores and small shops, and throughout every other area of society, conflict is becoming an increasingly obvious trend.[21]

To counter that trend, he and others advocated – with only moderate success – broadened government involvement in dispute resolution, relief measures, and oversight of industry.

As the decade advanced and international problems became more prominent, both workers and bosses modified their rhetoric. Proponents of "Japanist" labor unions that favored the notion of labor–management "fusion" in the name of national unity and strength gradually won shopfloor support. By the mid-thirties they were displacing the older unions that had defined labor as an interest group that could rightfully bargain with management on the basis of legal equality. Industrialists, meanwhile, tailored their rhetorical defense of business interests in response to the charges of capitalist greed that came from workers, rural folk, the military, government officials, and intellectuals of all persuasions. They emphasized patriotic goals, denied that self-interest motivated them, and insisted that their profits served the nation. And thanks to their power and connections they succeeded in thwarting most government efforts to intervene in workplace disputes.

As the country plodded further into war during the late thirties, the rhetoric of harmony intensified. Intellectuals became more and more interested in European fascist social organization as a model for Japan to utilize. Thus Ryū Shintarō, an economist and sometime participant in the Shōwa Kenkyūkai discussions that advised Prime Minister Konoe Fumimaro, wrote in 1937 that Japan must "progress beyond the productive power of Japanese capitalism" and that the present-day "laws of Germany and Italy seem to point the way for the future Japan."[22] In much the same spirit, officials espoused "labor–management oneness" and set up agencies to promote it.

Labor problems persisted, however. And more and more regulations, inspired in part by labor shortages in the rapidly expanding industrial sector, attempted to control workers and increase production.[23] According to a report of 1938:

> Entrepreneurs will offer anything as bait to attract workers, from higher pay to payment of worker debts on their behalf. A worker with even a little skill is constantly ready to move and doesn't give full attention to his job ... [When factories need more workers, they] pirate them from both small local factories and other large competitors ... [but because the labor shortage is chronic] the people thus "stolen" are pirated once again.

The desire for harmony evidently had not erased all devotion to self-interest.

Industrial problems of this sort persisted, and around 1941 the officially sponsored national labor organization declared that:

> Labor management should not be a mere exchange relationship in Japan, where the family system is so important, but it should focus attention on the family and respect the family system both in the ideology of the "enterprise as one family" and through family allowances.

It was a formulation that embedded labor relations in the grand Meiji vision of the realm as a family, stable and harmonious under its paternalistic emperor-father. It also conformed to the enduring agrarianist ideal of the self-reliant, household-based, harmonious village as foundation of the *kokutai*. As the energetic agrarianist Tachibana Kōsaburō put it in an essay published in 1935:

> The village community is based on the family structure, and the state is based on both... nothing will suffice to protect the people's true mutual livelihood except village communalism and the family system.[24]

Moreover, the vision of labor–management relations as a family affair found a fitting juridical expression in the family as defined by the Meiji legal codes, which granted great authority to the household head. Company bosses, as legitimately paternal figures, were to regard their employees as their children and treat them with proper affection.

As the country sank deeper into war, more and more skilled workers were drafted. Their replacements – in the end mainly disabled veterans, boys, girls, women, convicts, and forced labor from the colonies – proved even less satisfactory. Shortcomings in workplace efficiency, output, and coordination persisted until American strategic bombers, employing the most up-to-date industrial technology, "solved" the problem by destroying the factories and incinerating the cities.

ARTICULATE CULTURE

During the decades after 1914, even while Japan as a whole wrestled with the political and social ramifications of industrialization, the producers of articulate culture were addressing the same agendas.

Regarding the mechanics of cultural production, the central story is that of growing scale and richness. We noted the burgeoning school enrollments above. In addition, book publishers expanded the size of their printings dramatically and managed, despite government restrictions on "left-wing" thought, to produce 20,000 to 30,000 new titles a year even during the later thirties. By then film makers were turning out about 500 feature films annually plus documentaries, newsreels, and other shorts. The circulation of major newspapers was roughly triple that of 1914 while the roughly 3,000 registered periodicals of 1918 swelled to 11,000. Stage shows were touring the country, and the 3,500 radios in use in 1922 grew exponentially to six million by 1940.

This expansion in cultural output and consumption started closing the gap between avant garde Tokyo and the "old fashioned" hinterland. For one thing the Kamigata region, and Kyoto in particular, revived as a cultural rival to Tokyo. In part it did so by fostering its image as the repository and guardian of Japanese "tradition," and hence of ethnic self, a quality that rulers and pundits celebrated with ever more stridency as the decades advanced. More broadly the expanding cultural production gave expression to a new popular culture and fostered its dissemination throughout the realm. In essence this was an industrial-age, urban, middle-class culture addressed mainly to young adults. It included – along with the spread of radio listening, cinema, stage shows such as the Takarazuka Revue, and popular music – the proliferation of cafés and the appearance of department stores, art exhibits, and exhibitions that displayed and made generally available the creations of "modern civilization" and industry.

With society's increased complexity, the agendas of cultural commentary came to represent more diverse groups and to contain more varied viewpoints, doing so despite the perdurable impulse, which we saw in chapter 15 when examining political discourse, to reduce issues to either/or categories, notably "East and West." But what is perhaps most striking about the articulate culture of this period is the extent to which its creators assumed Japan's irrevocable engagement with the world. Although commentators rarely alluded to the country's new-found dependence on a global resource base, that fundamental change in material circumstance had become an unspoken premise of most cultural discourse, and what was left for debate was the question of how best to handle that worldly engagement.

The analytical categories of Marxism, which adherents treated as universalistic rather than culture-bound, enjoyed great vogue during the twenties. They fostered lively new perspectives on Japanese and Asian history: e.g., on the character of Japanese "feudalism;" on whether the Restoration was or was not a true "bourgeois revolution." They also inspired new interpretations of current social problems and, as a corollary, gave birth to a new "proletarian" literary genre and associated trends in drama and art. During the thirties, however, authorities hammered the "left" into silence, and social commentary came to be grounded almost completely in the East/West ethno-cultural dyad. Especially evident in political discourse, the dyad also informed much other cultural output, with creative artists consciously wrestling with the interplay of "old and new," "East and West." They employed avant-garde styles, articulated notions of what one might call the "counter-modern," and explored creatively the possibilities of their diverse disciplines.

CREATIVE LITERATURE

Creative literature – poetry and literary criticism, but prose fiction in particular – blossomed in the years after the Russo-Japanese war, and it continued to develop vibrantly thereafter, with certain main trends standing out. One trend was the proliferation of newer literary styles; another, the rise of a "mass" or popular literature.

The emergence of a popularly based literature was made possible by the earlier-noted spread of schooling and by the appearance of affordable writings. In particular, inexpensive, mass circulation newspapers that serialized new works of fiction were well established by the 1920s. In addition, low-priced editions of books became available from 1925 onward, after major publishers started producing multi-volume anthologies that sold hundreds of thousands of copies apiece. These developments, which underwrote the literary flowering, also lay at the heart of most critical debate.

Poetry and literary criticism. Poetry, to note it briefly, continued to flourish, with practitioners of older poetic styles, notably *haiku* and *tanka*, still debating proprieties of form and content. During the thirties many poets and their coterie publications favored current literary fashions that included the Dadaism then popular in Europe. Most notably, founders of the Nihon Rōmanha (Japan Romantic School), a movement that aspired to develop an up-to-date, aesthetically sophisticated, distinctively "Japanese" cultural voice, promoted poetry as the literary form of choice. One Rōmanha poet sought to realize "Japanese poetry as something alive today, as [something that] must experience the present." Another commentator saw in the Rōmanha's emergence "the rise to power in Japanese literary circles of poetic spirit."[25] It was a view that accorded nicely with the prominent role poetry had long enjoyed in Japan's literary tradition. And in a way that these authors may not quite have intended, poetry did indeed "experience the present," with poets, like writers of prose, generally producing works that spoke to the day, whether in peace or in war, in ways that were acceptable to the nation's rulers.

Literary criticism, much of it by authors of prose fiction, flourished. Some essays were carried in the partisan coterie magazines, while others were published, much more lucratively, in general interest magazines such as *Bungei shunjū* and *Chūō kōron*, with their broad "middlebrow" circulation. Pundits engaged in "roundtable discussions" (*zadankai*) that usually were amiable in tone. They wrote independent essays (*zuihitsu*), and they carried on heated, even bitter, literary disputes (*ronsō*) that argued the merits of different genres, authors, orientations, and works.

One of the most noteworthy issues in the literary punditry of the day reflected the rise of a popular press. Its rise presented littérateurs with both opportunity and problem: opportunity to prosper as never before by reaching a readership of unprecedented size, but a problem of professional self-esteem. To elaborate, for a long time, and especially during later Tokugawa when *gesaku* flourished, prose fiction had been viewed as a vulgar art, not at all estimable in the manner of poetry or the classical diary. However, Meiji-era literary figures had discovered that in Europe prose fiction was an honored genre, one that addressed the better classes, the literate few. Clearly, to be an honored author in the European manner was preferable to being a despised writer of *gesaku*, and that preference, as noted in chapter 14, found expression during later Meiji in the rise of Naturalist writing, the aesthetic self-consciousness of *Shirakaba* authors, and the appearance of the "I novel," or *shishōsetsu*, the confessional literary style whose gritty "realism" and "truthfulness" were contrasted to the shallow inventiveness and utter implausibility of *gesaku*.

The rise of a broad readership threatened the new-found respectability of prose writers because the general public favored stories that were lively, inventive, entertaining, and emotionally engaging: i.e., in the tradition of *gesaku*. To preserve "literary standards" in the face of this new enticement to vulgarity, during the 1920s critics attempted to articulate a distinction between "pure" and "mass" literature. The former spoke mainly via coterie magazines to the so-called *bundan*, that small, largely self-absorbed world of authors, critics, and refined readers that had emerged in Tokyo before 1914 and flourished thereafter. The latter appeared in serialized form in major newspapers and middlebrow magazines and in cheap editions of books. In practice, the most successful authors wrote for both mass-circulation and coterie publications, their income from the former buying them time to produce works that addressed their fellow littérateurs.

As the 1920s advanced, critics debated the issue of pure vs. mass literature, mainly arguing over definitions and the relative worth of the two types. By the later thirties the two categories were sufficiently fixed so that separate literary prizes were awarded annually to honor the best "pure" literature (the Akutagawa Prize) and the best "mass" literature (the Naoki Prize).

During the thirties, as writers increasingly felt impelled to cope with the political pressures of the day, literary disputes included some particularly savage exchanges between critics of differing persuasion. With more and more authors speaking in support of government policy, however, others were forced to adapt or fall silent lest police, public, or publishers take notice. An outpouring of chauvinistic literary commentary accompanied the glorious early months of the Pacific War, but by 1944–5 the quantities were shrinking and the tone growing more shrill and uncertain as reverses and calamities piled atop one another until unarguable defeat silenced even the most perfervid believers.

Prose fiction. While critics busily chattered, the authors of prose fiction continued building on Meiji precedents, particularly those of the Naturalist and *Shirakaba* writers, who did so much to create the "I Novel," with its single-minded attention to the narrator and his perception of affairs. Natsume Sōseki's premature death in 1916 robbed the world of a remarkable talent, but a number of the late-Meiji writers remained active through the twenties and thirties. Nagai Kafū, "the last of the *gesaku* writers," produced several beautifully elegiac stories set in pre-industrial Tokyo.[26] Shiga Naoya completed *An'ya kōro*, one of the most celebrated I Novels. And several other *Shirakaba* and Naturalist authors continued to write.

The well known Tanizaki Jun'ichirō, whose writings pigeonhole no more easily than Sōseki's, was perhaps the most versatile literary figure of the day. He is celebrated mainly for his fictional works, historical and contemporary, short and long, which embodied his "taste for the perverse, the sinister, the ingeniously wrought." He was also, however, a playwright, critical essayist, translator of foreign works, producer of a modern reading of *Genji Monogatari*, poet, letter-writer, and creator of a film score. During his early years Tanizaki was an enthusiast of European literature, but after fire destroyed his "western-style" house in Yokohama during the 1923 earthquake, he abandoned the Tokyo literary scene for the Kansai, where he came to celebrate the superiority of Japanese culture. In 1927 he declared:

> I am not sure just how to describe it, but I can sense in the Orient something
> special and different from the Occident, not only in literature and art but in

everything, from politics, religion, and philosophy down to the happenings of ordinary daily life and the small details of clothing, food, and shelter.

His new appreciation for things Japanese and his sense of the East/West issue were captured with particular effectiveness in *Tade kuu mushi* (Some Prefer Nettles, 1929). In the story a pseudo-cosmopolitan young man gradually loses interest in his stylish, modern wife in favor of her father's doll-like concubine and the images of puppet theatre she evokes, especially when the unhappy couple visits her father's old fashioned house in Kyoto.

Tanizaki's literary omnicompetence was shared by the less well known Satō Haruo, who was noted for his explorations of "unconscious drives, strange mental states, and irrational events" and for his stress on "freedom of the imagination and the primacy of art."[27] Satō wrote diverse types of poetry, works of literary criticism, translations from Chinese and European authors, a couple of I novels, works of fantasy and mystery, futuristic and psychological novels, and scripts for plays and a motion picture. He also managed to create scandal in the *bundan* by taking up with, and later marrying, Tanizaki's actress-wife.

During the twenties "socialist realism" emerged, despite official harassment, as the most powerful literary trend of the day. In its rhetoric it championed literature for the masses and thus seemed to pose an ideological challenge to the advocates of "pure" literature. In practice, however, socialist realism appears to have functioned as another sectarian literary style. New coterie magazines carried poetry, short stories, and critical essays in which authors attempted to view affairs from the perspective of the struggling worker and to treat them in terms of class conflict. Perhaps because the writers commonly were young people of privileged background, however, their works rarely rang true. Nor did the doctrinal restrictiveness of the genre allow much creative freedom. Still, works by Kobayashi Takiji, particularly his *Kani kōsen* (The Factory Ship, 1928), spoke so compellingly about the hard lives of workingmen as to attract public interest and official displeasure. A government roundup in 1932 sent Kobayashi into hiding, but he was captured in 1933. Probably because he failed to cooperate with sufficient alacrity in the rehabilitative *tenkō* policy then being applied to "thought criminals," he died from police torture. Within a year of his death the badly battered proletarian literary movement stalled, not reviving until 1945.

A number of women authors were caught in the assault on proletarian writers because they employed much the same literary styles as males, producing proletarian works as well as I novels. Nevertheless, they were regarded by the *bundan* as a group apart, "women writers" (*joryū sakka*), producers of "women's literature" (*joryū bungaku*), which, critics averred, was notable for its "sentimental lyricism and impressionistic, non-intellectual, detailed observations of daily life."[28] Despite that pigeonholing, literary women thrived. With the existence of a rapidly growing female readership, major newspapers began carrrying serialized fiction and other regular features aimed explicitly at women. And by the mid-1920s some fourteen women's magazines – including *Fujin sekai*, begun in 1906; *Fujin kōron*,

1916; *Shufu no tomo*, 1917; *Fujin kurabu*, 1920 – were, by one estimate, selling in aggregate over a million copies per monthly issue. The presence of this burgeoning market prompted many writers, particularly female authors, to cater to its interests.

Many women, however, seem to have found the proletarian genre most well suited to their interests and needs, as, for example, Nakamoto Takako. During 1932, between stints in detention for left-wing activism, she wrote "Tōmosu Daini Kōjō" (The Number Two Tokyo Muslin Factory), a serialized story of rising class consciousness among women workers at a textile plant. As the thirties advanced, Nakamoto and others, like male authors, faced jail time and underwent *tenkō*, in some cases eventually providing active support for the war effort.

Meanwhile, a number of the most celebrated women writers exploited the autobiographical quality of the I Novel to recount the hardships and disappointments of their lives and loves. Thus Hayashi Fumiko invested her *Hōrōki* (A Vagabond's Story, 1930) with a lively narrative style, a fine sense of irony, and a tone of bemused but compassionate appreciation for the travails of life among the lowly. Much to her delight the work became "an immediate and unexpected best-seller" that subsequently went through numerous editions.

The redoubtable Uno Chiyo may, like Satō Haruo, be less well known for her writing than for the scandals of her life, but her pieces captured the spirit of the I Novel so well that a woman critic of the mid-twenties could comment:

> The greatest flaw in works by women is that they do not strip themselves completely bare. But Uno, I feel, is exceptional. The women she creates are slovenly and deceitful, but they do not make me feel the least bit uncomfortable, perhaps because I can sense behind them the author's own candor and honesty.[29]

One of Uno's affairs provided grist for her *Irozange* (Confessions of Love, 1935), a compassionately ironic narrative of an artist friend's clumsily unsuccessful attempt at suicide.

During these decades works of historical fiction enjoyed popularity. Most notable were stories by the distinguished army doctor and author Mori Ōgai, who crafted two dozen works of historical fiction and biography during the decade prior to his death in 1922. The appeal of such works suggests how fully even the Tokugawa era had receded into a forgotten past. In early Meiji it had been an age to be repudiated; by the 1890s it constituted a heritage that aged survivors wished to preserve; by the 1920s it was a distant past to be recreated and thereby made accessible to the curious, the nostalgic, those seeking to rediscover the "real" Japan.

The mass market for literary works also envigorated the literature of mystery and imagination that Izumi Kyōka had favored. Rooted in stories and story-telling customs that dated back to Nara-period *setsuwa*, the genre also drew inspiration from the analogous traditions of Europe and America as seen in the works of Edgar Allen Poe. Poe's works so inspired Hirai Tarō that he adopted Poe's name, in the form of Edogawa Ranpo, and from 1925 on wrote mysteries and crime stories, often using European models, along with children's stories, essays, and other pieces. Akutagawa Ryūnosuke drew more heavily on domestic tradition, notably tales of the *Konjaku monogatari* collection, to write short works dealing with obsession and mystery (such as *Rashōmon* and *Hell Screen*), works of satire (such as *Kappa*), fairy tales, and critical essays. His writings, as the Akutagawa Prize for "pure" literature suggests, were – and still are – celebrated for their lucid and elegant style as well as their provocative insights into life.

Reflecting the rise of industrial science and technology, this literature of mystery and sleuthing quickly broadened to include science fiction. Edogawa himself crafted some short stories in this vein, as did Satō Haruo, and during the 1930s a number of other authors added to the corpus. Their works explored biological manipulation, bizarre gadgetry, environmental catastrophe, fantastic travel, Utopias, androids, Martians, and other futuristic elements, mingling them with quotidian and consciously "traditional" elements and commonly subordinating the "science" to some social agenda such as crime detection or political intrigue. These stories foreshadowed a postwar boom in the genre, but at the time they stood on the margin of the literary world.

The *bundan* was much more centrally affected by the "modernist" creative surge that swept up writers and artists in post-World War I Europe. Japanese writers translated works of the Dadaist, surrealist, and other modernist authors and tried their own hand at the styles. Inspired by the likes of James Joyce and Marcel Proust, they established their own new coterie magazines to promote new types of writing under new stylistic rubrics, notably the New Sensationalist School (*shin kankakuha*) and New Psychologist School (*shin shinrigakuha*). Yokomitsu Riichi was one of the most dedicated and successful practitioners of modernist writing, standing steadfastly against the proletarian insistence on social agenda and moral judgment and firmly for literary experimentation and the handling of style so as to evoke the sensations of life itself.

Most modernist writers, however, moved on to other styles because they found modernism unsatisfying or because of the changing political climate. Itō Sei, for example, emerged as a modernist during the thirties, but as the China war intensified, he began to favor the I Novel, seeing it as more purely Japanese. Writing in wartime, he reflected prevailing opinion when he declared:

> Japanese literature is in essence now undergoing a great process of purification. Never before in modern Japanese literary history has the pure voice of the race, the will of the race to fight, and the loyal spirit of the race been crystallized as they are in contemporary works of literature.[30]

It was a rhetoric he came to regret rather shortly.

Other modernist authors found more subtle ways to change course. Kawabata Yasunari, who was an early advocate of literary modernism, has been called "chief theorist" of the New Sensationalist School. Like others, however, he moved beyond it to develop a distinctive style celebrated for its verbal economy, powerful evocativeness, and finely honed sensibility. Establishing his reputation as a modernist with *Izu no Odoriko* (The Izu Dancer, 1926), he went on during the thirties to produce a number of profitable pot boilers along with more serious works, most notably the celebrated *Yukiguni* (Snow Country, initial version 1935–7). It is the non-story of a Tokyoite's dalliance at a hot spring resort, in which Kawabata evokes with the sparest of prose an extraordinarily haunting feel for physical scene and human sensibility. During the war he wrote a few works moderately supportive of the war effort but mostly revived his literary output after peace returned.

During the early thirties the government crackdown on left-wing activism had crippled proletarian literature, while other writers found the newly fashionable modernism alien and unsatisfying. A number of young authors, inspired by German romantic writings of the nineteenth century, discouraged by the crackdown at home, and dismayed by general trends of the day, including the rise of what they considered a vulgar popular fiction, began to advocate production of a Japanese literature that would achieve a "cultural renaissance." In 1935 they formed the earlier-noted Nihon Rōmanha and called for "the exaltation of the artistic disposition," and resurrection of "traditional artists" as means to "make manifest what is most sublime."[31] In following years the Rōmanha grew rapidly, coming to include a good many former Marxists, who found sanctuary in its rousing literary ideals.

By the late thirties most writers, whatever their stylistic preferences, were joining other intellectuals in giving at least passive support to their government's ventures abroad. Mindful of the choices that the law presented to "thought criminals," to left wingers most especially – namely, reorient (*tenkō*) or risk torture and worse – authors generally were able to redefine their positions. Some, such as Itō Sei and Satō Haruo, did so more vigorously; others more quietly, as Kawabata and Tanizaki, who cultivated their interest in Japanese classical letters and arts while offering little overt literary support to the war effort.

As the China Incident of 1937 deepened, finally growing into the Pacific War in 1941, the various literary groups were subsumed under government-sponsored organizations set up to foster the production of patriotic gore. Some writers found themselves being drafted into military service. Others had to continue working to survive. Some went abroad as special correspondents for Japanese newspapers and magazines while others were sent abroad by the government to build alliances with the intelligentsia in areas under Japanese control, most notably Southeast Asia. Like writers in the other belligerent states, most lent their talents to their government's cause until terminal disaster transformed the context of discourse.

THEATRE AND FILM

Live theatre.   In the hinterland local traditions of puppet theatre and *nō* continued to enjoy support, but the urban avant garde increasingly treated the forms as museum pieces. *Kabuki,* on the other hand, along with *rakugo* and other story-telling arts, remained vigorous, and newer theatrical forms – *shinpa, shingeki,* variety shows, and "all-girl revues" – acquired more visibility. Playwrights continued to translate and produce European dramas and write their own, with plays, love tragedies in particular, being staged most commonly in the romantic *shinpa* style until the 1920s. During that decade, however, the more realistic *shingeki* gained favor as serious drama while Takarazuka-style revues occupied the terrain of escapist romance. *Shingeki* plays reflected literary styles of the day, and through the thirties they and their European-inspired social realism dominated the "serious" stage.

One of the day's most influential playwrights was the versatile Osanai Kaoru. Back in 1907 he had established the coterie magazine *Shinshichō* (New Tides of Thought), mainly as a vehicle for drama theory and criticism and the introduction of European theatre. He translated and staged European dramas and wrote several of his own. In 1924, amidst the wreckage of post-earthquake Tokyo, he established Japan's first technically modern theatre, the Tsukiji Little Theatre. He also wrote Japan's first plays for radio presentation in 1925 and two years later prepared the first dialogues for talking film.

Osanai envisioned the Tsukiji Little Theatre as a place where *shingeki* could escape the influence of *kabuki,* with its gods, demons, and implausibilities, much as "pure" literature sought to escape the *gesaku* legacy, and thus become "the new national theatre of Japan." The enemy of *shingeki,* he declared in 1926, "is the traditional theatre, that is, *kabuki* drama … We must destroy *kabuki* patterns [and] create our own distinct theatre art, new and free."[32] It was a view that continued to inspire avant-garde dramatists well into the post-1945 era.

Cinema. The film industry reflected many of the trends seen in drama and literature, and by the 1930s the fields of prose, drama, and cinema were becoming entwined. Primitive, hand-cranked motion picture machines had come to Japan in the 1890s, and film making began in 1897. Silent film gained substantial popularity in the big cities before World War I, with *benshi* (live narrators) voicing dialogue and explaining the film while musicians added more aural context. The film-with-*benshi* genre was so quickly accepted because it slipped effortlessly into the long, indigenous tradition of *etoki* picture narrators, *nō* and *kabuki* choruses, puppet chanters, and *rakugo* story tellers. By the 1920s a handful of large film companies and scores of independent producers – mostly in Tokyo until the earthquake destruction of 1923 prompted their relocation to Kyoto and vicinity – were producing hundreds of feature films a year for *benshi* presentation in city theatres. In addition traveling projection units toured the countryside, but even during the thirties they were still using "ancient, often hand-cranked machinery and showed only the poorest and oldest silent films."[33]

Cinema, like the new drama and literature, was thus essentially an urban cultural form, but as such it flourished. By 1925 Japan had 813 movie theatres, all showing silent films, about half of which were domestic in origin, and that year they entertained 155 million paying customers. Ten years later, when two-thirds of the films were domestic creations and over half of them talkies, the theatres numbered 1,586 and counted over 200 million admissions.

In Japan, as elsewhere, talkies did not triumph easily. *Benshi* and musicians resisted displacement as best they could; the new technology was costly, and getting it to work right was a challenge. In 1932 a film critic, reviewing the newly released drama *Shanghai*, wrote of the character played by the popular actor Ōkōchi Denjirō, that he

> assumes a formal posture and speaks. We would like to think that the voice is coming from [Ōkōchi's] moving lips. Regretfully, though, we are inclined to think that it comes from somewhere around his backside, or perhaps around his navel.[34]

In time, happily, sound systems improved. And Ōkōchi, who gained great popularity in such comic and semi-comic roles as the "tough, cynical *rōnin* whose nihilism is more endearing than threatening" in the Tange Sazen film series, went on to a distinguished and lucrative acting career.[35] His memory was subseqently preserved at Ōkōchi Sansō, a lovely garden-museum overlooking the Katsura River and Tenryūji in Kyoto.

By the later thirties talkies had largely ousted *benshi* and musicians from the industry despite their resistance and the costs of retooling production facilities and theatres. As of 1940 Japan contained a well developed studio system, with ten major film companies (including Shōchiku, Nikkatsu, and Tōhō) complete with stables of directors and stars, studio lots, theatre chains, and fierce corporate rivalry.

Film content, meanwhile, was strongly shaped not only by foreign cinema, but also by *kabuki*, *shinpa*, and *shingeki*, which initially provided most subjects, actors, modes of acting, and principles of dramaturgy. Some of the most popular film topics were taken directly from *kabuki*: forty-five versions of the celebrated drama *Chūshingura* (the "47 *rōnin*") were filmed between 1907 and 1925 and additional ones in later years. Even the classic format of the *kabuki* program, a *jidaimono* together with a *sewamono*, was commonly replicated with a cinema double bill, a tandem screening of a period piece (*jidaigeki*), which commonly was a "samurai movie," and a contemporary work (*gendaigeki*). By the end of World War I, however, *kabuki* influence was waning as actresses replaced female impersonators (*onnagata*) and as more "realistic" swordplay, speech, acting, and sets became established.

Much as pundits spoke of articulate culture generally in dyadic terms of Japanese and Western, so the cinematic categories of *jidaigeki* and *gendaigeki* were perceived as "Japanese" and "modern," with the year 1868 marking the boundary between the two. In fact, however, cinema rapidly combined foreign and domestic attributes to achieve that "combination of East and West" (*wayō setchū*) commonly demanded by pundits. *Jidaigeki* remained the predominant type, but by 1930 film content included an array of genres devoted to dramatic tale telling, comedies, and sentimental love stories, as well as social commentary film inspired by 1920s socialist thought and *shingeki* drama.

The films being screened, whether of domestic or foreign origin, reflected and fostered the urban culture of the day, with its *moga*, its mass literature, and its racy consumerism. In 1929 they prompted one disgruntled gentleman to complain that "the modern 'talkie' or 'movie' consists almost always of leg-shows, crime, wild parties, cocktail drinking, and vulgarity." This "Westernism," he warned, "seems to be eating up all our good sense and to have destroyed all our better taste."[36]

His fears were soon eased. After the early-thirties' crackdown on radicalism, film makers toned down their offerings. Mostly they produced less censorship-prone human interest films that commonly explored family issues and life among the lowly, or escapist films whose heroes, Robin Hood-type samurai or gangsters (*yakuza*), triumphed over their evil tormentors and set matters aright.

During the later thirties, as the war in China intensified, authorities regulated cinema ever more strictly, defining criteria for "national policy films" (*kokusaku eiga*) and pressuring and enticing film makers to produce accordingly. The rulers urged them to do more shooting at studios and locations on the continent, sometimes in collaboration with Korean, Manchurian, and Chinese film makers, and to produce morally uplifting and inspirational propaganda films – such as the aforementioned *China Night* – that featured the glorious war, "Asian brotherhoood," and "Japanese spirit." In October 1940 an essay in the middlebrow *Chūō kōron* magazine explained the logic of government policy this way:

> Dramatic art must forget the old individualistic and class attitudes and must begin to realize that it has a cultural rôle to perform in the total program of our new national consciousness. Actors are no longer to serve a class but…the whole national entity…For this reason, the concentration of culture in the big cities should be eliminated.[37]

In that spirit the government upgraded the film projection equipment being used in the hinterland, thus finally bringing up-to-date "talkies," albeit largely works of propaganda, to the whole country.

In response to official pressure and inducements, film makers produced more serious works, with the comedic treatment of *jidaigeki* giving way to themes of *bushidō* honor, duty, and sacrifice; films highlighted the special virtues of "Japaneseness," as seen in art, architecture, and social norms. Some film makers, resentful of the meddling by amateurs, resisted this pressure by diluting almost beyond recognition the propaganda content of the commissioned films they produced. Others turned out nostalgic works on the Meiji era or screen adaptations of literary works, such as Uchida Tomu's 1939 film *Tsuchi* (The Soil). It was based on the powerful realist novel *Tsuchi* (1910) in which Nagatsuka Takashi explored the grim life of poor villagers. Such resistance notwithstanding, however, by and large the film industry of wartime Japan, like its counterparts in the other industrialized nations, ably produced motion pictures of mixed quality that affirmed government policy in the name of one or another high principle.

MUSIC AND ART

In the realm of musical arts the years before 1914 saw basic developments that were fleshed out in later decades. In visual arts change after 1914 was much more striking. The Meiji era had introduced oil paintings and the associated dyadic *nihonga/yōga* construct, as noted in chapter 14. After 1914, so much more complexity was introduced to the art world that the basic inadequacy of the *nihonga/yōga* dichotomy was unmasked, and that opened the way to a more creative universalism that blossomed later, in the wake of the Pacific War.

Musical arts. Much of the European musical legacy (genres, instruments, notation) had been introduced to Japan by 1914, and the process of combining indigenous and alien had begun. After World War I composers consciously sought to meld European and domestic musical sensibilities. Silent film provided a venue for musical experimentation, with the producers of accompanying music employing foreign and domestic instruments and musical forms eclectically to achieve the desired effects. Some composers employed the pentatonic scale, which closely resembled scales used in indigenous song. They used European and Asian instruments together and mixed foreign and domestic melodies. Musicians also improved their mastery of foreign genres. Choral and orchestral groups formed, and in 1930 the first fully Japanese-produced grand opera, Verdi's *La Traviata*, was presented at the Kabukiza in Tokyo. Within a few years a domestic opera company was putting on regular productions at Hibiya Hall, adjacent the Imperial Palace.

At a more popular level, as noted above, *kabuki* and its music continued to thrive, being supplemented by music halls – in Tokyo's Asakusa entertainment district most notably – that produced eclectic programs of song and dance. In schools choral singing flourished, with choral groups in women's schools largely singing American songs of the Stephen Foster sort while male choirs sang a European repertoire. And radio began supplementing the local festivals found throughout the country, bringing more varied musical fare to the hinterland. As war intensified during the later 1930s, military music flourished and stirring marches, replete with heroic imagery and chauvinist braggadocio echoed from bandstands, loudspeakers, and radio.

Visual Arts. In the fields of visual art, the story was somewhat more complex. In architecture, industrial-age technology continued to impose itself. The recently adopted brick and stone construction fared poorly in earthquake-prone Japan, but by the end of Meiji steel-framed and reinforced-concrete types of construction were emerging as preferred building methods, and they encouraged a spare, utilitarian style with minimal surface decoration. After World War I avant-garde architects of Europe and America, such as the Bauhaus group in Germany, exerted great influence, most especially on public urban construction. Domestic architecture retained its basic wood-plaster-tile format, but "western-style" rooms (*yōma*) with board floors, swinging doors, sofas, chairs, and tables became common among the urban well-off. And new forms of interior decorating, plumbing, and kitchen equipment appeared ever more widely.

Painters found their choices less firmly bounded. When Europe slid into war in 1913–14, some Japanese art students escaped the turmoil there by returning home, bringing back their newly acquired knowledge, which included awareness of the anti-realist trends, such as Fauvism and cubism, then beginning to sweep the continental art scene. Those trends continued in post-1918 Europe, when the even newer Dadaism, surrealism, and other avant-garde styles of visual (and literary) expression were being introduced to an embittered European intelligentsia that saw the certitudes of older realist cultural output as symptomatic of the elite arrogance that had culminated in four years of unspeakable suffering, unprecedented destruction, and incalculable slaughter.

In Japan, however, those older "realist" forms of art so bitterly rejected by European proponents of the new were the very heart of *yōga*. So the expressionist assault on realism constituted a repudiation of *yōga* by artists whose own works came to be categorized as *zen'ei bijutsu*, or avant-garde art. As a corollary the relatively straightforward Meiji-era Japanese/Western cultural dyad was transformed into a messy triangular field of artistic argumentation.

Moreover, many of the avant-garde painters were themselves found "guilty" of emulating European artistic precedents, which opened the way to energetic mutual criticism. Thus in 1924 the young Dadaist Murayama Tomoyoshi attacked a number of his peers for slavish followership. Most of their work, he lamented,

> is an imitation of spineless French imperial salon style boiled down from Picasso and Braque. There's nothing more shameless than this for the Japanese painting world … Oh mates, how far will you be slaves? It's as if you had been born slaves for generations.[38]

For Murayama, as for many in these debates, the issue of artistic creativity was thus grounded in the broader ethnic question of how to develop an art for the day that would be distinctively Japanese.

Within this context of variegated and conflict-ridden artistic production, the quest for individual expression and professional success gave rise during the twenties and thirties to a vigorous outpouring of richly diverse canvas art. As in the literary world, so in that of visual art, the twenties saw a flourishing of socialist realism as well as the appearance of Dadaist absurdism and related nihilist tendencies. And by the thirties the scientific fantasy of constructionism was appearing, and surrealist expressionism was coming into vogue.

One artistic sub-genre of these decades that merits particular attention is *bijinga* ("beautiful-woman art"). In social terms it was a facet of the growing visibility of women, but it also reflected the discourse on East and West and the quest for ethnically gratifying styles of artistic expression. A long-established Chinese artistic genre, and one best known in Japan from Edo-period courtesan prints, *bijinga* gained a new popularity from late Meiji onward.

One source of inspiration was the European "nude," a recently discovered art form that failed to elicit much Japanese favor, perhaps because it seemed more akin to the coarser forms of Edo-period erotic art (*shunga*; "spring pictures") than to the refined ideal of *bijinga*. Its particular shortcomings notwithstanding, the nude did demonstrate that "modern" art treated women as an important subject, so painters and print-makers continued to produce *bijinga*.

They created works for independent sale and provided illustrations and cover art for women's magazines, many of them portraying, "women of the bygone era in traditional costume and hair style."[39] *Bijinga* artists also introduced new stylistic techniques and imagery, however, some using the new ways as vehicle to celebrate the "oriental," as in Fujishima Takeji's 1924 series on women titled *Oriental Style*. "With a command of Western materials," he wrote, "I am trying to paint something distanced from the smack of things Western."[40]

Others aimed at a less ethnically defined goal. Thus a 1925 magazine illustration by Takabatake Kashō (figure 16.2) employed painting techniques eclectically to portray a globally generic schoolgirl whose "romantic yearning concealed by a melancholy air" suggests dreams that reach well beyond the world of "good wife, wise mother."[41] With the growth of women's schooling and female literacy, the market for images of progressive young women blossomed, and artists portrayed more adventurous, more individualized, and more self-possessed young women, in the process enriching the *moga* imagery of the day and commonly achieving that "combination of East and West" that critics sought.

On the other hand, insofar as *bijinga* gave expression to nostalgia for a feminine ideal that was being lost to the *moga* and all she represented, it shared the sensibility that welcomed historical fiction, prompted authors like Tanizaki to extol things Japanese, lamented the fate of the village community, denounced "Westernization," and celebrated the artistic heritage of Japan. Yanagi Sōetsu encouraged the preservation of folk arts most successfully, in 1926 cooperating with others to launch the Nihon Mingei Kyōkai (Japanese Folk Craft Association) and a decade later to establish a folk craft museum in Tokyo. There examples of ceramics, textiles, lacquerware, rope work, metalware, and myriad other craft objects were assembled, preserved, and displayed.

Even as Sōetsu and others labored to preserve Japan's "traditional" arts, *nihonga* itself was changing, influenced by trends of the day. By late Meiji some painters of *nihonga* were utilizing *yōga* techniques, and during the decades after 1914 water-color art acquired yet more variety. Print artists, too, continued to diversify their art. Wood-block carving remained the preferred technique, but artists experimented boldly, giving rise to the *soi disant* "New Print," whose innovative styles served to "combine East and West," as in the spare, stylized prints, often black and white, of Hiratsuka Un'ichi

Figure 16.2 Schoolgirl, by Takabatake Kashō, 1925. This illustration for the young women's magazine *Shōjo gahō* suggests the aspirations, uncertainties, and romantic idealism that the changing times encouraged among schoolgirls. The Takarazuka Revue also fed, and was fed by, those sentiments. *Source*: Mariko Inoue, "Kiyokata's *Asasuzu*: The Emergence of the *Jogakusei* Image," *MN* 51/4 (Winter 1996): 442.

(figure 16.3), the boldly rough-hewn prints of Munakata Shikō, and the soft, almost lyrical prints of Saitō Kiyoshi. After the Pacific War the works of these print artists would play a prominent role in the global art world as exemplars of "modern Japanese" artistic taste.

By the late thirties the army's military ventures were receiving artistic attention, and as war deepened, the government pressed artists into service along with other intellectuals. Some three hundred artists produced official war paintings, mainly *yōga*, which seemed more "realistic" and appropriate. Initially it was redolent with the images of national heroics until battlefield reverses led artists to present the horrors of combat in a gritty, ghastly

Figure 16.3 Old home of Koizumi Yakumo, by Hiratsuka Un'ichi, 1948. In this monochrome print of a town street scene, Hiratsuka uses single-point perspective to good effect even as he evokes "Japanese tradition," in particular the strength of domestic privacy and the ideal of intimacy with "nature," through the architecture, the closeness of entryways, and the neatness of the street with its open drain running beneath entryway flagstones. The town, however, is Matsue and the residence, now a museum, briefly that of Lafcadio Hearn ("Koizumi Yakumo"), Meiji-era foreign resident, teacher, "modernizer" of Japan, and explainer of things Japanese to the English-speaking world.

manner that has rarely passed the desk of the military censor. It did in this case, however, evidently because the censors felt that it conveyed effectively the grim, courageous sacrifice that soldiers were making and that civilians should therefore support to the bitter end.

[17] DRIFT TO DISASTER (1914–1945)

CHAPTER SYNOPSIS

THE DIPLOMACY OF DISORDER
DIPLOMATIC PROCESS
EMPIRE AS RESOURCE BASE: THE
1930s

INTO THE GLOBAL MAELSTROM
UPPING THE ANTE, 1939–1942
PAYING THE PRICE, 1943–1945

By the 1930s Japan was much larger, much more powerful, and culturally much more active than it had been in 1914. Thanks to striking growth in schooling, cinema, radio, other forms of communication, and socio-geographical mobility, the gulf between city and countryside, between Tokyo elite and rural everyman, seemed to be closing. As society and economy grew more elaborate, however, intersecting lines of social tension multiplied, reflecting thorny issues of class, status, gender, ideology, and institutional location. Social cohesion weakened and discontents multiplied and grew more fractious, which elicited more energetic efforts to maintain order and clarify communal values or "Japaneseness."

Even as life at home grew more complicated, worrisome, and unmanageable, Japan's leaders found the international order also growing more perplexing. The process of industrialization, with its associated shift from a domestic to a global resource base, drew Japan ever more deeply into the realm of international markets and politics. It was doing so, moreover, even as the Meiji-era imperialist order in Asia was disintegrating, giving way to a time of escalating diplomatic uncertainty and improvisation in which the initiatives of Japan's own leaders and would-be leaders contributed signally to the growing difficulty and danger.

THE DIPLOMACY OF DISORDER

By 1910 or so, as suggested in chapter 13, many Japanese observers had concluded that their country was making excellent strides in situating itself securely relative to both the "West" and "East Asia." The former accomplishment was evidenced in treaty revision and military–diplomatic triumphs; the latter, in the extent to which Asian, and particularly Chinese and Korean, reformers turned to Japan for model and guidance. With World War I and the collapse of the imperialist order in East Asia, however, regional order and the vision of a progressive East Asian ecumene rapidly disintegrated, their passage ill-concealed by the flutter of diplomatic agreements that dotted the teens and twenties or the government propaganda, academic rationalizations, and earlier-noted rhetoric about a "new order" that grew pronounced as the thirties advanced.

By then the outside world appeared far more hostile, much less manageable, and more deeply intrusive in domestic life. It complicated life not only directly as a set of increasingly difficult "foreign problems," but also indirectly because the domestic issues of most consequence, notably rural hardship, urban workplace conflicts, and business difficulties, were to an unprecedented degree shaped by global political and economic conditions. In consequence debates about seemingly domestic problems – unions, labor legislation, agrarian affairs, restless minorities, the alleged menace of socialism, liberalism, and materialism, the threat to *kokutai* and ethnic self – all became deeply entangled in questions of foreign policy and Japan's proper role in the world, East Asia most particularly.

Perhaps the vision of an East Asian ecumene was in any case destined to collapse in the face of nationalistic divisions, much as the vision of a Western or, more modestly, European ecumene repeatedly dissolved into war and slaughter. In any case, its collapse was assured by the narrowly self-serving criteria that shaped so much of Tokyo's actual policy throughout the period 1914–45 and by the generally heavy-handed and oftimes brutal implementation of that policy. The resulting failure of policy makers to forge a stable East Asian ecumene, or otherwise to assure Japan's access to the global resource base that its industrial character required, undercut attempts by intellectuals to fashion an image of Japan's proper place in the world, a place that would fit "the trends of the times," as phrase-makers liked to put it.

Instead, politicians and pundits alike came increasingly to perceive of Japan as isolated, unfairly excluded from the charmed circle of the Powers, whose white racial character had been reaffirmed with particular clarity in the years around World War I. That sense of isolation exacerbated domestic tensions and reinforced the desire for firmer control of East Asia and for articulation of a rationale to justify that control.

DIPLOMATIC PROCESS

Turning again to narrative, the Chinese revolution of 1911, which unseated the Ch'ing, threatened to rupture the imperialist order in China. However, the Powers, having a shared interest in minimizing the extent of change, were able to work together in support of the relatively accommodating strongman Yüan Shih-k'ai, even assembling a major international loan to prop up his regime in 1913. After the Europeans became bogged down in their own quarrels, however, that stabilizing context was lost and the process of political change in China grew much more disorderly, providing Tokyo with unprecedented challenges and opportunities. Successive cabinets launched initiatives to expand Japanese influence in China, particularly in Manchuria and environs, as well as in the Pacific. In the process they broadened Japan's resource base but also deepened foreign resentment and added complications to domestic politics.

To elaborate, the terms of the Anglo-Japanese Alliance gave Japan's leaders pretext to enter the European war, and they chose to do so because of the opportunities it had suddenly opened up to army and navy leaders. Army brass had long viewed adjacent continental regions as the area of key strategic importance and Russia as the primary foreign rival, a view reflected in the two earlier wars and in ongoing policy in Korea and Manchuria. Participation in the war against Germany would give them opportunity to seize German colonies on Shantung Peninsula, notably the port of Tsingtao, thus strengthening their position in the region.

Naval leaders saw things differently. Following the stunning victory off Tsushima in 1905, in which Japan's battle fleet destroyed twelve Russian capital ships and several destroyers and other vessels at the cost of three torpedo boats, Japanese commanders came to view the oceanic regions south of Japan as the preferred realm for extension of national influence because of their richness of resources and because success there would redound mainly to the navy's credit. However, American naval leadership, burdened since 1900 with the task of maintaining American imperial access to the Philippines as well as Hawaii, concluded from the outcome at Tsushima that the Japanese navy was the main threat to their Pacific dominion, and they planned and war-gamed accordingly. For the naval leadership in Tokyo, therefore, the American navy became a primary challenge, and the acquisition of mid-ocean bases a desirable objective.

When war erupted in Europe in August 1914, Tokyo found itself with an unexpected opportunity to advance the interests of both army and navy by simply seizing the German territories in Shantung and the west-central Pacific (Micronesia). As Foreign Minister Katō Kōmei put it at the time, participation in the war would provide "the opportunity to sweep up bases in Eastern waters and to advance the Empire's position in the world."[1]

Wartime diplomacy.   With London's reluctant acquiescence, Tokyo declared war on Berlin, and Imperial forces promptly seized the Kaiser's assets in China and the Pacific. Naval units secured Micronesia, pleased to control territories that lay between Hawaii and the Philippines. As an internal navy memorandum put it, the islands of Micronesia could

> fill a most important position as a link between Japan and the East Indies, the Philippines, New Guinea, and Borneo, ... [thereby serving] as stepping-stones to the treasure houses of the southern regions.

Diplomats subsequently secured European acceptance of Japan's presence in the island chains due north of those German colonies that Australia and

New Zealand had seized. After the war these arrangements were fitted into the League of Nations' system of "Mandates," which prescribed rules for governing newly acquired colonies.

Developments in China were much more important, at least in terms of the next twenty-five years. There, as it became apparent in late 1914 that the Europeans were fully occupied at home, Tokyo began applying policy initiatives reminiscent of those earlier used in Korea. Government leaders presented treaty proposals, most notably the Twenty One Demands of January 1915, that offered material assistance to the regimes of Yüan and others in return for greater access to raw materials and diverse other concessions, some of which entailed further inroads on Chinese sovereignty. They then negotiated accords with other Powers (including Russia in the summer of 1916 and the United States late in 1917) that secured some degree of international acquiescence in the new arrangements.

These initiatives scored some gains, mainly commercial, but they also provoked outbursts of Chinese resentment and contributed to heated political infighting at home. Then the Russian Revolution in 1917 and Soviet negotiations to end Russian participation in the European war led to allied invasions of Russian territory that were intended, more or less, to recommit Russia to the war against Germany and, if all went well, to crush the Bolsheviks. That scheme enabled Japanese military commanders, acting with unprecedented disregard for the opinion of civilian authorities in Tokyo, to commit large forces to the Siberian portion of the allied venture. Their hope was to acquire the northern half of Sakhalin Island and, in some ill-defined way, expand Japan's role in continental Northeast Asia. The armistice in 1918 deprived this whole interventionist enterprise of diplomatic legitimacy, but Japanese military commanders refused to withdraw when the other Powers did, sitting tight in Siberia despite international criticism and pressure from higher authorities in Tokyo.

Other developments were also muddying the diplomatic waters. In 1917 Chinese leaders had declared war on Germany as a step toward renegotiating earlier treaty concessions to the Powers and as a means of countering Japanese influence during the anticipated peace negotiations. Spokemen for Korean national interests also tried to advance their cause by lobbying among the Powers and in 1919 by mounting massive protest demonstrations against the Japanese colonial administration. Reliable statistics are unavailable but in those demonstrations millions of Koreans participated all across the peninsula and in Manchuria, which led to an armed crackdown, the arrest of 26,000 or more, and an unknown number of deaths, perhaps in the thousands. Meanwhile the racially discriminatory policies of Australia and the United States were offending cognizant Japanese and prompting Tokyo to call for an international declaration of racial equality. By 1919, in short, the diplomatic scene was far more messy than it had been five years earlier.

The 1920s. In several venues – the Versailles Conference to settle issues left over from World War I, the Washington Conference of 1922 to negotiate new military and diplomatic agreements in the Pacific–East Asian region, and bilateral Sino-Japanese and Russo-Japanese negotiations – diplomats resolved many of the outstanding issues by 1923. However, a complicated and intransigent set of foreign-related problems still faced Japan's leaders as they struggled to rebuild Tokyo after its destruction by earthquake that September.

Closest to home, authorities in Tokyo had rejected the 1919 demands for Korean independence. Nitobe Inazō, academic, diplomat, and international explainer of things Japanese, provided an appropriate rationale for that rejection by employing ideas that echoed the "Westerner's" catechism for the Orient:

> with a firm conviction that Japan is a steward on whom devolves the gigantic task of the uplifting of the Far East, I cannot think that the young Korea is yet capable of governing itself.[2]

So in Korea the underlying issue of hated alien rulers remained, scarcely mollified by Tokyo's less repressive colonial policies of the 1920s. Indeed, the hatred was worsened by the continuing economic exploitation, the persistent ill will between Japanese and Koreans, and the savage police, mob, and media attacks on Korean residents in Japan during the panic that followed the Kantō earthquake.

Other intersocietal problems also persisted. Despite Tokyo's seizure of the moral high ground on racial equality, and despite Chinese support for the cause at Versailles, their view was rejected, primarily at the behest of American and Australian delegates, and a few years later further discriminatory legislation was enacted in both countries, most notably the American immigration bill of 1924, which explicitly proscribed Japanese entrants. Finally, the Siberian Expedition, not fully resolved until 1925, had only deepened Russo-Japanese distrust, overlaying the older great-power rivalry with ideological tension regarding Soviet communism. Moreover, the episode badly embarrassed the army leadership in Tokyo, laying up domestic resentments and professional frustrations for the future.

In China, meanwhile, Japan's military and commercial advantages had become greater than ever, despite the return of Tsingtao to China in 1922, and so had the resulting hostility. Chinese ethnic consciousness, which had been called into widespread existence by a century of humiliation at foreign hands and by consequent ideological mobilization, was being skillfully harnessed by the nationalist movement that Chiang Kai-shek was gradually taking over from its founder, Sun Yat-sen. By the summer of 1928 Chiang's armies had swept northward across China, defeating rival warlords from Canton to Peking, reunifying the country and asserting its right to sovereign independence. As his forces advanced, they had sporadic run-ins with foreign troops, including Japanese. And by its nature his movement was beginning to pose a serious threat to a range of foreign commercial and diplomatic interests, most fatefully those in Manchuria.

Chiang's successful consolidation of power brought Japanese leaders, and especially those with the deepest commitment to Japan's continental position, face to face with the implications of the piecemeal changes that had been undercutting the imperialist order since 1914. In particular, arrangements made by the Powers at the Washington Conference, together with a number of *ad hoc*, bilateral adjustments, foreshadowed the dissolution of the treaty system that had assured Japan's access to Chinese raw materials and markets. Those actions also suggested that the Powers were prepared to sacrifice Tokyo's interests to accommodate a resurgent China. That this trend jeopardized the Japanese position in Manchuria was obvious; that it ultimately threatened the rest of the empire, particularly Korea and Taiwan, was clear to anyone familiar with East Asian history and conscious of the deep Korean hostility toward Japanese control.

In short, Chiang's success, together with the burgeoning Chinese national consciousness that undergirded it, threatened to undo core achievements of the revered Meiji era, much as foreign demands of the 1850s and 1860s had threatened basic arrangements that late Tokugawa leaders had ascribed to the sacred founders of the *bakuhan* order. Accordingly, in a mood akin to the *sonnō jōi* activism of the 1860s, those with the greatest stake in the preservation of Meiji triumph, notably military men and those ideologues most devoted to notions of imperial virtue and Japan's Asian mission, viewed the future with alarm and devised increasingly radical and risky strategies to forestall calamity and advance their cause.

The shape of things to come was prefigured in June 1928 when middle-ranking officers of the Kwantung Army assassinated Chang Tso-lin, the Manchurian strong man. In preceding years Kwantung Army leaders, working mainly through organs of the South Manchurian Railway, had developed a substantial economic investment in Manchurian mining and commerce, and they and Chang had managed to collaborate to mutual advantage. However, as Chiang Kai-shek gained strength, Chang became more deeply embroiled in Chinese warlord politics, which threatened the Kwantung Army's intention that Manchuria remain detached from the rest of China. So he was slain, the assassins hoping that their actions would prod superiors in Tokyo to adopt more ambitious policies to separate Manchuria from China and that Chang's heir and successor would prove a more malleable collaborator. Tokyo, however, chose to repudiate and punish the offenders. Worse yet, the heir proceeded to recognize Chiang's regime as the legitimate government of China, thereby linking Manchuria more closely than ever to a unified China. Furthermore, he fostered Chinese railroad and harbor development that challenged Japanese dominance in regional trade.

The onset of global depression in 1929 then added a major new cause for alarm. In terms of foreign relations, the central problem of the depression was its effect on textile exports, which paid for so much of Japan's steadily growing raw material imports: whereas silk and cotton goods had constituted about half the country's exports in 1913, they had swollen to about two-thirds by 1929.

However, silk prices had started dropping in the mid-twenties as cheaper rayon goods became available. Then the depression slashed by two-thirds the value of the remaining silk market, devastating the Japanese countryside and complicating trade policy. Concurrently, the primary export market for cotton goods, which was China, was becoming problematic. Cotton mills there, especially those operated by Japanese firms in the treaty ports, were cutting into it, and soon those Japanese mills, too, began to be threatened by vigorous Chinese boycotts of Japanese goods. By the late twenties the boycotts were prompting Japanese textile manufacturers to demand that their government "send troops to China."[3]

The concern over trade was heightened when Chiang's government began negotiating with the Powers to recover tariff autonomy. That endeavor threatened to erode Japan's China market even further once the domestic textile industry within China was able to expand under the shelter of tariff barriers and the boycott of Japanese products. In May of 1930 Sino-Japanese negotiations yielded a compromise on the tariff issue, defusing it for the moment, but for Tokyo the broader trajectory of affairs remained worrisome.

The 1930s. By 1930 these several real and anticipated reverses in foreign affairs had combined with domestic difficulties to create in Japan a mood opposing any further signs of "capitulation" to foreign "demands," and the effects of that mood soon became evident. Most immediately a newly negotiated agreement on American, British, and Japanese naval limits was widely seen in Japan as injurious to the nation's security and esteem, and the Hamaguchi cabinet, which had negotiated it, came under severe criticism from an opportunistic alliance of out-of-power Seiyūkai rivals, proponents of greater naval strength, and alarmed patriots. The naval agreement was ratified in October 1930 in the face of acrimonious opposition, and the protests culminated in November in the Prime Minister's mortal wounding by an indignant young civilian.

Meanwhile plotting among military officers and civilian extremists was intensifying, most importantly among officers of the Kwantung Army, including the brilliant but stunningly impolitic Lieutenant Colonel Ishiwara Kanji. In September of 1931 Ishiwara and his fellow officers launched a violent military conquest of Manchuria – an area larger than Britain, France, Germany, and Italy combined. They overran it in a few months and established the state of Manchukuo, a client regime under close army control. They were able to do so despite Chinese resistance, noisy international protests, and half-hearted attempts at containment by leaders in Tokyo. Starting in 1933 Kwantung Army officers employed diverse, dubious tactics to extend their influence into adjoining regions of northeast China in a semi-coordinated attempt to expand the resource base and market area of the new Manchurian industrial state that they were building as rapidly as possible.

A statement of October 1931, reportedly given by Ishiwara to his fellow officers to justify their newly initiated conquest, touches several of the concerns exercising politically conscious Japanese of the day.

> In Japan there is no world view, no world policy at present. We have no administration that can carry out Japanese interests in the world. Since the World War it's just been a case of the millionaires and profiteers seeking to preserve the status quo. Everywhere people just look out for themselves. Some want money, some want medals, others want titles. That's the situation in Japan today.

That's why the cry for a "Shōwa Restoration" has been raised! But before trying to reform Japan we must solve the Manchurian problem. If the army turns aside it won't be just a case of throwing away Manchuria; we'll be forced back to the Japanese territorial limits at the beginning of the Meiji period. Let the government and central army headquarters do what they will, the Kwantung Army is going to carry out its sacred mission. We must reach a basic solution to the Manchurian problem, even if temporarily it means giving up Japanese nationality. With firm decision on this policy, the only way is to advance together.[4]

If the old, internationally sanctioned, imperialist order were dead, a new autarchical form would take its place, with or without consent of the incompetents in Tokyo. And once that was achieved, Japan's larger task could be addressed. As Ishiwara put it a few months later:

It is only by bringing about Japanese-Manchurian cooperation and Japanese-Chinese friendship that the Japanese people can become rulers of Asia (*Tōa no ōsha*) and be prepared to wage the final and decisive war against the various white races.

And rationales for this venture were easily available, as in this English-language apologia of 1932:

Is it too extravagant to say that these half-dozen different races of Orientals now gathering in Manchukuo may be mixed and fused in due course and develop a freshly vigorous type of nation, as has been done on the North American continent?[5]

Inclusivistic rhetoric notwithstanding, little in the Kwantung Army's *modus operandi*, particularly its policies of land acquisition and colonial labor exploitation, really encouraged the growth of an East Asian racial/cultural ecumene capable of countering that of the "Westerners." A better analogy would have been European emigrant dealings with indigenes of the Americas, Africa, and Australia.

Indeed, whatever the intent of ideologues of East Asian brotherhood, the main thrust of Japanese continental policy had become a *de facto* attempt to "Balkanize" China, thereby transforming the older East Asian configuration with its large China and small Japan into a new configuration with a small China and large Japan. To that end those making actual policy worked to establish one or another form of Japanese control in Manchuria, Mongolia, and the adjacent provinces of China proper. And to make that control permanent, they promoted – to only modest effect – Japanese immigration to the region and "assimilation" of the indigenous populace into Japanese culture. It was a Herculean task, probably impossible under any circumstances, and shortly ruined by the extension of warfare in new directions.

EMPIRE AS RESOURCE BASE: THE 1930s

What Kwantung Army leaders could and did do with considerable success was build an industrial economy to serve their political purposes. The "millionaires and profiteers" whom they most despised were the *zaibatsu*, the giant industrial conglomerates that had emerged during preceding decades, so when they created Manchukuo and began developing their own vision of an autarchic industrial order, they purposely excluded major *zaibatsu* from participation. They preferred their own system of entrepreneur–government collaboration on the ground that,

> In view of the evils of an uncontrolled capitalist economy, we will use whatever state power is necessary to control that economy.

On the government side that policy involved, most notably, the Kwantung Army, South Manchurian Railway, and Bank of Chōsen; and on the entrepreneurial side, select industrialists, most famously Ayukawa Yoshisuke, whose company, Nippon Sangyō Kabushiki Kaisha (Nissan) became the prime collaborator with the Manchukuo regime. Under the aegis of these institutions, total Japanese investment in Manchuria rose from 1.6 billion yen in 1931 to 3 billion in 1937 and further in the next few years. Mining efforts yielded gold and other minerals, a sharp increase in coal output, and a doubling of iron ore production. Manufacturing initiatives doubled pig iron production, created from scratch a steel industry that produced 430,000 tons in 1937, and erected other industries that produced cement, chemicals, and diverse other products.

Ishiwara and others might well derive satisfaction from their industrial achievements in Manchuria, but it was also clear that their chosen diplomatic strategy of empire building was facing far greater obstacles than had that of Meiji leaders. Nevertheless, in part because the industrial powers, Japan included, were trying to cope with global economic disorder and political distrust by erecting tariff and other trade barriers against one another, the strategy of empire building retained its appeal and showed results in terms of international trade.

To elaborate, by 1930 Korea and Taiwan provided nearly two-thirds of Japan's imported foodstuffs, including four-fifths of rice imports and two-thirds of sugar. They also provided oil, minerals, and lumber. Karafuto yielded lumber and pulp, maritime products, and coal, and during the thirties it became a major source of petroleum. The former German colonies in Micronesia provided phosphates for fertilizer, explosives, and other uses, together with copra and sugar, which Japanese entrepreneurs and settlers produced on coconut and cane plantations. Whereas colonial commerce had been about 10 percent of Japan's total overseas trade in 1913, in 1929 it was roughly 20 percent, and by the later 1930s, fully 25 percent.

During the 1930s, as the Kwantung Army overran Manchuria and extended its influence into northern China, more of Japan's leaders came to view more and more of Asia as potential or quasi-colony. Whereas government policy had earlier spoken of Japan (including Korea) and Manchuria as a collaborative unit, in October 1933 cabinet leaders expanded the area to include China, resolving that:

> Our goal is to realize concert and mutual help between Japan, Manchuria, and China under Imperial leadership and, in this way, to secure

permanent peace in Asia and contribute to the promotion of peace throughout the world.[6]

Foreign trade reflected this empire-building trend. The value of trade with Europe declined in relative importance while that with Asia rose sharply, as table 17.1 reveals. Asia was especially important as an export market, but it was also providing essential raw materials, notably foodstuffs from the colonies, coal and iron from Northeast Asia, and oil, iron ore, rubber, and vegetable fibers from Southeast Asia. Because of the rapidity of Japan's industrial expansion, however, North America continued to play a major role as a source of raw cotton, petroleum products, lumber, iron, steel, copper, fertilizer, and machinery. It also remained a key export market for silk which, despite its sharply reduced price, was still an important hard currency earner because its production required almost no imports, in contrast to cotton goods and most other fabricated items.

By 1936 Japan had largely recovered from the depression, and its imports of machinery and raw material had grown substantially. The American silk market remained depressed, but exports to Asia (63 percent of all exports that year) helped offset the trade deficit to North America. So much of the gain from Asia was plowed back into the expansion of industry in Manchukuo and environs, however, and into the ceaseless expense of imperial expansion and rule, that the overall trade balance remained in the red, though sharply less so than in the late twenties. Moreover, very little of the overall economic growth translated into betterment of the general public because so much consisted of increases in war-related production.

Foreign trade had thus become more centered in Asia and in empire. It had also become more industrial in character, with two-thirds of imports being raw materials while finished goods declined in volume, save for technically complex machinery and motor vehicles. Exports had become predominantly manufactured goods, with textiles, largely cottons, being of lessened importance but still constituting 58 percent of total value in 1936. The textile exports were supplemented by an extraordinary array of consumer goods as well as growing quantities of machinery and electrical

Table 17.1 Foreign trade by select regions, 1893–1936

Year	1893	1913	1936
All Countries	174	1,511	7,226
Asia (all)	64	773	4,200
(Korea & Taiwan)	–	149	1,769
United States	34	311	1,450
Europe (all)	68	367	638
(United Kingdom)	33	156	220

Note: Figures in millions of yen; exports plus imports.
Sources: Extrapolated from the more complete table in William W. Lockwood, *The Economic Development of Japan, Growth and Structural Change* (Princeton: PUP, 1954), p. 395.

equipment. Whereas Japanese vessels had carried about 50 percent of foreign trade in 1913, by the mid-thirties they carried nearly all of the expanding colonial business and about 70 percent of the country's other overseas trade.

As a proportion of overall national production, foreign trade was growing but remained modest. By one estimate it rose from about 6 percent in 1890 to 15 percent by 1914, holding at around 20 percent during the twenties and thirties. However, it consisted of materials critical to the general economy, not luxuries for the privileged classes. By 1936 Japan was obtaining from the colonies and elsewhere the following:

20% of rice and beans
35% of fats and non-fossil oils
60–80% of iron and steel materials
90% of superphosphate fertilizer
100% of cotton, wool, and rubber.[7]

Moreover, about 75–80 percent of petroleum came from abroad. The dreams of empire builders notwithstanding, significant portions of these necessities – and other statistically less noticeable current needs, to say nothing of yet-to-be-discovered future needs – could not be obtained from an Asian empire, no matter how big or well managed. For better or worse, industrial Japan was infrangibly tied to its global resource base.

The deepening Japanese inroads into China during the mid-1930s provoked more and more Chinese outrage. In 1937, public anger finally forced Chiang Kai-shek to abandon his established policy of trading space for time: yielding concessions to the Kwantung Army while readying his own forces for the struggle and, in the interim, attempting to suppress the growing Chinese Communist movement of Mao Tse-tung. Because of this policy shift, in July of that year a minor collision between Japanese and Chinese troops near Peking (the Marco Polo Bridge Incident), escalated willy nilly into all-out war. Chiang's troops were unable to hold their own, but negotiations repeatedly failed, and over the next three years fighting resulted in gradual Japanese conquest of most of northeast China, the Yangtse River region, and coastal enclaves south to Indochina.

Chiang managed to survive, and during 1940, as the conflict ground on indecisively and as Europe was again dissolving into war, Japan's frustrated leaders were concluding that they must modify their policy. They could settle their China venture satisfactorily and prepare themselves for whatever was to emerge from the newest European catastrophe, they decided, only by bringing Chiang to his knees. To that end they must isolate him from outside supporters, whether Soviet or Anglo-American, and assure themselves sufficient raw material to do the job. How best to go about those conjoined tasks, however, was unclear.

INTO THE GLOBAL MAELSTROM

In many ways, as chapters 15 and 16 have shown, the decades to 1940 were the most vibrant in Japan's entire history, thanks to possibilities embedded in industrial technology and social organization and the global intellectual engagement that came with it. These possibilities had depended, however, on the immense energy boost that Japan, like other industrializing societies, gained from the use of fossil fuels, and by the 1930s the nation was encountering painful complications in establishing a global resource base that would assure it the requisite fossil fuels and associated raw materials.

Until 1939 those complications were largely confined to East Asia despite the global scope of the Great Depression, the intelligentsia's penchant for grand theorizing about Japan and the world, and the noisy diplomatic bruhaha that surrounded the Kwantung Army's conquest of Manchuria in 1931–2 and the fighting that erupted in 1937. In the summer of 1939, however, a cluster of developments substantially globalized the context within which Japan's leaders debated policy. Over the next two years international complications so escalated that in 1941 those leaders resolved to solve their "China problem" and address the broader global situation by challenging the United States, Britain, and other European Powers for domination of the western Pacific and all of Asia south and east of Mongolia. The disposition of Siberia they left contingent on the outcome in those other regions. In consequence of this radical expansion in the field of strategic planning, the disorderly and opportunistic longer-term Japanese empire-building activity in East Asia became linked to the much more recent conquest activity of Adolf Hitler. In the process it transformed the separate turmoil of Europe and East Asia into the global maelstrom of World War II.

In their expanded enterprise Japan's war planners of 1941 hoped that rapid military gains would lead to an acceptable negotiated settlement. In practice, however, military success only bred ambition that silenced all talk of negotiation. Then reverses in the latter part of 1942 gave rise to military obduracy that precluded any serious efforts at a diplomatic settlement. From 1943 onward military reverses multiplied, which did spark feeble Japanese efforts to seek a settlement, but those same reverses gave enemy leaders less and less reason to entertain any sort of compromise and more and more opportunity to punish Japan severely and rearrange the East Asian political map to their own satisfaction.

In the end, Japan's leaders induced their subjects to fight to exhaustion. Only when obscene amounts of irreplaceable natural resources had been squandered, only when uncountable millions of men, women, and children of myriad nationalities lay dead, maimed, and missing all across Asia and the Pacific, only when Japan lay in ruin, its navy and merchant marine sunk, its army crippled, its economy a shambles, its populace hungry and wretched, and its cities (see figure 17.1) burned to the ground, two of them reeking of

Figure 17.1 Nagasaki after the atomic bombing. Photographs of fire-bombed cities reveal comparable scenes of utter devastation. The atomic blasts were different in their lack of immediate forewarning, but primarily in their longer-term destruction of health and social well-being. *Source*: William Craig, *The Fall of Japan* (New York: The Dial Press, 1967), p. 144.

radioactivity – only then did military leaders acknowledge their failure and the war finally end. *Sengoku* at its worst was not even the palest foreshadowing of what had transpired.

UPPING THE ANTE, 1939–1942

In 1939 events far and near combined to begin the reorientation of strategic thinking in Tokyo. The conflict that had erupted at Marco Polo Bridge, which Japanese proponents had envisioned as another short, victorious war, continued to drag on. Chiang Kai-shek had escaped defeat and was refusing to capitulate, while Chinese guerrilla resistance in the countryside and popular hostility everywhere confounded Japanese attempts to consolidate the areas they purported to control. The burden of prosecuting the war was also injuring efforts to industrialize the empire and, worse yet, was straining and distorting the domestic economy. From 1937 onward it forced the treasury to export gold to pay for imports, and by 1939 it was creating scarcities of civilian goods and producing hardships that were fomenting more and more discontent with government performance and prompting deeper disputes over both domestic and foreign policy.

Global complications. The China quagmire not only created problems at home; it also was helping to embroil Japan in greater difficulties abroad. Least serious at the moment was a collision with the British. For decades they and the Japanese had collaborated, however uncomfortably, in the maintenance of imperialist "rights" in China, but in May 1939 a minor police incident in Tientsin led to a harsh confrontation between Japanese military forces and local British authorities. The collision made it clear that prosecution of Japan's war aims was hardly compatible with preservation of Britain's imperial concessions in China. The incident did not escalate, however, because other developments deterred both sides. London became preoccupied with the aggressive maneuvering of Nazi Germany, which culminated in Hitler's September invasion of Poland and Britain's consequent declaration of war against the Third Reich.

Events also drew Tokyo's eyes away from Tientsin. In July Washington notified Tokyo (in response to Japanese extension of the war into southern China) that it was abrogating its treaty of trade and navigation. Although not an immediate problem, the decision meant that after six months the US could unilaterally halt all commerce with Japan, thus depriving the Tokyo leadership of its single most important source of oil and metals and thereby threatening its capacity to maintain industrial production, to say nothing of waging war on the continent.

Of much more immediate concern, a major military confrontation that had erupted in May pitted the Kwantung Army against powerful Soviet armored forces at Nomonhan on the western border of Manchuria. During a summer of large-scale warfare Japanese units were severely mauled, with casualties numbering some 18,000. And the army's tactics, strategy, and equipment were thoroughly discredited, to the particular dismay of militant officers.

While Soviet firepower was sobering Kwantung adventurists, Soviet diplomats were confounding Tokyo leaders. For three years the German-Italian-Japanese Anti-Comintern Pact had given Tokyo a nominal link with Berlin against Moscow, but the Russo-German Non-Aggression Pact of August 1939 stripped Tokyo of that diplomatic fig leaf. It revealed, just when Tokyo badly needed a military counterpoise to Moscow and just when the Anglo-American powers were displaying more resolute hostility, that Japan's one powerful diplomatic ally lacked reliability. Coming atop so many other problems, that embarrassing discovery toppled the government and spurred the Kwantung Army to arrange a settlement at Nomonhan. Combined with the evidence of growing Anglo-American antipathy and, most importantly, the Nazi conquest of continental Europe, the diplomatic fiasco and military humiliation of 1939 led Japanese leaders into basic reconsideration of their foreign policy as a whole.

For two years this general situation persisted – an unwinnable war in China, increasingly difficult domestic conditions, and a global scene growing ever more chaotic and unpredictable – and Tokyo's policy twisted and turned as leaders argued fruitlessly over strategic choices. The heart of their problem, as seems clear in retrospect, was that they could not prevail in China. However, military leaders had too much self-esteem and institutional pride invested in the enterprise to retreat. Moreover, the fear shared by many of them, probably with justification, that the loss of China would ultimately mean loss of the entire empire, stiffened their resolve, depriving the government of almost all space for diplomatic maneuver.

Tokyo vs. Washington. Maneuver room was further narrowed by foreign actions and attitudes. In a story of escalating move and counter-move that has been told too often and too well to bear repeating here, Tokyo extended its war-making into French Indochina with the dual intentions of isolating Chiang Kai-shek and improving its own access to the raw materials essential to a sustained war effort. American leaders, alarmed at Hitler's successes in Europe and wishing to preserve Southeast Asian rubber, oil, metal, and other resources for themselves and anti-Nazi forces, tried to stymie the further extension of Japanese power, hoping thereby to keep Tokyo's armies bogged down in China if they refused to withdraw.

These conflicting strategic designs of Tokyo and Washington were quickly wrapped in legitimizing rhetoric. In Japan talk of a "new order" for East Asia grew into rhetoric about a Greater East Asia Co-Prosperity Sphere (Dai Tōa Kyōeiken). It was touted as Japan's contribution to a post nation-state system of regional spheres of domination: Japan leading Asia; the United States with its Monroe Doctrine dominating the Americas; Germany over Europe; the USSR supreme in the Eurasian heartland – or maybe split between Germany and Japan.

Washington invoked a different rhetoric. From the time of Woodrow Wilson leaders there employed the phrase "national self-determination" to define a key plank of their foreign policy. Because Washington had long since tabooed such self-determination within its own jurisdiction, the phrase's application elsewhere maximized the chance that the United States, with its immense area and resources, would emerge as the world's largest and most powerful industrial state for the foreseeable future.

The rhetorical postures of both governments addressed the basic industrial-age issue of global resource base. Tokyo's concept of regional spheres did so directly. It presumed (incorrectly, it appears in retrospect) that most, if not all, the resources needed by each regional hegemon could be found within its own sphere, freeing each of dependence on the others. The Washington advocates of national self-determination dealt with the issue on a global scale through the notion of the "Open Door," the insistence that merchants in all nation-states should have equal legal access to trade everywhere. It was a position the United States had advocated for decades: it not only favored traders based in resource-rich America but also was an economical strategy for insisting on American access to global trade opportunities while leaving to others most of the cost of establishing and militarily enforcing the claimed trading "rights."

These two visions of the future, both securely anchored in perceived national self-interest, were scarcely compatible. American rhetoric, when applied to

East Asia, was unacceptable to Tokyo. It could only mean that Japan must remain a small island state, that Koreans could legitimately demand independence, and that China could justifiably insist on changes in the political status of Taiwan and Manchuria. These changes ultimately would enable an industrialized China to tower over all other states in East and Southeast Asia, Japan included. Whether such a China would then subscribe to the American vision was not an issue that Washington had to address in 1941.

Tokyo's notion of regional spheres was equally anathema to Washington, its own Monroe Doctrine notwithstanding. Most immediately, Tokyo's policy and rhetoric suggested an Asian future that Washington could not welcome because of its implications for trade. Even more troubling was the linkage of developments in East Asia to those in Europe. Whatever the nature and scope of Adolf Hitler's ambitions, American leaders clearly preferred a Europe divided into small nation-states to a unified behemoth, especially one characterized by the vicious illiberalism of the Third Reich. Even if Anglophone ethnicity did not induce Washington to favor London over Berlin, Hitler's tactics and goals were intrinsically obnoxious to American leaders, who became especially displeased with Japan when Tokyo appeared to abet the Hitlerian project.

In particular, the September 1940 tripartite "Axis" pact between Japan, Germany, and Italy – which was clearly, if not explicitly, intended to deter Washington's involvement in the fighting in Europe or Asia – upset American leaders. It presented Washington with the classic threat of a two-front war, the prospect that had seemed to face Tokugawa leaders back in 1808, with the British at Nagasaki and the Russians in Ezo. American leaders, like bakufu officialdom then, found the threat thoroughly alarming. When Chiang Kai-shek learned of the new Japanese alliance with Germany and Italy, he noted in his diary:

> This is the best thing that could have happened to us. The trend toward victory in the war of resistance has been decided.[8]

Recognizing that an ally of Hitler was *ipso facto* an enemy of Washington, Chiang felt sure that with Tokyo tied to Berlin, Washington would, one way or another, end up his ally.

Choosing Charybdis. To the extent that Tokyo and Washington insisted on the positions they were embedding in legitimizing rhetoric, conflict was by 1941 becoming inescapable. During that year the confrontation unfolded. In April Tokyo arranged, despite bitter internal disagreements, a neutrality pact with Russia that complemented the Axis pact of the preceding autumn. As 1941 advanced, it expanded its military operations in China and French Indochina, pressed ahead with Manchuria's industrialization, and continued trying, with little success, to improve the performance of the domestic economy by tightening political control. Washington, meanwhile, had become deeply engaged in supporting London's resistance to Berlin and was making good progress on a massive program of rearmament. It was strengthening its military capabilities in the Philippines, was offering token support to Chiang, and had sharply restricted the export of metals and other matériel of war to Japan.

Meanwhile, Tokyo's long-standing internal debate about the relative merits of an "advance" northward into Soviet territory or southward into the Southeast Asian region continued to flourish. As the neutrality pact implied, however, by the spring of 1941 government policy, insofar as it was settled, gave precedence to the latter, primarily because the raw materials required by war and industry lay to the south, mainly in Dutch and British colonial areas. That policy survived the temptation to invade Siberia after Hitler attacked Russia in June 1941. And it was reinforced at the end of July when the movement of Japanese troops into southern French Indochina led American and British leaders and the Dutch exile regime in London to freeze all the Japanese assets they controlled and to halt all oil exports to Japan.

With that blockage of oil, policy debates in Tokyo narrowed sharply because the issue at stake had been reduced to its fundament: within a year the military would lack the fossil fuel necessary to continue fighting effectively. Attempts to discover compromise positions notwithstanding, the choices in fact had been dramatically simplified: either abandon the struggle to dominate China or quickly gain access to sufficient oil by whatever means was required.

In acrimonious discussions Tokyo leaders struggled during the summer and autumn of 1941 to find a way between the Scylla of retreat and the Charybdis of expanded war. Prime Minister Tōjō Hideki revealed the group's sense of affairs when he declared:

> Two years from now we will have no petroleum for military use; ships will stop moving. When I think about the strengthening of American defenses in the southwestern Pacific, the expansion of the U.S. fleet, the unfinished China Incident, and so on, I see no end of difficulties ... I fear that we would become a third-class nation after two or three years if we merely sat tight.[9]

In the outcome Tōjō's cabinet rejected the choice of retreat. And that decision eliminated all likelihood that Washington could be induced to reopen the oil spigot.

In consequence policy debate moved from grand strategic alternatives to narrow tactical analyses: how best to seize the Dutch East Indies and their oil wells. Analysts quickly concluded that the project must involve war not only with the British, who were well entrenched in Malaya, with its rubber plantations, but also with the Americans. They were expanding their military position in the Philippines, could interdict naval movement to the south, and would, it was presumed, stand by the British. So planning focused on the question of how best to cripple Anglo-American war-making capacity in the Asia-Pacific region long enough to secure the Indies and throw up a defensible perimeter around the western Pacific and Southeast Asia.

Hence the decision to attack the enlarged American fleet at Pearl Harbor, overrun the Philippines, seize Singapore, and drive the British westward into India. There, it was hoped, an Indian nationalist movement would destroy the remaining British position, ruining London's presence east of Suez.

Hitler, presumably, could take it from there, enabling Tokyo to negotiate a compromise with an isolated Washington facing powerful navies on both coasts. Considerations of weather, together with the current rate of oil consumption, dictated that the military moves commence before the arrival of winter, and even shorter-term factors made December 8 the optimal date to launch combat operations.

During the autumn Japanese and American diplomats played their pathetic *pas de deux* to its clumsy end, and on December 7, Hawaii time, the carnage began. Thanks to meticulous training, vigorous execution, and the good luck essential to all successful military ventures, the early operations mostly worked out well. By the spring of 1942 Japanese forces had attained their main strategic objectives and controlled most of the areas they intended to seize throughout the western Pacific and Southeast Asia (see Map 1). Having upped the ante, Japan's leaders and many subjects looked forward to reaping the benefits of military triumph.

PAYING THE PRICE, 1943–1945

Warfare is not a leisurely gentleman's game. Almost as soon as Tokyo announced its successes, reverses began to occur. Major naval battles, most notably the contest for Midway Island in early June 1942, went disastrously awry, and during 1943 the enemy took the offensive, mainly in the Pacific. There a year of "island hopping" brought American amphibious forces from the vicinity of Guadalcanal in the Solomon Islands, just east of New Guinea, northward to Saipan, halfway to Tokyo and well within bombing range of Japan's cities. Combat reverses continued thereafter; enemy submarines decimated surface shipping; embattled governments in Tokyo changed, and air raids steadily intensified.

In January 1945 iron bombs gave way to the much more effective incendiaries, and Japan's cities were consumed, one after another, even as enemy operations overwhelmed Japanese garrisons scattered across Southeast Asia. Flame throwers, suicide charges, and *kamikaze* aircaft sorties added to the battlefield carnage, but leaders in Tokyo still failed to seize opportunities – most notably Germany's capitulation in May – to seek a cessation of hostilities. Finally in August, after Hiroshima and Nagasaki had been ravaged by atomic bombs and the Russians had entered the war, the emperor ordered his military chiefs to accept the fact of defeat. They had bungled, he implied, their planning "erroneous and untimely." Couching his argument in terms that trumped the rhetoric about *kokutai*, "holy war," military honor, and the duty of the imperial subject, he opposed the army's calls for a homeland defense to the death:

> To subject the people to further suffering, to witness the destruction of civilization, and to invite the misfortune of mankind, are entirely contrary to my wishes.

With bitter reluctance, but having no better ideas, the military chiefs obeyed, and despite last-minute attempts to thwart the imperial order, the war ended.

By then the scale of devastation visited on the Japanese people by their leaders' horrific miscalculations had grown astronomically. Whereas Nomonhan had claimed 18,000 casualties in 1939, by December 1941 combat deaths in China had risen tenfold to 185,000, and by war's end in 1945 they had risen another tenfold to about 1,800,000 dead and disappeared. Total deaths for Japan, both combatant and non-combatant, numbered nearly 2,700,000, while wounded survivors, civil and military, totaled nearly a million, and millions more were seriously ill with tuberculosis and other diseases.

In many other ways, as well, the cost of war began early and rose dramatically thereafter. Individual experiences varied greatly, of course, depending on a person's age, wealth, location, and so forth, but in general a state of irksome deprivation that gradually intensified from 1937 through 1943 gave way during the war's last year or two to a condition of ruinous loss and devastation.

Deprivation.   In contrast to America, where the war, despite its initial worrisome possibilities, brought an economic revival that ended the Great Depression and put everyone to work, in Japan the depression had largely been overcome before 1937. So from the beginning the general public reaped little benefit from the struggle. Rather, because Tokyo was waging war on a shoestring, so to say, from the very outset the fighting in China precipitated restrictions and scarcities at home. Later, as military gains turned to losses and the enemy's capacity to inflict injury escalated, the civilian cost rose proportionately.

Almost from the start the government recognized that the war in China required sacrifices at home, and its measures of economic and social mobilization strove to elicit them. In early 1938 Tokyo leaders explained their first general mobilization law this way:

> the special characteristic of modern wars is that they are wars of national strength. To achieve the objectives of the war, we must...mobilize our entire resources, both physical and spiritual; it is not enough merely to provide sufficient munitions... [The country must] do its utmost to make people's livelihoods secure and harmonize the various aspects of national life necessary for prosecuting the war.[10]

One of the necessary aspects of war was dying in battle, and in the spring of 1939 government leaders moved to assuage the spirits of the multiplying war dead and their grieving kin by reorganizing the country's Shintō shrines. They expanded and rationalized their system of memorial shrines, retitling the regional Shōkonsha as Gokoku *jinja*, tightening their linkage to Yasukuni Shrine, and in 1940 providing government funding for the conduct of their shrine ceremonies.

For the remainder of the war Tokyo labored to sustain both "physical and spiritual" support for the war. It promoted press censorship and propaganda output, as in the art, film, and literature industries earlier noted. And it fostered the formation of community councils, neighborhood associations, and factory organizations to transmit and reinforce government propaganda, maintain morale, contain dissidence, and provide local mutual assistance.

At broader social levels some intellectuals and reformist leaders pointed to European fascism as a model for Japan, and government leaders, partially inspired by that thought, tried to reorganize the polity by dissolving the political parties and combining them into one nationwide patriotic organization. They also tried to tighten military control of the civilian government, notably the Diet and the several ministries of state, and through these organs to strengthen military control of industry. In the end, however, civil bureaucrats and industrial magnates were able to prevent almost all but cosmetic changes in organizational control. So military leaders had to be content with a patchwork of arrangements that enabled them, after a fashion, to direct most output to military purposes. They did succeed in expanding military production, achieving that goal in part by expanding total industrial output but primarily by shifting labor and plant from civilian to military purposes.

Because the war was being prosecuted on such a limited industrial foundation, scarcities began to emerge almost at once. Inflation appeared in 1937, roughly doubling prices by 1941 despite government attempts to control rents, wages, and prices. Rationing of gasoline began in the spring of 1938, but as a result, demand for charcoal rose, and in 1940 it too began to be rationed. By then copper for civilian use was nil, cotton was being rationed, along with sugar and matches, and rice was in short supply. By then, too, diverse luxuries, including public entertainment, and the use of cosmetics, permanent waves, and elegant clothing were being restricted or had been tabooed.

After Pearl Harbor the trends toward scarcity, control, and communal organization accelerated. By May 1944, reported the *Asahi* newspaper,

> everything from the distribution of cotton thread, socks, and toilet paper to repairing shoes, umbrellas, and pots and pans is being carried out by the neighborhood associations [as is] everything from buying national bonds, collecting money for postal savings and insurance, and tax payments to delivering the mail.

With so many men off to war, women were handling many of these tasks, but what little they had to distribute was controlled by higher authorities.

Overseas, meanwhile, the government was trying to organize its new imperial possessions. Tokyo promoted the rhetoric of Asian brotherhood and developed an elaborate governing apparatus in which civilian and military officials from Japan supervised collaborating locals. As Tōjō explained it to the Diet during the triumphant days of January 1942:

> we have in mind to bring under our power those areas which are absolutely indispensable for the defence of Greater East Asia and to deal with the others in accordance with traditions and the culture of every race.[11]

In line with that approach, the areas with the most valued resources, the Indies and Malaya in particular, were kept under more direct military control. The less essential areas, notably Burma and the Philippines, were scheduled, in theory at least, to become more autonomous.

A grand assemblage of delegates from the empire gathered in Tokyo in the autumn of 1943 to celebrate the escape of Asian peoples from

Euro-American domination, to declare their unity in the Greater East Asia Co-Prosperity Sphere, and to define their mutually shared principles and goals. In fact, however, military reverses came so quickly that the short-term needs of warfare dominated policy abroad, and the rhetoric of good will was soon lost amidst harsh demands for resources, labor, and other forms of military cooperation. That situation was epitomized by the cruel impressment of "comfort women," mainly Korean and Chinese, to contain the incidence of venereal disease among and rapine by imperial forces.

Devastation. Disintegration of the empire was soon matched by devastation at home. With the onset of sustained strategic bombing in 1944, urban conditions began to deteriorate rapidly. Because goods were so scarce and the official distribution system so pervasive, black markets in a broad range of goods had already appeared, and by that summer their prices were averaging about ten times the legal level. By November black market rice prices were far higher than that, and during following months they soared several fold. This inflation assured that large numbers of urban people could afford only the sharply reduced rations legally available, and malnutrition became widespread, which fostered the spread of various diseases and set the stage for an epidemic of tuberculosis.

The growing hardship of urban life contributed to discontent by casting into sharper relief the harsh disparity in circumstances of the general populace and privileged elites, particularly those of the military and industry. Meanwhile factory workers were becoming acutely frustrated by the lack of essential materials, the intense pressure to meet tight schedules, and the ineptitude of so much replacement labor, notably youth, prisoners, and conscripted foreigners. These conditions provoked more frequent strikes, work stoppages, absenteeism, industrial sabotage, and shoddy workmanship.

Despite intensifying labor scarcity and malperformance, Japan's leaders did much less to exploit their female population – apart from denying women consumption privileges and encouraging "volunteer" work in neighborhood associations – than did the enemy powers. Their preference for leaving women at home reflected the established ideals of woman as "good wife, wise mother" and the household as society's foundation, and it was reinforced by the military's wish for more manpower in future. To that end the government began forming, even before Pearl Harbor, marriage counseling centers intended "to make young women recognize motherhood as [their] national destiny" and thus to increase the birth rate.[12] The earlier lamentations about "overpopulation" had given way, it appears, to a wish to populate the newly acquired empire and its guardian army. In fact, however, the policy bore little fruit, and later, as the war turned sour and life grew chaotic, birth rates dropped precipitously.

During 1945, even as the empire was being lost, incendiary raids by American bombers brought death and destruction to the homeland. By that spring, the B-29 squadrons were large enough to mount attacks in which hundreds of bombers dropped thousands of tons of incendiaries on Japan's cities, night after night, methodically incinerating them and later returning to destroy surviving target areas.

Under this battering morale plummeted and more and more people began holding the government responsible for their predicament.[13] A police report of March 1945 noted that in the public at large,

> indignation against the ruling class has been shown in criticisms of military strategy and misrepresentation of the attitude of military circles. Others speak ill of government measures and government communiques. They explicitly assume a hostile attitude toward the government circles. Some others dare to speak of class antagonism.

A few weeks later an official fretted about the signs that even in the hinterland, "the germination of an impending class struggle is a real matter for anxiety."

By then dogs were rare, so many having starved or been eaten. And swaths of housing were being demolished to create fire breaks around war-making facilities. Evacuation of the cities was in progress, with children in particular being moved to rural safety. Some adults left the cities voluntarily before being bombed out; many more did so afterwards of necessity. By war's end about 10,000,000, nearly a seventh of the entire population, had fled the burnt-out cities for rural areas, the exodus facilitated by the fact that many of these people were recent immigrants to the cities and still had rural relatives and family friends who would, however unhappily, take them in.

The terror inflicted by the bombing can be surmised, but by then the grinding hardship of wartime had created a general sense of resignation and dogged readiness to cope, as suggested by this comment on people caught in an air raid:[14]

> There is not much excitement. The only voices you hear, are those of mothers calling for their children, or children calling their parents.

As survivors became refugees, they "were silent and calm, but the horror they went through reflected in their faces."

By war's end about 42 percent of Japan's urban industrial area was destroyed and upwards of half the total area of the largest cities was incinerated. During the summer of 1945 military leaders launched a preposterous program to arm male and female civilians of all ages with bamboo spears to meet the enemy on the beaches, but before such madness could be implemented the end came. The Americans and their allies had won; the Japanese lost. For Americans decades of prosperity followed; for Japanese, years of grinding poverty, dogged reconstruction, and eventual affluence.

Well over a half century of effort had been reduced to rubble; dreams of grandeur destroyed. In the process the vision of empire had also been discredited, along with its proponents. Ironically, however, as we note in chapter 18, it was a variant form of the Japanese vision of spheres rather than the American view of autonomously interacting nation-states that was to prevail for the next half century, the era of the "Cold War" as it was known. And it was within the parameters of this global order that Japan recovered and tried to build a new system for securing the natural resources essential to a more fully developed industrial order.

[18] ENTREPRENEURIAL JAPAN: POLITICS AND ECONOMY (1945–1990)

CHAPTER SYNOPSIS

THE DIPLOMATIC CONTEXT

SURVIVAL AND REDIRECTION (1945–1960)
FORGING NEW ARRANGEMENTS

ACCEPTING THE NEW ARRANGEMENTS

SHŌWA GENROKU (1960–1990)
GROWTH
POLITICS

To start where the story of Imperial Japan ends, the emperor was innocent of exaggeration on August 15, 1945 when, in explaining via radio the government's decision to surrender, he observed to the general populace that "the war situation has developed not necessarily to Japan's advantage."[1] In fact the magnitude of disadvantage was so stupendous that it eventuated in two major changes and a host of ancillary modifications in the character and functioning of Japan's industrial order. At the same time, however, despite the express wish of fanatics on both sides of the war, Japanese society did survive defeat, and many basic characteristics and trends of preceding decades persisted, continuing to shape affairs down to 1990 and beyond.

The more immediately visible of the two major changes was the discrediting of Japan's military leadership and destruction of its military organization. That outcome, initially the result of wartime failure, was sustained by the second major change, the collapse of the "empire-as-resource-base" strategy, which had for decades justified a mighty military establishment.

These changes enabled other segments of the prewar ruling elite, notably political partymen, bureaucrats, and industrialists, to take charge of the country – under the temporary oversight of a conquering foreign army – and to redirect government policies and society's energies in directions more agreeable to themselves. Most importantly they had to devise alternatives to the imperial strategy of resource acquisition, but doing so took years. In the meantime they implemented, initially under pressure from their foreign overseers, a broad array of modifications in domestic statutes and institutional arrangements while tailoring political verbiage to accommodate the victors' predilections. Whereas the Meiji Constitution of 1889, the Imperial Rescript on Education of 1890, and the civil, criminal, and commercial codes that were promulgated in the years around then had spelled out the structure, ideals, and rules of procedure that shaped Japanese development prior to 1945, new documents spelled out new ideals and arrangements following defeat, and these provided society's basic guidelines thereafter.

The historical experience framed by those guidelines unfolded within a diplomatic context that was considerably changed from that of preceding decades. That context, the Cold War as it was known, shaped mightily the strategies and tactics employed by the Japanese as they rebuilt their war-ruined industrial order, revived its cultural life, and re-established its ties to the outside world. That national effort yielded the richly textured, multi-layered history of entrepreneurial Japan.

Viewed narrowly as political narrative, the story of entrepreneurial Japan was a story of forced adaptation and continual maneuver, little of it decisive, and much of it not particularly edifying. Viewed more broadly as politico-economic history, however, it was a story of growth and change that can – granting the usual caveats about the porosity and conditionality of chronological divisions – be treated sequentially in terms of a postwar period (1945–60) in which society was essentially dealing with the consequences of defeat and a subsequent period (1960–90) marked by economic dynamism, rapid social change, and attempts to deal with the ramifications of those conditions.

The story of these decades as social history, to foreshadow chapter 19, was most strikingly one of deep and rapid change in rural–urban relations. But it was also a story of gradual change in matters of urban geography, gender, and minority status. At a more basic level, one encounters a story of ecological change as the environmental consequences of industrialism became more pronounced and, as a corollary, Japan deepened its demands and effects on the global ecosystem.

Finally, at the representational level of arts and letters (chapter 20), these decades yield a story of a widely shared "middlebrow culture" that took shape and became the cultural core of present-day Japan. More narrowly, it is the narrative of an intelligentsia that continued initially to argue old agendas but as years passed increasingly addressed new ones created by the changing times. It is also, however, a story of new departures in the intercon-nected realms of artistry, departures that placed Japan's creative writers, musicians, and theatrical and visual artists solidly in the flow of industrial-age global history.

THE DIPLOMATIC CONTEXT

Japan's experience after 1945 was strongly shaped by its global diplomatic context. In essence the prewar situation, in which the late nineteenth-century Eurocentric imperial order was disintegrating and rival industrializing regimes were trying to strengthen themselves at the expense of others, gave way within three years of war's end to a period of sustained global stalemate, the Cold War. That contest pitted a powerful, Washington-centered political sphere against a much weaker, Moscow-centered sphere, while regimes in still-unindustrialized regions (mainly Southeast and South Asia, the Middle East, Africa, and Latin America) did their best to maneuver advantageously between the two.

To adumbrate the more germane aspects of this context, whereas most of the rest of the industrial world lay in ruin in 1945, the United States emerged from World War II with unmatched and unprecedented military capability, a greatly expanded industrial plant, immense agricultural capacity, rich natural resources, and huge reserves of bullion and foreign currency. The only serious counter-force was the Soviet Union (USSR), whose geographical size and surviving military–industrial power enabled it to establish and maintain for nearly half a century a general boundary, known by its critics as the "iron curtain," beyond which American might could not be effectively projected. The rivalry between these two unequal colossi was sustained by an arms race of unprecedented magnitude and cost, intensive alliance-building and control, and sometimes-risky political maneuver. And it was legitimized by a vigorous ideological rhetoric in which each side presented the other as evil incarnate and itself as the model for industrial society's future.

Because the United States was the predominant force in Japan's defeat and excluded the USSR from a significant role in the country's occupation, Japan emerged from defeat on the American side of the iron curtain and had to build its future within the American-dominated sphere. For many of Japan's leaders that was – given the choices – a welcome outcome: for decades they had feared the specter of Communism and viewed Russia as a major threat, and as defeat loomed in 1944–5, they became increasingly concerned to end the war before the Russians were able to enter and avenge earlier insults. Given Tokyo's understanding of the American elite's attitude toward "socialism," surrendering to the Americans seemed the best way to forestall Russian advances.

Endless affronts and irritants notwithstanding, inclusion in the postwar American sphere was made all the more agreeable to Japan's new leadership by the way Washington managed its dominion. Because the USA emerged from the war with such immense wealth and power, Washington's earlier rhetoric, noted in chapter 17, about "national self-determination" and the "open door" continued to serve American interests very well and became central to American Cold War propaganda. Gussied up with attractive phrasing about free trade, democracy, and human rights, this rhetorical posture provided Washington with a rationale for opposing other empire builders while nurturing allies and collaborators, minimizing its own burdens of imperial administration, and asserting and abetting the right of American entrepreneurs to pursue their business wherever they wished within the American sphere.

For Tokyo this diplomatic posture meant that once Japan was shorn of empire and aggressive capability, the Americans accepted in principle its "right" to be rehabilitated as a sovereign nation whose entrepreneurs could engage in foreign trade. It was a posture that gave Japan access, within the American sphere at least, to the requisite global resource base. It accommodated the interests of Japan's new leaders and eventually proved, with some painful exceptions, advantageous to the Japanese populace as a whole, down to 1990 at least. The major constraint that the Americans imposed on Japan related to the larger Cold War rivalry, namely the discouraging of Japanese entrepreneurial activities in the Soviet (within a few years, Sino-Soviet) sphere. Cold War tension also helped justify a partial revival of Japanese military capacity despite widespread resistance from the Japanese public, and it led within Japan to restraints on labor activism and the suppression of "left-wing extremism."

Within this larger context of American pre-eminence, and with the notion of empire in ruin, Japan's revamped ruling coalition of political partymen, bureaucrats, and industrialists adopted the entrepreneurial strategy of trade championed by the Americans (and long favored by many Japanese businessmen) to gain access to the resources that would enable Japan to rebuild devastated infrastructure and press on with industrialization. That strategy ordinarily favors societies with rich capital reserves and the most advanced technologies, which Japan in the years after 1945 utterly lacked, but through hard work, frugality, and shrewd calculation those disadvantages were overcome to give the island nation decades of unprecedented material growth and prosperity.

SURVIVAL AND REDIRECTION (1945–1960)

Widely suffering from exhaustion and malnutrition, the Japanese public in August 1945 was torn between powerful grief over the lost cause and equally powerful relief that the bombing, slaughter, and sleepless nights had ended. With the wartime propaganda apparatus silenced, apprehension about possible atrocities by the occupying army soon eased despite the influx of some 300,000 conquering troops and a rich assortment of carpetbaggers. However, hunger, illness, and brutal hardship continued for months. By the autumn of 1946 a good harvest and an inflow of relief supplies from abroad eased the food crisis, but because of the massive urban destruction, lack of raw materials, collapse of infrastructure, and general confusion, economic recovery did not really get under way until about 1948. By then the sustained hardship, which could no longer be justified as sacrifice for a heroic war effort, was generating discontent and protest that was expressed in vigorous labor agitation, acts of violence, radical social analysis, and shadowy criminality.

Meanwhile the victors were pressing ahead with their political agenda, and over the course of three years or so they initiated a wide range of legal and institutional changes. During the 1950s, even as the Japanese were rebuilding their economy, the government and public alike actively contested particulars of the new order, with that contestation reaching a bitter climax in 1960. At that juncture, however, after an alarming flirtation with domestic upheaval, disputants tempered their tactics, and leaders and led alike generally put the past behind them. Although older agendas continued to spur reflection and rhetorical posturing, most social energies focused on tasks of the day and the challenge of coping with problems arising from contemporary socioeconomic change.

FORGING NEW ARRANGEMENTS

Officially the administration of defeated Japan was a joint effort by the allied victors. In fact, "the Occupation," as it is commonly known, was an American enterprise led by the American general Douglas MacArthur, whose firm sense of imperium was embodied in the title of his office: Supreme Commander for the Allied Powers (SCAP). Despite the large size of MacArthur's army, however, few of its members had the linguistic or cultural knowledge necessary to govern Japan, so SCAP left most of Japanese officialdom in place and exercised its control through the existing structures of administration, from emperor and central state organs to local leaders and mail carriers.

In certain ways the Occupation's leadership reminds one of the builders of the Kwantung Army's 1930s client state, Manchukuo. In particular, SCAP, like them, pursued policies designed basically to advance home-country interests while insisting on the benevolence of its motivation. Whereas the Japanese in Manchuria from the outset exploited the region for Japan's strategic and industrial advantage, however, the Americans' initial goal was to assure that Japan would never again be capable of posing a military threat to the United States. Later, as the Cold War took shape, and especially after Mao Tse-tung established the People's Republic of China in October 1949, American policy sought to assure that Japan would dutifully support Washington against its new challengers.

At the same time, however, much as some of Manchukuo's builders aspired to create a model society, one that would subsequently enable them to renovate and purify the *kokutai* of Japan proper, so some SCAP officials initally saw Japan as a place where noble reforms could be implemented to serve as a model for further New Deal-like changes in America. And just as Manchurian reform evaporated in the face of war, so the Occupation's reformist ideals faded as the Cold War soured America on "left-wing" ideas in general, prompting Washington to treat Japan not as a site for social engineering but as a political supporter to be strengthened for new struggles.

Initially Occupation policy reflected both themes, *Realpolitik* and reformism. The ideological postulate that enabled occupiers to pursue the two conjointly was the happy thought that democracies of the Anglo-American sort constitute singularly peace-loving regimes. The best way to forestall future Japanese aggression, it was held, was to democratize the country along those lines, an idea whose irony Native Americans and many colonial peoples surely could appreciate. Seeing Imperial Japan's military adventurism as the result of a malign alliance of militarists, aristocrats, corporate giants, rural landlords, and a populace indoctrinated with chauvinistic propaganda, the occupiers believed that a peace-loving Japan would be more certain if the alliance were dissolved and its parts reformed. Militarists were to be punished and eliminated and the titled aristocracy abolished. The great industrial combines (*zaibatsu*) were to be broken up and labor unions encouraged. Landlords were to be brought to heel and rural tenantry and poverty overcome. And the educational system was to be changed in both structure and content.

War crimes trials identified and punished thousands of those held accountable for the war and some of its excesses, with about 940 being executed. Purges removed another 220,000, mostly former military officers, from positions of authority in government, business, education, and the media, while thousands of other people resigned from responsible positions before being examined. The remnants of the military system were dissolved, equipment destroyed, and some six million military and civilian personnel repatriated from the former empire (while about 1.5 million Koreans departed Japan for Korea). The empire itself was dismantled. Taiwan and Manchuria went to the Chinese; Korea was divided between American and Russian armies of occupation; Karafuto and the Kuriles came under Russian control; the Ryukyu, Bonin, and most other Pacific island areas fell to the Americans, while Southeast Asia reverted awkwardly to its former European colonial masters. Subsequently several of those changes were modified, but save for the Ryukyu and Bonin chains, Japan never recovered its lost empire.

In conjunction with the loss of empire, plans were drafted to have Japan pay heavy reparations to regions injured by the war. However, the country's economic difficulties and the Cold War-related shifts in American policy delayed their implementation. Some years later, when Tokyo restored its diplomatic and trade relationships, it agreed to pay more modest reparations to several aggrieved Asian governments.

To transform Imperial Japan into a peace-loving democracy, SCAP drafted a new constitution that replaced the prewar rhetoric about imperial virtue and diligent subjects with the vocabulary of peace, liberty, and popular sovereignty. The document stripped the emperor of his independent wealth and all but ceremonial authority. It subordinated the cabinet to an elected bicameral Diet and dissolved the Meiji aristocracy by depriving some 900 families of their titles. It extended voting rights to women and enhanced women's marital rights. It strengthened a wide range of civil liberties and recognized labor's right to organize. It distanced the judiciary from government administrative organs, reduced police power, and in general tried to broaden public control of government.

In the most direct juridical move to prevent future Japanese aggression, Article 9 of the new constitution explicitly proscribed military forces: "land, sea, and air forces, as well as other war potential, will never be maintained. The right of belligerency of the state will not be recognized."[2] Much as the planned reparations fell victim to changing times, however, Article 9 was eventually compromised by government acts and court rulings, greatly to Washington's relief, and a small but powerful 180,000-man Japanese military force became established by 1954. It maintained state-of-the-art military technology thereafter and by the 1990s had grown into a force of nearly 250,000.

The core reform plank that SCAP pursued least vigorously was dissolution of the *zaibatsu*. These giant, family-centered combines, the likes of Mitsui,

Mitsubishi, and Sumitomo, which Washington initially viewed as key contributors to Japan's policy of aggressive warfare, were earmarked for a thorough break-up. Planning proceeded slowly, however, possibly because American industrialists and their allies in government perceived no serious competitive potential in those war-ruined remnants and because they were not keen on setting a precedent for such intrusive government "meddling" in business affairs. In any case, before much "*zaibatsu* busting" could be implemented, Occupation policy began to shift. Primarily because of the escalating Cold War, Washington began to view Japan's economic recovery as a top priority, and the break-up of large corporate structures, like the payment of reparations, came to be seen as an obstacle to that policy. In consequence, although new laws on corporate organization and stock holding were put into effect, only a few major combines were reduced in scale. And a few years later most of them reconsolidated, joining other newly-risen businesses to constitute the corporate giants that became so prominent in Japan's burgeoning, post-1960 economy, powerhouses capable of competing globally with their rivals in other industrial societies.

The shift in Occupation policy toward business was accompanied by a shift in attitude toward labor unions. Initially SCAP had encouraged unionization, and the prewar labor movement revived rapidly, with union membership growing dramatically to around five million by the end of 1946. From about 1947 onward, however, SCAP's support began to cool as labor organizations continued to grow and became more fractious in their salary demands and their claims to a role in managing enterprises. Both SCAP and Japanese government leaders regarded the labor actions as disruptive of economic recovery and bothersome to the task of governance, and doubtless many saw in them a threat to the "rights" of enterprise owners. Moreover, labor rhetoric seemed supportive of the Soviet position in the propaganda battles of the nascent Cold War.

In response to the disruptions and rhetoric SCAP imposed restraints on union activity, particularly in the public-service sector where the recently established right to strike was rescinded. And in 1949 it launched a broad purge of communists and other "radicals" in labor, education, and the media. During the fifties more moderate unions arose with business encouragement, and union leaders dropped most of their revolutionary Marxist rhetoric. From the 1960s onward, as the economy flourished, labor militancy declined along with union influence on politics and business.

Far more than *zaibatsu* busting and the early fostering of unionism, SCAP's initial policies toward landlordism and education left enduring marks on Japan. Agricultural landlords, to take their case first, proved to be much easier targets than the *zaibatsu*. Whereas corporate giantism has everywhere blossomed as industrialism has advanced, rural landlordism has declined, giving way to large-scale agrobusiness, small-time agricultural dilettantism, and residual family farming. By the 1920s, as noted in chapter 16, village landlordism was already beginning to lose its attractiveness near major urban centers, and the influence of landlords in government was declining. Indeed, by the 1930s officials in Tokyo were developing land reform plans of their own. Most landlords, moreover, held only modest amounts of land, generally less than four hectares (ten acres), so when the occupiers moved to redistribute land to tenants, they encountered little effective resistance.

In the land reform that was enacted in 1946, absentee landlordism was abolished and resident landlords were required to sell all acreage above specified limits. Skyrocketing inflation rapidly rendered the stipulated sale prices meaningless, with the result that in actuality tenants acquired land for a pittance in a process of *de facto*, nationwide expropriation that in retrospect seems positively "un-American." Under these circumstances land changed hands rapidly even though some tenants felt uneasy about acquiring land from neighbors and former betters in such a dubious manner. Doubtless many realized, moreover, that if higher authority could transfer land to them so cheaply, it could also take it away without much ado. In the outcome, by the time Cold War tensions were reorienting Washington's priorities on industry and labor, land reform was too far advanced to be undone. By August 1950 some 4.7 million acres of land had changed hands, and whereas 46 percent of Japan's arable had been worked by tenants in 1945, under 12 percent was by 1950 and 9 percent by 1955.

Several factors perpetuated the new landholding arrangements. Initially the high demand for food helped newly propertied farmers avoid the tenantry trap, and agronomic change in following years helped sustain rural prosperity for decades. Moreover, in contrast to unionization, which had fostered political activism that both Washington and Tokyo feared, land reform produced a welcome outcome: a conservative rural populace that generally favored the Occupation-inspired changes. Thanks to the slowness of electoral redistricting, the political clout of those newly landed farmers persisted for decades despite the dramatic decline in their numbers that came with renewed access to food imports and greater agronomic efficiency. So, agitation by landlords notwithstanding, political leaders remained supportive of the land settlement, providing farmers with diverse subsidies that helped maintain rural well-being while preserving their own electoral foundation. In consequence tenantry never re-emerged as a social problem and the Occupation's land reform policies survived almost intact to play a basic role in shaping Japan's agriculture and society down to 1990 and beyond. Indeed the very success of the reform in creating a countrywide population of small holders eventually came to be seen as a major factor thwarting agricultural "rationalization" and increased productivity per farmer.

Like land reform, educational reform accommodated "the trends of the times" and had an enduring impact. Before the war Japan's educational system had kept growing, but demand for more advanced schooling persistently exceeded the space available. SCAP reformers, spurred by an ideal of academic equal opportunity that has always eluded Americans at home, replaced Japan's complexly structured, career-oriented schooling system with a uniformitarian 6–3–3-year hierarchy of elementary and secondary schools that would supposedly enable all students to prepare for more advanced education if they so wished. Curricular changes replaced the old indoctrination in *kokutai* thought with a new indoctrination in American notions of democracy and individualism. And institutional changes shifted control of the schools from central to local governing bodies. After the Occupation ended in 1952, much control of schooling was recentralized, but only with great difficulty and at the cost of highly ideologized struggle between central political authorities and "leftist" teachers' organizations. The uniformitarian hierarchy remained largely intact, however, and little of the old imperial ideology reappeared. Moreover, the trend toward ever more schooling continued, giving Japan one of the world's most highly educated citizenries and one of the world's largest systems of higher education.

By 1950 SCAP leaders had long exhausted their portfolio of ideas and lost their reformist zeal. American attention had largely shifted from left-over issues of World War II to problems of the nonce, especially the Cold War. That reorientation was abruptly accelerated in June 1950 by eruption of the Korean War, when leaders of North Korea sent armies south to unify their divided country by force of arms and the United States responded by mobilizing an international army to thwart the effort.

By that November North Korean forces had been pummeled and driven back into their own territory and their country nearly overrun. That sharp reversal of fortune prompted intervention by the recently established People's Republic of China, which had no wish to see another Japan-like presence directly overlooking its northeastern regions. The conflict then degenerated into a bloody Sino-American stalemate in which success was measured in body counts rather than miles of advance. By mutual consent troops of the slowly reviving and lightly armed Japanese armed forces were not thrown into the fighting, although Japanese reportedly provided some shipping assistance, and finally in 1953 a ceasefire ended the pointless carnage.

By then, however, the conflict, together with its savage Cold War backdrop, had intensified the Japanese desire to escape American control, with its perceived risk of bloody entanglement in new wars. The situation also heightened American desire that Japan rebuild and rearm enough to assist the United States in defending the northeast Asian corner of its global sphere. Those ill-fitting considerations led to fuller rearmament and in 1951–2 to concurrent negotiation of a multilateral peace treaty and a bilateral US–Japan security pact. The two agreements tied Japan closely to the United States and perpetuated the American military presence there even as they officially ended the Occupation and proclaimed Japan an independent sovereign state.

ACCEPTING THE NEW ARRANGEMENTS

During the years of Occupation Japan's leaders attempted to cope with issues of the day and initiate planning for the future while maneuvering as best they could to protect vested interests in the face of unwanted demands from SCAP above and the newly energized labor movement below. After months of paralysis political and business leaders gradually regained their footing, and by 1949 the shrewd, energetic, and cantankerous Prime Minister Yoshida Shigeru had emerged as the leader most able to work with SCAP while retaining a domestic power base.

Recovery. As political leadership stabilized, national reconstruction continued. Initially, with the empire gone, the economy in a shambles, the merchant fleet crippled, and SCAP proceeding with its *zaibatsu* busting and its plans to ship surviving industrial facilities abroad as war reparations, Japanese planners focused on devising means to survive on the archipelago's own resources. They soon realized that under those constraints reconstruction must focus on the most critical tasks. Late in 1946 the economist Arisawa Hiromi, a key figure in the planning, explained government policy this way:

> since it is not possible to raise the production level of all goods evenly ... we are handling the problem by concentrating our priorities on raising production of the unique basic raw material, coal ... Our pressing need is to raise production rapidly in this basic sector and use that as a lever to increase the general level of production.[3]

Accordingly, during the next few years, and despite continual debate and infighting, authorities followed a policy of "priority production." They channeled their limited supply of foreign currency into the purchase of up-to-date equipment for select industries (namely, coal, fertilizer, and electricity production, and later steel and ship building) and provided them with "badly needed supplies of labor, steel, cement, electric power, timber, and other goods."

They encouraged primary production by fostering agricultural mechanization and agronomic improvements. As a result rice production, which had fluctuated around 9,000,000 metric tons during the 1930s, expanded to some 12,000,000 by 1955, stabilizing at about that level for the next three decades. During the fifties officials and community leaders promoted the rehabilitation of woodlands devastated by wartime and postwar clearcutting. They provided subsidies and other assistance to targeted industries and, together with the general public, pressed ahead with the reconstruction of cities, factories, and economic infrastructure. Slowly their efforts reduced the army of unemployed and underemployed, raising standards of living and improving public health and morale.

Well before the Occupation ended, Tokyo planners had redefined their goal from a Japan that could survive on its own resources to a Japan that would be able to export enough goods to pay for the imports required by industrial development. That shift, which meshed with SCAP's new-found interest in a revitalized Japan, realigned Tokyo's thinking with the fact of industrialism's dependence on a global resource base. Accordingly, groups of businessmen and technical specialists began going abroad again to acquire up-to-date technology and pursue private trade.

When Yoshida left office in 1954 after six years as Prime Minister, he had much reason to feel good about his accomplishments. The Occupation was history, and economic recovery was well underway, the Korean War having provided a powerful spur by creating a sustained demand for Japanese goods and services and a steady influx of foreign currency. Even after the ceasefire was arranged in 1953, that situation persisted thanks to the reconstruction of South Korea and the maintenance there of large residual military forces. By 1955 Japan's overall economy had regained its mid-1930s level of output.

The issue of nuclear warfare. Yoshida was a career diplomat whose goal was to rebuild Japan and reaffirm its independence as soon as possible, so the treaties of 1952 marked a great personal triumph for him. For most Japanese, however, the end of Occupation changed life very little. The gains from economic recovery were inequitably distributed; much was consumed rebuilding industry and infrastructure, and for most people living conditions remained difficult.

Furthermore, the continuing harsh tensions between the United States and the "Soviet bloc," particularly the People's Republic of China, sustained a high level of public unease over Japan's diplomatic posture as an affiliate of the Americans. Some saw it as pitting themselves against "fellow Asians," while others regarded it as aligning Japan with the enemies of "progressive historical forces." That unease was reinforced by political fallout from the atomic blasts at Hiroshima and Nagasaki.

To explain that last phrase, whereas survivors of "regular" strategic bombing were able to rebuild and get on with their lives, little fearing hidden future disabilities, survivors of nuclear bombing all too often were left with inescapable memories of unspeakable horror. In one of the less gruesome recollections, a woman, who was five when the bomb fell, observed:

> Black smoke was billowing up and we could hear the sound of big things exploding...Those dreadful streets. The fires were burning. There was a strange smell all over. Blue-green balls of fire were drifting around. I had a terrible lonely feeling that everybody else in the world was dead and only we were still alive.[4]

More cruelly, those exposed to nuclear radiation in 1945 kept discovering new complications as years passed, with dismaying numbers falling painfully ill and dying one after another while others were continually tormented by grievous disfigurement and fears for the future. The Occupation had been able to suppress most information about the aftereffects of nuclear bombing, but with its end information became much more widely available, which gave rise to heightened concern about the broader implications of nuclear-age warfare.

Concurrently, as Moscow pressed ahead with atomic weapons development, Washington deployed nuclear-tipped, tactical, surface-to-surface "Honest John" missile launchers to Korea. And in 1954 the American program of nuclear weapons testing in the Pacific enflamed affairs when a group of Japanese fishermen were sickened by radioactive fallout from a blast at Bikini Atoll in the Marshall Islands. Those developments suggested that however bad the 1945 bombing may have been, worse was in store, and that American policy should, therefore, be opposed.

That sentiment was reinforced, no doubt, by residual anger at the outcome of the Pacific War, by resentment of the continuing presence of well-fed, well-housed, well-off foreign troops who were largely exempt from Japanese jurisdiction, by anger at recurrent incidents involving those troops and their bases, and by the American government's hostility to all things "socialistic," including Japanese efforts to rebuild trade with China. These factors galvanized the Japanese left, generated a vigorous anti-war and anti-nuclear weapons movement that intensified domestic political conflict, and spurred production of anti-nuclear literature, theatrical productions, art, and – most famously – the 1954 animated film *Gojira* (Godzilla), in which a mutant monster emerged from the radioactive sea to ravage Tokyo until a heroic Japanese scientist drove it back to its lair.

Other issues.   Given the difficulties of the day, it is unsurprising that public discontents were rife and openly expressed during the 1950s. A broad array of issues was addressed, but in their entirety they constituted, one might say, a socialization to the outcome of the Pacific War. By the early 1960s a broad – though certainly incomplete – consensus had taken shape regarding Japan's new global position, its *modus operandi* in that position, and the structure and operation of domestic society as rearranged by SCAP and modified during the fifties.

Getting to that consensus was not easy. The arguments over Japan's global position, whether couched in the well-worn dyadic terms East and West or in Marxian terms of progressive socialist vs. reactionary capitalist forces, centered on whether Japan should function as a collaborator in American policy, an opponent of that policy, or a neutral aloof from the Cold War quarrel. In the end, participation in the Washington-centered economic sphere proved so advantageous to the new ruling coalition that, however strong the "nuclear allergy" or the discontent with American performance, policy strayed no farther than cautious moves to "normalize" relations with the Soviet bloc, moves that were executed during the mid-fifties, along with Japan's entry into international trade organizations and the United Nations.

Debates over the domestic settlement were equally rancorous. In a series of political initiatives, successive prime ministers tried, with varying degrees of energy and effectiveness, to centralize control of government and education, to strengthen industry's power *vis-à-vis* unions, and to modify what they regarded as various excesses in SCAP reform. In the face of sometimes violent objection (by local groups, opposition politicians in the Diet, labor unions, housewives, and the intelligentsia), Tokyo strengthened its control of prefectural and local government, recentralized the administration of police, further restricted labor's right to strike, and tightened its control of teachers, textbooks, and curriculum while restoring the central funding of education. It tried with less success to restore the role of Shintō in public life and modify parts of the 1947 Constitution. And it completely failed in repeated efforts to amend or delete Article 9, having to settle for *de facto* rearmament and the legal cover provided by a loose judicial interpretation of the Constitution.

By late in the decade domestic tensions were extremely high despite the accelerating rate of economic recovery and the slowly receding American presence (by 1960 US troop strength in Japan was down to 48,000). One source of tension was the seemingly endless stream of government initiatives that the dominant factional coalition of conservatives – identified after 1955 as the Jiyūminshutō or Liberal Democratic Party (LDP) – was able to pursue despite the angry opposition of aggrieved interest groups and ideologues. Another was the continual frustration of opposition Diet politicians and their supporters, mainly socialists of one sort or another. They were weakened by internal divisions and, perhaps even more, by a political rhetoric that alarmed not only big business and its political allies but also many small shop keepers and recently-landed farmers. That outcome thwarted their efforts to turn widespread discontent with the LDP into electoral victory, leaving them permanently out of power.

Yet another factor that exacerbated domestic tensions was the governing style of Kishi Nobusuke, who became Prime Minister in 1957. Having been a career official with deep ties to the Manchukuo regime, Kishi had been jailed as a major war criminal but then released by the Occupation. Given to an abrasive, uncompromising style of leadership and still wedded to a number of prewar ideals, he managed to unite more diverse groups against the government than did any other post-1945 leader before or since.

Then two developments at decade's end – a labor strike at the Miike coal mine in Kyushu and Kishi's renegotiation of the US–Japan security treaty – linked domestic tensions to the international context in ways that drew nearly every interest group of consequence, as well as people of every doctrinal persuasion, into political action, most of them in opposition to Kishi's administration.

Coal vs. oil. The problem at the Miike coal mine grew out of the changing global fossil-fuel situation. Tokyo's initial postwar energy policy, as noted above, had been to foster domestic coal mining, and annual output had risen from the 1946 low point of 20 million metric tons to nearly 52 million in the years around 1960, almost equaling peak wartime production. Japan's mines mainly yielded coal of low quality, however, and reserves were small and the coal seams difficult and dangerous to work. Consequently, many coal users found imports preferable in both price and quality.

Furthermore, not all fossil fuels proved equally useful. Leaders of the steel industry, who had long been dissatisfied with domestic coal, complained as early as 1950 that "the root cause of our inability to bring prices down is the high cost of coal." They went on to explain:

> heavy oil has a higher fuel efficiency than coal, it is easier to regulate the heat level
> of oil than of coal, if we use oil it reduces the amount of fuel we need, equipment
> and transport are simpler, it requires fewer of our employees to handle it.[5]

For them oil, whether imported or not, was preferable to coal.

In that view the steel makers were prescient. By then the most fully mechanized regions of the world, mainly in Europe and North America, preferred oil to other fossil fuels. Having expanded their oil consumption tremendously during preceding years, however, and having squandered their own reserves on inefficient usage and industrial-age warfare, they needed new sources of fuel. Most importantly, they encouraged ruling elites in the Middle East to provide oil by developing the still-untapped fields of that region. Those fields, which began coming on line in 1947, proved to be immense, and the resulting production soon was so great that it gave industrial users a vast, new source of fuel whose price dropped steadily as the fifties advanced.

Japan's leaders, recognizing that oil was in most ways preferable to coal and would be essential to further industrialization, and knowing that their own reserves were nil, moved to become a major buyer in this new market. Japanese oil men, most of whom were collaborating with major foreign oil companies, set about developing up-to-date refining facilities. Indeed, a government report of 1956 cited "the high degree of automation and continuity of the various [refining] processes, [which probably make them] the most highly automated of all manufacturing operations in the country." As oil's prospects brightened, those of coal mines and miners dimmed.

The use of Middle Eastern oil also created a role for large, ocean-going tankers, and the Japanese ship-building industry was well placed to meet the global demand for them. Having access to skilled but cheap labor in the still-large population of inadequately employed, and having just revitalized itself building a new merchant marine fleet for Japan, it rapidly became dominant in the production and export of super tankers. That outcome further energized the economy and generated foreign currency to pay for more fuel imports.

As domestic coal mining lost its attractiveness during the fifties and Middle Eastern oil was becoming available on terms that encouraged its use, government and industry leaders shifted to a policy of phasing out coal production in favor of imported energy supplies. The shift was hesitant, however, because of an enduring desire to minimize foreign fuel dependence and lingering doubts about oil's long-term promise – prescience indeed! In the late 1950s the question came to a head when Mitsui Mining Company, owner of the Miike mine, decided to cut back the mine's operations and slash its work force. The miners' union, aware of the larger trend that Miike foreshadowed, resisted fiercely and in 1959 a bitter strike ensued. By one report some 15,000 union activists trekked to Miike to support the 14,000 strikers while Kishi's government deployed some 13,000 riot police to counter them.[6]

The miners stayed out for a year despite sporadic violence, a split in their union, and the combined pressure of government and business. But in the end the company prevailed. Under cover of a compromise mediated by Kishi's successor, Ikeda Hayato, the Miike operation shrank, starting the process of withering that within a decade closed 580 of Japan's 682 mines and shrank the mining force by 80 percent to 52,000 miners. By 1990 fewer than 8,000 worked the archipelago's residual coal fields. And despite dramatic increases in output per miner due to mechanization, coal output had by then fallen from fifty million metric tons to around seven million. With that shift in energy policy Japan acquired a much more desirable mix of fossil fuels, but it also became more completely dependent on foreign sources of energy, and, as a corollary, on the export sales to pay for it.

The Treaty crisis. Even as the bitter struggle at Miike was making both international commerce and Japan's ruling classes look as heartless as 1930s critics had portrayed them, Kishi brought to the center of public attention the vexatious issues of US–Japan relations and Japan's position in the global political arena. He did so by undertaking to renegotiate the US–Japan security treaty. His goal was to establish greater diplomatic equality between the two parties while retaining Japan's position as a close adherent to US policy. But where he saw a more balanced relationship in the making, a broad coalition of others saw an agreement that would entangle Japan more deeply in American foreign policy, threatening to foster remilitarization at home and Japanese military involvement in American adventures abroad.

Despite months of intense and widespread protest and uncommonly powerful opposition within the Diet, Kishi pressed ahead with his treaty proposal. Then in late April 1960 his critics, students in particular, were galvanized by news that the authoritarian president of South Korea, Syngman Rhee, who was seen by many dissidents in Japan as an instrument of "American capitalist imperialism," was toppled from office by protests that culminated in a week of student-centered public demonstrations. Hoping to replicate that feat, Kishi's opponents responded to his persistence in May by precipitating two days of stormy violence inside the Diet while some 15,000 protesters milled around outside. When Diet members who opposed the treaty proposal boycotted the proceedings, Kishi arranged its hurried midnight ratification in their absence. That maneuver secured his treaty, but the public was enraged. Opposition grew, and a month later the crowd of demonstrators around the Diet reached some 300,000, while a massive strike by six million workers disrupted the economy.

Rural areas, which continued to benefit from the postwar settlement and LDP farm policy, were relatively unperturbed by the bruhaha in Tokyo, but in towns across the realm the postwar political order seemed more at risk than ever before. To save themselves and the system that served their interests so well, leaders of the ruling conservative coalition eased Kishi out of office. In his stead they turned to Ikeda Hayato, another career bureaucrat, but one of very different personality, a bluffly handsome man of great charisma, shrewd political instincts, and an overwhelming interest in economic growth.

Projecting an image of sincere modesty, Ikeda urged compromise and reconciliation. Most importantly, as illustrated in his handling of the Miike strike, he smoothed labor's relationship with government–industry leadership. During the fifties labor pressure had induced Tokyo to pursue modest improvements in workplace conditions, and following the Miike settlement Ikeda and other leaders made further attempts to better labor relations by expanding unemployment insurance and helping fired workers find new jobs. Those measures, together with more conciliatory policies by management in matters of workplace procedure and worker input, served further to weaken the more radical unions and strengthen those that would collaborate with industry to promote gains in worker productivity through workplace rationalization and technological adaptation.

More broadly, Ikeda encouraged the public to focus its energies on the processes of economic growth and material betterment. Adopting the slogan "income doubling" to suggest that very soon everyone's material standard of living would become much higher, he directed public attention away from the global political issues that Japan could not really control anyway to domestic economic trends which, as he well knew, were proceeding very favorably if people would only notice. His efforts bore rich fruit. The turmoil of 1960 had sobered enough people high and low so that LDP bosses and their opponents proceeded more cautiously. Political activists drew back from violent confrontation, and rhetoricians cooled their commentary. Moreover, the public, as Ikeda hoped, did turn its attention to the business of economic growth and the benefits it would presumably bring to society as a whole, and rapid commercial expansion during the next several years did in fact bring much of the general public substantial material benefits, at least in the short run.

By the early 1960s, then, Japanese society had largely come to terms with the facts of defeat and redirection, both domestic and global. Discontents and disagreements certainly persisted in following years, but they remained relatively modest. The general consensus seemed to be that the postwar institutional order was legitimate and deserving of support even if particular policies, politicians, and political groups were found wanting. In the spring of 1960 that outcome had not seemed at all assured.

SHŌWA GENROKU (1960–1990)

For the Japanese people as a whole, the three decades after 1960 were arguably the best in their entire history – or at least the best since 1915. They were characterized by unusually rapid economic growth and rising standards of living, with the complications, costs, and benefits of that growth becoming the primary items of the political agenda. Political process was, as a corollary, essentially a story of systems maintenance and *ad hoc* problem resolution.

The public perception of the age as one of exceptionally good fortune – good fortune that in the nature of things was probably fleeting, too good to last, and thus a source of regret for its anticipated transience as well as gratitude for its bounty – was reflected in the pundits' reference to it as "Shōwa Genroku." That reference invoked the popular, if somewhat erroneous, image of the Genroku period (1688–1704) as the short but glorious heyday of Tokugawa urban culture and affluence, after which came the hardships of the eighteenth century. Fittingly, 1989 marked the end of Shōwa Genroku in two senses: Shōwa *tennō* died that year, after the longest reign (1926–89) in Japanese history, and the decades of boom gave way to the longest, most intractable, most damaging economic downturn since the Pacific War.

GROWTH

Japan's main growth trends during Shōwa Genroku were all continuations of earlier ones: growth in population, production, productivity per capita, fossil fuel consumption, and global interdependence. Thanks to several domestic and foreign factors, however, most of those trends were notably more pronounced than during earlier decades.

Demographics. The trajectory of population growth changed only modestly. Before the Pacific War, even as empire builders had invoked the spectre of overpopulation to justify their enterprises, the government had actively thwarted efforts at family planning and birth control. After defeat, however, with millions repatriated from the empire, the economy in ruin, food and shelter inadequate, and illness and underemployment rampant, the government approved programs of birth control, primarily through abortion, in an effort to reduce a surging post-surrender birth rate. In following years that program, which accommodated the strongly felt desires of many people, achieved appreciable results, as indicated by table 1 in Appendix A.

However, improvements in diet and public health had a greater, contrary effect, enabling Japan's people to live longer (about 47 years in 1935; 68 in 1960; 78 in 1990). In consequence, as figure 13.1 (p. 327) indicates, the population continued to grow at an historically unprecedented speed: the roughly 32,000,000 of the later Tokugawa period, which had reached 70,000,000 by the later 1930s, zoomed past 100,000,000 in the 1960s, the growth not slowing appreciably until nearly 1990, when it stood at 123,600,000.

This surging population was sustained by a combination of imported foodstuffs and expanded domestic farm production. The imports were paid for by expanded industrial exports while domestic increases in food output were largely achieved, mainly during the 1950s–60s, through types of agronomic improvement that industrialization made possible. The intensive use of chemical fertilizer was of primary importance, but also the liberal use of herbicides and insecticides, field rationalization, seed improvement, crop diversification, and the more extensive multiple cropping permitted by greenhouses and plastic covering.

Growth factors. The heart of growth during Shōwa Genroku lay not in agriculture, however, but in the urban economy. A number of factors enabled industrial producers to increase their output and thereby exploit the expanding domestic market, as well as markets abroad. Most immediately, the rapidly expanding population continually provided more workers, and technological change in agriculture freed an ever larger proportion of them for other tasks, as we note more fully below. Of the many other factors one might mention, educational developments, social management practices, geography, technology, and global context merit particular attention.

The reformed and expanded education system was producing ever larger numbers of more highly trained and trainable young workers. To mention some salient figures, whereas less than 50 percent of students pursued formal education beyond the ninth grade in the early 1950s, over 90 percent were doing so by 1975 and over 95 percent by the 1990s. Even more dramatically, whereas some 240,000 students were enrolled in junior colleges and universities in 1950, the figure had nearly tripled by 1960. And during the next decade, as postwar baby boomers surged into college, it more than doubled again to a 1970 figure of 1,670,000. After 1975, as figure 18.1 indicates, the rate of enrollment growth slowed, having reached about half the total age group, a level comparable to that of other industrial societies. The number of women going beyond high school grew sharply during Shōwa Genroku, but through the 1980s a relatively high proportion continued, for reasons of

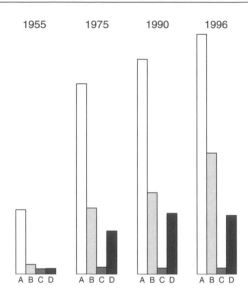

1955   1975   1990   1996

A B C D   A B C D   A B C D   A B C D

Figure 18.1 University and junior college enrollments, 1955–1996. (*a*=university males; *b*=university females; *c*=junior college males; *d*=junior college females.) *Source:* Figures calculated from *Japan Statistical Yearbook, 1998*, p. 702.

personal choice and family and social pressure, to enroll in junior colleges, which prepared them for marriage as well as work.

Meanwhile, the success of Japan's post-1960 rulers in defusing domestic discontents, even when done tardily, helped the country minimize a number of emotional and material costs that hampered other industrial and industrializing societies. Most importantly, perhaps, the harshest confrontations between labor and management had, as earlier noted, occurred by the early 1960s. As the economy boomed during Shōwa Genroku and as systems of production grew more complex and technologically sophisticated, a portion of the material benefit accrued to workers, and Japan's labor unions, like those in other, comparably developed industrial societies, became more sedate while declining in cohesiveness and political influence. After 1975 their membership stabilized at about 12.5 million, even as the work force continued to grow. As a result union membership as a percent of the labor force declined from the 1947 level of 55 percent to only about 25 percent by 1990.

Post-1960 Japan also managed to minimize harsh political wrangling, riots and their suppression, oppressive policing, endemic litigation, chemical addiction, social violence, and the imprisonment of large numbers of otherwise gainfully employable citizens. Whereas the United States, for the most notorious industrial-age example, had some 330,000 people in prisons and jails in 1972, a figure that mushroomed thereafter, hitting 1,800,000 by 1999, Japan had only about 45,000 to 50,000 incarcerated during the same period.[7]

Geography also gave Japan a competitive edge in global industrial competition. Lined with good harbors, and with its population mostly resident near the coast, it was able to achieve efficiencies of international transport that inland-oriented nations could not easily match. Also, because of Japan's acutely mountainous terrain, its population was densely settled on small patches of flat land. Lest the point be missed, note that by one official calculation, Japan around 1990 had a population density of some 1,500 people per square kilometer of habitable area, whereas West Germany had 360; France, 160; the United States, 50.[8] As a result of this exceptional density, every kilometer of material infrastructure – highway, railroad, electric and telephone line, sidewalk, street, subway, sewer, and water pipe – as well as every kilometer traveled by a mail carrier, policeman, fire truck, delivery van, or bus was able to serve far more people than equivalent services in those industrial societies where ampleness of level terrain has given rise to much greater urban sprawl and less efficient infrastructure and service systems.

The negative potential of this geographic context was reduced by the cultivation of behavioral norms that helped minimize social friction and by the miniaturization of much modern gadgetry. The development of commercial procedures that reduced the spatial requirements of material production and distribution, such as "just-in-time" parts supply and small-scale retailing, helped cope with terrain constraints. As did smaller trucks, automobiles, and other rolling stock, in many, many ways. So, too, did the prevalence of space-efficient forms of recreation. One thinks immediately of the ubiquitous *pachinko* parlor, a store front where vertical pinball machines are arrayed in rows, allowing players for a pittance to stand or sit elbow-to-elbow for hours of complete solitude, flicking their thumbs and watching the tiny, shiny metal balls jump and jitter their way down the glass-fronted mazes for the possible reward of candy, cigarettes, or such.

The archipelago's geographical character was turned to advantage when introducing up-to-date industrial technology. We noted in chapter 15 how select areas, such as the Kawasaki coastal strip on Tokyo's south side, had started developing into centers of diversified modern industry by the 1920s. After the Pacific War that trend accelerated, with the Kawasaki vicinity and several other harbor areas becoming some of the most densely industrialized pieces of real estate in the world. Indeed, the coastal development around Kawasaki was so intense that the port lost its geographical separateness, becoming part of a nearly uninterrupted industrial zone ringing Tokyo Bay. By the 1980s, two decades of intensive landfill activity had consumed about a fifth of the entire Bay, converting wetlands, by one count, into sites for "three steel works; thirteen oil refineries; six petro-chemical plants producing ethylene feedstock; twelve other chemical plants; ten shipyards; two automobile factories; and fourteen electric power stations," not to mention thousands of lesser shops.[9]

Japan's newest industrial zones also became increasingly "rationalized," most notably in the creation during Shōwa Genroku of huge integrated *konbinato*. These coastal sites, commonly built on salt marsh wetlands covered with landfill, combined wharf and warehouse areas for inbound raw materials with electric generating facilities, refineries and storage fields for fuel oil, industries such as steelworks, chemical plants, and shipyards that used the raw materials and energy, and finally wharfage and rail heads for loading the outbound finished products.

The several segments of these *konbinato* maximized their technological modernity by license, purchase, and invention of new devices and procedures. Refineries acquired cracking equipment that would handle ever-lower (and hence cheaper) grades of crude oil; electricity producers shifted from coal to oil and in the sixties developed thermal power plants that could burn the crude directly. Similarly, as steel makers erected major new facilities, mostly during the decade after 1955, they installed the most efficient equipment they could find, complete with complexly integrated, computer-controlled systems and flow-through production lines that took in ore at one end of the plant, moved it through the stages of processsing via huge blast furnaces and continuous casting lines to produce strip steel of highly controlled quality that emerged from the other end of the plant where it could be loaded directly onto ship, railway, or truck for transport to its destination.

As these brief comments on technology suggest, the bureaucrats and business leaders who played key roles in this industrial expansion had developed by Shōwa Genroku a broad sense of what their task entailed. Besides providing education and training, as earlier noted, they fostered worker efficiency and dedication through diverse incentives and means of indoctrination. Emphasis on quality control and cost containment strengthened the global market appeal of their products. Attention to efficiencies in factory design, energy consumption, and so forth, as well as the expeditious use of electronics, miniaturization, robotics, and other new industrial technology, helped assure Japan during these decades a strong competitive position in world markets.

The ability to function successfully in world markets was crucial because it was Japan's participation in the Washington-centered economic sphere that enabled it to import much cutting-edge technology while gaining access to fossil fuels and other raw materials as well as the export markets to pay for them. As the Sino-Soviet bloc lost internal coherence and vitality, moreover, and as Cold War attitudes softened despite the fervor of ideologues on both sides, Japan's leaders were able to extend their trading activity behind the iron curtain, slowly developing commerce with China, the USSR, and their affiliated states. Also, Japan's own lack of empire, together with its marginal role in the American sphere, enabled it to minimize the diversion of resources to military matters, despite recurrent counter-pressure from Washington.

The capacity of the ruling coalition of partymen, bureaucrats, and industrialists to operate relatively freely in this postwar global context helped them avoid or resolve destructive trade conflicts. Most strikingly, perhaps, as Japanese producers outperformed foreign competitors in field after field, causing the latter to turn to their governments for protection via import restrictions of one type or another, Japanese producers sidestepped the restrictions by constructing and operating factories abroad, thereby becoming domestic manufacturers, as in the case of automobile production in America and Europe. Less visibly, as other industrializing societies, notably South Korea, Taiwan, and parts of South and Southeast Asia, developed their capacity to outsell Japan in particular product areas, such as shipbuilding, textiles, or simpler electronics, Japanese leaders escaped a number of fruitless and destructive trade rivalries by phasing out uncompetititve domestic production, trying to do so in ways that minimized the damage to work force and community, and hence to the LDP electoral base.

Energy sources. The leaders of entrepreneurial Japan recognized the importance of these several competitive advantages because they realized that a rapidly growing portion of Japan's consumables were imported, were made from imported materials, or were fabricated using imported fuel. Back in 1890, as earlier noted, Japan's foreign trade bore the earmarks of an "undeveloped" country, being characterized by manufactured imports and raw material exports. By 1914 the balance was clearly shifting, and by the thirties Japan had become significantly dependent on imported foodstuffs (including the yield from pelagic fisheries) and was beginning to develop a need for imported fossil fuel, most critically oil for military use.

Following defeat, government policy emphasized energy autarchy and sought to maximize domestic food production and coal output. But during the fifties policy changed, and by Shōwa Genroku the situation was radically altered: over 90 percent of exports were manufactured goods, and imports consisted of about 80 percent raw materials (foodstuffs, fossil fuel, and other) and 20 percent manufactured goods and machinery.[10] And pelagic fishing had also expanded, further deepening the citizenry's dependence on offshore energy supplies.

The increase in industrial-age (non-foodstuff) energy consumption is particularly striking. During the decades 1960 to 1990, such consumption quintupled, rising from 952 trillion kilocalories to 4,663 trillion.[11] That was a rate of increase some 1.63 times faster than for the world as a whole.[12] Table VII in Appendix A indicates how thoroughly that increase depended on imports: whereas domestic energy production furnished nearly 79 percent of the total Japan consumed in 1955, by 1990 it yielded only about 17 percent.

That was not the preferred outcome. The early postwar hope that domestic coal could fuel the future had soon faded, but nuclear power had emerged as a great new basis for energy independence. During the war Japanese scientists had unsuccessfully attempted to develop nuclear weapons, and as the 1950s advanced, even when the anti-nuclear movement was at its height, atomic energy attracted the interest of scientists and government planners. To the former it stood as a great new scientific frontier; to the latter, an energy source that could minimize dependence on fuel imports. Ground was broken for Japan's first nuclear power plant in 1956, and the plant (situated on the coast at Tōkaimura, some 110 km northeast of Tokyo) came on line in 1965. The 1970s energy "shocks," which we note below, gave impetus to the program, and by the early 1990s over forty reactors were in operation at seventeen sites, producing more than 25 percent of the nation's electricity.

The use of atomic power slowed Japan's rapidly growing need for imported fossil fuel, but it did not provide the energy independence that government planners had sought. They envisioned a series of breeder reactors that would reprocess fuel and minimize the need for uranium imports, but by the 1980s technical problems, along with growing public alarm at the risks of fusion technology, led to abandonment of most of the plan. Earlier efforts to develop an indigenous fission technology had also foundered, forcing Japan to rely on imported American nuclear equipment. And mishaps abroad, notably the Chernobyl disaster of 1986 in the USSR, together with troublesome events and practices at nuclear sites in Japan, heightened public opposition to nuclear power of any sort.

In the outcome Japan's nuclear industry depended on imported machinery as well as imported fuel, and official enthusiasm for atomic energy, which had peaked during the seventies, gradually cooled, leading to delays in construction, scaled-back plans, and reluctant acknowledgment that the atom was not the key to energy autarchy. Rather, by 1990 the promise of nuclear power was giving way to the problems of where to store accumulating nuclear waste in an earthquake-ridden archipelago and what to do with radioactive nuclear plants once they were decommissioned, problems familiar to other industrial societies.

Even in terms of coal, Japan's most ample fossil fuel, the growth in import dependency was stunning, as table VIII in Appendix A shows. During the fifties, it will be recalled, Japan's leaders had decided to slash domestic coal production in favor of a mix of imported fuels. Coal, however, remained useful for some functions, and by 1990, as a consequence, the total tonnage consumed was roughly double that of fifty years earlier. However, instead of being nearly self sufficient in coal, Japan was 90 percent dependent on its import.

That change in coal provisioning was closely linked to changes in the generation of electricity. During prewar decades, as noted in chapter 15, hydropower had provided an ever-larger share of Japan's electricity. Initial postwar electric-power construction projects attempted to continue that trend, but by 1955 the effort was failing. Remaining dammable rivers were remote, and construction and power transmission costs were prohibitive. Moreover, projects were repeatedly bogged down by jurisdictional disputes as electric companies that serviced major cities tried to exploit distant watersheds at the expense of local folk. In consequence construction shifted to thermal power plants that could be built cheaply on the coast near cities and in *konbinato*, where ocean-going vessels could unload their cargo of fuel almost directly into giant furnaces. With that shift in generator policy, electricity supplies grew like topsy, but at the cost of sharply increased dependence on imports.

Regarding other fossil fuels, the tonnage of gas-carrying vessels rose ninefold between 1970 and 1990, and during the eighties gas displaced coal and oil as the main fuel for generating electric power. By the nineties both nuclear fuel and liquified nitrogen gas were rapidly gaining on coal as major sources of power, but as of 1990 oil remained the predominant source of overall industrial energy. As table VII in Appendix A shows, its role in energy production peaked during the 1970s, but around 1990 it still provided nearly half the total, in striking contrast to a mere 14 percent in 1955. And lest we forget, the oil was essential not only for energy but also for myriad industrial products, notably plastics, rubber, asphalt, fertilizer, pharmaceuticals, and diverse other chemicals. As table IX in Appendix A reveals, Japan's crude oil imports grew a hundred-fold during the half-century after 1940, when the question of oil availability first emerged as a *casus belli*.

Trade and industrial output. Even as this massive importation of fuel made possible a dramatic increase in industrial output, it also made essential a commensurate increase in exports. Prudence dictated, furthermore, that reserves of foreign currency or bullion be accumulated to cover import needs in times of export decline, whether that be caused by political, economic, or other misfortune. During the 1950s, as the economy rebuilt, Japan ran a continual trade deficit that forced it to delay badly needed imports of machinery and other supplies, but during the sixties it turned that situation around and since 1965 has enjoyed nearly uninterrupted surpluses. Indeed, those surpluses so increased the nation's currency reserves that during the 1980s Japan became a major holder of foreign securities and Japanese entrepreneurs became active investors in an array of overseas properties.

Meanwhile several factors kept foreign competition in Japan's domestic markets under control. Initially, when war-ravaged Japanese industry lacked the capacity to compete, formal import controls minimized the inroads of foreign producers, few of whom considered bombed-out Japan a market worth cultivating anyway. From the 1950s onward authorities gradually relaxed the formal restrictions, often in response to foreign pressure: as of 1960 nearly 500 product categories were subject to import restrictions; by 1975 the number had plummeted to 29, and by 1987, to 23, nearly all agricultural.

Even during Shōwa Genroku, however, many foreign producers continued to show little serious interest in the Japanese market, making minimal attempts to design products that would accommodate its particular needs and wants. Equally damaging, many foreign producers misperceived the idiosyncratic business practices of their own society as universal norms of the industrial world and did little to gain the language and cultural knowledge needed to move effectively in the Japanese marketplace. And the many foreign firms that tried to market goods they had on hand in the manner to which they were accustomed commonly encountered a seemingly endless array of frustrations, some because of their own ignorance, others due to consumer indifference, and yet others because of purposeful obstruction by Japanese industrial and governmental interest groups.

These diverse problems notwithstanding, ever more fast-food chains and other foreign businesses became established during Shōwa Genroku. Domestic producers were generally able to flourish, however, sustained by a rapidly expanding indigenous market while they learned how to operate abroad. In consequence they had sufficient time to develop the external markets necessary to support the imports of raw materials and other goods and services that sustained both the growing population and its rising level of consumption per capita.

Table 18.1 Indicators of industrial growth, 1960–1990

Item	1960	1990
Manufacturing employment (1,000s)	8,169	11,788
Gross National Product (mil. ¥, 1985 prices)	66,769	407,156
Electricity generated (mil. kw hours)	115,497	857,272
Inland freight transport (mil. ton-kilos)	138,901	546,785
Crude steel production (mil. metric tons)	22,138	110,339
Iron and steel exports (1,000 metric tons)	2,313	16,735
Four-wheel vehicle production (1,000s)	482	13,487
Four-wheel vehicle exports (1,000s)	39	6,165
Television set production (1,000s)	3,577	15,132
Television set exports (1,000s)	45	7,598
Electronic computer production (1,000s)	0	3,292

Sources: Figures assembled from *Japan Statistical Yearbook 1962, 1977, 1996, passim*, and Yano Tsuneta Kinenkai, ed., *Nippon, A Charted Survey of Japan 1994/95* (Tokyo: Kokuseisha, 1994), *passim*.

One must stress the qualitative importance of this foreign trade because in quantitative terms it remained a smaller portion of gross national product than in prewar years, which tends to conceal its utter essentiality for the well-being of entrepreneurial Japan. Thanks to the massive expansion of domestic consumption during Shōwa Genroku and to the high value-added character of Japan's technologically sophisticated exports, foreign trade remained in the 10–15 percent range of GNP as against 20 percent during the thirties. Without that 15 percent, however, and most fundamentally without the gigantic fossil fuel energy boost that it permitted, there would have been no Shōwa Genroku boom for later generations to recall with nostalgia.

Myriad statistics reveal the magnitude of industrial expansion that Japan experienced during these years. Table 18.1 lists just a few indicator items.

This massive expansion in industrial output, achieved with such a modest increase in factory work force, translated into notable gains in material standard of living. It not only eased the substantial pent-up, postwar demand for better housing, urban infrastructure, and creature comforts that still existed in 1960, but also provided a supply of goods and services that expanded even more rapidly than the population. The result was a considerable rise in consumption per capita, as shown in figure 18.2, which also indicates the similarity in Japanese and American trajectories since the 1950s. Furthermore, the increased output provided exports enough to cover imports and build up the earlier-noted cushion – an excessively plush cushion, some argue – of foreign currency reserves. In short, for at least forty years Japan found the entrepreneurial strategy for securing a global resource base far more satisfactory than it previously had found the strategy of empire building.

POLITICS

The politics of Shōwa Genroku were heavily shaped by the economics of entrepreneurial industrialism, and it is a story that illustrates wonderfully well why politicians in office love "peace and prosperity." In a manner that

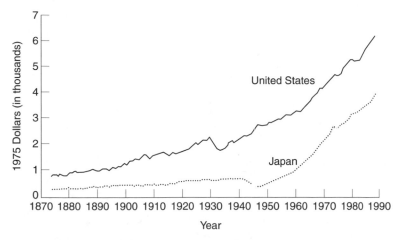

Figure 18.2 Trends in real consumption per capita, Japan and US, 1874–1988. Standards of living rose more rapidly in the USA prior to 1930, but from 1950 through the 1980s the two moved upward nearly in parallel, although Japan narrowed the gap slightly. *Source*: Andrew Gordon, ed., *Postwar Japan as History* (Berkeley: UCP, 1993), p. 260.

reminds one of how seventeenth-century prosperity helped the new Tokugawa regime perpetuate itself, the material benefits of nearly uninterrupted boom were spread widely enough through the general public to secure broad support for the established order. Discontents persisted, of course, but they were severely fragmented and localized, failing to generate the sort of broad-ranging opposition that Prime Minister Kishi had managed to elicit in 1960. Under these conditions, the LDP coalition of conservative politicians, with its ties to business and bureaucracy, held together into the 1990s.

The LDP held together, but it did so despite diverse problems of the day, sharp personal rivalries, minimal creative energy, an accumulating legacy of corruption, and a decline in public approval that is evident in figure 18.3. Those trends suggest another historical comparison: much as early Tokugawa and Meiji were times of dynamic, influential leadership that gave way to later years of political ineffectuality, so the LDP as decades advanced seemed less and less able to shape affairs.

Domestic problems. The tenor of domestic political tensions is suggested by issues that involved students, farmers, day laborers, and victims of industrial pollution.

During the later 1960s, as Washington bogged down in a land war in Vietnam – much as Tokyo had done in China three decades earlier – LDP leaders were able to exploit the American need for collaboration to regain administrative control of the Ryukyu and Bonin island chains. They were not, however, able to escape public disapproval of Washington's policy toward Southeast Asia, particularly its use of military bases in Japan. Instead the Vietnam issue became entangled in other developments to produce among intellectuals and students an intense and outspoken hostility to Washington's performance and Tokyo's acquiescence in it.

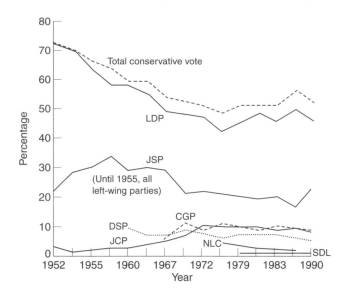

Figure 18.3 Trends in House of Representatives elections, 1952–1990. LDP = Liberal Democratic Party; DSP = Democratic Socialist Party; JSP = Japan Socialist Party; CGP = Clean Government Party; JCP = Japan Communist Party; NLC = New Liberal Club; SDL = Social Democratic League. The LDP lost strength steadily until the later 1970s, but the JSP had little success in recruiting the defectors. Most went to the proliferating minority parties, whose pressure added to government paralysis without creating a viable alternative to LDP rule. *Source*: Andrew Gordon, ed., *Postwar Japan as History* (Berkeley: UCP, 1993), p. 428.

By then the first postwar generation of students was in college, a generation conscious of the hardship and emotional turmoil that accompanied defeat as well as the hopes and dreams associated with early postwar rhetoric about peace, democracy, human rights, and the heady promise of socialism. What they found in college, however, was overcrowding, uninspiring classes, and the prospects of a humdrum future as low-level employees working at tedious tasks, essentially proletarians when viewed from the Marxist intellectual milieu that surrounded them.

Even those in the fields of science and technology, who had every reason to picture themselves as the cutting edge of human advance, saw an unappealing future, viewing science and technology as, "a tool of the oppressive technocratic regime, under which the university scientist exists merely as a rank and file employee."[13] Their sense of predicament reminds one of late Meiji youth, as noted in chapter 14, even though the deeds of their parents' generation cast a very different shadow across their lives than deeds of the glorious Meiji founders had cast over the lives of their offspring.

The personal discontents of this student generation seem to have combined with the public resentment of American policy and the intelligentsia's dismay over the faltering promise of socialism to precipitate a period of intense student protest activity. Although the students received little support from the public at large, during 1968–9 their activism in the name of peace, social justice, and academic reform disrupted 115 colleges of various sorts. Their actions paralyzed a number of schools, including the most prestigious, and finally prompted the government to deploy large numbers of riot police, who restored order to university life with remarkably few broken heads. The contrast with prewar police work was striking – to the outside observer, at least. In following years student activism rapidly declined, by 1971–2 being most visible in the violent actions at home and abroad of a handful of extremists whose deeds thoroughly alienated the general public.

By then, however, student discontent had also played a role in one of the longest drawn out conflicts of Shōwa Genroku, that arising from the government's 1966 decision to build a new international airport to accommodate Japan's rapidly expanding involvement in the global economy. The taking of farm land near Narita, a town east of Tokyo, provoked resistance from the 350 or more farm families whose holdings were threatened, and by 1968 their protests were being reinforced by brigades of well organized, highly motivated students. The sometimes violent confrontations between police and airport opponents received extensive media attention and elicited broad public sympathy for the farmers. That sympathy did not translate into broad public opposition to the planned airport, but it did force the government to proceed more slowly and in the end to settle for a single-runway arrangement that subsequently became severely congested as Narita grew into one of the world's half dozen busiest airports. The dispute raged on for years and in time became a more-or-less pro forma symbol of righteous opposition to the dominant values and policies of the day. It also echoed widespread regret for the agricultural society that was disappearing as industrialism raced ahead.

Less dramatic but just as enduring as this struggle over the sacrifice of farmers and farm land to the needs of air-age society was another problem created by the economic boom that began in the fifties and accelerated during the sixties. That was the swelling number of irregularly employed day laborers, who worked mainly in shipbuilding and construction projects but also as supplemental labor in diverse other enterprises. Many were troubled men, frequently alcoholic, often single or separated from kin, ill educated, or of minority status. Assigned to jobs by labor sub-contractors who commonly had gang (*yakuza*) ties, the men often were callously treated, poorly paid, given dangerous tasks, and denied job security and most fringe benefits. During the construction boom of the sixties their numbers grew rapidly, and the wretched slum areas where they lived, such as the San'ya district in northeast Tokyo, became crowded, prompting more and more of the men to seek shelter elsewhere about the cities. Occasional riots and demonstrations pitted the laborers against local police and detachments of riot police, but the confrontations eventually spurred local governments and agencies to make gestures of assistance. As Shōwa Genroku advanced, the problem of harshly exploited day labor was also eased by the sustained demand for workers, which improved wages until the onset of recession around 1990.

Even as the anger of day laborers was upsetting political tranquillity, another unwelcome aspect of industrialism reappeared on the scene: environmental pollution. As we note more fully in chapter 19, during the 1960s several forms of pollution, but most horrifically incidents of poisoning caused by industrial waste discharge, generated heated legal and political contention. Mainly during the seventies the government tardily developed more regularized mechanisms for mediation and compensation, stronger restrictions on polluting activity that eliminated much of the identified problem by 1980, and somewhat stronger laws on environmental protection. More subtle, more intractable, and more far-reaching environmental problems continued to fester, however.

Trade problems. As the issues of the Vietnam War, student discontent, Narita, day labor, and pollution slowly receded from the political foreground during the early seventies, Tokyo leaders encountered a series of trade-related difficulties that were partially precipitated by the speed and magnitude of Japan's industrialization. By then American industry had lost many of the political, economic, and technological advantages that in 1945 had made "free trade," meaning minimally regulated international trade, seem so attractive, and Japanese industry had emerged as its most formidable competitor. The American capacity to compete abroad was further injured by Washington's fiscal mishandling of the costly war in Vietnam and concurrent domestic programs, which stoked severe inflation. In a series of moves intended to address these problems, the American President Richard Nixon pressured Tokyo to trim its exports to the US, textiles in particular, and he unilaterally reversed US diplomatic policy toward China by recognizing the government in Beijing as legitimate. He also repudiated the postwar yen/dollar exchange rate of 360 to 1 and forbade the export of American soybeans.

These actions, known collectively as the "Nixon shocks," alarmed Tokyo, making leaders and led alike more aware than ever before of the highly vulnerable quality of their new affluence. As matters worked out, however, Japan coped with their effects within a few years, primarily through diplomatic nimbleness and rigorous self discipline.

To elaborate briefly, the textile dispute, which was an early instance of a type of trade quarrel that erupted repeatedly as the competitive positions of particular industries waxed and waned, was resolved by *ad hoc* compromises and, subsequently, a managed shrinkage of Japan's textile industry. The reversal of US policy in China prompted Tokyo, which thitherto had reluctantly abided by the American posture of non-recognition, to move briskly in reversing its own position. Following that reversal, Japanese businessmen found themselves far freer than before to pursue trade with China, and in following years they outstripped all others, including the Americans, in developing that commerce.

Because of the American dollar's central role in international currency transactions, Nixon's decision to end the fixed dollar/yen ratio seemed to threaten Japan's export capacity, and hence its ability to pay for essential imports, by pricing Japanese goods out of foreign markets. Within a few years, however, most exporters overcame that difficulty, mainly by cutting production costs and accepting lower profit margins, and in the outcome they compelled foreign competitors to improve their own efficiency. Meanwhile the windfall of cheaper dollars, which was the other side of the shift in exchange rates, made it easier for Japanese to accumulate foreign-currency reserves and purchase imports.

In the critical area of oil, however, that import gain proved short-lived. Japan had by then become a major oil user, as noted above, and it obtained about 80 percent of its supply from the Middle East. In 1973, and again in 1978–80, Middle Eastern regimes used their oil as a weapon in regional conflicts, creating market scarcities and driving up the price from about $2 a barrel in 1973 to around $30 by 1980, before it fell back toward earlier levels. Japanese industry responded to the price jumps by improving fuel efficiency and developing alternative energy sources, nuclear power plants most notably, and in the outcome it preserved its capacity to operate in the international marketplace. That outcome is suggested by the trajectory of Japanese exports to the USA, as seen in figure 18.4.

Finally, Nixon's freeze on soybean exports sent a shock wave through Japan because soy was a basic staple of the diet and over 90 percent of the supply came from America. Washington's action abruptly reminded the Japanese of how quickly and seriously a foreign food embargo could threaten them. All the alarums and horrendous implications notwithstanding, however, Washington quickly reversed its soybean decree, evidently because the financial hurt to American soy producers, wholesalers, and exporters translated into political injury for Washington leaders more quickly and effectively

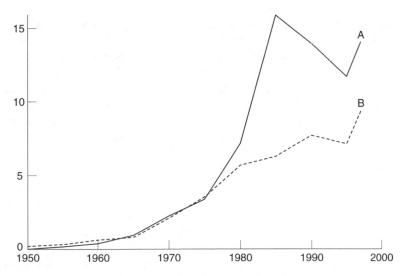

Figure 18.4 Trends in Japan–US trade, 1950–1997 (in trillions of yen, at 5-year intervals). A = exports to US; B = imports from US. Japan's bilateral trade balance with the US shifted from chronic deficit during the fifties through a decade of general balance, 1965–75, to a state of chronic surplus as Shōwa Genroku advanced, doing so despite major changes in currency exchange rates and reductions in formal import restrictions. With the onset of Heisei recession, the trade gap narrowed. *Source*: Based on figures in *Japan Statistical Yearbook 1962*, p. 257; *1972*, p. 294; *1999*, pp. 408–11.

than they had anticipated. In the outcome what had appeared to be, potentially at least, the worst of these several foreign trade crises proved the most fleeting and least consequential. And it had little subsequent effect on Japan's food policy: whereas the country had been about 60 percent dependent on soybean imports in 1950, it was at least 95 percent dependent by 1970 and remained at about that level thereafter.

Corruption and the Fisc. As the LDP became more entrenched during the sixties, as industrial growth raised the stakes in commercial success, and as perturbations in the marketplace became more severe and frequent, illegal dealings became more common and their scale larger. The several trade imbroglios of the early seventies exacerbated affairs, as did the ambitious developmental schemes of Tanaka Kakuei, who was Prime Minister from 1972 through 1974 and major LDP power broker for much longer. His proposals for situating industries widely about the hinterland, as a way to ease problems of urban crowding and rural economic decline, led to intense land speculation, a surge of inflation, a flurry of corrupt bargains between business and political interests, and embarrassing revelations in the press. The upshot of these trends was a series of major scandals that tarnished one LDP administration after another during the 1970s and 1980s, fostering factional conflict within and public disgust without.

By then the LDP faced another problem as well. During the early boom years the government had enjoyed annual budget surpluses that gave it the best of all fiscal worlds: a debt service rate that dropped to 0.2 percent in 1965 and did not rise to the 3 percent level until 1973 even as the rate of taxation by the central government was declining (from 16.4 percent of national income in 1953 to 11.7 percent in 1975).[14] By 1975, however, the most rapid economic growth was a thing of the past; the "Nixon shocks" had complicated affairs, and inflation was accelerating. LDP leaders tried to cope with their domestic difficulties, and thereby retain electoral support, by adopting diverse meliorative policies, notably farm price supports and a brace of social programs designed to benefit workers, the aging and otherwise vulnerable, and industries facing difficulties. The broader trend is suggested by social security expenditures, which rose thirteen-fold between 1970 and 1990 to exceed 53 trillion yen.

These social policies combined with the declining rate of fiscal growth to throw the budget into deficit: the debt service rate exceeded 10 percent in 1980 and 20 percent in 1987, finally forcing LDP leaders to confront the red ink. During the eighties they began selling ("privatizing" in the *parlance du jour*) such government assets as Japan National Railways and Japan Airlines while attempting to hike taxes and whittle away at welfare and support programs. They trimmed budgets for university expansion, for research projects, for nuclear power development, for environmental protection, and for a host of other ventures.

Unsurprisingly these moves angered interest groups and alienated voters. The exceptional popularity of Nakasone Yasuhiro, Prime Minister, 1982–7, together with a recklessly speculative boom (the so-called bubble economy), concealed the LDP's erosion for a time. However, following a string of hurtful events – Nakasone's departure from office in 1987, the eruption of a major new scandal in 1988, the emperor's death in 1989, and the collapse of the boom starting that year – the conservative coalition fell apart, demoralized and discredited. That outcome left Japan's government in the hands of a series of weak, short-lived, caretaker administrations formed by *ad hoc* factional coalitions whose only source of strength was the absence of effective rivals. Shōwa Genroku had come and gone.

[19] SOCIETY AND ENVIRONMENT (1945–1990)

CHAPTER SYNOPSIS

SOCIAL ISSUES
THE DECLINE OF AGRICULTURE
ASPECTS OF URBANIZATION
MATTERS OF GENDER
MINORITIES
RELIGION

ENVIRONMENTAL ISSUES
POLLUTION
DOMESTIC FORESTS
RESOURCE DEPLETION

The speed of entrepreneurial Japan's economic growth and the extent of change in the public's material well-being have prompted innumerable pundits to write of the country's postwar "economic miracle." More trenchant observers have noted that these material gains were accompanied by equally noteworthy social and ecological complications. The problems noted in chapter 18 of disgruntled students, day laborers, farmers displaced by Narita Airport, and people poisoned by industrial waste, were but hints of trends and tips of icebergs of discontent and difficulty that deserve more extended scrutiny.

SOCIAL ISSUES

The year 1960 provides a convenient breaking point in treating the politico-economic history of entreprenurial Japan, being the moment when primary concern with defeat and its political consequences gave way to emphasis on new issues and agendas, mainly economic. In terms of social history, however, the topics that seem most noteworthy relate to longer-term ramifications of industrialization itself. These topics include agriculture's role in society, aspects of urbanization, gender and minority relationships, and the condition and role of religion. As earlier chapters have attested, these topics generated concern, commentary, and varying levels of legislation during the prewar decades, and they generally reappeared or became more pronounced after 1945, especially during the decades of Shōwa Genroku.

THE DECLINE OF AGRICULTURE

Almost by definition industrialization entails the transformation of agriculture from society's central productive activity to a highly marginalized one and, as a corollary, the shift of society's spatial center of gravity from the rural community to the city. Most fundamentally industrialization has marginalized agriculture through the use of fossil fuels and non-organic energy sources. Their use destroyed the near-monopoly position of farm-produced energy supplies, mainly foodstuffs, while the awesome array of technological changes that their use has facilitated enabled an ever-larger proportion of the population to pursue non-farm employment.

Numerous statistics show that the marginalization of Japanese agriculture began in the Meiji era, but it accelerated after the Pacific War, particularly during Shōwa Genroku. Whether measured in human labor time or in terms of its economic contribution, agriculture was still a considerable part of society and economy until the 1950s, as figure 19.1 indicates. By 1990, however, it was reduced to a minor role, roughly 5 percent of the national totals – and still shrinking.

The sharp decline in farming's role after 1950 notwithstanding, the process was remarkably orderly and of only intermittent public concern, usually when some farm interest group assembled in Tokyo to placard and demonstrate outside the Diet in protest of some government policy or other. Mindful of the rural misery and political tension precipitated during the 1920s and thirties by increased rice imports from the empire and decline in the silk export market, one wonders how agriculture's more recent and more pronounced shrinkage was accomplished with so little evidence of public

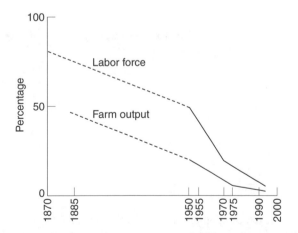

Figure 19.1 Trends in agricultural labor force and output as percentage of national totals, 1870s–1990s. The sustained prewar decline in agriculture's role in Japan's economy accelerated sharply during the 1950s, and by the 1990s it had reduced farming to a minor element in the total economy. *Source*: Figures calculated from Yano Tsuneta Kinenkai, ed., *Nippon, A Charted Survey of Japan 1994/95* (Tokyo: Kokuseisha, 1994), pp. 60, 121.

pain. How was it, to take the specific issue of silk, that whereas a 33 percent decline in the value of exports wreaked havoc on farmers during the decade 1921–31, a 68 percent decline in total silk output between 1960 and 1990 left farmers better off?

A simple answer presents itself: when farm work no longer paid, other jobs were available, as figure 19.2 suggests. Although agricultural mechanization made much farm labor superfluous (the number of motorized tractor-tillers zoomed from about 64,000 in 1955 to 2,500,000 by 1965, peaking at 4,400,000 in the mid-eighties, as larger riding tractors replaced walking tillers), between 1947 and 1990 Japan created 28 million new jobs in industrial-age areas while losing some 13 million in agriculture and forestry. Farm mechanization did not, therefore, create a large population of unemployed. Moreover, many of those who quit farm work appear to have done so as much from choice as necessity. Most older farmers were able to stay on, or even return to farming after a career in other work, while the young could and did abandon the tiller's life.

One still wonders, however, why that massive shift of villagers to dependence on non-farm employment was not accompanied by the rise of fetid, hughly sprawling, trouble-spawning urban and suburban labor slums such as have existed in so many places, from early nineteenth-century London to present-day cities on other continents. Certainly there was some dislocation. The decline of agriculture, as well as the shuttering of coal mines, did, after all, help create the earlier-noted population of slum-dwelling, urban day laborers. By global standards, however, the scale of things was modest.

The key factor is that the shift to non-farm work did not dislodge people from their homes. Whereas some 5.5 million homes were officially listed as

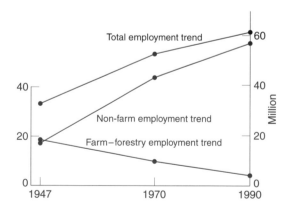

Figure 19.2 Select trends in employment, 1947–1990. The decline in farm and forestry employment after 1947 was more than offset by the 3-fold rise in non-farm jobs, which enabled Japan to sop up the postwar jobless, unemployed rural workers, and the rapid population growth of the period and, during the 1980s, still have jobs for "guest workers." *Source:* Figures calculated from *Japan Statistical Yearbook, 1950,* p. 36; *1996,* p. 88. But also see *Japan Statistical Yearbook, 1996,* p. 84. Japan's agricultural statistics are notoriously tricky because so much farm work is done on a part-time basis by family members.

farm households during the 1920s, the number rose after 1943 as cities went up in flame, and in 1960 there still were 6 million, the number not falling below 5 million until the mid-seventies, or 4 million until 1990.

Certainly one factor sustaining the numbers of farm households was the reluctance of farmers to sell their homesteads because of personal attachments, the difficulty of finding comparably satisfactory housing elsewhere, and the extremely high market value of the adjoining land, which made it a valuable buffer against future hard times. And – just as importantly – they did not need to sell them. Instead large numbers combined non-farm work with part-time farming in ways that allowed them and their families to stay in their homes, making the transition to industrialism a much more gradual shift than it might have been or than national employment and output figures seem to imply that it was.

The reasons so many farm families could stay put even as they shifted to non-farm employment are to be found primarily in Japan's geography and secondarily in government policy. Geography eased the shift to industrial society in a number of ways. The clustering of Japan's human population on the archipelago's small patches of flat land put most rural people within relatively easy reach of town and city, enabling them to commute to diverse, non-farm jobs, both full- and part-time, in construction, manufacturing, and commerce. Commuting was further facilitated during Shōwa Genroku by rapid improvement of roads and the proliferation of motor vehicles, which more than offset declines in rural bus and rail service. Moreover, ill-managed urban sprawl rapidly spread industrial-age employment opportunities out into the countryside. And, finally, because farms were small, mechanization permitted their operation on a part-time basis that combined the part-time farmer's weekend input with other household labor as needed during the week.

Abetted by their geographical circumstances, more and more farmers took off-farm jobs, and by 1990 only about 15 percent of them were still engaged in full-time farming. So few farmed full-time because they could not afford to do so and need not try. Tables IV and V in Appendix A, which suggest the changing economics of farming, indicate why that was so. The statistics reveal, in essence, that as decades advanced, the costs of farming consumed a larger portion of receipts, while the residue of profit covered a declining portion of the farm family's household budget, falling from about 60 percent, on average, during the later 1950s to a quarter or less by the nineties. When one considers, furthermore, that a large percentage of those farm receipts were for rice and that for most of this period rice support policies maintained the farmer's selling price at a substantially higher level than market demand would justify, the decline in real profitability was even greater.

However, other income increasingly covered household expenses and, for many part-time farmers, even some of their farm costs. Most importantly, non-farm earned income, mainly salaries and wages, emerged during Shōwa Genroku as the predominant source of wealth for most farm families. But secondarily, grants and annuities, including retirement income for aging farmers, acquired a fiscal importance that surpassed farming proper during the 1980s.

These grants and annuities were elements in a broader government policy of supporting agriculture. As it developed, the policy in Japan, as in other industrial societies, encompassed a rich array of programs designed to sustain agricultural production and prosperity and, as *quid pro quo*, the politician's job. As recently as 1990 an LDP Diet member noted the political logic of the relationship:

> It is often said that, unlike in the past, the LDP gets only 10 per cent of its votes from farmers. But they are not like salarymen. They are shrewd. And the Nōkyō [farmers' cooperatives] near large cities have financial resources in abundance. You cannot win an election if they are against you.[1]

For that reason, he concluded, one needs to support agricultural interests.

The heart of agricultural policy was support for rice prices, mainly by restricting imports, regulating the wholesale purchase price, storing surpluses, and when they grew onerous paying farmers to reduce paddy acreage. In part this rice policy reflected the lobbying power of agricultural interests, but in part it accommodated ethnic notions of Japanese rice's special virtue, and in part it bespoke the enduring wish to maximize Japan's self-sufficiency in a basic foodstuff.

Tokyo's rice policy drew considerable criticism over the years, to some degree from urban interests seeking lower food prices but mostly from academic ideologues of *laissez faire* and those foreign business interests wanting greater access to the Japanese food market. Nevertheless, and despite ancillary costs that we note below, rice policy, along with diverse other agricultural programs, did ease the pain of Japan's adaptation to industrialism by helping farm families to remain at home even as they transmogrified from agricultural households into participants in an urban industrial world.

In its entirety the semi-managed shrinking of agriculture's role in Japan had a broad range of consequences. Over the decades large numbers of poorly endowed, intermontane hamlets, and hence several hinterland prefectures, declined in population, some localities being entirely abandoned. A substantial amount of farmland also disappeared, with some 20,000–25,000 hectares being lost annually in the years around 1990. A small portion of that arable reverted to woodland as isolated villages shriveled or died and as farmers abandoned tiny, infertile, poorly accessible fields whose tillage had ceased to be economically feasible. Some fields simply were fallowed and left idle. Far more of the arable, however, was lost to the myriad forms of urban sprawl, including residential, commercial, and industrial structures, more and wider roads and railroads, recreation facilities, and all sorts of storage space. Attempts to offset the losses through creation of new farmland were minimally successful, in part because there was little incentive for either government or entrepreneur to undertake reclamation work, but more basically because little potentially productive arable existed, short of leveling bedrock mountains with nuclear-strength charges.

Where agriculture did continue, the extremely intensive techniques employed by farmers in their struggle to turn a profit and compete with imports produced widespread soil and water pollution. The extremely heavy use of chemical fertilizers and pesticides was particularly hurtful, with the early 1990s fertilizer-use rate of 387 kilograms per hectare standing higher than nearly all other countries, whether industrialized or not, and far above the United States' rate of 100 kg/ha.[2]

Closer to the heart, if less worrisome to the mind, agriculture's shrinkage made it difficult for more and more young farmers to find wives because so few young women envisioned the lifestyle of semi-agriculture as more attractive than that of city or suburb. Would you, after all, rather pull weeds on a sweaty summer's day or punch a computer in an air conditioned office? This situation prompted a few farmers to seek brides abroad, far more to pursue other careers, and some to resign themselves to bucolic bachelorhood.

Turning to a less lamentable topic, the change in farming's position altered the role of rural society in the urban imagination. Before the Pacific War, as noted in chapter 16, hardship in the countryside touched the nation directly, shaping political action, fostering anger and unrest, and finding rhetorical expression in agrarianist (*nōhon shugi*) writings. And many of those engaged in *nōhon shugi* activism had close ties to the countryside. By Shōwa Genroku, however, when a new surge of interest in village life appeared, it was a very different phenomenon. The *furusato* or "native village" boom, as it was called, was essentially a romantic urban indulgence and a tourist-industry promotional strategy that celebrated folk song and dance, old houses, rustic food, and happy images of simple, hard-working, virtuous peasant families. Farm people, with their machinery, up-to-date houses, partially protected markets, and non-farm jobs, had little to do with it, although they accepted with gracious good humor, one supposes, the tourist *yen* that came their way when city folk ventured out to rediscover their imagined roots.

Whereas prewar *nōhon shugi* had involved serious political business, that is to say, the *furusato* boom was in essence a cultural anachronism. Village life, once the heart of Japanese society, had been marginalized, elevated to the museum-like status enjoyed by "the family farm" in other industrial societies.

ASPECTS OF URBANIZATION

Urbanization involved noteworthy trends in several areas: demography, land use, residential housing, family composition, and spatial mobility.

Demographics. Entrepreneurial Japan witnessed a striking increase in city size and a radical shift in the balance between urban and rural population numbers. That trend had been proceeding gradually since the Meiji period, and by 1940 some 29 percent of Japan's population lived in cities of 100,000 or more while 32 percent were in towns and villages of fewer than 5,000 residents. During the 1950s the rate of urbanization accelerated, as table II in Appendix A indicates, and by 1990 nearly 60 percent lived in cities of 100,000 or more while fewer than 2 percent lived in the small communities.

The figures are, however, a bit deceiving. Over the years a large number of villages were, for a mix of reasons, combined administratively or absorbed into neighboring urban centers. That process, which we noted in chapter 15 when treating Ikegami Chinpei of Okayama, climaxed during the 1950s, as table II reveals, in a massive spate of consolidations, after which few independent small towns and villages remained. The process exaggerated the rate of real spatial concentration because it meant that millions of people who appear to have relocated to larger towns did not in fact move a centimeter. Nevertheless, towns and cities throughout the archipelago did really become more densely settled as the population grew and families abandoned more isolated dwelling sites. Thus it appears that between 1960 and 1990 about 300 towns and villages that initially numbered over 5,000 inhabitants lost enough members to fall below the 5,000 line.

The bulk of postwar urban growth occurred in cities of 300,000 inhabitants and up, especially those of a million or more. Whereas Japan had only two 7-digit cities, with a combined population of 3.4 million, in 1920, and four, with 12.4 million, in 1940, by 1990 there were eleven totaling 25.3 million. Ten of the eleven, moreover, were situated along the venerable Tokyo-to-Shimonoseki urban corridor. There the major nodes of settlement attained gargantuan proportions, most notably the Tokyo metropolitan region, which came to sprawl across much of the Kantō plain and to hold about a quarter of Japan's entire population.

Land use. As cities grew, both before and after the Pacific War, they sprawled outward, overrunning adjacent towns and villages, with urban planning and zoning laws having only modest effect in determining the location of industrial, commercial, and residential neighborhoods. In consequence clusters of apartments, single-family dwellings, factories, and other business establishments rose cheek by jowl amidst residual farmsteads more commonly than in Euro-America, where venerable traditions of stone and brick architecture seem to have entrenched the notion of construction as permanent and therefore properly subject to preventive community control. In Japan, perhaps because a sense that structures are temporary and land use subject to later change prevailed through centuries of wooden construction, industrial-age urbanization has been less constrained by zoning regulations.

Other factors, notably land taxes, capital-gains taxes, and tenantry laws, also contributed to the mixed-use character of city neighborhoods. As in other industrial societies, tax regulations sheltered farmers from higher residential tax rates, enabling them to keep their small fields in production even as adjacent areas gave way to urban sprawl. Tax regulations also made it advantageous for corporations to retain idle property pending future use, while tenantry laws restrained landlord freedom to evict tenants and convert property to more immediately profitable uses. In consequence existing land usages persisted on many parcels, even as surrounding areas were undergoing rapid change, with more and more of them sprouting large ferro-concrete structures whose costliness and durability assured that once in place they, too, would not change soon. In the outcome the close spatial mingling of diverse, modern-day structures and functions persisted through Shōwa

Genroku. And it did so despite growing problems of noise, traffic, air pollution, and so forth that elicited public complaints and protests.

Residential housing. Urbanization also entailed major changes in residential housing, in a word, "crowding." It manifested itself in two principal ways, in the "stacking" of people in high-rise structures and their "packing" in small and closely arrayed houses. Basically these trends reflected the normal industrial-age phenomena of rapid population growth, expanded spatial needs and wants per capita, and the clustering of ever more people in urban nodes, trends that everywhere have combined to yield striking increases in land prices, especially in cities.

In Japan, however, the stacking and packing was intensified by topography and tectonic instability: the relative dearth of flat land heightened the intensity of demand on usable areas, and the risk of earthquake damage slowed the development of high-rise construction. In addition – and in Tokyo particularly, with its immense and multi-faceted appeal, which drew immigrants from throughout the archipelago and abroad – the pressure to stack and pack was heightened by the above-noted tax and tenantry arrangements, which kept considerable urban acreage from being converted to residential use. During the later 1980s those conditions helped generate an immense temporary spike in land prices, which produced a wide range of disruptive effects that continued to reverberate well into the nineties.

In Japan as elsewhere, probably the historically more important of the two trends was stacking, the shift from an essentially horizontal to a highly vertical deployment of people. Technological advances eased the earlier concern about earthquakes early in Shōwa Genroku and, as a consequence, architectural restrictions were modified and multi-story buildings gradually proliferated and grew taller. Nevertheless, as of 1990 the stack arrangement was still only partially in place: 77 percent of housing was separate dwellings in 1958; 60 percent still was in 1990. And the public still favored the latter: over 80 percent of interviewees in a 1990 poll preferred separate dwellings to apartments.[3] Still, the trend was clear. Whereas single-family dwellings and one- or two-story apartment houses increased by only 50 percent (1.5 times) in the twenty-five years 1968–93, three- to five-story apartments grew by 5.9 times, and those of six stories and more increased by 58.4 times. As a corollary trend, whereas only 8 percent of dwellings were ferro-concrete structures in 1968, 28 percent were by 1993.

The massive, ferro-concrete apartment complexes that were erected after the war to house more and more of the rapidly swelling urban populace were for the most part drab, walk-up structures of standard design that were full of cramped quarters. They evoked considerable public distaste but stayed full *faute de mieux.* As decades passed, however, and the material level of living improved, newer high-rise apartments and condominiums became larger, more comfortable, and more diverse – at least for the more favored classes.

Meanwhile urban single-family houses remained small and densely packed. The older norm of small, wood-frame houses lining dusty village and town streets provided the spatial model for the tidy, tightly packed, single-dwelling neighborhoods that came to characterize much of the new suburbia. That norm also set the standard for dwelling size, although average house dimensions gradually increased, enlarging, by one estimate, from about 74 square meters in 1968 to 90 in 1990. But houses remained small by the standards of most other industrial societies, "rabbit hutches" in the words of one oft-quoted European visitor.

Houses in the hinterland were appreciably larger than those in cities, Tokyo in particular. But everywhere the modest gains in size were more than offset by accumulations of modern gadgetry and furniture, which effectively reduced the open space in most dwellings, making them feel smaller than ever. The growing disparity between the housing people could afford and what they aspired to (and evidently felt they deserved) generated growing dissatisfaction. By the mid-eighties, with the spike in land prices seeming to destroy all hope of more spacious housing in future, surveys showed that a majority of respondents, a gradually enlarging majority, was deeply disgruntled. The mood did not favor incumbent politicians.

Family composition. In Japan, as elsewhere, industrial-age urbanization and residential stacking and packing were accompanied by a decline in family size. Households became smaller as birth rates declined: whereas families averaged about three children apiece as recently as the early 1950s, by 1990 the average was roughly half that. Moreover, as swelling numbers of retired elderly chose to live alone or were kept at a distance by sons and daughters (most of whom lived in cramped urban quarters with spouse, children, and the clutter of modern gadgetry), the relative number of three-generation households also declined. The change, however, was slow. As of 1985 about 65 percent of those over 65 were still living with a son or daughter, in part because many people adhered to the notion that mature children ought to care for surviving parents, in part because alternative society-wide systems of elderly care were only partially developed, and in part because housing costs were prohibitive.

Spatial mobility. Urbanization also led to more residential mobility as workers repeatedly moved to new job sites, large companies moved personnel from branch to branch, and upwardly mobile families moved from smaller to larger apartments and houses. Furthermore, because of Japan's heightened dependence on a global resource base and engagement in the global marketplace, the increase in spatial mobility was not limited to Japan proper. Rather, it acquired during Shōwa Genroku a substantial international component.

The technological change that made this last development possible, needless to say, was the rise of air travel, specifically intercontinental, commercial jet service, which flowered during the sixties. Airline travel to and from Japan increased 100-fold during Shōwa Genroku to exceed ten million passengers in 1990. The affluence of the age enabled large numbers of Japanese to vacation abroad, making them the most common foreign tourist nationality in various parts of the world. Meanwhile more and more Japanese lived and worked overseas, some staying for years with their families, raising children who became fluent in the local language and at least as comfortable abroad as back in Japan. Yet others in growing numbers went abroad to pursue research and schooling.

Those global travelers then brought back to Japan new perspectives and new wants, which moved subtly into the larger society via commentary and demonstration effect. Alien influence also entered the country through foreign students, tourists, employees, military personnel, goods and their marketers, and communication links: film, satellite television, telephone, electronic mail, and so on. In short, much as industrialization slowly enmeshed rural areas in the nation's urban world, so it enmeshed Japanese society as a whole in the culture of global industrial life – whether it be *sushi* in London, doughnuts in Kyoto, or hot tubs, Zen, soccer, synthesizer music, and advertising flimflam all around.

MATTERS OF GENDER

Besides reconfiguring agriculture's role, urban arrangements, household composition, and human mobility, the rise of industrial society reshaped gender relations. By the 1970s, as noted in chapter 18, both men and women were completing much more schooling than ever before, but a substantial proportion of the women finished their schooling with two years of college while nearly all college men completed four, a distinction that reflected and helped sustain other gender-based dissimilarities of experience. The key issue of note was the work place, but other matters also command our attention.

Women and work. In Japan, as everywhere, industrialization reshaped employment patterns, doing so in two basic ways: the work place became, in the main, separated from the dwelling site, and the varieties of employment grew astronomically.

The separation of residence from work place was not, of course, entirely an industrial phenomenon, but it became standard practice with the rise of factory and office work. In Japan it appeared from late Meiji onward, but it advanced most rapidly during Shōwa Genroku: whereas 34 percent of dwellings were still associated with farming, fishing, commerce, or artisan-scale production in 1958, the figure in 1993 was only 5.6 percent.

"Gainful work," meaning income-producing employment, is everywhere a matter of necessity as much as choice. But as Tsuda Umeko noted in 1915, it is the key to a person's "economic independence" and hence to choice in other facets of life. As gainful work became separated from home life, however, it was mostly men who went out to the job and thus gained access to life's new choices, while women generally stayed home as their dependants.

In Japan, as elsewhere, that pattern was less pronounced at lower social levels, as evidenced most notably in the textile industry, where from the outset women predominated because the work was viewed as a variant of the established sericulture that for generations had been "women's work." Even in the thread mills, however, it appears that women generally saw employment as service to their natal household or as a short-term, money- and experience-gaining prelude to marriage. They were housed on-site in a pseudo-familial setting, with management at all levels male-dominated, while the women were limited to manual tasks. Moreover, most left as soon as they could afford to do so, if not sooner. Few women worked in the mills – or at any of the other menial jobs that generated income – from anything resembling genuine choice.

From the very outset of industrialization, it is clear, a few women in all societies aspired to more active social roles and career choices. However, because the available wage work was so unsatisfying, the separation of household from job and "women's work" from "men's work" may initially have been reasonably acceptable to most. Insofar as men brought home adequate income, women, or at least married ones, were able to focus on home making and child rearing, spared the added burden of gainful but dirty and dangerous drudgery.

Gradually, however, conditions changed, and with them, attitudes. Declining birth rates and the proliferation of household appliances made domestic work less time-consuming and exhausting, and possibly less fulfilling. Concurrently, as industrial technology and organization became more complex and choices of career and work routine more varied and attractive, it became increasingly apparent that the overall trend in work/home relations was benefiting men far more than women. As that realization spread, the stage everywhere was set for women to demand that the initial industrial-age gender arrangement be renegotiated.

In the case of Japan, a few young women of the better classes were already objecting to the new arrangements by later Meiji, as noted in chapter 14. However, it was after 1945, and especially during the boom years of Shōwa Genroku, as birth rates dropped, household appliances proliferated, jobs diversified, urbanization spurted ahead, and income and educational levels ascended, that women began to enter the urban job market in large numbers predominantly as an act of choice rather than necessity. As they did so, they discovered, as have women elsewhere, that employers commonly viewed them as an auxiliary labor force to be fitted in where convenient. Male workers, meanwhile, often perceived them as unwelcome competitors. In line with these views, those who controlled the work place implemented an array of stratagems to protect their own interests, engaging in gender-based hiring, paying, and promoting; invoking age restrictions, physical requirements, and time-in-rank; maintaining "glass ceilings," "old boy networks," and so forth.

The response to this situation in Japan was emergence of a women's movement demanding that the advantages of industrialization be shared more equitably. For several reasons, however, this response was not as aggressive as in some places. Most obviously, perhaps, the gender conflict over jobs and careers was mitigated by the striking change in job availability. The early postwar condition of massive under-employment changed rapidly during the 1950s, giving way during Shōwa Genroku to a chronic labor scarcity that provided job opportunities, even if not very good ones, for almost anyone wishing to work. Women were one of the main beneficiary groups of that shift, especially from the 1970s onward as service industries blossomed, creating more and more higher-skill positions for them.

The fight for work-place change may also have been softened by a widespread concern to minimize overt social conflict, along with the fact that many jobs and careers remained stressful and not very appealing anyway. More importantly, one suspects, the above-noted expressions of male-interest politics were reinforced by variants of the prewar rhetoric about "good wife, wise mother." That rhetoric was not entirely unwelcome to many women because in its own way it in fact helped give many of them a social position of considerable strength, status, and satisfaction.

To elaborate that last point, more than in most industrial societies, housewives in entrepreneurial Japan came to enjoy – and to be burdened with – nearly complete control of their household operation and budget; the care, discipline, and schooling of their children; and maintenance of their family's status in the community. As a corollary to those functions, many played a considerable role in determining their husband's wardrobe, appearance, and social performance. This housewifely role as guardian of home and family in turn undergirded the prominent role of women as leaders and activists in issues of consequence to homemakers and to society more broadly. These included the issues of air, water, and noise pollution, food and other product quality, questions relating to education and public safety, prostitution and other morals-related matters, recycling, nuclear energy, American military bases, and rearmament; i.e., most of the newsworthy citizen issues of the past half century.

Finally, although mothers of young children found themselves fully occupied with household obligations, they also discovered that, as the children grew, their housewifely role left them freer to pursue their own interests, whether in schooling, travel, part-time work, or recreation with friends. And that boon in the later years was doubly valuable because of the striking increase in longevity. Thanks in great part to sharply lower infant mortality rates (39.8 per thousand in 1955; 4.6 in 1990), but also to declines in deaths associated with childbirth and communicable disease, women born in 1990 had a life expectancy of about 82 years, compared to 68 for those born back in 1955 (and 43 in 1925). In the outcome, most women of Shōwa Genroku seem to have measured their sense of worth and fulfillment not by the size of their own paycheck but in terms of the quality of domestic life they could provide their families and the accomplishments of their children.

This constellation of factors, male and female, produced a so-called "M-shaped" female employment pattern that was more pronounced in Japan than in most contemporary industrial societies. Young, single women went to work after school but commonly quit at marriage or late pregnancy. Later, after their children were partially grown, they returned to work, usually on a part-time basis. Employers and male workers welcomed this pattern because it provided a cheaper, more flexible, and reliable work force that did not compete with men in terms of pay, promotion, authority, or status. That M-shaped pattern meant, however, that the range of life choices open to women was still less than that of men, a fact reinforced by the earlier-noted male dominance in four-year colleges. So dissatisfaction with employment arrangements persisted.

During the 1980s, as a more broadly arched feminist movement came into being, a major thrust of its activism was work-place change. The effort eventuated in 1986 in a law mandating equal employment conditions. The law was only hortatory in nature, however; lacking punitive stipulations, it had little immediate effect. So as of 1990, the striking gains of Shōwa Genroku notwithstanding, gender relations in the work place still fell short of the expectations of many women, particularly younger, more educated ones.

Other gender issues. Given the centrality of homemaking to their lives, women were keenly interested in questions of childrearing. During the seventies they mounted strong and effective resistance to government attempts to trim the abortion rights they had acquired in the late 1940s. They were less successful, however, in efforts to persuade government to authorize sale of contraceptive pills.

Meanwhile, "women's lib" groups were proliferating, and in a 1980 interview Atsumi Ikuko, founder of the journal *Feminisuto* (Feminist), framed the overall issue of gender this way:

> Generally men's role is the production of materials outside and women's role lies in the production of life at home ... [However,] Japanese feminist theory considers that both are equally important. Men should be more involved in the production of life, and women, in the production of materials ... The current feminist movement aims at the kind of society in which woman can not only be economically independent but also be free to choose the way she wants to live.[4]

This set of aspirations was evinced during the eighties in a vigorously growing feminist movement that embraced a broad set of projects and issues:

> women's health and reproductive rights, sex discrimination in the workplace, alternative ways of working, child care, challenges to the marriage system, media sexism, feminist arts and publications, protest against war and environmental exploitation, representation in politics, aging, violence against women, and sexual harassment.[5]

It was an ambitious agenda, one that even Fukuda Hideko surely would have found daunting.

The movement gave rise to "feminist debates," a rash of topical writings, and the proliferation of courses and programs on Women's Studies, particularly in women's colleges. It encouraged more extensive networking by women in the professions and better organized and more effective lobbying against gendered work and household arrangements. And it led to the election of a small but growing number of women candidates to local and higher-level political office.

Gains were made in many areas, but a good many women still found their household situations unsatisfactory. The older "mother-in-law problem" that once had generated much unhappiness among young wives eased during Shōwa Genroku as nuclear-family households became more common. And the proliferation of household appliances eliminated much tiresome work. However, husbands, with their hard-driving jobs, assumed domestic tasks less readily than many wives, with their greater education and aspirations, wished. And with fewer grandparents in residence and more husbands working away from the house, parental tasks devolved more fully on mothers, which meant that the "free time" they enjoyed thanks to their modern gadgetry was largely given over to semi-attentive and tedious supervision of children. Lamented one young mother in 1989:

> I don't mind so much when I'm doing the housework! But when it's finished, I long to have some time to myself but the children won't let me... There are so many things I'd like to be doing! Even though I tell myself repeatedly that it won't last for ever, I can't help thinking that I shall never be able to make up the time I've lost.[6]

This mood among young wives was contributing to the declining birth rate, was spurring feminist efforts at change in work place arrangements, and was encouraging a change in male attitudes toward domesticity.

MINORITIES

Like women, the archipelago's minorities – notably *burakumin*, Korean and Chinese residents, unskilled immigrants, Ainu, and Ryukyuans – found their lives changing as industrialization forged ahead.

Burakumin. The members of pariah communities, who continued to face discriminatory attitudes after the war, revitalized their prewar organization and their strategy of openly and directly confronting abusive words and deeds. They also pressured government to take remedial action. During the sixties, as the economy bloomed and Tokyo found that it had money to spend, leaders began responding to the pressure, in 1969 producing legislation that allocated funds to improve streets, schools, clinics, and housing in *burakumin* communities and to provide rent subsidies and other assistance to poorer families there.

Gradually *burakumin* found better-paying jobs, which enabled more and more of their community's younger members to acquire more education, skills, and connections, becoming more mobile and marrying and settling more freely outside the community; in toto, a decline in the old disadvantages. Gains in job benefits did not always keep abreast of higher costs of living, however, and the changes came much too slowly for activists. Moreover, incidents of discrimination and confrontation continued to occur, which during the eighties prompted the government to organize educational programs, lectures, and films to counter discrimination by employers and others.

The government procrastinated, however, when *burakumin* leaders called for laws to criminalize discrimination, arguing that punishment would only "drive discriminatory consciousness underground and harden it."[7] So grievances remained. As one *burakumin* educator put it in 1991, in a litany of issues recognizable from other industrial societies:

> We face discrimination at work, in school, and in marriage ... We are ten times more likely to be on welfare than the general population. We are twice as prone to illness. Half of all *burakumin* live in public housing ... Our children drop out of school at a high rate. As a people we have been vilified, shunned and segregated.[8]

For most *burakumin*, as for many women, the gains of Shōwa Genroku did not suffice.

Resident Koreans. The Shōwa Genroku boom also affected Japan's registered foreign residents. Like *burakumin*, the roughly 650,000 Koreans found theirs a painfully conflicted situation; indeed, it seemed to be the most complicated human story of the day. From the late forties onward they were divided factionally – and for many, bitterly – between those sympathetic to the North Korean regime and those oriented to the South. Most especially those affiliated with Chongryun, an "organization of 'overseas nationals' of North Korea loyal to Kim Il Sung," were isolated from the larger Japanese community, schooled separately, and encouraged to live as independently of Japanese society as possible.[9]

Chongryun members were the most deeply isolated, but nearly all Korean residents found themselves torn between their wish to live, thrive, and be fully accepted in Japan and their wish to preserve Korean ethnic identity as evinced in their names, language, and such cultural attributes as food and clothing. Unsurprisingly perhaps, that cluster of sentiments was accompanied, especially among older and less successful resident Koreans, by a strong distrust of the Japanese populace, a distrust too often repaid with disrespect and discriminatory conduct. They also looked suspiciously at government organs that were unresponsive to their ethnic desires and that seemed neither very interested in nor very capable of redressing their social and material grievances.

Nevertheless, like *burakumin* they did benefit from the affluence of Shōwa Genroku. Whereas they had worked mainly as rag and scrap collectors, manual laborers, and agricultural and fishery workers before 1960, by the 1980s the majority were working as white-collar workers and skilled laborers, although often in small firms rather than large, in real estate sales, and as "money lenders, sales clerks in wholesale and retail trades, catering service workers, taxi and lorry drivers, and clerks in entertainment businesses."[10]

Those employment changes brought many resident Koreans higher standards of living. They permitted more to attend college and by 1990 were contributing to increased rates of naturalization and inter-marriage with Japanese. As those trends advanced, younger members of Chongryun became disillusioned, and the organization lost size, strength, and coherence.

More Korean residents became sympathetic to the thriving society in South Korea (to which in any case 97 percent traced their ancestral roots, whatever their current political affiliation), and more could envisage eventual integration in the Japanese community as an acceptable prospect.

Resident Chinese. Like Koreans, Chinese had long lived in Japan. During the Edo period the most visible were the 2,000, and sometimes substantially more, who lived and worked in Nagasaki. Their numbers swelled during the 1860s when Chinese, working as servants and business employees, accompanied Europeans into Yokohama, Kobe, and the other foreign trading enclaves. By late Meiji, when Japanese authorities again controlled the treaty ports, over 5,000 Chinese were reportedly resident in the country. In subsequent years the number fluctuated with the vicissitudes of warfare and diplomacy, but there always were far fewer Chinese than Koreans. Indeed, perhaps the most noteworthy aspect of this population was how little it seems to have concerned the authorities, especially when compared to *burakumin* and Koreans. An early-Meiji attack on opium smuggling gave way to a mild late-Meiji concern with left-wing political activism, and following the 1923 earthquake Chinese in the Tokyo–Yokohama vicinity suffered along with Koreans. By and large, however, unofficial Chinese organizations appear to have provided sufficient social structure so that life in the Chinese communities was orderly and generally benign in the eyes of Japanese officialdom.

After 1945, as well, many fewer Chinese than Koreans lived in Japan, and Japanese officials and people perceived them as much less of a "problem." Some 35,000 remained after postwar repatriation, about half from Taiwan and half from the mainland. Able to present themselves to the Occupation as members of the victorious side, resident Chinese, and particularly those with better Japanese language skills, were able to move advantageously in the social space between victor and vanquished, serving Occupation troops and exploiting black market opportunities. By the fifties affairs were stabilizing and thereafter the Chinese communities in Tokyo, Kobe, and other cities grew slowly as more legitimate career opportunities developed.

Like Koreans, however, Chinese residents became split politically, with some supporting Chiang Kai-shek on Taiwan and others backing Mao Tse-tung's Peoples' Republic of China. During the 1970s, when resident Chinese numbered over 65,000, Japan's decision to recognize the Peoples' Republic spurred many to seek Japanese citizenship lest they be deported to mainland China. Their fears proved groundless, however, and during the later eighties the numbers of resident Chinese grew rapidly as students and laborers flowed into the country, legally and illegally, in response to the booming economy and Tokyo's interest in building its international reputation as a world leader in technology and modern progress.

Unskilled foreigners. As foreshadowed by that last sentence, the other most notable population entering the work force of entrepreneurial Japan was the foreign-born. Before the Pacific War, Korea had provided a large, transient force of unskilled laborers; during later Shōwa Genroku, when the domestic supply of workers for unattractive jobs grew scarce, people of diverse origins, but Southeast Asians in particular, entered Japan to work.

Initially the influx was heavily female, with young women entering the "water trades" – as entertainers, night club and bar hostesses, and prostitutes – that Japanese women were finding less and less acceptable. During the later eighties they were followed by large numbers of males. Many of these foreign workers arrived illegally, took jobs unauthorized by their visas, or overstayed their visa limits. As of 1990, by one estimate, there were some 600,000 of these "undocumented" workers, mainly in the manufacturing and construction sectors.[11]

Like Koreans before the war, and like migrant workers in other industrial societies, these people often found themselves filling the least desirable positions, their disadvantages reinforced by the language barrier, pervasive consciousness of ethnic distinctiveness, and widespread belief within Japan that the country was too crowded to serve as a job mecca for immigrants. For employers, on the other hand, cheap, vulnerable labor had its advantages, and women in particular were put into the sleazier parts of the water trades by bosses who commonly were affiliated with Japanese or foreign criminal organizations.

By 1990 government officials were so troubled by the ill-controlled ingress that they revised laws on immigration to create legal loopholes legitimizing the presence of an unskilled foreign labor force. One statute allowed "trainees" to enter and stay legally, even though the so-called training programs that employers provided often were thin cover for poorly paid employment. Another statute turned the notion of ethnic "Japaneseness" to advantage, distinguishing those of Japanese ancestry from other foreigners and allowing the former to "return" to their putative homeland. That device enabled some 150,000 Latin Americans, mostly from Brazil, to work in Japan legally, where they tended to get better jobs than did foreign workers of other ancestries. As long as the economy flourished, these loopholes enabled large numbers of workers to enter legally while others continued to arrive and remain illegally, but a business downturn could quickly throw larger numbers out of work, leaving them more desperate, and hence more of a social "danger," than ever.

Ainu and Ryukyuans. Long resident at the extremities of Japan, Ainu and Ryukyuans continued to experience difficulty in finding a satisfactory place in industrial-age society. The roughly 20,000 Ainu of Hokkaido, as noted in chapter 16, had by the 1930s lost much of their ethnic distinctiveness as a result of two centuries of sustained socioeconomic intercourse with Wajin (as Japanese residents of Hokkaido had been known in Tokugawa times). But a cluster of factors – exposure to Wajin disease, the loss of independent livelihood, the persistence of prejudice and discriminatory behavior among Wajin, and the overarching government commitment to Hokkaido's development regardless of the cost to Ainu culture – had combined to exact a heavy toll on Ainu well-being and self-esteem.

The government-affiliated Ainu Kyōkai of the 1930s had tried to better Ainu circumstances, and by then slowly improving educational arrangements were increasing Ainu fluency in Japanese language and culture and producing a small but growing number of Ainu intellectuals and activists committed to improving their people's circumstances. After the war ended, leaders reactivated their Association (renamed Utari Kyōkai in 1961) and revived their 1930s agenda of social advancement.

During the years of recovery, however, disparities in the situation of Ainu and Wajin persisted, with the former continuing to suffer from widespread prejudice. Despite generations of intercourse that had reduced genotypic distinctions, in mainstream Japanese eyes an Ainu was Ainu by "blood," although physical appearance also served as a marker. As one Ainu bitterly put it during early Shōwa Genroku:

> even when Ainu blood is only a small proportion of your actual blood, if you have an Ainu face you will surely be treated in general as Ainu. Where can we go, we Ainu who have been left hanging in mid-air?[12]

As in other societies marked by similar ethnic relationships, with the prejudice came discriminatory behavior, disadvantage, demoralization, and dysfunction.

In the 1960s, when, as noted above, Japan's first postwar generation of students was emerging from school into community life and the work force, young Ainu activists were among them. Much more aggressively than their predecessors they (and supportive Wajin students) began to demand that problems be addressed and long-standing wrongs righted. By 1970 activists, mainly in Tokyo, had organized to advance Ainu welfare by promoting a sense of "Ainuness" and an ideal of Ainu "liberation." They drew on the tactics of *burakumin* leaders who challenged directly and vigorously any Japanese acts and commentary that they regarded as racist. They found inspiration in the liberation movements of "indigenous peoples" in the Americas, Europe, and elsewhere, and they criticized the widespread Ainu practice of trying to "pass" as Wajin. They opposed industrial development plans that threatened Ainu fisheries and other interests. They criticized unwelcome non-economic behavior, whether it be displays of "primitive" Ainu culture aimed at tourists, or the continuing manifestations of daily-life prejudice that Ainu children encountered at school, that workers faced on the job, or that was reflected in official treatments of Japanese history and the lingering official insistence that Japan was a "homogeneous" society lacking ethnic minorities.

In place of "Japanization," they sought to unify and mobilize "the Ainu nation." They devised a flag for their nation and taught and displayed Ainu arts, crafts, customs, and language for the pleasure and instruction of Ainu rather than tourists. They rewrote history so as to celebrate Ainu rather than Wajin triumphs in "the Ainu homeland" (Ainu Moshiri). In the late 1970s Yūki Shōji, Ainu activist and head of the Utari Kyōkai, expressed the sense of Ainu nationhood this way:

> Ainu Moshiri was the Mother Earth that formed Ainu culture, and this remains unchanged to this day. The Gods in whom the people believe have not left

Ainu Moshiri for ever. The present situation where magnificent ethnic ceremonies are carried out every year in various regions, and prayers are offered
respectfully to the Gods of Nature, is confirming Mother Earth, Ainu Moshiri,
as the territory, albeit spiritually, of our people.[13]

The legislative substance of this vision was spelled out in 1984 when the
Utari Kyōkai drafted an elaborate new proposal for laws to criminalize acts
of discrimination, secure rights of Ainu language, culture, and schooling, and
promote Ainu economic and political rights. The activist Narita Tokuhei
revealed a political strategy for advancing that agenda when he spoke to an
assemblage of *burakumin*:

> [We] are now editing our history, claiming our rights, understanding our iden-
> tity, beginning to walk for ourselves. As we advance our work, we can gain soli-
> darity with the Buraku Liberation movement, the movement of Koreans in
> Japan, the physically handicapped, the women's movement, and various citi-
> zens' movements.

Coalition politics, it was hoped, could achieve what autonomous action
could not.

In response to this political agitation, which rivals of the ruling LDP tried
to turn to advantage, the government reaffirmed its commitment to the principle that Ainu and Wajin were one people, all "equal Japanese citizens under
the law."[14] They implemented more measures to improve Ainu well-being,
funneling funds through the Utari Kyōkai to blunt discontent and strengthen
the hand of "integrationists."

During the 1980s a combination of factors that was slowly benefiting ethnic relations – the Shōwa Genroku boom, expanded government assistance,
Ainu self-improvement, and generational change – blunted the Ainu nationalist movement and stalled action on the reform proposals of 1984. Instances
of Wajin prejudice remained troubling, but as of 1990 many Ainu had in fact
moved into the mainstream of Japanese life, were married to Wajin, and
wished to see their children thrive in mainsteam life. The majority felt minimal attraction to Ainu separatism, and little in the demographics suggested
that "nationhood" could be more than a transitional rhetorical stance, a
source of pride in one of the several historical legacies that went into the
making of industrial-age Japan.

At the other end of Japan, meanwhile, the million-odd Ryukyuans seemed,
on the face of it, to have a much better chance of achieving a viable nationhood. At the dawn of the Tokugawa era, it will be recalled from chapter 9,
the hitherto independent Ryukyuan Kingdom had been subjugated by
Satsuma. Following the Sat-Chō coup of 1868, the surviving semi-
autonomous Kingdom was absorbed into the Meiji political order, with the
northerly portion of the archipelago assigned to Kagoshima Prefecture and
the portion from Okinawa southward designated Okinawa Prefecture.

From then until the Pacific War Tokyo adhered to the assimilationist
vision for Ryukyuans that it applied to Ainu, and the Ryukyuan people found
their language and culture treated by "mainlanders" with much the same mix

of curiosity and disdain that Ainu experienced. Their economic condition also remained difficult, by 1935 prompting some 42,000 to leave Japanese jurisdiction entirely. Another 50,000 sought their fortunes in Japan proper or in Micronesia and other colonies, where they commonly ended up holding the least desirable jobs available to immigrants.

Defeat in 1945 proved particularly horrific for Okinawans because of the appallingly bloody battle there. The island chain then came under American military domination, not being officially "returned" to Japan until 1972, long after the Occupation proper had ended and Japan had embarked on its period of dynamic economic growth and change. The American military presence had proven exceedingly burdensome, especially on Okinawa proper, but as eager as most Ryukyuans were to escape American control, many were also displeased with the restored Japanese rule, which was implemented with little reference to Ryukyuan desires.

Even with Tokyo in charge again after 1972, the islands remained peripheral to the Shōwa Genroku boom. They did, however, benefit indirectly via government spending, expanded tourism, and remittances from the large number of Ryukyuans who took jobs on the mainland. Some Ryukyuans nurtured resentment at continuing disadvantages and discrimination, and among the intelligentsia, at least, there persisted into the nineties an enduring sense of frustration as an under-appreciated, semi-colonial people whose ethnic traditions and historical legacy of self-rule and cultural accomplishment failed to receive proper respect.

RELIGION

During the decades to 1990 religion – its status, condition, and social role – only sporadically generated public concern. The general tranquillity on matters theological reflected in part the official openness to religious diversity that characterized the age and in part the country's economic trajectory, which offered a sense of well-being to many and hope to others. But in part it reflected the long-established legacy of "combinative" thought, which tended to mute doctrinal fanaticism even as it gave the public a broadly shared religious praxis. In addition the very modest sense of religion as a "problem" may have reflected the fact that the day's most pressing concerns (about diplomacy, ethnicity, gender, and material well-being) lay to considerable degree beyond religion's purview. "Religion," of course, is a word of many meanings, but the topics that seem to merit brief comment here are the vicissitudes of religious institutions and their relationship to the state, and the character and role of religion as popular faith and practice.

Regarding institutions.   In Meiji Japan, as noted earlier, Buddhist temples had been stripped of all governmental affiliation. Diverse new religious movements had been redefined as Buddhist or Shintō sects, and non-sectarian Shintō shrines (fully 90 percent of the total) had been defined as non-religious entities, with major ones receiving government financial support. Subsequently sporadic conflicts over church–state relations troubled a few intellectuals and a few religious leaders, but the general public continued to practice religion with little notable change from earlier generations despite the escalating political rhetoric about Japan's unique Shintō legacy and divine mission.

During the Occupation SCAP redefined all Shintō shrines, including those that memorialized war dead (Yasukuni and its affiliated Gokoku *jinja*), as instruments of a forbidden state religion. It dissolved the government office that administered them and denied them public funds. After 1952 political leaders periodically made gestures to reaffirm a special linkage between Shintō and government, particularly on behalf of Yasukuni Shrine. However, the gestures elicited noisy protests from diverse religious interest groups, and the SCAP interpretation of church–state separation remained essentially intact throughout Shōwa Genroku.

The fate of Shintō shrines, as well as that of Buddhist temples, was determined less by government policy than by socioeconomic developments. During the hard years of recovery temples and shrines of all sorts deteriorated, being inadequately supported by donations of the faithful, income from land rents and other entrepreneurial sources, and, in the case of celebrated establishments, by exploitation of their market value as tourist attractions and sites for motion pictures. Subsequently, however, they shared in the affluence of Shōwa Genroku, benefiting from high land prices, the booming tourist trade, and widespread public interest in preserving the artifacts of "traditional culture," of which shrine and temple buildings and treasures were among the most celebrated.

As a result institutional Buddhism and Shintō as a whole flourished anew. Due to decades of village consolidation the 175,000-odd Shintō shrines of 1879 had by the 1940s shrunken by 50 percent, and during the fifties another 10,000 were disestablished as more villages merged. Thereafter, however, the number held steady at about 80,000 shrines, while Buddhist temples continued to number about 75,000.

On the margin of institutional religion stood the "New Religions" (*shin shūkyō*). Some of these sectarian movements, including the Kurozumikyō, Konkōkyō, and Tenrikyō mentioned in chapter 11, emerged late in the Edo period. Many more, including a few of Christian derivation, arose from Meiji onward, mostly appearing in rural areas. During the hard years after 1945 they enjoyed considerable popularity, but in Shōwa Genroku, as the rural population dwindled and employment shifted to industrial-age work sites, many lost adherents even as other, more urban oriented, doctrinally exciting, and technologically up-to-date sects arose and prospered, the *soi disant* "new New Religions."

As institutions, a few of these New Religions flourished, acquiring and retaining sufficient followers to erect major central temples and numerous branches and to develop seminaries, priesthoods, bodies of doctrine, splendid ritual, and detailed praxis. Others, however, were local and transient and achieved only modest formalization. Indeed, most experienced great fluctuation in membership, and as of 1990 only six of the forty-odd major new sects claimed a million or more members, while several claimed fewer than

100,000. And those figures, scholars agree, overstate significantly the actual number of committed adherents.

Regarding praxis. These new movements are noteworthy less as institutions than as expressions of popular religiosity. Unsurprisingly, given that they arose within the existing religious milieu, they shared many qualities of the older syncretic legacy. They did, however, have distinctive attributes that merit note because those underlay their special appeal. Commonly founded by charismatic women, these New Religions mostly minimized the distance between priest and follower. They recruited members vigorously and enmeshed them in sustained congregational activities. As adumbrated by one scholar, their teachings

> promise followers "this-worldly-benefits" in the form of healing, solution of family problems, and material prosperity. In ethics they emphasize family solidarity and qualities of sincerity, frugality, harmony, diligence, and filial piety.[15]

In that spirit they promoted faith healing, helped the aged, provided personal counseling to the troubled, and offered blessings to benefit dwellings and their inhabitants, both living and dead.

Proponents of these teachings stressed the importance of each member's self-cultivation. By improving oneself, it was argued, one contributed to the commonweal: to "happiness, health, social stability, abundant harvests, and regular succession of the seasons." And the means to this end was dedicated practice of those disciplines taught by the sect, it being reasoned that rigorous attention to discipline would strengthen character, produce a better person, and thus empower one to live a more worthy, more fruitful, more prosperous life, thereby contributing to the larger goal of a well ordered cosmos.

This sense that one's own performance benefited others and helped sustain the natural order was, of course, an idea of hoary ancestry, and in entrepreneurial Japan it retained its appeal in the older as well as the newer religions. Thus around 1980 a priest of Kinpusenji – a venerable branch temple of Enryakuji, the Tendai headquarters on Mt. Hiei, and a center of mountain ascetic practice in the Shugendō tradition – declared:

> First reflect on yourself, repent your faults, and correct yourself so as to develop the great and powerful mind of *jiri rita* [the process whereby benefiting oneself helps others].

In so doing, he went on, you will pursue "world peace and great harmony among all people," save others from suffering, and "help them in their wishes."[16]

Of the several new religions, by far the most visible was Sōka Gakkai, which blossomed after the war and persisted through Shōwa Genroku as a substantial religious presence. Grounded in the doctrines of Nichiren's Hokkeshū, Sōka Gakkai began during the 1930s in the religious exposition of Makiguchi Tsunesaburō. It survived official persecution during the war and after 1945 grew rapidly under Makiguchi's successors, becoming a national, and subsequently international, movement. It did so through forceful prose-lytizing, careful institutional development, the maintenance of intense con-gregational participation, and the promotion of ideas gratifying to the faithful. In 1964 the group founded its own political party, Kōmeitō, which elected members to local and prefectural office and to the national Diet and thereafter played a generally middle-of-the-road role between the LDP and Socialist opposition. By then Sōka Gakkai had an estimated membership of some fifteen million, of whom perhaps a third were active participants, and it maintained its religious and political presence thereafter.

A number of the other New Religions lost adherents during Shōwa Genroku, even while "new New Religions" were emerging as the most dynamic movements of the day. Characterized by some as "new age" reli-gions, they rejected the centrality of doctrine and focused their attention instead on the cultivation of individual spirituality. They held that individuals must, in the words of one scholar,

> search and discover their own inner being, develop their own spirituality, and bring about their own spiritual transformation. For such personal purposes, techniques such as meditation, ascetic training, bodywork, and psychotherapy are offered as forms of practice and combined with the study of ancient mysti-cism, archaic religions and myths and shamanistic rituals, and psychological theories.[17]

While expressing considerable skepticism about the claims of "scientific truth," proponents of these new movements reflected the contemporary fas-cination with science fiction, demons, aliens, and monsters of the *gojira* sort by taking inspiration from the hoary legacy of omnipresent spirits. Varying with the sect, they employed diverse amulets and rituals to elicit godly com-passion and guard against spiritual possession, and they practiced exorcism to expel unwanted spirits and regain good health.

While embracing venerable religious ideas, however, these newer move-ments were more urban in orientation than the older New Religions and more ready to employ electronic and other media to promote their creeds and recruit followers. In 1987 an observer explained the success of Kiriyama Seiyū, founder of Agonshū, one of the most dynamic of these movements, in this way:

> Kiriyama Seiyū consciously interprets Buddhism into a language that young people can relate to – thus the satellite broadcasts, the modern temple building, his friendly sermon and his approachable manner. All this adds up to a user-friendly religion appropriate to the needs of the modern Japan.[18]

It was a religion fit for the day; how durable it would prove remained to be seen.

Religion served a number of purposes, but for most people praxis was not tightly bound to any particular doctrine. It included practicing select austeri-ties, turning to fortune tellers and mediums for guidance, acquiring and deploying religious amulets or in other ways seeking godly intercession for a safe birth, a gentle death, success in school or work, highway safety, or other boon; and participating in such more-or-less religious ceremonies as visiting ancestral graves, performing New Years rituals, or going on pilgrimages.

A growing number of younger women were adopting the practice of memorial rites (*mizuko kuyō*) for aborted fetuses, doing so even as techniques of birth control improved and the abortion rate dropped. (Official statistics report a decline from 1,170,000 abortions in 1955 to 457,000 in 1990, although the actual drop may be less due to under-reporting.[19]) The growing popularity of fetal rites seemed to reflect changes in the logic of abortion. During the hard postwar years women had, in their own view, terminated pregnancies for the sake of others and were thus innocent of selfish motivation, but during Shōwa Genroku they did so more and more for the sake of their own desires, an expression of selfishness that presumably could give rise to an angry fetal spirit needing and deserving propitiation. That mood was exploited from the 1970s onward by religious entrepreneurs who offered to perform rituals that would honor the fetus, counter its vengeful spirit, and thus put the woman's mind at ease.

Most temples, meanwhile, functioned primarily as memorial sites for the dead, and temple priests served mainly as ritualists for the conduct of funerals and memorial services. As life span lengthened during Shōwa Genroku, a growing number of people, especially women, came to fear the prospect of a long, sickly old age of dependence on their children or others, and in response to this fear, more and more turned to temples to pray for a healthy life and prompt death that would spare them that outcome.

Despite the many services temples offered, organized religion per se was not widely admired nor subtleties of creed understood. During Shōwa Genroku only about a third of the public claimed to subscribe to a religious belief, although most acknowledged some temple affiliation, with many people retaining ties to their family's household temple, whatever its sectarian character, as for example Jōdo Shin or Sōtō Zen. Few, however, showed much interest in its teachings.

The tendency to preserve old ties notwithstanding, the mobility of the age weakened or severed the links of many to ancestral temples and burial grounds. However, the syncretistic legacy facilitated transfers, enabling the young and mobile to maintain some semblance of older practices and beliefs. At-home prayers and rituals tended to be abandoned, the trend encouraged no doubt by cramped housing that left little space for low-priority fixtures such as wall altars. In response the makers of such altars developed miniature ones that were acceptable to many, and during the 1980s some three-quarters of households still reported possessing a Shintō or Buddhist altar or both. Even businessmen found it useful to erect small shrines at their places of business to secure such godly blessings as might accrue. And religious ritual continued to grace many urban activities, such as when a Shintō priest purified a construction site prior to ground-breaking or blessed a new building when the ridgepole was installed, thereby making it a fit abode for the incoming *kami*.

One after another the local festivals (*matsuri*) and religious occasions that had enriched village life shrank and were abandoned or got reworked into celebrations of local culture or tourist-oriented events that appealed to a sense of ethnic nostalgia in the *furusato* vein. For many participants and observers, however, the deities were still compassionate and capable of furnishing aid, and unhappy or angry spirits of the deceased remained a danger to be assuaged. In short, throughout the decades of entrepreneurial Japan the public continued to affirm its identification with its combinative Buddhist/Shintō legacy even though the faith weighed lightly and identity and participation were more *pro forma* and ethnic in character than an expression of firm doctrinal commitment.

ENVIRONMENTAL ISSUES

In Japan, as elsewhere, industrialization brought consequences for the ecosystem, mostly harmful. Whereas industrialism's environmental impact in its very earliest stages was local (*vide* the 1890s Ashio copper mine incident), it broadened and transcended state boundaries as fossil fuel use accelerated, factory output expanded and diversified, chemical usage proliferated, human population mushroomed, and human dependence on a global resource base deepened. By 1990 the environmental impact of industrialization reached from pole to pole and it had become increasingly difficult to distinguish particular industrial societies as the source of specific environmental hurts because all in greater or lesser degree were contributing to all the major forms of damage. Nevertheless, some points of note in the case of entrepreneurial Japan merit consideration.

POLLUTION

Following the Ashio mine affair, industrial pollution continued to worsen as mining, chemical production, and other manufacturing generated more toxic effluents and residues. However, the instances of environmental injury and despoilation were sufficiently scattered and small in scale to escape escalation into national political issues. Instead of major, Ashio-like protests, they elicited local demands for compensation and industrial measures to appease critics by controlling local pollution, most notably through the use of tall smokestacks that sent pollutants elsewhere. There also were occasional expressions of alarm from the intelligentsia, but World War II came and went and Japan began experiencing the rapid growth of Shōwa Genroku before industrial pollution again burst onto the scene as a major bone of contention.

During the sixties, in tandem with the industrial boom, several forms of socially objectionable pollution – noise, vibrations, ground subsidence, foul odors, and construction that blocked out sunlight, as well as air and water pollution – became causes of complaint, especially in highly urbanized areas.[20] They derived from diverse sources: industries, transportation devices, electricity-generating facilities, farms, and households. It was, however, a number of horrific, local incidents of industrial poisoning that proved particularly traumatic, the most notorious being the Chisso Corporation's poisoning with industrial mercury of Kyushu's Minamata Bay, its marine life, and thence people in the locality. The poisoning there had begun back in 1908, but it worsened sharply during the 1950s, finally goading victims to protest.

One of the key elements in Japan's industrial triumph lay at the heart of much of this pollution. That was the *konbinato*, a type of integrated industrial site erected along the shore, especially in the Inland Sea, that concentrated diverse polluting activities at fixed spots. The problem manifested itself as early as 1959, when the *konbinato* at Yokkaichi, in Ise Bay southwest of Nagoya, was still new. Its petrochemical processing and other activities led to "pollution of the air by sulfur oxides, smoke and various dust particles; noise and vibration; and offensive odors."[21] The noxious output precipitated an epidemic of respiratory troubles in the vicinity, sharply higher death rates, and devastation of fishing grounds, leading in turn to citizen protests, law suits, and a long, ugly legal struggle against industrial interests and their government allies.

Finally, in 1969, after several incidents of this sort had revealed the magnitude of the problem, the government recognized some 73,000 people as victims of the major incidents of industrial poisoning. To obtain that recognition and subsequent aid and redress, however, victims' families had had to mobilize in protest; only after years of deepening illness; long, costly, frustrating litigation; and public demonstrations did they finally overwhelm the resistance of polluting industries, their bureaucratic allies, and indifferent politicians.

By 1970 these pollution battles had given Tanaka Shōzō and the Ashio affair a historical visibility they had previously lacked. And during the early seventies the citizen effort pressured Tokyo to establish an Environment Agency and legislate tighter pollution controls and other conservation measures. In the outcome the anti-pollution effort endowed Japan with new laws and institutions, a body of judicial precedent, and a small but growing environmentalist movement only a decade or so after such developments began to appear in other industrial societies.

By the late 1970s, however, the dramatic, headline-catching issues were gone, and public enthusiasm for environmental remediation had cooled, enabling industry to regroup sufficiently to weaken some pollution regulations and stall the development of others. In consequence during the 1980s, even as some of the more easily remediable problems abated, others continued to worsen and new ones to appear.

A particularly pervasive source of pollution was the internal combustion engine, which fouled air, water, and soil as it propelled ever more motor vehicles hither and yon. The numbers are stunning: 3,856 registered motor vehicles in 1917; 128,735 in 1937; 3.5 million in 1960; and a twelve-fold rise to 42 million in 1990.[22]

That spectacular growth in vehicle numbers reflected policy decisions of the 1950s. The system of train, trolley, and bus lines then crisscrossing Japan fitted nicely the country's topography and settlement patterns, but authorities failed to expand it rapidly enough to meet demand. Instead government and industry leaders, influenced no doubt by the American "model," decided to "supplement" their public transportation system with a fleet of privately owned motor vehicles. The appearance in 1959 of the first "citizen's car," the Nissan Corporation's Datsun Bluebird, symbolized that decision.

During Shōwa Genroku streetcar tracks were torn up, and throughout the country land was taken for roads and related uses. Construction proceeded, and a new network of controlled-access highways developed. In the outcome trolley systems died and rail and bus service was severely compromised, the trend masked by the contemporary success of the prestigious new "bullet trains" (*shinkansen*), which catered to major metropolitan nodes along narrow, predominantly urban corridors.

Enforcement of garaging requirements, driver qualifications, limits on vehicle exhaust emissions, and other constraints slowed somewhat the growth of truck and automobile use. However, the basic trend was that found elsewhere, with the shared corollary consequences of declining public transportation and deteriorating environment. In the outcome entrepreneurial Japan acquired the patterns of traffic congestion, pollution, exacerbated dependence on fuel imports, costly highway maintenance, and continual highway expansion that Americans in particular have come to know.

Other environmental concerns also arose. The rapid construction of nuclear power plants during the 1970s may have slowed the growth in consumption of air-polluting, resource-depleting fossil fuel, but it still energized an anti-nuclear environmentalist movement. The subsequent tapering off of that nuclear power boom did little to assuage fears because the problem of radioactive waste from power plants and other industrial and medical sources emerged during the 1980s. As of 1990 it was still an issue whose magnitude and intractability authorities were yet to appreciate fully.

Less worrisome to activists but more harmful in practice was the sharp increase in thermal energy production. Although the shift from hydropower to thermal generation allowed local ecosystems to survive that otherwise would have been submerged behind hydropower dams, it also meant that producers of electricity became major contributors to air pollution, wetlands destruction, and fossil fuel depletion.

Another concern was the soil pollution created by commercial, industrial, and intensive farm use of chemicals. This concern connected easily to the broader issues of agrarian decline and rural nostalgia, with their innuendoes of ethnic regret. Thus Inoue Hisashi, in his novel *Kirikirijin* (The People of Kirikiri, 1986), imagined a Japanese village, Kirikiri, which declares its political independence and repudiates modernity:

> In the country of Kirikiri the earth is a nostalgic color. Different from the whitish soil overstrewn with chemical fertilizers, this is a warm soft dark color, thanks to the droppings from stables and cow sheds and to human dung. This indeed is a place where human beings live.[23]

Such laments notwithstanding, urban nostalgia stood powerless against industrial-age agronomics.

Normal watershed and subsurface hydrology assured that soil pollutants would evolve into water pollutants, which then fouled Japan's rivers and lakes. These included potable water sources such as Lake Biwa, Japan's largest lake and the water supply for Kyoto city. Algal blooms there became so rich during Shōwa Genroku that they damaged the lake's marine life, and by 1990 Biwa's summertime water was only marginally potable despite vigorous remedial efforts by the Kyoto city water treatment system.

Because Japan's urban population and facilities were so heavily concentrated along the shoreline, pollutants wreaked particular havoc on coastal waters and wetland. Almost no coastline was exempt, but the worst pollution and biotic degradation appear to have occurred along the Inland Sea, where several huge *konbinato* buried large areas of wetland and then spewed out a witch's brew of effluents into surrounding air and waters. In Tokyo Bay most of the area's 15,000 fishermen had lost their livelihoods by the 1980s because of the Bay's pollution, which had destroyed biologically thriving wetlands and waters, transforming the Bay into a shrinking expanse of foul-smelling, badly polluted salt water.

Part of the wetland loss was due to landfill produced by solid waste disposal. Until the 1950s Japan was still celebrated for its frugality and recycling, with almost nothing going to waste, but the affluence of Shōwa Genroku brought the usual flowering of industrial-age, throw-away culture. That flowering was made all the more luxuriant by urban Japan's crowded conditions, which discouraged storage of the no-longer-used, and by the higher standard of living and labor costs, which made much entrepreneurial recycling uneconomic. Although some of this sharply increased solid waste was recycled or incinerated, much was barged to offshore sites for dumping. And much entered onshore landfill, whether directly, as ash from incinerators, or as sludge from sewage plants. Moreover, a growing amount was being dumped elsewhere illegally: 420 cases of that sort recorded by police in 1972; 8,853 in 1986. By 1990 a shortage of dump sites, together with public concern about the pollution that seeped from them, was presenting Japan with the same frustrating and costly problem of disposal that other industrial societies faced.

Wetland degradation was also accomplished by liquid waste. Waterborne effluents increased rapidly during Shōwa Genroku, maintaining pressure on the expanding system of sewage treatment plants. One major portion was industrial discharge, which was as varied in content as elsewhere, and which was mostly released, with or without treatment, into streams. As one student of the problem tartly noted, in a comment that could apply to any industrial society, "there is no end to the illegal discharge of industrial effluents into the sewers, especially after nightfall."[24] During the early 1970s, when the most notorious instances (the Minamata and other methyl mercury cases) were in the limelight, government studies revealed that water all along Japan's coast contained mercury contaminants. Doubtless other pollutants would have been found as well if appropriate inquiry had been made.

Another source of polluting effluent was household waste. Whereas earlier generations recycled kitchen and bodily waste as fertilizer material, in postwar decades more and more of it became sewage that was contaminated with solvents and other household chemicals. Although entrepreneurial Japan remained less fully committed to community sewage systems than most industrial societies, many were installed during Shōwa Genroku. As of 1990 about 40 percent of houses were connected to public sewers, and their effluent, carrying traces of more chemicals and pharmaceuticals with each passing year, flowed via urban treatment systems into streams where it joined industrial waste and traveled to the sea. There its broader ecological effects, like those of the solid waste in maritime dump sites, appeared slowly as ocean currents transported chemicals and buoyant solids elsewhere, mixing and disseminating ingredients with a grand indifference to the puny boundaries of state, language, and ethnicity.

Atmospheric pollutants move with equally great contempt for human boundaries. Japan's location off Northeast Asia assured that during Shōwa Genroku, even as worrisome amounts of continental air pollution began descending on the archipelago, the escalating emissions of Japan's own tailpipes and smokestacks mostly spread eastward over the Pacific, entering marine food chains before reaching terrestrial ones. As in other industrial societies, the scale of Japan's air pollution corresponded roughly to its level of fossil fuel usage. In addition, new types of industrial production kept introducing new contaminants to the air, although the rate of increase was slowed by improvements in exhaust technology.

DOMESTIC FORESTS

As the foregoing pages show, the story of pollution in Japan is a dreary one, largely because its essentials are so familiar to industrial peoples everywhere. The tale of entrepreneurial Japan's forests, on the other hand, may be the country's most interesting environmental story, precisely because of its ambiguities and atypicality. During the past century most of the archipelago's approximately 25 million hectares of woodland have been held as private woodlots or national forest (56 percent and 30 percent respectively in 1990, with the balance held by lesser governmental units), and contradictory forces have had mixed effects on both woodland categories.

To elaborate, later Tokugawa society had exploited its forests as fully as possible, but during the decades of Imperial Japan, a cluster of factors produced appreciable changes in woodland stand composition and gradual improvement in biological vitality. Private woodlots improved as more and more of them came into the hands of landlords who could afford to shield them from intensive scavenging and reforest them for future profit. Government woodland, as well, was gradually revitalized through sustained programs of harvest restriction and reforestation. (These gains, we should note in passing, were achieved at considerable cost to poorer villagers, and they contributed to rural hardship, political protest, and the *nōhon shugi* rhetoric and activism of the day.)

Meanwhile, the intensifying use of coal and chemical fertilizer slowed the growth in demand for wood fuel and mulch, two of the main products of private woodlots. And the growing demand for lumber that accompanied industrialization was largely satisfied, as noted in chapter 15, through exploitation of old-growth stands in Hokkaido, Karafuto, and other colonial regions. In consequence, as of the mid-thirties the forests of Japan proper may well have contained more timber stands and been less vulnerable to erosion than at any time since the seventeenth century.

Then, however, the Pacific War placed extreme demands on both government and private woodland as trees fell to aid the war effort and to take advantage of the black market in charcoal and other forest goods. Most of the serviceable stands that survived the war were then consumed during the later 1940s. The desperate postwar need for fuel wood and reconstruction lumber stripped government forest at government behest, while private woodland was harvested because market prices were so high and labor costs so low. Moreover, SCAP's land reform program, with all the rumors that preceded it, gave forest-holding landlords powerful incentive to harvest their trees before losing them. And following the reform, which deprived landlords of much rent-producing arable acreage, many cut and sold trees from their remaining woodlots as an alternative source of income. Never in Japan's history was so much woodland denuded so rapidly as during the decade to 1950. By then the country's forests were severely damaged, and problems of erosion and downstream silting and flooding were becoming acute.

During the fifties, however, with property rights resecured, the government stable, and the economy starting to revive, a massive and popular program of reforestation got underway. In the course of a decade professional and volunteer planters restocked forests from one end of the realm to the other, the effort peaking in 1954 when 394,522 hectares of woodland were planted to slips and seedlings.

Afforestation continued thereafter because even-aged, monoculture stands yield so much more wood per hectare and per hour of harvest labor than do natural stands. As a result the proportion of Japan's woodland devoted to plantation growth rose steadily, increasing from about 20 percent of the total during the 1940s to 40 percent by 1990. As plantation stands became larger and more widespread, of course, the risk of catastrophic epidemic disease or infestation increased. In general, however, good fortune held and the reforested areas flourished, producing all across the archipelago spectacular, park-like stands of *sugi* (cryptomeria), *hinoki* (Japanese cypress), and other market trees.

During Shōwa Genroku multiple, cross-cutting factors served, on balance, to leave most forest in place, growing but subject to declining maintenance. The pressure on woodland was eased by product substitution: the earlier-noted ferro-concrete in place of wood-frame construction; coal and oil instead of charcoal and fuel wood; chemical fertilizer in lieu of mulch material; and farm machines instead of draft animals, which reduced sharply the demand for fodder culled from woodlots. As farmers abandoned their customary fuel, fodder, and fertilizer harvest and found little other use for hillside woodlots or adjacent scraps of inferior arable, the areas reforested, some as merchantable timber but many others as wildlife-friendly mixed brush.

Other trends, however, were hurtful to woodland, one of those being its intensifying use for tourism and recreation. Environmental laws strove to protect rare upland species of vegetation against depredation by collectors and the careless, but escalating human activity at construction projects, ski resorts, holiday retreats, and camp sites, together with rising levels of ambient air pollution, compromised the botanical vitality of more and more woodland. These trends also proved destructive of animal life, as did the spread of plantation forestry, which reduced the acreage of mixed growth that provided food and shelter for assorted birds and animals. By the 1980s, several bird species and two mammal species were known to have become extinct in recent years while thirty-five and three respectively were known to be endangered. The rates of loss and decline among less esteemed creatures, including Japan's 6,000-odd plant species, are unknown.

Meanwhile, various government policies encouraged entrepreneurial wood production, and loggers helped sustain Japan's domestic timber yield by aggressively opening and harvesting less accessible forest areas. Output peaked during the sixties, however, and timber production declined thereafter despite the proliferation of vibrant new plantation stands and continuing growth in the demand for pulpwood and timber.

Thanks to the economics of the international lumber marketplace, that demand was met by a rapidly swelling volume of imports, as table VI in Appendix A indicates. To explain that outcome, from the 1970s onward merchants discovered that with the *yen* gaining value ($1.00 = 360 *yen* in 1970; 242 in 1980; 150 in 1990), it cost less and less to purchase timber on the global market (mainly from western North America and Southeast Asia) than it did to buy home-grown logs. Domestic labor costs had become so high and the difficulty of extracting timber from convoluted mountain ranges so great that the archipelago's beautiful, new timber stands were effectively priced out of most markets.

In consequence the plantation forests were left in place, and they continued to grow, providing travelers with aesthetic delights and year after year seeming to increase Japan's timber reserves. By 1990, however, new problems were beginning to appear, and during the nineties, as we note in the Epilogue, the woodland situation grew ever more ambiguous as stands aged and decayed.

RESOURCE DEPLETION

Broadly viewed, the story of entrepreneurial Japan's forests was one of biological change and stress. More narrowly, it was a tale of resource depletion and renewal. For most subsurface materials, the domestic story was a more unilinear one of depletion.

In our industrial age, depletion issues, like those of pollution, are fundamentally global, of course. At the global level, however, trends are easily masked by product substitution, the opening of new resource areas to exploitation, the use of political and economic power to secure particular short-term objectives, and, most importantly perhaps, the willful disregard of trends unfolding beyond one's immediate mental horizon. In the case of entrepreneurial Japan the non-forest resource issues of greatest consequence were those of subsurface materials and pelagic and terrestrial foodstuffs. These issues were only eliciting sporadic political attention before 1990, however (e.g., the Nixon soybean embargo), and need only be adumbrated here.

The awesome chemical and physical manipulation of metals and other materials made possible by fossil fuel use produced throughout industrial-age society a vast demand for a wide range of subsurface raw materials. The industries of entrepreneurial Japan obtained many of them, metallic and non-metallic alike, from domestic mines. But with a few exceptions quantities were modest, and even as demand grew, production declined, along with the mine-labor force. During the period 1960–90, the number of non-coal miners shrank by 88 percent, and in terms of mine output technological advances only partially offset the shrinkage.

Most centrally, iron ore remained a strategic industrial necessity, and growing imports compensated for declining domestic production, as table X in Appendix A indicates. Following two decades of explosive growth in imports, the demand for iron ore stabilized around 1980, and it then began to decline, due in part to reduction in those industries, such as shipbuilding, that were especially heavy users and in part to the transfer of fabricating work to overseas sites. By then, however, domestic ore supplies were essentially non-existent, and the industry was totally dependent on imports.

Turning to foodstuffs, as Japan's century of industrialization advanced, pelagic and overseas terrestrial sources became ever more essential. For assorted reasons Japanese whaling received unfavorable attention in the European and American media, but whaling was in fact a minor aspect of total maritime exploitation. In terms of seafood more broadly, its consumption as table fish, processed fish products, and animal feed rose steadily from the nineteenth century until the 1980s, as table III in Appendix A indicates. Through the 1970s a slowly falling number of fishery households was able to meet the growing demand by adopting more and more mass-harvesting techniques. During the eighties, however, the ecology and economics of global fishing began to change significantly, and imports started rising rapidly while the Japanese catch and catcher fleet started to decline.

Regarding terrestrial foodstuffs, the basic story of entrepreneurial Japan is that suggested by table 19.1, a story of sustained decline in self-sufficiency. To a degree this trend reflected shrinkage of Japan's arable (from 6.3 million hectares in 1960 to 5.2 million in 1990) as well as a considerable decline in grain double-cropping. However, those trends were more than offset, as noted earlier, by increased yield per hectare. The key factor increasing dependence on foreign food was population growth, which sharply outstripped the archipelago's capacity to produce foodstuffs. In addition, increased caloric intake per capita combined with a diversifying palate to create a market for foods not produced at home. Finally, foreign politico-economic pressures induced Tokyo to permit more and more imports despite the opposition of domestic agricultural interests.

Table 19.1 Levels of foodstuff self-sufficiency, 1960–1996 (in percentages)

Year	Calories	Cereals
ca. 1850	100	100
1960	79	82
1965	73	62
1990	47	30
1996	42	29

Sources: *Japan Statistical Yearbook 1999*, p. 272. Also Ohno Kazuoki, "Japanese Agriculture Today: The Roots of Decay," in Joe Moore, ed., *The Other Japan, Conflict, Compromise and Resistance Since 1945* (Armonk, NY: M.E. Sharpe, 1997), pp. 183, 197.

The decline in cereals self-sufficiency was dramatic, but in a sense it was misleading. Most of the imports were dry-field grains for use as animal feed (only a portion of which ultimately met human nutrient needs) while rice imports continued to be closely restricted. What was most striking, as other statistics reveal, was the ubiquity of decline in self-sufficiency: to some degree it affected nearly all categories of food – dry field grains, potatoes, beans, meat, fish products, fats and oils, fruit, and even vegetables. By the end of Shōwa Genroku more Japanese were eating better than ever before, but they were doing so on imported food. Whether the global conditions that permitted their comfort could be sustained remained to be seen.

By 1990, in short, the "economic miracle" of preceding decades had profoundly altered Japan's situation. The nation was far more dependent on its global resource base than in the prewar years when that issue had galvanized so much alarmist punditry and political action. And the associated problems of pollution were far more pronounced and pervasive. The social ramifications of industrialization were far more advanced, but to considerable extent society had come to terms with them. Neither the declining role of agricultural society nor the changes in domestic gender, ethnic, and religious relationships provoked the level of alarm and counter-pressure that had marked prewar decades. Finally, these diverse trends were all evident in the arts and letters of the day, as the following chapter will show.

[20] THE CULTURE OF ENTREPRENEURIAL JAPAN (1945–1990)

Behind the façade of political stability, as chapters 18 and 19 have shown, entrepreneurial Japan experienced deep and wide-ranging socioeconomic change. In the realm of cultural life, as well, much was in flux, so much in fact that an observant young man or woman of the year 1990 would in many ways have found the Japan of 1950 an alien, perplexing, and generally unattractive place. During the intervening decades industrial-age media acquired a much greater influence in the worlds of aesthetics, entertainment, and communication, doing more than ever before to shape the character and values of the public they addressed. And the cultural messages they delivered grew more diverse, more transient, and judgmentally more ambiguous.

The realm of creative arts and letters grew rife with experiment and discovery as artists addressed the implications of defeat and redirection; as the expanded and reformed educational system turned out new generations; as proliferating media exposed them to new experiences; as more and more young Japanese went abroad, by sea and later by air; and as new waves of foreign influence entered the country. Practitioners of the musical and visual arts proved most able to transcend prewar interpretive constructs, notably the East/West dyad, to find autonomous creative voice. But the worlds of literature, drama, and film also were stirred, especially during Shōwa Genroku, by experiments, initiatives, and productions that revealed how fully Japan's creative artists had become contributing participants in the global arts and letters of the day. The men and women of Meiji would have been amazed – and utterly flummoxed.

MEDIA AND MESSAGES

One major facet of the change between 1950 and 1990 was the expansion of what we earlier termed "an industrial-age, urban, middle-class culture" into a countrywide popular culture that reached from elite to *hoi polloi*, transcending the boundaries of class, gender, and geography, if not age. Another was the evolving character of highbrow cultural discourse, which moved well beyond the formulations of prewar decades.

CULTURAL MECHANICS AND THE MIDDLEBROW

In earlier chapters we noted the Meiji-era development of a new, up-to-date, high-brow culture that was urban, elitist, and strongly influenced by European arts and letters. It flourished in the midst of a predominantly rural society anchored in Tokugawa-era cultural precedents. By the 1920s, with urbanization, the spread of schooling, and the rise of mass marketing, mass newspapers, cheap books and magazines, radio, and film, a melding of those "high" and "low" cultures was becoming apparent among the rapidly growing urban middle classes, and by the thirties among hinterland folk as well.

After 1945, in the context of a society that war and defeat had leveled socially and economically as well as physically, the cultural conceits of the favored few fared poorly. On the other hand, music, art, drama, and writing that addressed a broader public flourished as performers, producers, publishers, pundits, authors, and others struggled to survive, rebuild careers, and give expression to their thoughts and feelings. Initially this cultural output centered in Tokyo, with its politico-economic primacy, but as the economy revived and life became easier, and as urbanization and industrialization surged ahead, it embraced the entire country, eventually reaching from Naha to Nemuro. By 1990 Japan had acquired a shared countrywide middlebrow culture whose vitality was sustained by the higher levels of schooling, ever more ubiquitous communication, and broader social experience of a much more mobile population.

During Shōwa Genroku mass marketers and mass-circulation media mingled and mangled Japanese and foreign customs, images, vocabulary, intellectual agendas, and material goods, in the process creating a consumer culture that did not easily segregate into high and low, urban and rural, new and old, "Western" and "Japanese." For the young, who were main consumers of this cultural output, the imagery of popular comic strips, animated films, television programs, and video games presented generic young people who toured the cosmos, overpowered the forces of evil, suffered the global pangs of heartbreak, and coped with adversities great and small. Popular music, which drew on every available aural legacy, was an eclectic din that ranged from raucous rock through Beatles and Beethoven to folk song, samisen, and sentimental ballad. Baseball thrived with a sprinkling of foreign players; Olympic Games came and went. By 1990 even *sumō*, that immensely popular and quintessentially Japanese sport, was touring abroad and counting foreigners among its most distinguished champions.

Differences persisted, of course, with working-class people preferring more "traditional" food, drink, art, and narrative entertainment while the more well-to-do displayed more "cosmopolitan" tastes. The cultural sophisticate might dress elegantly for a pricey concert of old standards by Tchaikovsky and Brahms while the working stiff listened on his transistor radio to *enka*, simple ballads of lonely nights, lost loves, and glories gone. But with proper lubrication, both could take microphone in hand and disport themselves creditably at a *karaoke* bar. Both could be found relaxing at the baseball game and *sumō* tournament, or pursuing finger exercises in the *pachinko* parlor. The suited classes might read the *Asahi shinbun* while *hoi polloi* took the *Yomiuri*, but the papers betrayed only modest dissimilarities in advertisements, news coverage, punditry, and prose usage. Meretricious indulgences, endlessly changing fads, and a steady rain of instantly forgettable neologisms notwithstanding, the middle ground of shared culture in Japan had become broader and more stable than at any time since the early nineteenth century.

Vehicles of culture. Changes in the means of cultural expression both reflected and facilitated the emergence of this broader middlebrow culture. Schooling, as noted above, became more widespread than ever, with more and more young people, women in particular, pursuing advanced education. As a result cultural producers had a larger, more plebeian, and more feminine consumer public to satisfy, which permitted continuing expansion of periodical and book production and sales: both newspaper circulation and the number of magazine titles roughly doubled during Shōwa Genroku while book output tripled, rates that continued to exceed population growth.

Beyond the print media, as noted in chapter 16, radio and film had emerged before the war as major vehicles of cultural expression, and after 1945 they continued in that role. The number of radio subscribers doubled in the fifteen years to 1960 while the number of cinemas quintupled to nearly 7,500. In them eight times as many domestic feature films were shown as in 1946. During Shōwa Genroku, however, radio and film were supplemented, and to significant extent displaced, by an immense boom in television viewing. Movie attendance plummeted nearly 90 percent during those thirty years; the number of cinemas dropped to 1,800, and the number of new feature films shrank by half, with the industry surviving by heavy reliance on imported films and pornographic titillation.

Meanwhile the 166,000 TV subscriber households of 1955 grew to nearly six million by 1960 and 33.5 million by 1990. And during the seventies and eighties the boom in air travel and the rise of electronic media (video, fax, e-mail, Internet etc.) added yet more avenues of cultural creativity, dissemination, and reception, further dissolving the urban/rural distinction and enmeshing the people of Japan in global culture more fully than ever before.

Folk arts. As these changes unfolded, they consigned some local folk traditions to oblivion while others were transformed into what one might call participatory museum events. During the postwar years of recovery many local festivals, whether in city neighborhood or small town, continued to flourish. They enabled temples and shrines to raise a little money and display a few icons. They provided young couples with opportunity to date and young men with occasion to carouse while permitting their elders to recall their own younger days and enjoy the survival of local customs. And they enabled the interested to take snapshots (and, a few decades later, to make videotapes of the curious goings on).

Especially from the 1960s onward, however, urbanization, heightened social mobility, and the spread of more commercialized culture, notably television and mass marketing, combined to erode genuine public interest in these local recreational traditions. Instead more and more festivals, local customs, and folk performing arts became grist for the mills of tourist agencies, town fathers, and professional organizations, both public and private, which sprang up to preserve "traditional" folk arts and culture. These organizations, which had antecedents in the prewar folklore preservationist efforts of people such as Yanagi Sōetsu, gradually "elevated" many local song, dance, and festival traditions to the status of officially sponsored folk-art displays that were by the 1980s being staged periodically, often in large, urban exhibition halls.

As in other industrial societies, government support of folk traditions was part of a broader program encouraging "native" arts and letters more generally. Much as the Meiji regime's chartering of Kokugakuin and Gakushūin universities was emblematic of its wish to preserve Japanese elite culture and society, so the postwar regime supported efforts to preserve classical theatre, folk arts, and other cultural accomplishments. Especially during the fiscally fat years of Shōwa Genroku national, prefectural, and local governments competed vigorously in matters cultural. As one administrator put it, local and prefectural leaders

> built cultural centers partly to show how wealthy they've become and partly to show the influence of prefectural and city officials over cultural affairs.[1]

Whatever their motives, Japan's leaders fostered programs to fund cultural research, instruction, and production. They built display and exhibition halls and established agencies to identify, preserve, and celebrate noteworthy cultural products and producers ("living treasures"), including esteemed potters, painters, actors, and musicians.

Kokusaika. In part tax-payer funded cultural projects thus aimed to preserve the skills and artifacts of ethnic heritage. But also in part the government's cultural initiatives sought to promote Japan's presence and enhance its performance in the global arena of industrial-age cultural competition. The most widely visible expression of that aim was the Japan Foundation, created in 1972 to fund a wide range of projects that would spread knowledge of Japan abroad while introducing useful foreign knowledge to the islands.

In numerous other ways, as well, Japan's leaders gave attention to the study of science, technology, and industrial society, particularly to the expansion of foreign studies in Japan's school system. Much as the Meiji regime had promoted the study of science and technology at its new imperial universities, so the postwar government created new institutions for research and study, most impressively a science-centered university that opened at Tsukuba north of Tokyo in 1974. During the 1980s, when this effort to promote Japan's global role reached its zenith, it was dubbed a policy of *kokusaika* or "internationalization."

Basically, of course, the "internationalization" of Japanese popular culture was a byproduct of the country's heightened dependence on a global resource base, with its corollary, noted in chapter 19, of sharply increased work, study, and travel abroad by Japanese and ingress of foreign people and goods to Japan. Government policy only reinforced the trend, in part by serving to legitimize it. Those developments combined with media activity to generate a massive, utterly unprecedented inflow of information about the outside world. And that information, however much it was manipulated in the process of internalization, gave most Japanese of 1990 a very different and much richer view of the world than their grandparents had during the 1940s.

HIGHBROW DISCOURSE

Among the intelligentsia more narrowly – that ill-defined population of authors, artists, pundits, playwrights, and professors who made their way through life as articulate observers and interpreters of the age – much cultural production, political commentary in particular, was couched in the established idioms of Marxist, "modernizationist," and East/West analysis. The Pacific War having lasted only a few years, post-1945 commentary, like postwar politics and business, was initially the work of those who had been active during the thirties, and intellectual agendas and interpretive perspectives reflected that continuity. In due course, however, generations changed, and by Shōwa Genroku new voices were advancing new agendas and perspectives in response to the changing times.

Frameworks of discourse. Immediately after the war some pundits settled for a simple, non-denominational repudiation of "militarism," assigning the blame for Japan's defeat to leaders of the uniformed services or to the very notion of military power itself. A much richer body of critical commentary was couched in the Marxist terms that earlier had gained academic respectability despite harsh suppression. The Marxist perspective became popular in the wake of defeat when about the only intellectuals not implicated in the failed war effort seemed to be those dedicated Communists who had been unable or unwilling to "convert" and give the venture at least tacit support.

Marxist thought was further vitalized for a time by postwar reforms and after 1947 by the rhetoric of Cold War warriors, with the Maoist triumph in China proving particularly inspirational. From the later 1950s onward, however, the persuasiveness of Marxist analysis was gradually undermined by a combination of factors. These included doctrinal quarrels among left-wing ideologues and activists in Japan, the official disfavor they encountered, the gradual spread of prosperity within Japan, unpleasant discoveries about life in the Sino-Soviet sphere, and the sphere's decay and eventual disintegration.

Even during the heyday of Marxian analysis, the well-worn East/West ethnic construct still lay at the heart of much cultural discourse. However, the ambiguities that had always marked it were sharply heightened after 1945 because the term "West" came to be used in two basically disjunctive ways. In some contexts it identified, as previously, a presumed ethno-cultural ecumene grounded in earlier European and Greco-Roman experience, as distinct from "other" societies, most pertinently here the postulated "Asian" ecumene. In other contexts, however, and particularly among Anglo-American rhetoricians, "the West" functioned as a geopolitical term that referred to the Washington-centered political sphere, as distinct from the Moscow-centered (or Sino-Soviet) one.

Often commentators sloppily elided the two uses of the term. They then confused matters further by equating "Western" with "modern," essentially meaning "industrial," thereby creating a composite image that linked unequaled present-day politico-military muscle to claims of a uniquely important history and a semi-sacred role as the moral, social, and technological model for all humankind. Because of its multiple, ill-defined meanings, sometimes-sloppy usage, and self-serving pretensions, the term "Western" all too often functioned in global discourse, whether overtly or by innuendo, as a judgmental labeling device for praising or damning as the pundit deemed appropriate.

In entrepreneurial Japan the East/West construct was used in both its ethno-cultural and geopolitical senses, with the philosophically inclined tending to prefer the former while the pragmatically oriented generally employed the latter. Depending on the commentator's purposes and prejudices, therefore, Japan could be identified as a bona fide part of the "West," as a sort of marginal, honorary member, or as an outsider interacting with it.

Early assessments. As ambiguous as the discourse on East and West was, it was further complicated by each pundit's sense of how well Japan was doing *vis-à-vis* the "West." During the immediate postwar years Japanese commentators wrestled with the painful evidence that despite their country's best efforts the West, far from being driven out of Asia as wartime celebrants had announced, was back again, more oppressively than ever. It was there with an army of occupation, enforced reforms, former colonies resecured (momentarily), and later a sustained military presence and a diplomatic headlock that dictated Japan's policy even toward neighboring Asian societies.

For some the lesson in all this was that the people of Japan had to overcome their "Asiatic" mentality and become "the modern, democratic human type."[2] Others held to a contrary formulation – that the flaw lay precisely in Japan's emulation of the "West." That policy, it was suggested, had transformed the venerable realm into a monster that ravaged Asia, chattering virtue while splattering blood. It was an outcome that could be set right only by rediscovering and revitalizing Japan's own indigenous or "Asian" character.

Some scholars found it fruitful to revive the theme of "modernism" that had enjoyed academic favor in the later thirties. During the years of recovery such noted figures as the cultural theorist Kamei Katsuichirō and the venerable ethnologist Yanagita Kunio debated whether modernism merely constituted Westernization and whether it was desirable or not.

Kamei, as noted in chapter 15, was one of the Marxists who had shifted during the 1930s to the politically more acceptable Nihon Rōmanha posture of supporting things "Japanese" and "Asian," and he then participated in the late thirties debate on "overcoming modernity." In 1954, when the country was free of occupation censorship but still struggling with the effects of defeat, he wrote an essay in which he argued that:

> Japan, as everyone knows, was the first country in Asia to become "modernized," but it is not yet clear what meaning this modernization had for Asia. It is also a question whether Asian thought, which possesses strong traditions despite the repeated taste of defeat and a sense of inferiority before Western science, is doomed to perish without further struggle, or if it is capable of reviving in the twentieth century and contributing something which will enable us to surmount the present crisis.[3]

Yanagita, who had devoted decades of his life to documenting, celebrating, and advocating the preservation of Japanese folk culture, joined others in arguing more forcefully that Japan's traditions must be reinvigorated as prologue to developing a truly indigenous modernization. Others argued, even more radically, that Japan must reject the "modern" outright as the only way to preserve "Asian freedom and autonomy."[4]

Meanwhile the older China/Japan dyad also remained in use, but its character changed substantially. The original *kokugaku* agenda of Sino-Japanese cultural relations, which had become so tortured by the 1930s, evolved into a postwar discourse about two societies operating within the larger context of the Cold War conflict, mutually distrustful and burdened with a tragic recent relationship but having more reason than ever to overcome differences and find in their shared character as "Asians" common ground against the overweening "Westerners." Whether observers spoke in terms of modernity or of Sino-Japanese relations, that is to say, in the postwar years the commentary was at heart an expression of the debate about East and West and a reflection of the recent, catastrophic national failure.

Later assessments. In the wake of defeat a Japanese observer might thus desire the demise of "Asia," or he might lament it, but in either case its demise seemed to be in store. During the heady years of Shōwa Genroku, some commentators continued to argue that Japan's modernity was flawed, being essentially European, and that a truly Asian and hence adequate basis for that modernity had yet to be awakened. A more influential view, however, held that distinctively Asian, indeed uniquely Japanese qualities really underlay the country's economic success and thus its modernity.

This perspective is commonly identified as *Nihonjinron*, which one scholar has defined as "a broadly based ideological stance for Japan's nationalism."[5] Pundits and scholars in several disciplines attempted to identify or explain Japan's alleged distinctiveness by citing such diverse factors as Japan's weather, rice culture, language, or brain physiology, or particulars of society, such as methods of child rearing, Japan's supposed ethnic homogeneity or "purity," a presumed legacy of village culture that gave rise to a sense of "group loyalty," or a postulated preference for social and spiritual "harmony."

As this more optimistic assessment of national capability gained favor, especially among leaders of business and government, a process of lexical substitution began replacing the categories West and East with a different directional formulation, that of "North" and "South." In this construction Japanese stood shoulder to shoulder with West Europeans, North Americans, Australians, etc. as modernized "Northerners" looking out at a world of "Southerners" who were referred to variously as backward, underdeveloped, or industrializing societies. Not all Japanese commentators welcomed this newest strategy for distancing Japan from Asia. And some "Westerners," Anglo-Americans in particular, countered this exercise in boundary jumping by distinguishing between "early" and "late" developers, with their own societies happily occupying the former category, while Japan and nearly everyone else filled the latter.

In this body of politically charged, "in-group out-group" commentary the concept of "modern" served not only to redefine, neutralize, or even obviate "Western," but also to transvalue Marxian analysis by accepting its basic vision of historical progress while reworking some of its value judgements. As elaborated in an interpretation known as "modernization theory," the development of monetized commerce, wage labor, and entrepreneurial industrialism ("capitalism") did not lead to harsh class stratification, proletarian immiseration, and eventual revolutionary upheaval. Rather, it "rationalized" society, releasing human creative energies and producing heightened material standards of living and greater human freedom. It was a perspective that proved particularly salient and satisfying to those commentators who focused on matters economic, and unsurprisingly it flourished during the heady years of Shōwa Genroku.

MODES OF CULTURAL EXPRESSION

In those fields of cultural endeavour given more to creative aesthetic expression than social explication, perplexities and ambiguities persisted, not only during the years of defeat and recovery but even during the heyday of Shōwa Genroku. As elsewhere in the industrial world, one striking quality of Japanese output in these fields was the extent to which it obscured ethnic and disciplinary distinctions.

Creative artists of all sorts drew eclectically on indigenous and foreign cultural legacies to produce distinctive and original works of their own. Especially during the 1960s, they built on, and went well beyond, prewar "modernist" trends, combining literary arts, drama, music, visual arts (painting, pottery, sculpture, architecture), and filmic representation in a rush of "Happenings" and "Performances." In consequence, much as *emaki-mono* scrolls of late Heian defied our customary disciplinary categories of art and literature, Japan's postwar cultural output begs for new interpretive frames of reference, and as the following sections reveal, the categories of arts and letters used in previous chapters work awkwardly in examining trends and accomplishments up to 1990.

THE LITERARY ARTS

During the Pacific War, as noted in chapter 16, writers in Japan, as in the other belligerent states, had on the whole supported their country's war effort for reasons of choice and necessity, and defeat left many of them spiritually shattered as well as economically devastated. In the face of this outcome, and in the context of war crimes trials, purges, and a new covey of censors, some fell silent while others experienced another "conversion" (*tenkō*), whether from conviction, convenience, or a happy convergence of the two.

Gradually, however, conditions improved, morale revived, older authors became active again, and new voices began to be heard. Initially much work dwelt on war and defeat, but with the passage of time other topics prevailed, being addressed in works of fantasy and science fiction and novels about the world of business as well as more customary settings. Equally impressive was the proliferation of works by women authors.

War and defeat. The mental turmoil produced by Japan's radical reversal of fortune was particularly evident among literary figures, being nicely illustrated by the writer Takami Jun.[6] Back in 1933 police had tortured the left-wing proclivities out of him, and in an essay of 1943 he could declare that:

> We hundred million people must become a single whole, offer up our lives, and confront the danger to the nation.

The sacrifice proved unavailing, however, and two weeks after surrender, he noted in his diary:

> It seems as if speech, publication, assembly, association, and the rest are all gradually becoming free. A load has been lifted from my heart. I realize now that we were in the Middle Ages. The politics were those of the Dark Ages, the politics of terror.

As foreshadowed by Takami's words, writers generally welcomed a number of changes that the Occupation imposed: greater freedom of expression, fuller constitutional guarantees of individual rights, greater gender equality, repudiation of aggressive militarism, and rejection of much imperial mythology. So the outcome of defeat was a bittersweet package of hated and welcomed effects.

Creative writers thus found themselves with a powerfully compelling agenda – how to comprehend and survive the most horrific catastrophe in Japanese history – and an appreciably broadened space in which to address it. Their opportunity for expression was restricted somewhat by sporadically repressive Occupation regulations but mainly by the poverty of the day. Those constraints notwithstanding, within weeks of war's end, and long before the economy recovered, new magazines began to appear and new intellectual and literary groups to form, mainly in Tokyo. They unleashed a flood of prose and poetry, to say nothing of visual arts, theatrical works, and social and artistic commentary.

Much of the literary output dwelt on war and the misery of defeat, and authors initially avoided Occupation censorship by limiting themselves to recounting personal experiences and the social disorientation that war and defeat entailed. The *haiku* poet Katō Shūson included this entry from 1944 in an annotated collection of poems he published four years later:

> On May 23rd there was a large-scale air attack late at night. Carrying my sick brother on my back, I went wandering through the flames all night long in search of Michiko and Akio.
>
> > In the depths of fire
> > I saw how a peony
> > Crumbles to pieces.[7]

In the autumn of 1946 the proletarian poet Tsuboi Shigeji opened a long poem on the emperor's announcement of surrender with these two stanzas:

> His standard toppled,
> god's voice trickles
> from the radio –
> empty, quivering, sorrowful ...
> this moment an historic occasion.
>
> The pages of this fabricated myth
> closed this day,
> opening the people's eyes afresh
> to the harsh world.[8]

Such moments of terror and transformation nested in years of tedious struggle. In "Shin'ya no Shuen" (Midnight Feast), a work of fiction he published in 1947, Shiina Rinzō spoke for many when he had his main character declare in the face of cold, hunger, and the disagreeable people with whom he had to share his wretched living space,

> For me, enduring is the same thing as living. Enduring liberates me from all the "heavy" things. Besides, enduring lets me have that intoxicating feeling called indifference. But, leaving all that aside, isn't it true that in this world one hasn't got much choice but to endure?[9]

Enduring was far from easy, however, and the sense of loss, despair, and nihilism that the times inspired was captured with particular power in the novels *Shayō* (The Setting Sun, 1947) and *Ningen shikkaku* (No Longer Human, 1948) by the gifted but tormented author Dazai Osamu.

Other writers sought solace in nature, the immediacies of daily life, and the pursuit of craft or creed, or in images of a more gentle past. Most famously, perhaps, in 1948 Tanizaki Jun'ichirō published *Sasameyuki* (The Makioka Sisters), which he had written during the war, a long, loving evocation of the graceful, unhurried cosmos of Osaka's declining merchant aristocracy during the 1930s. Theirs was, as Tanizaki pictured it, an age in which the old and new lived comfortably together, creating a civilized world untormented by harsh disjunctions. The book was an immediate success, its tenor surely comforting to the many distraught by the hardship and uncertainty of their own day.

During the 1950s, as the economy recovered and society regained its footing, literary production kept growing and commentary broadening. Weekly magazines and cheap paperbacks proliferated. *Haiku, tanka,* and "new-style" poets debated literary forms and produced a wide array of verses. Novelists turned out reams of pulp literature for middlebrow magazines as well as a stream of more serious works that reflected diverse Japanese and foreign literary traditions and fashions of the moment. Literary critics engaged in vigorous polemics, ideological and idiosyncratic, launching anew into overheated prose about Japanese character and culture and their prospects as "modernization" proceeds, a topic that had been frowned on by the Occupation.

Itō Sei emerged as "the most conspicuous presence" in the literary world, his postwar reputation greatly enhanced after 1950 thanks to his criminal prosecution for translating *Lady Chatterly's Lover* into Japanese. Kawabata Yasunari also enjoyed great popularity and visibility as an international literary lion. But it was the much younger Mishima Yukio, one of the most gifted Japanese literary figures of the century, who rose to pre-eminence during the decade. Mishima is particularly celebrated for select works, such as his 1956 novel *Kinkakuji* (The Golden Pavilion). However, his most striking qualities as a writer may have been his familiarity with both Japanese and European literary traditions and his authorial omnicompetence as a master of both simple and complex narratives; historical, philosophical, and lyrical works (both "pure" and "pulp"), and diverse genres of plays and poems.

As Occupation taboos faded, the war and its legacy came to be treated in more diverse ways. Most memorable, perhaps, was the novel *Nobi* (Fires on the Plain, 1952) by Ōoka Shōhei, a harrowing representation of defeat, survival, and madness in the Philippines. Also during the fifties "A-bomb literature" emerged as a distinctive sub-genre of war writing. Together with related art and performance, it dwelt on the nuclear bombing of Hiroshima and Nagasaki and its human consequences.

For the bombing's survivors (known as *hibakusha*), writing was one means of trying to come to terms with that horrific moment and the bone-deep foreboding that it begot. Writing also was a means to reclaim their humanity by sharing their grief and terror with others, too many of whom tended to see them as "damaged goods" to be avoided and put out of mind. A woman from a village near Nagasaki allegedly put it this way:

> Nobody's going to marry those Nagasaki girls. Even after they reach marrying age, nobody's going to marry them. Ever since the Bomb fell, everybody's

calling them "the never-stop people." And the thing that never stops is their bleeding. Those people are outcasts – damned Untouchables. Nobody's going to marry one of them ever again.[10]

Few curses have ever weighed so cruelly.

More broadly A-bomb literature of the fifties reflected the earlier-noted tensions of the Cold War, nuclear testing, American foreign policy, and domestic contestation of the postwar settlement. For many writers it was an expression of anti-militarism and loathing for the carnage of modern war. In the hands of some it constituted a rebuke to Imperial Japan's political order as a whole, while others used it for more immediate partisan political advantage. But it also became a means of affirming ethnic worth, with commentary on the A-bombed cities functioning at one level as an assertion that Japan was a victim of the war, again a victim of "Western" violence, a nation with a serious claim to redress. At a more elevated level A-bomb commentary raised Japan to the status of global exemplar, a lesson for humankind trapped in the madness of the nuclear arms race: this is where you too are headed; this could happen to you; we know and you should pay attention.

During Shōwa Genroku the tragedies of Hiroshima and Nagasaki continued to receive literary, as well as artistic and theatrical, treatment. The most acclaimed work was Ibuse Masuji's *Kuroi Ame* (Black Rain, 1965), which Imamura Shōhei made into a powerful film in 1989. Ibuse tried to suggest the magnitude of the catastrophe by relating through a complex use of diary entries and flashbacks how the quotidian routines of life were transformed instantly into a hell of fiery, ghastly unrecognizability and how the resulting radiation sickness, and the public fear and loathing that it elicited, created for the victim a burden of grinding, inescapable worry and sorrow made bearable only by desperate hope and a strong sense of the ironic and absurd.

Science fiction and business novels. During the fifties the atomic bombings, subsequent nuclear weapons testing, and spread of knowledge about the genetic effects of nuclear radiation fed into the prewar legacy of science fiction and fantasy writing to produce the literary monster Godzilla (*gojira*) noted in chapter 18. Subsequently Godzilla and an array of other monsters, super-humans, and robots went on to terrorize humankind until being overcome, usually by one or another heroic Japanese effort. In the outcome Godzilla became one of the most enduring images in a host of popular stories, comic strips, feature films, and eventually video cassettes and games. Aimed primarily at the young, these works appealed to a global market and in due course became major items of cultural export.

During the 1960s science fiction blossomed as society prospered and the postwar baby-boom generation came of reading age. Collections of science fiction were published, a magazine devoted to it appeared, and the genre flourished throughout Shōwa Genroku. As in other industrial societies, it was replete with heroes and malefactors, earthly and cosmic aliens good and evil, every sort of technical gimmick and biological perversity, mysterious manipulations of time and space, and demons, spirits, and godly powers of every imaginable sort.

Science fiction flourished mainly as popular literature. Literary professionals, however, generally continued to view their craft in the prewar terms of pure and mass literature, and some authors of sci-fi works (and the fantasy genre more broadly), such as the prolific Abe Kōbō and Komatsu Sakyō aspired to treat the "serious" issues expected of pure literature. Throughout Shōwa Genroku works by Abe, Komatsu, the inventive Murakami Haruki, and numerous other authors addressed real and imagined ills of the present and future: personal alienation; loss of community; gender conflicts; insidious foreign menaces; abuses by mad scientists; technology run amok; the dangers of human enslavement and brutalization in an age of technocratic bureaucracy; and the environmental and human damage wrought by ruthless business practices, industrial giantism, and crass materialism.

That last phrase points up a type of popular fiction that emerged with commercial revival during the later 1950s, the so-called business novel. During Shōwa Genroku the genre flourished, providing insight into the mechanics and values of the business world. Commonly these works explored the more scabrous aspects of business, whether in particular industries, the stock market, or government agencies, and whether focused on figures of high or low status. They contained lively plots, sometimes centered on disasters in the making, and their story lines generally were driven by the mercenary or megalomaniacal motives of their characters, who might or might not be countered by other figures of greater integrity.

Women writers.   In vitality and diversity the literary output of women came to challenge that of men, a trend that reflected their expanding presence on the social and cultural scene. Basic factors facilitating this output were noted earlier: greater female schooling and literacy, the proliferation of media directed to them, their increased leisure time and discretionary income, and their expanding role and influence in the urban work place. In addition, one suspects that the mid-century catastrophe eroded male authority, and clearly postwar reforms permitted freer literary expression. Existence of the literary category *joryū bungaku* or "women's literature" may have encouraged women writers by assuring them a recognized, if restrictive, place in the profession. Finally, the feminist movement noted in chapter 19 gave women authors an empowering perspective and broadened agenda.

During the years of Occupation and recovery women writers generally found the I novel a useful vehicle for treating defeat, reconstruction, and recollection of earlier and better – or worse – times as experienced at the personal and family level. Some female characters, particularly in the works of socialist writers such as Miyamoto Yuriko, optimistically called for social change and justice. More commonly female characters, as in works by Enchi Fumiko and Setouchi Harumi, found within themselves the strength to persevere in the face of hardship and unfair treatment, usually by men.

During the 1960s, however, as a younger generation of women started appearing in print, the tenor of their writings began to change. As the disparity between prospect and aspiration of educated women became more pronounced and oppressive, older notions of forbearance gradually lost persuasiveness. By then critics were again actively dissecting the concept of the I novel, and women writers were more consciously engaging in the art of literary creation. They crafted more frankly fictional works and presented female characters who were more complex, more dissatisfied, and more openly critical of society's definitions of femininity and expectations for women.

Some women writers found in fantasy fiction a vehicle to express their desires and discontents. In Ōba Minako's 1976 short story "Yamauba no bishō" (The Smile of a Mountain Witch), her main figure gave expression to a wish for solitude and mental freedom that was becoming common to many female characters: she dreamed of escaping to the mountains where "there would be nobody to trouble her, and she would be free to think as she pleased."[11]

By the 1980s the small but vigorous feminist movement was providing a more richly nuanced ideology and agenda for women writers. The ideals of personal autonomy, social equality, and equal opportunity all provided authorial grist. Even the procrustean category of "women's literature" became an object of attack, its assertions about a distinctive female voice disputed, its social and judgmental implications laid bare, its very use decried as "demeaning, inappropriate, or simply archaic."[12] The gender ideals of the day also carried a price, however, and it showed up in the works of women writers. Their female characters struggled with the difficulties of divorce, single motherhood, alcoholism, and loneliness, even as they enjoyed their independence and the "freedom to envision new experiences."[13] The inseparability of life's wounds and wonders was as basic to their creative efforts, it appears, as it was to that of their male contemporaries or their predecessors in the age of Murasaki Shikibu.

DRAMA, DANCE, AND MUSIC

Theatre with its scripts is in part a literary art, and it shared the trends and qualities found in other literary fields. It is also, of course, a performance art that combines aural and visual means of communication, and as such it exploits the contributions of music, dance, and the plastic arts as well as literature. Perhaps because of this richness of expressive resources, drama proved to be a highly insightful recorder of, and commentator on, entrepreneurial Japan's passage. Together with music, dance, and art, moreover, it showed with particular clarity how fully Japan had by 1990 become a participant in industrial-age global culture.

Drama: the pre-war forms.   The term "traditional" drama refers essentially to *nō*, *kyōgen*, *kabuki*, and the puppet theatre. However, by 1945 even *shinpa*, a Meiji-era invention, was sufficiently venerable and stable in form to be widely perceived as a "traditional" theatrical form more akin to *kabuki* than to "modern" drama.

These several genres all survived the war, and as buildings were restored after 1945, old plays were again produced. Some new plays also appeared as writers such as Mishima Yukio tried their hand at making the stage a vehicle for their concerns. Some experimentation in dramatic style occurred; some classical actors worked in the newer types of drama, and techniques from classical drama were tried there. To considerable extent, however, the older theatrical forms, *nō* most firmly, adhered to their established dramaturgies, retained their distinctive qualities, and appealed to their own audiences.

During Shōwa Genroku higher levels of income and a renewed attention to things Japanese led to greater audience interest in the older drama. During the 1970s and 1980s, as local, prefectural, and national authorities promoted tourism, they built performance halls and provided financial support for drama troupes, much as they did for folk artists and other performers. New plays for both *nō* and *kabuki* continued to appear and be performed. Actors were busy; their numbers grew, and troupes toured at home and abroad. By 1990 *nō*, *kabuki*, and Japan's other classical forms of drama were being performed more widely before more people than ever in memory. And their influence continued to be felt in other forms of theatre. To considerable degree, however, they had also acquired the attributes of "national treasures," museum objects to be displayed in the spirit in which industrial societies in general parade those artifacts of their pre-industrial past that are thought to celebrate their ethnic particularity and excellence.

Save for this matter of supporting "the native tradition," however, issues of the day found more forceful expression in other, more recent forms of theatre. The postwar story begins with *shingeki*. It had come into prominence during the thirties, as noted in chapter 16, committed to "realism" and actively hostile to the demons, deities, and radically stylized speech and movement of *kabuki*. Thanks to its commitment to realism, its sense of social purposefulness, and its need for financial support, *shingeki* became closely linked to organized labor and the political left, mainly the Japan Communist Party (JCP), during the hard years of recovery. Under those circumstances it flourished, its "social realist" plays drawing audiences and enabling it to develop large troupes and sustain major theatres.

As Marxism lost its persuasiveness, however, and as television cut into theatrical audiences during Shōwa Genroku, *shingeki* survived by growing more eclectic and catering to more varied audience interests. Works by Mishima Yukio, Abe Kōbō, and others provided inventive new scripts, and troupes presented a diversity of productions, foreign and domestic, ranging from Greek tragedy to modern drama. As of 1980 about 133 *shingeki* troupes were active. Most were based in Tokyo, but they depended heavily on income generated by tours about the country, tours facilitated by the nationwide proliferation of handsome new performance halls. By touring, the troupes helped sustain Tokyo's image as the dynamic center of Japan's cultural life even as they fostered the commonality of national culture.

Drama: the new theatre.   The postwar successes of *shingeki* notwithstanding, by 1960 it was no longer on the cutting edge of theatre. To explain, even as the first "postwar" generation of students was making its way through college and entering young adulthood during the later fifties, the political left had fizzured. In 1960, when the combined forces of the left were unable, even with broad public support, to prevent either treaty revision or the shuttering of coal mines, many of the young were bitterly disillusioned with postwar democracy and the socialist establishment. With *shingeki* so closely linked to the "old left," as young radicals characterized the JCP and its associates, the embittered young denounced the troupes and their social-ist realism as fraudulent. They turned instead to street theatre and other experimental forms of drama to express their dismay at the way history was unfolding.

As the critic Tsuno Kaitarō explained that development, *shingeki* had become "a tradition in its own right."[14] The legacy of European drama that it represented:

> is no longer some golden ideal as yet out of reach. It is instead a pernicious, limiting influence. Beneath *shingeki's* prosperous exterior there is decadence. It has lost the antithetic élan that characterized its origins. *Shingeki* no longer maintains the dialectical power to negate and transcend; rather, it has become an institution that itself demands to be transcended.

Shingeki must be transcended, Tsuno argued, because it cuts Japan's play-wrights off from the sources of their tradition:

> Today we are seeking to reaffirm our tradition, but not as our predecessors did in the years leading up to the war … [We] are attempting to reaffirm our tradi-tion, even when we find it distasteful, in order to deal directly and critically with it. Our hope is that by harnessing the energy of the Japanese popular imag-ination we can at once transcend the enervating cliches of modern drama and revolutionize what it means to be Japanese.

The end product, one supposes, would be a Japanese person and theatre fit for a peaceable, intellectually vital, and globally integrated, industrial age.

During a decade of bold innovation young dramatists (mostly born ca. 1935–45) rejected the secular socialist agenda, realistic style, and linear narrative structure of *shingeki*. Fired by their discontent with *shingeki*, these avant-garde dramatists and their troupes toured the country, performing in tents, at open sites, or in local theatres. Some tried to draw their audiences into participation, audiences that mainly were people in their twenties. Especially during the later sixties little theatres proliferated and playwrights produced new plays in abundance.

In place of *shingeki's* agenda and dramaturgy, avant-garde dramatists res-urrected images of gods and transcendent forces, explored the interplay of human and supra-human elements, and revived the role of godly powers in effecting change and righting wrongs. They examined the inner demons of everyday people and the evil within us that lies there waiting to ravage the world. Thus Kara Jūrō, one of the seminal figures in this movement, scripted a series of "Manchuria" plays in which the pirate John Silver is transposed to

Korea during the heyday of Imperial Japan to sing the siren song of gold and glory in Manchuria, the immortal temptation that can lead to armageddon. The years of imperial conquest were not the part of Japan's historical legacy that playwrights usually treated, but Kara's approach did reflect the broader dramatic agenda of the day.

Whereas the script, and hence the playwright, had been viewed as the key element in *shingeki*, avant-garde theatre treated the actor and his or her performance as the play's critical ingredient. Most celebrated was the actor, director, and playwright Hijikata Tatsumi, whose father had bankrolled Osanai Kaoru's Tsukiji Little Theatre back in 1924. Hijikata founded the radical troupe Ankoku Butō in 1959, achieving fame for presentations in which his gaunt, wasted appearance conveyed with overwhelming power a sense of the devastation that life in industrial society can visit upon humankind. As the drama critic Senda Akihiko wrote of his 1972 performance in a play in which lovely *Songs of the Auvergne* filled the auditorium:

> Hijikata, in all his nakedness, like a beggar crouching to warm himself in the sun, seemed to become a squirming insect, only shifting his body slightly from time to time. And what poverty in this "flesh"! His ribs seemed to float to the surface of his chest, his legs only sinews, poles thrust forward; he appeared to be facing his own death as he dragged along his own weakened body…He really did manage to reveal to us "the eyes of the dying." Yet within those eyes shown the glitter of a rapture approaching intoxication.[15]

A performance to remember.

Emphasis on the actor's role facilitated the blurring of disciplinary lines, linking theatre to performance art and to minimally scripted musical "Happenings" and improvisational presentations. But during the seventies and eighties the young rebels of 1960 matured, the late-sixties student unrest passed, and "peace and prosperity" robbed political activism of its effectiveness. Gradually the differences between *shingeki* and avant garde blurred. Playwrights moved on from politically engaged drama to works that exploited the theatrical possibilities of fantasy, science fiction, and contemporary popular culture. They probed the inner self, explored – with and without humor – the pathos of life, and pointed up the futility of revolt, the self-deceptions of the mind, the boring emptiness of modern affluence, and the impossibility of escape. A few works even confronted aspects of the day's environmental problems. All in all it was not, as of 1990, a notably cheerful theatre, but it did measure the times; it was very much a theatre of the world, one that resonated richly with drama elsewhere.

Music and dance. Music and dance have long been linked to drama in Japan. Since the earliest records of sacred Shintō dance and courtly *bugaku* presentations and, later, *nō, kabuki* and the many forms of folk performance, drama in Japan has consisted of music, movement, set, and speech in diverse combinations. However, *shingeki*, and the nineteenth-century European dramaturgical practices that underlay it, did much to exclude music and dance from the theatre, reducing them to sometime elements and background effects, and they only regained modest theatrical functions in the avant-garde drama of Shōwa Genroku.

During these decades, save for its continuing role in "traditional" drama, the music–dance–drama linkage was primarily maintained at the broad margins of "legitimate" theatre. European-style operas and operettas and American-style musicals, whether presented by foreign or domestic troupes, provided venues for its expression. More importantly, variety shows and other theatrical organizations brought lively song–dance–drama spectacles to the stage for popular consumption. Most famously the Takarazuka Revue continued to grow, creating new troupes, expanding its schedule, shrewdly promoting its stars, and adapting its repertoire to the changing times. Aimed mainly at audiences of girls and young women, its gorgeous programs of song, dance, and skit won devout followings by nurturing dreams of exotic worlds and romantic realms of surpassing beauty and exquisite rapture.

Music did retain its role in dance performance. "Classical" European ballet, first performed in Japan in 1916, subsequently enjoyed an urban following, being augmented in the 1930s by newer forms of dance associated with "modernism." From the fifties onward foreign troupes presented diverse forms of dance in Japan, but the classics of Russian ballet remained audience favorites. Domestic dance troupes also formed and produced their own programs. During the sixties dance became boldly experimental, along with avant-garde drama, most famously in productions by Hijikata's Ankoku Butō. Older forms of Japanese dance also changed as writers, choreographers, and dancers experimented with new routines and styles. By 1990 the dance scene in Japan was marked by grand diversity, vitality, and engagement with global dance.

The success of these several performance genres notwithstanding, music's more celebrated accomplishments stemmed from its separate disciplinary development. During the years of recovery composers, conductors, and musicians revitalized the prewar project of mastering European musical techniques and styles, even as those were rapidly changing. Musicians absorbed and began to employ newer approaches to music, such as atonality and the Schōnberg twelve-tone system, and by Shōwa Genroku Japan's musical capabilities were having a global impact. Musical instruments manufactured in Japan commanded a worldwide market; the "Suzuki method" of musical instruction developed by Suzuki Shin'ichi gained considerable favor; Japanese musicians were studying, working, and teaching abroad.

It merits note that among those Japanese musicians abroad a substantial number were women. In entrepreneurial Japan the popular notion that young women should acquire artistic skills translated into a surge of interest in mastering piano, voice, violin, and other instruments. That surge resulted in what one scholar called a "remarkable feminization of the Japanese musical world."[16] And the level of technical skill attained by those musicians equipped them to compete widely for positions as ensemble players and even as soloists.

Within Japan some musicians continued to play "traditional" music of diverse sorts, to perform at concert, and train successors. However, the more dynamic facets of musical development lay elsewhere. Composers created a grand array of original compositions, most famously Takemitsu Tōru, who employed musical instruments and idioms with creative eclecticism and used modern synthesizer technology to produce works that enjoyed wide acclaim and transcended the old categories of Japanese and foreign. His works showed up in scores of films as well as stage plays, concerts, and recordings.

Meanwhile, musical performance flourished. Choral music, which had been essentially an in-school student activity before the war, became more common as labor unions and religious groups found in choral singing a means to boost group élan. Also foreign choral groups performed on tour, as did countless orchestras and musicians, and myriad sorts of singers. Domestic orchestras and soloists proliferated, acquiring distinction and presenting musical programs that during Shōwa Genroku moved beyond meticulous performance of European classics to diversified offerings that creatively combined old and new, domestic and foreign. Musical instruction became ubiquitous, and music became a staple of radio. Musical shows also appeared on television, with popular musical fare, as earlier noted, being varied and inventive, if sometimes a bit noisy for old ears.

PAINTING AND PLASTIC ARTS

Perhaps the most noteworthy trend in painting and the plastic arts was their transcendence of genre. Artists boldly combined painting, sculpture, architecture, and even dance, drama, and film. In the process they broke free of prewar stylistic categories and, to a degree, escaped the increasingly anachronistic East/West agenda those categories embodied.

Immediately after the war, with the official wartime art organization dissolved, artists, like musicians and the intelligentsia as a whole, addressed anew the themes of the 1930s. Revitalized professional organizations sponsored exhibits of jury-selected works that were classified according to the established categories of Western-style and Japanese-style painting (yōga, nihonga), sculpture, calligraphy, and crafts. During the fifties, however, as the economy lumbered back into operation, foreign artists and exhibitions, mainly French and American, flowed in and Japanese artists started going abroad again, and that exchange revealed the outdatedness of existing art styles and categories, helping give impetus to avant garde art.

The challenge to established art was promoted with particular enthusiasm by the Osaka artist Yoshihara Jirō. Urging his followers to "Create what has never been created before," at the end of 1954 Yoshihara founded an art group, the Gutai Bijutsu Kyōkai, and through it promoted "a bold and spirited anti-academicism" in art.[17] During the Gutai group's seventeen-year life its members produced and exhibited

> painting, sculpture, indoor and outdoor site-specific installations, action events, stage performances, experimental film and musique concrète, the Gutai journal, and related graphic arts.

This output reflected the Gutai ideal of art as creative expression that by its nature is spontaneous, transient, and unrestricted by procrustean disciplinary boundaries.

Other artists, however, were less willing to abandon their ethnic past. Some saw their task as rescuing the "true" Japanese artistic legacy from the distortions produced by the authoritarianism of Imperial Japan. The job of rectifying those distortions meant for some artists getting beyond the entire imperial history, which willy nilly propelled them back to pre-*ritsuryō* times. For some the quest led to Asuka, whose bucolic air and historical artifacts and associations could transport one to the world before *Man'yōshū*. There, wrote one pundit in 1953, you can

> understand the ancient people's creativity by seeing the traditional lifestyle of the people living there today. In Asuka you can find [the real Japan and its beginnings].[18]

Some journeyed further back in time to a celebration of Yayoi agricultural society. On the basis of archaeological excavation, especially that at the Toro site in Shizuoka Prefecture, artists viewed Yayoi communities as fundamentally peaceful, egalitarian, and democratic and the scene, moreover, of aesthetically inspiring wooden tools and other artifacts. For others, rejecting the imperial legacy led even farther back to the study of Jōmon culture, which largely meant pottery and the "primitive" innocence and *joie de vivre* that it supposedly reflected. In a curious way, the agenda of Edo-period *kokugaku* had found a new voice.

Whether spurred by appealing notions such as these, or by a simpler desire to perpetuate the artistry visible in so many established crafts, artists tried their hand at ceramics, calligraphy, water colors, flower arrangement (*ikebana*), and other arts, seeking to give them relevance for the new age. Thus during the fifties the multi-talented Teshigahara Sōfū established the Sōgetsu Art Center in Tokyo to promote flower arrangement (along with diverse other arts) for contemporary use: for example, giant-sized *ikebana* displays appropriate for such sites as public halls and hotel lobbies. Similarly the photographer Domon Ken, who gained fame in 1960 when a book of his photographs revealed the pathetic conditions endured by the children of coal miners, travelled about the country, photographing temples and other cultural properties both to record them for posterity and to show how their forms could still inspire creativity. Throughout Shōwa Genroku the role of "Japanese" artistic tradition in the present-day world continued to receive attention.

Other agendas also showed up in art. The war, and especially the atomic bombings, inspired a number of horrific paintings and other visual expressions of anguish. Subsequently the outcome of the 1960 treaty crisis, which frustrated and disillusioned so many 1950s radicals, prompted alienated artists to engage in expressions of grotesquerie and anarchistic revel. Live theatre may have been the art most powerfully shaped by that crisis, as noted above, but it also spurred visual artists to more radical experimentation, and during the sixties the ideals so vigorously espoused by Gutai were reflected in the creations of numerous young artists. These included exhibits of junk art, assemblages, and anti-art, and a proliferation of Neo-Dadaist "Happenings" and performance art events.

Throughout Shōwa Genroku a rich array of artists explored every sort of artistic expression. They influenced, and were influenced by, the newest trends elsewhere, especially those in New York City and Paris, where a number of them lived for varying periods of time. Most notable perhaps were the Mono-ha productions of the 1970s, inspired by the art teacher Saitō Yoshishige. These often consisted of temporary assemblages and installations that sought to highlight the qualities of material, the significance of site and context, and the transcience of form – themes that persisted through the 1980s.

In a sense the tensions that informed the art world of entrepreneurial Japan were most successfully resolved in the work of architects. Being thoroughly constrained by the materials of their craft, the needs of their clients, and the sites of their projects, they were forced to accept the avant-garde stress on materials, place, and the relationship of art to life. They had little flexibility in employing elements of architectural legacy, whether of Europe, Japan, or elsewhere, and out of these constraints architects such as Tange Kenzō and his protégé Isozaki Arata proceeded to design prize-winning buildings and complexes in Japan and abroad, arranging the stone, glass, concrete, and other materials with which they worked in ways that fitted their particular sites and purposes while still conveying an underlying sense of appropriateness for industrial society as a generic human order.

Well before 1990, entrepreneurial Japan's creative arts – music and architecture in particular – had thus become a significant element in the global cultural life of the day. Artists still addressed the question of how to give contemporary voice to a presumed Japanese artistic style and taste, but most did so with sufficient creative openness that the issue did not dominate their work as it had that of their predecessors. Instead it contributed to their creative efforts as individuals.

FILM AND VIDEO

The 1920s and thirties had been a period of striking vitality in Japan's newly developing cinema, and under government supervision film making continued right through the war. Most studios, being situated on the outskirts of Tokyo or in Kyoto, which was not bombed, were almost untouched by the incendiary attacks, and after Japan's surrender they continued shooting film footage with only modest interruption.

After SCAP got organized, Occupation censors forbade production of "feudal" films on samurai and such like, and late in 1945 they defined what constituted acceptable cinema. Within those guidelines film makers produced upbeat films that treated such themes as democracy, liberalism, women's rights, and academic freedom, along with others that wrestled more deeply with difficulties of the day and hardships of the unfortunate – or that slyly evaded SCAP taboos by cinematic sleight of hand. The number of new releases was small (67 in 1946; 97 in 1947; reaching 278 in 1952), but cinemas showed about as many foreign as domestically made films, and the industry flourished, the vicissitudes of particular studios notwithstanding.

Cinema's heyday.   With so many people underemployed, production costs were low while the potential audience was immense, the moreso because other forms of recreation were few and darkened cinema halls offered an alternative to overcrowded, unpleasant housing. Surviving cinemas were packed, and even as more were built and opened, audiences remained huge. Movie-going functioned essentially as a cheap way to escape the harsh nonce to a Japan that was dynamic, independent, and engaged in "normal" life, or via foreign films to exotic lands of opulence, comfort, and happiness.

With Occupation's end Japanese cinema entered what proved to be a halcyon decade. Freed from creative restraints, and with access to large and receptive audiences and such up-to-date technology as color film, wide screen, and improved sound, directors produced a wide variety of films and the industry boomed. Films on contemporary topics (*gendaigeki*) became more varied in theme and style, and film makers turned to the past more freely to produce period pieces (*jidaigeki*) of great diversity and appeal.

Directors commonly viewed their films as vehicles for social commentary and aesthetic expression that was quite at odds with the wartime cinema's ideals of unquestioning imperial loyalism, duty, and honor. Their films might dwell on the ambiguities of morality, reality or truth, or, more commonly, on the cruel exploitation of the weak by the strong, as prescribed by the principles of socialist realism. They explored the individual and social effects of abuse and oftimes had a hero, whether samurai, villager, or other worthy, rise to right the wrong or at least fight the good fight. The style was exemplified by two *jidaigeki*, the celebrated *Rashōmon* of 1950 (based on stories by Akutagawa Ryūnosuke) and *Shichinin no Samurai* (The Seven Samurai) of 1954, both by Kurosawa Akira, which brought their director international fame and favor.

Some directors found in the domestic plays of Chikamatsu Monzaemon a vehicle for agendas of the day. As the film critic Satō Tadao explained it:

> many directors suddenly turned towards Chikamatsu because he explored the idea of freedom in his works. Before the war and also during wartime, the pursuit of love was considered bad, and even a man and woman walking together on the street were frowned upon.[19]

The new morality favored open expression of affection, however, so celebrating love constituted a repudiation of Japan's "feudalistic" heritage and thus became a way to overcome it.

Gendaigeki served similar purposes. Thus Kurosawa's extraordinarily moving 1952 film *Ikiru* (To Live) explored questions about life's purpose by watching the quietly stubborn effort of a dying civil offical to persuade his city government to resist business pressure and instead turn a tiny plot of urban land into a little park where neighborhood children could play. Other directors transferred novels of prewar and postwar life to the screen, exploring issues of family life, gender, jealousy, greed, growing up, and so on.

Cinema also participated actively in the 1950s national debate on war and defeat. Some directors addressed the issue seriously. Thus, in films produced in 1956 and 1959 respectively, Ichikawa Kon probed questions of war, sanity, civility, ethics, and spirituality in film versions of the novel *Biruma no tategoto* (Harp of Burma) by Takeyama Michio and *Nobi* (Fires on the Plain), the earlier-mentioned work by Ōoka Shōhei. Some films, however, adopted a facile anti-war posture while others exploited the lingering popular wish to believe in the worthiness of the great enterprise – or at least to honor those who had done their dutiful best. Thus the advertising for a war film produced in 1957 claimed that it was,

> Not a record of Japan's defeat in the Pacific War, but a record of the glorious victories of the army, navy and air force. See the brave deeds of your fathers and sons. Free stills of any scene in which your relatives and friends appear. War wounded admitted free.[20]

Not a bad marketing ploy.

As the war-film genre suggests, while directors may have envisaged themselves as artists, the industry itself was engaged in commercial entertainment and, as elsewhere, the great bulk of film output reflected that fact. It included innumerable pot-boilers that enriched the studios, with films about sword-swinging samurai (*chanbara*), full of gusto and bravado, enjoying particular popularity. Comedies and movies about gangsters (*yakuza*) swaggering across the screen and aiding the aggrieved drew large audiences. Sex, also, proved marketable. Prewar cinema had tabooed even the lovers' kiss, but in line with the new morality, the first screen kiss – presented with considerable ill-ease – occurred in a 1946 film. By 1950 mere kisses were passé and bedroom scenes, sex, and nudity were well ensconced on celluloid and destined to flourish thereafter.

The later years.　Annual film output peaked in 1960 with 547 feature films. By then, however, television was gaining popularity and the film industry was on the edge of decline, much as in other industrial societies. As Shōwa Genroku advanced, studio bosses struggled to sustain profitability. They sought new investors, diversified into other commercial ventures, including television itself, and looked for advantageous foreign linkages. They closed unprofitable theatres, with the result that cinemas were by 1990 found almost solely in the larger cities. One after another their business empires – studios, chains of theatres, staffs, and stables of actors, directors, and other professionals – dissolved.

In the struggle to survive, studios developed an assortment of market tie-ins and advertising gimmicks. They experimented with musicals, animation, and other cinematic variations, and turned to blockbusters. They cranked out ghost, monster, and other science-fiction films, spawned sequels (the

1954 film *Godzilla* led to sixteen at last count), and milked popular series. They exploited the "box office potential" of popular actors and actresses, cultivated the youth market, produced films explicitly for export, and relied heavily on works of "soft porn" and not so soft porn. Finally, during the 1980s film makers found in video cassettes a new and lucrative market (as did pirates who challenged them for it) and in cinema multiplexes a promising arrangement for screening full-size film. By 1990, however, feature film production stood at 239, down 56 percent from its 1960 peak.

The financial grimness of Shōwa Genroku cinema notwithstanding, independent directors continued to function, competing with the surviving studios through independent production companies funded by commercial investors and assisted by the Art Theater Guild, an independent professional organization. A few, such as Kurosawa, continued to produce distinguished films and establish or maintain international reputations, although in appreciably reduced numbers.

During the sixties in particular, as this larger story of institutional decline was starting to unfold, a "New Wave" of younger directors emerged. Whereas 1950s film makers had treated politics from the "progressive humanist" perspective of the established Japanese "left," after the treaty crisis of 1960 these younger film makers adopted a much more nihilistic, disaffected stance and expressed it through commensurately inventive cinema techniques. Their films embraced the demons, deities, transfigurations, transcendent visions, and other anti-realist aspects of *nō* and *kabuki* that avant-garde dramatists were bringing to the stage. And they used these elements in treating with a caustic eye a wide range of historical topics and contemporary events and issues, including the hardships of Korean residents and others – day laborers, *burakumin*, and the victims of radiation sickness and mercury poisoning.

In a series of films Ōshima Nagisa, one of the most prolific and esteemed of these New Wave directors, defied convention, mocked political verities, and explored with an unsentimental eye the pathologies of human life, such as criminality, abusive behavior, and government excess. He experimented with various cinematic techniques, employed Kara Jūrō and his troupe in one movie and the music of Takemitsu Tōru in others. He addressed the issues of resident Koreans and treated sexual obsession with a candor that won international acclaim, if not official favor or box office success. One of Ōshima's most celebrated works was *Ai no koriida* (In the Realm of the Senses, 1976). In it he recreated a sensational incident of the 1930s to explore with unprecedented visual frankness a couple's "obsessive search for sexual ecstasy" and defiant rejection of the government assertion that their behavior, which placed personal wishes ahead of social duty, was immoral or criminal.[21]

By then the gangster genre, which had long treated *yakuza* in simple terms of good Robin Hood types battling the bad, had begun portraying gangster life as ugly, violent, and destructive. And the *jidaigeki* and *chanbara* so favored during the fifties had lost their immense popularity. New Wave film was, however, only a partial replacement for these storied genres. It remained a minority camera style and during the seventies a fading one.

As Shōwa Genroku advanced and public attention focused more and more on the problems accompanying affluence, mainstream cinema adapted to the changing times by absorbing New Wave approaches, rather as the larger theatrical community was appropriating elements of avant garde drama. The industry produced films that dwelt, whether as melodrama, satire, or social commentary, on issues of the day, including the changing role of women, family tensions, oppressed groups, the aging, and the afflicted. Thus during the sixties Teshigahara Hiroshi, son of Sōfū of *ikebana* fame, made film versions of novels in which Abe Kōbō probed industrial-age issues of personal identity, purpose, freedom, community, and alienation.

Other films continued to re-examine the war or other aspects of history, sometimes with an eye critical of the government or the elite more generally, in other cases to probe the vulnerability of humanity more deeply. Thus the 1986 film *Umi to Dokuyaku* (The Sea and Poison) by Kumai Kei examined a brutal instance of wartime "research" by an army medical unit. To critics of the film Kumai insisted that his goal was not to criticize the medical profession. Rather,

> Man has long been noted for loss of conscience when placed in extreme situations. I wanted to define, examine and describe this horror through the medium of film.[22]

More celebrated was Imamura Shōhei's earlier-noted 1989 version of Ibuse Masuji's novel *Black Rain*, which treated the A-bomb and its effects.

Cinematic treatments of nuclear warfare were no more compelling than those of other artistic genres, but film-making technology enabled producers to manipulate the topic more radically. Most notably, authors and animators created from the notion of genetic mutation and global anti-nuclear outrage the earlier-noted monster Godzilla. In the original 1954 film Godzilla had risen from the depths following the Bikini bomb blast, a horrific American-spawned mutant that proceeded to trash Tokyo – rather as the mythic *namazu*, the giant catfish of popular legend, had flapped his tail in earthquake-like irritation and accidentally ravaged Edo following Commodore Perry's naval *démarche* of a century earlier. At first treated as an evil creature symbolic of the nuclear menace, Godzilla was transmogrified by later film makers into a defender of Japan against malevolent monsters of diverse origins, whether vaguely American or Russian, hideous life forms spawned from industrial sludge, or the creations of a subterranean species or an intergalactic alien race.

Through these transformations the Godzilla of Shōwa Genroku became, along with a panoply of science-fiction robots, androids, and generic youth heroes, major figures in the new filmic technology of animation. And from cinema the figures moved easily into video cassettes and thence to video games. By 1990 they had became a major genre of global youth entertainment, their grim real-life origins largely forgotten.

Women and cinema. Actresses, like women writers, carved out a substantial professional role for themselves before the Pacific War, and they retained it during cinema's postwar heyday. Thus the film career of Yamaguchi Yoshiko, star of the wartime *China Night*, which we noted in chapter 16, continued for a time as she appeared in several films following a stint in live theatre. Subsequently she made a few films in the United States under the stage name Shirley Yamaguchi and wed the American sculptor Isamu Noguchi. Later she married again, to a Japanese diplomat and LDP confidante, and gave up her acting career. In 1974 she parlayed her visibility and connections into electoral victory in the upper house of the Diet, becoming one of a small number of elected women national legislators.

During the fifties, an array of successful actresses emerged on the scene, including such mega-stars as Kyō Machiko and Takamine Hideko. By then another accomplished wartime actress, Tanaka Kinuyo, had created a media uproar when, after a short visit to America, she emerged from her airplane at Haneda Airport and threw kisses to the crowd – a thoroughly un-Japanese thing to do. She survived the pundits' hammering, however, to become a film director, turning out scores of movies after her directorial debute in 1953.

Tanaka's success notwithstanding, in Japan, as elsewhere, film making remained essentially a man's field until well into Shōwa Genroku. In 1979 the actress-turned-director Kurizaki Midori made her first film, *Kurokami* (Black Hair), seeking in it to "portray women as only a female director could."[23] She subsequently turned out other films, but by and large female images in cinema remained products of the male imagination. Thus, as one reviewer tartly observed about movie treatments of A-bomb survivors (*hibakusha*), "disfigured, but not deathly ill, *hibakusha* women have never been depicted in Japanese films; keloid-scarred women ... do not make for a beautiful heroine, and keloids are not a fatal illness."[24] So females appear in them not as angry, disfigured women who must plod on through lives of bitterness and hurt but as embodiments of the "sad beauty" of life, models of "forbearance, dignity, and stoic endurance," images akin to those envisioned for "good wife, wise mother" and idealized "Japanese" womanhood. It was an image that conformed to neither real life nor the lives sought by socially conscious women of the day, and it provided grist for the mill of those demanding more diverse roles for women.

The Japan of 1990 was very unlike that of 1950. Thanks to decades of wide-ranging growth it was bigger, richer, more cosmopolitan, and globally more influential. It was also, however, politically more unwieldy, socio-economically more complex, vastly more dependent on the outside world, and much more deeply entangled in the global problems of pollution and environmental deterioration.

With the death of Shōwa *tennō* in 1989 Japan entered its present-day reign period, that of Heisei. As noted in chapter 18, Heisei began inauspiciously, with the government in disarray and the economy stumbling. How well Japan has fared since then and how its people's prospects appear today are the final topics for us to consider.

EPILOGUE: JAPAN TODAY AND TOMORROW

CHAPTER SYNOPSIS

IMMEDIATE ISSUES

THE LARGER PICTURE

THE GLOBAL RESOURCE BASE
DOMESTIC TRENDS

Japan today is one of the world's most highly industrialized societies, strikingly different from what it was a century or two ago. What distinguishes it most fundamentally from the archipelago's earlier agricultural order, we have suggested, is its heavy reliance on recently developed forms of energy, fossil fuels most centrally. As a key corollary it has become dependent on a global resource base for which it once had no need. These basic changes, in turn, have been accompanied by a host of others, technological, social, and environmental. As a whole, finally, these diverse changes have occurred during the "growth stage" of industrialism. Whether or when Japan (and the world) can (or should) enter an era of industrial stasis and sustainability may be for humankind the basic question that awaits answer as the twenty-first century begins.

There are innumerable ways of thinking about present-day Japan (or any society). All prove immensely frustrating, however, because all demonstrate the classical ecological truism that "everything is connected to everything else" and, as a consequence, that every premise requires careful scrutiny and every statement seemingly endless qualification. Lest we bog down hopelessly, it may suffice here to invoke again our initial categories of production, distribution, and representation, looking briefly at a selection of immediate issues that are essentially matters of distribution and representation, and then to reflect on more elemental issues of production, which have basic implications for the question of where industrial Japan may be headed.

IMMEDIATE ISSUES

The issues of the moment that are most evident globally are the persistent weakness of Japan's financial markets and the flaccid quality of political leadership. Internally, however, issues relating to agriculture, urban life, women, and minorities also command attention, as does the perdurable question of "East and West." And the matters of an aging population and declining birth rate elicit more notice than ever.

Politics and the economy. By the end of Shōwa Genroku, as noted in chapter 18, Japan's economy was slipping into a "post-bubble" recession, and it remained stalled throughout the nineties. With major banking institutions mired in debt, unemployment and underemployment rose and consumers exercised greater frugality. Recently signs of revival have appeared, but as of this writing, no one can say when or whether lively growth will resume. There is such uncertainty in part because the aftereffects of 1980s domestic mismanagement were complicated during the nineties by economic disorder elsewhere, most hurtfully in the "Pacific Rim" region with which Japan's economy is most deeply engaged. And recovery there has only begun.

This decade-long "Heisei recession" has been nearly as damaging to the ruling LDP coalition as the "peace and prosperity" of Shōwa Genroku was beneficial. During the nineties Japan's government has been led by a series of weak cabinets that generally have served at all only because rival factions are even weaker. With the government's earlier fiscal cushion long gone and its social commitments swollen by politicians scrambling to retain popular support, Tokyo has found itself ill-equipped to address either its domestic social and economic problems or the international problems that affect the country's well-being.

These international problems are diverse in character. Some are bothersome residual issues of the Pacific War, most grievously the matter of "comfort women" and compensation for cruelties to them that can never be undone. But other wartime atrocities also continue to roil the waters, whether done by or to the Japanese. And farther back in memory, more diffuse issues of callous colonial exploitation still complicate relations. Other problems relate to Japan's role in the United Nations, questions about its use of military power, and policies on terrorism, technology exports, and so forth.

More sustained and substantial problems stem from postwar trade, and they commonly are evinced, as they were throughout Shōwa Genroku, in charges and counter-charges of unfairness, dissembling, and disrespect. The rhetoric is interest-driven, but no matter how self-serving and calculated, the tone of righteous indignation that characterizes so much of it does reflect and reinforce ethnic tensions and distrust, encouraging rhetoricians to dredge up and air yet again hurts of long ago. These problems have been exacerbated by the imbalances and disorder that seem chronically to plague international trade. Although particulars – notably the identity of who directs preachy lectures at whom – have changed with the ebb and flow of fortune, the sustained recession of the nineties has been accompanied by friction and complaints that are as abrasive and acerbic as those that accompanied the boom of Shōwa Genroku. As of this writing, it seems more likely that the tensions will heighten than lighten as long as the Pacific Rim economies remain depressed. And beyond that lies the broader question of how Japan would fit into a world economy dominated by a unified European behemoth, a powerful North America, and an Asia centered on an industrialized China.

Domestically the basic distribution of power and privilege has remained unchanged despite the Heisei recession. In consequence the government serves the same business interests as before and so has compelling reason to avoid measures that would threaten those who have sustained it for nearly five decades. Hence policy has in all areas been marked by caution and half-measures, with the regime essentially waiting for the economy to recover in its own cyclical manner. Although innumerable foreign pundits and politicians presume to lecture Tokyo on its performance, their own track records lend their words little credence.

Town and country. In broader terms of agriculture's decline and urban, industrial society's rise to predominance, the nineties have witnessed a continuing shrinkage in the number of rural households and in agricultural employment, especially by women. In part these trends reflect the fact that the last generation able to recall a rural-centered culture is rapidly dying off, which makes it easier for successors to abandon their residual rural roles. And in part the shrinkage is occurring because the part-time farming arrangements of Shōwa Genroku have been severely challenged by urban career alternatives at home and by food imports from government-subsidized producers abroad, mainly in North America.

In the cities, meanwhile, the recession has slowed the trend to more luxurious housing. However, the other established trends – toward greater density of settlement, more multi-story stacking, and smaller households – continue.

Women and minorities. The feminist movement that gained visibility during late Shōwa Genroku has continued to flourish, at least in terms of participatory activity. Interest in academic Women's Studies continues to grow, and publications by, for, and about women continue to proliferate. Participation in fetal rites (*mizuko kuyō*) appears to be in decline, which suggests that young women are feeling more secure in their exercise of choice, and that feeling may strengthen further now that the government has finally, in the summer of 1999, authorized the sale of contraceptive pills. In addition, women have made more inroads into the political establishment. And while the recession has complicated affairs, they slowly expand their position in the urban economy.

Nevertheless, frustration with the "glass ceiling" persists, and other manifestations of male advantage continue to rankle, as does the modesty of legal remedies to gender discrimination. More young husbands give greater attention to household affairs today, but the change may be proceeding more slowly than in most comparably industrialized societies, and it is occurring more slowly than many women wish. Moreover, in Japan as elsewhere, not a few older males still call for women to submit graciously, in the prewar manner of good wife, wise mother.

The situation of minorities varies from group to group. Some among the small population of Ainu continue to promote Ainu nationhood, and language instruction has broadened. One suspects, however, that as long as the basic vitality of Japan's industrial society remains intact, demographic trends will work to undo those efforts, in due course integrating Ainu and Wajin and consigning Ainu culture to the sort of museum status now enjoyed by other pre-industrial rural cultures in Japan and elsewhere.

In the south, meanwhile, the much larger Ryukyuan population seems far better positioned to contemplate alternative futures that may or may not offer some degree of ethnic autonomy. Given the proximity of the Ryukyus to Taiwan and China, depending on how affairs develop on the Western Pacific littoral, one can envisage Ryukyuan leaders and people being enabled (or forced) to reconceptualize their community's relationship to Japan and other nearby states. In the meantime the American military presence continues to be a source of grievance, and Tokyo's acceptance of that presence sustains dissatisfaction with Japanese rule. The displeasure is softened, however, by Tokyo's greater readiness to accept symbolic expressions of Ryukyuan ethnicity and by its encouragement of greater public appreciation for the Ryukyuan historical legacy, postures adopted, no doubt, in hopes of weakening any secessionist impulse.

In the heartland, *burakumin* continue to evince a strong wish to move into the mainstream, probably because they have found in their legacy little autonomous culture to celebrate and much oppression, exploitation, and hardship to escape. Residual prejudice, conscious and unconscious, continues to complicate the task, and *burakumin* activists keep lobbying for formal criminalization of discriminatory conduct. As more and more young *burakumin* leave their communities, they become less supportive of these activist efforts, but their movement into the mainstream is still hampered by educational and economic disadvantages, which the current recession has exacerbated. If the economy revives and remains vigorous, however, one can expect more *burakumin* to acquire the schooling and employment that will equip them to move into the mainstream. And one suspects that generational change, sustained lobbying efforts, and continuing global interactions will slowly erode old prejudices, easing *burakumin* efforts to make that move.

More and more Korean residents are also finding a place for themselves in the general population. Younger Koreans today are much more disposed to engage actively in Japanese society than were earlier generations, and the Japanese government has recently facilitated that trend by becoming more responsive to Korean complaints. In 1991–2 it abolished routine finger-printing of permanent foreign residents, eliminated legal distinctions between the North and South Korea-oriented communities, eased restrictions on visas and name usage, and improved the coverage of social benefits. It has made some effort to address residual issues of the colonial and wartime period, not always gracefully. And incidents of violence against Koreans that once passed without comment or action now elicit editorial criticism, public protest, and police inquiry.

However, unresolved tension between the two Koreas and policy choices of the P'yŏngyang government continue to complicate affairs. Nor is there any sign that either Japan's leaders or the general public is prepared to reconceive Japan as a multi-ethnic or multi-lingual society. Since many Korean residents are still unprepared to abandon their "Koreanness" to become citizens of Japan, problems of economic and social discrimination persist. Even if the current economic slowdown gives way to renewed boom, therefore, one can expect these problems to resolve themselves only slowly.

Resident Chinese continue to maintain the low profile of recent decades, even though their numbers keep growing, reaching some 250,000 by 1999. Many are unskilled laborers, however, and like those from other countries, they have been buffeted by the economic recession.

Regarding these foreign laborers, whatever their country of origin, many have had to accept the more difficult conditions of the day because they have so little to return to in their homelands. Early in the nineties the recession nearly halted the inflow of additional unskilled migrants, but it remains unclear to what extent the existing immigrant population will slowly shrink, move into the mainstream (an outcome that may be most feasible for Latin Americans of Japanese ancestry), or survive largely as an underclass akin to the *burakumin* of earlier generations.

Aging and infancy. The issues of old age and birth rates are closely linked. Many commentators assert that a continually expanding population of young producers is necessary to support the growing population of seniors; *ergo*, more babies are needed. But the presence of this larger cohort of aged is one of several factors prompting young couples, and young women in particular, to limit family size. And thus far the pundits of procreation have proven less influential than the practitioners.

Human life expectancy in Japan continues to lengthen, in 1997 standing at 83.2 years for women and 77.2 for men. This sustained rise in longevity has created a large and rapidly growing population of Japanese elders whose productive capacity no longer matches its consumption needs, particularly in the form of medical attention. As elsewhere, the arrangements for handling this population are being developed in tandem with the numbers, resulting in a state of continual uncertainty, dissatisfaction, and finger pointing. Individual households – with their space limitations, their competing interest in more creature comforts, their fashionable ideal of personal gratification, and their uncertainty about the future – generally find the seniors an unwelcome burden and a constraint on prized choice. Social service agencies find that government funding is difficult to secure because of the regime's fiscal straits. And non-governmental agencies seem thus far to have found little attraction in elder care, given the economics of the business, especially among the lower classes. One suspects that for the elderly in Japan, as elsewhere, their personal situation will remain roughly commensurate with their economic circumstance as they face the unpleasantness of social marginalization and the terrors of terminal decline.

Turning to the issue of birth rates, most observers approach the question from the perspective of prevailing ideology, which still seems to presume the feasibility of unbounded socioeconomic growth. On that assumption a robust birth rate continues to be defined as a Good Thing because most of the dominant social groups want a rate that assures population increase. Thus, celebrants of the nation are concerned lest Japan lose its position as a Major Power. Tax collectors and the politicians and interests they bankroll want more taxpayers; employers want abundant labor at minimal cost; purveyors of health, education, gospel, gadgets, and good times want an endless – better yet a burgeoning – stream of consumers. Only the early industrial military's wish for ample cannon fodder is absent, replaced in Japan, as in other comparably technological societies, by reliance on manufactured instruments of destruction that are far easier to deploy than the armed hordes of earlier twentieth-century warfare.

This broad-based desire for more children notwithstanding, the young women whose cooperation is essential to their production are disinclined to help, in considerable part because they are disenchanted with the style of homemaking and child-rearing that awaits them and see other, preferable ways to use their time and energy. And a good many young husbands share the disinclination to beget. The wish to use their resources for alternative purposes, their concern about future uncertainties, and their capacity to avoid unwanted progeny have combined to convince many young women not to marry and many young couples to remain childless or have only one or two offspring. These tendencies have been reinforced by the continuing recession. The fretting and pressure of privileged males notwithstanding, there seems at present no reason to expect a renewed burst of baby-making in the absence of radical change of one sort or another.

East and West. Finally, at the level of representation, the trends of late Shōwa Genroku continue in the fields of literary, performance, and visual arts. In terms of rhetoric, ethnicity still finds ample expression in the well-worn East/West dyad, which seems to be enjoying a new moment of popularity in the world of punditry.

Within Japan some commentators still call for the vitalization of Japanese or Asian culture, values, or society as an alternative to an unattractive "Western" modernity. And others call for a more glowing treatment of Japan's past. Thus a group of senior academics who established in 1997 the Japanese Society for History Textbook Reform has denounced what it sees as a slavishly Eurocentric view of history, declaring that,

> because of the way in which Japanese history has been taught since World War II, our citizens have been deprived of the opportunity to learn about their culture and traditions, and no longer take pride in being Japanese.[1]

Elsewhere, as well, the East/West dyad thrives, perhaps because the economic downturn of the nineties has (as of this writing) appeared to be primarily a "far side of the Pacific" phenomenon that juxtaposes a tottering, fragmenting "Asia" against an economically consolidating, politically expanding "West," meaning centrally the European Common Market, but by extension the "Atlantic community" of NATO: Western Europe and North America. Under these circumstances pundits have quietly dropped the rhetoric about "North and South," folding Japan again into Asia, thus aligning region, "race," "culture," and global position more completely than at any time in recent decades. By its nature this is a fragile foundation for an interpretive perspective, but thanks to the notorious shortsightedness of punditry, it has for the moment given rise to an ethnicity-based rhetoric of considerable strength.

At an esoteric level some members of academia and their outliers in the world of commentary have embraced a "deconstructionist" or "postmodernist" rhetoric that seeks to transcend these procrustean categories. However, the qualities of abstraction and obscurantism that have characterized the discourse tend to limit its influence to small circles of the *cognoscenti*. Meanwhile the broader world of representation, as evidenced in most media chatter, film and video, official rhetoric, and general commentary, continues to employ the paradigm of progress and the established dyadic categories of ethnicity and, sometimes, class.

THE LARGER PICTURE

The basic productive functions that sustain industrial society are rooted, as noted earlier, in a global resource base that must satisfy myriad needs. For Japan, as for other societies, it is trends in that base and in the nation's capacity to draw upon its yield (through one or another combination of economic and political–military policies) that will most basically determine its future.

THE GLOBAL RESOURCE BASE

For the Japanese, as for everyone else, two elemental variables are shaping the value of their global resource base: pervasive depletion and heightened competition for what remains. The competition intensifies as the world's human population continues to soar and as more and more societies aspire to living standards matching those of the industrialized minority. Depletion results from the consumption of irreplaceable materials and destruction of the ecosystemic base of self-renewing biotic resources. This last process is achieved directly through habitat destruction and indirectly through ambient pollution, two processes of global scope that are steadily undercutting earth's biodiversity and biomass production. Within this framework one can examine the overseas facet of Japan's resource situation in terms of industrial fuels, foodstuffs, other overseas resources, and forest products.

Industrial fuels. Fossil fuels, the key factor permitting industrial society's emergence, are found under both land and sea. Their story is the familiar one of discovery, depletion, and further search. With the level of global fuel consumption increasing decade by decade, with one oil field after another being depleted, with exploration focusing on ever more remote sites, and with new technology being devised to extract residues once deemed too limited or inaccessible, and hence too costly, for recovery, it is becoming ever more clear that the fossil fuel regime of the past century is approaching its end. Pessimists foresee terminal scarcity of hydrocarbons starting to emerge within fifteen years or less while optimists believe global reserves will suffice for another quarter century or more.[2]

The recession in Asia reduced fossil fuel use and drove prices downward for a time, but that trend now seems to be reversing, and with economic recovery one can expect the longer-term pattern of accelerating global fuel consumption to resume. When world reserves start to diminish, the politics of oil exploration, development, and marketing will become more convoluted and dangerous and Japan's overseas sources of oil and gas will become problematic.

In place of depleted oil and gas supplies, widely scattered seafloor beds of methane hydrates, including some near Japan as figure Epilogue 1 indicates, are available for exploitation if the technology to recover them can be devised. Indeed, Japanese authorities, with their acute awareness of energy issues and their enduring desire to minimize Japan's vulnerability to vagaries elsewhere, are already exploring the potential of frozen gas hydrates in adjacent waters.[3] However, the release of gas from these hydrates may present environmental complications that dwarf those attributable thus far to other fossil fuels, and their use still seems at best to lie a bit over the horizon.

Nuclear energy remains a major alternative to fossil fuel, and global supplies of nuclear fuel are substantial, provided one has breeder reactors that permit fuel recycling. Unfortunately, whereas the global nuclear industry (governmental and entrepreneurial) has poured incalculable wealth into

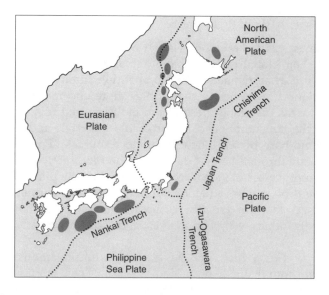

Figure Epilogue 1 Tectonic plates and suspected sites of methane hydrates around Japan. Japan's incessant tectonic activity reflects its location at the intersection of four major plates. Nearby accumulations of methane hydrates (shaded ovals) may provide a significant future fuel supply for the realm. *Source*: Based on fact sheet D-3 1998.2 from the Geological Survey of Japan.

developing nuclear weapons capability and energy-generating capacity, it has devoted a mere pittance to finding ways of rendering spent fuel and associated equipment non-radioactive or otherwise safe. In consequence the longer-term costs and dangers of nuclear fuel still leave it a highly problematic energy supply. In Japan the generating capacity of nuclear power plants has risen from nearly thirty-two million kilowatts to more than forty-three since 1990, as construction projects that were begun years ago come to completion. At present, however, there seems little likelihood that the country will increase its reliance on nuclear power very significantly in the foreseeable future, and the decommissioning of old power plants may in fact gradually reduce its role.

Renewable fuels are unpromising. The smoke from firewood is highly polluting, and other, higher-priority uses for wood already exceed global woodland's productive capacity. Moreover, areas devoted to growing wood cannot be otherwise used, and other crops have greater market potential. So firewood seems unlikely to develop into a source of consequence for Japan or other industrial societies. Corn, sunflower, and other vegetable oil can be used as industrial fuel, but arable acreage used that way cannot feed people, and global hunger, already an issue of concern, is likely to prevent the extensive use of arable to produce industrial fuel. Nor is trash likely to become a major fuel source since much of it will have other, more valued uses when recycled.

Other sources of power – hydro, solar, wind, geothermal, and tidal in particular – have modest promise as substitutes for or supplements to fossil fuels. Because of technical difficulties, social costs, or intrinsic limits of supply, however, they seem unlikely to provide other societies with additional quantities of energy sufficient to free up fossil fuels for export to Japan. Rather, they seem destined for the forseeable future to remain marginal in their roles, either globally or in Japan.

In short, the basic factor permitting the existence of industrial society – the immense boost supplied by non-food energy sources – evinces a problematic future. And it does so particularly for those societies, such as Japan, that are heavily dependent on imported fuels. Clearly energy policy will occupy a central role in shaping the country's global strategy and relations in future.

Foodstuffs. The other basic source of industrial society's energy, namely foodstuffs, can be treated in terms of their maritime and terrestrial origins. We foreshadowed the maritime story in earlier references to the nineteenth-century depletion of Atlantic cetacean stock by European and American whalers and the sustained Wajin overfishing of the Hokkaido herring run, whose harvest declined in prewar years and was abandoned during the early postwar period. Since then, prime fisheries all around the globe have been severely depleted.

Indeed, earth's maritime ecosystem is currently in a state of rapid deterioration thanks to global pollution, global warming, and the worldwide overfishing achieved by application of industrial-age search-and-harvest technology to a forager economy. Electronic search gear render the sea transparent and deprive many fish of the capacity to hide. Giant bottom trawlers transform verdant seafloor ecosystems into muddy deserts that repopulate slowly and sparsely: by one recent, possibly excessive estimate, such trawling "destroys a seabed area twice the size of the contiguous United States each year."[4] Long-line surface trawlers indiscriminately pick up whatever is in their paths, stripping large slabs of ocean of their macro-level biodiversity. And nowadays the mass harvesting of "secondary" species, many of which stand below desired table dishes in oceanic food chains, threatens to destroy yet more fisheries. In consequence of these trends, fishmeal for fertilizer and animal feed, as well as seafood for human consumption, must come from farther afield. It is more costly and of lower quality, forcing consumers to shift to other foods, commit more income to meals, or eat less.

The combination of spreading marine pollution and sustained over-fishing, which hitherto has produced only regional collapses of fish populations, now raises the strong possibility of much more far-ranging crashes, with all the incalculable ecological ramifications they will have. Despite growing conflicts among fishermen, fishing organizations, and governments as they scrap over declining resources, however, the looming danger has thus far produced within government and industry everywhere little more than token responses at best and vigorous denials at worst. Fish farming provides some relief, but the capacity of fish farms to expand is limited. Some entrepreneurs advocate massive conversion of ocean areas to managed fish rearing, but such monocultures are highly vulnerable to disease, and their merit remains to be demonstrated.

Regarding Japan's import of terrestrial foodstuffs, with global population burgeoning and people aspiring to better diets, demand for food grows, even as more and more arable land is shifted to urban uses. These trends lead to ever more land clearance and more intensive cultivation, and thence to worldwide depletion and pollution of top soil. Those outcomes, together with rising costs of fertilizer and machinery operation, work gradually and irregularly to force "rationalization" of provisioning – bulk processing, transport, and distribution; product substitution and modification; and the use of cheaper farm and food-processing labor. And where those measures do not suffice, the process pushes food prices upward, placing more and more global foodstuffs beyond the reach of more and more people. These processes can be expected to accelerate should the yield from pelagic fisheries start to plummet.

Insofar as foodstuffs move in response to market forces, Japan is reasonably well positioned for the foreseeable future: as is already happening, starvation will come to poor nations that are unable to importune or intimidate the wealthy well before it comes to the industrial powers, or at least to their more fortunate citizens. Under seriously straitened circumstances, however, it seems even less likely with food than with industrial fuels that market forces will prevail in the face of state, ethnic, and class interests. And then Japan's heavy dependence on food imports will become a more worrisome matter.

Other foreign resources. Japan today must import an immense array of other terrestrial raw materials, and the extent of global reserves varies tremendously. Subsurface materials disappear as they are extracted and consumed, of course, but substitution accommodates some losses and recycling slows rates of depletion. Some of these materials are already scarce; others, such as iron, aluminum, and limestone, are not – yet.

In the case of iron, thanks to a century of importing, Japan now has an immense supply of recyclable iron and steel embedded in its industrial infrastructure in the form of vehicles, structural steel, iron rails, and so on. However, that supply becomes available for reuse only slowly, partially, and at considerable cost. Moreover, much steel must leave the country again as exports that pay for food and fuel imports, so dependency on iron imports persists (see table X in Appendix A).

Forest products. The woodland harvest, which still has a wide array of industrial-age uses (*vide* this book), will become more scarce as global forests are consumed. As conifer stands on Siberian tundra are cut off, exposing the land's surface to sunlight, ever larger areas melt, allowing the soil to settle to the bottom and long-submerged water to rise and evaporate. In regions of unknown magnitude this process leaves lifeless salt flats whose surface particulates can then become airborne, with uncertain effects on downwind northeast Asia, Japan included. Tropical forests, which remain a major source of Japanese wood imports, are in process of being destroyed by fire, harvest, and conversion to other uses. How much these trends can be slowed or reversed is unclear, but evidence to date is not encouraging.

Most of the old-growth temperate-zone forests are long gone, but many secondary stands exist. Faster-growing species can be introduced, and many areas can be converted to plantation stock, whose rates of growth in future may well be spurred by global warming and higher levels of atmospheric carbon dioxide. These last gains are likely to be more than offset, however, by the impact of acid rain and other pollutants.

Moreover, the consumers of plantation yield must settle for less variety of product in an increasingly costly marketplace. Also, as earlier suggested, most areas that can grow plantation stands efficiently will be put to other, more lucrative uses as global population grows and urban needs swell. Furthermore, plantations, like fish farms and other monocultures, are highly vulnerable to disease and disruption. Most worrisome is the loss of biodiversity, which is roughly proportional to the extent of plantations and entails a global tradeoff whose implications are not yet understood. By one recent Swiss estimate, some 34,000 species of plants – about one eighth of all that are known – now appear threatened by extinction, and the list grows every year.[5]

As with foodstuffs and industrial fuels, for the foreseeable future Japan seems likely to be able to secure forest products. And recycling, product substitution, and the acceptance of inferior materials will continue to ease the problem. But here too, beyond the next several years the imponderables give ample cause for concern.

DOMESTIC TRENDS

Within this problematic global context the story of Japan's history continues to unfold. At the level of basic production, trends in domestic woodland and other select resources seem to merit brief comment.

Woodland. For millennia the well-watered, acutely mountainous topography of Japan's islands enabled their ecosystem to remain vibrant despite a long history of relatively dense human settlement and intensive exploitation. Even today, as Japan nears a full century of industrial change, those mountains still shelter a rich biota, to a degree confounding the best-laid schemes of those who have labored to turn the archipelago to immediate human advantage.

Admittedly, sustained urban pressure on the hinterland and intensified manipulation of terrain keep nibbling away at the woodland. Earth-moving equipment has already transformed many once-wooded terrace deposits into urban-use areas; conceivably, far more ambitious projects will follow. For now, however, Japan's woodland remains intact, nearly as much forested acreage officially recorded today as during the 1950s. And because most woodland is on steep hillsides, relatively little is compromised by suburban sprawl of the sort that is rapidly destroying forest integrity in much of North America.

As noted in chapter 19, Japan's woodland already contains a high proportion of plantation stands, and they are presently deteriorating. Too costly to harvest and too densely stocked to thrive at their present age, they have become subject to windthrow and snow breakage. The process ruins merchantable timber, but it also opens patches of hillside to sunlight, spurring mixed understory growth that is supportive of a richer faunal population. And on small farm woodlots, most of which are no longer exploited for fuel, fodder, and fertilizer material, plant life thrives and birds, animals, and other creatures become more varied and prolific. Indeed, in some places wild boar have become a nuisance to vegetable growers and the denizens of sprawling suburbia. Current trends are thus transforming Japan's woodland into messy, mixed, multi-aged forest of much reduced market worth but much greater long-term ecological value.

How long these trends will continue, however, is highly problematic. One suspects that global deforestation will eventually boost timber prices enough to make Japan's forests competitive again, which could lead to renewed harvesting and more widespread cultivation of even-aged, monoculture stands in lieu of the ecologically more desirable but commercially less efficient mixed forest. But perhaps not. Whether the current, unintended outcome of entrepreneurial Japan's forest policy constitutes the last hurrah of a vital ecosystem; whether poorly visible processes of terminal decay are already at work; whether the island nation's human population will adhere to ecologically defensible policies in future; or whether the dynamics of industrialism will ravage the realm – along with the rest of the world's woodland – is yet to be seen. Young readers may want to stay tuned.

Other domestic resources. Diverse subsurface resources survive in Japan. As earlier noted, however, few are of great economic value, and they do not include the crucial metals and fossil fuels, save for coal. Much of the coal is at present too costly and difficult to mine, but in a future, more impoverished global context, it may again become worth extracting despite its inferior quality.

Some of Japan's other domestic energy sources can be expanded. Hydropower is already well developed, but the social and environmental costs of new projects are becoming ever more prohibitive, so growth will be limited for the foreseeable future. Fully sustainable use of nuclear power awaits appropriate research and development. Solar energy has some promise despite the archipelago's relatively cloudy weather. Geothermal, wind, and tidal power seem to have greater potential, given Japan's geology, topography, and global placement. And if global warming brings the intensified atmospheric instability that climate modelers predict, wind and tidal energy sources may prove particularly useful.

Present technology renders most of these energy sources uncompetitive with fossil fuels, but future improvements in the former and scarcity of the latter will likely change that situation. It is important to remember, however, that none of these alternative fuels provides the myriad chemicals, fertilizers, plastics, and other products that fossil fuels supply, and without those materials industrial society as we know it cannot function.

Agricultural lands continue to shrink at the rate of about 20,000 hectares per year, most being converted to urban uses. And as Japan's part-time farming regimen decays, one can expect many of the scattered plots of farm land in and near cities to be lost to food growing. The remaining hinterland acreage will, no doubt, be subjected to more vigorous exploitation, with more use of plastic and greenhouses, more intensive application of chemical fertilizers to sustain soil nutrient value, more pesticides to control infestations, and the reopening of more marginal land at the expense of forest and fen. These agronomic techniques are costly, however, and until global food prices rise appreciably, they can succeed only if sheltered by government policies of one sort or another.

Coastal fishing, meanwhile, continues to be limited by supply constraints. And fish farming, while expanding, remains a very small part of the industry – about one percent of the total catch – its growth restrained by the scarcity of sufficiently unpolluted sites and by the costs and difficulties of technique. *In toto*, therefore, present trends suggest that the domestic maritime harvest will become a smaller part of Japan's food supply in future, increasing the nation's dependence on imports.

These several comments on the larger picture of Japan today suggest that the "growth" ceaselessly advocated by politicians, pundits, and the profit-driven, as well as its underlying ideal of progress – meaning limitless linear expansion in the scale of human activities – may be unsustainable. At this early point in the development of global industrial society, however, its future prospects are impossible to predict.

Industrialization is, after all, still in its infancy. Not only is much of the world still unindustrialized, but the use of fossil fuel and non-organic energy generally has only begun to expand rapidly: by one estimate global use of such energy stood at 2.7 billion metric tons as recently as 1960, rocketing to 8.0 billion by 1990.[6] Given the character and values of industrial society, powerful social forces will surely work to sustain that trajectory. And vast increases in energy use may in fact be attainable because many of the basic sources (nuclear, geothermal, wind, tidal, and perhaps most importantly, gas hydrates) have – for better or worse – yet to be seriously exploited.

That a world divided into the wealthy industrial few and the impoverished agricultural multitude cannot long endure seems too evident to belabor. But no one can yet say whether a fully industrialized world is capable of achieving a sufficient level of equity in the global distribution of privilege to maintain minimal social order while still leaving enough healthy space for the necessary minimum of biodiversity and biomass output (whatever that may prove to be) to assure humankind a viable ecological "niche."

Nor can one say whether the long-term rhythms of growth and stasis that marked earlier ages will reappear. From the rhetoric of pundits, politicians, and professional prognosticators, one could infer that industrial society is fundamentally a Ponzi scheme: if it fails to keep expanding, it withers, so endless growth is essential to survival. And that proposition seems to require that the earth function as an inflatable balloon.

Viewed from a broader biosystemic perspective, of course, the whole schema of growth and stasis may simply be a misperception based on temporal shortsightedness and arrant "speciesism." The global evidence to date suggests that by various criteria – biodiversity, biomass production, ecological resilience, energy transfers, space utilization – earthly life has for a long time (since the Mesozoic era perhaps?) been in overall terms a zero-sum game, more or less, with gains to some parts of the biosystem offset by losses to other parts. In recent times, growth in the human sector – whether of agricultural or industrial society, or possibly foragers – has been balanced, sooner or later, by shrinkage in other sectors of the biome. And in our own day, thanks largely to capabilities unleashed by use of fossil fuels, the price of extra human benefits in the present not only is paid for by other species but also can be, and is being, deferred, to be paid for by future generations.

Nevertheless, from a human-centered perspective the short-term advantages of industrialization are, for its beneficiaries, unprecedented in scale and range. And those advantages are amply visible in the case of Japan. Unsurprisingly, since it is beneficiaries who provide most of the documentation, these favorable aspects dominate the historical record and the historiographical discourse almost to the exclusion of the broader, more problematic dimensions of industrialism. And that state of affairs has to considerable extent been reflected in the pages of this volume.

If, however, the reigning ideal of progress is not sustainable, it may be that Japan's industrial society, like the forager and agricultural societies that preceded it, will evolve from a growth stage to one of stasis. Indeed, an impetuous observer might be tempted to cite recent trends in demography, levels of imports, industrial production, employment, and per-capita wealth to support such a proposition. Save for the trajectory of live births, however, these factors seem largely to reflect the recent economic downturn, and they provide no persuasive basis for longer-term prediction.

If nonetheless industrial society must evolve from growth to stasis, the young women of Japan, by declining to reproduce with sufficient vigor to please their elders, may inadvertently be steering their country in the direction of a sustainable future. Even if such be the case, however, some factors militate against that future being realized. Most immediately, the ideal of progress is as intact in Japan as elsewhere, important to the short-term well-being of those in power and at present not under serious challenge. Even environmentalists in Japan, as elsewhere, being mainly "middle class" beneficiaries of industrialism, are for the most part unprepared to reject core elements of that ideology.

More importantly, Japan today is not functioning with the high level of autonomy that marked its millennia as a forager and agricultural society. Rather, it is part of a semi-integrated global economic order, and its people are not free to pursue policies independently of trends elsewhere. Their destiny is not their own.

If industrial society's future lies in some form of stabilization and restraint, that outcome must be global. It may of necessity entail the displacement of today's ideology of growth with a commitment to humane stabilization and the articulation of social structures and values that enable such ideals to find expression in action. If so, only insofar as those young Japanese women are joined by their fellows in other societies can their purposeful managing of reproduction be first steps along a path to a future human order that will prove sustainable and satisfying, civilized in the best sense of the word.

Notes

1 Geology, Climate, and Biota

1 Parts of this chapter first appeared in my *Early Modern Japan* (Berkeley: UCP, 1993), ch. one.
2 Yutaka Sakaguchi, "Characteristics of the Physical Nature of Japan with Special Reference to Landform," in The Association of Japanese Geographers, ed., *Geography of Japan* (Tokyo: Teikoku-shoin Co. Ltd., 1980), p. 4.
3 H. Arakawa, "Three Great Famines in Japan," *Weather* (published by the Royal Meteorological Society, London), XII (1957): 211–12.
4 Fumiko Ikawa-Smith, "Chronological Framework for the Study of the Palaeolithic in Japan," *Asian Perspectives* 19/1 *Japanese Prehistory* (1978): 71, 74, 79.
5 Franz Heske, *German Forestry* (New Haven: YUP, 1938), p. 52.

2 From Origins to Agriculture

1 Matsuo Tsukada, "Vegetation in Prehistoric Japan: The Last 20,000 Years," in Richard J. Pearson et al., eds., *Windows on the Japanese Past: Studies in Archaeology and Prehistory* (Ann Arbor: Center for Japanese Studies, The University of Michigan, 1986), p. 39.
2 *Japan Foundation Newsletter* 25/4 (Dec. 1997): 6.
3 Richard Pearson, *Ancient Japan* (NY: George Braziller, 1992), p. 68.
4 For a recent treatment of the demographic issue, see Keiji Imamura, *Prehistoric Japan, New Perspectives on Insular East Asia* (Honolulu: UHP, 1996), pp. 155–60. Tsukada, p. 50, gives the figure 1–2 million for "Yayoi." Shūzō Koyama, "Jōmon subsistence and population," *Senri Ethnological Studies* 2 (1978), pp. 56–7, estimates a Jōmon peak of about 260,000 for ca. 2400 BCE, falling to 160,000 or so around 1200 BCE. Makoto Sahara, "Rice Cultivation and the Japanese," *AA* 63 (1992), citing Koyama, gives the figures 600,000 to 1,000,000 for the start of the Common Era (CE).

Introduction to Part II

1 By Kinai Basin, I refer to the watershed of the Yodo and Yamato rivers, not the five provincial political units (Izumi, Kawachi, Settsu, Yamashiro, and Yamato) of

the *ritsuryō* regime, as is commonly the case. The five provinces cover less territory than the Basin, excluding Ōmi and Iga provinces and the part of Tanba drained by the Ōi River, a major tributary of the Yodo.

3 POLITICAL CONSOLIDATION TO 671 CE

1 *Science News* 151/7 (February 15, 1997): 106–7.
2 Ryūsaku Tsunoda, tr. and L. Carrington Goodrich, ed., *Japan in the Chinese Dynastic Histories* (South Pasadena: P.D. and Ione Perkins, 1951), p. 24.
3 *Wajinden* is a portion of the supplemental segment of the *Wei chih* (History of the Wei Dynasty) that reported on the "barbarian" peoples of the Manchuria–Korea–Japan region. The *Wei chih* itself was a part of the *San-kuo chih* (History of the Three Kingdoms), which was compiled sometime during the years 280–297 CE by the historian Ch'en Shou. The quotations are from Tsunoda and Goodrich, *Japan in the Chinese Dynastic Histories*, pp. 8–16.
4 Tsunoda and Goodrich, *Japan in the Chinese Dynastic Histories*, p. 12.
5 See the discussion of marriage in Hitomi Tonomura, "Black Hair and Red Trousers: Gendering the Flesh in Medieval Japan," *American Historical Review* 99/1 (Feb. 1994): 135–8.
6 This quotation, and the following ones, are also from Tsunoda's translation of the *Wei chih* in Tsunoda and Goodrich, *Japan in the Chinese Dynastic Histories*, pp. 8–16.
7 William Wayne Farris, *Sacred Texts and Buried Treasures, Issues in the Historical Archaeology of Ancient Japan* (Honolulu: UHP, 1998), p. 25, and Gina L. Barnes, *Protohistoric Yamato, Archaeology of the First Japanese State* (Ann Arbor: The University of Michigan Center for Japanese Studies, 1988), p. 214.
8 See Farris, *Sacred Texts and Buried Treasures*, p. 114, for this viewpoint.
9 Joan R. Piggott, *The Emergence of Japanese Kingship* (Stanford: SUP, 1997), p. 31.
10 W. G. Aston, tr., *Nihongi* (Tokyo: Tuttle, 1972), Bk. 2, pp. 65, 66.
11 Piggott, *The Emergence of Japanese Kingship*, p. 95.
12 Aston, tr., *Nihongi*, Bk. 2, p. 123.
13 Aston, tr., *Nihongi*, Bk. 2, p. 203.

4 ESTABLISHING THE RITSURYŌ ORDER (672–750)

1 Joan R. Piggott, *The Emergence of Japanese Kingship* (Stanford: SUP, 1997), pp. 287–303, provides a valuable summary of written sources.
2 J. B. Snellen, tr., "Shoku Nihongi," *TASJ*, Second Series, Vol. 14 (1937) pp. 218–20. Another translation is in Piggott, *The Emergence*, pp. 188–9.
3 W. G. Aston, tr., *Nihongi* (Tokyo: Tuttle, 1972), Bk. 2, pp. 197–8.
4 Piggott, *The Emergence*, p. 155.
5 Aston, tr., *Nihongi*, Bk. 2, p. 369. For another translation, see Piggott, *The Emergence*, p. 154.
6 The following is a summary of the decree as given in Kōjirō Naoki's modern-language rendering of the *Shoku Nihongi*, Vol. 2 (Tokyo: Heibonsha, 1988), pp. 91–3.
7 Kōyū Sonoda, "Early Buddha Worship," in Delmer M. Brown, ed., *The Cambridge History of Japan, Volume 1, Ancient Japan* (Cambridge: CUP, 1993), p. 402.

8   Ryusaku Tsunoda et al., comps., *Sources of the Japanese Tradition* (NY: CUP, 1958), p. 106. For another translation, see Piggott, *The Emergence*, p. 259.

9   Tsunoda et al., comps., *Sources*, pp. 106–7.

10 John Whitney Hall, *Government and Local Power in Japan, 500 to 1700* (Princeton: PUP, 1966), pp. 73–4. The Japanese terms *kokuga*, *kokuchō*, and *gundan* are deleted here.

11 Piggott, *The Emergence*, p. 193.

12 Bruce L. Batten, "Provincial Administration in Early Japan: From *Ritsuryō kokka* to *Ōchō kokka*," *HJAS* 53/1 (June 1993): 109, quoting the *Ryō no gige* of 833.

13 Karl F. Friday, *Hired Swords: The Rise of Private Warrior Power in Early Japan* (Stanford: SUP, 1992), p. 14.

14 William Wayne Farris, *Heavenly Warriors, The Evolution of Japan's Military, 500–1300* (Cambridge, MA: HUP, 1992), p. 50.

15 On the scale of elite households, see William Wayne Farris, *Sacred Texts and Buried Treasures, Issues in the Historical Archaeology of Ancient Japan* (Honolulu: UHP, 1998), pp. 162–4, 224–7.

16 Dana Robert Morris, *Peasant Economy in Early Japan, 650-950* (Ann Arbor: University Microfilms International, 1980), p. 110, gives the 15 percent figure. A fine diagram of the tribute system is in Piggott, *The Emergence*, p. 200.

17 Horses and cattle were, it appears, only beginning to be employed as draft animals for pulling the Chinese-style, iron-tipped wooden plow (*karasuki*). Long known from the Heian period, the remains of a *karasuki* dating to ca. 650 CE were recently discovered at an inland site west of Kyoto. *Kyoto shinbun*, March 11, 1993.

18 Torao Toshiya, "Nara economic and social institutions," in *The Cambridge History, Vol. 1*, p. 424.

19 Piggott, *The Emergence*, p. 224.

20 William Wayne Farris, *Population, Disease, and Land in Early Japan, 645–900* (Cambridge, MA: HUP, 1985), pp. 65–6.

21 Different sources give different population figures. I have these, which seem to be the recently preferred numbers, from Conrad Torman, *The Green Archipelago: Forestry in Pre-Industrial Japan* (Berkeley: UCP, 1989), p. 172. A tabulation of population estimates appears in Hiroshi Kitō, *Nihon nisennen no jinkōshi* (Two thousand years of Japanese population history) (Tokyo: PhP, 1983), pp. 12–13.

22 Farris, *Population*, p. 106.

5   RITSURYŌ *ADAPTATION AND DECAY (750–1250)*

1   Ivan Morris, *The World of the Shining Prince* (NY: Alfred A. Knopf, 1964), p. 23.

2   G. Cameron Hurst, *Insei: Abdicated Sovereigns in the Politics of Late Heian Japan, 1086–1185* (NY: CUP, 1976), p. 68.

3   Helen Craig McCullough, tr., *Tales of Ise* (Stanford: SUP, 1968), p. 139. Michele Marra, *The Aesthetics of Discontent: Politics and Reclusion in Medieval Japanese Literature* (Honolulu: UHP, 1991), p. 45, cites this poem as evidence of Ariwara's embitterment at Yoshifusa's power.

4   Helen Craig McCullough, tr., *Ōkagami* (Princeton: PUP, 1980), pp. 190–1. The "present Emperor" of this passage is Go-Ichijō (r. 1016–1036).

5   Quoted in Hurst, *Insei*, p. 149. For more of Munetada's eloquence, see p. 152.

6 Translated in Minoru Shinoda, *The Founding of the Kamakura Shogunate, 1180–1185* (NY: CUP, 1960), p. 151.
7 Keiichi Miura, "Villages and Trade in Medieval Japan," *AA* 44 (1983): 56.
8 Jennifer Brewster, tr., *The Emperor Horikawa Diary* (a tr. of Fujiwara no Nagako, *Sanuki no Suke Nikki*) (Honolulu: UHP, 1977), p. 24.
9 Carl Steenstrup, "Hōjō Shigetoki's Letter of Instruction to His Son Nagatoki," *Acta Orientalia* 36 (1974): 426.

6 CLASSICAL HIGHER CULTURE (750–1250)

1 Nippon Gakujutsu Shinkōkai, *The Man'yōshū* (NY: CUP, 1965), p. 3. For another translation, see Ian Hideo Levy, *The Ten Thousand Leaves,* Vol. 1 (Princeton: PUP, 1981), p. 38, and Levy, *Hitomaro and the Birth of Japanese Lyricism* (Princeton: PUP, 1984), p. 25.
2 Yoshito S. Hakeda, *Kūkai: Major Works* (NY: CUP, 1972), pp. 145–6.
3 Hakeda. *Kūkai,* p. 227.
4 Ivan Morris, *The World of the Shining Prince: Court Life in Ancient Japan* (NY: Alfred A. Knopf, 1964), p. 124.
5 Mimi Hall Yiengpruksawan, "The Phoenix Hall at Uji and the Symmetries of Replication," *Art Bulletin* 77/4 (Dec. 1995): 649.
6 Terukazu Akiyama, "The Door Paintings in the Phoenix Hall of the Byōdōin as *Yamato-e*," *Artibus Asiae* 53/(1/2) (1993): 145.
7 William H. and Helen Craig McCullough, *A Tale of Flowering Fortunes* (Stanford: SUP, 1980), Vol. I, p. 11.
8 Ivan Morris, tr. and ed., *The Pillow Book of Sei Shōnagon,* Vol. 1 (NY: CUP, 1967), p. 57.
9 Helen Craig McCullough, *Brocade by Night, 'Kokin Wakashū' and the Court Style in Japanese Classical Poetry* (Stanford: SUP, 1985), p. 324.
10 Morris, tr., *The Pillow Book,* Vol. 1, p. 250.
11 Richard Bowring, tr., *Murasaki Shikibu, Her Diary and Poetic Memoirs* (Princeton: PUP, 1982), p. 133.
12 This and the next two passages by Shōnagon come *seriatim* from Morris, tr., *The Pillow Book,* Vol. 1, pp. 115, 250, 121.
13 Helen Craig McCullough, tr., *Kokin Wakashū, The First Imperial Anthology of Japanese Poetry* (Stanford: SUP, 1985), p. 146.
14 The quoted phrase is from Helen Craig McCullough, *Tales of Ise* (Stanford: SUP, 1968), p. 65.
15 Kiyoko Takagi, "Saigyō – A search for Religion," *JJRS* 4–1 (March 1977): 58. *Sakaki* leaves were waved by priests performing Shintō rituals. For an interpretation of how Buddhism and Shintō melded in the issue of "the Buddhahood of plants," with special reference to Saigyō's poetry, see William R. LaFleur, "Saigyō and the Buddhist Value of Nature, Part I," *History of Religion* 13/2 (Nov. 1973): 93–128, and "Part II," 13/3 (Feb. 1974): 227–48.
16 James C. Dobbins, *Jōdo Shinshū, Shin Buddhism in Medieval Japan* (Bloomington: Indiana University Press, 1989), p. 15.
17 The quoted fragments from *Mumyōzōshi* are from Michele Marra, "Mumyōzōshi, Part 3," *MN* 39/4 (Winter 1984): 419, 422, 423.
18 Laura W. Allen, "Images of the Poet Saigyō as Recluse," *JJS* 21/2 (Winter 1995): 94–5.

19 Yung-Hee Kim, *Songs to Make the Dust Dance, the* Ryōjin hishō *of Twelfth-Century Japan* (Berkeley: UCP, 1994), p. 40.
20 This is the phrasing of P. G. O'Neill, *Early Nō Drama* (London: Lund Humphries, 1958), p. 45.
21 Julia Meech-Pekarik, "The artist's View of Ukifune," in Andrew Pekarik, ed., *Ukifune, Love in The Tale of Genji* (NY: CUP, 1982), p. 176.

7 THE CENTURIES OF DISORDER (1250–1550)

1   Ann Bowman Jannetta, *Epidemics and Mortality in Early Modern Japan* (Princeton: PUP, 1987), pp. 68–9, quoting the *Hyakurensho*.
2   Kristina Kade Troost, "Common Property and Community Formation: Self-Governing Villages in Late Medieval Japan, 1300–1600" (Ph.D. dissertation, Harvard University, 1990), p. 75.
3   Haruko Wakita, "Towards a Wider Perspective on Medieval Commerce," *JJS* 1/2 (Spring 1975): 334.
4   Keiji Nagahara, "The Medieval Peasant," in Kozo Yamamura, ed., *The Cambridge History of Japan, Volume 3, Medieval Japan* (Cambridge: CUP, 1990), p. 335.
5   Kristina Kade Troost, "Peasant, Elites, and Villages in the Fourteenth Century," in Jeffrey P. Mass., ed., *The Origins of Japan's Medieval World* (Stanford: SUP, 1997), p. 99.
6   Barbara Ruch, "The Other Side of Culture in Medieval Japan," in *The Cambridge History, Vol. 3*, pp. 513–14.
7   Kozo Yamamura, "The Growth of Commerce in Medieval Japan," in *The Cambridge History, Vol. 3*, p. 347.
8   Scholars credit Kuroda Toshio with introducing the term *kenmon*. On its academic uses, see Mikael Adolphson, "Enryakuji – An Old Power in a New Era," in Mass, ed., *The Origins of Japan's Medieval World*, pp. 238–44.
9   George Sansom, *A History of Japan, 1334–1615* (Stanford: SUP, 1961), p. 141.
10 Akira Imatani, with Kozo Yamamura, "Not for Lack of Will or Wile: Yoshimitsu's Failure to Supplant the Imperial Lineage," *JJS* 18/1 (Winter 1992): 51.
11 The *tokusei* articles of 1441 are translated in Kenneth A. Grossberg, ed., *The Laws of the Muromachi Bakufu* (Tokyo: Monumenta Nipponica, Sophia University, 1981), pp. 99–102.
12 Michael Solomon, "The Dilemma of Religious Power: Honganji and Hosokawa Masamoto," *MN* 33/1 (Spring 1978): 57.
13 This and the next two quotations regarding Kyoto come *seriatim* from Mary Elizabeth Berry, *The Culture of Civil War in Kyoto* (Berkeley: UCP, 1994), pp. 89, 61, 165–6.

8 MEDIEVAL HIGHER CULTURE (1250–1550)

1   Donald Keene, tr., *Essays in Idleness, the Tsurezuregusa of Kenkō* (NY: CUP, 1967), p. 29.
2   Sumito Miki, "Essays and Journals in the Medieval Period." *AA* 37 (1979): 81. This work of 1349 is the memoir *Takemukigaki* by the court lady Hino Meishi (d. 1358).
3   Robert H. Brower, tr., *Conversations with Shōtetsu* (Ann Arbor: Center for Japanese Studies, The University of Michigan, 1992), p. 33.

4   Carl Steenstrup, "The Gokurakuji Letter," *MN* 32/1 (Spring 1977): 12.
5   Teiji Itō, "The Development of Shoin-Style Architecture," in John Whitney Hall and Takeshi Toyoda, ed., *Japan in the Muromachi Age* (Berkeley: UCP, 1977), pp. 237–8.
6   For illustrations, see chapter 6 of Mitchell Bring and Josse Wayembergh, *Japanese Gardens, Design and Meaning* (NY: McGraw-Hill, 1981).
7   Royall Tyler, *The Miracles of the Kasuga Deity* (NY: CUP, 1990), p. 291. Jōruri and Vulture Peak are the paradises of the Buddhas Yakushi and Shaka; the Mountain is Mt. Mikasa, overlooking Kasuga; Myōe is the distinguished Kegon priest, Myōe shōnin, 1173–1232; Toshimori is the official, Fujiwara no Toshimori, 1120–ca. 1180. Myōe and Toshimori are major figures in the scroll.
8   Gail Capitol Weigl, "The Reception of Chinese Painting Models in Muromachi Japan," *MN* 35/3 (Autumn 1980): 258.
9   Thomas Blenman Hare, *Zeami's style, The Noh Plays of Zeami Motokiyo* (Stanford: SUP, 1986), p. 16. The aristocrat was Go-Oshikōji Kintada (1324–1383).
10 Jin'ichi Konishi, *A History of Japanese Literature, Volume Three, The High Middle Ages* (Princeton: PUP 1991), p. 534.
11 Masakazu Yamazaki, "The Aesthetics of Transformation: Zeami's Dramatic Theories," *JJS* 7/2 (Summer 1981): 220.
12 The quotation is from Mary Elizabeth Berry, *The Culture of Civil War in Kyoto* (Berkeley: UCP, 1994), p. 272.
13 Robert E. Morrell, *Sand & Pebbles* (Albany: SUNY Press, 1985), pp. 19–20.
14 Kanetomo Yoshida (Allan G. Grapard, tr.), "*Yuiitsu Shintō Myōbō Yōshū*," *MN* 47/2 (Summer 1992): 153.
15 William M. Bodiford, *Sōtō Zen in Medieval Japan* (Honolulu: UHP, 1993), p. 181.
16 Berry, *The Culture of Civil War*, p. 153.
17 James C. Dobbins, *Jōdo Shinshū, Shin Buddhism in Medieval Japan* (Bloomington: Indiana University Press, 1989), pp. 112–13.
18 Minor L. Rogers, "Rennyo and Jōdo Shinshū Piety: The Yoshizaki Years," *MN* 36/1 (Spring 1981): 28.
19 Dobbins, *Jōdo Shinshū*, p. 142.
20 Michael Solomon, "Kinship and the Transmission of Religious Charisma: The Case of Honganji," *JAS* 33/3 (May 1974): 410.
21 Diana Y. Paul, *Women in Buddhism, Images of the Feminine in Mahāyāna Tradition*, 2d ed. (Berkeley: UCP, 1985), pp. 85–6.
22 Dobbins, *Jōdo Shinshū*, p. 127, quoting Nyodō (1253–1340).
23 James H. Sanford, "Mandalas of the Heart: Two Prose Works by Ikkyū Sōjun," *MN* 35/3 (Autumn 1980): 298.
24 Laurel Rasplica Rodd, "Nichiren and *Setsuwa*," *JJRS* 5/(2/3) (Jun–Sept. 1978): 162.
25 Margaret Helen Childs, *Rethinking Sorrow, Revelatory Tales of Late Medieval Japan* (Ann Arbor: Center for Japanese Studies, The University of Michigan, 1991), pp. 105–6, parenthetic passage added.

9   ESTABLISHING THE BAKUHAN ORDER (1550–1700)

1   David John Lu, *Sources of Japanese History*, Vol. One (NY: McGraw Hill, 1974), p. 176.

2   Shizuo Katsumata, "The Development of Sengoku Law," in John Whitney Hall et al., eds., *Japan Before Tokugawa* (Princeton: PUP, 1981), p. 122. Italics added.
3   Katsumata, "The Development of Sengoku Law," p. 122.
4   This and the next quotation come from Neil McMullin, *Buddhism and the State in Sixteenth-Century Japan* (Princeton: PUP, 1984), pp. 70, 153.
5   George Elison, *Deus Destroyed, The Image of Christianity in Early Modern Japan* (Cambridge, MA: HUP, 1973), pp. 115–18. See also, C. R. Boxer, *The Christian Century in Japan, 1549–1650* (Berkeley: UCP, 1951), pp. 146–8.
6   This quotation and the following fragments come from Mary Elizabeth Berry, *Hideyoshi* (Cambridge, MA: HUP, 1982), pp. 112–13.
7   Michael Cooper, comp., *They Came to Japan, An Anthology of European Reports on Japan. 1543–1640* (Berkeley: UCP, 1965), p. 87.
8   George Elison, "Hideyoshi, the Bountiful Minister," in Elison and Bardwell L. Smith, eds., *Warlords, Artists & Commoners* (Honolulu: UHP, 1981), p. 225.
9   The above fragments come from Berry, *Hideyoshi*, pp. 102–3.
10 Lu, *Sources of Japanese History*, Vol. One, p. 187.
11 Berry, *Hideyoshi*, p. 110.
12 Berry, *Hideyoshi*, p. 216.
13 Adriana Boscaro, tr. and ed., *101 Letters of Hideyoshi* (Tokyo: Sophia University, 1975), p. 31.
14 This quote and the following fragment are from Berry, *Hideyoshi*, p. 208.
15 Conrad Totman, *Tokugawa Ieyasu, Shogun* (South San Francisco: Heian International, 1983), p. 140. The advisor was Ishin Sūden.
16 Lu, *Sources of Japanese History*, Vol. One, p. 236.
17 Ryusaku Tsunoda et al., comps., *Sources of the Japanese Tradition* (NY: CUP, 1958), pp. 398–9.
18 This and the next two quotations come from Gary P. Leupp, *Servants, Shophands, and Laborers in the Cities of Tokugawa Japan* (Princeton: PUP, 1992), pp. 74, 149, 160.
19 This and the following quotation come from Cecilia Segawa Seigle, *Yoshiwara, The Glittering World of the Japanese Courtesan* (Honolulu; UHP, 1993), pp. 23–4, 31.

10   THE AGE OF GROWTH (1590–1700)

1   Kozo Yamamura, "Returns on Unification: Economic Growth in Japan, 1550–1650," in John Whitney Hall et al., eds., *Japan Before Tokugawa* (Princeton: PUP, 1981), p. 334. Yamamura also gives the figures 862,000 for 930 and 3,050,000 for 1874.
2   Michael Cooper, *They Came to Japan, An Anthology of European Reports on Japan, 1543–1640* (Berkeley: UCP, 1965), p. 283.
3   This and the next quotation come from Constantine Nomikos Vaporis, *Breaking Barriers, Travel and the State in Early Modern Japan* (Cambridge, MA: HUP, 1994), pp. 30, 42.
4   J. Mark Ramseyer, "Thrift and Diligence: House Codes of Tokugawa Merchant Families," *MN* 34/2 (Summer 1979): 225.
5   This quotation from Frois and the subsequent one from Rodrigues come in reverse order from Cooper, *They Came to Japan*, pp. 277–9, 281.
6   Takeshi Moriya, "*Yūgei* and *Chōnin* Society in the Edo Period," *AA* 33 (1977): 38–9.

7   Katsuhisa Moriya, "Urban Networks and Information Networks," in Chie Nakane and Shinzaburō Ōishi, eds., *Tokugawa Japan, The Social and Economic Antecedents of Modern Japan* (Tokyo: UTP, 1990), p. 98.

8   Donald H. Shively, "Popular Culture," in John Whitney Hall, ed., *The Cambridge History of Japan, Volume 4, Early Modern Japan* (Cambridge: CUP, 1991), pp. 736–7.

9   Nobuhiko Nakai, "Commercial Change and Urban Growth in Early Modern Japan," in *The Cambridge History, Vol. 4*, p. 556.

10 Donald Keene, *World Within Walls, Japanese Literature of the Pre-Modern Era, 1600–1867* (NY: Grove Press, 1976), p. 33. Italics added.

11 The quotations from *Seken munezan'yō* come *seriatim* from Ben Befu, *Worldly Mental Calculations, An Annotated Translation of Ihara Saikaku's Seken munezan'yō* (Berkeley: UCP, 1976), pp. 52–3, 38, 82.

12 The following fragments of quotation come from Nobuyuki Yuasa, tr., *Bashō: The Narrow Road to the Deep North and Other Travel Sketches* (Harmondsworth: Penguin, 1966), pp. 98, 105, 109, 113.

13 Tsutomu Ogata, "Five Methods for Appreciating Bashō's *Haiku*," *AA* 28 (1975): 49, translation by R. H. Blyth.

11   STASIS AND DECAY (1700–1850)

1   Eijiro Honjo, *The Social and Economic History of Japan* (originally published 1935; NY: Russell & Russell, 1965), p. 154.

2   Kozo Yamamura, "Returns on Unification: Economic Growth in Japan, 1550–1650," in John Whitney Hall et al., eds., *Japan Before Tokugawa* (Princeton: PUP, 1981), p. 334. Figures differ with one's sources. James I. Nakamura, *Agricultural Production and the Economic Development of Japan, 1873–1922* (Princeton: PUP, 1966), pp. 26, 43, reports only 2,623,000 *chō* of taxed paddy fields in 1880, which he adjusts upward by 9,000 *chō* to offset concealment.

3   Eiichi Kiyooka, tr., *The Autobiography of Yukichi Fukuzawa* (NY: CUP, 1966), pp. 115–16.

4   Conrad Totman, *The Green Archipelago, Forestry in Preindustrial Japan* (Berkeley: UCP, 1989), p. 75.

5   Thomas C. Smith, *The Agrarian Origins of Modern Japan* (Stanford: SUP, 1959), p. 56, footnote e.

6   Tessa Morris-Suzuki, *The Technological Transformation of Japan, From the Seventeenth to the Twenty-first Century* (Cambridge: CUP, 1994), p. 32.

7   J. R. McEwan, *The Political Writings of Ogyū Sorai* (Cambridge: CUP, 1962), p. 24.

8   This example is drawn from Jennifer Robertson, *Native and Newcomer, Making and Remaking a Japanese City* (Berkeley: UCP, 1991), pp. 80–93 and *passim*.

9   A particularly valuable contribution to the study of this somewhat nettlesome topic, with guides to earlier works, is Laurel L. Cornell, "Infanticide in Early Modern Japan? Demography, Culture, and Population Growth," *JAS* 55/1 (Feb. 1996): 22–50.

10 Smith, *The Agrarian Origins of Modern Japan*, p. 100, footnote 1.

11 David L. Howell, *Capitalism from Within: Economy, Society, and the State in a Japanese Fishery* (Berkeley: UCP, 1995), p. 50.

12 On this topic see Brett Walker, "Matsumae Domain and the Conquest of Ainu Lands: Ecology and Culture in Tokugawa Expansionism, 1593–1799" (Ph.D. dissertation, University of Oregon, Eugene, 1997).

13 Honjo, *The Social and Economic History of Japan*, p. 180.

14 Susan B. Hanley, *Everyday Things in Premodern Japan, The Hidden Legacy of Material Culture* (Berkeley: UCP, 1997), p. 67.

15 Takeo Yazaki, *Social Change and the City in Japan* (San Francisco: Japan Publications, Inc., 1968), p. 255.

16 Andrew L. Markus, "The Carnival of Edo: *Misemono* Spectacles from Contemporary Accounts," *HJAS* 45/2 (Dec. 1985): 509.

17 James W. White, *The Demography of Sociopolitical Conflict in Japan, 1721–1846* (Berkeley: Institute of East Asian Studies, University of California, 1992), p. 29.

18 Nakamoto Tominaga (Michael Pye, tr.), *Emerging from Meditation* (Honolulu: UHP, 1990), p. 57.

19 This and the next quotation from Shōeki come in reverse order from Toshinobu Yasunaga, *Andō Shōeki: Social and Ecological Philosopher in Eighteenth-Century Japan* (NY: Weatherhill, 1992), pp. 246, 271–2.

20 The quotations from Daini come *seriatim* from Bob Tadashi Wakabayashi, *Japanese Loyalism Reconstrued, Yamagata Daini's* Ryūshi shinron *of 1759* (Honolulu: UHP, 1995), pp. 129, 130, 133, 135, 140, 147–8, 157, 170, 36.

21 The quotations from Baigan come in reverse order from Robert N. Bellah, *Tokugawa Religion, The Values of Pre-Industrial Japan* (Glencoe, IL: The Free Press, 1957), pp. 158, 161. Italics omitted.

22 This quotation and the subsequent ones (from Teshima Toan) come *seriatim* from Janine Anderson Sawada, *Confucian Values and Popular Zen, Sekimon Shingaku in Eighteenth-Century Japan* (Honolulu: UHP, 1993), pp. 144, 88–9, 147, 32, 59.

23 Herman Ooms, *Tokugawa Ideology, Early Constructs, 1570–1680* (Princeton: PUP, 1985), p. 237.

24 Morris-Suzuki, *The Technological Transformation of Japan*, p. 29.

25 This and the following quotation come from Herman Ooms, *Tokugawa Village Practice* (Berkeley: UCP, 1996), pp. 287, 296. Italics added.

26 James L. McClain, "*Bonshōgatsu*: Festivals and State Power in Kanazawa," *MN* 47/2 (Summer 1992): 163–202.

27 Luke S. Roberts, "The Petition Box in Eighteenth-Century Tosa," *JJS* 20/2 (Summer 1994): 423.

12 CRISIS AND REDIRECTION (1800–1890)

1 Bob Tadashi Wakabayashi, *Anti-Foreignism and Western Learning in Early-Modern Japan. The New Theses of 1825* (Cambridge, MA: HUP, 1986), p. 60.

2 Bob Tadashi Wakabayashi, "Opium, Expulsion, Sovereignty: China's Lessons for Bakumatsu Japan." *MN* 47/1 (Spring 1992): 3.

3 Harold Bolitho, "The Tempō Crisis," in Marius B. Jansen, ed., *The Cambridge History of Japan. Vol. 5, The Nineteenth Century* (Cambridge: CUP, 1989), p. 146.

4 Conrad Totman, "Political Reconciliation in the Tokugawa Bakufu: Abe Masahiro and Tokugawa Nariaki, 1844–1852," in Albert M. Craig and Donald H. Shively, eds., *Personality in Japanese History* (Berkeley: UCP, 1970), p. 190.

5 The English-language versions of these treaties, with annotations, are given in W. G. Beasley, tr., *Select Documents on Japanese Foreign Policy 1853–1868* (London: Oxford University Press, 1955), pp. 119–22, 183–9.

6   Reinier Hesselink, "The Assassination of Henry Heusken," *MN* 49/3 (Autumn 1994): 344.

7   Anne Walthall, "Off With Their Heads! The Hirata Disciples and the Ashikaga Shoguns", *MN* 50/2 (Summer 1995): 148.

8   Samuel Hideo Yamashita, *Master Sorai's Responsals. An Annotated Translation of Sorai Sensei Tōmonsho* (Honolulu: UHP, 1994), p. 47.

9   Conrad Totman, *The Collapse of the Tokugawa Bakufu, 1862–1868* (Honolulu: UHP, 1980), p. 165.

10 M. William Steele, "Edo in 1868: The View from Below," *MN* 45/2 (Summer 1990): 142.

11 Helen Hardacre, *Shintō and the State, 1868–1988* (Princeton: PUP, 1989), p. 85.

12 Klaus Antoni, "Yasukuni-Jinja and Folk Religion, The Problem of Vengeful Spirits," in Mark R. Mullins et al., eds., *Religion and Society in Modern Japan, Selected Readings* (Berkeley: Asian Humanities Press, 1993), p. 122. Japanese terms are omitted.

13 David Anson Titus, *Palace and Politics in Prewar Japan* (NY: CUP, 1974), p. 317.

14 Donald H. Shively, "The Japanization of the Middle Meiji," in Shively, ed., *Tradition and Modernization in Japanese Culture* (Princeton: PUP, 1971), p. 85.

15 Ryusaku Tsunoda et al., comps., *Sources of the Japanese Tradition* (NY: CUP, 1958), pp. 646–7.

16 Tsunoda et al., comps., *Sources of the Japanese Tradition*, p. 644.

17 Mark E. Lincicome, *Principle, Praxis, and the Politics of Educational Reform in Meiji Japan* (Honolulu: UHP, 1995), p. 161.

18 George DeVos and Hiroshi Wagatsuma, *Japan's Invisible Race, Caste in Culture and Personality*, revised edn. (Berkeley: UCP, 1972), p. 33.

19 Sukehiro Hirakawa, "Japan's turn to the West," in *The Cambridge History, Vol. 5*, p. 433.

20 Kenneth B. Pyle, *The New Generation in Meiji Japan, Problems of Cultural Identity, 1885–1895* (Stanford: SUP, 1969), p. 151.

21 Material on Chinpei comes from Shōtokuhi Kensetsukai, comp., *Ko-Ikegami Chinpei kun ryakuden* (privately published, 1921), pp. 1–30 *passim*.

22 Figures extrapolated from James I. Nakamura, *Agricultural Production and the Economic Development of Japan, 1873–1922* (Princeton: PUP, 1966), pp. 43, 48.

23 Fumio Yoshiki, "How Japan's Metal Mining Industries Modernized," *Project on Technology Transfer, Transformation, and Development: The Japanese Experience* HSDP-JE Series (Tokyo: The United Nations University, 1980), p. 12.

24 Nisaburo Murakushi, "Technology and Labour in Japanese Coal Mining," *Project on Technology Transfer, Transformation, and Development: The Japanese Experience* HSDP-JE Series (Tokyo: The United Nations University, 1980), pp. 7, 21.

25 Andrew Gordon, *Labor and Imperial Democracy in Prewar Japan* (Berkeley: UCP, 1991), p. 22, footnote 14. Tessa Morris-Suzuki, *The Technological Transformation of Japan, From the Seventeenth to the Twenty-first Century* (Cambridge: CUP, 1994), p. 97, reports that by 1888 some 38,000 *jinrikisha* were operating in Tokyo alone, with proportionally comparable numbers in other towns and cities.

13 *Early Imperial Triumph (1890–1914)*

1   Kenneth B. Pyle, "The Technology of Japanese Nationalism: The Local Improvement Movement 1900–1918," *JAS* 33/1 (Nov. 1973): 54.

2 This information on Ikegami Chinpei is extracted primarily from the 30-page *Ko-Ikegami Chinpei kun ryakuden*, compiled by the Shōtokuhi Kensetsukai (Committee for erection of a memorial monument) (privately published, 1921), which drew heavily on Chinpei's multi-volume diary, and secondarily from the November and December 1920 issues of *Kami jihō*, the monthly newspaper of Chinpei's village, issues mostly devoted to his life and funeral. On Inukai, Okayama, and the Taishō Political Crisis more broadly, see Richard K. Beardsley et al., *Village Japan* (Chicago: UCP, 1959), pp. 424–34, and Tetsuo Najita, *Hara Kei in the Politics of Compromise, 1905–1915* (Cambridge, MA: HUP, 1967).

3 Richard Siddle, *Race, Resistance and the Ainu of Japan* (London: Routledge, 1996), p. 53.

4 John D. Pierson, *Tokotomi Sohō, 1863–1957, A Journalist for Modern Japan* (Princeton: PUP, 1980), pp. 232–3.

5 W. G. Beasley, *Japanese Imperialism 1894–1945* (Oxford: Clarendon Press, 1987), p. 77.

6 Peter Duus, *The Abacus and the Sword; The Japanese Penetration of Korea, 1895–1910* (Berkeley: UCP, 1995), p. 298, quoting Taguchi Ukichi.

7 This and the following quotation come in reverse order from Ramon H. Myers and Mark R. Peattie, eds., *The Japanese Colonial Empire, 1895–1945* (Princeton: PUP, 1984), pp. 69, 141.

14 EARLY IMPERIAL SOCIETY AND CULTURE (1890–1914)

1 Kenneth Strong, *Ox Against the Storm, A Biography of Tanaka Shozo: Japan's Conservationist Pioneer* (Tenterden, Kent: Paul Norbury Publications Limited, 1977), pp. 63–4.

2 F. G. Notehelfer, "Japan's First Pollution Incident," *JJS* 1/2 (Spring 1975): 364.

3 This quotation and that of Shōzō below come from Strong, *Ox Against the Storm*, pp. 74, 121–2.

4 Nimura Kazuo, *The Ashio Riot of 1907, A Social History of Mining in Japan* (Durham: Duke University Press, 1997), p. 38.

5 This and the following quotation come from E. Patricia Tsurumi, *Factory Girls: Women in the Thread Mills of Meiji Japan* (Princeton: PUP, 1990), pp. 56, 85.

6 Gary R. Saxonhouse, "Country Girls and Communication Among Competitors in the Japanese Cotton-Spinning Industry," in Hugh Patrick, ed., *Japanese Industrialization and Its Social Consequences* (Berkeley: UCP, 1976), p. 104. The words are those of Saxonhouse.

7 This and the following quotation come from Andrew Gordon, *The Evolution of Labor Relations in Japan, Heavy Industry, 1853–1955* (Cambridge, MA: HUP, 1985), pp. 36, 65. The speaker in the latter instance was Soeda Juichi of the Finance Ministry. Also cited in Byron K. Marshall, *Capitalism and Nationalism in Prewar Japan, The Ideology of the Business Elite, 1868–1941* (Stanford: SUP, 1967), p. 54, and Sheldon Garon, *The State and Labor in Modern Japan* (Berkeley: UCP, 1987), p. 26.

8 The two Chamber of Commerce quotations come from Marshall, *Capitalism and Nationalism in Prewar Japan*, pp. 57–8.

9 W. Dean Kinzley, *Industrial Harmony in Modern Japan, The Invention of a Tradition* (London: Routledge, 1991), p. 20.

10 Gordon, *The Evolution of Labor Relations in Japan*, p. 66, quoting a Mitsubishi shipyard executive in 1910.
11 Tsurumi, *Factory Girls*, p. 94.
12 Thomas R. H. Havens, *Farm and Nation in Modern Japan, Agrarian Nationalism, 1870–1940* (Princeton: PUP, 1974), p. 100.
13 Kenneth B. Pyle, "The Technology of Japanese Nationalism: The Local Improvement Movement 1900–1918," *JAS* 33/1 (Nov. 1973): 62.
14 This and the following quotation come from Sharon L. Sievers, *Flowers in Salt, The Beginnings of Feminist Consciousness in Modern Japan* (Stanford: SUP, 1983), pp. 38, 112.
15 This and the following quotation come from Masanori Nakamura, ed., *Technology Change and Female Labour in Japan* (Tokyo: United Nations University Press, 1994), pp. 63, 104.
16 Sievers, *Flowers in Salt*, p. 127.
17 Vera Mackie, *Creating Socialist Women in Japan: Gender, Labour and Activism, 1900–1937* (Cambridge: CUP, 1997), p. 65.
18 This quotation and the subsequent one, from Kunikida Doppo, come from Barbara Rose, *Tsuda Umeko and Women's Education in Japan* (New Haven: YUP, 1992), pp. 128, 139. In 1901 Tsuda changed her given name from Ume to Umeko.
19 Earl H. Kinmonth, *The Self-Made Man in Meiji Japanese Thought, from Samurai to Salary Man* (Berkeley: UCP, 1981), p. 271.
20 This and the following quotation come from Peter Duus, *The Abacus and the Sword; The Japanese Penetration of Korea, 1895–1910* (Berkeley: UCP, 1995), pp. 321, 322.
21 Kinmonth, *The Self-Made Man in Meiji Japanese Thought*, p. 211.
22 Peter Duus, "Socialism, Liberalism, and Marxism, 1901–1931," in Peter Duus, ed., *The Cambridge History of Japan, Vol. 6, The Twentieth Century* (Cambridge: CUP, 1988), p. 659.
23 F. G. Notehelfer, *Kōtoku Shūsui, Portrait of a Japanese Radical* (London: CUP, 1971), pp. 160–1.
24 Duus, "Socialism, Liberalism, and Marxism," p. 659.
25 Strong, *Ox Against the Storm*, p. 129.
26 Carol Gluck, *Japan's Modern Myths, Ideology in the Late Meiji Period* (Princeton: PUP, 1985), p. 176.
27 Havens, *Farm and Nation in Modern Japan*, p. 128.
28 The quoted fragment comes from Gluck, *Japan's Modern Myths*, p. 176.
29 Kenneth B. Pyle, "Meiji Conservatism," in Marius B. Jansen, ed., *The Cambridge History of Japan, Vol. 5, The Nineteenth Century* (Cambridge: CUP, 1989), p. 696.
30 The words are those of Gluck in her *Japan's Modern Myths*, p. 146.
31 Kenneth B. Pyle, *The New Generation in Meiji Japan, Problems in Cultural Identity 1885–1895* (Stanford: SUP, 1969), p. 190.
32 Donald Keene, *Dawn to the West, Japanese Literature of the Modern Era: Poetry, Drama, Criticism* (NY: Holt, Rinehart and Winston, 1984), p. 557.
33 James L. Huffman, *Creating a Public, People and Press in Meiji Japan* (Honolulu: UHP, 1997), p. 232. Circulation figures for journals come from pp. 60, 267, 315, 317.
34 James R. Bartholomew, *The Formation of Science in Japan* (New Haven: YUP, 1989), p. 122.
35 Keene, *Dawn to the West: Poetry, Drama, Criticism*, p. 241.
36 Keene, *Dawn to the West: Poetry, Drama, Criticism*, p. 233.

37 Edward Fowler, *The Rhetoric of Confession, Shishōsetsu in Early Twentieth-Century Japanese Fiction* (Berkeley: UCP, 1988), p. 192.

38 The fragments of quotation come from Ury Eppstein, *The Beginnings of Western Music in Meiji Era Japan* (Lewiston, NY: Edwin Mellen Press, 1994), pp. 52, 53, 64, 65.

15 LATER IMPERIAL POLITICS AND ECONOMY (1914–1945)

1 Michael Lewis, *Rioters and Citizens; Mass Protest in Imperial Japan* (Berkeley: UCP, 1990), p. 107.

2 The homeless, derelict, mentally defective, criminal, those under twenty five, and those unable to write the name of a candidate on the ballot were excluded, along with women.

3 Richard H. Mitchell, *Thought Control in Prewar Japan* (Ithaca: Cornell UP, 1976), p. 77.

4 David John Lu, *Sources of Japanese History* Vol. Two (NY: McGraw Hill, 1974), p. 117.

5 The two quoted fragments are from Richard H. Mitchell, *Janus-Faced Justice, Political Criminals in Imperial Japan* (Honolulu: UHP, 1992), pp. 55, 67. The first fragment is Mitchell's words; the second served as the title of Tanaka's parliamentary address of April 23, 1928.

6 Ben-Ami Shillony, *Revolt in Japan, The Young Officers and the February 26, 1936 Incident* (Princeton: PUP, 1973), pp. 34, 80.

7 Shillony, *Revolt in Japan*, p. 147.

8 This and the following quotation come from Mitchell, *Janus-Faced Justice*, pp. 88, 107.

9 Richard J. Smethurst, "The Military Reserve Association and the Minobe Crisis of 1935," in George M. Wilson, ed., *Crisis Politics in Prewar Japan* (Tokyo: Sophia University, 1970), p. 9.

10 Ryusaku Tsunoda et al., comps., *Sources of the Japanese Tradition* (NY: CUP, 1958), pp. 705–6.

11 Richard J. Smethurst, *A Social Basis for Prewar Japanese Militarism, The Army and the Rural Community* (Berkeley: UCP 1974), p. 25. See Tanaka's comments on pp. 22–3 for the following quotations.

12 George M. Wilson, *Radical Nationalist in Japan: Kita Ikki 1883–1937* (Cambridge, MA: HUP, 1969), p. 98.

13 The characterization of Kita is that of Shillony, *Revolt in Japan*, p. 76.

14 Kita's words are quoted from Wilson, *Radical Nationalist*, pp. 69, 82, 86.

15 The following quotations of Tachibana come from Thomas R. H. Havens, *Farm and Nation in Modern Japan, Agrarian Nationalism, 1870–1940* (Princeton: PUP, 1974), pp. 249, 258, 271–2.

16 Joshua A. Fogel, *Politics and Sinology, the Case of Naitō Konan (1866–1934)* (Cambridge, MA: HUP, 1984), p. 243.

17 Lincoln Li, *The China Factor in Modern Japanese Thought, the Case of Tachibana Shiraki, 1881–1945* (Albany: State University of New York, 1996), p. 82. The words are Li's paraphrase.

18 Kevin Michael Doak, *Dreams of Difference, The Japanese Romantic School and the Crisis of Modernity* (Berkeley: UCP, 1994), p. 101.

19 Kimitada Miwa, "Japanese Policies and Concepts for a Regional Order in Asia, 1938–1940," in James W. White et al., eds., *The Ambivalence of Nationalism,*

Modern Japan between East and West (Lanham, MD: University Press of America, 1990), pp. 151–2.

20 The quoted fragments come from Mori Tetsurō, "Nishitani Keiji and the Question of Nationalism," in James W. Heisig and John C. Maraldo, eds., *Rude Awakenings: Zen, the Kyoto School, and the Question of Nationalism* (Honolulu: UHP, 1994), pp. 318, 321.

21 Takafusa Nakamura, *Economic Growth in Prewar Japan* (New Haven: YUP, 1983), p. 185.

22 Masanori Nakamura, *Technology Change and Female Labour in Japan* (Tokyo: United Nations University Press, 1994), p. 126.

16   LATER IMPERIAL SOCIETY AND CULTURE (1914–1945)

1 Ryusaku Tsunoda et al., comps., *Sources of the Japanese Tradition* (NY: CUP, 1958), p. 796.

2 Barbara Rose, *Tsuda Umeko and Women's Education in Japan* (New Haven: YUP, 1992), pp. 149, 150.

3 Laurel Resplica Rodd, "Yosano Akiko and the Taishō Debate over the "New Woman," in Gail Lee Bernstein, ed., *Recreating Japanese Women, 1600–1945* (Berkeley: UCP, 1991), p. 190.

4 Mikiso Hane, *Reflections on the Way to the Gallows, Rebel Women in Prewar Japan* (Berkeley: UCP, 1988), pp. 126–7.

5 Margit Nagy, "Middle-Class Working Women During the Interwar Years," in Bernstein, *Recreating Japanese Women*, p. 205.

6 Rodd, "Yosano Akiko and the Taishō Debate," p. 194.

7 Vera Mackie, *Creating Socialist Women in Japan: Gender, Labour and Activism, 1900–1937* (Cambridge: CUP, 1997), p. 136.

8 Jennifer Robertson, *Takarazuka, Sexual Politics and Popular Culture in Modern Japan* (Berkeley: UCP, 1998), p. 7.

9 Miriam Silverberg, "The Modern Girl as Militant," in Bernstein, ed., *Recreating Japanese Women*, p. 247.

10 The next two quotations come from Mariko Inoue, "Kiyokata's *Asasuzu*: The Emergence of the *Jogakusei* Image," *MN* 51/4 (Winter 1996): 439, 440.

11 George DeVos and Hiroshi Wagatsuma, *Japan's Invisible Race, Caste in Culture and Personality*, rev. edn. (Berkeley: UCP, 1972), p. 44.

12 Young-Soo Chung and Elise K. Tipton, "Problems of Assimilation: the Koreans," in Tipton, ed., *Society and the State in Interwar Japan* (London: Routledge, 1997), p. 182.

13 Richard Siddle, *Race, Resistance and the Ainu of Japan* (London: Routledge, 1996), p. 136.

14 The two following quotations come *seriatim* from Henry Dewitt Smith II, *Japan's First Student Radicals* (Cambridge, MA: HUP, 1972), pp. 214, 201.

15 Mikiso Hane, *Peasants, Rebels, and Outcasts, The Underside of Modern Japan* (NY: Pantheon Books, 1982), p. 212.

16 W. Dean Kinzley, *Industrial Harmony in Modern Japan, The Invention of a Tradition* (London: Routledge, 1991), p. 50. The Diet member was Uehara Etsujirō.

17 George B. Bikle, Jr., *The New Jerusalem, Aspects of Utopianism in the Thought of Kagawa Toyohiko* (The Association for Asian Studies Monograph No. 30) (Tucson: University of Arizona Press: 1976), p. 131.

18 Andrew Gordon, *The Evolution of Labor Relations in Japan, Heavy Industry, 1853–1955* (Cambridge, MA: HUP, 1985), p. 175.

19 Sheldon Garon, *The State and Labor in Modern Japan* (Berkeley: UCP, 1987), p. 165.

20 Mackie, *Creating Socialist Women*, p. 125.

21 Kinzley, *Industrial Harmony in Modern Japan*, p. 126.

22 William Miles Fletcher III, *The Search for a New Order, Intellectuals and Fascism in Prewar Japan* (Chapel Hill, The University of North Carolina Press, 1982), p. 77.

23 The next two quotations come from Gordon, *The Evolution of Labor Relations*, pp. 158, 291–2.

24 Thomas R. H. Havens, *Farm and Nation in Modern Japan, Agrarian Nationalism, 1870–1940* (Princeton: PUP, 1974), p. 251.

25 Kevin Michael Doak, *Dreams of Difference, The Japanese Romantic School and the Crisis of Modernity* (Berkeley: UCP, 1994), pp. 34, 35.

26 This fragment, which is Keene's characterization (italics added), and the two quotations about and by Tanizaki are from Donald Keene, *Dawn to the West, Japanese Literature of the Modern Era, Fiction* (NY: Holt, Rinehart and Winston, 1984), pp. 431, 727, 756.

27 Elaine Gerbert, "Introduction," in *Beautiful Town, Stories and Essays by Satō Haruo*, tr. by Francis B. Tenny (Honolulu: UHP, 1996), p. 5.

28 This fragment and the one below about *Hōrōki* are from Joan E. Ericson, *Be a Woman, Hayashi Fumiko and Modern Japanese Women's Literature* (Honolulu: UHP, 1997), pp. 3, 57.

29 Rebecca L. Copeland, *The Sound of the Wind, The Life and Works of Uno Chiyo* (Honolulu: UHP, 1992), p. 31.

30 Keene, *Dawn to the West, Fiction*, p. 677.

31 Doak, *Dreams of Difference*, pp. xxiv, xxxv, xxxvii.

32 David G. Goodman, *Japanese Drama and Culture in the 1960s, The Return of the Gods* (Armonk, NY: M.E. Sharpe, Inc., 1988), pp. 5–6. Italics modified.

33 Joseph L. Anderson and Donald Richie, *The Japanese Film: Art and Industry*, Expanded Edition (Princeton: PUP, 1982), p. 146.

34 Iwamoto Kenji, "Sound in the Early Japanese Talkies," in Arthur Nolletti, Jr. and David Desser, eds., *Reframing Japanese Cinema: Authorship, Genre, History* (Bloomington: Indiana University Press, 1992), p. 314.

35 The quotation comes from Darrell William Davis, *Picturing Japaneseness: Monumental Style, National Identity, Japanese Film* (NY: CUP, 1996), p. 76. Italics added.

36 Davis, *Picturing Japaneseness*, p. 52, quoting a letter to the *Japan Times*.

37 Anderson and Richie, *The Japanese Film*, p. 135.

38 Alexandra Munroe, *Japanese Art After 1945: Scream Against the Sky* (NY: Harry N. Abrams, Inc., 1994), p. 42.

39 Inoue, "Kiyokata's *Asasuzu*:" 450.

40 John Clark, "Artists and the State: the Image of China," in Tipton, *Society and the State in Interwar Japan*, p. 75.

41 Inoue, "Kiyokata's *Asasuzu*:" 442.

17 DRIFT TO DISASTER (1914–1945)

1 This and the next quotation come, in reverse order, from Mark R. Peattie, *Nan'yō, The Rise and Fall of the Japanese in Micronesia, 1885–1945* (Honolulu: UHP, 1988), pp. 51, 324, footnote 6.

2 Stefan Tanaka, *Japan's Orient, Rendering Pasts into History* (Berkeley: UCP, 1993), p. 248.

3 Peter Duus, Ramon H. Myers, and Mark R. Peattie, eds., *The Japanese Informal Empire in China, 1895–1937* (Princeton: PUP, 1989), p. 326.

4 This and the next quotation come from Mark R. Peattie, *Ishiwara Kanji and Japan's Confrontation with the West* (Princeton: PUP, 1975), pp. 159, 166.

5 This and the next quotation from Kwantung army leaders come from Duus et al., eds., *The Japanese Informal Empire*, pp. 141, 426.

6 Shin'ichi Kitaoka, "Prophet Without Honor: Kiyosawa Kiyoshi's View of Japanese-American Relations," in James W. White et al., eds., *The Ambivalence of Nationalism, Modern Japan between East and West* (Lanham, MD: University Press of America, 1990), p. 173.

7 William W. Lockwood, *The Economic Development of Japan, Growth and Structural Change, 1868–1938* (Princeton: PUP, 1954), p. 75.

8 Ikuhiko Hata, "Continental Expansion, 1905–1941," in Peter Duus, ed., *The Cambridge History of Japan, Volume 6, The Twentieth Century* (Cambridge: CUP, 1988), p. 313.

9 This and the next quoted statement, by the emperor in 1945, come from Alvin D. Coox, "The Pacific War," in *The Cambridge History, Vol. 6*, pp. 336, 375.

10 This and the next quotation, from the *Asahi* newspaper, come from Thomas R. H. Havens, *Valley of Darkness, The Japanese People and World War Two* (New York: W.W. Norton & Co., 1978), pp. 11–12, 87.

11 F. C. Jones, *Japan's New Order in East Asia, Its Rise and Fall, 1937–45* (London: Oxford University Press, 1954), p. 332.

12 Havens, *Valley of Darkness*, p. 135.

13 The two following quotations come, in reverse order, from John W. Dower, *Japan in War and Peace, Selected Essays* (NY: New Press, 1993), pp. 114, 130.

14 Havens, *Valley of Darkness*, p. 183.

18 *ENTREPRENEURIAL JAPAN: POLITICS AND ECONOMY (1945–1990)*

1 David John Lu, *Sources of Japanese History*, Vol. Two (NY: McGraw Hill, 1974), p. 176.

2 Hugh Borton, *Japan's Modern Century* (NY: The Ronald Press, 1955), p. 493. A convenient side-by-side display of the Meiji and 1947 constitutions is at pp. 490–507.

3 This and the following quotation come from Laura E. Hein, *Fueling Growth, The Energy Revolution and Economic Policy in Postwar Japan* (Cambridge, MA: HUP, 1990), pp. 119–20.

4 Kyoko and Mark Selden, eds., *The Atomic Bomb, Voices from Hiroshima and Nagasaki* (Armonk, NY: M.E. Sharpe, Inc., 1989), p. xix.

5 This and the following quotation come from Hein, *Fueling Growth*, pp. 184, 205.

6 Benjamin Martin, "Japanese Mining Labor: The Miike Strike," in Jon Livingston et al., eds., *The Japan Reader 2: Postwar Japan* (NY: Random House, 1973), pp. 491, 493.

7 Figures for USA derived from *New York Times*, March 15, 1999, p. A13; Japanese figures from Sōmuchō tōkeikyoku, *Nihon Tōkei Nenkan 1998 (Japan Statistical Yearbook)* (Tokyo: Nihon tōkei kyokai), p. 777.

8 Yukio Noguchi, "Land Problems and Policies in Japan: Structural Aspects," in John O. Haley and Kozo Yamamura, eds., *Land Issues in Japan: A Policy Failure?* (Seattle: Society for Japanese Studies, 1992), p. 14. "Habitable land" excludes mountains, deserts, and lakes.

9 Yuzuru Hanayama, "Land Use Planning and Industrial Siting Policy," in Shigeto Tsuru and Helmut Weidner, eds., *Environmental Policy in Japan* (Berlin: Edition Sigma, 1989), p. 417.

10 Takafusa Nakamura, *The Postwar Japanese Economy, Its Development and Structure* (Tokyo: UTP, 1981), pp. 60–1.

11 *Japan Statistical Yearbook 1996*, p. 358.

12 Yano Tsuneta Kinenkai, ed., *Nippon, A Charted Survey of Japan 1994–95* (Tokyo: Kokuseisha, 1994). Calculated from tables on pp. 245, 246.

13 Shigeru Nakayama, *Science, Technology and Society in Postwar Japan* (London: Kegan Paul International, 1991), p. 132.

14 *Japan Statistical Yearbook 1960*, p. 429; *1996*, pp. 492, 504. Local taxes are separate: 5.8 percent in 1953; 6.6 percent in 1975.

19 SOCIETY AND ENVIRONMENT (1945–1990)

1 Kozo Yamamura, "LDP Dominance and High Land Price in Japan: A Study in Positive Political Economy," in John O. Haley and Yamamura, eds., *Land Issues in Japan: A Policy Failure?* (Seattle: Society for Japanese Studies, 1992), p. 47.

2 Yano Tsuneta Kinenkai, ed., *Nippon, A Charted Survey of Japan 1994–95* (Tokyo: Kokuseisha, 1994), p. 223.

3 Susan B. Hanley, "Traditional Housing and Unique Lifestyles: The Unintended Outcomes of Japan's Land Policy," in Haley and Yamamura, *Land Issues in Japan*, p. 196.

4 Kathleen S. Uno, "The Death of 'Good Wife, Wise Mother'?" in Andrew Gordon, ed., *Postwar Japan as History* (Berkeley: UCP, 1993), p. 314.

5 Kazuko Tanaka, "The New Feminist Movement in Japan, 1970–1990," in Kumiko Fujimura-Fanselow and Atsuko Kameda, eds., *Japanese Women: New Feminist Perspectives on the Past, Present, and Future* (NY: The Feminist Press, 1995), p. 349.

6 Muriel Jolivet, *Japan: the Childless Society? The Crisis of Motherhood* (London: Routledge, 1997), pp. 5–6.

7 Frank K. Upham, "Unplaced Persons and Movements for Place," in Gordon, ed., *Postwar Japan as History*, p. 331.

8 Mikiso Hane, *Eastern Phoenix, Japan Since 1945* (Boulder, CO: Westview Press, 1996), p. 148, italics added.

9 Sonia Ryang, *North Koreans in Japan: Language, Ideology, and Identity* (Boulder, CO: Westview Press, 1997), p. 11.

10 Hiromi Mori, *Immigration Policy and Foreign Workers in Japan* (NY: St. Martin's Press, Inc., 1997), pp. 160, 168.

11 Hiroshi Komai, *Migrant Workers in Japan* (London: Kegan Paul International, 1993), pp. 1, 82, 100.

12 Richard Siddle, "Ainu: Japan's Indigenous People," in Michael Weiner, ed., *Japan's Minorities, The Illusion of Homogeneity* (London: Routledge, 1997), p. 26.

13 This and the following quotation come from Richard Siddle, *Race, Resistance and the Ainu of Japan* (London: Routledge, 1996), pp. 176, 178.

14 Siddle, "Ainu: Japan's Indigenous People," p. 34.
15 This and the following quotation come from Helen Hardacre, *Kurozumikyō and the New Religions of Japan* (Princeton: PUP, 1986), pp. 5, 12.
16 Ian Reader, *Religion in Contemporary Japan* (London: Macmillan Press, 1991), p. 110. Kinpusenji is located in the mountainous Yoshino district of Nara Prefecture.
17 Susumu Shimazono, "New Religious Movements; Introduction," in Mark R. Mullins et al., eds., *Religion and Society in Modern Japan, Selected Readings* (Berkeley: Asian Humanities Press, 1993), p. 226.
18 Reader, *Religion in Contemporary Japan*, p. 219.
19 Eiki Hoshino and Dōshō Takeda, "Mizuko Kuyō and Abortion in Contemporary Japan," in Mullins et al., eds., *Religion and Society in Modern Japan*, p. 179, report the figures. Jolivet, *Japan: the Childless Society?*, p. 129, reports the reservations about their reliability.
20 Margaret A. McKean, *Environmental Protest and Citizen Politics in Japan* (Berkeley: UCP, 1981), p. 19.
21 Shigeto Tsuru, "History of Pollution Control Policy," in Tsuru and Helmut Weidner, eds., *Environmental Policy in Japan* (Berlin: Edition Sigma, 1989), p. 21.
22 Sōmuchō tōkeikyoku, *Nihon Tōkei Nenkan (Japan Statistical Yearbook)* (Tokyo: Nihon tōkei kyokai), *1962*, p. 227; *1996*, p. 372. The 1990 figure excludes about 18,000,000 "light" 2-, 3-, and 4-wheel vehicles, a category not distinguished in 1960.
23 Susan J. Napier, *The Fantastic in Modern Japanese Literature, The Subversion of Modernity* (London: Routledge, 1996), p. 165.
24 Junko Nakanishi, "Sewerage Policy and its Problems," in Tsuru and Weidner, eds., *Environmental Policy in Japan*, p. 314.

20 THE CULTURE OF ENTREPRENEURIAL JAPAN (1945–1990)

1 Thomas R. H. Havens, *Artist and Patron in Postwar Japan, Dance, Music, Theater, and the Visual Arts, 1955–1980* (Princeton: PUP, 1982), p. 85, quoting Kimura Hideo.
2 J. Victor Koschmann, "Intellectuals and Politics," in Andrew Gordon, ed., *Postwar Japan as History* (Berkeley: UCP, 1993), p. 400, quoting Ōtsuka Hisao.
3 Ryusaku Tsunoda et al., comps., *Sources of the Japanese Tradition* (NY: CUP, 1958), p. 901.
4 The words are those of Kevin Michael Doak, *Dreams of Difference, The Japan Romantic School and the Crisis of Modernity* (Berkeley: UCP, 1994), p. 145.
5 Harumi Befu, *Cultural Nationalism in East Asia, Representation and Identity* (Berkeley: Institute of East Asian Studies, 1993), p. 107.
6 The two comments by Takami come from Donald Keene, *Dawn to the West, Japanese Literature of the Modern Era: Fiction* (NY: Holt, Rinehart and Winston, 1984), pp. 877, 968.
7 Donald Keene, *Dawn to the West, Japanese Literature of the Modern Era: Poetry, Drama, Criticism* (NY: Holt, Rinehart and Winston, 1984), p. 164.
8 Tsuboi Shigeji (Robert Epp, tr.), *Egg in my Palm* (Stanwood, WA: Yakusha, 1993), pp. 122–3.
9 Keene, *Dawn to the West: Fiction*, p. 991.

10 Ōe Kenzaburō, ed., *The Crazy Iris and Other Stories of the Atomic Aftermath* (NY: Grove Press, 1985), p. 145.

11 Susan J. Napier, *The Fantastic in Modern Japanese Literature, The Subversion of Modernity* (London: Routledge, 1996), p. 84.

12 The words are those of Joan E. Ericson, *Be a Woman, Hayashi Fumiko and Modern Japanese Women's Literature* (Honolulu: UHP, 1997), p. xi.

13 Yukiko Tanaka, ed., *Unmapped Territories, New Women's Fiction from Japan* (Seattle, WA: Women in Translation, 1991), p. xvi.

14 The comments by Tsuno come from David G. Goodman, *Japanese Drama and Culture in the 1960s, The Return of the Gods* (Armonk, NY: M.E. Sharpe, Inc., 1988), pp. 7, 16. Italics added.

15 Senda Akihiko (tr. J. Thomas Rimer), *The Voyage of Contemporary Japanese Theatre* (Honolulu: UHP, 1997), p. 30.

16 Havens, *Artist and Patron in Postwar Japan*, p. 181.

17 This and the next quote come from Alexandra Munroe, *Japanese Art After 1945: Scream Against the Sky* (NY: Harry N. Abrams, Inc., 1994), pp. 83, 84.

18 Clare Fawcett, "Archaeology and Japanese Identity," in Donald Denoon et al., eds., *Multicultural Japan, Palaeolithic to Postmodern* (Cambridge: CUP, 1996), p. 64.

19 Keiko I. McDonald, *Japanese Classical Theater in Films* (Rutherford, NJ: Fairleigh Dickinson University Press, 1994), p. 72.

20 Joseph L. Anderson and Donald Richie, *The Japanese Film: Art and Industry*, Expanded Edition (Princeton: PUP, 1982), p. 268.

21 The quoted fragment is from Max Tessier, "Oshima Nagisa, or The Battered Energy of Desire," in Arthur Nolletti, Jr. and David Desser, eds., *Reframing Japanese Cinema, Authorship, Genre, History* (Bloomington: Indiana University Press, 1992), p. 70.

22 Keiko McDonald, "Japan," in John A. Lent, *The Asian Film Industry* (London: Christopher Helm, 1990), p. 57.

23 McDonald, *Japanese Classical Theater in Films*, p. 83.

24 Maya Morioka Todeschini, " 'Death and the Maiden': Female *Hibakusha* as Cultural Heroines, and the Politics of A-bomb Memory," in Mick Broderick, ed., *Hibakusha Cinema: Hiroshima, Nagasaki and the Nuclear Image in Japanese Film* (London: Kegan Paul International, 1996), p. 235. The quoted fragments that follow come from p. 231.

EPILOGUE: *JAPAN TODAY AND TOMORROW*

1 Japanese Society for History Textbook Reform, *The Restoration of a National History* (Tokyo, 1997), p. 31.

2 *Science News* 154/18 (Oct. 31, 1998): 278.

3 *Science News* 154/20 (Nov. 14, 1998): 312–14.

4 *Science News* 154/25 (Dec. 19, 1998): 388.

5 *Science News* 153/17 (April 25, 1998): 264.

6 Yano Tsuneta Kinenkai, ed., *Nippon, A Charted Survey of Japan 1994/95* (Tokyo: Kokuseisha, 1994), p. 246. The figures are "oil equivalents."

APPENDIX A: SUPPLEMENTAL TABLES

Note: The source of most of the data in these tables is identified here as *Japan Statistical Yearbook*, which refers to the bilingual annual compilation edited by Sōmuchō tōkeikyoku, *Nihon Tōkei Nenkan* (*Japan Statistical Yearbook*) (Tokyo: Nihon tōkei kyokai).

Table I Births, deaths, and rates, 1925–1996

Year	Live births	Deaths	Net gain	Birth rate	Death rate	Rate of infant mortality
1925	2,086	1,211	875	34.9	20.3	142.4
1950	2,338	905	1,433	28.1	10.9	60.1
1960	1,606	707	899	17.2	7.6	30.7
1975	1,901	702	1,199	17.1	6.3	10.0
1990	1,222	820	401	10.0	6.7	4.6
1995	1,187	922	265	9.6	7.4	4.3
1996	1,207	896	310	9.7	7.2	3.8

Note: Figures are in thousands and per thousand.
Source: *Japan Statistical Yearbook 1999*, p. 59.

Table II Population changes: city and village, 1920–1995

Year	Total population of Japan	In cities of 100,000 and up	% of total	In towns and villages of under 5,000	% of total	Number of towns and villages
1920	55,963	6,754	12.0	27,106	48.4	10,048
1950	83,200	21,327	25.6	20,671	24.8	6,669
1960	93,419	37,982	40.6	1,132	1.2	329
1990	123,611	72,353	58.5	1,960	1.6	629
1995	125,570	74,849	59.6	2,100	1.7	677

Note: Population in thousands.
Source: *Japan Statistical Yearbook 1999*, p. 36.

Table III Marine fisheries catch and supply, 1930–1996

Year	Catch	Net import*	Total supply**	Fishery households (1000s)
1930	3,136			
1955	4,659			
1965	6,381	−14	6,569	390
1975	9,573	102	10,125	324
1985	10,877	951	12,458	302
1990	9,570	2,744	13,244	258
1995	6,007	6,540	12,118	215
1996	5,974	5,645	11,923	205

Notes: Figures are in 1,000 metric tons.
  *Net import equals total import minus export.
**Total supply includes non-marine fishery catch.
Source: *Japan Statistical Yearbook 1999*, pp. 252, 258, 271.

Table IV Trends in agricultural receipts and costs of farm households, 1955–1996

Statistic	1955	1958	1970	1975	1990	1996
A. Farm receipts	372	306	985	2,081	3,002	3,801
B. Farm costs	117	109	477	935	1,839	2,413
C. Cost as % of receipts (B÷A)	31.5	35.6	48.4	44.9	61.3	63.5
D. Farm profit (A−B)	255	197	508	1,146	1,163	1,389
E. Family expenditures	313	324	1,225	2,650	5,504	5,730
F. Farm profit as % of expenditures (D÷E)	81.5	60.8	41.5	43.2	21.1	24.2

Note: Figures are in 1,000s of *yen*.
Source: *Japan Statistical Yearbook 1960*, p. 100; *1999*, p. 243.

Table V Trends in farm household income, 1955–1996

Statistic	1955	1958	1970	1975	1990*	1996
A. Total income	380	377	1,592	3,961	8,819	8,935
B. Farming income	255	197	508	1,146	(1,163)	1,389
C. (B as % of A)	67.1	52.3	31.9	28.9	16.2	15.5
D. Non-farm earned income	103	153	885	2,268	5,526	5,462
E. (D as % of A)	27.1	40.6	55.6	57.3	62.7	61.1
F. Annuities and grants	21	27	199	546	1,797	2,085
G. (F as % of A)	5.5	7.2	12.5	13.8	21.4	23.3

Note: Figures are in 1,000s of *yen*.
*The 1990 figures do not tally because the source gives the figure 1,430 for Farming income, although 1,163 is the correct figure for the calculation it employs: gross receipts minus expenditures.
Source: *Japan Statistical Yearbook, 1960*, p. 100; *1999*, p. 243.

Table VI Timber production and imports, 1950–1996

Year	Production	Imports
1950	20.3	0
1952	38.8	0
1955	42.8	2.5
1960	48.5	6.6
1965	49.5	16.6
1970	45.4	43.0
1975	37.1	62.2
1990	31.3	81.9
1996	23.8	90.3

Note: Figures are in million cubic meters.
Sources: *Japan Statistical Yearbook 1960*, p. 113; *1972*, p. 140; *1999*, p. 250. Total domestic wood production declined more sharply during Shōwa Genroku, falling from 75 million cubic meters in 1960 to 36 million in 1991, largely due to a dramatic drop in fuel wood consumption. *Nippon, A Charted Survey, 1994–1995*, p. 135.

Table VII Primary energy sources, 1955–1996

Year	Total energy	Domestic production*	Coal	Crude oil	LNG**	Nuclear
1955	644	508	311	88	–	–
1960	952	571	421	309	–	–
1975	3,435	445	602	2,436	66	57
1990	4,663	816	817	2,158	472	455
1995	5,208	982	899	2,452	567	655
1996	5,296	1,004	906	2,445	605	680

Notes: Figures are in trillions of kilocalories.
*Includes hydro-power and a few other minor sources as well as fossil fuels and nuclear power.
**LNG (liquified nitrogen gas).
Source: *Japan Statistical Yearbook 1999*, p. 356.

Table VIII Coal production and imports, 1930–1997

Year	Production	Imports	Exports
1930	31,376	2,693	2,131
1940	56,313	5,076	548
1960	52,607	8,595	14
1975	18,597	62,339	33
1990	7,980	104,835	–
1995	6,166	125,322	–
1997	3,974	132,473	–

Note: Figures are in thousand metric tons.
Source: *Japan Statistical Yearbook 1950*, p. 180; *1962*, p. 212; *1999*, p. 351.

Table IX Crude oil production and imports, 1930–1996

Year	Production	Imports
1930	317	570
1940	331	2,292
1950	328	1,541
1955	354	8,553
1960	593	31,116
1975	699	262,785
1990	655	238,480
1995	834	263,792
1996	840	267,489

Note: Figures are in thousand kiloliters.
Source: *Japan Statistical Yearbook 1952*, p. 170; *1962*, p. 215; *1999*, p. 350. In 1930 and 1940 small quantities were exported.

Table X Iron ore production and imports, 1930–1997

Year	Production	Imports
1930	246	2,261
1940	1,123	5,129
1960	1,218	10,280
1975	602	133,524
1980	477	134,828
1990	34	125,581
1995	3.0	120,521
1997	3.6	126,600

Note: Figures are in thousand metric tons.
Source: *Japan Statistical Yearbook 1960*, p. 200; *1962*, p. 213; *1999*, p. 294. In 1930 and 1940 small quantities were exported.

APPENDIX B: CHINESE WORDS: WADE–GILES AND PINYIN ORTHOGRAPHIES

Well-established, idiosyncratic usages are retained for a few well-known terms: Canton, Confucius, Hong Kong, Mencius, Peking until 1948, Sun Yat-sen, Taiwan.

This Appendix is based on the conversion table in Jonathan Spence, *The Search for Modern China* (NY: W.W. Norton & Co., 1990), pp. xxvi–xxvii.

The terms *Wajinden* and Wakō are Japanese pronunciations.

Word in Text	*Wade–Giles*	*Pinyin*
Ch'an	Ch'an	Chan
Chang Tso-lin	Chang Tso-lin	Zhang Zuolin
Ch'eng-Chu	Ch'eng-Chu	Cheng-Zhu
Chiang Kai-shek	Chiang Kai-shek	Jiang Jieshi
Ch'ing	Ch'ing	Qing
Chou	Chou	Zhou
Chu Shun-shui	Chu Shun-shui	Zhu Shunshui
Han	Han	Han
Hou Hanshū	*Hou Hanshū*	*Hou Han shu*
Kuomintang	Kuomintang	Guomindang
Laozi	Lao-tzu	Laozi
Liaotung	Liaotung	Liaodong
Liu Sung	Liu Sung	Liu Song
Lolang	Lolang	Luolang
Manchukuo	Manchukuo	Manzhuguo
Mao Tse-tung	Mao Tse-tung	Mao Zedong
Ming	Ming	Ming
Beijing	Peiching	Beijing
San-kuo chih	*San-kuo chih*	*San guo zhi*
Shanghai	Shanghai	Shanghai
Shantung	Shantung	Shandong
Sui	Sui	Sui
Sung	Sung	Song
Sungshū	*Sungshū*	*Song shu*
T'ang	T'ang	Tang
tao	tao	dao
Tientsin	T'ienchin	Tianjin
Tsingtao	Ch'ingtao	Qingdao
Wajinden	*Wojenchuan*	*Woren zhuan*

Wakō	Wok'ou	Wokou
Wei	Wei	Wei
Wei chih	*Wei chih*	*Wei zhi*
Wu	Wu	Wu
Yangtse	Yangtse	Yangzi
Yao	Yao	Yao
Yūan	Yūan	Yuan
Yūan Shih-k'ai	Yūan Shih-k'ai	Yuan Shikai
Zhuangzi	Chuang-tzu	Zhuangzi

APPENDIX C: GLOSSARY OF JAPANESE TERMS (EXCLUDING PROPER NOUNS)

akamatsu	Japanese red pine; *Pinus densiflora.*
akutō	"evil bands," lawless men, esp. of Kamakura period.
baiu	"spring rain," a seasonal occurrence in Japan.
bakufu	"tent government," shogunal governments at Kamakura, Muromachi, Edo.
bakuhan	elided form of "bakufu-and-han," cf. bakuhan taisei.
bakuhan taisei	"power structure of bakufu and daimyo domains," refers to Edo bakufu and daimyo domains (han) as a single governing system.
benshi	live narrator of silent films.
bijinga	"beautiful-woman art," a traditional category in East Asian art.
bikuni	Buddhist nun or mendicant woman, esp. of Heian–Kamakura periods.
biwa hōshi	lute-playing priest, esp. of medieval centuries.
bonshōgatsu	city festivals sponsored by lord of Kaga; later Edo period.
bugaku	court dance of ritsuryō period.
bugyōsho	magistrate's office of Edo period.
buke	"military house," or high-status samurai, esp. as distinct from court nobles of late Heian; cf. kuge.
bunbu	"civil and military arts;" ideal of well-rounded political mastery, esp. in Edo period.
bundan	"literary establishment" of modern Japan.
bunmei kaika	"civilization and enlightenment," a policy ideal of Meiji reformers.
burakumin	pariah status in modern Japan, derived from eta status of Edo period.
bushi	warrior; samurai status.
bushidō	"Way of the warrior," a concept of Edo period.
byōbu-uta	screen poem; a favored art form of Heian period; cf. uta-e.
chanbara	sword play; a movie full of sword fighting.
chanoyū	ceremonial tea drinking; an art form developed during Muromachi period.
chigaidana	split-level shelving; an element in shoin-style architecture.
chō	a measure of acreage: today, 0.99 hectares.
chōzen naikaku	"transcendental cabinet," a cabinet answerable only to emperor: a late Meiji political ideal.
chūsei	"medieval," essentially Kamakura–Muromachi periods.
daijō daijin	principal minister of ritsuryō government theory.
daijōkan	Council of State; senior official body of ritsuryō government.

daikan	district intendant; a civil office of Edo bakufu.
daimyō	"great name," regional magnates of medieval Japan; standardized during Edo period as officially enfeoffed holders of domains of 10,000 koku or greater putative yield.
daimyōjin	"divine rectifier," a term for imagined saviors and political champions of later Edo-period folklore.
daitōmai	hardy rice, a more cold-resistant rice introduced to Japan in late Heian period.
daiwa	"Great Wa"; an alternative reading of the kanji normally read Yamato.
dajōkan	*See* daijōkan.
dekasegi	working away from home; an employment pattern that became common in later Edo period.
dengaku	"field dances"; invocatory dances associated with rice planting on ritsuryō-era shrine-temple lands; a courtly entertainment by later Heian.
dōjin	"natives," a term applied to Ainu before Meiji period.
dōjin zasshi	"coterie magazine," small circulation highbrow magazines of later Meiji–Taishō period.
edokoro	court painters' office; an official post of ritsuryō–medieval period.
eejanaika	"ain't it grand," raucous celebration; an expression associated with some late-Edo public disturbances.
egoma	a species of Asian mint; *Perilla ocimoides*.
ehon	"picture book," a painting format of medieval period.
emakimono	"narrative picture scroll," a format for illustrated tales, esp. of late Heian–Kamakura periods.
enka	sentimental ballads sung in a distinctive keening voice; esp. in Shōwa Genroku period.
eta	hereditary outcast; a long-standing, semi-pariah status that was formalized in Edo period.
etoki hōshi	"picture-explaining priest," religious tale-telling itinerants, esp. of medieval period.
fudai	hereditary servant or retainer.
fudoki	"gazetteer," esp. written reports for Genmei tennō on conditions and resources in the provinces.
fuko	*See* hehito.
fukoku kyōhei	"rich country; strong army," a policy ideal of Meiji reformers.
funkyūbō	large burial mounds of Yayoi–Kofun periods.
furusato	"native village," romanticized urban image of rural Japan, popular during Shōwa Genroku period.
fusuma	wood-framed, sliding, opaque paper wall panel; element in shoin-style architecture.
gagaku	orchestral court music of the ritsuryō period, based on continental antecedents.
gekokujō	"those below toppling those above," a phrase characterizing sengoku political turmoil.
gendaigeki	"modern works," movies that treat post-1868 topics.
gesaku	"silly or light works," popular fiction of later Edo period.
geta	Japanese-style clogs.
gō	township; a legal entity in ritsuryō organization.
goen	imperial palace grounds in present-day Kyoto.

gojira	"Godzilla," movie monster; an A-bomb mutant; 1954 and later.
gokenin	vassals of Kamakura bakufu; minor vassals of Edo bakufu.
gosho	imperial palace in present-day Kyoto.
gozan	"five mountains," organization of major Rinzai monasteries in Kamakura–Muromachi periods.
goze	blind female story teller, esp. of medieval period.
gun	"district," subdivision of province, and, in modern Japan, prefecture.
gunken	"province-district," a Chinese term denoting a centralized polity; contrast with hôken.
gunki monogatari	"war tale," a genre of oral literature esp. popular late Heian to early Muromachi.
gun'yaku	military levy; required of vassals by their lords, esp. by Tokugawa shogun.
haikai	17-syllable verse (haiku), dating from seventeenth century.
haiku	*See* haikai.
hajiki	"Haji ware," daily-use earthenware, from late Yayoi onward.
hakama	formal menswear skirt.
hanbatsu seiji	"clique government," a pejorative label for Meiji regime, reflecting its origin in Sat-Chō conquest of 1868.
haniwa	funerary figurines of clay encircling elite tombs of Kofun period.
hatamoto	"bannermen," middling retainers of Tokugawa bakufu; ranked between gokenin below and fudai daimyo above.
hehito	"sustenance households," producer households assigned by court to temples and nobility as tribute sources during ritsuryō period.
heimin	commoner; a formal status category of Meiji period.
hibakusha	survivor of atomic bombing in Hiroshima and Nagasaki.
hijiri	a mendicant or itinerant Buddhist monk, esp. of Heian-Kamakura periods.
hinin	non-hereditary pariah status of Edo period.
hinoki	Japanese cypress; *Chamaecyparis obtusa*.
hiragana	Japanese syllabary, formed by extreme simplification of kanji.
hiratake	agaric (a mushroom); *Agaricus subfunereus*.
hōben	"expedient means," a Buddhist concept that relates optimal religious praxis to one's level of spiritual development.
hōken	decentralized or "feudal," a Chinese term denoting a decentralized polity; contrast with gunken.
hon-jaku	*See* honji suijaku.
honji suijaku	the theological principle of true nature and secondary manifestation, esp. favored in later Heian and medieval centuries.
hyakuin	"hundred-stanza verse," mature form of renga, esp. in Muromachi period.
hyōjun	"proper Japanese," a term denoting Tokyo dialect as standard Japanese; esp. from later Meiji period onward.
ichimon	Ashikaga kinsman; a political category of Muromachi bakufu.
ie	familial lineage group; a core social category from ritsuryō period onward.

igusa	a rush or sedge used to form tatami; *Juncus effusus*.
ikebana	flower arrangement; a venerable art form that flourished esp. from Muromachi period onward.
ikki	"of one mind," a term signifying communal unity of purpose, esp. associated with commoner disturbances in Muromachi and later Edo periods.
imayō	popular songs, esp. of later Heian period.
in	"retired emperor," esp. during later Heian–Kamakura periods.
insei	governing organ of the in, esp. during later Heian period.
jiban	political machine or bailiwick; refers to local political organizations in modern Japan.
jidaigeki	a "period piece" in cinema repertory; cf. gendaigeki.
jidaimono	a "period piece" in kabuki repertory; cf. sewamono.
jikatasho	farm manual; a type of practical agronomic treatise popular during later Edo period.
jingikan	central bureau in charge of religious affairs in ritsuryō period.
jinja	Shintō shrine.
jinrikisha	"rickshaw," a human-drawn, two-wheel passenger vehicle invented in early Meiji.
jisha bugyō	superintendents of shrines and temples; an office of Tokugawa bakufu.
jitō	"land steward," a title regularized by Kamakura bakufu to assure its vassals authority over land and people.
jitsugaku	practical learning; practicality; a philosophical principle of Chinese provenance favored during Edo period.
jiyū minken	"freedom and people's rights," a political posture of Meiji period.
jōmon	"cord markings," surface form defining pottery of Jōmon period.
joryū bungaku	"women's literature," a literary category of modern Japan.
joryū sakka	"women writers," an authorial category of modern Japan.
kabane	"bone rank," a political ranking system of Korean provenance used in pre-ritsuryō Japan, esp. sixth century.
kabuki	a popular theatre of Edo period; has persisted to the present.
kagami	"mirror," a term used in titles of historical works, mainly of later Heian and Kamakura periods.
kaisho	"meeting place," public assembly rooms of Muromachi-period mansions.
kamado	cooking hearth introduced to Japan during Yayoi period; enlarged in later centuries to provide better cooking facilities.
kami	Shintō deity; awesome presence.
kamikaze	"divine wind," esp. the typhoon (taifū) of 1281 that struck Mongol invaders; applied to aircraft suicide missions in waning months of Pacific War.
kan	Chinese-style volume; a folded-leaf, thread-bound type of book used in Japan since ritsuryō period.
kana	syllabary; modified kanji used to represent syllables of Japanese; cf. hiragana, katakana.
kanamajiribun	medieval writing style that employed both kana and kanji.
kana zōshi	simply written works, popular in late medieval and early Edo periods.
kanga	"Chinese style art," esp. favored in medieval and Edo periods.

kanji	"Chinese character," used to represent a word, rather than just a syllable.
kanjin	temple fund raising project, esp. late Heian-to-medieval period.
kanjōsho	finance office of Tokugawa bakufu.
kanpaku	regent to an adult emperor, esp. Hokke Fujiwara in Heian period.
kanrei	regent to an Ashikaga shogun in Muromachi period.
kanshi	"Chinese poetry," as distinct from Japanese; cf. waka.
karamono	"China goods," esp. as favored for display by Muromachi kenmon.
karaoke	recreational singing to pre-recorded accompaniment; flourished in Shōwa Genroku period.
kare sansui	dry landscape garden; a style favored esp. during Muromachi period.
katakana	Japanese syllabary, formed by using fragments of kanji.
kawata	hereditary pariah; term dating from Heian period; status regularized as eta in Edo period.
kazoku	hereditary peerage of Imperial Japan.
kebiishi-chō	special police agency, formed in early Heian.
ken	a linear measure; six shaku; today, 1.82 meters.
ken	prefecture; a territorial division of modern Japan.
kenmon	"powerful house," scholar's term signifying dominant groups, esp. in Muromachi period.
kikin	famine.
kimono	a dress-robe outfit.
kin	a measure of weight; today, 0.6 kg.
kindai	"modern," essentially Japan since 1868; or 1868–1945.
kinsei	"early modern," essentially Edo period.
ko	statutory household of ritsuryō landholding regulations.
kōbugattai	"union of court and bushi," a political category of 1860s.
kofun	"old tomb,' denoting pre-Taika era of elite tomb building; also tombs themselves.
kokka	a political term, variously denoting province, domain, realm, nation, or state, esp. during Edo period, and from Meiji onward, state, nation, or realm.
koku	a measure of volume: 180 liters of grain; 0.27 cubic meters of wood.
koku	*See* kuni.
kokubunji	*See* kokubunsōji.
kokubunniji	provincial nunnery of ritsuryō period.
kokubunsōji	provincial monastery of ritsuryō period.
kokudaka	putative crop yield of a field, village, or domain and hence, in Edo period, a measure of landed income.
kokufu	provincial headquarters of ritsuryō period.
kokugaku	"nativist learning," of the Edo period.
kokugakusha	scholar of "nativism," esp. of the Edo period.
kokugaryō	"provincial dominion"; imperial tax lands, esp. in later Heian period.
kokujin	"a provincial," local power holder, esp. in later Muromachi.
kokusaika	"internationalization," a policy ideal, esp. of Shōwa Genroku period.

kokusaku eiga	"national policy film," government-approved cinema of 1930s–40s wartime.
kokutai	"national polity" or "national essence," denoting, esp. in Imperial Japan, the realm's uniquely virtuous character.
kome shōgun	"rice shogun," an epithet applied to Tokugawa Yoshimune.
konbinato	integrated industrial site of Shōwa Genroku period; from Latin *combinare* via Soviet Russian *kombinat*.
kōri	district; a territorial category of ritsuryō period.
koto	zither; a large, resonant, multi-string, platform instrument played with a plectrum.
kubunden	a parcel of arable land as designated in ritsuryō regulations.
kuge	civil aristocrat, esp. of Heian period onward, as distinct from buke.
kumiai	trade association; flourished in Edo period.
kun	indigenous Japanese reading of a word represented by a kanji, as distinct from Japanized Chinese readings; cf. on.
kuni	locality, province, country, nation; a term of hoary Chinese provenance that reflects differing mental horizons; cf. kokka.
kuroshio	"Japan Current," a northward flowing ocean current that warms waters off southern Japan.
kusemai	a lively recitative dance style popular in fourteenth century.
kyōgen	brief farces included in nō programs; Muromachi period onward.
kyō-masu	a measure of volume, esp. for rice, standardized by Hideyoshi; about two liters.
machi	town, esp. from Muromachi period onward.
machi bugyō	city magistrate; government office of Edo bakufu.
machishū	"townsmen," burghers, esp. of sengoku period.
mandara	mandala; visual representation of sacred realm, whether Buddhist or combinative, esp. in late Heian and medieval periods.
mandokoro	administrative office of Heian noble household or fane.
mappō	"defiled latter age," of Jōdo doctrine, esp. in later Heian–Kamakura period.
matcha	powdered tea, used in tea ceremony, esp. Kamakura period onward.
matsuri	local festival.
matsutake	a mushroom; *Armillaria edodes*.
mikkyō	Esoteric or Tantric Buddhism; esp. Shingon, popular at Heian court.
miko	"shamaness," of combinative religious praxis, esp. in Heian period.
miyake	monarchical tribute lands, esp. of sixth century.
miyaza	membership bodies of local shrines, esp. Kamakura period onward.
mizuko kuyō	"fetal rites," rites of propitiation to fetal spirits, esp. during Shōwa Genroku period.
mizu mondai	disputes over water use, esp. for irrigation in Edo period.
moga	"modern girl," a polyvalent stereotype, esp. of 1920s.
monogatari	"tale," literary category, esp. of later Heian onward.
mura	village.
myō	units of land held by local men of influence, esp. later Heian period.

myōshu	local men of influence who held assigned properties (myō), esp. later Heian period.
myōshu shiki	contractual document assuring myōshu their myō.
nakama	trade association, esp. flourished in Edo period.
namazu	earthquake-causing subterranean catfish of folklore, esp. late Tokugawa period.
namu Amida butsu	"invoking Amida's name," mantra of Jōdo Buddhism, esp. late Heian onward.
namu myōhō rengekyō	"invoking the Lotus sutra," mantra of Hokke Buddhism, esp. later Kamakura onward.
nanbokuchō	"northern and southern courts," denotes bifurcated imperial lineage of early Muromachi period.
nenbutsu	"calling the Buddha," via the Jōdo mantra namu Amida butsu.
nenbutsu odori	"dancing the nenbutsu," a means to religious ecstasy, esp. of Ji sect in medieval period.
nengō	"year period," continental system of frequent calendrical name changes; adopted in seventh century and used thereafter; coterminus with imperial reigns after 1868.
nihonga	"Japanese painting," art category of late Meiji and onward.
nikki	"diary," literary category, esp. of later Heian onward.
ninennaku	"no second thought," ideal of automaticity in response to threats, applied to coastal defense in 1820s.
ningyō jōruri	puppet theatre, flourished in Edo period.
nō	type of drama; developed esp. by Zeami in early Muromachi period.
nōhon shugi	"agrarianism," rural advocacy, esp. in Imperial Japan.
nōhon shugisha	"agrarianist," an advocate of rural interests, esp. in Imperial Japan.
odoi	earthen rampart placed around Kyoto by Hideyoshi.
ofumi	pastoral letter, esp. the sort employed by Rennyo.
on	Japanized Chinese reading of a word represented by a kanji, as distinct from indigenous Japanese reading; cf. kun.
onbyakushō	"honorable peasant," honorific status label of Edo period.
onnagata	female impersonator, esp. in kabuki.
otogi zōshi	modern generic label for longer tales of medieval period.
oyashio	cold Chishima Current, which flows southward along Japan's coasts.
pachinko	upright pinball-machine game of modern Japan.
raigō	painting of Amida and his host descending to receive the believer; esp. in late Heian and Kamakura periods.
rakugo	style of popular comic-story telling, esp. of Edo period.
rangaku	"Dutch learning," esp. of later Edo period.
renga	linked verse, flourished esp. in Muromachi period.
ritsuryō	"penal and civil codes," esp. those developed from continental precedents in decades around 700 CE.
ritsuryō seido	"system of penal and civil codes" of ritsuryō period.

rōjū	"senior councillor," one of 4–5 members of Tokugawa bakufu's council of senior officials.
rōnin	masterless samurai of Edo period.
ronsō	"literary dispute," a journalistic form of intellectual combat in modern-day Japan.
ryōsai kenbo	"good wife; wise mother," a shibboleth connoting proper womanhood in Imperial Japan.
saibara	folk songs of Heian period.
sake	rice wine.
sankin kōtai	"alternate attendance," hostage system for daimyo in Edo period.
saraike	"saucer pond," shallow water-holding pond to supplement stream flow in irrigating paddy fields, esp. in late Heian-medieval periods.
sarugaku	light entertainments that evolved into tale-telling dance troupes by late Heian.
sarugaku nō	theatrical performance by sarugaku troupes, esp. early Muromachi period.
sasara	"bamboo whisk," beat by sekkyō bushi to establish tempo in medieval tale telling.
sashidashi	survey of land-use rights by examining pertinent land-use documents, esp. in later sixteenth century.
seihen	change of government; political crisis.
seiitaishōgun	"barbarian-subduing generalissimo," shogunal title used by three successive bakufu; derived from ritsuryō-period titles temporarily assigned to commanders of military expeditions.
seinendan	"youth group," esp. those officially promoted in Imperial Japan.
sekkyō bushi	type of medieval tale teller.
sengoku	"warring states," a term of Chinese derivation; in Japan refers to century of endemic warfare after 1460s.
sentō gosho	palace of imperial heir in present-day Kyoto.
sesshō	regent to a child emperor; esp. title appropriated by Hokke Fujiwara leaders in early Heian.
setsuwa	"anecdotal tale," a short prose form, esp. of Heian period.
sewamono	domestic drama, a genre of kabuki play; cf. jidaimono.
shaku	a linear measure; today, 30.3 cm.
shiki	functions (rights and duties), or the document specifying functions, of a participant in a shōen.
shikken	regency of Hōjō leaders in Kamakura bakufu.
shinden	architectural style for mansions of ritsuryō elite.
shinden	"new fields," branch village; suffix added when creating a new village as population grows and more land is cleared for cultivation.
shingaku	"heart learning," a means to wisdom, esp. fostered by Sekimon Shingaku movement in Edo period.
shingeki	"new drama," theatrical style based on European precedent, established in Imperial Japan.
shin kankakuha	"New sensationalist school," literary fashion of 1930s, based on European precedent.
shinkansen	"Bullet train," high-speed trains of Shōwa Genroku period.
shinōkōshō	"samurai–farmer–artisan–merchant," four-status socio-ethical hierarchy of Edo-period ideology.

shinpa	new hybrid drama style, flourished in late Meiji-Taishō period.
shinpan	"related household," Tokugawa term for cadet lineage of shogund line; cf. ichimon of Ashikaga.
shin shinrigakuha	"New psychologist school," literary fashion of 1930s, based on European precedent.
shin shūkyō	"new religion," a term for diverse creeds articulated from late Edo through 1930s; more recent ones called shin shin shūkyō.
shintaishi	"new-style poetry," verse based on foreign precedents, mainly European; esp. later Meiji onward.
shirabyōshi	female dancer-entertainer, esp. popular at late Heian court.
shishi	political activist, esp. of 1860s.
shishōsetsu	"I novel," literary form; emerged in late Meiji and flourished into Shōwa Genroku period.
shiso	a species of Asian mint; *Perilla frutescens*.
shizen shugi	"naturalism," literary style promoted in late Meiji period; in critique of gesaku.
shizoku	"gentry," title awarded to declassed samurai by Meiji rulers.
shōen	corporate estates; manorial lands, esp. of Heian period.
shoin	architectural style of Muromachi period; survives to today.
shōji	"sliding door," made of translucent paper on light wood frame; integral to shoin architecture.
shokunin	"tradesmen," emerged as identifiable social category in late medieval period.
shoshidai	Kyoto magistrate; senior Tokugawa official in Kyoto.
shōya	village headman; one of several terms so used in Edo period.
shunga	"spring pictures," erotic art, esp. of Edo period.
shūu	autumn rain; notably that from typhoons.
sō	self-governing village association of medieval period.
sōja	provincial Shintō administrative office of ritsuryō period.
sonnō jōi	"revere the emperor; expel the barbarian," political ideal and instrumental slogan of 1860s.
sueki	"Sue ware," high-fired, wheel-thrown stoneware introduced from continent during fifth century.
sugi	cryptomeria; *Cryptomeria japonica*.
suiboku	ink-line painting, introduced from continent, esp. during Muromachi period; also called sumi-e.
suijaku	*See* honji suijaku.
suiko	seed rice loan; an overseer's way to assure availability of seed rice at planting time, roughly fifth century onward.
sumi-e	*See* suiboku.
sumō	Japanese heavyweight wrestling.
sushi	diverse dishes based on vinegered, seasoned rice.
taifū	"typhoon," cyclonic storm of western Pacific; cf. hurricane.
taihei	"the great peace," laudatory term for Edo period.
tandai	resident representative of Kamakura bakufu in Kyoto.
tanka	"short poem," modern term for 31-syllable waka.
tatami	sedge mat; integral part of shoin architecture; emerged in Muromachi period; cf. igusa.
tenjinsama	spirit of Sugawara no Michizane; deity of Kitano and other Tenjin shrines; from later Heian onward.

tenka	"the realm," political concept favored from late sixteenth century onward.
tenka fubu	"Rule the Realm by Force," phrase credited to Oda Nobunaga.
tenkō	rehabilitation or conversion; police strategy of 1930s.
tennō	emperor of Japan; title in use since about 700 CE.
tōfu	soy-paste cake.
tokonoma	decorative alcove; element in shoin architecture.
tokusei	"act of virtuous rule," an edict of debt relief or cancellation; esp. from later Kamakura period.
tonseisha	recluse; esp. during late Heian and medieval periods.
ton'ya	merchant house; from medieval period; flourished in Edo period.
tozama	"outside lord," in medieval period, bushi leader external to one's band of vassals; in Edo period, daimyo lineages not sworn to Tokugawa before 1600.
tsuchi ikki	"solidarities of the locale," local rural organizations and their protest activity of Muromachi period.
tsuke shoin	writing alcove; element in shoin architecture.
uchi harai	"shell and repel," tactic for driving off foreign vessels, esp. in early nineteenth century.
uchi kowashi	"house smashing," form of urban protest in later Edo period.
uji	lineage group, esp. those favored by rulers from fifth century onward.
ujigami	deity of a lineage group.
uji no kami	chief of a lineage group.
ukiyo	"floating world," the pleasurable but evanescent life, esp. in Edo-period literature and arts.
ukiyo-e	"floating-world art," esp. of Edo period.
ukiyo zōshi	"floating-world tales," secular narrative literature, esp. of middle Edo period.
ume	plum; *Prunus mume*.
uta-e	poem art; a favored art form of Heian period; cf. byōbu-uta.
wabicha	"poverty tea," style of ceremonial tea drinking practiced by urban elites in sengoku period.
wabun	"Japanese-style writing," kana-syllabary type of writing favored by women of Heian court.
waka	"Japanese poem," as distinct from Chinese-style poem; esp. of ritsuryō period, but practiced thereafter; cf. tanka.
wakan renku	linked poetry that alternated stanzas of Chinese and Japanese verse; esp. during Kamakura period.
wakō	"Japanese pirates," piratical traders on East Asian littoral, esp. in Kamakura-Muromachi periods.
watakushi shōsetsu	*See* shishōsetsu.
wayō setchū	"combination of East and West," cultural ideal advocated in Imperial Japan.
yaku	use rights and duties *vis-à-vis* land and other matters, esp. in Edo period; cf. shiki.
yakuza	criminal gangs, esp. in twentieth century.
yamabushi	mountain ascetics, mainly of Shugendō tradition.

yamase	cooling effect of summer polar air over Tōhoku.
yen	modern coinage introduced in Meiji period.
yōga	"Western painting," art category of late Meiji onward.
yoki hito	"good people," self-appelation of Heian elite.
yōma	"Western style room," esp. in twentieth-century houses.
yonaoshi	"world renewal," term evocative of radical social change, esp. in late Edo period.
yūgei	gentlemanly accomplishments; cultural ideal of seventeenth-century Kyoto *cognoscenti*.
yūgen	"graceful elegance," in nō drama; aesthetic canon derived from older poetic ideal of subtle mystery.
za	licensed commercial groups, esp. of later Heian and medieval periods.
zadankai	"roundtable discussion," format for give and take among intellectuals; esp. in twentieth century.
zaibatsu	family combine; form of large-scale business organization; arose in late Meiji and flourished in 1920s and 1930s.
zaigō gunjinkai	military reservist association; flourished in Imperial Japan.
zen'ei bijutsu	"avant garde art," an art category of 1930s onward.
zuihitsu	"miscellany," a literary category, esp. of later Heian onward.

Appendix D: Supplemental Readings

Note: Other valuable works that deserve attention are cited in the endnotes of this volume.

Reference Readings

Basic bibliographies; Scholarly journals; Reference works; General works.

Basic bibliographies

Bibliographies relating to Japan are innumerable, but most are selective, specialized, and out of date. At present the most useful and current general bibliography on Japanese history is John W. Dower with T. S. George, *Japanese History and Culture from Ancient to Modern Times: Seven Basic Bibliographies*, 2d edn. (NY: Markus Wiener Publishing, 1995). It will lead one to more specialized bibliographies as well as reference works and secondary sources. The annual *Bibliography of Asian Studies* (Ann Arbor: Association for Asian Studies), although cumbersome to use, enables the diligent student to conduct an exhaustive search for materials in English (and some other European languages) on any facet of Japanese (or other Asian) history. The *BAS* is now available electronically, and in that form it is very convenient to use on the Internet.

Materials in Japanese are, of course, immensely more voluminous than those in English, and searches are commensurately more difficult. As a result selective bibliographies have proliferated, but they tend to be idiosyncratic in selection, to become obsolete quickly, and hence to miss much that a student may find useful. There are, however, two well-organized sources that will guide a reader to other bibliographies and reference works and also permit exhaustive searching on specific topics. One is the journal *Shigaku zasshi* (Tokyo: Tokyo Daigaku Bungakubu), edited by Shigakkai. Its monthly issues contain, in addition to scholarly essays, well organized listings of current scholarship in all fields of history (Japanese and foreign). And its thick May issue consists of critiques, by experts in the fields under review, of the past year's scholarly corpus. The other is the multi-volume *Nihon keizaishi dai (1–7) bunken* (Kyoto: Nihon Keizaishi Kenkyūjo of Osaka Keizai Daigaku, 1933–77), edited by Eijirō Honjō and his successors. Its successive volumes present in a well-organized topical order the published source materials and secondary scholarship of the several years since the preceding volume. A researcher can use the Honjō volumes to locate pre-1970 works, turning to *Shigaku zasshi* for more recent ones.

SCHOLARLY JOURNALS

The field of Japanese history is blessed with good scholarly journals. In Japanese, of course, the number is immense, as perusal of bibliographical citations in *Shigaku zasshi* will reveal. In English the most valuable journal is *Monumenta Nipponica*, which treats the subject broadly, although giving fullest attention to cultural history. Its essays are, as a rule, solidly researched, concise, well written, and of enduring worth. And until the late 1990s its book review coverage of English-language works was exceptionally complete, concise, and current. The *Journal of Japanese Studies* devotes a portion of its pages to historical topics in essays that most commonly are politico-economic in content and that tend to be longer than those of *MN*. The *Harvard Journal of Asiatic Studies*, like *JJS*, offers mostly longer essays, but with a greater focus on topics in cultural history. Only a portion of its space is devoted to Japan. *Acta Asiatica* presents the work of Japanese scholars in translation. Like *HJAS*, it covers more than Japan but frequently carries essays on Japanese history. The *Japanese Journal of Religious Studies* is a particularly valuable source for essays on topics in religious history, while *Transactions of the Asiatic Society of Japan* offers generally short pieces on diverse topics. The *Bulletin of Concerned Asian Scholars*, *Journal of Asian Studies*, *Journal of Asian History*, *Modern Asian Studies*, the *Japan Quarterly*, the *American Historical Review*, and numerous disciplinary journals in archaeology, art history, religious studies, economics, anthropology, and other fields carry occasional essays, some of them very valuable, on aspects of Japanese history. See the Dower and George bibliography cited above, pp. 427–30, for an extensive listing.

REFERENCE WORKS

The single most valuable English-language reference work on Japanese history remains the *Kōdansha Encyclopedia of Japan*, 9 vols. (Tokyo: Kōdansha, 1983). Changing intellectual priorities and perspectives make it less than wholly satisfying, particularly in its broader-ranging essays, and it is, of course, dated on recent developments. Nevertheless, it continues to contain the mother lode of reliable detail on innumerable historical topics. The titles of other, more specialized reference works can be gleaned from Dower and George, *Japanese History and Culture*, pp. 417–24. In Japanese, reference works are legion, but two major encyclopedias of Japanese history deserve citation: the beautiful *Nihon rekishi daijiten*, 22 vols. (Tokyo: Kawade Shōbo Shinsha, 1961), and the more recent *Nihonshi daijiten*, 7 vols. (Tokyo: Heibonsha, 1992–94). For biographical information, Nichigai Asoshietsu, comp., *Jinbutsu refarensu jiten*, 5 vols. (Tokyo: Kinokuniya, 1983) provides the most reliable birth and death dates and guidance to fuller citations in major biographical encyclopedieas. For death dates of notable people from 1995 onward, consult the annual volumes of *Asahi nenkan* (Tokyo: Asahi shinbunsha).

GENERAL WORKS

A major collection of essays that covers many aspects of Japan's history from origins to about 1960 is the *Cambridge History of Japan*, 6 vols. (Cambridge: CUP, 1988ff). As a whole it reflects the dominant intellectual perspectives of the 1960s–70s, and it has, as a consequence, become dated rather more rapidly than the *Kōdansha Encyclopedia*. Nonetheless it remains, primarily in the areas of elite political and economic history, a rich source of information and scholarly interpretation. Somewhat more dated, but still serviceable in many areas, is George B. Sansom's *History of Japan*, 3 vols. (Stanford: SUP, 1958–63), which follows the story from Japan's origins to the mid-nineteenth century. For a delightful visual safari through Japanese history, see the lavishly illustrated *Japan, A History in Art* (Garden City, NY: Doubleday, 1964), by Bradley Smith. Two useful collections of source materials in translation are the venerable *Sources of the Japanese Tradition* (NY: CUP, 1958), compiled by Ryusaku Tsunoda et al., and the recently updated *Sources of Japanese History* by David J. Lu, now titled *Japan: A Documentary History*, 2 vols. (Armonk, NY: M.E. Sharpe, Inc., 1996). Shorter textbook treatments of the history are numerous, and Dower and George, *Japanese History and Culture, passim*, lists most of them.

FURTHER READINGS FOR PART I

Geography; Forager culture.

GEOGRAPHY

As a discipline geography has fared poorly of late, much of it becoming scattered among such related disciplines as geology, anthropology, and economics. Perhaps for that reason the best general geography of Japan is still the badly dated *Japan, A Geography* (Madison: The University of Wisconsin Press, 1965) by Glenn T. Trewartha. A newer collection of technical essays is The Association of Japanese Geographers, ed. *Geography of Japan* (Tokyo: Teikoku-shoin Co., Ltd., 1980). Valuable essays on select topics in geography and paleo-geography also appear in various journals and collections of essays.

On geology more specifically, Takashi Yoshida, ed. *An Outline of the Geology of Japan*, 3d edn. (Kawasaki: Geological Survey of Japan, 1976), provides a concise discussion. A highly detailed technical study that reflects recent gains in geological understanding is Toshio Kimura et al., *Geology of Japan* (Tokyo: UTP, 1991). An abundance of splendid atlases and maps is available in Japanese, and a convenient English-language atlas is *Teikoku's Complete Atlas of Japan* (Tokyo: Teikoku-shoin Co., Ltd., 1977).

FORAGER CULTURE

The archaeological literature on Japan is rich. And new knowledge and interpretation keep appearing thanks to the energetic salvage archaeology that has accompanied Japan's frenetic construction activity of the past few decades. One consequence of the field's vitality, however, is that secondary works rapidly become dated. Still, the exceptionally succinct, thoughtful, and readable essay by Fumiko Ikawa-Smith, "Current Issues in Japanese Archaeology," *American Scientist* 68/2 (1980): 134–45, remains a valuable point of entrée. The most recent general text is Keiji Imamura's *Prehistoric Japan, New Perspectives on Insular East Asia* (Honolulu: UHP, 1996). A remarkable collection of twenty seven specialized essays is *Windows on the Japanese Past: Studies in Archaeology and Prehistory* (Ann Arbor: Center for Japanese Studies, Univ. of Michigan, 1986), edited by Richard J. Pearson. See also Pearson's *Ancient Japan* (NY: George Braziller, 1992). A helpful recent treatment of East Asian archaeology more broadly is Gina L. Barnes, *China, Korea and Japan: The Rise of Civilization in East Asia* (London: Thames & Hudson, 1993).

FURTHER READINGS FOR PART II

Early centuries; *Ritsuryō* period.

EARLY CENTURIES

The early centuries of dispersed agriculture are known mainly from archaeological sources. Besides pertinent portions of works cited above, a particularly revealing essay is "Yoshinogari: A Yayoi Settlement in Northern Kyushu," by Mark Hudson and Gina Barnes, in *MN* 46/2 (Summer 1991): 211–35. In his most recent work, *Sacred Texts and Buried Treasures: Issues in the Historical Archaeology of Ancient Japan* (Honolulu: UHP, 1998), William Wayne Farris reviews the historiography and current understanding of four hardy issues in this history: the identity of Yamatai, ancient Korean–Japanese relations, the scale and character of early Yamato capitals, and the significance of *mokkan*, or wooden-strip documents. See also the relevant essays in volume I of the *Cambridge History*.

Regarding written sources, pertinent portions of the Chinese chronicles are available in Ryusaku Tsunoda tr., and L. Carrington Goodrich, ed., *Japan in the Chinese Dynastic Histories* (South Pasadena: P.D. and Ione Perkins, 1951). For elite political process and foreign relations during the centuries ca. 500–697 CE, the translation of *Nihon shoki* by W. G. Aston, *Nihongi: Chronicles of Japan from the Earliest Time to A.D. 697* (reissued by Charles E. Tuttle, 1972), is of great use. Information on aspects of domestic society ca. 600–700 is available in the gazetteers (*fudoki*) recently translated by Michiko Y. Aoki, *Records of Wind and Earth* (Ann Arbor: AAS, 1997). A recent scholarly study of political history ca. 250–750, which includes a good listing of earlier works, is Joan R. Piggott, *The Emergence of Japanese Kingship* (Stanford: SUP, 1997).

RITSURYŌ PERIOD

For later centuries, written sources and secondary works proliferate, as perusal of Dower and George, *Japanese History and Culture*, reveals. And the newly issued volume 2 of the *Cambridge History* treats these centuries, particularly their political and institutional history, and provides guides to earlier works.

The foundational history of agriculture and the broader history of demographics and social process have received minimal treatment, doubtless because documentation is thin. William Wayne Farris, *Population, Disease, and Land in Early Japan, 645–900* (Cambridge, MA: HUP, 1985), is a pioneering exploration of the interplay among those variables during the eighth century. And Dana Morris, "Peasant Economy in Early Japan, 650–950" (Ann Arbor: University Microfilms, 1980), a Ph.D. thesis that, regrettably, has not been published, attempts a longer-term study of the classical economy's agricultural foundation. Thomas Kierstead sheds light on the operation of the late Heian fisc and its landed base in *The Geography of Power in Medieval Japan* (Princeton: PUP, 1992).

At higher political levels, a dated but still useful general study of political institutions that treats historical change as an internally driven, evolutionary process is John W. Hall, *Government and Local Power in Japan, 500–1700* (Princeton: PUP, 1966). William Wayne Farris's *Heavenly Warriors, the Evolution of Japan's Military, 500–1300* (Cambridge, MA: HUP, 1992), examines the linkage between changes in the economy and the organization and use of military power. Central politics of early and later Heian, respectively, are treated in Robert Borgen, *Sugawara no Michizane and the Early Heian Court* (Cambridge, MA: HUP, 1986), and G. Cameron Hurst III, *Insei, Abdicated Sovereigns in the Politics of Late Heian Japan, 1086–1185* (NY: CUP, 1976). And facets of dyarchy are explored in the several monographs and essay collections of Jeffrey P. Mass, most notably the volume of essays titled *Court and Bakufu in Japan* (New Haven: YUP, 1982).

Higher culture – arts, letters, and religious thought – has, with good reason, received the richest scholarly treatment of any topic area. A recent survey of the literary corpus that is unusually readable, thoughtful, comprehensive, and well organized is Donald Keene, *Seeds in the Heart: Japanese Literature from Earliest Times to the Late Sixteenth Century* (NY: Henry Holt, 1993). Keene's work will lead readers to the rich body of earlier studies. A severely dated but readable, and in some ways delightful, general introduction to Heian court culture that one uses for want of a more up-to-date alternative is Ivan Morris's *World of the Shining Prince* (NY: Knopf, 1964). Its interpretation of the age relies heavily, and not always critically, on Murasaki Shikibu's great fictional masterpiece *Genji monogatari* (*Tale of Genji*). Two translations of the *Genji* – an older one by Arthur Waley (reissued by Random House in 1960); a newer one by Edward Seidensticker (NY: Knopf, 1976) – are available, together with a rich ancillary scholarly corpus. In particular one might mention Doris G. Bargen, *A Woman's Weapon, Spirit Possession in the Tale of Genji* (Honolulu: UHP, 1997), whose bibliography will lead to earlier works. Among the many other fine translations and scholarly works on classical higher culture, perhaps the most revealing is William H. and Helen Craig McCullough, *A Tale of Flowering Fortunes*, 2 vols. (Stanford: SUP, 1980), a translation of *Eiga monogatari* that gives readers a remarkable entrée to the court life of its time. One should note the book's appendices and maps, which provide a rich sense of context.

On classical religion, a general work with a good bibliography is the new edition of Joseph M. Kitagawa, *Religion in Japanese History* (NY: CUP, 1990). A work that examines, in a looser chronological manner, the role of religion in society is Ichiro Hori, *Folk Religion in Japan, Continuities and Change* (Chicago: UCP, 1968). A number of admirable monographs, as cited in Dower and George, *Japanese History and Culture*, pp. 72–84, have enriched our understanding immensely. Thus, Yoshito S. Hakeda, *Kūkai, Major Works* (NY: CUP, 1972), is a valuable study of a distinguished theologian. And Alan G. Grapard, *The Protocol of the Gods, A Study of the Kasuga Cult in Japanese History* (Berkeley: UCP, 1992), is the most fully developed expression of recent attempts to understand classical religion's role as an institutional element in Heian society.

Classical art and architecture have also received valuable attention. Pertinent chapters of the grand old treatise by Robert Treat Paine and Alexander Soper, *Art and Architecture of Japan*, rev. edn. (London: Penguin Books, 1981), remain a basic point of departure, and Penelope Mason, *History of Japanese Art* (NY: Harry N. Abrams, 1993), offers a well illustrated update. Several monographic studies, short and long, flesh out – or revise the interpretation of – particular details. Two recent ones merit note. Elizabeth ten Grotenhuis, *Japanese Mandalas, Representations of Sacred Geography* (Honolulu: UHP, 1999), is a thoughtful, richly illustrated work with a very helpful bibliography; Mimi Hall Yiengpruksawan, *Hiraizumi, Buddhist Art and Regional Politics in Twelfth-Century Japan* (Cambridge, MA: HUP, 1998), situates its study of art and architecture in the sociopolitical culture of the day.

Music and dance have also been treated, though much less extensively than art. For music, a descriptive introduction is Shigeo Kishibe, *The Traditional Music of Japan* (Tokyo: The Japan Foundation, 1966). A delightfully revealing study of late Heian musical lyrics and their cultural content and context is Yung-Hee Kim, *Songs to Make the Dust Dance: The* Ryōjin hishō *of Twelfth-Century Japan* (Berkeley: UCP, 1994), whose bibliography will lead to earlier works.

FURTHER READINGS FOR PART III

Medieval; Early modern; Early Meiji.

Historians, being predominantly interested in elite politics, generally segment the centuries of intensive agriculture (dated here 1250–1890) in terms of political chronology. Most studies fall within segments designated "medieval" (*chūsei*: Kamakura/Muromachi), "early modern" (*kinsei*: Azuchi-Momoyama/Edo), or "early Meiji," and that arrangement is perforce followed here.

MEDIEVAL

Elite politics, including foreign relations, have been explored in great detail. A sustained narrative treatment is available in Sansom's *History of Japan*, mainly in volume 2. Aspects of political organization and process are detailed in the earlier-noted *Government and Local Politics* by Hall, in several other book-length monographs cited in Dower and George, *Japanese History and Culture*, pp. 37–44, and in the recent volume by Andrew Edmund Goble, *Kenmu: Go-Daigo's Revolution* (Cambridge, MA: HUP, 1996). See also pertinent essays in the *Cambridge History*, vol. 3; Jeffrey P. Mass, ed., *The Origins of Japan's Medieval World: Courtiers, Clerics, Warriors, and Peasants in the Fourteenth Century* (Stanford: SUP, 1997), and John W. Hall and Takeshi Toyoda, eds., *Japan in the Muromachi Age* (Berkeley: UCP, 1977). A richly discursive examination of life and politics in Kyoto during the century after the Ōnin War is Mary Elizabeth Berry, *The Culture of Civil War in Kyoto* (Berkeley: UCP, 1994).

The medieval economy has received far less attention, although somewhat more than that of Heian. Broad integrations of demographic trends, changes in agricultural technology, and commercial-political developments are only beginning to appear in English, as seen in essays by Keiji Nagahara and Kozo Yamamura in the *Cambridge History*, vol. 3, pp. 301–95. One of the most promising studies to date is the unpublished Ph.D. dissertation of Kristina Kade Troost, "Common Property and Community Formation: Self-Governing Villages in Late Medieval Japan" (Harvard University, 1990). Its contents are suggested by her essay, "Peasants, Elites, and Villages in the Fourteenth Century" in Mass, ed., *The Origins of Japan's Medieval World*, pp. 91–109, cited above. A more closely focused study of economic change is *Community and Commerce in Late Medieval Japan, The Corporate Villages of Tokuchin-ho* (Stanford: SUP, 1992), by Hitomi Tonomura. Medieval fisheries remain unstudied, and only a brief overview of forest trends is available in chapter 2 of Conrad Totman, *The Green Archipelago, Forestry in Pre-Industrial Japan* (Berkeley: UCP, 1989).

Tonomura has also been a pioneer in the study of women in medieval Japan, a subject on which information is scarce, most of it pertaining to the favored few. See her essay, "Re-visioning Women in the Post-Kamakura Age," in Mass, ed., *The Origins of Japan's Medieval World*, pp. 138–69, whose notes and bibliography will lead to other pertinent works. See also Barbara Ruch, "The Other Side of Culture in Medieval Japan," in *The Cambridge History*, vol. 3, pp. 500–43.

Cultural history of the medieval elite has been richly treated, with numerous fine works examining facets of literature, art, drama, and religion. As entries in Dower and George, *Japanese History and Culture*, *passim*, indicate very nicely, the Nō drama, like the earlier *Tale of Genji*, has been a focus of much scholarship, and the tea ceremony, trends in residential architecture, and garden design have also received attention.

On religion, and Buddhism in particular, William M. Bodiford, *Sōtō Zen in Medieval Japan* (Honolulu: UHP, 1993), examines a major development, and his bibliography will guide one to earlier studies, including James C. Dobbins's *Jōdo Shinshū, Shin Buddhism in Medieval Japan* (Bloomington: Indiana University Press, 1989). On medieval Shintō, Mark Teeuwen, *Watarai Shintō, An Intellectual History of the Outer Shrine in Ise* (Leiden: Research School CNWS, 1996), provides a critical study of rhetoric and a bibliography of earlier works.

Prose and poetry of the era have been studied more fully of late, as exemplified by two recent works: Virginia Skord, tr., *Tales of Tears and Laughter, Short Fiction of Medieval Japan* (Honolulu: UHP, 1991), and Robert H. Brower, tr., *Conversations with Shōtetsu* (Ann Arbor: Center for Japanese Studies, The University of Michigan, 1992). For broader coverage of the literature, see the earlier-cited work by Keene, *Seeds in the Heart*, and for a discursive interpretation, Michele Marra, *Representations of Power: The Literary Politics of Medieval Japan* (Honolulu: UHP, 1993). On broader social implications of cultural production see the above-noted essay by Barbara Ruch in *Cambridge History*, vol. 3, and her "Medieval Jongleurs and the Making of a National Literature, in Hall and Toyoda, *Japan in the Muromachi Age*, pp. 279–312.

EARLY MODERN

The surviving documentary record on early modern Japan is substantially greater than that of the medieval centuries, and secondary scholarship reflects the difference, as evidenced by entries in Dower and George, *Japanese History and Culture*, pp. 43–48, 100–38. Volumes 4 and 5 of the *Cambridge History* contain lengthy essays on a broad range of topics. A recent overview of the history is Conrad Totman, *Early Modern Japan* (Berkeley: UCP, 1993), which cites specialized works and bibliographical references in its footnotes and its bibliographical essay, pp. 567–77. A number of those studies are also cited in endnotes of this volume; suffice here to note salient works that have appeared since *Early Modern Japan* was prepared.

As a whole the focus of scholarship on early modern Japan has shifted from political to social agendas. And those works that address politics now focus not on the "center," the *bakufu*, but on the "periphery" and on a "bottom up" approach to political relationships. Thus Philip Brown, *Central Authority and Local Autonomy in the Formation of Early Modern Japan, The Case of Kaga Domain* (Stanford: SUP, 1993), emphasizes the level of autonomy retained by leaders of Kaga domain. Herman Ooms, *Tokugawa Village Practice: Class, Status, Power, Law* (Berkeley: UCP, 1996), looks at ruler-ruled and superior-inferior relations from the latter's perspective. And two new works – Luke S. Roberts, *Mercantilism in a Japanese Domain, the Merchant Origins of Economic Nationalism in 18th-Century Tosa* (Cambridge: CUP, 1998) and Mark Ravina, *Land and Lordship in Early Modern Japan* (Stanford: SUP, 1999) – examine politico-economics in daimyo domains.

The issues of social tension and conflict that Ooms examines are also treated in two quantitative analyses by James W. White: *The Demography of Sociopolitical Conflict in Japan, 1721–1846* (Berkeley: Institute of East Asian Studies, University of California, 1992), and *Ikki: Social Conflict and Political Protest in Early Modern Japan* (Ithaca: Cornell University Press, 1995).

Ooms's work also gives us new insights into village life more broadly, while Arne Kalland, *Fishing Villages in Tokugawa Japan* (Honolulu: UHP, 1995), offers a rich sense of such villages in northern Kyushu. Also on fisheries, David L. Howell, *Capitalism from Within: Economy, Society, and the State in a Japanese Fishery* (Berkeley: UCP, 1994), explores the central role of the herring catch in Ainu–Japanese relations from Tokugawa through Meiji times. In other areas of primary production, Edo-period mining has still not received close attention, but Conrad Totman, *The Lumber Industry in Early Modern Japan* (Honolulu: UHP, 1995), examines aspects of forest output in the context of commercial history.

Howell's is one of three recent works that examine trade and regional interactions. Constantine Nomikos Vaporis, *Breaking Barriers, Travel and the State in Early Modern Japan* (Cambridge, MA: HUP, 1994), explores the Edo-period highway system and its diverse and changing social and economic roles. And Kären Wigen, *The Making of a Japanese Periphery, 1750–1920* (Berkeley: UCP, 1995), illuminates the role of geographical determinants in shaping the local impact of Tokugawa-Meiji economic change in a mountain-girt region of central Japan.

Wigen's work, like that of Kalland, also illustrates the broader ecological perspective that is starting to inform scholarship on early modern Japan. Interest in demographic issues, which generated lively scholarship during the 1970s and eighties, has, however, diminished. Ann Bowman Jannetta published two essays on mortality rates in successive issues of *Population Studies* 45 (1991): 417–36 and 46 (1992): 427–43, and a newer essay by Laurel L. Cornell, "Infanticide in Early Modern Japan? Demography, Culture, and Population Growth," *JAS* 55/1 (Feb. 1996): 22–50, is particularly valuable for both its contents and its bibliography.

The "center" has not been entirely ignored, but recently scholars have studied Edo's society more than its polity. Aspects of the city are examined in several essays in James L. McClain et al., eds., *Edo and Paris, Urban Life & the State in the Early Modern Era* (Ithaca: Cornell University Press, 1994). Kokichi Katsu, *Musui's Story, The Autobiography of a Tokugawa Samurai*, translated by Teruko Craig (Tucson: University of Arizona Press, 1991), reveals less-than-Confucian aspects of samurai life in nineteenth-century Edo, and Gary P. Leupp, *Servants, Shophands, and Laborers in the Cities of Tokugawa Japan* (Princeton: PUP, 1992), explores major segments of the urban lower class. In *Male Colors, the Construction of Homosexuality in Tokugawa Japan* (Berkeley: UCP, 1995), Leupp examines Edo's tradition of recreational bisexuality, particularly its expression in commercial literature and art. Cecilia Segawa Seigle, *Yoshiwara, The Glittering World of the Japanese Courtesan* (Honolulu: UHP, 1993), focuses on the heterosexual world of Edo's famous licensed quarter, its organization, operation, and evolution, its elegant cultural image, and its not so elegant social character.

Seigle's work reflects another welcome trend in this scholarship, the emergence of studies focused on women. Kikue Yamakawa, *Women of the Mito Domain, Recollections of Samurai Life*, translated by Kate Wildman Nakai (Tokyo: UTP, 1992), offers a richly rewarding look at Mito and its samurai women around the 1860s. Several essays in Gail Lee Bernstein, ed., *Recreating Japanese Women, 1600–1945* (Berkeley: UCP, 1991), treat aspects of women's experience during the Edo period. Also, the subject matter of Susan B. Hanley, *Everyday Things in Premodern Japan, the Hidden Legacy of Material Culture* (Berkeley: UCP, 1997), pertains to women at least as much as to men.

Intellectual and cultural production, particularly of the eighteenth century, continues to receive attention. Samuel Hideo Yamashita, *Master Sorai's Responsals, An Annotated Translation of* Sorai sensei tōmonsho (Honolulu: UHP, 1994), adds to our corpus of Ogyū Sorai's writings, while Janine Anderson Sawada, *Confucian Values and Popular Zen, Sekimon Shingaku in Eighteenth-Century Japan* (Honolulu: UHP, 1993), enriches our understanding of Shingaku during its heyday in the later eighteenth century. A pair of recent works contain translations from two of the century's most iconoclastic thinkers: Toshinobu Yasunaga, *Andō Shōeki: Social and Ecological Philosopher in Eighteenth-Century Japan* (NY: Weatherhill, 1992), and Bob Tadashi Wakabayashi, *Japanese Loyalism Reconstrued, Yamagata Daini's* Ryūshi shinron *of 1759* (Honolulu: UHP, 1995).

Two recent literary studies jointly illustrate the enduring celebrity of the *Tale of Genji* and the rise of a commercialized popular culture during the Edo period. James McMullen, *Genji gaiden: the Origins of Kumazawa Banzan's Commentary on the Tale of Genji* (Exeter: Ithaca Press, 1992), describes how Kumazawa, a celebrated samurai scholar, engaged in serious study of the *Genji* during the 1660s, employing it to illustrate pious Confucian virtues. Andrew Lawrence Markus, *The Willow in Autumn: Ryūtei Tanehiko, 1783–1842* (Cambridge, MA: HUP, 1993), is a biographical study of the popular samurai writer, Takaya Hikoshirō, who, using his pen name, gained fame and some fortune during the 1830s as the author of *Nise Murasaki Inaka Genji*, a commercially inspired, serialized lampooning of the *Genji*.

In the field of art history Joan Stanley-Baker, *The Transmission of Chinese Idealist Painting to Japan, Notes on the Early Phase (1661–1799)* (Ann Arbor, Center for Japanese Studies, the University of Michigan, 1992), merits note. It reveals the continuing influence of Chinese painting on Japan's art world, showing in yet another field the extent of foreign contact that persisted through the Edo period. That broader theme is also reflected in Marius Jansen, *China in the Tokugawa World* (Cambridge, MA: HUP, 1992).

EARLY MEIJI

A broadly conceived treatment of the Meiji Restoration that is still impressive in its breadth and judiciousness is W. G. Beasley, *The Meiji Restoration* (Stanford: SUP, 1972). More recently essays in Marius B. Jansen and Gilbert Rozman, eds., *Japan in Transition, from Tokugawa to Meiji* (Princeton: PUP, 1986), and several essays in volume 5 of the *Cambridge History* examine aspects of early Meiji. Because editors of the six-volume *Studies in the Modernization of Japan* (Princeton: PUP, 1965–1971) treated the Restoration as the start of modern Japan, many of the articles in that series, notably those in Donald H. Shively, ed., *Tradition and Modernization in Japanese Culture* (Princeton: PUP, 1971), deal with the early Meiji decades. And Dower and George, *Japanese History and Culture*, pp. 135–50 and *passim*, lists many more specialized studies.

The reformist mood of the early Tokyo intelligentsia, which has been one focus of English-language scholarship, is vividly apparent in William Reynolds Braisted, tr., *Meiroku zasshi, Journal of the Japanese Enlightenment* (Cambridge, MA: HUP, 1976). And the educational reform that this mood inspired is examined in Mark E. Lincicome, *Principle, Praxis, and the Politics of Educational Reform in Meiji Japan* (Honolulu: UHP, 1995), whose bibliography will lead readers to the many earlier works on this topic.

Studies of elite politics and politicians are numerous. The symbolic role of the Meiji emperor is richly explored in Takashi Fujitani, *Splendid Monarchy, Power and Pageantry in Modern Japan* (Berkeley: UCP, 1996). On the formation of the Meiji Constitution, two of many titles are the early study by George Akita, *Foundations of Constitutional Government in Modern Japan, 1868–1900* (Cambridge, MA: HUP,

1967) and more recently Junji Banno, *The Establishment of the Japanese Constitutional System* (London: Routledge, 1992), translated by J. A. A. Stockwin.

On public unrest, see Roger W. Bowen, *Rebellion and Democracy in Meiji Japan, A Study of Commoners in the Popular Rights Movement* (Berkeley: UCP, 1980). And on quieter, perhaps more consequential forms of public political engagement, see Neil Waters, *Japan's Local Pragmatists: The Transition from Bakumatsu to Meiji in the Kawasaki Region* (Cambridge, MA: HUP, 1983). On the political unease of middle Meiji, Kenneth B. Pyle, *The New Generation in Meiji Japan, Problems of Cultural Identity, 1885–1895* (Stanford: SUP, 1969), remains invaluable. The separating of Shintō and Buddhism is studied in James Edward Ketelaar, *Of Heretics and Martyrs in Meiji Japan, Buddhism and Its Persecution* (Princeton: PUP, 1990), and Helen Hardacre, *Shintō and the State, 1868–1988* (Princeton: PUP, 1989).

On the economy, a pioneering study of early Meiji industrial development is Thomas C. Smith, *Political Change and Industrial Development in Japan: Government Enterprise, 1868–1880* (Stanford: SUP, 1955). In the manner of the Princeton *Studies* and the Fujitani and Hardacre volumes, however, more recent works on industrialization usually treat early Meiji as prologue and follow the story proper well into the twentieth century. Many other facets of early Meiji, as well, are treated in works that carry their story beyond the 1890s. On the Meiji press, for example, James L. Huffman, *Creating a Public, People and Press in Meiji Japan* (Honolulu: UHP, 1997) follows the story through 1912. Similarly, studies of diplomatic history, and also works on social change and cultural production, often follow that pattern, and a number of those titles are cited below.

FURTHER READINGS FOR PART *IV*

Imperial Japan, 1890–1945; Entrepreneurial Japan, 1945–1990.

Works of historical scholarship – to say nothing of primary sources, studies in other disciplines, or the ephemera of punditry – are much more numerous for industrial Japan than for the longer, earlier segments of this history. Two recently updated survey text treatments are W. G. Beasley, *The Rise of Modern Japan* (NY: St. Martin's Press, 1990), and Peter Duus, *Modern Japan* (Boston: Houghton Mifflin, Co., 1998). A convenient introduction to diverse issues of the period is Harry Wray and Hilary Conroy, *Japan Examined, Perspectives on Modern Japanese History* (Honolulu: UHP, 1983). And essays in the earlier-noted Princeton *Studies in the Modernization of Japan* and in volume 6 of the *Cambridge History* treat aspects of the time at greater length.

Almost no historical studies address the broader ecological agenda of human-environment relations, but environmental pollution has received modest attention, as has the topic of technology and its effects. On the other hand, the corpus richly illuminates most of the established fields of inquiry: diplomacy and war; political structure, process, and thought; commerce and the economy; social relations and trends, and cultural production and consumption. Many monographs and essay collections cover both the pre- and post-1945 periods, and writers often – and properly – strive to highlight continuities between the two, but World War II continues in fact to loom large in the corpus as a watershed event, and works are so arranged here.

IMPERIAL JAPAN, 1890–1945

Japan's attempt to "out-empire" the European Powers challenged "Western" interests and *amour propre* so effectively as to make Japan's foreign relations a central area of

English-language scholarly inquiry. Although now somewhat dated, a still-valuable point of approach to the subject is James William Morley, *Japan's Foreign Policy, 1868–1941, A Research Guide* (NY: CUP, 1974). Scholars have continued to study such matters, as amply testified by the scores of recent entries in Dower and George, *Japanese History and Culture*, pp. 205–14, 249–345. Suffice here to mention five comparatively recent works that further illuminate Japan's role as empire builder: W. G. Beasley, *Japanese Imperialism, 1894–1945* (Oxford: Clarendon Press, 1987); Peter Duus, *The Abacus and the Sword; The Japanese Penetration of Korea, 1895–1910* (Berkeley: UCP, 1995); Mark R. Peattie, *Nan'yō, The Rise and Fall of the Japanese in Micronesia, 1885–1945* (Honolulu: UHP, 1988); Ramon H. Myers and Mark R. Peattie, eds., *The Japanese Colonial Empire, 1895–1945* (Princeton: PUP, 1984); and Peter Duus, Ramon H. Myers, and Mark R. Peattie, eds., *The Japanese Informal Empire in China, 1895–1937* (Princeton: PUP, 1989).

The wider diplomacy and the warfare of the years 1937–45 have also been extensively examined, and they continue to receive attention, both scholarly and polemical. English-language treatments of the Pacific War commonly focus on the English-speakers' side of affairs, but a concise and readable study of the Japanese role is Saburō Ienaga, *The Pacific War, 1931–1945, A Critical Perspective on Japan's Role in World War II* (NY: Pantheon, 1978). Thomas R. H. Havens, *Valley of Darkness, The Japanese People and World War Two* (NY: W.W. Norton & Co., 1978), explores wartime life in Japan itself, while other works, such as Ben-Ami Shillony, *Politics and Culture in Wartime Japan* (London: Oxford University Press, 1981); Haruko Taya Cook and Theodore F. Cook, eds., *Japan at War: An Oral History* (NY: The New Press, 1992); and Frank B. Gibney, ed., *Sensō: The Japanese Remember the Pacific War, Letters to the Editor of Asahi Shinbun* (Armonk, NY: M.E. Sharpe, 1995), illuminate facets of the home front and provide recollections of wartime experiences.

Domestic political processes in Imperial Japan have also been studied in depth. On the imperial institution itself, see David Anson Titus, *Palace and Politics in Prewar Japan* (NY: CUP, 1974), and the earlier-noted *Splendid Monarchy* by Fujitani. Mainstream party politics is explored by three older works: Tetsuo Najita, *Hara Kei in the Politics of Compromise, 1905–1915* (Cambridge, MA: HUP, 1967); Peter Duus, *Party Rivalry and Political Change in Taishō Japan* (Cambridge, MA: HUP, 1968); and Gordon Mark Berger, *Parties out of Power in Japan, 1931–1941* (Princeton: PUP, 1977).

The authoritarian state has received much attention, as in two recent studies: Richard H. Mitchell, *Janus-Faced Justice: Political Criminals in Imperial Japan* (Honolulu: UHP, 1992), and Elise K. Tipton, *The Japanese Police State: Tokkō in Interwar Japan* (Honolulu: UHP, 1991). The political "left" is examined in a number of works, including George O. Totten, *The Social Democratic Movement in Prewar Japan* (New Haven: YUP, 1966), and Robert A. Scalapino, *The Japanese Communist Movement, 1920–1966* (Berkeley: UCP, 1967).

On political thought, an excellent study of later Meiji ideology is Carol Gluck, *Japan's Modern Myths, Ideology in the Late Meiji Period* (Princeton: PUP, 1985). A solid study of a major constitutional thinker is Frank O. Miller, *Minobe Tatsukichi, Interpreter of Constitutionalism in Japan* (Berkeley: UCP, 1965). On varieties of "radical" thought, see F. G. Notehelfer, *Kōtoku Shūsui, Portrait of a Japanese Radical* (London: CUP, 1971); Germaine Hoston, *Marxism and the Crisis of Development in Prewar Japan* (Princeton: PUP, 1986); George M. Wilson, *Radical Nationalist in Japan: Kita Ikki 1883–1937* (Cambridge, MA: HUP, 1969); and William Miles Fletcher III, *The Search for a New Order, Intellectuals and Fascism in Prewar Japan* (Chapel Hill, The University of North Carolina Press, 1982).

Rural society and its trends are the focus of several studies. Two works that illuminate village life are the novel *Tsuchi* by Takashi Nagatsuka, translated by Ann Waswo as *The Soil, A Portrait of Rural Life in Meiji Japan* (London: Routledge, 1989), and the scholarly monograph by John F. Embree, *Suye Mura, A Japanese Village* (Chicago: UCP, 1939), a careful ethnography of a village in 1930s Kyushu (see also *The Women of Suye Mura* cited below). On rural social change, see the earlier-cited work by Kären Wigen, *The Making of a Japanese Periphery, 1750–1920*, and Ann Waswo, *Japanese Landlords, The Decline of a Rural Elite* (Berkeley: UCP, 1977). On the politics of "agrarianism," consult Thomas R. H. Havens, *Farm and Nation in Modern Japan, Agrarian Nationalism, 1870–1940* (Princeton: PUP, 1974). The rural economy is examined by James I. Nakamura, *Agricultural Production and the Economic Development of Japan, 1873–1922* (Princeton: PUP, 1966); Penelope Francks, *Technology and Agricultural Development in Pre-war Japan* (New Haven: YUP, 1982), and Richard J. Smethurst, *Agricultural Development and Tenancy Disputes in Japan, 1870–1940* (Princeton: PUP, 1986).

Economic development more broadly has received much attention. A concise survey with useful statistical tables is the old but solid work by G. C. Allen, *A Short Economic History of Modern Japan, 1867–1937* (London: George Allen & Unwin Ltd., 1946). For more detail overall, see the magisterial, old treatment by William W. Lockwood, *The Economic Development of Japan, Growth and Structural Change, 1868–1938* (Princeton: PUP, 1954), and more recently Takafusa Nakamura, *Economic Growth in Prewar Japan* (New Haven: YUP, 1983). William Miles Fletcher III, *The Japanese Business Community and National Trade Policy, 1920–1942* (Chapel Hill: The University of North Carolina Press, 1989), examines the evolution of overall policy within the organized industrial elite, and several recent works examine particular industries and issues, as Dower and George, *Japanese History and Culture*, pp. 157–74, reveals.

The environmental effects of industrialization have received little treatment, save for the notorious Ashio pollution affair of the 1890s. The pioneering book-length work on that topic is Kenneth Strong, *Ox Against the Storm, A Biography of Tanaka Shōzō: Japan's Conservationist Pioneer* (Tenterden, Kent: Paul Norbury Publications, 1977). A useful forerunner collection of studies can be found in the "Symposium: The Ashio Copper Mine Pollution Incident," *JJS*, 1/2 (Spring 1975): 347–407.

The history of technology, though more developed, is still a pioneering field. James R. Bartholomew, *The Formation of Science in Japan* (New Haven: YUP, 1989), sheds light on the rise of institutions of scientific research, which ultimately are essential to sustained technological change. Tessa Morris-Suzuki, *The Technological Transformation of Japan, From the Seventeenth to the Twenty-first Century* (Cambridge: CUP, 1994), explores the longer story of technological change. And the essays in Erich Pauer, ed., *Papers on the History of Industry and Technology of Japan*, 3 vols. (Marburg: Förderverein Marburger Japan-Reihe, 1995), introduce readers to diverse topics, as do the valuable but hard-to-find paperback booklets of the *Project on Technology Transfer, Transformation, and Development: The Japanese Experience* (Tokyo: United Nations University, ca. 1979–81).

The ideology of industrialization is concisely examined by Byron Marshall, *Capitalism and Nationalism in Prewar Japan, The Ideology of the Business Elite, 1868–1941* (Stanford: SUP, 1967), and more recently by W. Dean Kinzley, *Industrial Harmony in Modern Japan, The Invention of a Tradition* (London: Routledge, 1991). On social ramifications of industrialization, see Hugh Patrick, ed., *Japanese Industrialization and Its Social Consequences* (Berkeley: UCP, 1976); William Johnston, *The Modern Epidemic: A History of Tuberculosis in Japan* (Cambridge, MA: HUP,

1995); and Masanori Nakamura, ed., *Technology Change and Female Labour in Japan* (Tokyo: United Nations University Press, 1994).

The rise of industrial labor has received valuable monographic treatment, as in Kazuo Nimura, *The Ashio Riot of 1907, A Social History of Mining in Japan* (Durham: Duke University Press, 1997); E. Patricia Tsurumi, *Factory Girls: Women in the Thread Mills of Meiji Japan* (Princeton: PUP, 1990); and two works by Andrew Gordon – *The Evolution of Labor Relations in Japan, Heavy Industry, 1853–1955*, (Cambridge, MA: HUP, 1985), and *Labor and Imperial Democracy in Prewar Japan* (Berkeley: UCP, 1991).

The development of a modern school system and the concerns of students are treated in several works. Byron Marshall, *Learning to be Modern, Japanese Political Discourse on Education* (Boulder: Westview Press, 1994), surveys educational developments from late Tokugawa onward, and Marshall's bibliography will lead readers to earlier titles. On student ideals and discontent in particular, see Earl H. Kinmonth, *The Self-Made Man in Meiji Japanese Thought, from Samurai to Salary Man* (Berkeley: UCP, 1981); Donald T. Roden, *Schooldays in Imperial Japan: A Study in the Culture of a Student Elite* (Berkeley: UCP, 1980); and Henry Dewitt Smith II, *Japan's First Student Radicals* (Cambridge, MA: HUP, 1972).

The roles and experiences of women are treated in several works. On feminist activism see Sharon L. Sievers, *Flowers in Salt, The Beginnings of Feminist Consciousness in Modern Japan* (Stanford: SUP, 1983), and Vera Mackie, *Creating Socialist Women in Japan: Gender, Labour and Activism, 1900–1937* (Cambridge: CUP, 1997). For translations of the writings of several notable women, consult Mikiso Hane, *Reflections on the Way to the Gallows, Rebel Women in Prewar Japan* (Berkeley: UCP, 1988). Several essays in Janet Hunter, ed., *Japanese Women Working* (London: Routledge, 1993), look at women workers, and Tsurumi, *Factory Girls*, cited above, gives us insight into the world of textile workers. For a rich view of rural women's lives, see Robert J. Smith and Ella Lury Wiswell, *The Women of Suye Mura* (Chicago: UCP, 1982). Dower and George, *Japanese History and Culture*, pp. 232–37, lists numerous other titles, including Kristina Ruth Huber, *Women in Japanese Society: An Annotated Bibliography of Selected English Materials* (Westport: Greenwood Press, 1992).

Minorities have received treatment in a number of fine works, as citations in Dower and George, *Japanese History and Culture*, pp. 242–4, evidence. The earliest major work on *burakumin*, and still one of the best, is George DeVos and Hiroshi Wagatsuma, *Japan's Invisible Race, Caste in Culture and Personality* (Berkeley: UCP, 1966; rev. edn., 1972). Several works have examined Koreans in prewar Japan, most recently Michael Weiner, *Race and Migration in Imperial Japan: The Limits of Assimilation* (London: Routledge, 1994). A fine new contribution on the Ainu is Richard Siddle, *Race, Resistance and the Ainu of Japan* (London: Routledge, 1996). And the socially oppressed are treated more generally in Mikiso Hane, *Peasants, Rebels, and Outcastes, The Underside of Modern Japan* (NY: Pantheon, 1982).

Turning to cultural production and consumption, an incomparable introduction to the modern literary corpus is Donald Keene, *Dawn to the West, Japanese Literature of the Modern Era*, 2 vols. (NY: Holt, Rinehart & Winston, 1984), which treats writers of fiction, poetry, drama, and literary criticism through the 1960s. That source will also guide readers to the rich body of translations and scholarly studies that antedated it. Three more recent works that treat aspects of the literature are Tomi Suzuki, *Narrating the Self: Fictions of Japanese Modernity* (Stanford: SUP, 1996); Kevin Michael Doak, *Dreams of Difference, The Japan Romantic School and the Crisis of Modernity* (Berkeley: UCP, 1994); and Edward Fowler, *The Rhetoric of Confession, Shishōsetsu in Early Twentieth-Century Japanese Fiction* (Berkeley: UCP, 1988). On women writers, the bibliography in Joan E. Ericson's graceful and thoughtful *Be a Woman, Hayashi Fumiko and Modern Japanese Women's Literature* (Honolulu: UHP, 1997) will direct readers to earlier works, as will Claire Zebroski Mamola, *Japanese Women Writers in English Translation: An Annotated Bibliography*, 2 vols. (NY: Garland Press, 1992).

The musical and visual arts of these decades, and particularly those that were not purposeful continuations of indigenous artistic traditions, have received relatively little treatment in English. A brief survey of the musical history is William P. Malm, "The Modern Music of Meiji Japan," in the earlier-cited Shively, ed., *Tradition and Modernization in Japanese Culture*, pp. 257–300. And in *Six Hidden Views of Japanese Music* (Berkeley: UCP, 1986), Malm describes older musical styles that continue to be used in modern Japan. A recent study of one facet of music in early Meiji is Ury Eppstein, *The Beginnings of Western Music in Meiji Era Japan* (Lewiston, NY: Edwin Mellen Press, 1994).

On art history a dated but still usable survey is Hugo Munsterberg, *The Art of Modern Japan, From the Meiji Restoration to the Meiji Centennial, 1868–1968* (NY: Hacker Art Books, 1978). The problematic art category *"nihonga"* is richly and thoughtfully examined in Ellen P. Conant, *Nihonga, Transcending the Past: Japanese-Style Painting, 1868–1968* (St. Louis: The Saint Louis Art Museum, 1995). Select essays in Alexandra Munroe, *Japanese Art After 1945, Scream Against the Sky* (NY: Harry N. Abrams, 1994), add valuable insights and detail on the newer artistic departures of prewar decades.

On theatre, see the relevant chapters of Keene's *Dawn to the West*. Cinema, which was strongly influenced by indigenous theatrical precedents, has been richly studied. A major work is Joseph L. Anderson and Donald Richie, *The Japanese Film: Art and Industry* (Princeton: PUP, 1982), an expanded edition of a pioneering 1959 study. Two recent, more specialized studies are Keiko I. McDonald, *Japanese Classical Theater in Films* (London: Associated University Presses, Inc., 1994), and Darrell William Davis, *Picturing Japaneseness: Monumental Style, National Identity, Japanese Film* (NY: CUP, 1996).

ENTREPRENEURIAL JAPAN, 1945–1990

Integrative historical studies of the postwar decades are only beginning to appear, perhaps because for so many historians the period is not "history" at all: depending on one's year of birth, more or less of the era constitutes "current events," the present day. Even the redoubtable bibliographical compilation by Dower and George, *Japanese History and Culture*, is of less help beyond the 1950s.

A cluster of textbooks on postwar Japan has recently appeared, and these volumes reflect the pioneering quality of their authors' projects. Dennis B. Smith, *Japan since 1945, The Rise of an Economic Superpower* (NY: St. Martin's Press, 1995), is a concise history of Japan's postwar economic recovery and boom. Paul J. Bailey, *Postwar Japan, 1945 to the Present* (Oxford: Blackwell Publishers, 1996), is a more detailed politico-economic history. Gary D. Allinson, *Japan's Postwar History* (Ithaca: Cornell University Press, 1997), is a broader, integrative social history. Mikiso Hane, *Eastern Phoenix, Japan since 1945* (Boulder: Westview Press, 1996), which is a broad ranging, topically organized, fact-laden work, is the most detailed of the four, has the fullest bibliography, and suffers from the greatest problems of internal repetition and inconsistency. Three recent collections of scholarly essays on diverse topics are Carol Gluck and Stephen R. Graubard, eds., *Shōwa, The Japan of Hirohito* (NY: W.W. Norton & Co., 1992); Andrew Gordon, ed., *Postwar Japan as History* (Berkeley:

UCP, 1993); and Joe Moore, ed., *The Other Japan: Conflict, Compromise, and Resistance Since 1945*, new edn. (Armonk, NY: M.E. Sharpe, 1997).

Perhaps the aspect of these decades that stands out most clearly in general texts is the sheer magnitude of socioeconomic expansion and change. That magnitude is apparent in the myriad statistical measures one can glean from the large, annual, bilingual compilation by Sōmuchō tōkeikyoku, *Nihon tōkei nenkan* (Japan Statistical Yearbook) (Tokyo: Nihon tōkei kyokai, 1950ff). It is the most comprehensive of a host of official statistical compilations that are available for scholarly use. Secondary works, mainly by economists, anthropologists, sociologists, and students of government, also make rich use of statistical information of many sorts.

Turning to particular topics, the wartime experience that generated the most intense commentary after the fact was the atomic bombing of Hiroshima and Nagasaki, which gave rise to a considerable historical, social, and scientific scholarship, an array of literary, dramatic, artistic, and cinematic representations, and an outpouring of ephemeral polemics pro and con. A valuable collection of writings from those on the ground is Kyōko and Mark Selden, eds., *The Atomic Bomb: Voices from Hiroshima and Nagasaki* (Armonk, NY: M.E. Sharpe, 1989). Many other materials are conveniently grouped together in Dower and George, *Japanese History and Culture*, pp. 338–42.

Japan's foreign relations since 1945, lacking the excitement and visibility of earlier decades, have received only modest attention from historians, and then mainly in terms of trade relations or sporadic diplomatic incidents that reflect the painful residues of empire and war. For a sampling of the literature, see the bibliographical entries in Hane, *Eastern Phoenix*, pp. 235–6.

The period of Occupation, on the other hand, has been exhaustively treated, as the immense listing in Dower and George, *Japanese History and Culture*, pp. 373–411, reveals. An early but solid narrative work is Kazuo Kawai, *Japan's American Interlude* (Chicago: UCP, 1960), and a more recent collection of essays is Robert E. Ward and Yoshikazu Sakamoto, eds., *Democratizing Japan: The Allied Occupation* (Honolulu: UHP, 1987).

Political structure and process have also received detailed treatment, as titles in Hane, *Eastern Phoenix*, pp. 238–40, show. A recent study of Shōwa *tennō* is Stephen S. Large, *Emperor Hirohito and Shōwa Japan: A Political Biography* (London: Routledge, 1992). A broad-gauge description of rule by the Liberal Democratic Party during its heyday is Nathaniel B. Thayer, *How the Conservatives Rule Japan* (Princeton: PUP, 1969). Three more recent studies are Susan J. Pharr, *Losing Face; Status Politics in Japan* (Berkeley: UCP, 1990); Richard H. Mitchell, *Political Bribery in Japan* (Honolulu: UHP, 1996); and a collection of essays by Gary Allinson and Yasunori Sone, eds., *Political Dynamics in Contemporary Japan* (Ithaca: Cornell University Press, 1993).

Business and the economy have also been a central focus of study, oftimes polemical, as the list of titles in Hane, *Eastern Phoenix*, pp. 236–8, suggests. A good study of developments up to the heyday of Shōwa Genroku is Takafusa Nakamura, *The Postwar Japanese Economy, Its Development and Structure* (Tokyo: UTP, 1981). A major and wide-ranging collection of essays on myriad aspects of economic life is Yasusuke Murakami and Hugh T. Patrick, eds., *The Political Economy of Japan*, 3 vols. (Stanford: SUP, 1987–92).

Resource issues in the immediate postwar years are examined in Laura E. Hein, *Fueling Growth, The Energy Revolution and Economic Policy in Postwar Japan* (Cambridge, MA: HUP, 1990). On social ramifications of coal's decline see a fine new study by Suzanne Culter, *Managing Decline, Japan's Coal Industry Restructuring and Community Response* (Honolulu: UHP, 1999). The domestic politics of energy supplies, but not the broader resource issues, are treated in Richard J. Samuels, *The Business of the Japanese State, Energy Markets in Comparative and Historical Perspective* (Ithaca: Cornell University Press, 1987). On science and technology, in addition to the earlier-cited work by Morris-Suzuki, *The Technological Transformation of Japan, From the Seventeenth to the Twenty-first Century*, see Shigeru Nakayama, *Science, Technology and Society in Postwar Japan* (London: Kegan Paul International, 1991).

The social change that engulfed rural Japan after 1950 is nicely evoked in the delightful work by Ronald P. Dore, *Shinohata, A Portrait of a Japanese Village* (NY: Pantheon, 1978). A more recent study of rural change is Jackson H. Bailey, *Ordinary People, Extraordinary Lives, Political and Economic Change in a Tōhoku Village* (Honolulu: UHP, 1991). Economic issues lying behind this change are treated in Yūjirō Hayami, *Japanese Agriculture Under Seige, The Political Economy of Agricultural Policies* (London: MacMillan Press, 1988), and John O. Haley and Kozo Yamamura, eds., *Land Issues in Japan: A Policy Failure?* (Seattle: Society for Japanese Studies, 1992).

An old but charming evocation of changes imbedded in Japan's postwar urbanization is Edward Norbeck, *Changing Japan* (NY: Holt, Rinehart, & Winston, 1965; 2nd edn., 1976). Two revealing studies of urban life during the early days of postwar affluence are R. P. Dore, *City Life in Japan, A Study of a Tokyo Ward* (Berkeley: UCP, 1958), and Exra F. Vogel, *Japan's New Middle Class, The Salary Man and His Family in a Tokyo Suburb* (Berkeley: UCP, 1963). Jennifer Robertson, *Native and Newcomer, Making and Remaking a Japanese City* (Berkeley: UCP, 1991), explores urbanization over the longer term in a suburb of Tokyo. A recent look at urban life near Kyoto is Eyal Ben-Ari, *Changing Japanese Suburbia, A Study of Two Present-Day Localities* (London: Kegan Paul International, 1991).

On blue- and white-collar labor in post-1945 Japan, two works from the heyday of economic growth are Robert E. Cole, *Japanese Blue Collar, The Changing Tradition* (Berkeley: UCP, 1971), and Thomas P. Rohlen, *For Harmony and Strength: Japanese White-Collar Organization in Anthropological Perspective* (Berkeley: UCP, 1974). Two recent works that shed light on workers' lives and employment conditions after the heyday are Christena L. Turner, *Japanese Workers in Protest, An Ethnography of Consciousness and Experience* (Berkeley: UCP, 1995), and Edward Fowler, *San'ya Blues, Laboring Life in Contemporary Tokyo* (Ithaca: Cornell University Press, 1996).

Minorities continue to receive attention. A valuable recent work that treats several groups is Michael Weiner, *Japan's Minorities, The Illusion of Homogeneity* (London: Routledge, 1997). The noteworthy new minority of recent years is foreign unskilled workers, and several works examine them, notably Hiroshi Komai, *Migrant Workers in Japan* (London: Kegan Paul International, 1995). On Ainu, the earlier-cited work by Richard Siddle, *Race, Resistance and the Ainu of Japan*, is especially helpful. A valuable collection of essays on Koreans in postwar Japan is Changsoo Lee and George DeVos, eds., *Koreans in Japan: Ethnic Conflict and Accommodation* (Berkeley: UCP, 1981), and a wonderfully revealing study of a segment of that population is Sonia Ryang, *North Koreans in Japan: Language, Ideology, and Identity* (Boulder: Westview Press, 1997).

Studies of women continue proliferating to good effect. A delightful glimpse of rural women's life is Gail Lee Bernstein, *Haruko's World, A Japanese Farm Woman and Her Community* (Stanford: SUP, 1983). Unsurprisingly, most works now focus on urban women, who are the overwhelming majority, as reflected in the recent study by Sumiko Iwao, *The Japanese Woman: Traditional Image and Changing Reality* (NY: The Free Press, 1993). A fine collection of recent essays is Kumiko Fujimura-Fanselow and Atsuko Kameda, eds., *Japanese Women: New Feminist Perspectives on the Past,*

Present, and Future (NY: The Feminist Press, 1995). On women in the political world, see Susan J. Pharr, *Political Women in Japan, The Search for a Place in Political Life* (Berkeley: UCP, 1981). On women at home, see Anne E. Imamura, *Urban Japanese Housewives, At Home and in the Community* (Honolulu: UHP, 1987). On the issue of fetal rites (*mizuko kuyō*), see Helen Hardacre, *Marketing the Menacing Fetus in Japan* (Berkeley: UCP, 1997), whose bibliography will lead to the few earlier studies. And on women and child rearing in recent years, see Muriel Jolivet, *Japan: the Childless Society? The Crisis of Motherhood* (London: Routledge, 1997).

Women and the work place has been a topic of particular interest. Three recent studies that will lead readers to older works are Mary C. Brinton, *Women and the Economic Miracle, Gender and Work in Postwar Japan* (Berkeley: UCP, 1993); Glenda S. Roberts, *Staying on the Line, Blue-Collar Women in Contemporary Japan* (Honolulu: UHP, 1994); and Yuko Ogasawara, *Office Ladies and Salaried Men, Power, Gender and Work in Japanese Companies* (Berkeley: UCP, 1998).

Environmental issues of recent decades have received only modest scholarly treatment in English, mainly in regard to pollution and its effects on the human population. A useful recent collection of essays on select incidents is Jun Ui, ed., *Industrial Pollution in Japan* (Tokyo: United Nations University Press, 1992). For book-length treatments see Margaret A. McKean, *Environmental Protest and Citizen Politics in Japan* (Berkeley, UCP, 1981), and more recently Akio Mishima, *Bitter Sea: The Human Cost of Minamata Disease* (Tokyo: Kosei Publishing Co., 1992). The politics of environment vs. development are illuminated by Jeffrey Broadbent, *Environmental Politics in Japan* (Cambridge: CUP, 1998). A valuable collection of essays that cast a broader environmental net is Shigeto Tsuru and Helmut Weidner, eds., *Environmental Policy in Japan* (Berlin: Edition Sigma, 1989).

Turning to intellectual and cultural facets of the history, matters of ethnicity and "East-and-West" generated much rhetoric over the years, and a recent study of *Nihonjinron* is Kosaku Yoshino, *Cultural Nationalism in Contemporary Japan: A Sociological Enquiry* (London: Routledge, 1992). Two collections of essays that reflect the recent flurry of "postmodernist" analyses are Masao Miyoshi and H. D. Harootunian, eds., *Japan in the World* (Durham: Duke University Press, 1993), and Charles Wei-hsun Fu and Steven Heine, eds., *Japan in Traditional and Postmodern Perspectives* (Albany: State University of New York Press, 1995).

Religion has received considerable attention. Ian Reader, *Religion in Contemporary Japan* (Honolulu: UHP, 1991), treats current practice, and his endnotes and bibliography identify earlier works. The essays in Mark R. Mullins et al., eds., *Religion and Society in Modern Japan, Selected Readings* (Berkeley: Asian Humanities Press, 1993), illuminate many aspects of religious practice today.

The postwar literary world has received much study. Donald Keene's earlier-cited *Dawn to the West*, deals with works into the sixties, and it lists the rich earlier scholarship on authors of that day. Several recent studies and translations introduce more recent writings. To sample fiction of the 1970s–80s, consult Helen Mitsios, *New Japanese Voices, The Best Contemporary Fiction from Japan* (NY: Atlantic Monthly Press, 1991). Two works that treat fantasy and science fiction are Robert Matthew, *Japanese Science Fiction, A View of a Changing Society* (London: Routledge, 1989), and Susan J. Napier, *The Fantastic in Modern Japanese Literature, The Subversion of Modernity* (London: Routledge, 1996). On business novels, see Tamae K. Prindle, tr., *Made in Japan and Other Japanese "Business Novels"* (Armonk, NY: M.E. Sharpe, 1989), and Ikkō Shimizu, *The Dark Side of Japanese Business: Three "Industry Novels"* (Armonk, NY: M.E. Sharpe, 1996), which Prindle translated.

Two good collections of translated works by women writers are Yukiko Tanaka and Elizabeth Hanson, eds., *This Kind of Woman, Ten Stories by Japanese Women Writers, 1960–1976* (Stanford: SUP, 1982), and for fiction of the 1980s, Yukiko Tanaka, ed., *Unmapped Territories, New Women's Fiction from Japan* (Seattle, WA: Women in Translation, 1991). Other translations of recent fiction are listed in Hane, *Eastern Phoenix*, pp. 244–6.

From ancient times, as we noted in discussing classical and medieval culture, performance artists have combined visual, musical, and dramatic arts with dance to produce theatrical performances, and in recent decades, particularly during the 1960s, that combining of representational genres flourished. This picture is evident in the richly informative essays of the earlier-cited Munroe, *Japanese Art After 1945, Scream Against the Sky*.

Two recent works on theatre that will lead readers to other studies are Benito Ortolani, *The Japanese Theatre: From Shamanistic Ritual to Contemporary Pluralism* (Leiden: E. J. Brill, 1990; paperback Princeton: PUP, 1994), and Akihiko Senda, *The Voyage of Contemporary Japanese Theatre* (Honolulu: UHP, 1997), translated by J. Thomas Rimer. Two studies that illuminate the current status of folk drama are Barbara E. Thornbury, *The Folk Performing Arts, Traditional Culture in Contemporary Japan* (Albany: SUNY Press, 1997), and Jane Marie Law, *Puppets of Nostalgia, The Life, Death, and Rebirth of the Japanese Awaji Ningyō Tradition* (Princeton: PUP, 1997). A revealing study of the institutional context for this flourishing cultural output is Thomas R. H. Havens, *Artist and Patron in Postwar Japan, Dance, Music, Theater, and the Visual Arts, 1955–1980* (Princeton: PUP, 1982).

On cinema, a number of insightful works have appeared recently. In addition to portions of the volumes cited above for prewar decades, see Arthur Nolletti, Jr. and David Desser, eds., *Reframing Japanese Cinema: Authorship, Genre, History* (Bloomington: Indiana University Press, 1992), and David Desser, *Eros Plus Massacre, An Introduction to the Japanese New Wave Cinema* (Bloomington: Indiana University Press, 1988).

Index

1 Index sub-entries are listed chronologically rather than alphabetically.
2 Consult the Glossary for English equivalents of Japanese terms not listed in the Index.
3 For Japanese persons, birth and death dates, as well as common alternative names, are given where known.
4 Author, date, and common translations are listed for Japanese literary works and movies.

KEY TERMS: consult these entries for guidance to other entries in each category.

Culture: *See* literature; middlebrow culture; performance arts; religion; visual arts
Ecology: *See* biosystem; disease; energy; pollution; population
Economy: *See* agriculture; commerce; economic fluctuations; industry; labor; media; transportation
Government: *See* foreign relations; military organization; political consolidation; political institutions; political thought; regionalism; taxation
Society: *See* education; minorities; population; social conditions; social structure; villages; women